Invitation to Public Speaking

Sixth Edition

D0070884

Invitation to Public Speaking

Sixth Edition

Cindy L. Griffin

Colorado State University

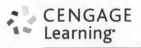
CENGAGE
Learning·

Australia • Brazil • Mexico • Singapore • United Kingdom • United States

CENGAGE
Learning·

Invitation to Public Speaking, Sixth Edition
Cindy L. Griffin

Product Director: Monica Eckman

Product Manager: Kelli Strieby

Content Developer: Lisa Moore

Marketing Manager: Sarah Seymour

Content Project Manager: Dan Saabye

Art Director: Melissa Falco

Manufacturing Planner: Doug Bertke

IP Analyst: Ann Hoffman

IP Project Manager: Kathryn Kucharek

Production Service: MPS Limited

Compositor: MPS Limited

Text Designer: Liz Harasymczuk Design

Cover Designer: Red Hangar Design

Cover Image: Andrew Toth/FilmMagic/
Getty images

"National Geographic," "National Geographic
Society" and the Yellow Border Design are reg-
istered trademarks of the National Geographic
Society® Marcas Registradas

Design Element: arzawen/Shutterstock.com

2018, 2015, 2012 Cengage Learning

ALL RIGHTS RESERVED. No part of this work covered by the copyright herein
may be reproduced or distributed in any form or by any means, except as
permitted by U.S. copyright law, without the prior written permission of the
copyright owner.

Unless otherwise noted, all art is © Cengage Learning.

For product information and technology assistance, contact us at
Cengage Learning Customer & Sales Support, 1-800-354-9706.

For permission to use material from this text or product,
submit all requests online at **www.cengage.com/permissions.**
Further permissions questions can be emailed to
permissionrequest@cengage.com.

Library of Congress Control Number: 2016947575

Student Edition:
ISBN: 978-1-305-94808-2

Loose-leaf Edition:
ISBN: 978-1-305-94818-1

Cengage Learning
20 Channel Center Street
Boston, MA 02210
USA

Cengage Learning is a leading provider of customized learning solutions
with employees residing in nearly 40 different countries and sales in more
than 125 countries around the world. Find your local representative at
www.cengage.com.

Cengage Learning products are represented in Canada by
Nelson Education, Ltd.

To learn more about Cengage Learning Solutions, visit **www.cengage.com.**

Purchase any of our products at your local college store or at our preferred
online store **www.cengagebrain.com.**

About the Author

Cindy L. Griffin is a professor emeritus of communication studies at Colorado State University. She received her BS from California State University, Northridge, her MA from the University of Oregon, and her PhD from Indiana University. She teaches public speaking; gender and communication; contemporary rhetorical theory; feminist rhetorical theory; communication, language, and thought; and rhetoric and civility. A proponent of service learning, instersectionality, civic engagement, and civility, she integrates these ideas and assignments into her coursework and research. In addition to her teaching and research, she has published numerous articles, books, and book chapters, served as editor of the journal *Women's Studies in Communication,* and is a member of the Women's Studies faculty at CSU. She and her husband, Mike Harte, live in Fort Collins, Colorado.

Michael J. Harte

National Geographic Explorers Who Contributed to *Invitation to Public Speaking*, Sixth Edition

Invitation to Public Speaking is the only public speaking textbook to work collaboratively with the National Geographic Society, highlighting the central role of public speaking in our work, professional interactions, and even our social lives. Our innovative collaboration with the National Geographic Society allows us to showcase and explore the ways that National Geographic Explorers—scientists, researchers, artists, educators, and activists—use public speaking skills to carry out their work, develop professional and personal relationships with others, and share their discoveries and research with the larger public.

Through the text, these National Geographic Explorers invite you into their world to demonstrate in what way they use public speaking skills to achieve their goals, enhance their success, and help them continue in their exploratory journeys. Look for the National Geographic SPEAKS and National Geographic TIPs in the chapters.

Chapter 1: Thomas Taha Rassam Culhane

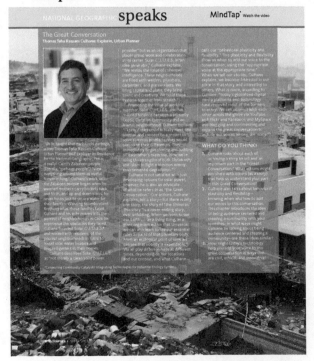

Chapter 2: K. David Harrison

Chapter 3: Becca Skinner

Chapter 4: Raghava KK

Chapter 5: Barrington Irving

Chapter 6: Josh Thome

Chapter 7: Albert Yu-Min Lin

Chapter 8: Alexandra Cousteau

Chapter 9: Gregory D. S. Anderson

Chapter 10: Wade Davis

Chapter 11: Asher Jay

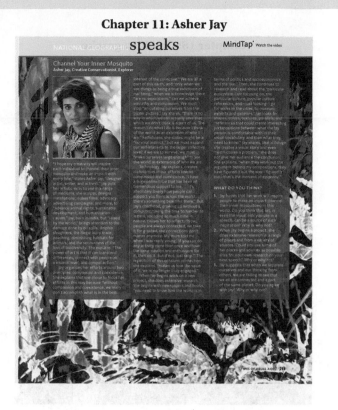

Chapter 12: Sylvia Earle

Chapter 13: Aziz Abu Sarah

Chapter 14: Shabana Basij-Rasikh

Chapter 12: Sylvia Earle

Chapter 11: Asher Jay

Chapter 15: Sol Guy

Chapter 16: Chad Pregracke

MindTap° Appendix: Dino Martins

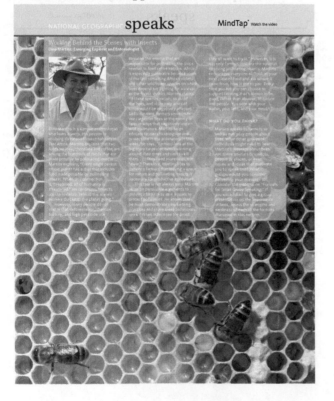

Chapter 13: Aziz Abu Sarah

Brief Contents

Contents

5 | Gathering Supporting Materials 79

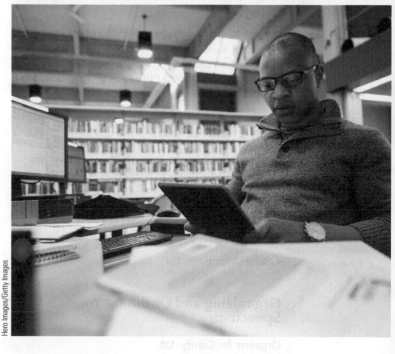

6 | Developing and Supporting Your Ideas 103

7 | Organizing and Outlining Your Speech 127

8 | Introductions and Conclusions 157

Bloomberg/Getty Images

Andrew H. Walker/Getty Images Entertainment/Getty Images

Ben Baker/Redux

16 | Speaking on Special Occasions **315**

Preface

Our best public speaking courses focus their efforts on teaching students the skills needed to speak effectively in public settings and to deliberate with one another on important issues. Most existing texts focus primarily on informational and persuasive speaking, often also preparing students to give speeches that entertain or celebrate others. *Invitation to Public Speaking* includes this focus, but also introduces students to *invitational* speaking, a type of speaking that links directly to public deliberation and that is becoming increasingly common in our societies.

In invitational speaking, speakers enter into a dialogue with an audience to clarify positions, explore issues and ideas, or share beliefs and values. When we speak to invite, we want to set the stage for open dialogue and exploration of ideas and issues—we want to come to a fuller understanding of an issue, regardless of our different positions. This speech type is introduced when other speech types are defined and discussed, and is included in discussions of the speechmaking process throughout the text.

This emphasis in *Invitation to Public Speaking* on the interconnections between the speaker and the audience reminds students that they speak to and for an audience. Students are, therefore, encouraged to consider their audience at every step of the speechmaking process. This audience-centered approach also reminds students of the responsibilities associated with speaking publicly and the importance of advanced planning and preparation. Plus, it seems to ease some of the familiar speech anxiety students have, because it turns their attention toward speech preparation and effective communication with others and away from the performance aspect of public speaking.

Invitation to Public Speaking also encourages students to see public speaking as a meaningful and useful skill beyond the classroom by expanding the range of venues for public speaking. The text prompts students to speak not only in required classroom speaking situations but also when they are asked to do so (for example, in the workplace) and when they decide to do so (perhaps as voices of their communities). Thus the text exposes them to the wide range of situations that encourage us to contribute to the public dialogue.

In this expanded context, public speaking reflects the many changes that have been taking place in our society, changes that call for an exploration of many perspectives. When framed as a public deliberation and dialogue, public speaking emphasizes the right to be heard and the responsibility to listen to others. As such, *Invitation to Public Speaking* explores public speaking in relation to a modern definition of eloquence in which differences, civility, narratives, visual aids, and even self-disclosure play a larger role than they tend to in traditional rhetoric.

In addition, the text's pragmatic approach—in combination with other numerous dynamic, real-life examples—allows working students to design speeches with their employment settings in mind. In this way, the text helps students view public speaking as a layering of skills and issues rather than as a series of actions existing in isolation. Although the speaking process is presented systematically and in discrete steps, the end result is a smooth integration of material and speaking techniques.

Finally, the text's audience-centered approach, combined with a focus on ethics and integration of diversity, helps students better understand their audiences so they can establish credibility and communicate effectively.

Features of the Book

National Geographic Partnership

We continue our partnership with the National Geographic Society in the sixth edition. Working in partnership with the National Geographic Society helps frame the invitational approach to public speaking as public deliberation and dialogue, encouraging students to see themselves as significant contributors to their larger communities and as able to add their voices to important dilemmas we face in our world today. National Geographic photographs throughout the book provide added visual enrichment to the pages that help reinforce the real-world application of the explanations presented, and the skills taught, in the chapters.

See the What's New in The Sixth Edition Section for a description of additional ways this National Geographic partnership enhances *Invitation to Public Speaking* such that students can study and explore the ways individuals are using their public speaking skills around the world in hands-on and tangible ways to effect change. These public and professional dialogues are about complex issues that affect us all.

Extensive Coverage of Civility and Civic Engagement

By emphasizing the "how" and the "why" of public speaking, *Invitation to Public Speaking* demonstrates the impact that participating in public dialogue and deliberation can have on students' lives and communities. Civility and the importance of civic engagement are emphasized throughout the book. For example, Civic Engagement in Action boxes, included in many of the chapters, highlight the ways in which students, average citizens, and celebrities have used their public speaking skills to affect the public dialogue in meaningful and satisfying ways. Students can look to these vignettes as examples of how to apply public speaking and civic engagement to their own lives as they become more active members of their communities. Even the photo captions emphasize the importance of civic engagement and civility in the public dialogue. The text's thoughtful attention to these issues continually reminds students of the important role that public speaking plays in our diverse society.

Focus on Skills

Invitation to Public Speaking prepares students to give speeches and enter the public dialogue via a solid, pragmatic, skills-based foundation in public speaking. Beginning with Chapter 2, "Effective Listening," and continuing through Chapter 11, "Visual Aids," each chapter guides students through specific speech construction, delivery, or strategy steps. The text provides straightforward instruction in speechmaking that is based on the author's classroom experience and knowledge of students' expectations for skill training.

Practicing the Public Dialogue boxes provide assignable exercises that expose students to each component of the speechmaking process and gives them strategies for tackling the informative, invitational, persuasive, and special occasion speeches found in Chapters 12, 13, 15, and 16. Speech models included throughout the text are consistent with the principles presented.

In addition, Review Questions conclude each chapter and give students the opportunity to further hone their skills. These questions range from straightforward true–false statements to activities that require more research, student involvement, and reflection.

Quick-Start Guide: Ten Steps to Entering the Public Dialogue

Sometimes, students can feel overwhelmed just thinking about adding their voices to the public dialogue. They may wonder where to begin. They may be uncertain about how to organize their efforts. They may not know if they have completed all the steps of speech preparation. *Invitation to Public Speaking* includes a quick-start guide that is designed to help them track their process from topic selection to delivery. Presented as ten steps to entering the public dialogue, this guide will help them organize their efforts, feel more confident, and deliver successful speeches. Students can use this guide as they prepare and complete each of the assigned speeches, and also as a study prompt for their exams. Instructors might find it a useful overview of the process that they can walk students through at the beginning of the course.

Speaking Venues and Service Learning

Invitation to Public Speaking covers a variety of speaking venues and provides ample opportunity to incorporate a service learning component into the course. Chapter 1, "Why Speak in Public?" offers students a comprehensive view of public speaking as public dialogue and discusses speaking when someone is asked to speak, decides to speak, or is required to speak. In addition, the *Invitation to Public Speaking* Instructor's Resource Manual provides a definition of service learning and instruction for how to use service learning projects as a source for speech topics, speech research, and possibly an environment for delivery.

These options allow students and instructors to step outside the speech classroom if they desire, and take the public speaking skills taught and learned in the classroom into their communities. However, the text's flexible organization allows instructors who do not want to include service learning to easily maintain the traditional classroom-based speaking situation throughout the term. If instructors choose to stay with the traditional classroom speech format, the service learning information can be used simply to prompt students to select and deliver speeches that address larger social issues and dilemmas.

Expansive Coverage of Speech Types

Some courses emphasize particular types of speeches, but *Invitation to Public Speaking* was specifically developed to cover and support the entire array of public speaking types. The text's coverage of multiple speaking forms invites students to discuss audience centeredness and difference, as well as the ways that speakers can acknowledge, incorporate, and respond to difference with respect and integrity.

Beginning with the "Quick-Start Guide, Ten Steps to Entering the Public Dialogue" (pages xxx–xxxii), the text presents a synopsis of five types of speaking: informative, invitational, persuasive, speaking on special occasions, and in the appendix that is available through Mind speaking in small groups. Each type of speech previewed in the quick start is covered in depth in Chapters 12 through 16 and the appendix on group speaking, and is given equal attention with regard to examples and tips in Chapters 2 through 11, furthering the text's goal of preparing readers for public speaking in a range of venues beyond the classroom.

Coverage of Social Diversity

Through reviewer-praised examples and discussion of key concepts, the text makes a comprehensive yet subtle integration of social and cultural diversity. *Invitation to Public Speaking* offers meaningful coverage of diversity by exploring culture and speaking styles; cultures, identities, and listening styles; speaking to diverse audiences; and language, identities, and culture. Our partnership with National Geographic enhances this feature, as Explorers share with students the importance of social diversity, cultural awareness, and sensitivity in the work they do.

Rather than isolate issues of diversity into separate chapters, *Invitation to Public Speaking* presents ideas and issues of diversity in examples, discussions, National

Geographic tips and stories, activities, and exercises throughout the text. In the process, the text provides sufficient information so that instructors and students can explore together the implications of social diversity and the importance of developing layers of knowledge about difference.

Coverage of Ethics

Ethical issues are discussed throughout the text to help students understand how ethical considerations affect every aspect of the speechmaking process. For example, the importance of practicing ethics in regard to listening, Internet research, interviewing, reasoning, citing sources, and in informative, invitational, and persuasive speaking are covered thoroughly. In addition, select chapters feature Ethical Moment boxes, which highlight ethical dilemmas related to the public dialogue. These ethical dilemmas bring in both iconic figures, such as Martin Luther King Jr. and Barack Obama; contemporary social issues and practices such as graffiti and YouTube, and everyday individuals, like students and citizens. Many of our National Geographic Explorers also address the importance of ethical choices and considerations in the work they do. This array of opportunities for conversations about ethical public speaking assists students in linking real ethical dilemmas to their own lives and professional goals.

Coverage and Use of Relevant Technology

Invitation to Public Speaking was written with technology use in mind. Thoughtful integration on nearly every page continually helps students understand the links between the text and technology. The text not only covers technology as it relates to speechmaking but also incorporates the use of technology as a powerful learning tool. The Internet and online databases are discussed as tools for speech topic selection, research, and support, while presentation technology such as Microsoft PowerPoint, Prezi and Google Slides, and Internet downloads are presented as a resource for creating professional visual aids. Each chapter points students to relevant websites, video clips of student and professional speakers, and other online activities that can be accessed via the online resources for *Invitation to Public Speaking*.

What's New in the Sixth Edition?

- **National Geographic Speaks features in every chapter**

Our collaboration with the National Geographic Society is expanded in this sixth edition with National Geographic Speaks features in every chapter. National Geographic Explorers—scientists, researchers, linguists, artists, educators, activists, and more—include Gregory D. S. Anderson, Shabana Basij-Rasikh, Alexandra Cousteau, Thomas Taha Rassam Culhane, Wade Davis, Sylvia Earle, Sol Guy, K. David Harrison, Barrington Irving, Asher Jay, Raghava KK, Dino Martins, Chad Pregracke, Aziz Abu Sarah, Becca Skinner, Josh Thome, and Albert Yu-Min Lin. These case studies, developed from interviews and research, showcase the importance and centrality of ethical and civil public speaking in the work of these nationally recognized explorers. Questions at the end of each case study prompt students to reflect on these Explorers' public speeches and the ways in which a particular strategy might also become a part of their own public speaking skill set.

- **Updated Public Speaking Tips from National Geographic Explorers**

Alexandra Cousteau, Thomas Taha Rassam Culhane, Barrington Irving, Aziz Abu Sarah, and Becca Skinner continue to provide students with hands-on support for researching and giving speeches. Interviews with these nationally known researchers, explorers, and scientists provide the substance for these tips. These tips help students apply the skills taught in the book, showcase the real-life application of these skills by nationally recognized experts, and even offer students hands-on and practical advice for researching, rehearsing, and giving speeches. These tips enliven every chapter of the book.

- **Public Speaking in the Workplace**

Our new "Public Speaking in the Workplace" feature explores and showcases the various kinds of public speaking that actually take place in our professions. These features help students see that the skills they are learning in their public speaking course carry over into their professional lives and can benefit them enormously in getting, keeping, and advancing in their jobs and careers.

Eight chapters explore the following topics: Top Ten Skills Employers Seek; Are There Advantages to Diversity?; Conducting Interviews; Different Generations Can Equal Different Styles of Communicating; How Your Public Speaking Skills Can Help You Keep That New Job; Managing those Nerves; How Much Public Speaking Will You Do?; and Tips for Job Interviews. Each feature engages students in the exploration of various facets of public speaking as it occurs in the workplace and assists students in getting that job, keeping that job, and advancing in their professions.

- **Updated Chapter 5, "Gathering Supporting Materials," and Chapter 11, "Visual Aids"**

Chapter 5, "Gathering Supporting Materials," has been streamlined and updated to reflect the process of research in today's online world. The ethical dilemmas created by today's access to so much data are addressed, as are the most effective approaches to conducting research. In Chapter 11, "Visual Aids," new material reflecting Internet software, downloads, and applications has been added. Chapter 11 also contains a streamlined discussion of how to create professional and ethical visual aids and what to show on them.

- **Updated Ethical Moment features**

Ethical public speaking remains a central focus of *Invitation to Public Speaking*, sixth edition. Updated Ethical Moment features help students explore and reflect on the implications of offensive language, careful reasoning, nonverbal communication, and social media. National Geographic Explorers such as Shabana Basij-Rasikh, Wade Davis, Alexandra Cousteau, Sylvia Earle, Aziz Abu Sarah, and Thomas Taha Rassam Culhane also urge students to consider the ethical implications of their choices throughout the process of crafting and giving a speech. These features are placed strategically in chapters, helping students link the content they are reading to contemporary ethical dilemmas. Chapters in the sixth edition also maintain their emphasis on the importance of considering the ethical implications of each step of the public speaking process.

- **Enhanced coverage of technology**

The ways technology influences the public speaking process also remain central to this sixth edition. This edition offers many updates throughout related to the use and importance of technology and the innovations that continue to change the way we speak in public—how technology helps us with research, preparation, or presentation, among other things. For example, Chapter 1, "Public Speaking Is Influenced by Technology," has been updated and continues to enrich the "What Is Ethical Public Speaking" section. Many of our National Geographic Explorers— Sol Guy and Josh Thome, K. David Harrison and David Anderson, Albert Yu-Min Lin, Asher Jay, and Raghava KK, for example—also challenge students to consider the importance of, and opportunities provided by, technology in public speaking.

- **New and updated examples and research**

Throughout the book, examples have been updated to include more that students will recognize and relate to. In addition, research has been updated throughout the book as appropriate.

MindTap®

- ***Invitation to Public Speaking* now comes with MindTap.**

MindTap represents a new approach to a customizable, online, user-focused learning platform. MindTap combines all of a user's learning tools—readings, multimedia, activities, and assessments—into a singular Learning Unit that guides students through the curriculum based on learning objectives and outcomes. Instructors personalize the experience by customizing the presentation of these learning tools to their students, even seamlessly introducing their own content into the Learning Unit via "apps" that integrate into the Mind-Tap platform.

Unique to MindTap Speech is "Practice and Present"—an online video submission and grading program that allows for individualized feedback and provides a digital environment for public speaking students to practice their skills and get meaningful feedback from their instructor and peers.

Also included are Interactive Video Activities and Speech Builder Express 3.0™—a tool that coaches students through the entire speech organization and outlining process.

Through the use of assignable and gradable interactive video activities, polling assignments, study and exam preparation tools, MindTap brings the printed textbook to life. Students respond enthusiastically to the readspeak, highlighting, search, and dictionary features available on MindTap. Student comprehension is enhanced with the integrated eBook and the interactive teaching and learning tools that include:

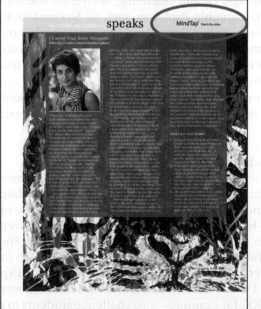

- Sample speech videos
- Sample speech outlines and note cards
- An online speech organizing and outlining tool
- An online speech practice and presentation tool
- Web Connect links
- Practicing the Public Dialogue prompts
- Study aids such as glossary flash cards and review quizzes
- Additional Civic Engagement and Ethical Moments boxes
- And much more

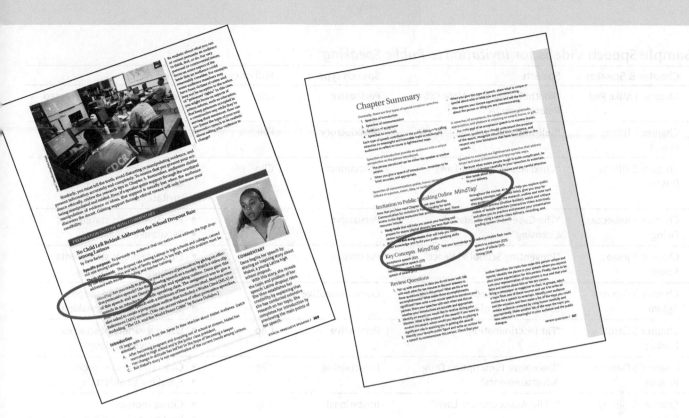

YouSeeU

- With **YouSeeU**, students can upload video files of practice speeches or final performances, comment on their peers' speeches, and review their grades and instructor feedback. Instructors create courses and assignments, comment on and grade student speeches, and allow peer review. Grades flow into a gradebook that allows instructors to easily manage their course from within MindTap. Grades also can be exported for use in learning-management systems. YouSeeU's flexibility lends itself to use in traditional, hybrid, and online courses.

Outline Builder

- **Outline Builder** breaks down the speech preparation process into manageable steps and can help alleviate speech-related anxiety. The "wizard format" provides relevant prompts and resources to guide students through the outlining process. Students are guided through topic definition, research and source citation, organizational structure outlining, and drafting note cards for speech day. The outline is assignable and gradable through MindTap.

Speech Video Library

- **Speech Video Library** gives students a chance to watch videos of real speeches that correspond to the topics in *Invitation to Public Speaking*. Each chapter begins with a vignette that builds directly on a video of a student speech available in MindTap, allowing for a quick preview of the chapter topics and skills. The text also includes several prompts to watch the video of the sample student speeches that accompany this book. Students find these prompts near the ends of Chapters 3, 8, 9, 12, 13, 14, 15, and 16.

   Each video is accompanied by a speech activity that provides a full transcript so viewers can read along, the speech outline—many in note card and full sentence form, and evaluation questions so students are guided through their assessment. While viewing each clip, students evaluate the speech or scenario by completing short-answer questions and submitting their results directly to their instructor.

Sample Speech Videos for *Invitation to Public Speaking*

Chapter & Speaker	Speech	Speech type	Full or clip	Related topics
Chapter 1 Mike Piel	"Foothills Gateway: Vote YES on Referendum 1A"	Persuasive	Clip	• Remaining audience centered • Persuasive speaking
Chapter 1 Tiffany Brisco	"Self-Introduction"	Introductory	Full	• Giving your first speech • Speeches of self- introduction
Chapter 2 Tiffany Brisco	"Child Abandonment Laws"	Invitational	Clip	• Encouraging effective listening • Invitational speaking
Chapter 3 Rebecca Ewing	"The Case for Graduated Licensing"	Persuasive	Clip	• Effective thesis statements • Persuasive speaking
Chapter 3 Jesse Rosser	"Preventing School Violence"	Persuasive	Clip	• Effective thesis statements • Persuasive speaking
Chapter 3 Ogenna Agbim	"This Is Dedicated . . . : A Tribute to the Women of History"	Commemorative	Full	• Speech topic and purpose • Special occasion speaking
Chapter 5 Carol Godart	"Fat Discrimination"	Persuasive	Clip	• Using a variety of sources • Persuasive speaking
Chapter 5 Damien Beasley	"Deceptive Prescription Drug Advertisements"	Entertaining	Clip	• Oral citation of source • Speaking to entertain
Chapter 5 Tiffany Brisco	"Child Abandonment Laws"	Invitational	Clip	• Citing sources • Invitational speaking
Chapter 6 Chelsey Penoyer	"11 Lives a Day: Youth Suicide in America"	Informative	Clip	• Using narratives • Informative speaking
Chapter 7 Lisa Alagna	"Breast Cancer Awareness"	Invitational	Clip	• Deductive reasoning • Invitational speaking
Chapter 7 Brent Erb	"Stay on Designated Hiking Trails"	Persuasive	Clip	• Causal reasoning • Persuasive speaking
Chapter 8 Cindy Gardner	"U.S. Flag Etiquette"	Informative	Clip	• Organization of main points • Informative speaking
Chapter 8 Jeff Malcolm	"History of Fort Collins, Colorado"	Informative	Clip	• Chronological organization • Informative speaking
Chapter 8 Katy Mazz	"Why Pi?"	Informative	Full	• Speech organization • Informative speaking
Chapter 9 Brandi Lafferty	"Feeding the Wildlife: Don't Do It!"	Persuasive	Clip	• Story in an introduction • Persuasive speaking
Chapter 9 Mike Piel	"Foothills Gateway: Vote YES on Referendum 1A"	Persuasive	Clip	• Preview in an introduction • Persuasive speaking
Chapter 9 Mike Piel	"Foothills Gateway: Vote YES on Referendum 1A"	Persuasive	Clip	• Conclusions • Persuasive speaking
Chapter 9 Chelsey Penoyer	"11 Lives a Day: Youth Suicide in America"	Informative	Clip	• Credibility in conclusion • Startling conclusion • Informative speaking
Chapter 10 Brandi Lafferty	"Feeding the Wildlife: Don't Do It!"	Persuasive	Clip	• Casual style of speaking • Persuasive speaking
Chapter 10 Stacey Newman	"Fallen Soldiers"	Commemorative	Clip	• Language techniques • Special occasion speaking
Chapter 11 Eric Daley and Shelley Weibelt	"Mountain Biking in Colorado" (Eric) "Preserving Our National Resources" (Shelley)	Persuasive	Clip	• Comparison of written and conversational styles • Persuasive speaking

Sample Speech Videos (continued)

Chapter & Speaker	Speech	Speech type	Full or clip	Related topics
Chapter 11 Brandi Lafferty, Amy Wood, Carol Godart, and Hans Erian	"Feeding Wildlife: Don't Do It!" (Brandi) "Voting Age" (Amy) "Fat Discrimination" (Carol) "No More Sugar" (Hans)	Persuasive	Clip	• Comparison of delivery methods • Persuasive speaking
Chapter 12 Cindy Gardner	"U.S. Flag Etiquette"	Informative	Clip	• Use of object as visual aid • Informative speaking
Chapter 12 Tony D'Amico	"Springtime for Musicians"	Communication analysis	Clip	• Use of a poster as visual aid
Chapter 12 Carol Godart	"Fat Discrimination"	Persuasive	Clip	• PowerPoint presentations • Persuasive speaking
Chapter 12 Chelsey Penoyer	"11 Lives a Day: Youth Suicide in America"	Informative	Clip	• PowerPoint presentations • Informative speaking
Chapter 12 Joshua Valentine	"The Dun Dun Drum"	Informative	Full	• Use of visual and audio aids • Informative speaking
Chapter 13 Rachel Rota	"Tap"	Informative	Full	• Informative speaking
Chapter 13 Chung-yan Man	"Chinese Fortune Telling"	Informative	Full	• Informative speaking
Chapter 13 Elizabeth Lopez	"The Three C's of Down Syndrome"	Informative	Full	• Informative speaking
Chapter 13 Shana Moellmer	"The African Serval"	Informative	Full	• Informative speaking
Chapter 14 Shelley Weibel	"Cloning Endangered Animals"	Invitational	Clip	• Condition of equality • Invitational speaking
Chapter 14 Melissa Carroll	"Education in Prisons"	Invitational	Clip	• Condition of self-determination • Invitational speaking
Chapter 14 Amanda Bucknam	"Funding for HIV/AIDS in Africa and the United States"	Invitational	Full	• Invitational speaking
Chapter 14 Cara Buckley-Ott	"Creationism versus the Big Bang Theory"	Invitational	Full	• Invitational speaking
Chapter 14 David Barworth	"Federal Minimum Wage"	Invitational	Full	• Invitational speaking
Chapter 14 Courtney Felton	"Four-Day School Week"	Invitational	Full	• Invitational speaking
Chapter 14 Jennifer N. Dragan	"Bilingual Education"	Invitational	Full	• Invitational speaking
Chapter 15 Courtney Stillman	"Light Pollution"	Persuasive	Clip	• Persuasive organizational patterns • Persuasive speaking
Chapter 15 Brent Erb	"Stay on Designated Hiking Trails"	Persuasive	Clip	• Immediate action (solutions) • Persuasive speaking
Chapter 15 Brandi Lafferty	"Feeding Wildlife: Don't Do It!"	Persuasive	Clip	• Causes • Persuasive speaking
Chapter 15 Dana Barker	"No Child Left Behind: Addressing the School Dropout Rate among Latinos"	Persuasive	Full	• Persuasive speaking

Sample Speech Videos (continued)

Chapter & Speaker	Speech	Speech type	Full or clip	Related topics
Chapter 15 Renee DeSalvo	"The U.S. and the World Peace Crisis"	Persuasive	Full	• Persuasive speaking
Chapter 15 Hans Erian	"No More Sugar!"	Persuasive	Full	• Persuasive speaking
Chapter 15 Maria DiMaggio	"You Have My Deepest Sympathy: You Just Won the Lottery"	Persuasive	Full	• Persuasive speaking
Chapter 15 Jessica Fuller	"Colorado Prison Reform: A Solution to Reduce Recidivism and Overcrowding"	Persuasive	Full	• Persuasive speaking
Chapter 15 Carol Godart	"Fat Discrimination"	Persuasive	Full	• Persuasive speaking
Chapter 15 Amanda Konecny	"Stop Animal Testing"	Persuasive	Full	• Persuasive speaking
Chapter 16 Tara Flanagan	"My Grandfather, John Flanagan Sr."	Commemorative	Full	• Special occasion speaking
Chapter 16 Brandon Perry	"Water"	Commemorative	Full	• Special occasion speaking

Civic Engagement and Ethical Moments Library

The following library of Civic Engagement in Action and Ethical Moment boxes is featured in the Speech Communication MindTap for *Invitation to Public Speaking*. These boxes are in addition to the Civic Engagement in Action and Ethical Moment boxes that appear in this new edition of the text.

Civic Engagement in Action Boxes

Subject	Title	Synopsis
Ishmael Beah	"A Boy Soldier Tells His Story"	Ishmael Beah's story about his experiences as a boy soldier in Sierra Leone inspires him to speak out for the rights of children around the world.
George Clooney and Don Cheadle	"In What Area of Your Life Do You Wield Influence?"	Actors use their influence to bring attention to humanitarian causes around the world.
Shauna Fleming	"A Million Thanks"	Freshman Shauna Fleming organized a massive letter-writing campaign to show appreciation for soldiers in the military.
Margaret Gibney	"I Always Believed Things Would Change"	At the age of 13, Margaret Gibney of Belfast, Ireland, wrote a letter to British Prime Minister Tony Blair to request peace. Her letter, and subsequent work for peace, caught the attention of the world's leaders.
Rodolfo "Corky" Gonzales	"Say What You Got to Say and Say It Directly"	Former boxer Corky Gonzales became a leading voice in "one of the most influential and controversial Chicano civil and humanitarian rights organizations" of the 1960s.
Aung San Suu Kyi	"To Care Is to Accept Responsibility"	After Kyi's Democratic Party wins a national election, Kyi spends 15 years under house arrest in Myanmar before she is allowed to take office.
Daniel Lubetzky	"Food for Peace"	Entrepreneur Daniel Lubetzky uses food as a vehicle for speaking out against the violence in the Middle East.
Matt Roloff	"Against Tall Odds"	Star of TLC's *Little People, Big World*, Matt Roloff raises awareness about the lives of little people in mainstream America.
Lori Weise	"To the Rescue"	Inspired by the relationship of a homeless man with his dog, Weise founded a rescue for abandoned city dogs that provides support for the homeless and their pets.
Wingspread Summit on Student Civic Engagement	"The New Student Politics"	Students assert that they can use both politics and other, nontraditional means to campaign for positive change in their communities.

Ethical Moment Boxes

Subject	Title	Synopsis
Animal Liberation Front	"How Graphic Is 'Too Graphic'?"	Do the militant actions and graphic images used by the animal rights group Animal Liberation Front go too far in persuading the public that the abuse of animals should be stopped?
Barry Bonds	"When Must We Speak?"	Barry Bonds's testimony about his use (or not) of steroids in 2003 raised the issue of what our ethical obligations are when we're required to speak.
Angelina Grimke	"Must We Listen to Others?"	In 1838, American activist Angelina Grimke broke the law to speak out about the wrongs of slavery and the importance of the vote for women.
Don Imus	"Did Don Imus Go Too Far?"	How far is too far regarding humor that makes fun of others?
Marilyn Manson	"What's in a Master Status?"	Shock rocker Marilyn Manson uses his image to challenge audiences.
The Patriot Guard Riders	"Free Speech and Reasoning"	The actions of the Westboro Baptist Church and the Patriot Guard Riders at the funerals of soldiers killed in combat raise questions about free speech and responsibility.
Cindy Sheehan	"What Are Good Reasons?"	Mother-turned-peace-activist Cindy Sheehan's participation in the public dialogue inspires praise and criticism.
Larry Summers	"What Evidence Should a Speaker Use to 'Provoke a Debate'?"	Former Harvard University president Larry Summers sparks controversy with his statements about women versus men in the fields of math and science.

Additional MindTap Study Tools

Flashcards is a classic learning tool. Digitally reimagined, Flashcards detect the chapter a student last opened, then shows cards for that chapter.

Flashnotes.com is an online marketplace full of study guides, notes, flash cards, and video help created by students, for students.

Merriam-Webster Dictionary enriches the learning experience and improves users' understanding of the English language.

Notebook Integrating Evernote technology is an app that aggregates student annotations and notes into a single consolidated view.

ReadSpeaker Text-to-speech technology offers varied reading styles and the option to select highlighted text to reinforce understanding.

NetTutor® staffed with U.S.-based tutors and facilitated by a proprietary whiteboard created for online collaboration in education.

Sharing and Collaboration

 Google Docs Instructors and students share dynamically updated text documents, spreadsheets, presentations, and PDFs.

 Inline RSS Feed Send timely, valid feeds to students—within the Learning Path or as a separate reading—with the option to add remarks.

Kaltura Simple video, audio, and image uploading tools opens a wealth of instructional, testing, and engagement opportunities.

 Web Video Easily incorporate YouTube videos as a separate viewing activity within the Learning Path or directly within a reading assignment.

 ConnectYard This MindApp social media platform fosters communication among students and teachers without the need to "friend" or "follow" or join a social network.

Additional Resources for Instructors

Instructor's Resource Manual. The Instructor's Resource Manual provides a comprehensive teaching system. The Instructor's Manual contains tips and tools, including suggested teaching goals, sample course schedules, in class activities, service learning opportunities, speaking assignments, performance evaluations, and suggestions for using technology in the classroom. Included in the manual are suggested assignments and criteria for evaluation, chapter outlines, and in-class activities. PowerPoint slides also are included.

Instructor Companion Website. The password-protected Instructor Companion Website includes Computerized Testing via Cognero®, ready-to-use PowerPoint® presentations (with texts and images that can also be customized to suit your course needs), Join In for Turning Point Clicker questions, and an electronic version of the Instructor's Manual. Visit the Instructor Website by accessing **http://login.cengage .com** or by contacting your local sales representative.

The Teaching Assistant's Guide to the Basic Course. Written by Katherine G. Hendrix, University of Memphis, this resource was prepared specifically for new instructors. Based on leading communication teacher-training programs, this guide discusses some of the general issues that accompany a teaching role and offers specific strategies for managing the first week of classes, leading productive discussions, managing sensitive topics in the classroom, and grading students' written and oral work.

Instructor Workbooks: *Public Speaking: An Online Approach, Public Speaking: A Problem-Based Learning Approach, and Public Speaking: A Service-Learning Approach for Instructors.* Written by Deanna Sellnow, University of Kentucky, these instructor workbooks include a course syllabus and icebreakers; public speaking basics such as coping with anxiety, learning cycle, and learning styles; outlining; ethics; and informative, persuasive, and ceremonial (special occasion) speeches.

***Teaching the Invitational Speech Resource Guide* and Accompanying Video and DVD.** This resource, featuring an introduction by author Cindy L. Griffin, shows you how to effectively teach the invitational speech to your students.

Cengage Communication Video and DVD Library. Cengage's video and DVD series for Speech Communication includes Student Speeches for Critique and Analysis as well as Communication Scenarios for Critique and Analysis.

Videos for Speech Communication 2016: Public Speaking, Human Communication, and Interpersonal Communication. These videos provide footage of news stories from BBC and CBS that relate to current topics in communication, such as teamwork and how to interview for jobs, as well as news clips about speaking anxiety and speeches from contemporary public speakers, such as Michelle Obama and Hillary Clinton.

ABC News DVD: Speeches by Barack Obama. This DVD includes nine famous speeches by President Barack Obama, from 2004 to present day, including his speech at the 2004 Democratic National Convention; his 2008 speech on race, "A More Perfect Union"; and his 2009 inaugural address. Speeches are divided into short video segments for easy, time-efficient viewing. This instructor supplement also features critical thinking questions and answers for each speech, designed to spark class discussion.

Guide to Teaching Public Speaking Online. Written by Todd Brand of Meridian Community College, this helpful online guide provides instructors who teach public speaking online with tips for establishing "classroom" norms with students, utilizing course management software and other eResources, managing logistics such as delivering and submitting speeches and making up work, discussing how peer feedback is different online, strategies for assessment, and tools such as sample syllabi and critique and evaluation forms tailored to the online course.

Service Learning in Communication Studies: A Handbook. Written by Rick Isaacson and Jeff Saperstein, this is an invaluable resource for students in the basic course that integrates or will soon integrate a service learning component. This handbook provides guidelines for connecting service learning work with classroom concepts and advice for working effectively with agencies and organizations. It also provides model forms and reports and a directory of online resources.

Digital Course Support. Get trained, get connected, and get the support you need for the seamless integration of digital resources into your course. This unparalleled technology service and training program provides robust online resources, peer-to-peer instruction, personalized training, and a customizable program you can count on. **Visit http://www.cengage.com/dcs/** to sign up for online seminars, first days of class services, technical support, or personalized, face-to-face training. Our online and onsite trainings are frequently led by one of our Lead Teachers, faculty members who are experts in using Cengage Learning technology and can provide best practices and teaching tips.

Custom Chapters for *Invitation to Public Speaking.* Customize your chapter coverage with bonus chapters on impromptu speaking, civic engagement, and service learning. You can access these chapters online within the Instructor Website, or you can order print versions of the student text that include the extra chapter of your choice. Contact your local sales representative for ordering details.

Flex-Text Customization Program. With this program you can create a text as unique as your course—quickly, simply, and affordably. As part of our flex-text program, you can add your personal touch to *Invitation to Public Speaking* with a course-specific cover and up to 32 pages of your own content—at no additional cost.

Cengage Learning Testing, powered by Cognero. Accessible through **cengage. com/login** with your faculty account, this test bank contains multiple-choice, true/false, and essay questions for each chapter. Cognero is a flexible, online system that allows you to author, edit, and manage test bank content. Create multiple test versions instantly and deliver through your LMS platform from wherever you may be. Cognero is compatible with Blackboard, Angel, Moodle, and Canvas LMS platform.

Acknowledgments

I believe writing and scholarship are both individual and collaborative efforts. Acknowledging the individuals who assisted me throughout the process of writing this book is one small way of recognizing that collaboration and thanking those who offered invaluable assistance and endless support. To Monica Eckman, product director; and Greer Lleuad, senior content developer, two key individuals in the early stages of this project, I express my deepest and heartfelt appreciation. For their invitation to embark on this journey, their incredible vision and talent, their endless guidance, support, kindness, and laughter, I am honored and grateful. My writing process and life are richer because of the two of them. To Kelli Strieby, product manager; Daniel Saabye, senior content production manager; Janine Tangney, managing content developer; Leslie Taggart, senior content developer; Lisa Moore, content developer; Erin Bosco, associate content developer; Sarah Seymour, marketing manager; Ann Hoffman, IP (Intellectual Property) rights analyst; Kathy Kucharek, IP (Intellectual Property) project manager; Marissa Falco, senior art director; and Ed Dionne, our compositor, I express my sincerest thanks. These amazing people shared their talents, time, and energy, enhancing the book every step of the way. They also generously offered insight, wisdom, and expertise in response to my never-ending requests and questions.

To Dr. T. M. Linda Scholz, associate professor at Eastern Illinois University, and Dr. Jennifer Emerling Bone, Instructor of Communication, Leeds School of Business, University of Colorado; friends in every way and collaborators on various aspects during various stages of this book, I am forever indebted. Their excellent ideas and insights, love and support, steady stream of laughter, smiles, and hugs, and willingness to test out the early versions of this book in their own classes are acts of courage and connection that never went unnoticed or unappreciated. The speeches of their students grace the chapters of this book, which reflect not only the talents of those students but also the extraordinary skill Linda and Jennifer possess as teachers. I am lucky to have them in my life.

To Kristen Slattery, Matt Petrunia, Anne Trump Evans, and Beth Bonnstetter, lecturers and former graduate students at Colorado State University, many, many thanks. Their hours and hours in the library, on the Internet, and in my office assisting me with research in the early stages of the life of this book are invaluable. Working with the four of them gave me confidence and the assurance that the ideas in this book are supported by the very best of scholarship, both historical and contemporary.

Many thanks to all the reviewers of this sixth edition and also to those who reviewed the fifth edition. Their feedback and support of this book have been invaluable. They are Sharon Askew, Halifax Community College; Karl Babij, DeSales University; Constance Berman, Berkshire Community College; Ellen Bland, Central Carolina Community College; Kendra Bolen, Mountwest Community College; Ferald Bryan, Northern Illinois University; Tim Chandler, Hardin-Simmons University; Linda Crumley, Southern Adventist University; David J. Eshelman, Arkansas Tech University; Gina Firenzi, San Jose State University; Tonya Forsythe, Ohio State University; Patrick Gagliano, Newberry College; Gary Graupman, Taft College; Larry Haapanen, Lewis-Clark State College; Patricia Hill, University of Akron; Shaorong Huang, University of Cincinnati, Blue Ash College; Dejun Liu, Prairie View A&M University; Laurie Metcalf, Blinn College; Laura Morrison, College of the Albemarle; Daryle Nagano, Los Angeles Harbor College; Rasha Ramzy, Georgia State University; Tiffany Sarkisian Rodriquez, California State University, Fresno; Nedra Shamberger, Ocean County College; Kim Smith, Bishop State Community College.

And a warm thank you to all the reviewers, focus group participants, and class testers of the first, second, third, fourth, fifth, and sixth editions who are too numerous to list here.

Thanks also to former and current Colorado State University faculty, lecturers, graduate students, and special-appointment faculty Cara Buckley, Kathleen Creamer, Erin Cunningham, Ian Dawe, Brian DeVeney, Tomas Dunn, Savannah Downing, Alicia Ernest, Holly Gates, Katie Gibson, Jeremy Grossman, Bill Herman, Jeffery Ho, Lori Irwin, Keli Larson, Derek Lewis, Jill Lippman Mellott, Katheryn Maguire, Jeremy Mellott, Kaile McMonogal, Beth Myers-Bass, Sonja Hollingsworth, Kirsten Pullen, Raena Quinlivan, Virginia Ramos, Sabrina Slagowski-Tipton, Mark Saunders, Heather Landers, Allison Searle, Elizabeth Sink, Jamie Skerski, Kristin Slattery, Jessie Stewart, Derek Sweet, Elizabeth Terry, Elisa Varela, Toni-Lee Viney, and Elizabeth Williams, who at various times (and sometimes without even realizing it) shared speech ideas, outlines, assignments, and stories that add to the depth and strength of this project.

Many thanks also to their students, whose speeches are found in pages of this text. And a very special thanks to Mary Triece of the University of Akron, not only for her invaluable class-test feedback but also for so graciously providing us with the speeches of some of her students, which are also incorporated throughout this text.

And, finally, a sincere thank you to my public speaking students and to the students from other parts of the country whose voices enhance this text, for their creativity, flexibility, and talents.

Without a doubt, the strongest collaborative force in my life comes from my family. My husband, Mike Harte; my son, Joseph Griffin-Harte, and my daughter-in-law, Kari Griffin-Harte; my sisters, Tracy Zerr and Wendy Stewart; my brother, John Griffin; and my extended family, Jana Webster-Wheeler, Scott Wheeler, and Joseph and Marissa Wheeler keep strong and steady the flame that fuels my energy. Their unending love and support have enriched this project and reminded me daily that the public dialogue is enhanced by our willingness to listen to others and by our commitment to speak as clearly and honestly as possible. To them, I offer my love and thanks, and the acknowledgment that their care for me gives me great strength and peace.

—*Cindy L. Griffin*

Quick-Start Guide

Ten Steps to Entering the Public Dialogue

Whether your speaking goal is to inform, invite, persuade, speak to a small group, or give a special occasion speech, you can use these ten steps for giving speeches as a guide and helpful tool as you prepare your presentations.

STEP 1

Determine your topic and your purpose (or reason) for speaking.

Do you want to know more about something (a political issue, an event in history, a person, place, or thing)? Are you actively involved in something (an art or skill, a club or group, a blog or message board)? Select a topic of public relevance based on your interests or skills, or sit with paper and pen or at a computer and **brainstorm (Chapter 3)** ideas you can link to the public dialogue.

After you've chosen your topic, consider whether your **general purpose** might be to invite, inform, persuade, or entertain your audience. Then determine your **specific purpose (Chapter 3)**. A *specific purpose* presents your exact goals and helps you refine your topic as you move forward with your speech. Identify your specific purpose in your **thesis statement (Chapter 3)**. Your thesis statement allows you to state, in a single sentence, the content of your speech, including the main idea of your speech and your main points.

Example:
Here's how Missy expressed her specific purpose and thesis statement for her speech "The Mysterious World of Hiccups":

Topic:
Hiccups

General purpose:
To inform

Specific purpose:
To inform my audience of the "anatomy" of a hiccup.

Thesis statement:
Hiccups, or involuntary spasms of the diaphragm, are most often caused by food, beverages, and medicines but can be cured easily with a few simple techniques.

Crafting your specific purpose and a fully developed thesis statement at the beginning of the speechmaking process provides you with a specific and focused plan for your speech.

STEP 2

Analyze your audience.

As a speaker you always want to stay **audience-centered** and ethical **(Chapter 4)**. Because your audience will be composed of diverse individuals, you want to consider their perspectives carefully. Analyze your audience by asking yourself these questions:

- Who is my audience?
- What are their interests, views, and experiences?
- Why would my audience be interested in this topic?
- How do they feel about this topic?
- What previous experience might they have with the topic?

The audience is your reason for speaking, so you must consider them in each step of your speech preparation process.

STEP 3

Identify your main points.

Your **main points** should reflect your **thesis statement (Chapters 3 and 7),** and they are the most important **claims**, arguments, or concepts in your speech **(Chapter 6)**.

Example:
For example, in Missy's speech about hiccups, she used her specific purpose and thesis statement to develop the following main points:

I. Hiccups are involuntary spasms of the diaphragm that cause the space between the vocal cords to close suddenly and make a peculiar sound.

II. Hiccups are most often caused by the foods we eat, the beverages we drink, and the medicines we ingest.

III. Mild cases of hiccups can be cured with a few simple techniques.

She identified these main points by breaking her thesis down into her primary ideas (definition of hiccups, causes of hiccups, cures for hiccups) and asking herself how she could elaborate on those ideas.

STEP 4

Gather your supporting materials.

As you gather **supporting materials** from the library, Internet, interviews, and personal experiences **(Chapter 5)**, look for the following types of information so that you can develop your ideas ethically and effectively **(Chapter 6)**.

Examples:
Specific instances used to illustrate a concept, experience, issue, or problem.

Helpful hint: *Examples help you clarify a point or argument, specify the nature of something, or support your explanation.*

Narratives:
Stories that recount real or fictional events.

Helpful hint: *The characters, events, and settings of narratives can help draw an audience into your speech, and can illustrate, develop, or clarify a claim you are making. Narratives can be very short or longer, and they can be told in segments over the course of the speech or told at one interval.*

Statistics:
Numerical summaries of facts, figures, and research findings.

Helpful hint: *Statistics numerically quantify, estimate, measure, and represent events, issues, positions, actions, beliefs, and the like.*

Testimony:
The opinions or observations of others.

Helpful hint: *Testimony, often in the form of quotations, can come from an authority, an average person who has relevant experience with your topic, or from your own experiences.*

Definitions:

Statement of the exact meaning of a word or phrase.

Helpful hint: Definitions help clarify claims and ideas, especially when new terminology is introduced or when a topic is controversial or emotional.

STEP 5

Organize your ideas.

You are now ready to **organize your speech (Chapter 7)**. The three most basic components of almost every speech are the introduction, body, and conclusion.

Start with the **introduction** of the speech **(Chapter 8)**. Introductions set the stage for a speech and should accomplish four objectives:

- Introduce you and your topic to the audience.
- Capture the audience's attention and get them interested in or curious about your topic.
- Establish your credibility.
- Preview the main ideas of the speech.

Example:

In her speech on hiccups, Missy followed these four principles to come up with the following introduction:

I'm here today to share information about one of life's great mysteries. No, I'm not referring to Stonehenge or the Great Pyramids, but to something everyone in this room has experienced: hiccups! Yes, I'm talking about the mysterious world of hiccups, which seem to be a universal occurrence *(introduces topic)*. However, although this mystery is universal, hiccups appear to serve no physiologic function *(catches interest)*.

I recently was blessed with an overwhelming occurrence of the hiccups, and this sparked my interest and curiosity in the subject *(establishes credibility)*. This "blessing" caused me to do some research and investigation, during which I discovered some interesting information about hiccups *(establishes credibility)*. I would like to share this information with you today. Specifically, my focus will be on three aspects of hiccups that I find especially informative. First, I'll explain the anatomy of a hiccup, or what a hiccup is and how it occurs. Second, I'll explain the three most common causes of hiccups, which are food, beverages, and medicine. Third, I'll share some simple techniques for curing those milder cases of hiccups *(previews main points)*.

The **body** of the speech **(Chapter 7)** is the longest part of a speech and contains the information you have gathered to develop your main ideas. There are many ways to organize your main ideas. Remember, your main ideas should follow a systematic, logical, or natural progression that supports and develops your thesis statement. The most common **organizational patterns (Chapters 12, 13, and 15)** are chronological, spatial, causal, problem-and-solution, and topical. There are two basic rules you can follow to organize your ideas:

Rule 1:

Identify your main ideas and arrange them according to (1) which ideas must be discussed before others and (2) which ideas will most interest the audience.

Rule 2:

Link your ideas together with words and phrases called **connectives (Chapter 7)** that help you transition, introduce, preview, or call attention to your main points.

The **conclusion** of a speech **(Chapter 8)** brings closure to your ideas, and it is often the shortest part of your speech. In your conclusion, you want to accomplish two things:

- Signal to the audience that you are finished.
- Summarize or restate your thesis statement.

Example:

Let's take a look at the conclusion to Missy's speech:

So, now you see that there is more to learn about the mysterious world of hiccups than you might have imagined. In this speech, I've shared some very enlightening information about what a hiccup is, the reasons hiccups occur, and the process of curing them *(signals end of speech)*. Now, if someday you find yourself in the mysterious world of hiccups, you'll be well prepared to fight back with several of the remedies you've heard about today *(summarizes thesis)*.

STEP 6

Outline your speech.

Preparing your **outline (Chapter 7)** can help you organize your ideas, discover missing points or arguments, and determine whether the speech is balanced and within your time limits. Your outline should include:

- Speech title.
- Specific purpose.
- Thesis statement.
- Clear labels for introduction, body, connectives, and conclusion.
- Consistent pattern of symbols and indentation (roman numerals for main points, capital letters for subpoints, Arabic numerals for sub-subpoints, and lowercase letters for sub-sub-subpoints: I, A, 1, a).
- At least two supporting subpoints under a main point.
- Approximately equal development of points and subpoints.
- Source citations listed in a Works Cited section.

See **Chapter 7, pages 146–148**, for an example of an effective **preparation outline**.

Speakers also often create a speaking outline (a shorter version of their preparation outline) to use when they deliver their speeches. A speaking outline (or note cards) is a condensed version of the preparation outline and includes the following:

- Keywords and phrases only—not the full text of your speech
- Clear, legible, and large font or handwriting
- Cues for delivery, such as "make eye contact," "pause," "slow down," "look up," "show visual aid"
- Correct pronunciation of words or names you stumble on
- One- or two-word prompts for stories, examples, and concepts you tend to forget

See **Chapter 7, pages 152–153**, for an example of note cards and a **speaking outline**.

STEP 7

Create visual and other presentational aids.

Presentational aids (Chapter 11) can take many shapes and forms, including images, lists of ideas, diagrams, objects or models, and charts or maps. They help you gain and maintain audience attention, explain and clarify ideas, increase your persuasiveness, and enhance your credibility. They can also help reduce your nervousness. Here are some tips to help you decide what kind of presentational aid to use for different types of information:

- For a series of names, key features, or procedures, use a *list*.
- For steps in a process, use a *flow chart, model, or Internet download*.
- For the structure of a group, use an *organizational chart*.
- For comparison of quantities at a specific time, use a *bar graph*.
- For trends over time, use a *line graph*.
- For relative sizes of parts of a whole, use a *pie graph*.
- For comparison of quantities, use a *picture graph or model*.
- For the physical layout of a place, use a *map*.

STEP 8
Consider language and figures of speech.

Because you will probably use different styles of speaking for different audiences and different speaking goals **(Chapter 9)**, ask yourself the following questions as you select the language style for your speech:

- What types of vocabulary, imagery, and rhythms best match my audience, topic, and goals?
- Have I included vocabulary, imagery, and rhythms that draw my audience into my speech and help me express my ideas vividly and appropriately?
- Do any of the vocabulary, imagery, and rhythms have the potential to offend, hurt, or alienate my listeners?
- What vocabulary needs to be defined, explained, or illustrated by examples?
- Am I speaking at a level appropriate for my audience?
- Have I omitted slang, euphemisms, or other unfamiliar or inappropriate words and phrases?
- Have I paraphrased confusing or highly technical terms and phrases?

STEP 9
Practice your speech.

Always **practice your speech** before you deliver it **(Chapter 10)**. So that you'll be very familiar with your speech before you give it in front of an audience, follow these steps:

- Begin your practice sessions alone. *At first, practice only segments of your speech.* For example, try getting the introduction down,

then the body, and then the conclusion. You may even find it useful to break down the body by practicing each main point separately.

- *Make notes on your speaking outline* to help you remember your material and delivery techniques. If you plan to use presentational aids, practice using them until you can manage them easily as you speak.
- Once you've practiced each segment of your speech individually, *practice the speech as a whole*. Try practicing in front of a mirror. Go back and *rehearse the places where you stumble* or get lost. Make sure your presentational aids work as planned.
- Before you give your speech, *practice it three to six times from start to finish*, depending on the level of spontaneity or polish you want in your speech.
- Finally, *practice your speech in front of an audience*. Rehearsing your speech in front of your family or friends is a great way to gain some practice and get feedback on your presentation.

STEP 10
Give your speech.

The final step in the speechmaking process is a reminder to relax and give your speech with confidence **(Chapter 10)**. Here are some guidelines for managing your voice, gestures, posture, facial expressions, and presentational aids as you give your speech:

- Visualize a successful speech before you deliver it.
- Know your introduction well so you can begin your speech feeling confident.
- Use your notes as prompts and as a source of security.
- Make eye contact with audience members during the speech.
- Remember to breathe, gesture naturally, and pause as needed during your speech.

Final Hints

If you take the time to select a relevant topic, gather your supporting materials, and organize your speech, you can minimize some of the nervousness that most people feel with public speaking. The more you practice, the more confident you will feel on your speaking day. And if you **listen respectfully** to the speeches of your classmates, they probably will listen respectfully to you **(Chapter 2)**.

Good luck, and have fun!

1 | Why Speak in Public?

- Identify the influence of culture on speaking styles

- Differentiate between public speaking and other kinds of communication

- Discuss the most common reasons for nervousness associated with giving a speech

- Summarize the six techniques for reducing speech-related nervousness

IN THIS CHAPTER, YOU WILL LEARN TO:

- Describe civility and explain its relationship to the public dialogue

- Summarize the power of ethical public speaking

H ave you ever been moved by the words of a public speaker? If so, you are not alone. Most of us have left at least one public speech or lecture feeling different about the world, about the issues that concern us, and even about ourselves.

MindTap Start with a quick warm-up activity and review the chapter's learning objectives.

Tom Merton/Caiaimage/Getty Images

▲ When we enter the public dialogue we engage others in a conversation about issues and ideas that are important to us. In this chapter, you will be introduced to the public dialogue, ways to stay ethical, and techniques for building your confidence as a public speaker.

This book is designed to get you started as a public speaker. It will help you successfully and ethically add your voice to the many public conversations and debates of our democratic society. In these pages, you will learn about a range of settings where public speaking occurs and a variety of reasons for speaking. The chapters that follow break down the components of the public speaking process into discrete steps, which you will follow in crafting your own speeches. As you gain confidence in using these techniques, you can adapt them to your real-life speaking experiences at work and in your community. You'll find that you will speak in any number of instances to provide instructions, explain procedures, share information, encourage or influence decisions, and more.

Public speaking is a learned skill that gets more rewarding as our experience with it grows. No one was born a public speaker. Every speaker had to learn how to give effective speeches—even renowned speakers such as Abraham Lincoln, Martin Luther King Jr., Michelle Obama, and the many others you will read about in this text. The more you practice this new skill, the more quickly you will feel you are a competent speaker. With care and diligence, you will find that you can add your own voice to the public dialogue in positive ways.

This chapter introduces you to the power of ethical public speaking and the differences between public speaking and other forms of communication. It invites you to consider the opportunities you will have to speak publicly and to recognize the importance of learning the basic skills necessary to do so successfully and effectively. When we consider the power these actions have to shape lives, we begin to gain a sense of the challenges, responsibilities, and thoughtfulness that go into designing, delivering, and listening to effective public speeches.

Even skilled speakers like President Barack Obama had to learn how to give effective speeches. Here, the president speaks at his inauguration on January 20, 2013, an event that affected the entire nation. Even if you didn't hear his speech, do you think you have been influenced by it? In what way?

Justin Sullivan/Getty Images News/Getty Images

MindTap®

Read, highlight, and take notes online.

civility: Care and concern for others, the thoughtful use of words and language, and the flexibility to see the many sides of an issue.

The Power of Ethical Public Speaking

When you speak publicly, you have the power to influence others. With every speech you give, you make choices about the kind of influence you will have. All of us are familiar with hostile public arguments and debates. We are used to politicians taking partisan stances on issues and "doing battle" with their "opponents." Such debates turn social policy questions into "wars" as groups position themselves on either side of the "dispute," offering "the solution" while negating the views of the "other" side. We even watch, read about, or listen to people engaging in hostile or threatening exchanges over their differences.

Angry opposition may be a common style of public speaking today, but there are other ways to influence people when you give speeches. As you've watched and listened to combative exchanges, you may have heard some call for more civility in public exchanges. The word *civility* comes from a root word meaning "to be a member of a household." In ancient Greece, *civility* referred to displays of temperance, justice, wisdom, and courage. Over time, the definition has changed only slightly, and in public speaking, **civility** has come to mean care and concern for others, the thoughtful use of words and language, and the flexibility to see the many sides of an issue. To be civil is to listen to the ideas and reasons of others and to give "the world a chance to explain itself."[1] To be uncivil is to show little

TOP TEN SKILLS EMPLOYERS SEEK

The Association of American Colleges & Universities reports that it is not your major, necessarily, that increases your chances at getting a great job, but, rather, obtaining the skills necessary to perform well in our dynamic and ever changing workplaces. To assist college students, the Association publishes its "Top Ten Things Employers Look for in New College Graduates." You might be surprised at how central communication and public speaking are to this list.

The "Top Ten" list includes the following: (1) clear and appropriate communication; (2) working well in teams; (3) writing and speaking well; (4) thinking clearly about complex problems; (5) analyzing problems and developing solutions; (6) understanding our current global environment; (7) creativity and innovation; (8) applying skills in new settings; (9) understanding numbers and statistics; and (10) strong ethics and integrity.

As this list suggests, employers are seeking what are called "soft skills" and employees with soft skills are excellent communicators: they work well in teams as well as on their own; they are able to be flexible in a wide range of situations and circumstances; they are strong critical thinkers and seek to understand diverse perspectives; and, finally, they are creative and able to engage in effective interactions with other people, whether face-to-face, in writing, or giving a speech.

Fortunately, this book breaks down these skills for you so that you can appreciate and acquire them. You can use your new understanding of what communication is and the processes involved in communicating effectively with others to assist you not only in securing a job, but keeping it and performing well.

---

respect for others, to be unwilling to consider their ideas and reasons, and to be unwilling to take responsibility for the effect of one's words, language, and behaviors on others.

Deborah Tannen, author of *The Argument Culture: Moving from Debate to Dialogue,* offers a compelling description of many people's views about the incivility that characterizes much of our present-day public debates.[2] She explains that in an argument culture, individuals tend to approach people and situations with a me-against-you frame of mind. Because they see each issue, event, or situation as a contest, they begin with the idea that the best way to discuss any topic is by portraying it through opposing positions, rallying to one side of the cause, and attacking the other side. Although conflict and disagreement are familiar parts of most people's lives, the seemingly automatic nature of this response is what makes the argument culture so common today.

Tannen and others concerned with the argument culture recognize that there are times when strong opposition and verbal attack are called for.[3] Nevertheless, this form of communication isn't the only way people can discuss issues, offer solutions, or resolve differences. We can view public speaking not only as engaging in a public argument but also as participating in a public dialogue.

A dialogue is a civil exchange of ideas and opinions between two people or a small group of people. The **public dialogue** is the ethical and civil exchange of ideas and opinions among communities about topics that affect the public. To participate in the public dialogue is to offer perspectives, share facts, raise questions, and engage others publicly in stimulating discussions.[4] When we enter the public dialogue, we become active and ethical citizens who participate in our nation's democratic process, and consider the needs of others in our communities as well as our own needs. The ethical dimension of our participation in the public dialogue becomes apparent when we participate in the global dialogue, speaking about issues that affect the entire world, such as human rights, hunger, access to medical care, and the environment. To be an **ethical public speaker**, you must consider the moral impact of your ideas and arguments on others when you enter the public dialogue.

Giving a speech is a natural way to enter the public dialogue because it gives us a chance to clearly state our own perspectives and to hear other people's perspectives.

public dialogue: Ethical and civil exchange of ideas and opinions among communities about topics that affect the public.

ethical public speaker: Speaker who considers the moral impact of his or her ideas and arguments on others when involved in the public dialogue.

Many reform efforts proposed by the U.S. government have been a matter of public debate recently, such as proposals to reform health care, immigration laws, and the financial system. These complex, far-reaching efforts have sparked passionate and sometimes contentious dialogue. How difficult do you think it would be to respond civilly to an audience that doesn't seem open to your topic? What could you do to make your audience receptive to your views?

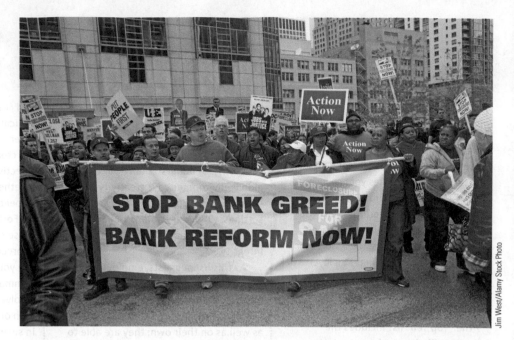

Jim West/Alamy Stock Photo

Practicing the Public Dialogue | 1.1

CHOOSE A CIVIL, ETHICAL APPROACH TO PUBLIC SPEAKING

Make a list of five topics you might use for a speech in this class. How does each topic contribute to the public dialogue? Now identify how you might discuss each of these topics in a civil, ethical way. For example, would it be more ethical to approach one of your topics from a two-sided perspective and another from a multisided perspective? Why do you think so? Save these as possible topics for your in-class speeches.

MindTap

Learn more about what the public dialogue is and how your participation in this unending conversation can help shape your community.

In this sense, giving a speech can be like participating in an ongoing conversation. Kenneth Burke describes this conversation as follows:

> Imagine that you enter a parlor. You come late. When you arrive, others have long preceded you, and they are engaged in a lively discussion, a discussion too passionate for them to pause and tell you exactly what it is about. In fact, the discussion had already begun long before any of them got there, so that no one present is qualified to retrace for you all the steps that had gone before. You listen for a while, until you decide that you have caught the tenor of the argument; then you put in your oar. Someone answers; you answer them; another perspective is shared. The hour grows late; you must depart. And you do depart, with the discussion still vigorously in progress.[5]

Throughout this book, you will encounter the power of civil and ethical public speaking. As you engage with this power yourself, you should always strive to give speeches that help clarify issues and stimulate thinking even as you inform, persuade, or invite others to consider a perspective. Although you may have strong views on issues, a civil and ethical approach to public speaking often is the most productive way to present those views.

Culture and Speaking Style

Culture often has a significant effect on communication. Whether culture derives from our nationality, race, ethnicity, religion, work environment, peer group, or even gender, we cannot ignore its influence on our communication with other people. When we give or listen to speeches, we bring our cultural norms and styles with us. Consider a few examples of ways that culture influences public speaking:

> The traditional West African storyteller, called the *griot*, weaves a story with song and dance, and enlivens a tale with all sorts of sound effects. He or she changes the pitch to suit the characters and the action and adds all kinds of popping, clicking, clapping sounds to dramatize the events of the story. The members of the audience respond like a chorus. They interpose comments at convenient intervals, add their own sound effects, and sing the song of the tale along with the griot.[6]

To this day, poets are held in the highest esteem in Arab societies. The Arab poet performs important political and social functions. In battle, the poet's tongue is as effective as is the bravery of the Arab people. In peace, the poet might prove a menace to public order with fiery harangues. Poems can arouse a tribe to action in the same manner as the tirade of a demagogue in a modern political campaign. Poetry frequently functions in a political context to motivate action, and, as such, it is accorded as much weight as a scholarly dissertation.[7]

The late Texas governor Ann Richards's speaking style [was] dominated by the use of inductive and experiential reasoning, folk wisdom, and concrete examples and stories as the basis for political values and judgments. A favorite line she often use[d] [was], "Tell it so my Mama in Waco can understand it." Her accessible style . . . encourage[d] audience participation and reduce[d] distance between the speaker and audience.[8]

These examples come from cultures that may be different from your own or may be familiar to you. What they suggest is that the ways we approach a public speech often reflect our cultural backgrounds.

Research on cultural styles of communication helps explain some of these differences. In general, many white males, for example, are comfortable with the direct, competitive style of interaction found in public presentations. Because white males have held more public offices and positions of power in the United States historically, it makes sense that their preferred style of communication has become the norm for public speaking. However, there are many other communication styles. African American men, for example, tend to be more comfortable with a complex style of speaking that may be competitive but is more subtle, indirect or exaggerated, intense, poetic, rhythmic, and lyrical. Hispanic or Latino males usually reject the competitive style, favoring a more elegant, expressive, or intense narrative form of public communication. Similarly, Arab American males tend to use an emotional and poetic style (poets often respond to and interpret political events in Middle Eastern countries and rely on rhythm and the sounds of words to express their ideas).[9]

Other research suggests that in most Native American cultures, framing an issue from a two-sided perspective is rare. Many Native American cultures welcome multiple perspectives and discourage competition, preferring cooperation when discussing important matters. In addition, a more circular and flexible style of presentation is common, as is the use of stories, humor, and teasing to explain ideas or teach beliefs. In many Native American cultures as well as some Asian and Asian American cultures, direct eye contact is a sign of disrespect, and publicly proving that someone else is wrong is considered a serious insult.[10]

The research on styles of speaking specific to women is slight. We do know that, in general, African American and Hispanic or Latina women may use a style of speech

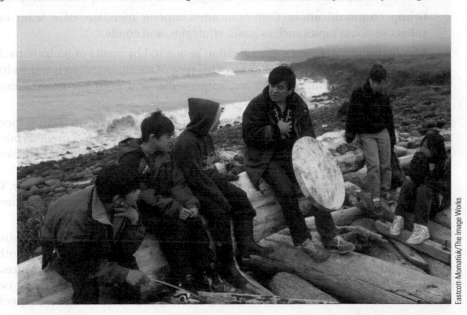

Eastcott-Momatiuk/The Image Works

The elder is a well-respected storyteller in Native American culture. Is storytelling a style of speaking familiar to you? What style, or combinations of styles, of speaking do you think you'd like to use in a speech?

similar to the lyrical, rhythmic, or poetic style used by the males of their cultures, but it may be more collaborative than adversarial. White and Asian American women seem to share this sense of comfort with collaboration but do not often incorporate the poetic or lyrical forms into their speaking. In general, we also know that women from many different cultural backgrounds tend to incorporate a personal tone and use personal experiences and anecdotes alongside concrete examples as evidence; they establish a connection and common ground with their audiences in their public speeches.[11]

In reading about these differences, you may have recognized your own culture's influence on your style of communication. These differences suggest there is more than one way to approach public speaking. Public speaking can occur when we argue with others or take sides on an issue. It can take place when we connect, collaborate, and share stories or humor with our audience. It also happens when speakers use various styles of language or delivery. To enter the public dialogue is to recognize the many different styles of speaking and to use those that fit you and the audience best.

So much of our time is spent communicating with others that we often forget to consider what it takes to be a good communicator. This class will help you learn important communication skills that you can use as you speak publicly and with your friends.

intrapersonal communication: Communication with ourselves via the dialogue that goes on in our heads.

interpersonal communication: Communication with other people that ranges from the highly personal to the highly impersonal.

group communication: Communication among members of a team or a collective about topics such as goals, strategies, and conflict.

mass communication: Communication generated by media organizations that is designed to reach large audiences.

public communication: Communication in which one person gives a speech to other people, most often in a public setting.

What Is Ethical Public Speaking?

Every day, we are bombarded with information from computers, televisions, radios, newspapers, magazines, movies, billboards, and even logos on clothing and cars. Bosses, teachers, friends, and family also fill our days with words, sounds, symbols, and conversations. Researchers estimate that we spend as much as 70 to 80 percent of the day listening to others communicate. In fact, so much communication crosses our paths every day that this era has been called the *information* age. Where does public speaking fit into this environment? Consider the following sources of communication in which we can engage:

Intrapersonal communication: Communication with ourselves via the dialogue that goes on in our heads.

Interpersonal communication: Communication with other people that ranges from the highly personal to the highly impersonal. Interpersonal communication allows us to establish, maintain, and disengage from relationships with other people.

Group communication: Communication among members of a team or a collective about topics such as goals, strategies, and conflict.

Mass communication: Communication generated by media organizations that is designed to reach large audiences. This type of communication is transmitted via television, the Internet, radio, print media, and even the entertainment industry.

Public communication: Communication in which one person gives a speech to other people, most often in a public setting. This speech has predetermined goals and is about a topic that affects a larger community. In public speaking, one person—called the speaker—is responsible for selecting a topic and focus for the speech, organizing his or her ideas, and practicing his or her delivery. The *speaker* is also responsible for acting ethically and for responding to audience questions and feedback.

Unlike casual conversations with friends and family, public speaking contains a structure and purpose that add a level of responsibility not found in most other everyday interactions. Similarly, the ability of the audience to respond directly sets public speaking apart from mass communication. And unlike private conversations with oneself or with friends, public speaking is directed at specific groups of people and is designed to be shared with those outside the immediate audience.

From these definitions, we can see that public speaking is unique because the responsibility for the organization, delivery, and flow of communication falls mostly on one person. However, if we think of public speaking as participating ethically in the public dialogue, additional differences between public speaking and other forms of communication emerge.

Public Speaking Creates a Community

We often think of public speaking as an individual act. We imagine one person standing in front of a group of people presenting information to them. We forget that public speaking occurs because individuals belong to a community and share social relationships. We speak publicly because we recognize this connection. When we share ideas and information ethically and consider questions and possibilities with others, we are creating a civil community. We recognize we are "members of a household," and even if we disagree with members of that household (our audience), we acknowledge that we are connected to them. We create a community when we speak because we are talking about topics that affect us and each member of the audience.

At times, we may forget our connections to others and think our interests and needs are not important to society. However, we are members of a larger social community, and when we make our voices heard, we recognize the need to stimulate the public dialogue, to answer the claims or statements of those who have spoken before us, and to offer our audience ideas for consideration and discussion.

Public Speaking Is Audience Centered

Public speaking also stands apart from other forms of communication because speakers recognize the central role of their audience. Speakers speak to audiences, and without them, we are not engaged in public speaking. Moreover, in public speaking, the makeup of the audience directly influences the speaker's message. Consider the following scenarios:

> Su Lin's older brother was recently almost hit by a car while riding his bike across town. Upset by motorists' lack of awareness, Su Lin wants to speak out at the next city council meeting to argue for motorist education programs.

> Gretchen's brother recently had a near miss while riding his bike across town. Upset by motorists' lack of awareness, Gretchen has decided to give a speech on motorist safety in her public speaking course.

> Arturo rides his bicycle to work every day and has persuaded many of his coworkers to do the same. He recently had a near miss with a distracted motorist, and he wants to speak to his coworkers about what they can do to stay safe while riding to work.

The audiences in these three scenarios dictate the choices each speaker will make. Each of the audiences—the city council, the public speaking class, and the other cyclists—has different positions, beliefs, values, and needs regarding cyclist safety. City councils have financial limitations, time constraints, and voter preferences that Su Lin will need to consider. Gretchen's classmates, unless they are cyclists, may not readily see the relevance of her concerns and may also resent any efforts to curb their driving habits. At Arturo's workplace, the other cyclists probably also worry about their own vulnerability and wonder whether riding to work is really worth the risk.

These three examples suggest that public speaking is distinctly **audience centered**, or considerate of the positions, beliefs, values, and needs of an audience. To be audience centered is to keep your audience in your mind during every step of the public speaking process, including your research, organization, and presentation.

Public speaking is also audience centered because speakers "listen" to their audiences during speeches. They monitor audience *feedback*, the verbal and nonverbal

audience centered: Considerate of the positions, beliefs, values, and needs of an audience.

The Great Conversation

Thomas Taha Rassam Culhane: Explorer, Urban Planner

Mark Thiessen/National Geographic Creative

"We're taught that garbage is garbage," states Thomas Taha Rassam Culhane, Urban Planner and Explorer-in-Residence for the National Geographic, but is it really? Cairo's Zabaleen people (literally, "garbage people") "view everything around them as useful for something." Culhane's work with the Zabaleen people began when he watched mothers carry buckets back and forth, and up and down stairs, for seven hours just to secure water for their families. Wanting to understand firsthand what these families faced, Culhane and his wife moved into the poorest of neighborhoods in Cairo to experience the obstacles they faced. Culhane founded Solar C³.I.T.I.E.S.* and worked with residents of the poorest neighborhoods in Cairo to install solar water heaters and biogas digesters in their homes.

Culhane describes Solar C³.I.T.I.E.S. as "not merely a clean solar power provider" but as an organization that places group work and collaboration at its center. Solar C³.I.T.I.E.S. is "an idea generator," Culhane explains. "We realize the value of collective intelligence. These neighborhoods are filled with welders, plumbers, carpenters, and glassworkers. We bring capital and plans; they bring talent and creativity. We build these systems together from scratch."

Promoting the value of working together, Solar C³.I.T.I.E.S. also has reduced tensions between a primarily Coptic Christian community and an Islamic neighborhood. Culhane explains: "I knew if they could actually meet one another and connect on a project to solve common problems, they would overcome their differences. They immediately began sharing and building on each other's expertise. Now we're using the strengths of both Christianity and Islam to fight a common enemy: environmental degradation."[12]

Culhane is not satisfied with just developing options for solar power, however; he is also an advocate of what he refers to as "the Great Conversation." Our actions, Culhane explains, tell a story—but there is only one story, the story of "the Universe." This story "is a never-ending story, ever unfolding. When we learn to see our Earth . . . as a living thing, as a giant organism within that Universe, we can also learn to see our essential roles as parts of that planetary body. From an ecological point of view we can see that nobody is expendable." We all play different roles at different times, depending on our locations and our context, and what Culhane calls our "behavioral plasticity and flexibility." This plasticity and flexibility show us when to add our voice to the conversation, using the "appropriate voice at the appropriate time." When we tell our stories, Culhane explains, we become *interested* in our place in that story and *interesting* to others. What is more, according to Culhane, "today's globalized digital media platforms and technology have removed most of the barriers to entry! We can connect with each other across the globe via YouTube and Flickr and Facebook and MySpace and blogging and commenting and expand the great conversation to include our voices among the many."[13]

WHAT DO YOU THINK?

1. Culhane talks about each of us having a story to tell and an important part in the "Great Conversation." What actions might you share with others (as a story) that help us understand your part in this Great Conversation?

2. Culhane also talks about behavioral plasticity and flexibility— knowing when and how to add our voices to this conversation. This chapter introduces the idea of being audience centered and creating a community with your speeches. In what ways might Culhane be talking about being audience centered and creating a community—are these ideas similar?

3. How might today's technology help you add your voice to this great conversation in ways that are civil, ethical, and innovative?

*Connecting Community Catalysts Integrating Technologies for Industrial Ecology Systems.

Ed Kashi/VII Photo Agency/Corbis

Can Breaking the Law Be Ethical?

On April 12, 1963, civil rights activist Martin Luther King Jr., and fellow activists were arrested for intentionally disobeying an Alabama Supreme Court injunction against public demonstrations. While in solitary confinement that day, King read a letter published in the *Birmingham News* by eight white Birmingham clergymen who asked the activists to work through the courts for the change they sought rather than protesting in the streets. In their letter, the clergy accused King and other civil rights advocates of "failing to negotiate," "using extreme measures," and "choosing an inappropriate time to act."

King responded with his "Letter from Birmingham Jail," which explained his unsuccessful attempts to negotiate with unwilling merchants and economic leaders of Birmingham, his conviction that "one has a moral responsibility to disobey unjust laws," and his unwillingness to wait any longer for freedom. In his letter, King made the point that "Injustice anywhere is a threat to justice everywhere" and went on to suggest that "We are caught in an inescapable network of mutuality, tied in a single garment of destiny. Whatever affects one directly affects all indirectly."

WHAT DO YOU THINK?

1. Do you think King acted ethically when he broke the law by disobeying the Alabama Supreme Court injunction? Why or why not?
2. Do you think the Birmingham clergy were correct in labeling King and other civil rights advocates as extremist and unwilling to negotiate? Why or why not?
3. Do you think King was correct when he wrote that we are "caught in an inescapable network of mutuality"? What might be the ethical implications of this claim? How does this idea relate to the discussions about public dialogue in this chapter?

signals an audience gives a speaker. Audience feedback often indicates whether listeners understand, have interest in, and are receptive to the speaker's ideas. This feedback assists the speaker in many ways. It helps the speaker know when to slow down, explain something more carefully, or even tell the audience that she or he will return to an issue in a question-and-answer session at the close of the speech. Audience feedback assists the speaker in creating a connection of mutual respect with the audience.

Public speaking differs from other forms of communication not only because it is done in front of an audience but also because of the ways the speaker relates the ideas of the speech to the audience.

Public Speaking Is Influenced by Technology

Whether it is the research we do, the tools we use to design our visual aids, or the presentational tools we have at our fingertips, the public dialogue is richer and more complex because of the technology we use. Search engines not only help us find the latest information but also sort through decades of research and discussion quickly. The images and sounds we can share with our audiences are appealing and compelling, yet they must also be used cautiously so as to not shock or offend our audience unnecessarily. And in the "smartest" of classrooms or lecture halls, we can move through a speech with extraordinary polish, shifting images and text like magicians. The benefits of our technologically enhanced lives as speakers cannot be denied. Yet with all this richness comes increased responsibility to our audiences. The public dialogue is improved when we use technology ethically, responsibly, and meaningfully. Unlike a quick text, tweet, or Facebook post, technology differs from other forms of communication in that it must be used thoughtfully, strategically, and with care.

Public Speaking Encourages Ethical Dialogue

A final difference between public speaking and other kinds of communication is that public speaking sets the stage for the ongoing conversation Kenneth Burke described earlier in this chapter. For this conversation to be meaningful, the speaker must present ideas ethically with fairness and honesty. This ethical aspect of speaking means that the speaker is responsible for framing the conversation, or dialogue, honestly and for laying the foundation for future discussions. Public speaking encourages ethical dialogue because speakers want the people who hear the speech to engage others—and perhaps even the speaker—in a conversation about the topic or issue after the speech is given. Public speaking encourages this ethical dialogue because the speaker is interested in presenting ideas fairly, in discussing issues openly, and in hearing more about them from the audience.

A Model of the Public Speaking Process

Consider the following components of the public speaking process as it has been discussed thus far (Figure 1.1 can help you visualize this process):

Speaker: A person who stimulates public dialogue by delivering an oral message. The speaker researches the topic of the speech, organizes the material that results from the research, presents the message, and manages discussion after or, in some cases, during a speech. Throughout this process, the speaker is civil, considering the needs and characteristics of the audience.

Message: The information conveyed by the speaker to the audience. Messages can be verbal or nonverbal. For example, a speaker giving a speech about her recent experiences in the military would use words to describe those experiences and facial expressions and gestures to convey the various aspects of those experiences. Most of our messages are intentional, but sometimes, we send an unintentional message, such as an unplanned pause, a sigh, or a frown that conveys an idea or a feeling we had not planned to communicate. When we speak, we convey messages by **encoding**, or translating ideas and feelings into words, sounds, and gestures. When we receive the message, we are **decoding** it, or translating words, sounds, and gestures into ideas and feelings in an attempt to understand the message.

Audience: The complex and varied group of people the speaker addresses. Because of the ethical and audience-centered nature of public speaking, the speaker must consider the positions, beliefs, values, and needs of the audience throughout the design and delivery of a speech.

speaker: Person who stimulates public dialogue by delivering an oral message.

message: Information conveyed by the speaker to the audience.

encoding: Translating ideas and feelings into words, sounds, and gestures.

decoding: Translating words, sounds, and gestures into ideas and feelings in an attempt to understand the message.

audience: Complex and varied group of people the speaker addresses.

Figure 1.1   A model of the public speaking process

Context

noise

noise

noise

Channel

Message

Feedback

Channel

noise

noise

Speaker

Audience

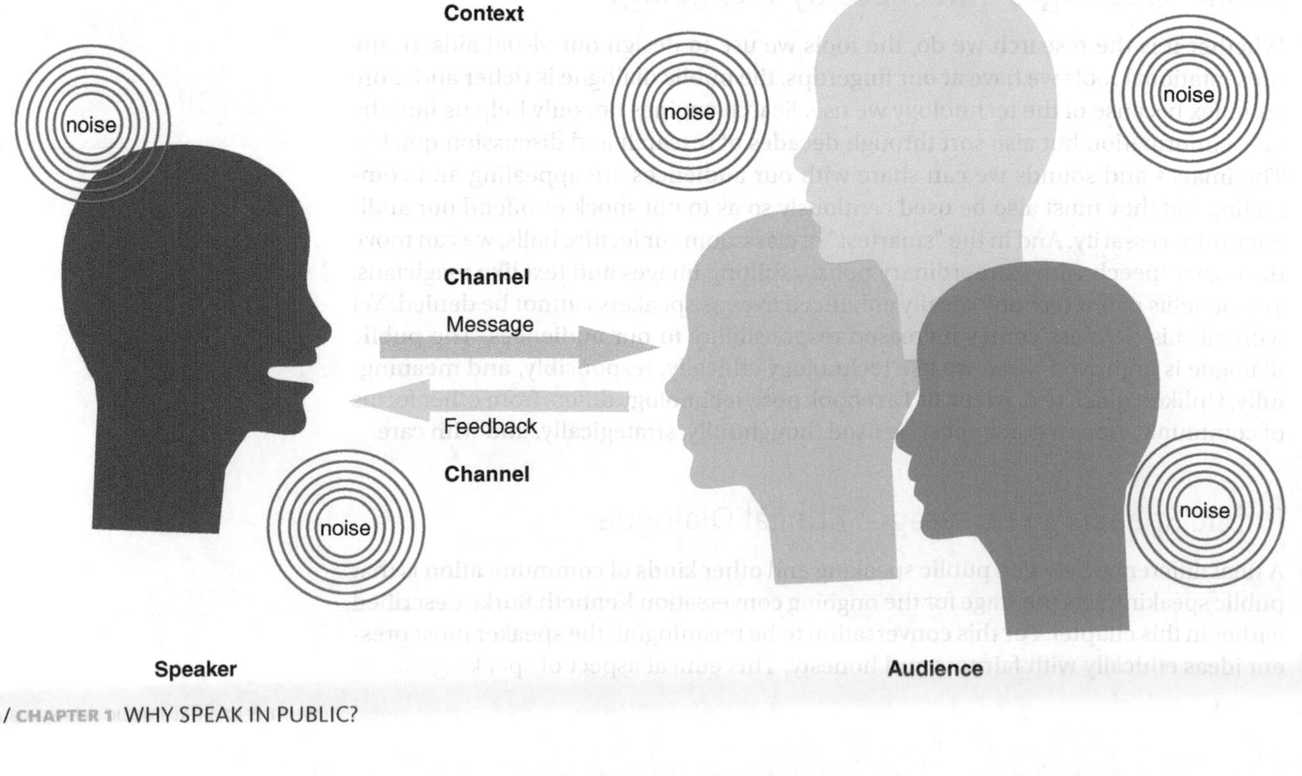

Channel: The means by which the message is conveyed. A message can be conveyed through spoken words, vocal tone and gestures, and visual aids. The channel might include technology like a microphone, or smartphone, a YouTube clip, Prezi, or PowerPoint slides.

Noise: Anything that interferes with understanding the message being communicated. Noise may be external or internal. External noise—interference outside the speaker or audience—might be construction work going on outside the classroom window or a microphone that doesn't work in a large lecture hall. Internal noise—interference within the speaker or audience—might be a headache that affects one's concentration or cultural differences that make it hard to understand a message.

Feedback: The verbal and nonverbal signals the audience gives the speaker. Feedback from an audience indicates to the speaker the need to slow down, clarify, respond to questions, alter delivery, and the like.

Context: The environment or situation in which a speech occurs. The context includes components such as the time of day and the place the speech is given, the audience's expectations about the speech, and the traditions associated with a speech. For example, a commemorative speech would likely be given in a formal setting, such as during a banquet or at a wedding reception. A speech given to classmates or coworkers might be given in a very informal setting, such as in your classroom, or in a formal meeting room at work.

Although we describe each component separately, they are interconnected. Notice that the speaker is both a "speaker" and a "listener," sending a message but also attending to feedback from the audience. The audience members also have a key role, reducing external and internal noise whenever possible and listening to the message so they can contribute to the discussion that may occur when the speech is finished.

Practicing the Public Dialogue | 1.2

CONSIDER THE UNIQUE ASPECTS OF PUBLIC SPEAKING

Choose one of the five speech topics you identified in Practicing the Public Dialogue Activity 1.1. Think about giving a speech on this topic in class.

- What are two ways your speech could create a sense of community with your audience?
- What are two ways you could stay audience centered while speaking about this topic?
- What are two ways your cultural background might affect your speaking style when giving a speech about this topic?
- What are two ways your speech could encourage dialogue with your in-class audience or with your campus community?

Save this topic and analysis to possibly use for an in-class speech later in the course.

MindTap

Learn more about how to analyze an audience and stay audience centered. In addition, watch a video clip of a student speaker, Mike Piel, as he makes a relevant connection with his audience and remains audience centered. As you watch Mike speak, consider the strategies he uses to communicate the importance of his topic to his audience. What does Mike say to connect his topic to his audience?

Building Your Confidence as a Public Speaker

Even the most experienced speakers get a little nervous before they give a speech, so it is normal that you might feel a bit nervous, too. One reason we become anxious is that we care about our topic and our performance. We want to perform well and deliver a successful speech. Another reason we might be nervous before a speech is because we fear the unknown; we anticipate the speaking event and imagine that it will be stressful long before we actually give the speech. These are also normal, and it is helpful to know that there are ways to build your confidence as a speaker and reduce some of the nervousness you might feel.

Our nervousness before a speech is often called **communication apprehension**, "the level of fear or anxiety associated with either real or anticipated communication with another person or persons."[14] Communication apprehension can take two forms. People who are apprehensive about communicating with others in any situation are said to have **trait anxiety**. People who are apprehensive about communicating with others in a particular situation are said to have **state or situational anxiety**. To help reduce your nervousness, take a moment to consider whether you are trait anxious or state anxious in communication situations. Do you fear all kinds of interactions or only certain kinds? Most of us experience some level of state anxiety about

channel: Means by which the message is conveyed.

noise: Anything that interferes with understanding the message being communicated.

feedback: Verbal and nonverbal signals an audience gives a speaker.

context: Environment or situation in which a speech occurs.

communication apprehension: Level of fear or anxiety associated with either real or anticipated communication with another person or people.

trait anxiety: Apprehension about communicating with others in any situation.

state or situational anxiety: Apprehension about communicating with others in a particular situation.

some communication events, such as asking a boss for a raise, orally evaluating another's performance, or introducing ourselves to a group of strangers. This is quite normal.

Most people also experience some level of state anxiety about public speaking. This is called *public speaking anxiety* (PSA), the anxiety we feel when we learn we have to give a speech or take a public speaking course.[15] You can build your confidence and reduce some of your PSA by following the tips provided in this section. However, if you are extraordinarily nervous about giving speeches, see your instructor for special assistance about your fears.

Knowing why we become nervous before a speech can help us build our confidence. Research suggests that most people's state anxiety about public speaking exists for six reasons. Many people are state anxious because public speaking is:

1. *Novel*—we don't do it regularly and lack necessary skills as a result.
2. *Done in formal settings*—our behaviors when giving a speech are more prescribed and rigid than usual.
3. *Often done from a subordinate position*—an instructor or boss sets the rules for giving a speech, and the audience acts as a critic.
4. *Conspicuous or obvious*—the speaker stands apart from the audience.
5. *Done in front of an audience that is unfamiliar*—most people are more comfortable talking with people they know. Also, we fear that audiences won't be interested in what we have to say.
6. *A unique situation in which the degree of attention paid to the speaker is quite noticeable*—audience members either stare at us or ignore us, so we become unusually self-focused.[16]

It helps to know that research also suggests people are usually nervous only about specific aspects of public speaking. When people ranked what they fear while giving a speech, here's what they said:[17]

Trembling or shaking	80%
Mind going blank	74%
Doing or saying something embarrassing	64%
Being unable to continue talking	63%
Not making sense	59%
Sounding foolish	59%

When we combine this research, a pattern emerges that helps us understand our nervousness. Because public speaking is novel and usually done in a formal setting, our nervousness can make us shake or tremble. Then, when the spotlight is on us as the speaker, we fear our minds will go blank, we will say something embarrassing, or we will be unable to continue talking. Finally, we often don't know our audience well, which can make us fear evaluation, not making sense, or sounding foolish more than we ordinarily would. As you can see, some of our nervousness is legitimate. Even so, we can get past it and build our confidence as speakers.

The suggestions offered here should help you build your confidence and turn your nervous energy to your advantage.

Do Your Research

One way to build your confidence before giving a speech is to prepare as well as you can.[18] Careful preparation will help you feel more confident about what you will say (and what others will think) and ease fears about drawing a blank or not being able to answer a question. Speakers who research their topics thoroughly before they speak feel prepared. As a result, they tend to be much more relaxed and effective during their presentations.

tip
National Geographic Explorer

Courtesy of Becca Skinner.

BECCA SKINNER, Explorer, Photographer

How you deal with any nervousness that you may experience before you talk?
I get so nervous before I speak. I think breathing really deep has always helped me. Then I also remember that people want to be there to listen to what I'm saying. And so the fact that they're interested, and that I have something to say that might inspire someone or engage someone really gives me a little bit more confidence to go stand and talk in front of a large group of people. But breathing is, I think, really key, and not to feel rushed is also important. It's okay if I'm not talking constantly; I try to remember to just sit back and let people look at the photos for a minute.

One thing I really like to do in my presentation to make it easier is make people laugh; I think once people laugh I feel better and I kind of loosen up. That might not apply to every public speaking event, but I think that starting off with something to make you a little bit more comfortable is one tip.

I think people need to remember that everyone gets pretty nervous, or a lot of people get nervous, and so your audience sympathizes with you. They're not there to critique you and judge you and make your time miserable. They're there to hear what you have to say.

Practice Your Speech

You can build your confidence and reduce the nervousness associated with the formality of a speech by practicing. And the more times you practice, the more confident you can become. Here is an example of how this can be done.

Randy was terrified to give his first speech. His instructor suggested a solution he reluctantly agreed to try. Feeling a little silly, Randy began by practicing his speech in his head. Then, when no one else was home, he began to present his speech out loud and alone in his room. He then stood in front of a mirror and delivered his speech to his own reflection. After several horrifying attempts, he began to feel more comfortable. Soon after, he began to trust his speaking ability enough to deliver his speech to his older sister, whom he trusted to be kind and constructive. First, he asked her to simply listen, so that he could practice in front of a real person. After doing this a few times, he asked her to give him honest feedback and to share her suggestions and comments with kindness. Finally, he practiced once more in the clothing he planned to wear and delivered his speech in his kitchen, which he arranged so it resembled, as closely as possible, his classroom.

When speakers practice their speech before they give it, they become more familiar with the process of speaking and the formality of the situation. As they gain comfort by practicing alone, they can move to rehearsals before an audience. They also have time to make changes in their presentation and to smooth out the rough spots before they actually give the speech. This practice is part of a process known as **systematic desensitization**, a technique for reducing anxiety that involves teaching your body to feel calm and relaxed rather than fearful during your speeches. This technique can help you give successful speeches and build your confidence, thus breaking the cycle of fear associated with public speaking. Talk to your instructor if you'd like to learn more about this technique.[19]

systematic desensitization: Technique for reducing anxiety that involves teaching your body to feel calm and relaxed rather than fearful during your speeches.

Have Realistic Expectations

A third way to build your confidence is to set realistic expectations about your delivery. Few speakers sound or look like professional performers. When real people give real speeches, they sound like real people who are invested in their topic and speech. So rather than worry about delivering a flawless performance, adjust your expectations to a more realistic level.

Remember, speakers pause, cough, rely on their notes for prompts, occasionally say "um," and even exhibit physical signs of nervousness, such as blushing or sweating. As we give more speeches, these "flaws" go away, become less noticeable, or we learn to manage them effectively. Here are a few realistic expectations for beginning speakers:

- Take a calming breath before you begin your speech.
- Remember your introduction.
- Strike a balance between using your notes and making eye contact with your audience.
- Make eye contact with more than one person.
- Gesture naturally rather than hold on to the podium.
- Deliver your conclusion the way you practiced it.

Practice Visualization and Affirmations

Sometimes, we increase our nervousness by imagining a worst-case scenario for the speech, and these images often stay in our minds. We've set up what is called a *self-fulfilling prophecy*: if you see yourself doing poorly in your mind before your speech, you set yourself up to do so in the speech. There are two ways to turn this negative dynamic around and build your confidence as a speaker: visualization and affirmations.

visualization: Process in which you construct a mental image of yourself giving a successful speech.

Visualization. **Visualization** is a process in which you construct a mental image of yourself giving a successful speech. Research on the benefits of visualization suggests that one session of visualization (about fifteen minutes) has a significant positive effect on communication apprehension.[20] The techniques of visualization are used by a wide range of people—athletes, performers, executives—and can range from elaborate to quite simple processes. For public speakers, the most effective process works like this.

Find a quiet, comfortable place where you can sit in a relaxed position for approximately fifteen minutes. Close your eyes and breathe slowly and deeply through your nose, feeling relaxation flow through your body. In great detail, visualize the morning of the day you are to give your speech.

You get up filled with confidence and energy, and you wear the perfect clothing for your speech. You drive, walk, or ride to campus filled with this same positive, confident energy. As you enter the classroom, you see yourself relaxed, interacting with your classmates, full of confidence because you have thoroughly prepared for your speech. Your classmates are friendly and cordial in their greetings and conversations with you. You are *absolutely* sure of your material and your ability to present that material in the way you would like.

Next, visualize yourself beginning your speech. You see yourself approaching the place in your classroom from which you will speak. You are sure of yourself, eager to begin, and positive in your abilities as a speaker. You know you are organized and ready

Emily Cook, a member of the U.S. freestyle ski team in 2014, uses visualization during her training as well as competition. Cook includes all of her senses when she visualizes her aerial jumps, hearing the crowd, seeing the lights, feeling the wind, and even solving potential problems. What kind of detail might you include as you visualize your next speech?

to use all your visual aids with ease. Now you see yourself presenting your speech. Your introduction is wonderful. Your transitions are smooth and interesting. Your main points are articulated brilliantly. Your evidence is presented elegantly. Your organization is perfect. Take as much time as you can in visualizing this part of your process. Be as specific and positive as you can.

Visualize the end of the speech: It could not have gone better. You are relaxed and confident, the audience is eager to ask questions, and you respond to the questions with the same talents as you gave your speech. As you return to your seat, you are filled with energy and appreciation for the job well done. You are ready for the next events of your day, and you accomplish them with success and confidence.

Now take a deep breath and return to the present. Breathe in, hold it, and release it. Do this several times as you return to the present. Take as much time as you need to make this transition.[21]

Research on visualization for public speakers suggests that the more detail we give to our visualizations (what shoes we wear, exactly how we feel as we see ourselves, imagining the specifics of our speech), the more effective the technique is in building our confidence and reducing apprehension. Visualization has a significant effect on building our confidence because it systematically replaces negative images with positive images.

Affirmations. Speakers sometimes undermine their confidence through negative self-talk; they listen to the harsh judgments many people carry within themselves. When we tell ourselves, "I'm no good at this," "I know I'll embarrass myself," or "Other people are far more talented than I am," we engage in negative self-talk. We judge ourselves as inferior or less competent than others. Although it is natural to evaluate our own performances critically (that's how we motivate ourselves to improve), negative self-talk in public speaking situations often is unhelpful. When our internal voices tell us we cannot succeed, our communication apprehension only increases.[22]

To build your confidence, however, and counter the negative self-talk that might be going on in your head before a speech, try the following technique. For every negative assessment you hear yourself give, replace it with an honest assessment reframed to be positive. This technique, sometimes called **cognitive restructuring**, is a process that builds confidence because it replaces negative thoughts with positive thoughts called affirmations.[23] **Affirmations** are positive, motivating statements. They are very helpful in turning our immobilizing self-doubts into realistic assessments and options. Consider the following examples.

Negative	Positive
I'll never find an interesting topic.	I can find an interesting topic. I am an interesting person with resources. I have creative ideas.
I don't know how to organize this material.	I can find a way to present this effectively. I have a good sense of organization. I can get help if I need it.
I know I'll get up there and make a fool of myself.	I am capable of giving a wonderful speech. I know lots of strategies to do so.
I'll forget what I want to say.	I'll remember what I want to say, and I'll have notes to help me.
I'm too scared to look at my audience.	I'll make eye contact with at least five people in the audience.
I'm scared to death!	I care about my performance and will do very well.
I'll be the worst in the class!	I'll give my speech well and am looking forward to a fine presentation. We are all learning how to do this.

Practicing the Public Dialogue | 1.3

BUILD YOUR CONFIDENCE ABOUT GIVING A SPEECH

With another member of your class, make a list of what makes each of you feel nervous about public speaking. Now sort this list into categories that reflect your view of yourselves as speakers, your audience, the process of developing your speech and presentational aids, and delivering your speeches. Identify which aspect or aspects of the public speaking process generate the most anxiety for each of you. Discuss which techniques for easing public speaking anxiety presented in this chapter might work best for each of you.

MindTap®

Learn more about managing your nervousness about speaking in class.

cognitive restructuring: Process that helps reduce anxiety by replacing negative thoughts with positive ones, called affirmations.

affirmations: Positive, motivating statements that replace negative self-talk.

AP Images/Evan Dyson

Kai Degner, OrangeBand
executive director

At lunch one day in 2003, a group of friends at James Madison University decided to try to engage students, faculty, staff, and administrators in a meaningful discussion about one important issue: the war in Iraq. They didn't want a rally, protest, or debate. Instead, they wanted "a community-wide conversation." For one week, the students passed out simple bands of orange fabric that could be tied to a backpack or jacket to symbolize a desire to talk about the war. They wanted to spark the question "What's your OrangeBand?" and invite conversation about the war.

"WHAT'S YOUR ORANGEBAND?"

Five weeks later, more than 2,000 students, professors, and community members had chosen to wear OrangeBands, attend forums, and discuss their views. Dialogue soon turned to a number of other core issues, and the question became "What's your OrangeBand today?" In 2004, the nonprofit OrangeBand Initiative, Inc., was formed; by 2010, OrangeBand had coordinated dozens of forums and several action campaigns designed to facilitate conversations on a wide range of topics, and inspired more than 10,000 OrangeBand wearers.

The organizers think OrangeBand taps into three things that people are hungry for:

- **Civil discourse (respectful conversation).** There is desire out there to talk about issues we care about with other people and to try to learn from them when we disagree rather than dismiss and disrespect them.

- **Social capital (community).** OrangeBand is not just about having a conversation with someone but also about feeling connected to them. The "relationship building aspect of a quality

conversation on an important topic" is just as important as the conversation itself.

- **Civic engagement (citizenship).** Whether we call it getting involved, citizenship, or civic responsibility, OrangeBand taps into a desire to participate in democracy. When OrangeBand conversations start up, talking quickly turns to taking action.

OrangeBand chapters or groups are springing up across the nation, and the organization has only one rule: "to be successful in providing a neutral space for dialogue, the organization must remain neutral itself. We vigorously work to protect this political impartiality by inviting people of diverse perspectives to participate on staff and in our forums." OrangeBand is "not interested in advocating for any particular stance"; rather, the goal is to "generate a better understanding of why a person thinks" what she or he thinks.[24]

🔗 YOU CAN GET INVOLVED

MindTap® Learn more about OrangeBand and how to get involved.

Positive affirmations build confidence because they reframe negative energy and evaluations and shed light on your anxieties. To say you're terrified is immobilizing, but to say you care about your performance gives you room to continue to develop your speech. It is also a more accurate description of what is going on inside. Affirmations can assist you in minimizing the impact of your internal judgments and, along with visualization, can help build your confidence about public speaking.

Connect with Your Audience

A final way to build your confidence is to connect with your audience members—getting to know them in class or gathering information about them before a more formal speaking situation. As you prepare your speech, identify what you know about them, the ways you are similar to your audience, and the ways you might be different. The similarities may be as general as living in the same town or working for the same company or as specific as sharing the same views on issues. Whatever the level of comparison, finding out about your audience reminds you that we all share many aspects of our daily lives. This helps you see that, despite differences, we do share similar views and experiences.

You can also build your confidence by being a good member of the audience when others are speaking. Although this might seem unusual, ask yourself the following questions: When you are listening to a speech, do you make eye contact with the speaker? Do you sit with an attentive and alert posture, taking notes or showing interest in the presentation? Do you ask relevant questions of the speaker when the speech is over or offer constructive comments if you have the opportunity to evaluate his or her performance? Speakers who fail to behave as engaged and interested audience members often fear the very same response to their speeches.

One way to overcome this fear of disrespectful audiences is to behave as an audience member as you would want others to behave when you speak. Doing so helps establish rapport (if you are kind to a speaker, she or he likely will respond similarly to you). It also helps you learn about how to put together and deliver an effective speech.

The solutions offered in this section may help you reduce some of the speech anxiety so common to beginning public speakers. Preparing, practicing, being realistic, visualizing and affirming, finding connections, and modeling appropriate audience behavior are options that even experienced public speakers use to build their confidence. Learning to relax while giving speeches enhances your ability to contribute to the public dialogue.

Chapter Summary

Ethical public speaking is powerful.

- Speeches have the power to influence people and to shape actions and decisions. The ideas expressed in speeches enter and shape the public dialogue for years to come.

- The public dialogue is the open and honest discussion that occurs among groups of people about topics that affect those groups. It allows speakers to offer perspectives, share facts, raise questions, and engage others in stimulating discussions. When we join that dialogue, we rely on and respond to these earlier speakers.

Culture can influence our public speaking style.

- Your speaking style is shaped by your culture as well as your gender.

- As you enter the public dialogue, you will be exposed to speaking styles different from your own. This range of styles is essential to the health of the public dialogue, and understanding these differences assists you in responding civilly to others.

Civil, ethical speakers participate in the public dialogue productively.

- Participating in this dialogue civilly means you must display care, respect, thoughtfulness, and flexibility.

- Participating in this dialogue ethically means you must consider the moral impact of your ideas on your audience and contribute to the public dialogue in productive ways.

Public speaking is unique.

- Public speaking has a structure, purpose, and role that are different from the other types of communication we engage in regularly: intrapersonal, interpersonal, group, and mass communication.

- Public speaking places a lot of responsibility on the speaker, seeks to address issues that affect the larger community, and relies heavily on one speaker to convey a message. It also creates community, is audience centered, and encourages ethical and civil dialogue in ways that other types of communication do not.

- The model of the public speaking process highlights the role of the speaker and explains the message, audience, and channel as well as the influence of noise and feedback.

Several methods can help build your confidence about public speaking.

- Research your speech topic thoroughly so you feel confident about the material and are prepared to answer questions.

- Practice your speech to work out any problems with it and to feel comfortable giving it in front of an audience.

- Have realistic expectations about your delivery so you don't feel you have to give a perfect presentation.

- Visualize yourself giving a successful speech, and replace any negative self-talk with positive affirmations.

- Find points of connection with your audience. Model good behavior when you are an audience member so you establish rapport with the people who may be members of your audience.

Invitation to Public Speaking Online MindTap

Now that you have read Chapter 1, use your MindTap Communication for *Invitation to Public Speaking* for quick access to the digital resources that accompany this text. These resources include:

- **Study tools** that will help you assess your learning and prepare for exams (digital glossary, key term flash cards, review quizzes).
- **Activities and assignments** that will help you hone your knowledge and build your public speaking skills throughout

the course, as well as help you explore public speaking concepts online (web links), give you step-by-step guidance through the research, outline, and note card preparation process (Outline Builder), watch and critique videos of sample speeches (Interactive Video Activities), and allow you to practice and present your presentation online using a speech video delivery, recording, and grading system (YouSeeU).

Key Concepts MindTap   Test your knowledge with online printable flash cards.

affirmations (15)
audience (10)
audience centered (7)
channel (11)
civility (2)
cognitive restructuring (15)
communication apprehension (11)
context (11)
decoding (10)
encoding (10)
ethical public speaker (3)
feedback (11)
group communication (6)

interpersonal communication (6)
intrapersonal communication (6)
mass communication (6)
message (10)
noise (11)
public communication (6)
public dialogue (3)
speaker (10)
state or situational anxiety (11)
systematic desensitization (13)
trait anxiety (11)
visualization (14)

Review Questions

1. Who are the most compelling speakers you have encountered? Why did they speak? Did they decide, were they asked, or was it required? What issues did they discuss? How do these issues relate to the public dialogue discussed in this chapter? What made these speakers such strong presenters?

2. This chapter presented Deborah Tannen's notion of the argument culture. What is your perception of this culture? Have you been exposed to public communication as an argument? What were your reactions to this kind of interaction? If the people engaged in this interaction were to communicate civilly, what specifically would change?

3. Make a list of issues you find interesting and have followed for some time. Who spoke publicly on these issues? If you don't know who gave speeches on the issues, spend time finding several of these speeches. How do these speeches affect your own positions on these issues? How did this activity shape your perception of the unending conversation discussed in this chapter?

4. What cultural or gender influences do you think will become (or already are) a part of your speaking style? Are these similar to those discussed in this chapter? If they are different, identify the differences and how they affect communication. Discuss this topic in your public

speaking class so that you and your classmates begin with a recognition of the differences you will encounter as you all give speeches.

5. Set aside fifteen minutes of alone time the day before your first speech. Take time to visualize that speech as the process is described in this chapter. Go through each step carefully and in detail. Do not rush or overlook any aspect of the speech process. After you give your speech, compare having visualized the speech and your level of nervousness to a situation in which you were nervous but did not visualize. Was the visualization helpful in reducing your nervousness? Why or why not?

6. Either alone or with a friend, list or discuss the negative self-talk you use to describe your ability to give speeches. Identify the specific negative phrases you use and turn them into positive affirmations. Be realistic in reframing your negative self-talk into positive self-talk using the examples in this chapter as a guide.

7. As you listen to other students give their speeches, see if you can find similarities and differences between them and you. This will help you find points of connection with your audience, one of the techniques for reducing your nervousness before a speech. It will also help you stay audience centered.

2 | Effective Listening

IN THIS CHAPTER, YOU WILL LEARN TO:

- Explain why listening to others is important

- Recognize the reasons we sometimes fail to listen to others

- Create an environment that helps your audience listen to your ideas

- Apply strategies for becoming a more careful, critical, and ethical listener

- Understand how your roles as a speaker and as a listener are related

MindTap° Start with a quick warm-up activity and review the chapter's learning objectives.

Can you recall the last speech you heard? How much of its content do you remember? Now think of the last presentation you gave. How much of that information did you want your audience to remember? Is it inevitable that listeners lose so much information? As speakers, we definitely want our audiences to retain the information we worked so hard to present. And as listeners, most of us want to make the time we spend listening more profitable. In this chapter, you'll learn about how you listen as an audience member, why our listening sometimes fails, and how to listen carefully, critically, and ethically. You'll then explore how, as a speaker, you can listen to your audience and adapt to their needs, helping them listen to your speech more effectively.

Richard Levine/Alamy Stock Photo

▲ When we listen to other people, we communicate that we are willing to enter a conversation with them, even though our views may be quite different. These differences can be challenging, so in this chapter you will explore the many ways we can listen effectively to the different views present in our public dialogue.

Why Listen to Others?

Listening to others is a powerful act of communication. When we listen to others, we confirm their humanity, presence, and worth. When we listen and **confirm**, we recognize, acknowledge, and express value for another person. So central is the act of listening that philosopher Martin Buber claimed in the 1920s, "A society may be termed human in the measure to which its members confirm one another."[4] Note that listening is different from hearing. **Hearing** refers to the vibration of sound waves on our eardrums and the impulses that are then sent to the brain. When you listen to someone, you do more than simply receive sound waves—you actively engage with the information you hear.

To confirm others by listening to them is not necessarily to agree with them or even to be persuaded by them. **Listening** is the process of giving thoughtful attention to another person's words and understanding what you hear. By listening to another's words, you recognize those words as expressions of that person's experiences, values, and beliefs. If we are to participate in the ethical and civil public dialogue of our communities and make a space for others to do so, we must listen. If we are to be effective public speakers and audiences, we must also understand why we sometimes fail to listen.

Gilbert Carrasquillo/Getty Images Entertainment/Getty Images

One of former President Bill Clinton's strengths as a speaker is his ability to confirm others. In what ways does Clinton appear to be confirming his audience here?

DID YOU KNOW?

Did you know? In your public speaking class and at work . . .

- Over the course of one public speaking class, you may speak for a total of twenty to thirty minutes.
- In a class of thirty students, you'll listen to speeches for a total of ten to fifteen hours.
- In the workplace or as a member of a community group, most of your presentations will only last between ten and thirty minutes.
- Most likely, you'll spend much more of your time in an audience listening to others.[1]
- In an average day of communicating, you'll spend 55 percent of the time listening, followed by speaking, reading, and writing.[2]

Did you know? About listening and presentations in general . . .

- After a ten-minute oral presentation, the average person understands and retains only 50 percent of the information presented.
- Forty-eight hours after the presentation, those same listeners retain only 25 percent of the information.[3]

Why We Sometimes Fail to Listen

Why do we ignore some messages but tune into others, opening ourselves up to new ideas and ways of thinking? Why do we willingly confirm some people but refuse to consider confirming others? Similarly, why are we sometimes surprisingly good at understanding some speakers but unable to follow others? Listening researcher Michael Nichols explains that we sometimes fail to listen because "the simple art of listening isn't always so simple." Rather, it is often work. The "sustained attention of careful listening—that may take heroic and unselfish restraint. To listen well we must forget ourselves" and give our focused attention to another.[5]

As listeners, we fail to focus our attention for three reasons: listener interference, speaker interference, and an inability to get beyond differences. **Interference** is anything that stops or hinders a listener from receiving a message. Interference can be external to the listener (auditory or visual distractions) or internal (distracting thoughts or feelings). As you read this section, see if you recognize some of your own weaknesses as a listener or as a speaker.

Listener Interference

You may be surprised to learn that most challenges to listening stem from poor listening habits. Consider the following list of bad listening habits. Can you identify times you've done some of the following?

- Think you're not interested in the subject before the speech really gets going.
- Assume you know what the speaker is going to say before it's even said.
- Get so focused on the details that you miss the bigger point.
- Adopt a passive physical stance—slouching, reclining, making no eye contact.
- Adopt a defensive physical stance—turning away, crossing arms, making hostile eye contact.
- Pay attention to distractions—or create them yourself.
- Be so preoccupied with the messenger that you miss the message.
- Tune out difficult information.

tip
National Geographic Explorer

AZIZ ABU SARAH, Explorer and Cultural Educator

Tell us about an experience where active listening made a difference in one of your speaking engagements. For example, did someone in the audience tell a story that you listened to that changed your thinking or how you made your next presentation?

When we speak to groups or individuals, the most important thing is to be able to listen—and not only to the words. We have to listen to what is behind the words. We use active listening because there's an emotional component to what people are saying. So we listen to why they are upset, why they're angry, why they're ashamed, why they're sad or happy about what was just shared. And by doing that we avoid a lot of fights and unproductive conversations.

For example, when I was speaking in an Israeli classroom just a couple months after a suicide bombing had happened, I was speaking with an Israeli partner of mine. We told our stories and how we should try to overcome anger, bitterness, and hatred and begin to work together. But one of the students was very, very angry. And he interrupted us throughout the speech and was pretty verbally violent. And so we stopped, and we asked him to tell us what was bothering him. And eventually he shared that his uncle was in a suicide bombing just a couple months earlier, and he was very angry, and he had never met a Palestinian before. I was the first Palestinian he had met, and all his anger just came at me. He shared how he was just waiting to get a chance for revenge. But we started this conversation, and it ended up going on for a couple of hours, and we just listened. We listened to his position, and we learned where he was coming from, and we heard his pain. I think he needed somebody from the other side to yell at. And for me, that was fine. I think he needed to get all his emotions out, because after that we ended up having a very productive conversation. And at the end of our conversation, he said that he—although he was confused because he had a chance to say everything he wanted to say and because we listened—was not as angry as he was earlier. And without us listening to the emotions and the pain, I think that would have been impossible to get to that point.

- Tune out information you don't agree with or argue with the speaker's message in your own mind.
- Prepare your response while the speaker is speaking.
- Daydream or pretend you are listening when you really aren't.

At one time or another, most of us have fallen into many of these habits. We may think we've heard all there is to hear on a subject, so we begin daydreaming or simply pretend to listen. We become so enamored of or so frustrated with a speaker that we forget to listen to the content of a speech. We find the material too challenging or difficult to understand, so we give up listening, begin talking to the person next to us, or even open the newspaper and begin to read. Although we might want to blame the speaker for these lapses in listening, we really are responsible for practicing these bad habits. We will learn how to replace these bad habits with more productive ones later in this chapter.

Speaker Interference Caused by Information

As speakers, we can create speeches that are "listenable," speeches that help our audiences focus and pay attention. A **listenable speech** is considerate and delivered in

confirm: To recognize, acknowledge, and express value for another person.

hearing: Vibration of sound waves on our eardrums and the impulses then sent to the brain.

listening: Process of giving thoughtful attention to another person's words and understanding what you hear.

interference: Anything that stops or hinders a listener from receiving a message.

listenable speech: Speech that is considerate and delivered in an oral style.

an oral style. This type of speech uses words meant to be heard (oral style) rather than words meant to be read (written style).[6] **Considerate speeches** help our audience process information. Listeners generally stop listening, or become frustrated, when we present information that is overly complicated, challenging, or simple.

When we share ideas that are too complicated, audiences can have difficulty following our line of reasoning. We've probably all heard speakers who try to explain complicated procedures or tell detailed stories in too short a time. When audience members don't have the time or the knowledge to absorb a speaker's ideas from the beginning of a speech, they may just give up listening. Similarly, when our ideas seriously challenge an audience's belief systems, the audience can get caught up in the differences in values and lose sight of the point we are trying to make. This is particularly true when the speaker's topic brings up strong emotions, such as in speeches about polarizing social issues or traumatic events.

On the other hand, when we present stories or arguments that are too simple, our audiences may become bored and stop listening. Consider the following example: Katherine, a graduating senior, was the student speaker at her recent college graduation. Recognizing that graduation is a time of huge transition and uncertainty but also a time of excitement, she decided to read lengthy passages from one of her favorite books, Dr. Seuss's *Oh, the Places You'll Go!* After a while, people stopped listening to her speech because the language was too simple. Her audience began to shift and shuffle, to lose interest, and to strike up small side conversations while she was speaking. Although it can be interesting and meaningful for adults in short passages, *Oh, the Places You'll Go!* is written for children. Thus, Katherine's speech on change and the excitement of the unknown used too much language that was overly simple for college graduates and their families.

Speaker Interference Caused by Language

Another way we can help our audience listen is by reducing interference caused by language. Listening can fail simply because the speaker's language is unclear. The language may be too formal or technical, too casual, too noninclusive, or too cluttered.

Formal or technical language. Most of us have heard the following phrases or sayings many times in our lives. Can you recognize them?

- Scintillate, scintillate, asteroid minific.
- Members of an avian species of identical plumage congregate.
- Surveillance should precede saltation.
- Pulchritude possesses a solely cutaneous profundity.
- It is fruitless to become lachrymose over precipitately departed lacteal fluid.
- Freedom from encrustations of grime is contiguous to rectitude.
- Eschew the implement of correction and vitiate the scion.
- It is fruitless to attempt to indoctrinate a superannuated canine with innovative maneuvers.
- The temperature of aqueous content of an unremittingly ogled saucepan does not reach 212 degrees F.
- All articles that coruscate with resplendence are not truly auriferous.[7]

You may not recognize these common sayings because they are expressed in very formal and technical language. In some situations, this style of language may be quite appropriate, but most audiences stop listening when the speaker's language is more formal or technical than they can understand. These ten very formal sentences simply say:

1. Twinkle, twinkle, little star.
2. Birds of a feather flock together.
3. Look before you leap.
4. Beauty is only skin deep.

considerate speech: Speech that eases the audience's burden of processing information.

5. Don't cry over spilled milk.
6. Cleanliness is next to godliness.
7. Spare the rod and spoil the child.
8. You can't teach an old dog new tricks.
9. A watched pot never boils.
10. All that glitters is not gold.

A specific type of language that is often too technical is **jargon**, language used by a special group or for a special activity. You've probably used jargon if you play sports (a bogey is a type of score in golf) or are a member of a specialized group (in the military, a bogey is an unidentified, possibly hostile, aircraft). You also may have used jargon on your job to identify processes or objects specific to your occupation (truck mechanics know a bogie is a type of wheel assembly used in some automotive trucks). Jargon can be confusing because your audience may not know what a particular word means. As a speaker, use jargon only if it will help your audience better understand your message.

Casual language. Language also can be difficult to listen to if it is too casual. We often fall into our familiar, everyday language patterns, which can be too informal for our audience. Three types of commonly used casual language include slang, colloquialisms, and euphemisms. **Slang** is an informal nonstandard vocabulary, usually made up of arbitrarily changed words. A **colloquialism** is a local or regional informal dialect or expression. A **euphemism** substitutes an agreeable or inoffensive expression for one that may offend or suggest something unpleasant. When our language is too casual, audiences might not be able to follow the main ideas of the speech, or they become confused or uncomfortable. Either way, they stop listening to our message. Consider these examples:

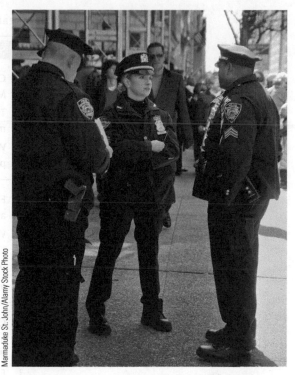

Marmaduke St. John/Alamy Stock Photo

Police officers use jargon to communicate efficiently with one another. How might these police officers describe this scene to someone who isn't a police officer? What jargon do you use in your profession that you might need to explain to an audience?

Slang:	EIL5: Explain it like I'm 5.[8]
	(Used when you need a simpler explanation than the one just given)
	DAE: Does anyone else?
	(A prefix for a question you are asking when you want to know if anyone else does the same thing or thinks the same way)[9]
Colloquialism:	Keep me in the loop.
	(Keep me informed as things unfold)
Euphemism:	There's going to be too much collateral damage.
	(There will be too many accidental deaths.)[10]
	Her friend is in a correctional facility.
	(Her friend is in a jail or prison.)[11]

In some settings, such as at a party with your friends, casual language is easily understood. However, in public speaking settings, translate slang, colloquialisms, and euphemisms into expressions an audience is more likely to understand. Because our language changes so rapidly, today's slang, colloquialisms, and euphemisms can rapidly drop from use. Some casual language may even be offensive to some members of an audience, causing them to stop listening or to focus on the speaker's language rather than the speaker's ideas. Or it may be very confusing to people from cultures other than your own. Remember, when audience members are confused or offended by your language, they won't hear the message you want to send.

Noninclusive language. Listening can break down when you use noninclusive language, or words that seem to refer only to certain groups of people. Such language

jargon: Technical language used by a special group or for a special activity.

slang: Informal nonstandard vocabulary, usually made up of arbitrarily changed words.

colloquialism: Local or regional informal dialect or expression.

euphemism: Word or phrase that substitutes an agreeable or inoffensive expression for one that may offend or suggest something unpleasant.

Table 2.1 Research on Gender-Inclusive Language

YEAR	STUDY
1973	Children were asked to select photographs for textbook chapters titled "Urban Man" and "Man in Politics" or "Urban Life" and "Political Behavior."
	The children nearly always chose pictures of men when the titles included the male nouns.
	When the titles were not specifically male oriented, children chose more pictures that contained both women and men.[12]
1984	First grade through college students were asked to write a story about an average student.
	When the researchers used the word *he* to describe the assignment, only 12 percent of the students wrote a story about a female.
	When researchers used "he or she," 42 percent of the students wrote stories about females.[13]
1995	College students were asked to fill in the blanks to sentences such as, "Before a judge can give a final ruling, ____," and "Before a doctor can make a final diagnosis, ____."
	Even though women today participate in almost all aspects of public and professional life, students chose predominantly masculine pronouns to finish the sentences.[14]
1996, 1998	Subjects were asked to read a report written in the style of a newspaper article about a meeting of athletes and a meeting of scientists.
	When neutral and masculine pronouns were used in the report, the subjects described both events as being attended predominantly by men.
	When the events were given a female context (a meeting of gymnasts versus hockey players, a meeting of nutritionists versus geophysicists), the subjects described the events as being attended by only slightly more women.[15]
2008	Students in England, France, and Germany assigned predominantly male images to sentences containing supposedly generic masculine pronouns.
	Again, this confirms the overriding power of pronoun choice to influence perceptions.[16]

excludes people who are not in the "in group" and who are likely to be offended by and tune out speakers who use it. A common example of noninclusive language is language that describes only men ("All men are created equal," for example), and not both men and women ("All people are created equal," for example). **Gender-inclusive language** remedies this exclusion, and is one of the simplest ways you can improve listening. Research indicates that when we use noninclusive nouns and pronouns, listeners visualize men far more often than they do women or men and women together (see Table 2.1).

Noninclusive language also includes language that does not acknowledge cultural diversity. **Culturally inclusive language** respectfully recognizes the differences among the many cultures in our society. Although it may seem obvious that we need to consider diversity when we speak to diverse audiences, at times our language does not reflect our attention to diversity.

A common example of language that is not culturally inclusive is **spotlighting**, the practice of highlighting a person's race or ethnicity, sex, sexual orientation, physical disability, and the like during a speech. Speakers who spotlight describe a lawyer as a Hispanic lawyer, a doctor as an Asian American doctor, and a friend as an African

gender-inclusive language: Language recognizing that both women and men are active participants in the world.

culturally inclusive language: Language that respectfully recognizes the differences among the many cultures in our society.

spotlighting: Practice of highlighting a person's race or ethnicity (or sex, sexual orientation, physical disability, and the like) during a speech.

American friend. Spotlighting is most common among members of the dominant culture in a society, and it marks differences as being unusual. Consider the following examples:

The jury includes five men and two African American women.

The panel includes three professionals and a disabled lawyer.

The meeting is going to be chaired by a Hispanic professor and a university administrator.

He's a talented gay artist.[17]

Spotlighting identifies people thought to belong to a special, and hence an unusual, category. As a result of spotlighting, differences get marked as abnormal, slightly strange, or surprising. A speaker using culturally inclusive language would describe the people in these examples as five white men and two African American women (or as seven people), four professionals (a lawyer is professionally employed), two employees of the university (or a Hispanic professor and a white administrator), and a talented artist.

Sometimes, speakers fail to be culturally inclusive when they neglect information that acknowledges important cultural differences. Using culturally inclusive language helps a speaker tell the whole story. For example, in his speech on equity in the workplace, Howard used culturally inclusive language by including statistical information beyond the familiar "a woman earns about 83 cents to every dollar a white man earns." He told his audience that Asian American women earn approximately 78 cents to every dollar an Asian man earns, and Hispanic and African American women earn approximately 90 and 89 cents, respectively, to every dollar their Hispanic and African American male counterparts make. This culturally inclusive language recognized important cultural differences that gave Howard's audience more insight into this complex topic.[18]

Using culturally inclusive and gender-inclusive language communicates to an audience that you are aware of the diversity in our society and of the influence of culture. Your speech becomes more listenable because audiences gain a more holistic view of an issue. Your goal as a speaker is to connect with your audience and to share your ideas with them, so make listening as easy as possible. Using language that includes all members of your audience assists you in doing just that.

Verbal clutter. Sometimes, audiences have a difficult time listening to a speaker because of **verbal clutter**, extra words in sentences that don't add meaning. Even though listeners can mentally process far more words than speakers can speak per minute (the average speaker speaks at a rate of 125 to 175 words per minute, but a trained listener can process 350 to 450 words per minute), verbal clutter impedes listening because listeners must process words that are unnecessary or redundant.[19]

Examples of verbal clutter are such common words and phrases as "you know," "it's like," "I'm like," "um," "and all," and "stuff like that." These small additions to a speech, although commonly used in casual conversation, distract listeners and add no useful meaning.

Similarly, descriptions loaded with adjectives and adverbs act as verbal clutter. Hard to spot sometimes, we often use this type of verbal clutter when we try to create vivid descriptions. Consider the following cluttered sentences and their uncluttered alternatives.

Cluttered:	Good, effective public speakers use carefully selected and chosen words, sentences, and phrases, correctly and accurately.
Uncluttered:	Skilled speakers present their ideas clearly.
What's improved?	A few strong words are used rather than several adequate, but less focused, words.
Cluttered:	If nothing else, he was first and foremost, above all, a man of considerable honor and principled integrity.
Uncluttered:	Above all, he was a man of integrity.
What's improved?	The redundant words have been edited out (for example, honor and principled), leaving a focused message.

verbal clutter: Extra words that pad sentences and claims but don't add meaning.

The Problems with Offensive Language

Politicians from both sides of the House and Senate, as well as governors, mayors, and political hopefuls, are sometimes known for their racially offensive and sexist comments. Although Donald Trump, as an example, may be notorious for offensive speech, he is not the only political hopeful or elected official to utter offensive remarks. Indeed, his anti-Muslim statements during his presidential campaign in 2015, in which he called for a "complete shutdown"[20] of our country's borders to prevent any person who was Muslim from entering the United States, were problematic, as was his suggestion in 2013 that when men and women serve together in the military, sexual assault should be "expected."[21] But Trump is not alone in his ability to make offensive statements. Consider the following:

> In 2013, a governor explained our nation's "mediocre" educational system as the fault of women: "I think both parents started working. And the mom is in the workplace."

> In 2013, during a hearing regarding sexual assault in our military, a senator remarked, "The young folks coming in to each of your services are anywhere from 17 to 22 or 23. Gee wiz, the hormone level created by nature sets in place the possibility for these types of things to occur."[22]

At a 2012 campaign stop, a presidential hopeful slandered African American individuals with his statement regarding welfare programs, explaining he "didn't want to make 'black people's lives better by giving them somebody else's money.'"

In 2012, a House representative shared his perspective on sexual assault and abortion by explaining, "if it's a legitimate rape, the female body has ways to try to shut that whole thing down."

These examples can help us understand some of the effects of offensive speech on our audiences and the importance of our language choices. As a result of these comments, many of these individuals lost considerable credibility, as well as their campaigns, and many others were not reelected. Although some people may have agreed with or supported these statements, the statements reflect an unwillingness to listen to the public dialogue and to enter that conversation with respect and civility. Offensive statements can cause members of our audience to feel alienated and unwelcome. They also hinder our reasoning process.

WHAT DO YOU THINK?

1. Who do you think might feel respected and welcome by these comments? Who might feel disrespected and unwelcome?
2. Select one or two of these offensive statements and see if you can find the arguments or ideas being advanced. What are the arguments? Are they clear?
3. Do you think you can rephrase these statements so that they are more civil and ethical? What would you say differently so that an audience might be better able to listen to them?

The uncluttered sentences are much easier on the ears. They hold our attention and focus our listening efforts. Without the clutter, audiences have a far easier time listening for our main points and ideas. But how much clutter do you really want to eliminate? Notice the differences in the level of clutter in the next three examples:

Cluttered: At some point during the day, every single day of her life, no matter the weather or the distractions, she would make the long, steep trek three miles one way to the distant, far-off waterfall.

Less cluttered: At some point during the day, every day of her life, she made the three-mile trek to the waterfall.

Uncluttered: Every day, she hiked three miles to the waterfall.

Notice that some of what might be called "clutter" in one speech adds richness and detail to another, setting a particular tone or mood. Go back and reread the cluttered example. If we simply took out the words *distant, far-off*, we might have a nice description for a commemorative speech or a speech of introduction. But in a persuasive or informative speech, the focus might be on the daily hike to a waterfall, not on the characteristics of the woman. Thus, the less cluttered or uncluttered versions might make the point far more effectively.

Table 2.2 How Differences Can Prevent Listening

DIFFERENCE	HOW IT AFFECTS LISTENING
Speech style	Accents, tonal and rhythmic qualities, stuttering, nonnative speakers of a language, and gendered speech differences affect listening. When we see these differences as strange, funny, or inappropriate, we often have trouble paying attention to the message.
Background and occupation	Differences in race, ethnicity, nationality, regional upbringing, religion, education, occupation, and economic status can affect listening. When we see these differences as right or wrong, we forget to be open to the value of other experiences and influences and often stop listening.
Appearance	Styles of dress, height, weight, hair, body adornment, and even a speaker's posture affect listening. Audience members sometimes have difficulty listening because they are so focused on the speaker's appearance that they cannot focus on the message.
Values	When a speaker holds values that are different from members of the audience, listening sometimes is difficult. When listeners are so convinced that certain values are "worthy" and "good" and others are "wrong" and "bad," they rarely listen to understand why that position makes sense to the speaker.

Ask yourself two questions when you want to eliminate verbal clutter. First, do the words you use help develop your argument or make more work for listeners? Second, how many words in your speech are redundant?

Speaker Interference Caused by Differences

Differences between a speaker and an audience can also cause problems with listening. Although we are all similar in many ways, none of us exactly matches our audience in appearance, mannerisms, values, or background. When we are faced with differences, we sometimes see them in terms of a hierarchy (such as seeing a person of a certain age or sex as more trustworthy or credible than another person). When we see differences in this way, we become preoccupied with questions of right and wrong and have trouble focusing on what a speaker is saying. Table 2.2 shows some of the ways speakers and audiences are different and the ways those differences can prevent effective listening.

How do we minimize our differences, or explain and account for them, so audiences and speakers can more easily confirm one another? We can go a long way toward that goal by defining *difference* as meaning simply *different,* as not the same but still worth listening to. Thus, we can open up the possibility for listening that confirms others rather than listening that means we must agree with everything they say.

Although listeners are responsible for interference caused by differences, as speakers we also contribute to this listening problem. Here are a few ways we can minimize the impact of differences:

- Acknowledge and explain differences in speech styles or appearance. Act as an interpreter for the audience, explaining what those differences mean.

As a member of an audience, what about this speaker might cause interference for you as a listener? What could you do to reduce this interference? What could the speaker do?

AGfoto/Alex Rowbotham/Alamy Stock Photo

Practicing the Public Dialogue | 2.1

HELP YOUR AUDIENCE LISTEN TO YOUR SPEECH

Find a partner in your speech class. With your partner, choose a topic that both of you would be interested in giving a speech about. Imagine that each of you is going to give a speech to your classmates on a different aspect of this topic, and that you want to ensure that each speech is listenable. With your partner, identify information you could use that would be too complex for the audience. Next, identify language you could use that would be too technical, too casual, or non-inclusive. What information and language could you use instead that would be more audience centered? Now, each of you write a short paragraph about your topic with as much verbal clutter included as you can. Then rewrite that paragraph, taking out the clutter. Share your paragraphs with each other. Were you each successful in reducing the clutter? What else might each of you do as a speaker to stay audience centered and create a listenable speech?

MindTap®

Learn more about one remedy for a specific kind of noninclusive language, gender-neutral language.

- Explain your background and how it affects your position or presentation of information. In this way, you become a source of information regarding your differences, not just someone unusual or unfamiliar.
- Invite others to consider your values without attempting to persuade.
- Assume an invitational stance that attempts to confirm the audience as well as offer your own perspective. (See Chapter 13 for more about invitational speaking.)

Even though differences can seem like permanent obstacles to listening, both audiences and speakers must recognize that difference is the foundation of a healthy public dialogue. Once we invite dialogue rather than monologue, we encourage the exchange of ideas, information, perspectives, and even creative solutions to many of the dilemmas we face. Both audiences and speakers are responsible for creating this healthy dialogue, and a public speaking course is an excellent place to practice listening and speaking in ways that confirm and respect differences.

Technology Can Help or Hinder Listening

Perhaps the biggest hindrance to listening, when we think of technology and public speaking, is equipment failure. Our best-laid plans can become meaningless when we cannot get equipment to work, access material online, or even adjust the lights or sound to our satisfaction. It takes time to remedy these failures, and our messages may be lost or disorganized. Audiences are accustomed to instant images, instant access, and instant fixes, and when speakers cannot create the kind of listening environment an audience expects, their communication can be less effective. As a speaker, take careful stock of what is available to you, check to be sure it's in working order before the speech, and always have a backup plan to help your audience listen should your technology fail.

Audience-Centered Listening

As listeners, we can improve our skills and increase the amount of information we retain. In the process, we will also become better speakers. In fact, the listening strategies you'll read about in this and the next two main sections involve listening for many of the components you will incorporate later into your own speeches.

How to Listen Carefully

One of the most important obstacles to overcome as a listener is your own interference, or the bad habits discussed earlier in this chapter. However, if you learn to listen carefully, these bad habits are relatively easy to minimize. A **careful listener** overcomes listener interference to better understand a speaker's message. To minimize your own bad listening habits and reduce interference, try the following strategies:

- **Listen for the speaker's purpose:** Determine the speaker's goal. Is the speaker attempting to introduce, inform, invite, persuade, or commemorate? What are you being asked to learn, consider, think, or agree to?

careful listener: Listener who overcomes listener interference to better understand a speaker's message.

- **Listen for the main ideas:** Identify each of the speaker's main points or arguments. Are there two, three, or more main points or arguments? How does the speaker connect each main point or idea? How well can you follow the development of the ideas? Try to find a relationship among the main ideas by listening for previews before main ideas, transitions, connectives from one idea to the next, and summaries that follow main ideas.

- **Listen for supporting evidence and sources:** What kind of evidence does the speaker use to support ideas—narratives, personal experiences, statistics, comparisons, or expert testimony? Does the speaker use enough evidence, and does it help the speaker make the argument?

- **Write down new words, ideas, and questions:** Write down any unfamiliar words, phrases, or ideas. Keep notes as you listen, writing down main points and important ideas. Write down your questions so you remember what to ask the speaker at the end of the speech.

- **Listen for the conclusion:** Listen to see if you can discover the moment the conclusion begins. How does the speaker summarize the main points? Does the speaker end by telling a story, asking the audience to participate in some action, or using a quotation?

- **Offer nonverbal feedback:** Listen by sitting in an upright (but relaxed) posture. Engage the speaker by making eye contact (if it is culturally appropriate). Use other culturally appropriate nonverbal cues, such as smiles of encouragement and head nods that signal understanding and attention.

ANTHONY WALLACE/AFP/Getty Images

Does it seem that some members of this audience are not listening carefully? What nonverbal cues give you the impression that one person is paying less attention than another? Do you recognize your listening habits in any members of this audience?

How to Listen Critically

To listen critically to a speech is to check it for accuracy as you listen, assessing the strengths and weaknesses of the speaker's reasoning and supporting materials. Note that listening critically is different from listening to judge or find fault with a message. Rather, **critical listeners** listen for the accuracy of a speech's content and the implications of a speaker's message. Critical listeners remain open to new ideas, but they also listen carefully to how speakers develop those ideas into arguments. In addition, they consider the impact of a speaker's ideas on the immediate audience as well as the larger community.

To help you listen to speeches critically, ask yourself the questions in Table 2.3 and then follow the suggested guidelines. Asking these questions will help you assess a speaker's claims and arguments before you make decisions about their value or strength.

When we listen critically, we allow for dialogue because we avoid making quick decisions about good and bad, right and wrong. Listening critically encourages us to ask questions about ideas so we are better able to respond to claims and explore issues with others.

How to Listen Ethically

Listening ethically encourages audiences to pay attention to the moral implications of a message. Ethics refers to the study of moral standards and how those standards affect our conduct. When we speak of ethics, we are talking about the moral principles we use to guide our behaviors and decisions. An **ethical listener**, then, considers the moral impact of a speaker's message on one's self and one's community. Ethical listeners attend to the standards and principles advocated by a speaker. To listen ethically, listeners must suspend judgment, assess the information they hear, and at times respond to the speaker's message.

critical listener: Listener who listens for the accuracy of a speech's content and the implications of a speaker's message.

ethical listener: Listener who considers the moral impact of a speaker's message on one's self and one's community.

Table 2.3 Guidelines for Critical Listening

QUESTION	GUIDELINE
How fully has the speaker developed an idea? Is something left out, exaggerated, or understated? Does the speaker use sound reasoning? Are claims based on fact or opinion (see Chapter 14)?	Speakers must develop all major arguments fully rather than present them without explanation and development. Speakers should not exaggerate arguments or understate their importance. Major ideas should be supported by evidence in the form of examples, statistics, testimony, and the like.
What sources do the speaker rely on? Are they credible? How are they related to the speaker's topic? Will the sources benefit if facts are presented in a certain way (see Chapter 6)? For example, is the tobacco industry arguing that smoking isn't harmful?	Speakers must use credible sources that are as unbiased as possible. Speakers must cite sources for all new information. Sources should be cited carefully and with enough detail so the audience knows why the source is acceptable.
Are the claims the speaker makes realistic? What are the implications of those claims? Who is affected by them? In what way? Has the speaker acknowledged these effects, or are they left unstated? Are there other aspects of the issue the speaker should address (see Chapter 4)?	Speakers must make realistic and logical claims and acknowledge different perspectives. They must also acknowledge those affected by their arguments and acknowledge the effects of their proposed solutions. When speakers take a position, they must not present their position as absolute or as the only one possible.
How does this speech fit with what I know to be true? What is new to me? Can I accept this new information? Why or why not (see Chapters 4 and 14)?	When speakers make claims that go against your personal experience, see if you can discover why. Sometimes, the answer lies in cultural differences or in a speaker's research. Try to be open to different views of the world while at the same time assessing the speaker's evidence and reasoning objectively. Before you reject a speaker's claims, engage the speaker in a civil discussion to find out why your perspective differs.
What is at stake for the speaker? How invested is the speaker in the topic and the arguments being made? How will the speaker be affected if the audience disagrees (see Chapters 1, 4, and 14)?	All speakers are invested in some way in their topics and arguments. However, some arguments benefit a speaker more than anyone else. Identify the speaker's motives so you can better understand why she or he is making particular claims.

Practicing the Public Dialogue | 2.2

Listen critically to the next speech you hear and ask yourself the questions in Table 2.3. When you listen critically, do you find you better understand the speaker's position and retain more information than when you don't listen critically? Are you able to engage the speaker in the question-and-answer session more meaningfully? Now listen critically to your own speech before you give it in class. Ask yourself the first two groups of questions in Table 2.3. Are you satisfied with the arguments you make and the sources you cite? How do you think your audience will respond to the last three groups of questions?

MindTap˙

For more practice listening critically to speeches, select one or two political speeches and evaluate them using the questions in Table 2.3.

Suspend judgment. Ethical listeners suspend judgment throughout a speech. To gather as much information as they can, they are willing to listen to a speaker's message, without assigning "right" or "wrong" to it, until the speech is complete and they've had adequate time to evaluate its arguments. Ethical listeners consciously avoid reacting immediately to a statement they disagree with. This allows them to take in the speech's complete message and not jump to conclusions before the speaker is finished. And when they hear the complete message, they can contribute to the public dialogue in more informed ways.

Consider an example. Two students are listening to a speaker on their campus argue for free speech and the right of hate groups to say or print anything they want. Early in the presentation, the speaker says, "It's our constitutional right to express ourselves; this country was founded on that principle. Two hundred-plus years later, I argue we are guaranteed the right to say anything we want to anyone."

Let's Listen While We Still Can
K. David Harrison, Explorer and Linguist

Jeremy Fahringer

K. David Harrison is a linguist and leading specialist in the study of endangered languages. In addition to acting as co-leader of the Enduring Voices project with National Geographic Fellow Gregory Anderson, Harrison co-stars in the 2008 documentary film *The Linguists*. This film has been screened at the Sundance Film Festival and on college campuses across the United States. *The Linguists* is described as:

a fantastic little film that follows professors David Harrison and Gregory Anderson as they crisscross the globe on a mission to document languages on the verge of extinction. From the depths of Síberia to the high reaches of Bolivia, the pair is relentless in their goal, displaying a remarkable

patience for interviewing deaf nonagenarians who are frequently the only surviving speakers [of a language]. . . . A two-man mission to document the world's endangered tongues becomes a fleet-footed study of human communication and its limitless structural and functional possibilities.[23]

Harrison believes there are many reasons to preserve vanishing languages. Most of the world's languages do not use writing; instead, they rely on their oral languages. Oral societies use cognitive skills and memory techniques to store information, and we can learn a lot by listening to them.[24] These languages teach us how "ancestors calculated accurately the passing of seasons without clocks or calendars. How humans adapted to hostile environments, from the Artic to Amazonia."[25] Yet preserving languages requires work. Designated "last speaker" of the Chemehuevi tribe of Arizona, Johnny Hill, Jr., says many children of his tribe claim they want to learn the language, "but when it comes time to do the work, nobody comes around." This leaves Hill feeling linguistically isolated. "There's nobody left to talk to, all the elders have passed on, so I talk to myself . . . that's just how it is."[26]

Harrison and his team are willing to do the work of helping to preserve dying languages because they believe it to be the most consequential social trend for coming decades because "what they know—which we've forgotten or never knew—may some day save us." Harrison and Anderson are listening. Harrison says, "We hear their voices, now muted, sharing knowledge in 7,000 different ways of speaking. Let's listen while we still can."[27]

WHAT DO YOU THINK?

1. If listening to others is a crucial part of the public dialogue, why might preserving language be a central part of this listening process?
2. Although our differences can cause difficulties in listening to others, how might Harrison and his team's efforts to preserve linguistic differences actually reduce the difficulties caused by cultural differences?
3. What types of speeches might you give that engage Harrison's ideas of "listening while we can"? Would you consider one of these as a speech to give in this class? Why or why not?

Sange Degio/Living Tongues Institute; Enduring Voices Project

Practicing the Public Dialogue | 2.3

LISTENING CAREFULLY, CRITICALLY, AND ETHICALLY

Using the Speech Evaluation Checklist for this activity, evaluate any of the following speakers: one of your instructors, a public figure, a student speaker giving one of the speeches featured in the MindTap, or someone else speaking publicly. Bring your completed checklist to class and discuss the strategies you used to be a careful listener and the ways that listening critically and ethically helped you evaluate the strength of the speaker's ideas and claims.

Speech Evaluation Checklist

Speaker _____ Topic _____

Introduction

_____ Is the purpose of the speech clear? What is the purpose?

_____ Does the speaker establish credibility?

_____ Are the topic and purpose relevant to the audience?

_____ Does the speaker preview the speech?

_____ Does the speaker present ideas that might require me to suspend my judgment while I listen? Identify those ideas.

Body

_____ Are the main points clearly identified? What are the main points?

_____

_____

_____

_____ Are the main points fully supported? Why or why not?

_____ What might be the moral impact of the main points on me and other people?

_____ Are the sources credible? Why or why not?

_____ Is the reasoning sound? Why or why not?

_____ Are other perspectives addressed?

_____ Is the speech listenable? Why or why not? (Consider language, organization, and interference.)

At what points do I suspend judgment to listen ethically and effectively?

_____

_____

Conclusion

_____ Does the speaker signal the end of the speech?

_____ Does the speaker summarize the main points?

_____ Does the speaker appear open to dialogue about the topic?

Discussion

What questions would I like to ask the speaker? _____

What information would I like clarified? _____

What would I like the speaker to talk more about? _____

What would I like the speaker to think more about? _____

What information do I have that I want to share with the speaker?

_____

_____

One listener rushes to judgment and says, "That's ridiculous. How can he say that? People don't have the right to say anything they want whenever and wherever they want. That's harassment, and we don't have the right to do that to anyone!"

By rushing to judgment, this listener may stop listening altogether or may focus on a response to the speaker rather than listening to more of what the speaker has to say. By doing so, she may miss the speaker's later claim that our right to express ourselves also guarantees that we can freely criticize hate speech, a freedom not all societies enjoy.

Now consider a student who listens ethically, suspending judgment to listen to the full message: "Wow, that sounds extreme to me, but maybe he's got a reason for making that claim. Let me see if I can understand why he makes such a strong statement."

Even though this student disagrees with the speaker, he's willing to put aside his disagreement until he's heard all the speaker has to say. Thus, he'll have an easier time following the speaker's ideas, confirming them, and responding intelligently to them. Suspending judgment does not mean that we as listeners sit passively without scrutinizing whatever a speaker says. You can still question and disagree with a speaker's message. Suspending judgment is simply a tool to help you listen more effectively and take in a speaker's entire message.

Assess information and respond to the speaker's ideas. Ethical listening also requires that listeners assess a message (listen critically) first and then respond to the speaker's ideas. When ethical listeners respond to a speaker's ideas, they participate in a constructive dialogue with a speaker. Even if they do not agree with a speaker's position, ethical listeners join the public dialogue so they can better understand a position, explore differences, and share their own views. In their attempts to understand, ethical listeners recognize, acknowledge, and show value for others, even if their positions are vastly different from the speaker's.

Speakers as Listeners: Staying Audience Centered

Although this chapter has focused extensively on how we as members of an audience can improve our listening skills, speakers are also listeners. In front of an audience, speakers do more than produce a steady stream of words. They listen to their audiences during the presentation by monitoring their expressions, posture, feedback, and level of attention. Speakers use this information to adapt to audience needs throughout the speech by slowing down or speeding up, taking more time to explain, omitting information, or adding extra examples to clarify. In Chapter 4, you'll learn more about your relationship to your audience. Here we'll focus on how you can listen effectively to your audience.

When you give a speech, remember that audience members bring with them many bad listening habits. What follows are some examples of problematic audiences and ways you can counter their bad habits to help them listen better.

Audiences Who Think They Aren't Interested

Sometimes, audience members appear uninterested in your speech from the start or seem to assume they already know what you will say.

- **Here's how you can address this behavior:** Make your introduction and first main points compelling, innovative, and attentive to your audience's particular biases.
- **Here's an example of a speaker who addressed this behavior successfully:** Genet began his speech by saying, "You say you already know. You say, 'There's nothing new here!' You might even be thinking, 'This will never happen to me,' and maybe—just maybe—you're right. But what if you're wrong? What if you're probably wrong? Are you willing to be the two out of three who didn't listen?" After this introduction, he had the full attention of the class and was able to maintain their attention throughout his speech on alcohol and drug addiction.

MindTap°

To see another student speaker attempt to gain her audience's attention in her introduction, watch the video clip of Tiffany Brisco. What does she say in her introduction that makes it easy for her audience to listen to her speech?

A group of New Hampshire environmental activists disrupted Hillary Clinton's town hall-style campaign stop in 2015, silencing Clinton with both a chant and a banner that said "act on climate change!" If you were interrupted by speakers such as these activists, which of the strategies for responding to disruptions might you use?

Melina Mara/The Washington Post/Getty Images

Audiences Who Are Distracted or Disruptive

Some audience members may slouch, fail to make eye contact, and daydream. Others make or attend to distractions.

- **How you can address this behavior:** Ask questions of the entire audience or of particular members. Or ask the audience to complete an activity related to your topic, such as making a list or jotting down what they already know about the topic. Bring particularly disruptive people into your speech verbally or by bringing them to the front of the audience for a legitimate reason (for example, to give a demonstration or to record discussion ideas on a whiteboard). Note that you want to be careful about singling out audience members. Make sure you aren't embarrassing people or making the rest of the audience feel uncomfortable.

- **An example of a speaker who addressed this behavior successfully:** Noticing that several of his audience members were reading the newspaper during his speech, Seth paused midsentence to catch his audience's attention and said, "You know, I bet that whatever's in that paper isn't as current or relevant to our lives as my next point. Because, at this moment in time, our government is spending billions of dollars to cover up . . . ," and he continued with his topic. At that point, he had the full and respectful attention of the audience.

  Sometimes, audience members are distracted by the speaker—by how he or she dresses, unusual hair styles, differences in speech styles, and so on.

- **How you can address this behavior:** Explain the distraction. In addition, be sure to dress appropriately for the speaking situation. Chapter 10 explains how personal appearance affects the way audiences see you.

- **An example of a speaker who addressed this behavior successfully:** Angelique, a student with a strong accent, shared with her audience that she was from the Dominican Republic. She explained that her husband kept trying to correct her accent, but she told him, "It's my accent and I like it." Sharing this story in the introduction of her speech made her audience laugh and helped reduce the focus on her accent. It also helped her audience listen to her message.

Approaching this type of situation with good-natured humor can go a long way toward reducing distractions and resistance to your message. It can also help audience members feel that you value them.

THE LISTENING PROJECT: WHAT DOES THE WORLD THINK OF AMERICA?

How well do you think you can listen to what others think of you? Asking the question, "What do you think of America?" four "listeners" traveled to fourteen different countries to hear the answers. Carrie Lennox (seventh-grade history teacher), Bob Roeglin (corrections), Bao Phi (spoken word artist and poet), and Han Shan (trainer of grassroots youth activists) traveled around the globe to ask common people "What's wrong and what's right with America?" They made a commitment to be curious and to listen to the answers, and the result is the documentary and award-winning film *The Listening Project*.

The producers of the film explain: "We had our own very strong feelings about the Unites States and its place in the world. How do you set that aside? How do you set aside your own personal views and really try to go out and very objectively talk to people and be able to really listen?"—especially regarding views with which you might not agree. But the producers and the "listeners" made that commitment. Here is a little of what they heard, when they asked, "When I say 'America' or 'American,' what's the first thing that pops into your head?"

> There is a Japanese saying: To criticize is to help . . ."
> "America really influences the world . . ."
> "America is what gives to you with one hand and then takes away with both."
> "I love America, and I hate America."
> "Most Americans don't understand how we live where we live and what is going on. We are not a terrorist people."
> "In America, there is a sense that if you've got drive and ambition, you can make it."
> "America's role has always been to try and make peace."
> "You have always been so much involved with wars."
> "The Greeks and the Romans—America should learn from history."
> "The world is one, one, two, three: there we all are."
> "Does it really make you so happy to drive home in your Beemer and go out again in your Lexus?"
> "There is a saying: 'God has given you two ears and one mouth to listen more than speak.'"

WHAT DO YOU THINK?

1. What listening skills do you think *The Listening Project* listeners might have used to really listen to the people they spoke with?
2. Have you been in a situation in which you listened to things you agreed with and did not agree with? What listening strategies did you use?
3. If you could go around and ask people a question with a commitment to hearing answers you might not agree with, what would that question be?

Audiences Who Are Confused

You can use a number of strategies to help audiences who appear confused by the information in your speech.

- **How you can address this behavior:** Slow down and explain with more detail. Reduce your number of main points. Alter your language to be more inclusive, less complex, or even less simple. Improvise visual aids: use an available flip chart or whiteboard or ask someone from the audience to demonstrate your ideas.
- **An example of a speaker who addressed this behavior successfully:** When Marilyn saw her audience looking confused, she outlined her main points on a whiteboard and jotted down key words and phrases. The audience applauded her efforts and acknowledged that her speech was much easier to follow with a visual map.

Audiences Who Plan Their Responses Rather than Listen

Sometimes, particular audience members appear to be planning their responses to you during your speech.

- **How you can address this behavior:** Both verbally and nonverbally acknowledge their eagerness to participate, and approach it as a positive sign of interest.
- **An example of a speaker who addressed this behavior successfully:** When Hallie watched a member of her audience react with dismay to one of her claims and then fidget and sit on the edge of his seat, she knew she had to respond somehow. She acknowledged his desire to respond by saying, "I see I've struck a chord with some of you. If you'll hang on to your questions and hear me out, I'd love to hear your reactions at the end of the speech." Her resister relaxed a bit and was able to put his opposition

aside long enough to listen to her full arguments and reasons. The conversation at the end of the speech was lively and dynamic, and both Hallie and the audience member benefited from it.

In Chapter 4, you will discover other excellent ways to help your audience listen to you. As a speaker, when you listen to your audience, you make your message more listenable and memorable, and you make it easier for your audience to give you the attention and respect you deserve.

Chapter Summary

We listen to others for very important reasons.

- We listen to others so we can confirm their ideas and enter the public dialogue in ways that are intelligent and rewarding.
- Listening is one of the most important communicative acts.

We sometimes fail to listen.

- Bad listening habits cause listener interference, which stops or hinders us from receiving messages.
- Our failure to listen well is also caused by speaker interference due to information, language, or other differences in style, background, appearance, and values.

There are many ways to improve our listening.

- To listen carefully, listen for supporting evidence and for the speaker's purpose, main ideas, and the links between ideas. Take notes and write questions you have for the speaker. Provide positive nonverbal feedback. Listen for the conclusion of the speech, and review the material you have just heard.

- To listen critically, assess the strengths and weaknesses of a speaker's reasoning and evidence, and remain open to new ideas and information.
- To listen ethically, listen for the moral implications of a message.
- Ethical listeners practice two listening behaviors: (1) suspending judgment and (2) assessing and responding to the speaker's ideas.

Speakers are also listeners and can adapt their messages so their speeches are listenable.

- When you give a speech, listen to your audience for signs of disinterest, hostility, or opposition.
- Also listen to make sure your style and mannerisms aren't confusing or distracting.
- Finally, listen for signs that your audience is confused by the information in your speech.

Invitation to Public Speaking Online MindTap®

Now that you have read Chapter 2, use your MindTap Communication for *Invitation to Public Speaking* for quick access to the digital resources that accompany this text. These resources include:

- **Study tools** that will help you assess your learning and prepare for exams (digital glossary, key term flash cards, review quizzes).
- **Activities and assignments** that will help you hone your knowledge and build your public speaking skills throughout

the course, as well as help you explore public speaking concepts online (web links), give you step-by-step guidance through the research, outline, and note card preparation process (Outline Builder), watch and critique videos of sample speeches (Interactive Video Activities), and allow you to practice and give your presentation online using a speech video delivery, recording, and grading system (YouSeeU).

Key Concepts MindTap® Test your knowledge with online printable flashcards.

careful listener (28)
colloquialism (23)
confirm (20)
considerate speech (22)
critical listener (29)
culturally inclusive language (24)
ethical listener (29)
euphemism (23)
gender-inclusive language (24)

hearing (20)
interference (20)
jargon (23)
listenable speech (21)
listening (20)
slang (23)
spotlighting (24)
verbal clutter (25)

Review Questions

1. Identify the times you have listened to confirm others. Were you able to recognize, acknowledge, and express value for another individual? Did you do this verbally or nonverbally? Now identify the times you listened with judgment. What are the differences between the two types of listening? Do you prefer one to the other? Why?

2. Monitor your listening for a day and write down five ways your listening failed. How might you change these bad listening habits?

3. Attend, watch, or listen to a speech given by someone very different from you. Pay attention to how you manage the listening interference that comes from differences. Can you listen nonjudgmentally? Can you accommodate different speech styles, mannerisms, dress, and backgrounds? How are you able to listen even though differences may be present?

4. What kinds of slang, jargon, or euphemisms do you use in your everyday interactions at school, at work, or at home? Make a list of some of the unique expressions you use and define each word or phrase on your list. Now think about your next speech topic and your audience. What would be the benefits or the drawbacks of using slang, jargon, or euphemisms in your speech?

5. Review the definition of ethical listening. What is the role of ethical listening in the public dialogue? Do you believe it is your responsibility to listen ethically? Do you think you can suspend judgment and listen to assess and respond to the information? Explain your answers.

3 | Developing Your Speech Topic and Purpose

IN THIS CHAPTER, YOU WILL LEARN TO:

- Recognize the ways context influences your speaking goals

- Select audience-centered speech topics

- Explain the process of brainstorming

- Design clear statements of purpose for your speeches

- Formulate the thesis statement of your speeches

For more than 50 years, student groups in the United States and other countries have publicly asked political leaders to act with integrity and morality. In 1962, Students for a Democratic Society issued the Port Huron Statement, a "living document" that condemned the Cold War, racism, and poverty, and identified students as "agents of social change." The Occupy Wall Street movement reiterates many of those claims, questions the morals of our leaders, calls for "participatory democracy," and has served as an inspiration for student-led movements in Tunisia, Egypt, and several countries in the Middle East. Student protests in 2015 against racial discrimination at the University of Missouri sparked protests at other college and university campuses across the country, "forcing higher education administrators to take

MindTap® Start with a quick warm-up activity and review the chapter's learning objectives.

WOJTEK RADWANSKI/Getty Images

▲ Because there is no shortage of important issues to discuss in today's complex and interconnected world, selecting a topic for a speech can be challenging. In this chapter you will find strategies for choosing relevant topics, narrowing your speaking goals, and focusing your ideas.

another look at racial misunderstandings."[1] Inspired by the Freedom Riders of the early 1960s, and selling for 25 cents in 1962, the Port Huron Statement is described as having "a power and excitement rare to any document," and as having "dignity in its language, persuasiveness in its arguments."[2]

Whether or not you've followed the voices of today's student protesters, heard the term *participatory democracy*, or are familiar with the Freedom Riders or the Port Huron Statement, you can use the public speaking skills you develop in this class to participate in our public dialogue. This chapter will help you select interesting and relevant topics for your speeches, topics that reflect the concerns of our world and that help us sort through complex issues. This chapter will also help you determine the best way to frame a topic so you fulfill your speaking purpose and what you want to accomplish with your speech.

Successful public speaking is usually the result of careful planning and forethought rather than any so-called intuitive or natural speaking ability. No doubt, we can and do find ourselves in front of audiences without much advance notice. However, we are more likely to find ourselves speaking on topics we care about after we've had time to prepare our ideas. Although preparation means work, careful planning before you speak helps you choose speech topics and then narrow them and your purpose to accommodate three speaking contexts: when you decide to speak, when you have been asked to speak, and when you are required to speak.

MindTap®

READ, highlight, and take notes online.

How Context Influences Your Speaking Goals

There are many different contexts for speaking—formal or informal settings, large or small audiences, serious or lighthearted issues, and so on. Identifying the context in which you speak publicly will help you understand the connection between why we speak publicly and what we speak about.

Deciding to Speak

The most common reason to speak is because we find an issue so important or our experience so relevant that we decide to speak about it. This is also perhaps the most powerful reason people become public speakers. Throughout history, people used a variety of platforms to share their opinions and ideas. They spoke in churches and town halls, at street corners, in town squares or centers, and on wooden soapboxes. So important was the power of public speech in shaping opinions and influencing actions that until the 1850s, legislation in the United States prevented certain people, such as women, from speaking publicly.

Mass media and journalists may be viewed as the voice of the people, yet, individuals are inserting their own voices into public discussions and stimulating important discussions at a rapid pace. Today, people use blogs, Twitter, Facebook, YouTube, and more to participate in public discussions. In educational settings, we give class presentations and participate in student government. In social gatherings, we debate current issues or offer toasts and congratulations to others. In business and professional meetings, we evaluate ideas and create plans. And in community forums, we discuss local issues, and assess their impact on the environment, population growth, education, and the like.

When people decide to speak, as students throughout history have, they generally speak about issues central to their lives and well-being. To decide to speak publicly is to decide you can offer an audience important knowledge or a valuable perspective.

Personal Stories after Natural Disasters
Becca Skinner: Explorer, Photographer

Courtesy of Becca Skinner.

Rebecca Skinner is from Wyoming, and attended the University of Wyoming, where she majored in Social Work. For Skinner, photography became more than a hobby when, in the fall of 2010, she won a grant from her university to travel to New Orleans to photograph the rebuilding after Hurricane Katrina. Then, as a National Geographic Young Explorer, she traveled to Banda Aceh, Indonesia, to photograph rebuilding efforts after the 2004 tsunami in the Indian Ocean. In Indonesia, she found it "most challenging" to try to document seven years of rebuilding in one short month on location. Since then, she has spoken about her expeditions to varied audiences, from small groups of third-graders to large audiences of potential Young Explorer candidates.

Her talks feature her photographs, which she selects to suit the particular group or occasion. As someone who majored in social work, she is concerned about people's lives, and she realized that, through her photography, she could tell the personal stories of people whose lives were affected by natural disasters. She says,

> Studying social work in school has made me really passionate about giving a voice to people who feel they cannot be heard. Through both my tsunami and Hurricane Katrina photo projects, I've realized that post-natural disaster communities are often forgotten about or pushed aside in the wake of more recent news stories. I strongly believe that how a community recovers (or does not recover) is just as important as the disaster itself. Photographically documenting these communities and individuals seems to give personal stories and experiences a voice through an artistic and tangible venue.

Skinner says she is a "really visual person," and she selects her photographs to tell particular stories that are tailored to her audience. For example, when she gave a presentation to a group of third graders, her talk focused not on natural disasters, but about the process of photography; she selected both "good" and "bad" photographs, and engaged the students in a discussion of what they liked or didn't like about the photos. For older audiences, she talks about the people she met and tries to convey both individual and community stories of disaster and rebuilding; her stories also describe how she makes connections across cultures through her photography. In Indonesia, she photographed the top of a mosque that had been carried nine miles from a village and landed in the middle of a rice paddy. She said, "I went that night and all the stars were out, and so I have a picture of the top of this mosque in a rice field with all of the stars overhead, and that picture to me was very special," because it reminds her of the people she met, their stories, and their resilience.[3]

WHAT DO YOU THINK?

1. Skinner turned her hobby, photography, into a way to raise awareness, advocate for change, and stimulate public discussion and dialogue. What interests of your own, or your classmates, could be used in a similar way to stimulate the public dialogue on important issues?

2. The severity of recent natural disasters has made this phenomenon a common topic in our public deliberations. What are the different aspects of natural disasters that you might consider developing into a speech, and what would your purpose be in giving a speech on natural disasters?

Courtesy of Becca Skinner

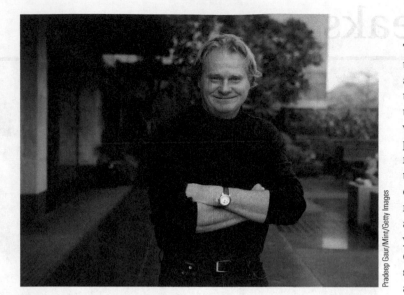

Pradeep Gaur/Mint/Getty Images

National Geographic Explorer Wade Davis explains, "Individuals have had, literally, their careers transformed by a single TED Talk. So, have something important to say, that the world needs to hear—I mean, that is the essence of communication" (personal interview, December 14, 2015).

Being Asked to Speak

To be asked to speak is probably the most flattering context for a public speaker. When we are asked to speak, we are asked to share important experiences, our expertise, or our perspectives with others. When we are asked to speak, we are recognized as experts or at least as people who have information others want. As you move through life, you might find you are asked to speak in educational settings, at service clubs, or at formal or professional gatherings. But remember that although you may be considered an expert, you'll be a more successful speaker if you follow the principles of speech preparation discussed in this book. Expertise in a particular subject area does not always guarantee you are an expert at giving speeches.

Being Required to Speak

Being required to speak can be a regular part of our lives. For example, you're now taking a public speaking course that requires you to give speeches. But outside the public speaking class, you may have a job that requires public speaking, such as in marketing or as a tour guide. Occasionally, you may have to fulfill a civic or legal obligation, such as speaking before a Senate hearing or as part of a jury.

When you are required to speak, you often must follow strict guidelines. For example, in a professional setting, you likely will have a limited amount of time to speak and a very specific speaking goal. In a typical public speaking assignment, you may be asked to give an informative speech that is three minutes long, cites two sources, and includes a visual aid. Although we may not like required public speaking, learning to give speeches in a public speaking course can be invaluable. If you view a classroom speaking requirement as an opportunity to prepare for other speaking contexts, you can make the most of the time you spend in class. In a public speaking course, you are given structure and guidance that can help you improve your presentational skills and participate in the public dialogue.

These three contexts—deciding, being asked, and being required to speak—are the reasons people enter the public dialogue. Understanding how you become a public speaker is the first step in preparing a successful presentation. Once you recognize why you are speaking, you can turn your attention to selecting and narrowing your speech topic and deciding on your purpose for speaking.

Choosing Your Speech Topic

Your **speech topic** is the subject of your speech. Selecting a topic for a speech can be a very creative and energizing part of putting a speech together. With a little systematic thought and inventive organization, speakers often come up with a wide range of interesting speech topics. By now, you've probably discovered in your public speaking course that you need to choose a topic of interest to both you and your audience. The steps described in this section will help you find interesting and relevant speech topics for your required speeches. When you decide or are asked to speak, your topic is usually predetermined. Your task in these contexts is to make sure you understand your topic fully. You can do this by asking yourself several questions, which are discussed at the end of this section.

speech topic: Subject of your speech.

tip

National Geographic Explorer

BECCA SKINNER, Explorer, Photographer

How do you practice your speech? Do you stand in front of a mirror or do you have somebody tape you, or how have you practiced?

I have had someone tape me before. I read my presentations to my dog, honestly. If I mess up, she doesn't care and I can start over. But most of the time, I've been alone in a hotel room, or in my own room or in my car and I'll just keep practicing. I'll keep saying it out loud. Talking in front of a mirror has never felt really comfortable for me. Even being taped wasn't really comfortable for me, so I think just repeating my talk by myself or with my dog to help.

The Classroom Setting

Before you can select an appropriate and interesting topic for your assigned speech, you must consider the requirements of your assignment. Assigned speeches usually have several constraints because they are presented in a classroom setting:

- *Preselected purpose.* An instructor usually tells you to give a particular type of speech, such as a speech to inform or persuade. You do not have the freedom to select your speech purpose, and you must select a topic compatible with the purpose.
- *Time limits.* Class size determines speech length; your instructor wants to make sure all students in class have time to give their speeches. Classroom speeches often last only a few minutes, and you may be penalized for going over time. You must select and narrow your topic to satisfy the assignment's time limits.
- *Highly structured assignment.* You're usually asked to incorporate several specific speech components. You may be required to cite a specific number of outside sources, use visual aids, incorporate a specific style of language, or use a particular organizational pattern. The structure of an assigned speech often influences topic selection.
- *Instructor as an audience.* You give your classroom speeches to an instructor who is already a skilled public speaker. You must select a stimulating topic that your instructor, who has listened to many other speeches, will appreciate.
- *Class members as an audience.* Your classmates may become the best audience for you as a beginning public speaker. They also are learning the ropes of public speaking, and they will appreciate your diligent efforts. But they can also be a challenge because they are also searching for interesting topics, so try to avoid commonly used topics.

So how do you select a manageable, interesting, and dynamic topic for your required speeches? The process takes a bit of planning and effort, but you will discover that you have a wealth of usable ideas once you organize your thoughts about who you are, what you know, and what issues and events capture your own attention.

Choosing Your Topic and Staying Audience Centered

One of the most basic ways to select a topic for a required speech is to make a list of your interests and give a speech about one of them. In this section, you'll discover that with some care and time, you can build on this basic process to come up with unique and interesting slants on topics that at first may seem uninteresting.

In a public speaking classroom, the first step in selecting a topic is to outline the requirements of the speech assignment. Write down your speech requirements at the

Radius/SuperStock

Public speaking instructors and students might hear eighty or more speeches in a single course. Try to think about who is in your audience and select your speech topics carefully so that your speech stands out.

top of your computer screen page or a piece of paper. Your assignment might look like this:

> Informative purpose; four minutes long; three to four sources; one statistic; one of the following: metaphor, analogy, narrative, or alliteration; inclusive language.

The second step is to match your interests or expertise to these requirements.

Matching your interests to a speaking assignment. Before you can match your interests to a particular assignment, you must determine what they are. Divide your interests into the following categories: what you like to do, what you like to talk about, and what you would like to know more about.

Most people can identify many activities they like to participate in. Make a list of them, including those that seem serious as well as playful or silly. Try to be as detailed as possible. Krista, a twenty-three-year-old college senior, likes to do the following:

- swim, run, cycle
- play soccer, volleyball, tennis, and Frisbee golf
- snowboard, skateboard, and hike
- watch television and movies
- Facebook
- spend time with her friends
- coach children in sports during the summer
- get good grades
- stay up late
- eat pizza, hamburgers, anything barbecued, and some vegetables

With a little adjustment and creativity, any of these interests could be turned into an interesting informative topic. Krista could inform her audience about any of the following:

- the top ten medal-earning swimmers in the world
- the history of marathon running
- how to play Frisbee golf
- who invented skateboards
- the longest-running television sitcom
- the first chat room on the Web
- gender differences in friendship styles
- the relationship between grades and annual income
- medical research on optimal sleeping patterns
- the origins of pizza

These are just a few of the many informative topics Krista could speak about, all relevant to her instructor, her classmates, and the public dialogue.

Another good way to find speech topics is to take inventory of what you like to talk about. To do this, ask yourself the following questions:

- When do you find yourself participating in discussions?
- When do you feel like you have a lot to say about an issue but don't speak up?
- What topics do you raise in conversations?
- What topics do you repeatedly return to or seek more information about?

For example, Keenan loves to talk about basketball. He could turn this very broad topic into a dynamic speech by going beyond the obvious. What does he love about the sport? Is it the players' skill, the strategy of the game, the politics of athletics, or the behaviors of sports fans? He could fashion a speech out of any of these topics:

- evolution of basketball as a sport
- advantages and disadvantages of starting children in the sport at a young age
- money behind the game
- balance between athletic talent and game strategy
- role of sports fans in supporting individual teams

With some creativity and effort, Keenan could turn his love of basketball into an informative, invitational, or persuasive speech.

Issues, events, people, and ideas you are curious about also often make excellent speech topics. You could give a speech that informs others of a particular event, or you could persuade them to participate in that event. If you are intrigued by a famous person, you could give a commemorative or informative speech about that person's life and accomplishments. If you are curious about a place, an idea, an object, or an animal, you could explore it with others in an informative or invitational speech. If you participate in an activity or have always wanted to do so, you could give a persuasive, informative, or invitational speech about it. Speeches that grow out of a speaker's curiosity often capture the attention, interest, and curiosity of an audience as well.

Matching your expertise to a speech assignment. *Expertise* can be an intimidating label, but whether or not we realize it, almost everyone is an expert in some area of life. Some people are experts in obvious ways, such as playing a musical instrument, painting, or computer programming. Other people are experts in less obvious ways. They may have an unfailing sense of direction, know the right gift to buy for any occasion, or tell hilarious jokes. Dynamic speech topics can come from your own skills and talents. Consider the following examples:

- Tomás is an excellent cook. He decides to give an informative speech on the differences between traditional Bolivian and Spanish foods.
- April is fluent in American Sign Language. She decides to give a speech persuading her audience to learn a second language.
- Rachael comes from a family of artists. She decides to give a speech inviting her audience to support the arts.
- Gardner is a mechanic. He decides to give a commemorative speech on nineteenth-century French inventor Gustave Trouvé, the creator of the first automobile powered by electricity.

These are interesting speech topics about activities or skills that may seem mundane to the person who has them. You can identify areas in which you may be considered an expert by asking yourself the following questions:

- What comes naturally to me?
- What runs in my family?
- Do I often get compliments when I do a particular thing?
- Do others repeatedly ask me to take the lead, take care of some situation, or solve a problem for them?
- Have I ever had special training or lessons?
- Have I spent years studying, practicing, or doing something?
- Do I have degrees, certifications, licenses, or other markers of my accomplishments?

If you answered yes to any of these questions, you may be an expert in some area that would make an interesting topic for a required speech. Although not all of our experiences make us experts, you might find you have expertise because of an event you've witnessed or an environment you've been in. Consider these possibilities:

- Did you live or grow up in another country?
- Did you play sports in high school or college?

- Is there something about your family that is unique or unusual?
- Have you had unexpected or momentous experiences in your life?
- Have you been exposed to different cultures, religions, and philosophies?

Situations like these can generate short speeches that satisfy the requirements of an assignment, capture the attention of your instructor and classmates, and relate directly to the public dialogue. A few final tips: As you translate your experiences into speech topics, be certain you can talk about them easily without getting upset or revealing more than you are comfortable with. And note that although you might know a lot about a topic, you should still research it to discover interesting aspects about which you might be unaware.

Brainstorming

Brainstorming is the process of generating ideas randomly and uncritically, without attention to logic, connections, or relevance. This process requires you to free-associate rather than plan, and it is often used as a problem-solving strategy in business settings. Brainstorming can be an effective tool for coming up with speech topics in required speaking situations, and you can use this technique by yourself, in pairs, or in groups. Here are some tips for successful brainstorming:

- Let your thoughts go where they will. Don't censor yourself or others. Allow all ideas, even those that seem trivial or odd.
- Write down your ideas quickly. Don't worry about spelling or punctuation, and abbreviate whenever you can.
- Keep your list handy over the course of several days, and add to it as new thoughts come to you.

You can approach brainstorming in several ways: by free association, by clustering, by categories, and by technology.

Brainstorming by free association. Brainstorming can be as unstructured as sitting at your desk with a pencil and paper, or at your computer with a blank screen, and recording all ideas that come to your mind. Although it might take a moment for the first idea to come to mind, more will follow in rapid succession.

Brainstorming on a computer is especially effective because many people can type faster than they can write in longhand. When you record your ideas quickly, your thoughts also flow quickly. If you use a computer, consider starting by free-associating with the computer screen turned off. Sometimes, the blank screen allows you to free-associate without the pressure of filling up a blank page. At other times, seeing your ideas on the screen stimulates your thinking and spurs additional ideas.[4] After only a minute, a typical free association list might look like this:

> hands, keyboard, letters, movement, running, wind, kites, children, play, laughter, skinned knees, Band-Aids, nurses, hospitals, sterile, feral cats, tiger, cougars, wilderness, encroachment, farming, ranching, cows, cowboys, rodeos, circus, clowns, entertainment, containment, buckets, garage, car, war, peace, hostility, conflict, harm, warm, cold, snow skiing, skis, lifts, chairs, dining rooms, meals, holidays, families, celebration, gifts.

A free association list can go on and on until you run out of ideas. When you're trying to come up with a speech topic, try to spend at least several minutes brainstorming by free association to generate as many ideas as possible. Once you've compiled your list, explore it to determine if one of your ideas might be an appropriate speech topic. The free association list here could generate the following interesting speech topics:

- the inventor of Band-Aids
- what to do when you encounter a feral cat
- different kinds of clowns
- how different countries celebrate holidays or the starts of new seasons

brainstorming: Process of generating ideas randomly and uncritically, without attention to logic, connections, or relevance.

Bryan Busovicki/Shutterstock.com

Using a busy image like this as a basis for brainstorming can yield a lot of good ideas for speech topics. What possible topics come to mind when you consider the details of this photo? Can you narrow your ideas down to one interesting topic that would interest your audience and contribute to the public dialogue?

If brainstorming by free association doesn't generate the kinds of topics you think might make an interesting speech, other techniques might help.

Brainstorming by clustering. Clustering is a visual way to brainstorm. Write down an idea in the center of a piece of paper and then draw four or five lines extending from it. At the ends of these lines, write down other ideas that relate to your first idea. Then extend lines from these new ideas to even more ideas. Let's take a look at Jeret's clustering diagram. He began scuba diving at a very young age, so he used this as his general idea and developed the cluster of ideas in Figure 3.1.

Brainstorming by categories. Most speeches given in public speaking classrooms are about concepts, events, natural phenomena, objects, people, places, plans and policies, problems, and processes. As you've probably noticed, these topics represent different categories. Brainstorming by categories is an excellent way to generate a speech topic, and it provides more structure than free association or clustering. To brainstorm by categories, list the following nine categories on your computer screen or a piece of paper. Then list five or six different words under each

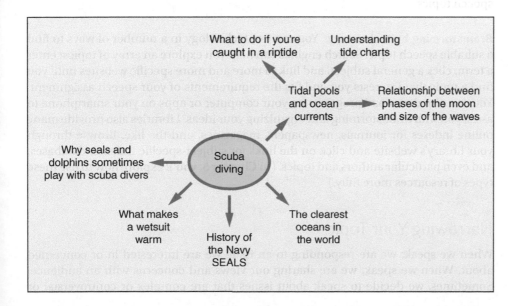

Figure 3.1 Cluster diagram

The figure shows that from scuba diving, his general idea, Jeret was able to branch out to many additional ideas. Brainstorming by clustering is a good way to generate speech topics because it gives some structure to the brainstorming process without limiting your possibilities too much.

heading that fit into the indicated categories. Two students working together came up with this list:

Concepts	Events	Natural phenomena
socialism	Hurricane Sandy	tornadoes
tourism	Stop Online Piracy Act	eclipses
sustainability	Internet Blackout	monsoons
astrophysics	Walk for the Cure	geysers
dieting	Mardi Gras	mudslides
long-distance relationships	Inti Raymi (Incan Festival of the Sun)	glaciers
	Atlanta Hawks' Jason Collins's coming out	**Places**
Objects		my hometown
cell phones		Machu Picchu
guitars	**People**	Germany
cars	Barack Obama	China
films of M. Night Shyamalan	Aamir Khan	Tanzania
Japanese teapots	Tiger Woods	Stonehenge
mountains	Marissa Mayer	
	Roya Mahboob	**Processes**
	Sonia Sotomayor	brewing beer
		building a house
Plans and policies	**Problems**	preparing a meal
universal health care	terrorism	debating versus dialoguing
government stimulus plans	sexism	making electricity
gun control	racism	
sex education	cancer	
censorship laws	obesity	

If none of the words you write down immediately strikes you as a good speech topic, select one or two and use free association or clustering to narrow your scope, generate new ideas, or frame the topic in a way that is interesting and fits the requirements of your assignment.

Similarly, if none of your brainstormed topics catches your interest, link several of them together. Can you find a connection among Mexico, India, and your hometown? What about these locations and tsunamis or earthquakes? How about laptops, espresso machines, and theme dining? Linking any of these topics, randomly or with purpose, gives you additional opportunities to develop interesting speech topics.

Brainstorming by technology. You can use technology in a number of ways to find a suitable speech topic. Search engines can help you explore an array of topics: enter a term, click a general subject, and link to more and more specific websites until you find a topic that interests you and fits the requirements of your speech assignment. You can also download programs on your computer or apps on your smartphone to assist you with brainstorming and organizing your ideas. Libraries also provide many online indexes for journals, newspapers, magazines, and the like. Browse through your library's website and click on the links for subject-specific indexes, databases, and even particular authors and topics. (In Chapter 5, you'll explore how to use these types of resources more fully.)

Narrowing Your Topic

When we speak, we are responding to an issue we are interested in or concerned about. When we speak, we are sharing our views and concerns with an audience. Sometimes, we decide to speak about issues that are complex or controversial or

CIVIC ENGAGEMENT In Action

"I HAD NO IDEA THAT ANYONE WAS LISTENING"

Wangari Maathai (1940–2011), the daughter of a sharecropper father and a farmer mother, was often considered something of a first lady. She is the first woman from East and central Africa to earn a Ph.D. (in biological sciences); the first woman to become a department chair of the University of Nairobi; the first president of the African Union's Economic, Social, and Cultural Council; and the first African woman to earn a Nobel Peace Prize.

Maathai began her impressive career as an environmental and political activist in the 1970s. As part of her work with the National Council of Women of Kenya, Maathai established the Green Belt Movement in response to her conversations with rural women about their concerns over water, energy, and nutrition. Seeing the connections between the clear-cutting of forests and the diminished quality of life for many in Kenya, she began to lead high-profile campaigns to save Kenya's forests and protect its green spaces. Working with thousands of other women, she planted trees to replenish the soil, protect the watersheds, provide fuel, and enhance nutrition. "If you understand and you are

Patrick Robert/Corbis News/Corbis

disturbed," she said, "then you are moved to action. That's exactly what happened to me."

The government responded to the movement by harassing Maathai and many other women, holding them in jail and sending them death threats. At one point, Maathai was labeled a "mad woman" and beaten almost to death. However, these setbacks did not stop her. By the late 1990s, the government had abandoned its illegal deforestation and development plans and,

to date, more than 30 million trees have been planted throughout Kenya. However, when Maathai received the Nobel Peace Prize in 2004 for her work with the Green Belt Movement, she was surprised. She said, "I had no idea that anyone was listening."

As the Green Belt Movement's official website states, the movement has evolved into "one of the most prominent women's civil society organizations, . . . advocating for human rights and supporting good governance and peaceful democratic change through the protection of the environment." Maathai explains this evolution by saying, "When you start working with the environment seriously, the whole arena comes: human rights, women's rights, environmental rights, children's rights—you know, everybody's rights. Once you start making these linkages, you can no longer do just tree-planting."[5]

⟲ YOU CAN GET INVOLVED

MindTap If you'd like to learn more about the Green Belt Movement and how you might contribute to its work in Kenya and around the world, and for information about other organizations that work to conserve the environment, go to your MindTap for *Invitation to Public Speaking*.

---

issues that are multifaceted and with long histories. When selecting your topic, take a moment to ask yourself the following questions:

- What *exactly* is the topic of my speech? If I have decided to speak, or if I'm required to speak, what specific topic do I want to talk about? If I have been asked to speak, what specific topic does my audience want to hear about?
- Can I discuss this topic in the time allowed, or do I need to narrow or broaden my scope? Is there some aspect of this topic that I might be better able to cover in the time allowed?
- Who is my audience? What is my relationship to my audience? If I've decided to speak, am I qualified to speak about this topic? Will my audience see me as qualified? If not, could I change my topic or strengthen my qualifications in some way? If I've been asked to speak, why am I qualified to speak about this topic?

These questions will help you focus and narrow your topic so it is appropriate for your speaking situation. They'll also help you better understand why you want to speak or why you've been asked to speak and what you're most qualified and prepared to speak about.

Practicing the Public Dialogue | 3.1

GENERATE A LIST OF POSSIBLE SPEECH TOPICS

Make a list of what you like to do or want to know more about. Make this list as detailed as you can, including what you find yourself discussing with friends or what people say you're good at. Now brainstorm additional topics using one of the techniques you read about in this chapter. Next, organize the topics you've listed by categories to help you see connections among your topics and possibly generate more. If you are doing a service learning project in your speech class, make a list of possible topics related to your volunteer experience. Choose ten possible speech topics for your next speech. Set them aside for now.

Whether you take inventory of your interests and skills, use brainstorming techniques, decide what you are motivated to speak about, or are given a topic to speak about, recognize that you are capable of generating any number of speech topics. With a little bit of creativity and organization, you can come up with speech topics that are interesting and relevant to the public dialogue.

Articulating Your Purpose

There are many different types of speaking: speaking to inform, invite, or persuade, and speaking on special occasions and in small groups. For each of these speaking types, the speaker has a different goal: to inform, invite, persuade, or to introduce, commemorate, and accept. These are the goals we focus on in this chapter. Note that as a speaker in or as part of a small group, your speaking goal generally falls into one of these six categories. As such, we'll save the discussion of small group speaking's unique components until the appendix at the end of this book.

Speaking goals can be explained in terms of general purposes and specific purposes. The **general purpose** of a speech is its broad goal: to inform, invite, persuade, introduce, commemorate, or accept. The **specific purpose** is a focused statement that identifies exactly what a speaker wants to accomplish with a speech. Let's take a look at how you use each of these purposes to organize your thoughts about your speeches.

General Speaking Purposes

Suppose you want to speak about organic farming. You could speak about many aspects of this topic. Without knowing your purpose for your speech, it can be difficult to know where to begin. Do you describe organic farming, what it is, and who practices it (informative)? Do you ask your audience to explore the impact of organic farming on the environment and the average family's grocery bills (invitational)? Do you attempt to convince your classmates that organic farming is the most efficient type of farming (persuasive)? Do you commemorate organic farming or something about it (commemorative)? Your first step toward answering these questions is to determine the overall goal for your speech, or your general purpose:

> To *inform:* describe, clarify, explain, define
>
> To *invite:* explore, discuss, dialogue, understand
>
> To *persuade:* change, shape, influence, motivate
>
> To *introduce:* acquaint, present, familiarize
>
> To *commemorate:* praise, honor, pay tribute
>
> To *accept:* receive an award, express gratitude

Notice that each of these overall goals is quite different from the others. For example, the goal of acquainting is different from the goal of praising, which is different from the goal of clarifying. So by determining your general purpose, you begin to find a focus for your speech.

Specific Speaking Purposes

Once you determine your general purpose, you must then determine exactly what you want to communicate to your audience, or your specific purpose. Specific speaking purposes help you narrow the focus of your speech. A specific purpose states

general purpose: Speech's broad goal: to inform, invite, persuade, introduce, commemorate, or accept.

specific purpose: Focused statement that identifies exactly what a speaker wants to accomplish with a speech.

exactly what you want to accomplish in the speech. To understand the importance of a speech's specific purpose, consider Greg's speaking situation.

Greg tutored fourth graders in an after-school math homework program, and he'd found a way to teach math skills through sports. This experience prompted his interest in several topics for a speech. Greg became interested in innovative approaches to teaching math skills, as well as the link between exercise and learning. He decided he wanted to talk about the link between exercise and academic success because he could find more details and research on that topic. He knew he wanted to convince his classmates of this link, so he decided to give a persuasive speech, but he needed to focus his topic even more.

Greg now needed to develop a specific-purpose statement. How did he do this? First, he identified his **behavioral objectives**, the actions he wanted audience members to take at the end of his speech. After some thought, he decided that he wanted his classmates to change their view of the link between exercise and learning. On his laptop he wrote, "I want my classmates to believe differently about the connection between activity and learning." His next step was to narrow the focus of his behavioral objective even further. He needed to define what he meant by "believe differently." After some thought, Greg decided that he wanted to persuade his audience that schools should retain or enhance their physical education programs rather than cut them, because of the link between enhanced learning and exercise. With this focus, he now could begin to gather the evidence he needed to make his case.

Table 3.1 shows more examples of general and specific purposes. Notice the differences between them. From the six general purposes, you could generate specific purposes for at least twelve very different speeches.

When stating your specific speaking purpose, remain audience centered and state your specific speaking purpose clearly. Begin your statements with the infinitive phrases to *inform, to invite, to persuade, to introduce, to commemorate, or to accept.* These phrases clearly indicate what your general purpose is and what you hope to accomplish with your speech. Compare the following correct and incorrect statements of purpose:

These individuals are part of a Japanese self-defense martial art (Shorinji Kempo) demonstration at the Powell Street Festival, in Vancouver, British Columbia. See if you can write three different specific-purpose statements (to inform, invite, or persuade, for example) for a speech related to this photo. Now compare them with those of your classmates. Are they clear and specific enough so that the audience knows what to expect?

Correct	Incorrect
To introduce Master Cho and three of his most noteworthy accomplishments to my audience.	Master Cho's talent.
To inform my audience of the history of martial arts in the United States.	I'm going to talk about martial arts.
To invite my audience to explore ways we could support physical education in schools.	Supporting physical education.
To persuade my audience that practicing martial arts is an excellent form of exercise.	The martial arts are good for you.

Notice that the incorrect statements are unfocused and don't indicate the overall goal of the speech. Although it may seem that the incorrect statements leave greater room for a speaker's creativity, they are too vague to be of much help when you prepare your speech. For example, the statement "Master Cho's talent" functions better as a speech topic than a statement of purpose. The statement "I'm going to talk about martial arts" won't help the speaker focus on a particular aspect of martial arts and prepare a manageable speech. Nor will it give an audience a sense of what direction the speech will take. Similarly, the phrase "supporting physical education" doesn't indicate the speaker's speech goal at all. In contrast, each of the correct statements provides you with a focused, solid framework from which to prepare your speech, and each lets audiences know what they can expect to hear in your speech.

behavioral objectives: Actions a speaker wants the audience to take at the end of a speech.

Table 3.1 General and Specific Speaking Purposes

GENERAL PURPOSE	SPECIFIC PURPOSE
To inform	To inform my audience of the services offered by our campus counseling center
	To inform my audience of the process of planting, harvesting, and preparing organic produce
To invite	To invite my audience to consider the merits of the three martial arts experts who have been interviewed to teach at our school
	To invite my audience to explore the implications of turning the city's abandoned municipal lot into a clean, safe skate park
To persuade	To persuade my audience to use the services offered by our campus counseling center
	To persuade my audience to buy organic produce
To introduce	To introduce my audience to Dr. A. J. Johnson, director of our counseling center
	To introduce my audience to today's schedule for our tour of the Martial Arts Center
To commemorate	To commemorate for my audience my grandparents and the values they taught me during my summers on their organic farm
	To commemorate for my audience Wong Fei-Hung, one of the first well-known masters of the martial arts
To accept	To accept an award from my employer for our highly successful peer-counseling program
	To accept the city council's Outstanding Community Project award for my efforts at constructing a clean, safe skate park in the city's abandoned municipal lot

Keep your audience in the forefront of your mind. Remember, you are speaking to and for a particular audience, and you research and organize your speech with this fact in mind. Your specific purpose should clearly reflect the presence of your audience. To this end, be sure your specific-purpose statement includes the words my audience or a more specific synonym. Compare the following correct and incorrect statements of purpose:

Correct	Incorrect
To inform my audience of the process of planting, harvesting, and preparing organic produce.	The methods of growing organic produce.
To invite my coworkers to consider altering our current training program.	Shall we alter our training methods?
To persuade my audience of the importance of growing and eating organic fruit.	We should grow and eat organic fruit.
To commemorate for my audience Native American hero Chief Joseph, peacemaker and humanitarian.	Chief Joseph was a Native American peacemaker and humanitarian.
To accept and express my gratitude to the city council and my neighbors for the Outstanding Community Project award.	Thank you for this Outstanding Community Project award.

Notice how the correct examples encourage you to reflect on the makeup of your audience in ways that the incorrect examples do not. The words "my audience," "the city council and my neighbors," and "my coworkers" encourage the speaker to focus on a specific group of people with particular traits and characteristics, not on some unspecified entity.

As you begin to organize the materials for your speech, write your general and specific statements of purpose at the top of all your research notes. Like any good road map, clear statements of purpose help you select and navigate the path toward putting the final touches on your presentation.

Stating Your Thesis

So far in this chapter, you've explored how context affects your speaking goals, how to select a speech topic, and what your general and specific purposes are. Now you are ready to take the final step to complete this initial part of the speech preparation process. Every successful speech has a *thesis statement,* sometimes called a *central idea.* A **thesis statement** summarizes in a single declarative sentence the main ideas, assumptions, or arguments you want to express in your speech. It adds focus to your specific purpose because in a thesis statement you state, in a single sentence, the exact content of your speech.

Note that the thesis statement is closely related to the specific purpose. Recall that the specific-purpose statement indicates what you want your audience to understand or do as a result of your speech. The thesis statement helps you accomplish this goal by allowing you to state in a single sentence the specific ideas you will cover in the speech. The thesis statement helps you identify the main ideas of your speech, which will become your main points for the speech (Chapter 8).

Let's look again at some specific-purpose statements to see how they relate to thesis statements (see also Table 3.2):

Specific purpose: To inform my audience of the different belts in the martial arts

With this statement, Oscar claims it is useful to understand the different belt levels in the martial arts. To focus his speech on a manageable aspect of this topic, he must

Practicing the Public Dialogue | 3.2

WRITE A GENERAL-PURPOSE STATEMENT AND A SPECIFIC-PURPOSE STATEMENT

With three or four other students in class, look over the lists of topics you selected in Practicing the Public Dialogue 3.1. Select one or two topics from each person and write a general-purpose statement and a specific-purpose statement for each. Consider which topics would work best for informative, persuasive, invitational, or commemorative speeches.

MindTap®
You can use Outline Builder to help you create these statements.

thesis statement: Statement that summarizes in a single declarative sentence the main ideas, assumptions, or arguments you want to express in your speech.

Table 3.2 General and Specific Purposes and Thesis Statements

INFORMATIVE SPEECH	
General purpose	To inform
Specific purpose	To inform my audience of the three most important ways to avoid getting lost while traveling
Thesis statement	The three simple ways travelers can avoid getting lost are to carry maps, plan out the route beforehand, and ask directions from knowledgeable sources.
General purpose	To inform
Specific purpose	To inform my audience about where to seek shelter during a tornado
Thesis statement	When a tornado strikes, seek shelter in a storm cellar, a fortified storm closet, or your bathtub.
INVITATIONAL SPEECH	
General purpose	To invite
Specific purpose	To invite my audience to explore ways to support the arts in our community

(Continued)

Table 3.2 (Continued)

Thesis statement	The arts have played a very important role in my life, enhance the quality of life in any community, and I'd like to explore with my audience whether or not there are simple ways to support them.
General purpose	To invite
Specific purpose	To invite my audience to explore the reasons for and against retaining the death penalty in our state
Thesis statement	I'd like to describe the many benefits and drawbacks of retaining the death penalty in our state and then explore with my audience whether this punishment is still appropriate for serious crimes.

PERSUASIVE SPEECH

General purpose	To persuade
Specific purpose	To persuade my audience to spay or neuter their pets
Thesis statement	Spaying or neutering pets is easy and affordable, and it helps prevent having to put down thousands of unwanted kittens and puppies each year.
General purpose	To persuade
Specific purpose	To persuade my audience to learn a second language
Thesis statement	When we learn a second language, not only do we learn to appreciate the culture of the people who speak that language, but also we increase our understanding of our own culture.

determine exactly what he wants the audience to know about the martial arts belt systems. He considers what he is asked most often about this topic. Thus, his thesis statement looks like this:

> **Thesis statement:** In the three most common schools of martial arts in the United States—judo, karate, and tae kwon do—the black belt is the most esteemed belt level among the slightly differing belt systems.

With his thesis statement, Oscar considers how much common knowledge there is about the martial arts as well as what people are most curious about. In addition, his thesis statement summarizes and previews two main points:

1. Judo, karate, and tae kwon do are the most common schools of martial arts in the United States.
2. Each school has a slightly different belt system, but the black belt is the most esteemed belt level in all the schools.

Consider a second example:

> **Specific purpose:** To persuade my audience to eat healthy organic fruit

This statement makes the claim that organic fruit is good for you. To persuade your audience to eat it (what you want to accomplish), you must refine this statement to explain why eating organic fruit is good for you (what you will say to accomplish your goal). In explaining why, your thesis statement begins to take shape:

> **Thesis statement:** Because organic fruit does not contain the dangerous chemicals found in nonorganic fruit, it is far healthier for people to eat and better for the environment.

Practicing the Public Dialogue | 3.3

WRITE A THESIS STATEMENT

In a small group or as a class, choose five of the topics you wrote purpose statements for in Practicing the Public Dialogue 3.2. Write a thesis statement for each. Is your thesis statement a single declarative sentence? Does it state the main ideas, assumptions, or arguments you want to express in your speech? Review the completed thesis statements and select the one for the speech you're most interested in. Why do you like this one more than the others? Does it best fit the assignment your instructor has given you, your audience, or your own personal preferences?

MindTap®

You can use Outline Builder to help create your own thesis statement. In addition, watch the video clip of Jesse Rosser, as he delivers his thesis statement.

This thesis statement indicates that the speech will consist of three main points:

1. Organic fruits do not contain dangerous chemicals.
2. Organic fruits are healthier to eat than nonorganic fruits.
3. Organic fruits are grown in ways that are safe for the environment.

Some instructors like to divide a thesis statement into two sentences: one that states your thesis (your main idea) and one that lists the main points of your speech (your preview). You can read a more detailed discussion of previews in Chapter 8.

The clarity and focus you get when you develop your thesis statement and main points guide your research efforts and supporting materials, your reasoning, and your organizational patterns (Chapters 5, 6, 7, and 14). Use your thesis statement in combination with your general and specific statements of purpose to help you identify your main points. You can then move to the next steps of putting your speech together.

STUDENT SPEECH WITH COMMENTARY

This Is Dedicated . . . : A Tribute to the Women of History
by Ogenna Agbim

Specific Purpose: To commemorate important women in history who have come before my generation

Thesis Statement: Throughout history, women's struggle for equality has provided opportunities for women today, and the women of the past deserve our recognition.

MindTap If you have been assigned a speech in your class, such as an introductory, narrative, or commemorative speech, you can use the following speech as a model. Ogenna gave this speech in an introductory public speaking class. The students' assignment was to give a two- to four-minute speech commemorating an important person or important people in their lives. Notice that even though this speech was required, Ogenna chose a topic that is different enough to keep her audience engaged and listening. Watch a video clip of student speaker Ogenna as she delivers her speech. As you watch Ogenna speak, notice how her passion about the topic affects her delivery.

Introduction

This is dedicated to all the women out there who have gone through the struggle: You're not going through it alone; it's our time to shine. Ladies, don't you hang your heads low. I can see you're feeling bad because you're trying to make it on your own. Ladies, it seems everything for us has gone wrong, but if you believe in me, you will find bad times will pass you on. It's our time to shine. We've been down for much too long. But we have to combine, and we have to keep moving on. We have to combine, and we have to keep moving on.

Body

I want to ask every woman gathered here today to stand up. You, you, and you. My women in front, my women in the middle, and my women in back. If no one has told you, it's your time to shine. You've been down for much too long. For the last couple of hundred years, we women: What have we not endured? We've been slaves, we've been seen through the earth's eyes in every way but our own. We've been told how to act, and how to behave, and what makes us beautiful, and what doesn't. Hundreds of years we've spent, and decades of years, fighting for equal pay and equal opportunities and voting rights. We've supported our men, and our families, our brothers and sisters. Through it all, we haven't been appreciated. We haven't been honored, both entirely appreciated and honored

COMMENTARY

Ogenna catches her audience's attention with a dedication, setting a tone of optimism and recognition. She also uses rhyming language ("pass you on," "much too long") and repetition ("We have to combine, and we have to keep moving on") for effect and emphasis.

By identifying the women in her speaking environment specifically as members of her audience, Ogenna makes the speech relevant to them.

Ogenna continues to draw her audience in by tracing some of women's experiences in history. She also helps her audience listen to her speech by using language that creates pleasing rhythms, such as alliteration ("priceless piece," "happy hearts").

By using specific women in history as examples, Ogenna fulfills her specific purpose and supports the claims she made in her thesis statement that women throughout history have paved the way for women today and deserve to be commemorated.

As she reminds her audience of the significance of past accomplishments and brings herself back into the speech, Ogenna begins to bring her speech around full circle, transitioning from women of history to women of today.

Ogenna concludes her speech with a memorable quote by a famous woman of today, author and poet Maya Angelou, who is especially appropriate because she's written extensively about her own history.

enough. And without crying a river still we stand. As you stand, you represent a priceless piece of the voice that was never heard. You stand for the opportunities missed. You stand for the oppression where our happy hearts were broken and for the things that make us who we are—and made us dismissed. For what you've been through for me, and for us all, I thank you. Without you today, where would we all be?

Now for my ladies who took a stand, take a seat for the future. As I have said, it's our time to shine. Take a front seat and count your accomplishments. Take a seat and view the laws that have been passed because of women. Take a seat and watch every seed women have planted in the concrete grow into beautiful roses. Women, we salute you. We are proud of you. You are an inspiration. You are our mentors, you are our saviors, our motivation, and I commend you. Bessie Coleman, the first African American woman to fly a plane; Zora Neale Hurston, first African American woman graduate of Barnard College; and you, Eleanor Roosevelt, who broke the rules in 1933 for women to be allowed in press conferences; Rosa Parks; Toni Morrison: With so many other women to name, the branches you have built over time will forever give me light to shine. You have been oppressed but have risen as organization presidents, artists, dancers, and dreamers that have led your way and mine. Women, your small steps are like giants in history. Forever you will be a heroine to those you never thought you would touch, and you will be a heroine for saving us throughout the drowning madness.

Women, you motivate me in this age to become a better woman, because without your contributions, today there may not have been a history for me. There may have been no gateway for me to college, and in music, in sports, in politics, and so very much more.

Conclusion

Ladies, it is your time to shine. Your efforts never go unnoticed, at least not in my eyes. Your small impacts make a huge impact on us all, even if it's one body at a time. To my women out there, if you ever find yourself going through a struggle, remember to keep your head held high. You're not going through it alone. We have been down for much too long. But like Maya Angelou once said, "We rise, we rise, we rise." And from this day forward, it is our time to shine.

Chapter Summary

Understanding the context in which you speak will help you prepare effective speeches.

- When you decide to speak, you do so because an issue is so important that you feel drawn to speak out about it.
- When you are asked to speak, you do so because you have been asked to share information with others.
- When you are required to speak, you do so because you are obligated to give a speech.
- Although you are required to speak in your public speaking class, it is more likely you will decide or be asked to give speeches in the future.

When you choose a speech topic, consider the purpose of your speech, your time constraints, and your audience.

- If you are giving a speech in a classroom setting, also consider the specifics of your assignment.
- Choose a speech topic by taking stock of your interests (e.g., what you like to talk about or what people say you're good at) or by brainstorming with a variety of methods: free association, clustering, categories, or using technology.
- Narrow the focus of your speech by matching your interests and expertise to your speech assignment.

Determine the general and specific purposes for your speech.

- Most often, the general purpose for your speech will be to inform, to invite, to persuade, to introduce, to commemorate, or to accept.
- Identify your specific purpose by stating exactly what you want to accomplish with your speech.
- Write specific-purpose statements so your speaking purpose is clear, keep the audience in the forefront of your mind, and use definitive and complete sentences.

Write your thesis statement.

- Your thesis statement is a single declarative sentence that summarizes the main points of your speech.
- Thesis statements indicate what you want to say in your speech to accomplish your speaking goal. They also preview the content of your speech for your audience.

Invitation to Public Speaking Online MindTap°

Now that you have read Chapter 3, use your MindTap Communication for *Invitation to Public Speaking* for quick access to the digital resources that accompany this text. These resources include

- **Study tools** that will help you assess your learning and prepare for exams (digital glossary, key term flash cards, review quizzes).
- **Activities and assignments** that will help you hone your knowledge and build your public speaking skills throughout

the course, as well as help you explore public speaking concepts online (web links), give you step-by-step guidance through the research, outline and note card preparation process (Outline Builder), watch and critique videos of sample speeches (Interactive Video Activities), and allow you to practice and present your presentation online using a speech video delivery, recording, and grading system (YouSeeU).

Key Concepts MindTap° Test your knowledge with online printable flash cards.

behavioral objectives (51)
brainstorming (46)
general purpose (50)

specific purpose (50)
speech topic (42)
thesis statement (53)

Review Questions

1. Use the strategies suggested in this chapter to make a list of four different speech topics you might like to speak about. How do you think the classroom setting would affect what you would say about these topics? What would you do to make these topics suitable for a classroom setting?

2. Rewrite the following incorrect specific-purpose statements so they are correct:

   a. To give 10 percent of your annual income to charity
   b. Barack Obama
   c. Olympic gold medals
   d. Natural disasters
   e. Isn't the level of water pollution in our local river too high?

3. Make a list of speech topics you might decide to speak about. For each topic, identify why you've decided to speak and who your audience would be. How might your reasons for speaking and your audience affect what you say about your topics? Write a general-purpose and a specific-purpose statement for at least one of these topics. Is this a speech you might give in your speech course? Why or why not?

4. Practice writing a general and a specific statement of purpose for a speech on each of the following topics: relief efforts in Haiti, mandatory military service, bilingual education, or hybrid cars. Now write a thesis statement for each of these possible speeches and identify the main points for each. Could you choose one of these topics for your next speech? Why or why not?

4 | Your Audience and Speaking Environment

IN THIS CHAPTER, YOU WILL LEARN TO:

- Analyze the various components of an audience.

- Conduct a demographic audience analysis.

- Adapt to an audience that is both a group of diverse people and a unique community.

- Identify the influence of a speaking environment on an audience.

- Formulate strategies for adapting to audience expectations for a speech.

When you give a speech, you add your voice to the public dialogue. To engage in a **dialogue** is to interact, connect, and exchange ideas and opinions with others. When you engage in the public dialogue, you recognize that the speaker and the audience are equally important; both have opinions, feelings, and beliefs. To be a successful public speaker, you must acknowledge these realities and listen carefully to your audience before, during, and after your speech.

MindTap Start with a quick warm-up activity and review the chapter's learning objectives.

Diaophoto.org/Alamy Stock Photo

▲ The people in any audience will be a complex mixture of individuals, usually holding a range of beliefs, values, attitudes, and expectations. Because your audiences are so important to you as a speaker, in this chapter you will explore what being audience centered means and find strategies for communicating effectively with your audience.

One of the most effective ways you can listen to your audience is by adopting an audience-centered perspective. To be **audience centered** is to acknowledge your audience by considering and listening to the unique, diverse, and common perspectives of its members before, during, and after your speech. Being audience centered does not mean you must compromise your message to appeal to your audience. Nor does it mean that you can use your knowledge of the audience to manipulate its members. Rather, being audience centered means you understand the positions and perspectives of your audience so you can craft an appropriate, listenable message.

But what is an audience? We often use the term *audience* without much thought. We prepare our speeches with our "audience in mind," we want to "persuade our audience" of something, and we "sit in the audience" as we listen. In terms of public speaking, **audience** is defined as a complex and varied group of people that a speaker addresses. Although this definition is simple, we recognize that audiences are far more complex than the definition suggests. Modern audiences are composed of groups of diverse people exposed to endless messages from the media, their workplaces, their families and friends, and many other sources. Despite all these demands on the listening time of a group of highly diverse people, you can learn a number of skills to help you address an audience effectively.

In Chapter 2, you learned how to listen to your audience during a speech to better respond to its needs. In this chapter, you will build on those skills and learn how to best understand your audiences by exploring what an audience is, why there are different types of audiences, how speaking environments affect audiences, and how you can apply what you learn about your audience and speaking environment to help others listen to your speech.

MindTap®

Read, highlight, and take notes online.

Considering an Audience as a Group of Diverse People

Have you ever noticed that for each similarity you have with someone, you also find a difference? Perhaps you and a friend love action films, popcorn, and state-of-the-art theaters. Yet one of you loves a bargain matinee, to sit up close, and to pour on the butter, whereas the other is happiest settling in the balcony for the late-night show with no butter at all. You are similar, yet you are different.

People are unique for a variety of reasons that relate to some combination of culture, upbringing, experiences, personality, and even genetics.[1] Like you and your moviegoing friend, no two people are alike, and this uniqueness sets us apart and makes us interesting. But groups of people are often similar to one another in many ways. As public speakers, how can we give a speech that takes into consideration an audience's conflicting differences and similarities? How can we understand the different ways our complex identities intersect and influence who we are? First, try to consider how your audiences view the world by analyzing its members' master statuses and their standpoints.

Master Statuses

Groups of people share common experiences, perspectives, and attitudes because they occupy certain master statuses. **Master statuses** are significant positions a person occupies within society that affect that person's identity in almost all social situations.[2] A person's master statuses might include race or ethnicity, sex or gender, physical ability, sexual orientation, age, economic standing, religion or spirituality, and educational level. They could include positions in society like being a parent, child, or sibling, being employed or unemployed, and so on, if those positions affect someone's identity in almost every social situation. Here's how one public speaking

dialogue: Interaction, connection, and exchange of ideas and opinions with others.

audience centered: Acknowledging your audience by considering and listening to the unique, diverse, and common perspectives of its members before, during, and after your speech.

audience: Complex and varied group of people the speaker addresses.

master statuses: Significant positions occupied by a person within society that affect that person's identity in almost all social situations.

ARE THERE ADVANTAGES TO DIVERSITY?

Although we regularly hear the concepts of "diversity," "accepting diversity," and "appreciating diversity" in our workplaces, classrooms, communities, and our media, what does "diversity" actually mean? Diversity in the workplace can be defined as "differences among people with respect to age, class, ethnicity, gender, physical and mental ability, race, sexual orientation, spiritual practice, and public assistance status," as well as primary languages spoken.[3] However, diversity also includes "a wide variety of other differences, including work experience, parental status, educational background, geographic location, and much more."[4] When we "accept diversity," or "embrace diversity," we acknowledge, understand, accept, value, and celebrate "the variety of experiences and perspectives that arise" from these differences.[5] In short, a diverse workplace encompasses the range of social positions, identities, and abilities, and makes the most of these diverse elements.

What does the valuing of diversity add to a workplace? Numerous studies show that the more diversity in a business or organization, the better off the workplace and its workers. According to Kim Abreu, a recruiting trends analyst at Glassdoor, and Sophia Kerby and Crosby Burns, of the Center for American Progress,[6] here are just a few of the benefits derived from diverse workplaces:

1. **A more qualified workforce.** Recruiting from the best of the best means that companies are "more likely to hire the best and brightest in the labor market." Where talent is crucial, hiring from "the largest and most diverse set of candidates" only makes sense.[7]

2. **Lower employee turnover.** When companies lack diversity, hostile and unpleasant environments (however unintentional) often drive talented people who feel like they "don't fit in" away. In fact, businesses with little diversity see the higher turnover rates than those with diverse employees.

3. **More creativity and innovation.** Workplace teams that include individuals from different backgrounds and experiences often "come up with more creative ideas and methods of solving problems."[8]

4. **A larger share of the market.** Workers with diverse "backgrounds and experiences . . . can more effectively market to consumers from different racial and ethnic backgrounds, women, and consumers" from different sexual orientations and identities. "Diversifying the workplace helps businesses increase their market share."[9]

5. **More competitive in our globalized world.** When businesses and organizations welcome diverse employees, they become more competitive in our "global economy by capitalizing on the unique talents and contributions that diverse communities bring to the table."[10]

student, Miranda, described her master statuses and how they influenced her life and speaking experiences:

> I have many master statuses. I am a daughter dedicated to her family and her family values. I am forever a student, always craving new knowledge. I am a first-generation student, boldly going where no one else in my family has gone before—college. I am a Mexican American living life for my ancestors. Last but not least, I am curious, always searching for new adventures in life. All of this makes up who I am and affects every decision I make each day, from what clothes I choose to wear to the books I choose to read. It also affects what topics I choose to speak about and how effectively I listen to other speakers.

A status is a *master* status when it profoundly influences a person's identity and the way he or she is perceived by others. Whether or not we intend to, we often respond to other people based on one or more master statuses. For example, teenagers with rumpled and baggy clothes are often treated differently in a grocery store than neatly dressed adult mothers with children. Whether or not our assumptions about these people are correct (teenagers will cause problems, mothers are responsible and will manage their children), we categorize and respond to people based on the positions they hold in society.

Master statuses affect our view of the world because we make judgments based on them, and hence we see some master statuses as more valuable than others. For example, whether or not we are comfortable acknowledging such differences, American culture tends to rank whiteness, heterosexuality, and masculinity higher than darker skin color, homosexuality, and femininity. Because the first three statuses are considered more valuable, they are generally rewarded with higher salaries, more acceptance and protections, and more personal freedoms, whereas the last three, on average, receive lower salaries, less acceptance and fewer protections, and greater threats to physical safety.[11]

Practicing the Public Dialogue | 4.1

WHAT ARE YOUR MASTER STATUSES?

Take a moment and list all of the identities you have that you would consider "master." Now write a paragraph like Miranda did explaining how those master statuses influence who you are, how others see you, and how they might affect you as a speaker. Share this with a classmate to see if his or her perceptions of you match the description you wrote.

Standpoints, Attitudes, Beliefs, and Values

The impact of different treatment because of master statuses can affect an individual's **standpoint**, the perspective from which a person views and evaluates society. Members of your audiences have different standpoints because they have different master statuses and thus different experiences. For example, teenagers often see life as unfairly biased against them, and mothers often see the world as expecting them and their children to behave perfectly in all situations.

Note that although master statuses can have a powerful influence on a person's view of the world, they do not *determine* a person's standpoint. For example, not all women believe they need to have children to fully experience womanhood, just as not all men believe their masculinity is weakened if they are not the primary breadwinner for their families. In addition, we all occupy numerous master statuses throughout our lives, and each influences us in different ways. For example, although we maintain our ethnicity throughout our lives, if we move to a new country, adapt to a new culture, and learn a different language, our experience of our ethnic identity can evolve. Moreover, we all move from young to old and experience changing family and job roles, shifting from child to parent, unemployed to employed, and so on.

Our standpoints influence our attitudes, beliefs, and values. An **attitude** is a general positive or negative feeling a person has about something. Attitudes reflect our likes and dislikes, our approval or disapproval of events, people, or ideas.[12] A **belief** is a person's idea of what is real, not real, true, or not true. Beliefs are more conceptual than attitudes and reflect what we think we know about the world. A **value** is a person's idea of what is good, worthy, or important. Our values reflect what we think is an ideal world or state of being. Values help us determine whether we think a person, idea, or thing is acceptable in our worldview.[13]

Conversations, debates, and arguments held as part of the public dialogue are heavily influenced by the different attitudes, beliefs, and values that result from our different standpoints and master statuses. In particular, attitudes, beliefs, and values are often influenced by our cultural backgrounds. All cultures have unique ways of explaining and organizing the world. Audience-centered speakers recognize these different worldviews and guard against ethnocentrism. **Ethnocentrism** is the belief that our own cultural perspectives, norms, and ways of organizing society are superior to others. When we hold ethnocentric views, we see other cultures as odd, wrong, or deficient because they do not do things the way we do. Speakers who let ethnocentric views come through in their speeches run the risk of alienating audience members who do not hold similar views.

To be audience centered, speakers must consider the significant influence of master statuses, standpoints, attitudes, beliefs, and values on audiences. When speakers take these factors into consideration, they increase their chances of giving effective speeches.

Demographic Audience Analysis

How does recognizing your audience's master statuses and standpoints help you become a better, more ethical speaker? By using master statuses as guideposts for crafting your speech, you can try to anticipate the potential impact your speech topic, language, and so on might have on your audience. Are members of your audience first-year high school students or seniors in college? Are they of a certain ethnicity? What types of jobs do they hold? Are they grandparents? What are their educational backgrounds? How might each of these master statuses influence the standpoints of your audience members? Once you've answered these types of questions, you can consider the attitudes, beliefs, and values of your audience more completely. This will help you adapt the message of your speech to your audience.

A common way to determine the master statuses of an audience is to conduct a **demographic audience analysis**, an analysis that identifies the particular

---

standpoint: Perspective from which a person views and evaluates society.

attitude: General positive or negative feeling a person has about something.

belief: Person's idea of what is real, not real, true, or not true.

value: Person's idea of what is good, worthy, or important.

ethnocentrism: Belief that our own cultural perspectives, norms, and ways of organizing society are superior to others.

demographic audience analysis: Analysis that identifies the particular population traits of an audience.

Mark Thiessen/National Geographic Creative

tip
National Geographic Explorer

T. H. CULHANE, Explorer and Urban Planner

What beliefs or values are important to consider about your audience before you speak to them?

I try to find out what expectations, background experiences, and prejudices my target audiences have. Some audiences are really tough, so I do get nervous at times and, yes, I've had some "failures to communicate." For example, I thought the idea that you can turn your wastes into energy and fertilizer and produce your own electricity from the available sunlight—doing it yourself—would have universal appeal. But it doesn't always. For example, after a very successful speech in Cairo, we were flown in to deliver a keynote to a group in Abu Dhabi. The slides that I showed and the music that I used, along with the experiences I related, didn't resonate with the audience at all. I could sense misunderstanding and tension growing in the room. It turned out that it was because seeing slums and poverty was upsetting to the audience even though I thought my message was, as ever, hopeful and intended to be inspiring. I always speak about how we are climbing together to co-create a better civilization, but while the audience had some wealthy philanthropists in it, most of the people didn't feel very motivated or comfortable having to see what "the other 90%" have to go through and how they live. Some people actually felt guilty, depressed, or even threatened by what I showed. In these cases, I have to find a way to get back to some common ground and move my speech into the comfort zone of the audience and make them feel good about their role in society. One has to be alert to cues from the room—body language, smiles and frowns, when people laugh, when they cough, when they look at you, and when they look away or at each other. You learn to read the room and you adapt. One way I was able to pull through this event was to introduce the audience to a concept my father introduced me to: the idea of "The Great Conversation". We humans have been sharing stories for centuries that have helped us to progress, and most of us are fascinated by and willing to listen to stories of "the other" if our own story is also acknowledged as important. Some of us who have had the privilege to be an active part of that great conversation believe that no human being should be excluded from it, but not everyone feels that way. Not everyone believes in our vision of democracy. The trick for me has been to find common ground with whomever I'm speaking to, listen deeply to their perspectives, and help them see how hearing about other's can improve their own lives. So now, rather than just lecturing, I ask questions and involve the audience more. That almost always works better.

Courtesy of TH Culhane

population traits of an audience. These traits, or demographic characteristics, include age, country of origin, ethnicity and race, physical ability or disability, family status (parent, child), religion, and gender (male or female). You can gather demographic information by interviewing your audience personally, through a survey, or by researching the Internet. Using the Internet is best when you want to find information about a large general group of people, such as the citizens of a town, county, or region. However, to gather targeted information about your specific audience, you must interview your audience directly or conduct a survey.

You can conduct a demographic analysis before your speech by asking your audience to fill out a survey that asks about demographic information and attitudes, beliefs, and values. Surveys ask two primary types of questions: open ended and closed ended. An **open-ended question** allows respondents to answer in an unrestricted way. An example of an open-ended question is "What are your reactions to the president's economic reforms?" People asked this question are free to respond with any answer they like. A **closed-ended question** requires respondents to choose an answer from two or more alternatives. Examples of closed-ended questions are "Do you

open-ended question: Question that allows the respondent to answer in an unrestricted way.

closed-ended question: Question that requires the respondent to choose an answer from two or more alternatives.

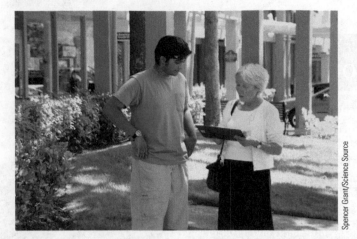

Spencer Grant/Science Source

Surveys are an excellent way to gather information about your audience's attitudes, beliefs, and values. What kind of information would you want to gather about your audience? Would you use open-ended or closed-ended questions to obtain this information?

support the president's attempts at economic reform?" (requires a yes or no answer) and "On a scale of 1 to 5, with 5 indicating the highest support, how do you rate the president's success at economic reform?" (requires one rating of five possible alternatives).

When you construct your survey, follow these guidelines:

- Keep your survey short (one or two pages).
- Keep your questions short and focused on one idea at a time.
- Use clear and simple language.
- Keep your own biases out of the survey.
- Provide room for respondents to write their comments.

Keep your speaking goals in mind as you construct your survey. What would you like your audience members to do or know after you've given your speech? Do you want them to understand a concept or a process? Explore an issue? Take some action? Appreciate another person? Whatever your goal, conducting a thorough and accurate analysis of your audience will help you accomplish your goals in a civil and ethical manner.

Remember that your primary goal in analyzing your audience is to give an ethical, audience-centered speech. Although master statuses can be powerfully influential, people can experience them in very different ways. Speakers must understand that we are all unique, that we experience life differently, and that we grow and change over time. When conducting a demographic analysis and considering master statuses, it can sometimes be easy to forget individual differences and resort to stereotyping. A **stereotype** is a broad generalization about an entire group based on limited knowledge or exposure to only certain members of that group. Stereotyping is harmful because we make assumptions based on incomplete information. It may seem comforting to predict certain behaviors based on a stereotype, but we can usually find many exceptions to any stereotype. Remember, an audience is a collection of people with unique experiences and personalities, and you cannot lump all members into one universal category.

Practicing the Public Dialogue | 4.2

CONDUCT A DEMOGRAPHIC AUDIENCE ANALYSIS

To learn about the group of people who make up your classroom audience, conduct a demographic analysis before your next speech. Using the information you gather, identify your audience's master statuses, standpoints, attitudes, beliefs, and values. As you prepare your speech, remain flexible about the influences of master statuses on your audience and do what you can to avoid stereotyping.

MindTap°

You can download a Demographic Audience Analysis form online. To see an example of a speech given by a student who used her demographic audience analysis to determine how thoroughly she needed to explain her topic to her audience, watch Chung-Yan Man's speech "Chinese Fortune Telling."

Considering an Audience as a Community

Although audiences begin with individuals who bring various standpoints to a presentation, they rapidly become a community of people joined together in some way, if only temporarily. Understanding how an audience comes together as a temporary community helps speakers stay audience centered.

Voluntary Audiences

Just as speakers decide something is significant enough to speak out about, people come together as audiences because they find something significant enough to listen to. These audiences are voluntary: they have chosen to be present. Examples of voluntary audiences are the delegates who attend the Democratic and Republican national conventions every four years. Public celebrations and commemorations, such as Super Bowl victories or the return of a famous person to a hometown, also bring audiences together voluntarily. And tragedies, like a terrorist attack or school shooting, often draw people together.

stereotype: Broad generalization about an entire group based on limited knowledge or exposure to only certain members of that group.

Sensitivity Toward Others

Raghava KK, Explorer

JAIN MIMISH/National Geographic Creative

"My art looks at issues from multiple perspectives to help open minds, inspire tolerance, and engender empathy. You can appreciate other viewpoints even if you don't accept them," explains internationally acclaimed artist, Raghava KK. "Everyone has a bias. What can be transformational is creative expression that allows many different biased perspectives to coexist simultaneously. When you see the world through other people's eyes, you have a richer understanding of who you are and why people do what they do."

Born in India, and leaving school at the age of sixteen, KK's life as a professional artist began in the world of cartooning and later expanded to a range of venues, including painting, sculpture, film, performance, and installation. He explains, "I like to question the way information is delivered," and we have to view knowledge as an active process of engaging. To help him accomplish that questioning and engaging, and to continue to communicate multiple perspectives through his art, he has, once again, expanded, and entered into the realms of interactive technology. KK has created picture frames that turn his paintings into touch screens. People can "touch" his paintings by pressing or tapping on the frames. Each touch changes the image, through a process of digital projection, and the painting is "reinvented by each person who interacts with it."

Another of KK's projects is an iPad picture book for children and a new genre he calls "shaken stories." The picture book, which children and parents "read" on their iPad, takes up our notions of "family." He explains how: Every time children and their parents "shake the screen, a new definition of 'family' appears. Mom, dad, and child; two dads and kids; two moms and kids, single parents" and so on. KK explains why: "I created this book because I wanted to expose my own children to many perspectives at an early age." KK shares, "I grew up in the bubble of a very traditional Indian family and only saw one point of view. It was only when I started to travel that I was exposed to different realities. And I realized that there is no one truth, there are many truths and that it's important for me to contextualize what is true and real for me but also to be willing to question the most basic assumptions that I have."

But, really, he states, "life is mysterious and we are constantly learning." Communication, effective communication, requires "empathy," "responsibility," "acknowledging bias," and "sensitivity toward others," and the question is "are we getting better and better" at these things?[14]

WHAT DO YOU THINK?

1. Raghava KK suggests that we can appreciate the viewpoints of others, even while we do not agree with them. Discuss what you think he means by this.
2. Do you think it is possible to appreciate the views of others with whom you do not agree? How might (or do) you do this?
3. KK calls for empathy, responsibility, acknowledging bias, and sensitivity toward others. How do these communication skills fit into the process of analyzing your audience?

Raghava KK

The need to listen unites people with various master statuses and standpoints. This means that most audiences are quite diverse. As a result, they may agree or disagree with a speaker or with one another. Although it is tempting to think that voluntary audiences are easier for speakers to address, this is not always true. Consider city council meetings, where community members hold vigorous debates about school funding, land development, and similar topics. However, voluntary audiences usually have an active interest in your topic. This fact certainly works to your advantage as a speaker, and staying audience centered will help you deliver your message effectively, no matter what your speaking situation.

Involuntary Audiences

Just as speakers are sometimes required to give a speech, people sometimes form an audience because they must. These audiences are involuntary: they might prefer not to be present. Examples of involuntary audiences are students in required public speaking courses and employees in mandatory business meetings. Some involuntary audiences have little or no interest in your topic. Thus, they may display open hostility toward you and your topic or a disconcerting lack of attention and involvement. For example, in your public speaking class, some of your classmates would rather not hear about certain topics because of their own strong beliefs, yet they are forced to sit and listen. Others seem only to stare blankly at you. Still others ignore you and e-mail or text while you are speaking. Unfortunately, you may encounter the same behaviors in your professional and social worlds; some audiences attend a speech only because their job requires it or because of family or social obligations. However, with a little forethought and effort, most involuntary audiences can become a productive part of the public dialogue.

For a speaker who faces an involuntary audience, being audience centered may mean the difference between an ineffective and a successful speech. Before you give your speech, talk with the person who asked you to speak. Discover why your audience is required to attend. Or at the beginning of your speech, ask audience members why they've been asked to listen to you. Then address those issues in your speech. For example, if you are presenting to an audience that is part of a mandatory training program, ask about the rationale for the training, the goals of the training, and what your audience hopes to gain by the training. Knowing this information will help you design and present a message that is relevant and useful.

Similarly, if an audience opposes your topic, learn why so you can confirm (Chapter 2) and be confirmed by an involuntary audience. Before you speak, ask audience members to write down their concerns and pass them to you or gather this information several days before. The feedback you receive will help you thoughtfully address an audience's concerns, frustrations, or resistance. This audience-centered approach opens up dialogue rather than forces ideas on people. You let audience members know you are working to understand them as you ask them to do the same for you.

Finally, if you are speaking to an involuntary audience, use a little **empathy** by trying to see and understand the world as another person does. What would motivate you to listen to a topic you disagreed with or a presentation you were required to listen to? If you adopt this empathic, audience-centered approach, your involuntary audience may be delightfully surprised by your presentation and welcome you as a speaker.

So far, you've discovered you must consider both the individual and collective nature of audiences, you've explored why audiences come together, and you've learned how you can engage an involuntary audience. Audience-centered speakers keep all these factors in mind as they prepare and present their speeches. In the next section, you'll learn techniques to help you manage your speaking environment effectively.

Practicing the Public Dialogue | 4.3

DETERMINE WHETHER YOUR AUDIENCE IS VOLUNTARY
OR INVOLUNTARY

Consider the audience of a speech you might give sometime in the near future. Are listeners there voluntarily, present because they are interested in your topic and want to hear what you have to say? Or are they there against their will, present because they have to be? If it is a voluntary audience, adapt to audience members by identifying the various perspectives they have about your topic. If it is an involuntary audience, discover why and adapt your speech to better suit its needs. What are some ways you can communicate your empathy for your listeners?

---

empathy: Trying to see and understand the world as another person does.

Considering Your Speaking Environment

Before audience-centered speakers give a speech, they must discover as much as they can about their **speaking environment**, or where and when they will speak, so they can manage their speaking situation with relative ease. Effective speakers must consider such situational factors as the size of the audience and the physical arrangement of the speaking site, the availability of technology, the time of day they'll be speaking, where their speech falls in a series of presentations, and the length of time they have to speak.

Size and Physical Arrangement

The size of an audience and the physical arrangement of a speaking situation may seem like minor matters, but they can have a powerful effect on a speaking environment. You can enhance your ability to connect with your audience if you consider these matters carefully before your speech and adapt to them during your speech. Consider the following example:

> I found [him] alone in an empty basketball locker room moments before he was to speak before a crowd of six thousand at Arizona State University, calmly sipping tea. "Your Holiness, if you're ready . . ."
>
> He briskly rose, and without hesitation he left the room, emerging into the thick backstage throng of local reporters, photographers, security personnel, and students—the seekers, the curious, and the skeptical. He walked through the crowd smiling broadly and greeting people as he passed by. Finally passing through a curtain, he walked on stage, bowed, folded his hands, and smiled. He was greeted with thunderous applause. At his request, the house lights were not dimmed so he could clearly see his audience, and for several moments he simply stood there, quietly surveying the audience with an unmistakable expression of warmth and good will. For those who had never seen the Dalai Lama before, his maroon and saffron monk's robes may have created a somewhat exotic impression, yet his remarkable ability to establish rapport with his audience was quickly revealed as he sat down and began his talk.
>
> "I think that this is the first time I am meeting most of you. But to me, whether it is an old friend or new friend, there's not much difference anyway, because I always believe we are the same; we are all human beings. . . ."[15]

It might seem that a large audience, a group of journalists and security guards, and a wide stage would mean distance and disruption for a speaker, but not necessarily. Despite these potentially difficult physical settings, the Dalai Lama stayed audience centered by engaging with his audience personally. He asked that the house lights be left on, and he took the time to make eye contact with his audience, acknowledging a connection to each audience member. He took advantage of his setting rather than letting it control him. But how does a speaker do this?

To establish rapport with our audiences, we must consider the dynamics of audience size and physical arrangement before we speak, and we must adjust to any changes immediately before or during our speech. To stay audience centered with respect to size and place, ask yourself the following questions:

- How many people will be present?
- Will they stand or be seated?
- Where will they stand or sit?
- From where will I be speaking?
- Does this arrangement help or hinder the speaking environment I wish to create?
- What adjustments will I want to make before the presentation begins?
- What will I do if I cannot make these adjustments?
- What kinds of adjustments might I make during a presentation if I want to alter the environment?

speaking environment: Time and place in which a speaker will speak.

Strong speakers take stock of their environment before they begin to speak. What questions might you ask yourself to prepare to speak in this environment? If you're planning to use technology, what will you do to make sure your speech is successful even if your technology fails?

You probably won't be able to change the size of most audiences, but you should be able to work with the physical setting to create the kind of speaking environment you want. Consider whether you want to stand or sit, where you want your audience to sit (for example, in rows, in a circle, on chairs, on the floor), and how these decisions will affect your ability to connect with your audience. Ideally, you would make arrangements to establish your speaking environment ahead of time, as well as plans to make adjustments during your speech as needed. Remember, your speaking goal is to connect with your audience before, during, and after the speech.

Technology

Technology refers to the tools speakers use to help them deliver their message. Technology can be as elaborate as a computer and LCD panel or as simple as a pen and a flip chart. Table 4.1 presents a list of technologies speakers typically use. When you're thinking of using technology for your speech, stay audience centered by asking yourself the following questions:

- Have I asked what types of technology will be available for me to use?
- Do I have time to prepare the materials I need to use that technology?
- Do I have the time to practice using the technology?
- Have I worked out any glitches?
- Am I prepared to speak if the technology fails?
- Am I sure that my decision to use or not use technology helps me create the kind of environment I want?
- Does the technology help me communicate my messages clearly?
- Does it enhance my speech or detract from it?

Note that audience-centered speakers use technology to do more than simply enhance or project their message. They also make a commitment to their audience to

Table 4.1 Technologies for Speakers

NONELECTRONIC TECHNOLOGIES	ELECTRONIC TECHNOLOGIES
Podiums	Microphones
Tables or easels for displays	Laptop computers, cell phones, and LCD projectors
Handouts	Overhead projectors and screens
Ink markers, whiteboards, and erasers	Presentational aids such as PowerPoint slides
Markers, pens, and flip charts	DVD and Blu-ray players
Tacks, pins, or tape	CD-ROM players

use that technology competently. Consider the importance of this commitment in the following example:

> Mike wanted to include several YouTube clips in his speech. He identified the clips he wanted a day or two before he spoke, and he figured he could just pull them up during his speech. When he set up his computer on the day of his speech, he had trouble getting Internet access because the network was not running smoothly that day. After several tries, he was finally able to log on. But he couldn't locate his YouTube citations easily because he had searched for them by subject and failed to record the URLs. Then, because he was not familiar with the projection technology in the room, he discovered the hard way that the volume on the projector had been turned up to its highest level. When he played his first clip, everyone in the audience winced and covered their ears.

Mike did what he could to recover, but after his speech, he felt he didn't really create the kind of environment he wanted. He wanted people to get excited by his material, but he felt they simply were just being patient with him instead.

In Chapter 10 you will learn more about presentational aids that rely on technology. Remember, although technology is a tool that can help you give a more effective speech, it has its drawbacks. If your speech relies on technology to be effective but the technology you need is not available when you arrive to speak, your presentation will be negatively affected. That's why you need to take the time to consider how to present your speech without technology. Putting this time into your speech before you give it will help you stay audience centered by keeping your attention focused on delivering your message to your audience in a way members appreciate.

Temporal Factors

Audience-centered speakers also consider issues of time, sometimes called *chronemics,* when they think about connecting with their audiences. Three important time considerations are the time of day you'll be speaking, where your speech falls in a series of presentations (will you speak first, last, or somewhere in the middle?), and how much time you'll have to speak.

Time of day. The time of day a speech is scheduled is significant. Take a moment to consider your moods throughout a day. Is your energy different in the morning than it is in the evening? How about before or after a meal? Just as our levels of energy are affected by the time of day, so too is the mood of an audience.

In the morning, audiences tend to be fresher, but they may also be anxious about the responsibilities they have that day. In the evening, audiences may be weary, tired from all the work they've done. Around lunchtime, they are hungry and preoccupied with getting some food, or they have just eaten and may be drowsy as their bodies work to digest food rather than your message. Let's consider Julia and how she adjusts her message about the services her product design company offers according to what time of day she speaks:

> *In the morning,* Julia begins by encouraging her audience to refill their cups of coffee and tea as she speaks. She then acknowledges the demands on listeners' time by speaking for fifteen minutes, asking them to participate in an activity for twenty minutes, and then breaking for fifteen minutes so they can check messages. When they reconvene, they follow up on the activity for about an hour.

> *After lunch,* Julia also engages her audience verbally because she knows their energy will be a bit lower than it was in the morning. When she speaks for longer than half an hour or so, she incorporates a break so audiences can check messages. If she speaks before lunch, Julia clearly defines her speaking schedule so her audience knows when they can expect to eat.

> *In the evening,* Julia acknowledges that it's the end of a workday that was probably very busy for most audience members. Rather than beginning by explaining the program, she immediately engages them verbally by asking them a few questions about a typical work-day that they can answer by raising their hands. This strategy keeps them connected to her in a more direct way—she knows they are probably tired, and she wants them to stay actively involved in the speech rather than sitting back passively.

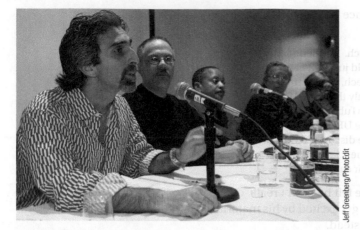

A daylong training that features a number of speakers is fairly common in the workplace. If you are asked to present at this kind of speaking event, consider your speaking order, or the place you occupy in a series of speakers.

Julia stays audience centered, regardless of the time of day, by acknowledging the audience's needs at specific times of the day and by organizing her presentations accordingly.

Speaking order. To be audience centered, you must also consider speaking order, or the place you occupy in a series of speakers. If you are the first speaker, you get the audience when members are fresh, listening more actively, and usually more willing to process your message. You also can set the stage for later speakers, make the first impression, and direct the audience's energy without interference by previous speakers. In addition, you connect with an audience before anyone else does, especially because audiences sometimes ask more questions of first speakers.

If you are the last speaker or near the end of a series, your audience may be tired and weary of processing the information presented by previous speakers. They will have had their attention pulled in lots of different directions, and they may be more inclined to tune out a speaker or leave than to sit and listen to another speech. Therefore, start by acknowledging previous speakers and the information they presented. Then try to use your speech to reenergize the audience and redirect their focus as needed. At the end of your speech, audience members may have asked previous speakers most of their questions, so don't be disappointed if they have none for you. Or be prepared to share the stage with previous presenters who will also be answering the audience's questions.

If you are in the middle, you have the advantage of a warmed-up audience that isn't yet anxious to leave, but such an audience is also able to compare the information in your speech to the information given in previous speeches. Thus, engage an audience by making connections to previous speakers. As needed, recast or reshape the audience's mood or tone so members are able to hear your message more effectively. At the end of your speech, keep in mind that the audience may ask questions that attempt to pull together information from prior speeches or to rectify discrepancies in claims. If you can help audiences synthesize the information from your speech and previous speakers' speeches, you stand a better chance of sticking in listeners' memories; people tend to remember beginnings and endings rather than what comes in the middle.

Length of speech. Students of public speaking often groan when an instructor sets a specific time limit to a speech and refuses to accept an infraction of that limit without penalty to the student. Why the strict time limits? What's the big deal? Time limitations, although invisible to the audience, are an important structural component of a speech.

When speakers exceed their time constraints, they communicate several things. If others are scheduled to speak after them, they communicate to their audience that their presentations are more important than those of the speakers who follow. If they are the only speaker, they communicate their lack of concern that audience members may have other places to be. Speakers who go over time limits also appear disorganized, suggesting they cannot prioritize material to fit into a predetermined time. In the same vein, a speech that is far too short suggests that the speaker has not prepared fully. Finally, speakers who do not prepare a speech that fits within time limits risk not being able to give their entire speech, which means their audience won't receive their complete message.

The responsibility for staying within time constraints falls on the speaker. When you agree to speak, find out how much time you will have for your

Practicing the Public Dialogue | 4.4

CONSIDER YOUR SPEAKING ENVIRONMENT

For your next speech, think about the size of your audience, the physical arrangement of the room, and the technology you want to use. What elements of your speaking environment will help you stay audience centered? What problems might come up during your speech? How could you solve them? Now consider the time of day you will give your speech, your speaking order, and the length of your speech. How will you work with these temporal factors to stay audience centered?

presentation and stay within that time frame. If your audience wants more of your information, they can ask you to continue, elaborate, or engage you later in a question-and-answer session. (Question-and-answer sessions are discussed at the end of this chapter.) If you decide to speak for far less time than you have been allotted, explain to the audience that you will only deliver a short speech to allow more time for discussion with the audience. If you do not know what your time limitations are and there are other speakers who want to speak, do some quick mental math: divide the total time for the event by the number of speakers, allowing time for questions and discussion. Remember, audience-centered speakers manage their time efficiently and responsibly; they create an environment in which audiences feel respected and appreciated. For more information about time limits, see Chapters 8 and 10.

Adapting to Audience Expectations

What expectations do you bring when you go to a ball game? When a friend takes you to dinner? When you attend a dance performance? When you watch a favorite television program or listen to a new song on your smartphone? We usually have certain expectations about how these types of activities and events will progress. For example, when we attend a ball game, we expect bleachers, announcers, players, referees, rules, a scoring system, and an end to the game. We expect the game to progress in a certain way, and we know when it doesn't progress properly.

When audiences attend public speaking events, they also bring their expectations. They expect speakers to perform in certain ways, expect public speaking events to follow a certain structure, and base their interpretation of a speaker's message on those expectations. Audiences have expectations about the credibility of the speaker, the form of a speech, and how the speaker interacts with the audience in discussions. Audience-centered speakers must address these expectations because audiences use them to help decide whether or not a speaker "did a good job."

Expectations about the Speaker

When audiences take the time to listen to a speech, they want the speaker to be competent (qualified) and credible (believable). You'll explore competence and credibility in more detail in Chapters 8 and 14, but here you'll learn how audiences use master statuses to assess whether or not a speaker is qualified and believable.

As you learned earlier in this chapter, master statuses are the positions people hold in society that affect their identities in almost all social situations. Whether or not we like it, once an audience identifies a speaker's master statuses, members usually form expectations about that speaker based on their beliefs concerning those master statuses. Consider Tim Wise, a nationally known speaker who addresses the topics of race and privilege. Wise, a white male, speaks about topics most audience don't expect a white man to speak about. As such, he opens his presentations with an explanation of his master statuses and how they affect his audience's view of him, as well as his ability to speak about difficult topics in particular ways. You can Google "Tim Wise" and watch his presentations on YouTube to see how he does this.

To understand what an audience might expect of you as a speaker, take a moment to identify your own master statuses. Are you a woman or a man? What is your age and physical state? What is your race and ethnicity? Do you have an accent or a particular style of speech? Will you acknowledge your marital status, parental status, or sexuality in your speech? What is your educational level? Are you often labeled or marked by society in a particular way? Your answers to questions like these will help you adjust to your audience's expectations of you as a speaker.

Tim Wise, speaking about issues of race and privilege, considers his audience carefully throughout his speeches.

"I WANTED TO UNDERSTAND"

If you conduct a Google search for award-winning actress Angelina Jolie, you'll get literally millions of hits, almost all highlighting her many children, her relationships with famous men, her sexy image, and her movies. However, many people outside the reaches of Hollywood know her primarily for her humanitarian work. Through her efforts as a goodwill ambassador for the United Nations High Commissioner for Refugees (UNHCR), she has assisted the United Nations in providing relief to more than 20 million refugees displaced by violence, war, and poverty around the world. She not only engages directly with the men, women, and children who are affected but also assists in building shelters for refugees, releases many journals that document her travel experiences, and visits U.S. detention centers so she can more effectively advocate for the reunion of families separated while escaping their home countries.

Jolie became interested in the plight of refugees after visiting Cambodia to film *Lara Croft: Tomb Raider*. "I started to travel and realized there was so much I was unaware of," she explains. "There were many things I hadn't been taught in school and daily global events I was not hearing about in the news. So I wanted to understand." Her belief in what the United Nations has always stood for—equality and the protection of human rights for all people—has resulted in her commitment to use her status as an A-list celebrity to learn as much as she can and speak out

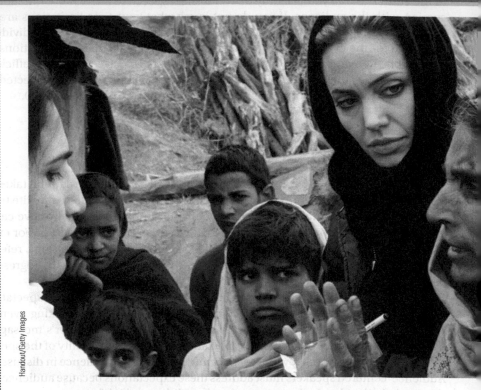

As the Goodwill Ambassador representing the United Nations High Commission for Refugees (UNHCR), actress Angelina Jolie (second right) listens to an earthquake survivor on her November 2005 visit to Jabel Sharoon, a remote village in Pakistan-administered Kashmir.

about the refugee crisis. For example, she says, "When I read about the 20 million people under the care of UNHCR, I wanted to understand how in this day and age that many people could be displaced."

Jolie's focus is on the humanity and heroism of those who have been forced to leave their homes and live in overcrowded and dangerous refugee camps: "What was really shocking was that every individual person you meet will tell you

that their immediate family was [affected]. Somebody's child was killed, somebody's husband. Someone was beaten. . . . You go to these places and you realize what life's really about and what people are really going through. . . . These people are my heroes."[16]

🔗 YOU CAN GET INVOLVED

MindTap Learn more about UNHCR and explore how you can get involved with global humanitarian issues.

Perhaps the most useful strategy for working with audience assumptions about master statuses is to simply acknowledge them. Master statuses do affect us, but help your audience move beyond them because they are not the totality of who we are. Speakers can use many nonthreatening phrases to help audiences move beyond their assumptions. They include phrases such as "I'm often asked that question," "Audiences generally assume," "As a woman (or other master status), people expect me to," and "Now, you might be wondering why someone like me is speaking on this topic today." Phrases that can help audiences shift their focus from unfamiliar styles or mannerisms include "Let me explain the symbolism behind the clothing I'm wearing today," "I'll be using an interpreter today and, as fascinating as they are to watch, I'd love it if you look at me as I speak and ask your questions directly to me," and "Even though I've lived in the United States for ten years now, the English language still stumps me at times. I hear it occasionally stumps some of you native speakers as well, so maybe we can help each other out with some of what we don't understand."

These kinds of phrases acknowledge, directly and kindly, that an audience's assumptions may prevent listeners from hearing a speaker's message. They also acknowledge differences in a positive way and encourage audiences to better understand those differences. As an audience-centered speaker, you certainly want to understand the positions of your audience, but you also want your audience to understand your positions. To help audiences understand you, encourage members to move beyond simply defining you by your master statuses and ask them to recognize you as a unique individual.

Expectations about the Form of a Speech

Communication scholar and theorist Kenneth Burke defines *form* as "the creation of an appetite" in the minds of an audience and the "adequate satisfying of that appetite." He suggests that a speech has form when one part of it leads an audience to "anticipate another part, to be gratified by the sequence."[17] That is, audiences expect a speech to follow a certain structural progression. For audiences with a Western cultural background, audiences often expect speeches to take the following form:

- The speaker will do most of the speaking or facilitating and share information the audience does not already have.
- The audience will listen during the speech and ask most of its questions at the end of the speech.
- Certain types of speaking will follow certain sequences. At the opening of an event, speeches of introduction are given; at public lectures, speeches of information, invitation, or persuasion are likely; at a celebration, speeches of commemoration or acceptance are given; and at business meetings, speeches take the form of presenting ideas, facilitating discussions, or gathering information.

To stay audience centered, do your best to recognize which form your audience will expect for your speech. Then try to follow that form or explain your reasons for altering it. If you don't, your audience's expectations will be violated, and members may react negatively to your speech. For example, if you are asked to commemorate a colleague, be sure to prepare a speech that praises the person and highlights her contributions. Even if you don't feel your colleague has contributed as much as the company thinks she has, try to focus on the positive aspects of your interactions with her so your speech is appropriate for the occasion. Don't take the opportunity to give a persuasive speech that tries to convince the audience your colleague isn't at all praiseworthy. By violating the form of a commemorative speech, you'll only frustrate your audience's expectations and make listeners feel uncomfortable. In our next example, the speaker doesn't follow the form he knows his audience expects, but he explains why he doesn't and so gives a successful speech.

Jeff Ho had been invited to speak to a class on communication and culture about representations of race in the media. An Asian American who had studied the subject fairly extensively, and a dynamic and engaging speaker, Jeff had often been asked to give similar presentations. As a result, he was quite familiar with his material and with his audiences' expectations about how he should present it. Students expected him to lecture and present facts and research so they could take notes. But he really wanted to connect with his audience and create a dialogue, so he decided to violate his audience's expectations.

When he began his presentation, he told the students that he knew they expected him to lecture and they were prepared to sit back and maintain a certain distance. He said, "I'm going to make it really hard for you to stay distant, because I can't be distant from the issue of race and the media—and neither can you. You see, how the media present us as individuals, as people engaged with one another, affects us too powerfully to pretend we can understand by simply listening to someone lecture for fifty minutes. So, I am going to tell you some of my stories, experiences, and perspectives, and I'm asking that you tell me some of yours during this time we have together."

Jeff's presentation was a huge success. His listeners understood why he violated their expectations of form because he explained why. In fact, he set up new expectations—the exchange of stories and experiences. He created a new appetite, which he satisfied during his time with them.

Expectations about Discussions

An important part of the public dialogue is responding to an audience when members ask questions or want to discuss the ideas you present. Speakers are often expected to make time for question-and-answer sessions at the end of a speech or to manage brainstorming sessions and discussions. This type of audience interaction can be challenging because when you share the floor with others, you lose some of the control you had when you were presenting, and you cannot always predict what will happen or what the audience will ask or say.

Despite the unpredictability of discussions and question-and-answer sessions, there are several strategies to stay audience centered and manage this flow of information effectively. First, consider why people ask questions. They usually ask because they want you to clarify points you raised, get more information about a position you advocate, satisfy their curiosity about an issue or an idea, identify or establish connections between ideas, or support or challenge you or the ideas you presented.[18] In addition to asking questions, audience members participate in discussions for many of the same reasons that they ask questions. They also may want to share specific information with the group, restate information in a way that may be easier to understand, or even dominate the conversation.

Identifying which of these reasons motivates someone to participate in a speaking event can help you enormously. If an audience asks you for more information or to clarify a point, try to recognize that members are interested in your topic and are not commenting on your ability to present information clearly. If listeners attempt to make connections between what they previously believed and the new information you've presented, help them make those connections rather than get frustrated because they just don't "get it." Similarly, when audience members try to organize their thoughts about a complicated topic, work with them rather than against them and perhaps incorporate their ideas into your plan for the discussion. If they try to dominate the conversation, set some time limits for each question and explain that, although their views are important, you want to hear from as many people in your audience as possible.

Recognizing what motivates an audience to attack or challenge a speaker is a particularly valuable tool. Addressing attacks or challenges from an audience during a question-and-answer session is often a speaker's greatest fear. When an audience attacks or challenges you, it is usually because they doubt the validity of your information or your credibility as a speaker. When you recognize why audiences do these things, you are more likely to respond appropriately rather than feel intimidated or engage in unproductive sparring. If you fear being challenged, or you watch others challenge a speaker, ask yourself the following questions:

- Which master statuses might challenge members of the audience?
- Why might those master statuses be a challenge?

tip
National Geographic Explorer

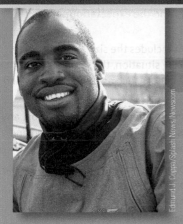

Edmund J. Coppa/Splash News/Newscom

BARRINGTON IRVING, Explorer, Pilot, Educator

How do you prepare for different types of audiences?
I get a briefing and learn what type of group I am speaking to; is this an education group, is this a nonprofit, is this a corporation? But when I arrive, I like to have the opportunity to sit in the audience, even if it's for fifteen to twenty minutes. Within that ten to fifteen minutes, I pretty much know who I'm talking to.

I know the core things about my speech; I'll talk about flying around the world, what were some of the challenges, what were some of the obstacles before and after. But there are different things I'll add on. If I'm talking to an education group, then I'll add on more educational pieces such as metrics and so forth that we have done with students.

What do you take into consideration when you're speaking to a group of younger students, elementary-school age?
Young people are your most challenging critics. The younger the audience, the harsher the criticism. So when you're dealing with elementary school students, middle school students, they're the worst because they'll immediately tell you if you did well or not. But at the same time, when you're talking to young students, it's hard for them to picture what you're saying because they're still kids. They're not adults. They haven't experienced life yet. So you have to paint a picture for children.

Kids in the first two to three minutes, they can tell who wants to be there, or who's been hired by their company to just be there. Kids have a great radar at reading the genuineness behind your talk.

What might you take into consideration when you're speaking to adults?
When I'm talking to adults, I try to share stories of not just inspiration, but stories that bring out the kid inside of an adult. You know, that young explorer or adventurer that's within them; everyone has that. And I'll also talk about critical things such as the future of education and so forth.

Robert Sullivan/AFP/Getty Images

- Are there ways I might address what is being challenged respectfully?
- Are there ways to share my (or the speaker's) expertise and credibility with the audience?

Often, when speakers can share their experience and credentials with an audience, they can build credibility. Audiences are more able to move beyond their assumptions and work with a speaker's ideas and suggestions as a result.

Despite the unpredictable nature of question-and-answer sessions, speeches that allow time for questions or incorporate discussion can be particularly rewarding for both audiences and speakers. In these speeches, speakers communicate that they're interested in the audience's thoughts, beliefs, and concerns. They also communicate that they want to interact with the audience to provide more information if necessary or perhaps learn something new themselves. They are engaging in a healthy public dialogue by making a space for conversation, confirmation, and the exchange of perspectives. For more information about question-and-answer sessions, see the appendix at the end of this book.

Chapter Summary

Audience-centered speakers consider several things about their audiences before, during, and after their speeches.

- An audience is a collection of people who have gathered to listen to a speaker's message.
- Audience members have various master statuses, standpoints, attitudes, values, and beliefs. You can gather this information by conducting a demographic audience analysis, a survey that provides information about the population traits of a particular audience.
- Audiences form a community, and it's important to acknowledge why people have gathered as an audience. Some audiences are voluntary and are interested in your topic and what you have to say. Other audiences are involuntary and are required to listen to you.

Audience-centered speakers also pay careful attention to their speaking environments and the expectations of their audiences.

- The speaking environment includes the size and physical arrangement of the speaking situation, the available technology, and temporal factors such as the time of day and the speaking order.
- You will be able to give a more effective speech in almost any environment if you assess the environment beforehand and adapt to it during your speech.
- Audience expectations focus on how qualified and believable the speaker is, the form of the speech, and the speaker's ability to lead discussions.

Invitation to Public Speaking Online MindTap

Now that you have read Chapter 4, use your MindTap Communication for *Invitation to Public Speaking* for quick access to the digital resources that accompany this text. These resources include:

- **Study tools** that will help you assess your learning and prepare for exams (digital glossary, key term flash cards, review quizzes).
- **Activities and assignments** that will help you hone your knowledge and build your public speaking skills throughout

the course, as well as help you explore public speaking concepts online (web links), give you step-by-step guidance through the research, outline and note card preparation process (Outline Builder), watch and critique videos of sample speeches (Interactive Video Activities), and allow you to practice and present your presentation online using a speech video delivery, recording, and grading system (YouSeeU).

Key Concepts MindTap Test your knowledge with online printable flash cards.

attitude (62)
audience (60)
audience centered (60)
belief (62)
closed-ended question (63)
demographic audience analysis (63)
dialogue (59)
empathy (66)

ethnocentrism (62)
master statuses (60)
open-ended question (63)
speaking environment (67)
standpoint (62)
stereotype (64)
value (62)

Review Questions

1. Identify the following statements as true or false:
   ____ A dialogue is simply taking turns in a conversation.
   ____ When preparing my speech, I need to think more about what I want to say than the background and experiences of my audience.
   ____ All cultures and subcultures have the same basic idea of how the world works.
   ____ Audiences will interpret my message in just the way I want them to.
   ____ To be audience centered, I must say only what the audience wants to hear.
   ____ Temporal and situational factors have little effect on my speech.
   ____ When I open up my speech for questions or discussion, I lose all control of the flow of communication.
   Each of these statements is false. Can you explain why?

2. Consider the times when as an audience member you held a very different standpoint from the other audience members. Consider the times you held a very similar standpoint to the other audience members. How did these situations affect your experience? Did the speaker address these differences or similarities? What was the effect of the speaker's actions?

3. Discuss with your classmates the differences between voluntary and involuntary audiences. In your public speaking class, you will speak to involuntary audiences. What strategies will you use as a speaker to communicate an audience-centered perspective to your audience?

4. Imagine you are giving a speech to introduce your audience to rock climbing and to encourage them to take up the sport. Describe how your speech might change for each of the following audiences:

   - Thirty sixth graders, voluntarily present

   - Thirty corporate executives, asked to attend by their bosses

   - Seven pregnant women and their partners, voluntarily present

   - Fifteen people over the age of sixty, voluntarily present

   - Twelve lower-income teenagers who are part of an environmental education program and quite frightened by the prospect of rock climbing

   - Your boss at the sporting goods store (you want her to invest more money in supplies for rock climbers)

   With your classmates, discuss the changes you would make in your approach, content, and presentation.

5. Consider the room in which your public speaking class is held. Describe the physical setting, options for the placement of speakers, time constraints, and other temporal factors. How is your audience limited or enhanced by these environmental factors? How are you limited or enhanced? Identify specific strategies you can use to enhance this environment so your audience is more open to your message and better understands it.

6. Do discussions and question-and-answer sessions make you nervous? If so, what are your biggest fears regarding these speech elements? Using this chapter as your guide, identify three ways you might ease some of your fears.

5 | Gathering Supporting Materials

....

IN THIS CHAPTER, YOU WILL LEARN TO:

- Explain the types of supporting materials you need for your speech.

- Evaluate the information you find on the Internet, in the library, and through personal interviews.

- Design and conduct research interviews.

- Apply several tips that will help your research efforts.

- Cite your sources for your speech ethically and effectively.

One of our primary responsibilities as public speakers is to provide audiences with accurate information. In addition to expressing our opinions on the topics we speak about, we must also provide facts, examples, and evidence. We can find this type of information, called *supporting material*, by consulting our own experiences and knowledge, by doing research over the Internet and at the library, or by interviewing the right people.

MindTap° Start with a quick warm-up activity and review the chapter's learning objectives.

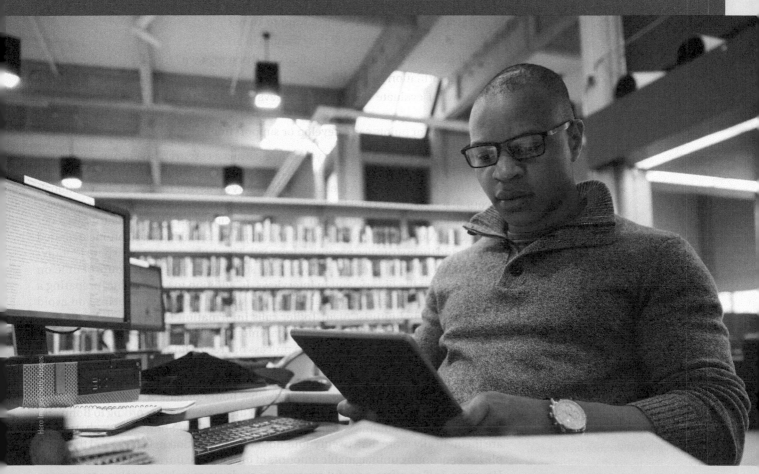

Hero Images/Getty Images

▲ Although we often think we are well informed on issues, in order to maintain an ethical public dialogue we still must gather supporting materials for our speeches. In this chapter you will explore the range of sources and places to do your research, ways to evaluate the accuracy of that information, and the ethics of including the information you find to support your ideas.

Conducting research may seem intimidating at first, but if you organize your efforts, the process should be efficient and productive—and in less time than you might imagine, you can fill notebooks and folders with an impressive range of supporting materials. Research not only ensures that your ideas and arguments are accurate and that your audience is appropriately informed but also that the insights it offers you on your subject can also keep you excited about your speech up until you deliver it and beyond.

This chapter will help you collect the supporting materials you need to enter the public dialogue successfully. You will learn how to organize your research efforts into three categories: (1) determining what types of information you need, (2) identifying where you can find this information, and (3) assessing the strengths and weaknesses of the information you find. If you approach your research in an organized way, you will spend your time productively, reduce your frustration, and increase your chances of finding excellent materials to support your ideas.

MindTap®

Read, highlight, and take notes online.

Determine What Types of Information You Need

Before you begin your research in earnest, take some time to organize your thoughts about what types of supporting material you already have and what types you still need. Start by asking yourself the following kinds of questions (note that in Chapter 6, we'll discuss examples, narratives, statistics, testimony, and definitions in detail):

- What examples and stories do I have?
- What statistics will my audience want to know?
- What kinds of testimony will they want to hear?
- What terms and phrases can I define clearly on my own?
- Is the information I already have accurate, relevant, and credible?
- How will I evaluate the accuracy, relevance, and credibility of the information I find?
- What ideas or points can I develop or support from my own experiences?

As you consider these questions, you can construct a **research inventory**, a list of the types of information you have and the types you want to find. A research inventory helps you focus your research efforts and identify areas that need special attention. It is your first step toward making the time you spend gathering materials productive.

Consider the sample research inventory in Figure 5.1. This inventory was developed by Alena, who gave a speech to her public speaking class on incarcerated parents and their struggles parenting from jail. The thirty minutes she spent identifying what information she had and what she still needed saved her hours of time on the Internet, in the library, and in interviews. In addition to saving time, preparing a research inventory before you start to gather supporting materials helps you avoid experiencing what futurist Alvin Toffler calls **information overload**. In his famous book *Future Shock*,[1] Toffler explained that information overload happens when we take in more information than we can process but realize there still is more information we must know.

Roger Bohn and James Short determined that in today's hypermediated world, North Americans consume more than twelve hours of data a day, not including watching television and using the computer at the same time. According to Bohn and Short, the use of "multiple simultaneous sources of information" means that "there are theoretically more than twenty-four hours of information in a day,"[2] and that people are consuming unimaginable amounts of information during their waking hours. However, Toffler offers a useful strategy for students of public speaking to manage

research inventory: List of the types of information you have for your speech and the types you want to find.

information overload: When we take in more information than we can process but realize there still is more information we are expected to know.

Speech topic: Incarcerated parents

General purpose: To invite

Specific purpose: I want to invite my audience to consider the issues regarding incarcerated parents and when they should or shouldn't be permitted to parent.

My audience is: My public speaking classmates

I currently have:

Examples and stories:
A story Li wrote from the juvenile corrections facility
Stories from Sandra Enos, _Mothering from the Inside_, 2001

Statistics:
The number of children in the U.S. who have parents in prison, and the number of mothers and fathers released each year to return home. (Silja J. A. Talvi, _Women Behind Bars: The Crisis of Women in the U.S. Prison System_, 2007)

Testimony:
My own experiences working with a correctional facility.

Definitions:

This information is relevant, accurate, and credible because:
The story really catches the emotion and sadness of kids with incarcerated parents.
The book, _Mothering from the Inside_, is foundational, and _Women Behind Bars_ is fairly current.

My audience will want to hear:

Examples of the following:
Specific examples of incarcerated parents.

Statistics for the following:
Statistics to illustrate the kinds of crimes and lengths of sentences that keep parents away from children.
Statistics to illustrate the different lengths of times fathers and mothers are separated from children.

Testimony about the following:
The experiences of mothers and fathers who are currently incarcerated.
The experiences of children with incarcerated parents and of parents who have been released.

Definitions of the following:
Kinship (who takes care of children when a parent is incarcerated)
Incarceration
Correctional facility

The kinds of sources they will find trustworthy are:
People who work in correctional facilities
Legal services
Periodicals and journals that publish articles on the impact of incarceration on families

I need to find the following information:
Specific definitions
More statistics, especially about the effects on families
More testimony (from a range of perspectives)

The kinds of technology I might use are:
Downloaded photos or images
Charts or graphs with statistics
Power point quotations from one of the children's stories

Sources for this information:
Library database
Government websites (statistics)
Websites about barriers incarcerated parents face
Possibly interview a local correctional officer

Figure 5.1 Sample research inventory

this overload: classify information so it fits into manageable units. This is what you do with your research inventory. You organize the information for your speech into two classifications: what you have and what you need. The next step is to determine where you'll find the information you need.

Notice that the last item on the Research Inventory Worksheet is "Sources for this information." Once you know what types of information you want, you can classify that information even further by identifying where you are most likely to find it. In the next few sections, you will explore four common sources of information: your own experiences and knowledge, the Internet, libraries, and personal interviews. Understanding how best to access information from these sources and what you can gather from each will help you evaluate each source's strengths and weaknesses.

Use Your Personal Knowledge and Experience

After reading Chapter 3, you probably recognized that you have personal, firsthand knowledge about several subjects that would make excellent speeches. After you've selected your topic, use this personal experience as a source of research. Before you begin other research, take a moment to consider what knowledge you already have about your topic. This knowledge can come from your own experiences and training, your family background, hobbies, job or profession, and even things you have read or observed.

For example, the information in Cindy's speech on folding the American flag (Chapter 7) relies on her personal experience in the military and with folding the flag during ceremonial events. Similarly, Carol used her personal experiences with being overweight as one of her sources of research for her speech on fat discrimination (Chapter 14). If you're interested in a topic but don't have personal experience with it, you can gain personal experience as part of your research. For example, suppose you wanted to give a speech about a particular agency in your community. You could visit that agency and observe someone for a day to get the personal experience you need.

Practicing the Public Dialogue | 5.1

PREPARE YOUR RESEARCH INVENTORY

Bring a copy of the Research Inventory Worksheet to class. With a partner, discuss the kinds of research you both need for your next speech as well as the types of research you already have. Discuss where you might find the research you need, and develop a timeline for gathering this material. Consider the advantages and disadvantages of your sources for the material you might find. Remember to consider your speech goals, your audience, and the need to vary your sources of information.

MindTap®

You can download the Research Inventory Worksheet online.

Identify the Technology You Might Use

Without a doubt, you will do most of your research using your computer, iPad, or other electronic device. With so much technology to use, it's important to consider what kinds of information might help you develop your ideas. Consider whether you want to take or download photos; use YouTube clips; share maps, figures, or tables; or use one of the many presentation tools (e.g., Prezi or PowerPoint slides) that are available. Make a list of possible types of technologies that can help you develop your ideas and arguments, and add them to the research inventory you are developing.

Search for Information on the Internet

Information found on the Internet is the most prevalent source of research for college students in the United States. For public speaking students, the Internet offers information on local, regional, national, and international events and issues. But how do we sort through the staggering array of ideas, opinions, claims, and arguments we find on the Internet and determine the accuracy and validity of this information?

tip
National Geographic Explorer

BARRINGTON IRVING, Explorer, Pilot, Educator

Can you tell us about the kind of supporting materials you use?

Yes, I will use numbers and statistics but not too many because no one will remember them. And that's the honest truth. Everyone will remember a personal story because, as human beings, we like to tell stories. Even if we're not great writers or great readers, we like to tell stories, right? So, I know that stories connect with a lot of people but it's also finding a balance. I will use evidence, and I will use statistics, but at the end of the day—unless you are specifically speaking at a conference where people are coming for that type of information, don't give too many statistics. That's because only one or two numbers will stay in someone's head.

So, for example, if I'm going to give statistics about, let's say, high school dropout rates, or the lack of student interest in science and math, I start off with a story that everyone can relate to, you know, such as, "Remember when you were young and as a kid, you'd have a toy car or whatever, and you'd run it off of the ramp of your parent's table, or off the chair? You were doing science and math. And what happened when you got to middle school and you stopped doing that? That's also when math and science stopped being cool, right?"

So, I'll use that story to open up the door to introduce statistics about academic achievement.

Let's look first at the ethics of doing your research on the Internet and then some ways you can evaluate this information to answer this question.

The Ethics of Internet Research

The Internet is not without its weaknesses. Because it is easy to access and open to anyone, information from every imaginable type of source is posted—and a lot of it may not be accurate. Many websites are maintained and regularly updated by reputable people, companies, and institutions, but just as many are not. Websites are regularly abandoned and thus are never updated by operators who lose funding or simply lose interest. As a result, websites range dramatically in accuracy, complexity, and usefulness. Many sites include information that is old, incomplete, or based on personal opinions and biases. In addition, identifying credible Internet sites can be difficult because many sites are well designed and look professional even if they're not.

Challenges like these place particular ethical responsibilities on you when you use the Internet to find supporting materials. Although the Internet can be an excellent source of information, you must use this tool properly to get information you can use ethically in your speech. To act in good faith with your audience, use only reliable and relevant information from the Internet and accurately credit the sources for this information in your speech. Knowing how to evaluate the quality of information you find on the Internet is crucial and ensures that you develop your speech ideas responsibly.

Evaluating Internet Information

Given the fluid nature of the Internet, how do you know whether a source you find there is one you can use in your speech? As you would with any other source of

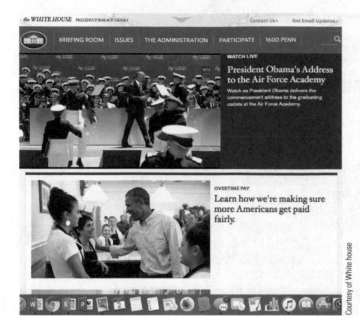

Courtesy of White house

Assess the information you see on the home page of the White House. Does the information on this site look current and complete? How reliable do you think the information on this site is compared with the information on, say, TMZ.com, a celebrity gossip site?

information, evaluate your data according to the following criteria.

Is the information reliable? Check the domain in the uniform resource locator (URL). Is it ".com" (a commercial enterprise that might be trying to sell something), an ".org" (a nonprofit organization more interested in services and issues than in commerce), an ".edu" (an educational institution), or a ".gov" (a government agency)? What bias might those operating the site have about your topic? Do they make any disclaimers about the information they post on the site? What makes this information reliable or not?

Is the information authoritative? URLs that include a tilde (~) often indicate that a single individual is responsible for the information on a website. Can you find the person's credentials posted on the site? Can you contact the person and ask for credentials? Can you find the person's credentials in any print sources, such as a *Who's Who* reference? Regardless of whether the material was authored by a single person, an organization, an institution, or a company, is the author an expert on the subject of the site?

How current is the information? Many web pages include a date that tells you when it was posted or last updated. If you don't see such a date, you may be able to find it in your browser's View or Document menu. If you determine that the website is current, is the time frame relevant to your subject or arguments? You may find great information, but if it doesn't relate to the time frame of your speech, it's not relevant or ethical to use.

How complete is the information? Much of the text posted on the Internet consists of excerpts from printed material, and what is left out may be of more use than what is included. For example, a site may contain one paragraph from a newspaper article, but that paragraph may not reflect the overall message of the article. If you want to use an excerpted portion of a printed work, you must locate the complete work to ensure you are using that material accurately.

Is the information relevant? Many interesting facts and stories appear on the web, but be sure those you use as supporting material do more than just tell a great story. Your information must help you develop your thesis (Chapters 3 and 6). Ask yourself whether the information fits your needs. Does it help develop your main ideas, or does it take you in a different direction?

Is the information consistent and unbiased? Is the information you find consistent with information you find on other sites, from printed sources, or from interviews? Can you find other sources to support the statements, claims, and facts provided by a website? If the information is inconsistent with other sources, then it may reflect new findings about a topic—but it also may reflect an unfounded or unsubstantiated claim. Many sites present only one side of an issue. To guarantee a less biased presentation and more comprehensive picture of your topic, explore a number of different sites and be sure to cross-check what you find against the information you obtain from more established sources such as books and other print documents. Be wary of outrageous or controversial claims that cannot be checked for accuracy or aren't grounded in reasonable arguments or sources.[3]

If you keep these six criteria in mind as you research your speech topic on the Internet, you'll be more likely to use supporting materials that are credible. Recall from Chapter 4 that you increase your chances for giving a successful speech by remaining audience centered, and audiences expect information that is reliable, authoritative, current, complete, relevant, and consistent. The Internet is certainly a source of much credible material, but it should be only one of many tools you use to gather materials for your speech.

Finding Information at the Library

The library is a very comprehensive tool for gathering materials. There you have access to librarians, databases, indexes, journals, magazines, newspapers, books, documents, and many other useful resources, including the Internet. These materials cover an extensive range of topics and time frames, and their sources are usually reliable, routinely evaluated, and systematically organized.

But libraries also have their weaknesses. Unless you are familiar with how libraries organize their materials, you can find yourself confused—and even lost. One library may not have the exact source you want, so you have to look for other sources or visit another library. Until you get to know them, libraries can seem quite foreign. However, once you understand the strengths and weaknesses of a library, you can easily combine Internet research with library research to gather a wide range of useful and credible materials for your speeches.

Orientations and Librarians

If you are new to library research or are unfamiliar with the library you will be using, schedule a tour of the library before you begin your research. Getting a library orientation may sound silly or boring, but it can save you countless hours wandering around a place you don't understand. Most orientations take about an hour, and they can give you the confidence you need to begin your research on the right foot.

Librarians are also excellent resources. Consider what a librarian is trained to know: how materials are cataloged or stored, what materials are on databases, how to search through databases, how to refine subject and word searches, where materials are located, and how to request materials from other libraries. These skills can be invaluable to someone who is looking for supporting materials for a speech. Surprisingly, though, many students ask a librarian for assistance only as a last resort. If you find yourself spending more than half an hour searching for materials you cannot find, ask for assistance. Remember, librarians won't do the work for you, but they can make the work you do much more efficient and fruitful. When you do seek a librarian in the course of your research, consider the following tips:

- *Fill out your research inventory before you begin your search and bring it with you to the library.* Refer to it as you work with the librarian.
- *Ask specific questions.* For example, rather than asking, "Where can I find information on incarcerated parents?" ask where you might find statistics on the number of children with incarcerated parents. Or ask where you can find testimony by social workers about the effects of incarceration on families or examples of the most common problems faced by families with one or both parents incarcerated.
- *Share the specifics of your assignment with the librarian.* "It's only a four-minute speech," "My instructor wants three sources from this year and two from within the last ten years," "My audience is a potential source of funding for my proposal," "I want a really dramatic story for my introduction," and so on. Information like this will give the librarian the same focus you have for your speech and will help you avoid information overload.
- *Treat the librarian with respect. Librarians are highly trained people whose specialty is finding information.* They are eager to help but only if you recognize their talents and worth.

Creatas Images/Jupiter Images

Don't be shy about asking librarians to help you navigate your school's library or find information. They love to help and can save you a lot of time in your search for supporting materials.

MindTap®

Access librarians at the New York Public Library online. You don't have to live in New York for these librarians to e-mail answers to questions you have about specific topics.

MindTap®

Learn more about call numbers and how they can help make your research more efficient.

Library Catalogs

A library's catalog allows you to search your topic by title, author, or subject in books, journals, magazines, and many other print and electronic materials. When you log into your library's home page, the catalog is one of the first headings you'll see. Library catalogs allow you to perform keyword and subject searches and will tell you the location of the book, magazine, or other material you want to find. Each page about a source indicates that source's call number, an alphanumeric code that indicates exactly where that material is stored in the library.

Keyword searches are helpful if you don't know the full title of the source you want. When you search with a word that you know is included in the title, search results will list all titles that include that word. Subject searches allow you to find all the sources that include information about a particular topic. For example, Lin's speech topic was road rage, and she wanted to know if any recent books or magazine articles had been written about her subject. She didn't have a specific author or title, so she searched on the subject of driving. This search produced far too many sources to look through. She then searched on a more specific term, road rage. The results of this search were much more manageable. (If your subject is more than two words, put quotation marks around the words: "road rage." The quotation marks tell the computer to search for the words together, not separately.)

Lin later used a Boolean operator to refine her search further. **Boolean operators** are words you can use to create specific phrases that broaden or narrow your search. Three of the most commonly used are AND, OR, and NOT. In her search for links on road rage, Lin used the Boolean operator AND to link her topic with the broader issue of antisocial behavior. As a result, she got a listing of sites on both road rage and antisocial behavior. If she had used OR, she would have called up a listing of sites on either road rage or antisocial behavior. If she'd searched on "road rage NOT antisocial behavior," she would have gotten only links to sites about road rage that made no reference to antisocial behavior. Boolean operators help you focus your searches to find as much or as little information as you need.

Databases and Indexes

Databases are collections of information stored electronically so they are easy to find and retrieve. They are useful research tools for several reasons. Computer searches are quick, saving you valuable research time, and they are efficient because you can search using keywords and subjects. Databases allow you to access materials from other libraries, and most can usually be accessed from any computer connected to the Internet. Sources are current because records can be entered into a computerized database as soon as they are available, and they are updated regularly. Finally, databases present their information in a format that is easy to copy.

But databases also have their drawbacks. The so-called logic of databases is sometimes hard to understand, so searches can yield false hits or citations unrelated to your topic. For example, a search for articles on "road rage" may yield articles on road construction and even anger-management techniques. In addition, many electronic databases (except catalogs) do not include older materials. So, if you are looking for historical trends, you will need to consult other sources of information.

You will find two kinds of databases in libraries. **Bibliographic databases** index publishing data for books, periodical articles, government reports, statistics, patents, research reports, conference proceedings, and dissertations. **Full-text databases** index the complete text of newspapers, periodicals, encyclopedias, research reports, court cases, books, and the like. Bibliographic databases help you find a specific source of information, such as the title of a journal article, and a full-text database provides the entire text of that item. Note that because full-text databases store so much text, they are more likely to yield false hits.

Some databases provide abstracts of documents. An **abstract** is a summary of the text in an article or publication. An abstract can be very useful because it tells

Boolean operators: Words you can use to create specific phrases that broaden or narrow your search on the Internet.

database: Collections of information stored electronically so they are easy to find and retrieve.

bibliographic database: Database that indexes publishing data for books, periodical articles, government reports, statistics, patents, research reports, conference proceedings, and dissertations.

full-text database: Database that indexes the complete text of newspapers, periodicals, encyclopedias, research reports, court cases, books, and the like.

you whether or not a document includes the information you need, which can save you from reading text you cannot use. Most abstracts are about a paragraph long, but some are longer. However long the abstract is, you need to track down the full text of the article or publication if you want to cite it in your speech. Abstracts help you find relevant sources, but they are not the sources themselves.

When you want to search through materials that are published regularly, such as magazines, newspapers, yearbooks, scholarly journals, and proceedings from conferences, an index can be very helpful. An **index** is an alphabetical listing of the topics discussed in a specific publication, along with the corresponding year, volume, and page numbers. Many indexes are computerized, but some libraries still rely on the print versions. You can find indexes from almost every academic discipline and area of interest. Figure 5.2 presents a list of commonly used indexes. Keep a few tips in mind when you search indexes for materials:

- Subject and keyword searches are crucial to finding what you want in an index, so be as specific and concise as you can.
- Indexes vary in how they classify topics, so a particular search term might not yield useful results from all indexes.
- You can usually find something on your topic in almost any index, so be sure you are searching indexes relevant to your topic.

InfoTrac and InfoTrac College Edition	Citations, abstracts, and full-text articles from thousands of magazines, journals, and newspapers.
LEXIS/NEXIS	Full-text database for legal, business, and current issues. Includes U.S. Supreme Court and lower court cases.
Academic Search Premier	Scholarly academic multidisciplinary database. Covers a broad range of disciplines, including general academic, business, social sciences, humanities, general sciences, education, and multicultural topics.
IngentaConnect	Indexes scholarly journals and delivers documents. A fee is charged for document delivery.
Readers' Guide to Periodical Literature	Indexes almost 300 popular and general interest magazines, including *The New Yorker*, *Newsweek*, and *National Geographic Traveler*.
DataTimes	Online newspaper database, including *Washington Post*, *Dallas Morning News*, and *San Francisco Chronicle*.
Christian Science Monitor	Indexes the *Christian Science Monitor International Daily Newspaper*.
New York Times Index	Indexes the *New York Times* newspaper.
NewsBank	Microfiche collection covering current events from newspapers in over 100 cities.
The Times Index (London)	Index to the daily *Times*, the *Sunday Times*, the *Times Literary Supplement*, the *Times Educational Supplement*, and the *Times Higher Education Supplement*.
Wall Street Journal Index	Emphasizes financial news from the Journal. Includes *Barron's Index*, a subject and corporate index to *Barron's Business and Financial Weekly*.
Washington Post Newspaper	Index of the newspaper from our nation's capital.

Figure 5.2   Indexes

abstract: Summary of the text in an article or publication.

index: Alphabetical listing of the topics discussed in a specific publication, along with the corresponding year, volume, and page numbers.

Government Documents

Government documents can help you make a well-informed contribution to the public conversation. They contain all kinds of useful information:

- Statistics on population, personal income, education, crime, health, and the like
- Information about social issues such as employment, hunger, teen pregnancy, and the environment
- Issues discussed in Congress, such as gun control, seat belts, and education
- Information about historical events, such as wars and elections
- Information on local issues, such as funding for public education or charter schools, land disputes, water rights, and so on
- Research sponsored by the government
- Maps, charts, and posters that you can download or photocopy to make excellent visual aids for your speeches (Chapter 11)

You can find government documents online, as well as in print, on CD-ROM or DVD, and on database indexes. Most government information now is available on the Internet thanks to a 1996 mandate by Congress to cease publishing government information in microfiche and paper formats.[4] To find this information on the Internet, check out USA.gov. This comprehensive website lets you search by subject or by agency.

Practicing the Public Dialogue | 5.2

RESEARCH AND EVALUATE INTERNET AND LIBRARY SOURCES

Bring the research you've found for your speech on the Internet and at the library to class. Share your research with the class and discuss whether your sources are credible, ethical, and audience centered and whether your research supports your speaking goals. Discard any information that does not seem ethical, reliable, authoritative, current, complete, relevant, consistent, or audience centered.

Evaluating Library Resources

Although the information in libraries is generally more reliable than materials on the Internet, you still must evaluate library sources and use them ethically. Not all the sources you find will be credible or appropriate for your particular speech and audience. Evaluate library sources by checking that the source is reliable, authoritative, current, complete, relevant, and consistent. For a summary of how to use Internet and library research to the best advantage, see Table 5.1.

Table 5.1 Internet and Library Research

USE THE INTERNET WHEN YOU . . .	USE THE LIBRARY WHEN YOU . . .
Want an overview of your topic	May want assistance with your search
Want the most current ideas	Want comprehensive materials
Want to explore less established sources	Want established sources
Want shortened versions of print documents	Want the full text of a document
Know your specific subject or URL	Want to review databases
Can verify the accuracy and credibility of the information found	Can evaluate the appropriateness and relevance of the information found

Build, Fly, and Soar
Barrington Irving: Emerging Explorer, Pilot, Educator

Raised in a low-income neighborhood in Miami, Barrington Irving's life changed when he met a pilot who asked him if he had ever considered becoming a pilot. Irving explains, at the age of fifteen, "I didn't think I was smart enough; but the next day he gave me the chance to sit in the cockpit of the commercial airplane he flew, and just like that I was hooked." Convinced he wanted to become a pilot, Irving turned down a football scholarship to the University of Florida in favor of flight school, which he paid for by doing odd jobs, including washing airplanes. After obtaining his pilot's license, he had another dream to pursue: to fly solo around the world.

To sponsor his dream, Irving approached various manufacturers asking them to donate parts for an airplane he wanted to build; more than fifty companies rejected him, before he found some who would help. With no weather radar, no de-icing system, and only $30 in his pocket, he took flight: "I like to do things people say I can't do." At age twenty-three, Irving became the youngest person and first African American ever to fly solo around the world.

Following his historic flight, Irving decided to help other young people achieve their dreams. "I was determined to give back with my time, knowledge, and experience." He founded a nonprofit organization, Experience Aviation, intended to increase the number of students in aviation, as well as other math and science-related careers. In his Build and Soar program, sixty students from failing schools built an airplane from scratch in ten weeks (which Barrington then flew on its test run). Irving states: "Kids want to be challenged, but today too many are bored and uninspired. I want to use aviation to excite and empower a new generation to become scientists, engineers, and explorers."

As a part of this effort, he created a "flying classroom" that enabled students to participate via technology in a three-part round-the-world flight: "the students and the educators voted on everything I did. So, for example, they determined the type of meals I ate or what path I took up a mountain, or what things I explored." Students in their classrooms saw, via webcast and blogs, both flights up to 45,000 feet and ground expeditions to locations like Machu Picchu, the Galapagos Islands, and the Pyramids of Egypt. Apps tracked adventures like tagging sharks, with ongoing location and water temperature data.

In the course of his adventurous life, Irving has learned to speak to audiences that vary from potential corporate sponsors to elementary school students. When he speaks to students who "aren't sure what they want to do with their lives," he tries to inspire them to have a dream, and to have the confidence to believe they can fulfill that dream. He says, "No matter what the challenge, the only one who can stop you is you." His own goal is to use aviation "to excite and empower a new generation to become scientists, engineers, and explorers." Barrington Irving flies high every day, with no limits to what he dares to dream.

WHAT DO YOU THINK?

1. Barrington Irving used his passions and his determination to pursue his goals. He now shares those goals with young people through his public speaking. What passions and goals do you have that others might be interested in learning about?

2. Irving is gathering the ideas and suggestions of students across the country through his "flying classroom." What other innovative ways can you identify to "gather material" for a speech?

3. If you were to gather those materials in innovative ways, how might you evaluate them for their appropriateness and strengths?

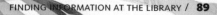

Conduct Research Interviews

Using the words of other people in a speech can supply important information, provide a sense of immediacy, bring abstract concepts and arguments to life, and make seemingly distant issues hit home. Therefore, including the results of an interview in your speech can be a powerful way to present your ideas. An **interview** is a planned interaction with another person that is organized around inquiry and response, with one person asking questions while the other person answers them.[5] Interviews require planning, and productive interviews involve more than simply asking a few questions. You must first decide whom you'll interview, then schedule the interview, decide what questions to ask, conduct the interview in a professional and ethical manner, and then follow up with a letter of thanks.

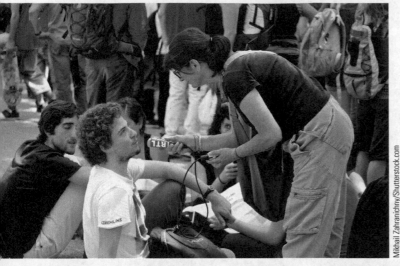

Mikhail Zahranichny/Shutterstock.com

Reporters often use interviews to gather information to be sure their stories are accurate and interesting. If you're planning to conduct an interview for your next speech, who might you interview? How could the information this person provides make your speech more interesting and relevant?

Determine Whom to Interview

Your first step in conducting interviews is to determine whom you want to interview. You can use several criteria to identify the best interview subjects for your speech. Who are the experts on your speech topic? Who has personal experience with the topic? Who will your audience find interesting and credible? Who has time to speak with you? Who do you have time to contact?

As you gather other supporting materials from the Internet and the library, also keep your eyes open for people in your area who might be excellent sources of information. If you have time, you might consider contacting people who live outside your area via e-mail or telephone. Choose interview subjects who have credentials and experiences relevant to your topic and thus can speak intelligently about it. A good interview subject might be a well-known expert or scholar, a head of an agency or company, someone on staff or in a support position, or a member of a community group, club, or organization.

Schedule the Interview

Although there are exceptions, most people are flattered when asked for an interview and will agree if you present yourself and your request respectfully. To ensure that a potential source sees you as credible and professional, take a moment to consider why you want the interview and why this person is an appropriate interview subject, what specific types of information you want to gather, roughly what questions you'll ask, and approximately how much time you want to spend with this person. When people are asked for an interview, they want to know the answers to all of these questions. Before you contact someone to request the interview, rehearse what you'll say a few times (like you would a speech) so you sound organized and professional. In your request, do the following:

- Identify who you are, providing your full name, where you're from (school, place of business), the public speaking course you're in, and your instructor's name.
- Specify the requirements of your assignment, such as its purpose, length, and topic.
- Describe why you've chosen to contact the person (for example, she's an expert in the field, he's the head of an agency).
- Request the interview, letting the person know how much time it will take and what kinds of questions you'll ask. Include two or three of your most important or engaging questions.

interview: Planned interaction with another person that is organized around inquiry and response, with one person asking questions while the other person answers them.

"I'M GOING TO HELP THESE KIDS"

Colombian singer Shakira may be one of the most driven people in the entertainment industry. Since 1995, she's released several best-selling albums (she's the highest-selling Colombian artist of all time), has won a couple of dozen major music awards (including two Grammy Awards), and collaborated with the South African group Freshlyground to sing the official song of the 2010 World Cup. Oh, and she also performed with superstars Stevie Wonder and Usher at President Obama's inaugural ceremonies in 2008.

But Shakira is also driven to succeed as a humanitarian. When she was eight years old, her father experienced some financial trouble and had to sell much of what her family owned. No longer were they living the comfortable middle-class life she was used to. "In my childish head, this was the end of the world." To help her see that their circumstances weren't as dire as they could be, her father took her to the park to see the homeless kids addicted to sniffing glue who lived there. "From then on, I gained perspective, and realized that there were many underprivileged children in my country. The images of those kids, with their tattered clothes and bare feet, have stayed with me forever. I said to myself back then,

AP Images/Alan Diaz

one day I'm going to help these kids when I become a famous artist."

She's certainly made good on that promise to herself. With the money she made from her first successful album, she founded the Pies Descalzos (Barefoot) Foundation, a Colombian charity that provides education and meals for impoverished Colombian children. Shakira also founded the ALAS Foundation (Fundacion América Latina en Acción Solidaria), an organization dedicated to launching "a new social movement that will generate a collective commitment to comprehensive early childhood development programs for the children in Latin America." In 2007, she used her humanitarian clout and persuasive skills to secure commitments of an impressive 200 million dollars for the ALAS Foundation from Mexican philanthropist Carlos Slim and U.S. philanthropist and conservationist Howard Buffett. In 2012, via YouTube, she asked her fans to help her build a school in one of the most impoverished neighborhoods in her

home country of Colombia, Cartagena, by "buying a brick," and in 2014, she opened that school.[6] As a goodwill ambassador for UNICEF, Shakira and her husband, Gerard Pique, threw a "charity baby shower for UNICEF ahead of the birth" of their second son in 2015, and raised more than a million pounds for that charity.[7]

Shakira decided to engage with her community because she wanted to help kids like those she saw in the park. But she also has a larger goal in mind, which she described in a 2008 speech at Oxford University about her humanitarian work in Latin America:

> Now I want to be clear about this, this isn't about charity. This is about investing in human potential. From an ethical point of view, from a moral point of view, it accomplishes a purpose. But also from an economic point of view, this could bring enormous benefits to all mankind. Universal education is the key to global security and economic growth.[8]

🔗 YOU CAN GET INVOLVED

MindTap Learn more about Shakira's Pies Descalzos Foundation,. You can also explore a nonprofit organization made up of artists and volunteers all over the world who raise awareness and secure funds for humanitarian causes.

Note that by describing the types of questions you'll ask, your interview subjects can determine whether they can answer them and if they need to prepare before you arrive. And by letting them know how long you'll need for the interview, they can schedule time for you.

Prepare for the Interview

Preparing for interviews often takes longer than conducting them, but the payoff of careful preparation is worth the extra time you spend. The two components of preparing for interviews are designing your questions and deciding how you will record your interview.

Designing interview questions. Take time with your interview questions because they are your guide for an interview. Showing up with a plan to "just see how it develops" may be a good strategy for meeting a new friend, but it usually does not get you what you need in an interview. Even seasoned interviewers plan their questions carefully before they begin an interview, and most of them also research their interview subjects extensively.[9]

Shel Israel, a media consultant and journalist has "conducted thousands of interviews, been interviewed hundreds of times," and "observed thousands of interviews from a neutral seat." Israel, writing for *Forbes*, offers nine tips for conducting interviews:

1. **Start slow, safe, and personal.** Begin with a question that will relax and focus the person you are interviewing. Ask them where they grew up or about their first job.
2. **Coax, don't hammer.** Although "shock jocks" might garner audiences, Israel suggests a softer approach to interviewing people. He offers NPR's Terry Gross as a model, advocating her very personal style to interviewing.
3. **Use open-ended questions.** Even if you have views and opinions different than the person you are interviewing, keep them to yourself and ask open-ended

questions. Israel shares that the job of the interviewer is to get the person to tell their "story and let the readers decide what they think of his or her ideas."

4. **Ask what you don't know.** When we ask what we don't know, Israel reports, we get surprises. "Surprises mean I have something that has not been previously reported," and that's great supporting material.
5. **Let them wander, but not too much.** Israel suggests that allowing people you are interviewing to talk about what they see is important to them, rather than trying to keep them focused on your questions, can lead to interesting material. Although this is risky, Israel states, "Sometimes it works, sometimes it does not."
6. **Interview in person rather than via e-mail.** E-mail answers feel scripted and stilted, explains Israel. It also

prevents you from asking that important follow-up question or probe that often gives you the best material.

7. **Be prepared.** Israel encourages interviewers to Google the person they are interviewing and gather as much information about them as possible before the interview. Go back three or four pages, he urges, to find forgotten information or "surprisingly interesting content that no one else has recently looked at."
8. **Listen, really listen.** The most important information comes from what people say, Israel explains, not what we ask. So, pay close attention to what your interviewee is saying and share that with your audience.
9. **Yes, there are dumb questions.** Ask about what's not on the person's bio or résumé. Your goal, Israel states, is to get new information and insights, not to find out what you already know.[10]

The goal of your interview questions should be to obtain information that you couldn't find through your Internet and library research. For example, in her speech on road rage, Lin couldn't find information about the personality profiles of people prone to road rage. When she interviewed a driving instructor, she asked him about his experiences with students who fell into road rage. Thus, she was able to get the information she needed.

Three kinds of questions are commonly used in interviews: open-ended questions, closed-ended questions, and probes. Most research on interviewing suggests that a combination of open-ended and closed-ended questions yields the best results. Open-ended questions give you more stories and details than closed-ended questions, but when you just need facts, there's nothing like a closed-ended question to prompt the specific answer you need.[11] A **probe** is a question that fills out or follows up an answer to a previous question. Probes are useful for obtaining more far-reaching or comprehensive answers. Table 5.2 provides examples and the advantages of each of these kinds of questions. (Open-ended and close-ended questions are also discussed in Chapter 4.)

Recording the interview. As you prepare for an interview, consider whether you want to tape-record your conversation or record it on paper. Both methods have advantages and disadvantages. On tape, you have a record of your exact conversation, but you have to comb through or even transcribe the whole thing to find the exact quotes you want, which can be time consuming. A tape recorder can also sometimes make an interviewee nervous and less prone to share stories and ideas. However, with a tape recorder, you are free to relax a bit during the interview and make more extensive eye contact because you aren't busy writing things down.

probe: Question that fills out or follows up an answer to a previous question.

Table 5.2 Examples and Advantages of Different Types of Interview Questions

QUESTION TYPE	EXAMPLES	ADVANTAGES
Open-ended questions invite a wide range of possible responses.	• How did you become a driving instructor? • What are your thoughts on this most recent form of legislation?	• Usually nonthreatening and so prompt interviewees to do most of the talking. • Do not restrict the form or content of an answer, and they allow interviewees to offer information voluntarily. • Encourage interviewees to pull together ideas, knowledge, and experiences in interesting ways.
Closed-ended questions invite brief, focused answers and allow an interviewer to keep tighter control of the direction of the conversation.	• How long have you been a driving instructor? • Do many of your students display road rage?	• Can be answered easily and quickly. • Encourage interviewees to give you specific information. • Result in shorter answers for you to process.
Probes are questions that fill out or follow up an answer to a previous question.	• ***Nonverbal:*** Head nods or questioning eyes that indicate interest and a request to continue. • Minimal ***responses:*** Slight vocalizations such as "Oh?" "Really?" "Um-hmm," and "Is that so?" • Direct ***requests for clarification:*** "Let me see if I've got this right. Did you say that . . . ?" or "Could you explain what those figures mean for our community?" • ***Direct requests for elaboration:*** "Why do you say you're angry about this new legislation?" or "When that first driver went crazy with you in the car, what was your reaction?"	• Allow you to take an initial question further than you'd planned. • Allow you to get a more comprehensive answer.

When you record your interview on paper, you have the advantage of being able to make notes about nonverbal aspects of the interview that may help you when you repeat a quote in your speech, and when it is over, you already have a written transcript of your conversation. However, because you are trying to record the highlights of what is said, it can be harder to relax and simply engage in a conversation with your interviewee. Whether you plan to take notes on paper or record on tape, ask your interviewee if you have permission to record your conversation.

Conduct the Interview

The guidelines for conducting interviews are essentially grounded in the rules of common courtesy, so they are not difficult to follow. Dress appropriately, show up on time for your interview, and begin by introducing yourself to your interviewee. Restate the purpose of the interview and your speech assignment, and request permission to record the interview. Start with questions that will put the interviewee at ease and then follow those with your most important questions. As the interview progresses, remember that although you are having a conversation with your interviewee, you need to listen more than you talk; you are there to get the other person's perspectives and ideas.

At the end of your interview, ask your interviewee if she or he would like to add any information. You may get a piece of information or a story you did not think to ask for directly but that fits into your speech perfectly. Finally, thank the interviewee verbally for his or her time, and be sure you have recorded names, professional titles, and addresses correctly so you can cite them accurately and send a letter of thanks.

Follow Up the Interview

Review your notes or transcribe your tape as soon after the interview as you can, filling in details that are fresh in your mind and spelling out abbreviations you might have used in recording words on paper. Make notes of ideas that came to you as you listened to your interviewee, such as places in your speech that a particular quote or story might go or ways you might use some of the interview information in your opening and closing comments. And remember, always send formal letters of thanks to your interviewees, communicating your appreciation for their time and willingness to share information with you. You might even share with them some of the interview material you've decided to include in your speech.

Ethical Interviews

Ethical interviewing means preparing for interviews, asking appropriate questions, using quotes and information honestly, including only what was said and staying true to the intention of the speaker, and giving credit to interviewees for the words and ideas you include in your speech. At times, it may be tempting to alter a statement, embellish a story, or change a number or example just slightly to fit your needs. However, if the public dialogue is to function in any meaningful way, we must present material that is accurate and true. Information is inaccurate even if it's been changed only slightly, and people cannot make rational and reasonable choices if they have incorrect information.

Of course, ethics also apply to interviewees. If an interviewee provides information that seems inconsistent with what your other research supports, take the time to double-check your own research and the credentials of your interview subject. Also ask your interviewee for documentation or sources that support unusual claims. If an interviewee provides information that is highly personal or would compromise the integrity or reputation of others, do not use that information in your speech. And, of course, if an individual shares something with you "off the record," that information should stay out of your speech and never be disclosed in conversations with others.

Conducting an ethical interview can be a detailed, time-consuming process. However, all your hard work will result in a conversation with someone who may give you the information you need to make your speech come alive. The supporting materials you gather from interviews also supplement and confirm the materials you find in your Internet and library research.

Research Tips

To make the research process manageable, remember to give yourself plenty of time and consider the following tips for doing research.

Begin by Filling Out Your Research Inventory

Take the time to fill out your research inventory so you can figure out and remember what you need. Update your inventory as you begin finding information and discovering other sources.

Take Notes and Download Copies

Keep careful, complete notes and records of sources to ensure you have accurate information. This will help you find the information again if you need to and will provide all the information you need to cite your sources correctly in your speech. Include in your notes the following information:

- For all sources, full name of the author; the title of the source (book, magazine, article, document, and so on); the edition, issue, or volume; the publisher (and some bibliography formats also require the place of publication); the publication date; and the page numbers or web address where you found the information.
- For Internet sources, the exact URL as well as the name of the website, the publication or posting date, and if the site may get updated or change, include the date you accessed it.
- For interviews, the full name of the interviewee, his or her title and place of business, and the date of the interview.
- The exact, complete phrases or words you are citing or quoting.

Amana images inc./Opus/Alamy Stock Photo

In addition to taking notes, download or photocopy and print pages of the more extensive material you want to cite, paraphrase, or quote. When you record a URL, make sure it is absolutely accurate. Any mistake, even a missing period or a misspelling, may lead to an incorrect site or a dead end, which is why with longer and more complicated URLs it can be worth your time to download or print the pages on which you find information. If a DOI (direct object identifier) or permalink is available, it will not change and should be included as the web address.

Finally, review your notes for completeness and accuracy by asking yourself these questions:

- Is the material *permanent*? This indicates whether you or a member of your audience can find the material again, especially if it comes from an Internet source.
- Is the material from an *authority*? This means that the source is not paid to promote the subject, is not self-published, or is not biased in other ways.
- Did you *include all the bibliographic details* you need for a hard-copy citation?

Avoid Plagiarism

Plagiarism is presenting another person's words and ideas as your own. In other words, plagiarism is stealing someone else's work and taking credit for it. This is a serious issue in public speaking because it's dishonest and detrimental to a healthy public dialogue. There are three types of plagiarism. **Patchwork plagiarism** is constructing a complete speech that you present as your own from portions of several different sources. **Global plagiarism** is stealing an entire speech from a single source and presenting it as your own. **Incremental plagiarism** is presenting select portions from a single speech as your own.

All three forms of plagiarism are extremely unethical. However, they are easy to avoid. As you do your research, avoid unintentional plagiarism by taking careful notes and accurately documenting the source of each idea. Remember to cite these sources in your speech, even if you are paraphrasing an idea or borrowing only one phrase. Sometimes, especially when researching on the Internet, you'll find that some of the basic information you need to cite a source is missing, such as the author's name. This doesn't mean you cannot use the source, but if you do, you still must cite it in your speech. Simply cite as much information as you can, such as the name of the site, the URL, or the name of the article. Also be sure to include as much of the citation as you can in your bibliography. (Note that if the author's name is not included on a website, you can use "Anonymous" instead.)

Consider the consequences of plagiarizing: loss of credibility, failing the assignment or course, and perhaps even expulsion from your school. The most obvious way to avoid plagiarism is simple: do your own work and give credit to others for their ideas and words.

Keeping your research well organized from the start helps you avoid plagiarism, prepare your preliminary bibliography, and cite sources appropriately when you give your speech. How will the research you use to support your next speech reflect your participation in the public dialogue?

plagiarism: Presenting another person's words and ideas as your own.

patchwork plagiarism: Constructing a complete speech that you present as your own from portions of several different sources.

global plagiarism: Stealing an entire speech from a single source and presenting it as your own.

incremental plagiarism: Presenting select portions from a single speech as your own.

Set Up a Filing System

As you gather information, it is tempting to put it all in one folder or let it sit on your desktop and wait to organize it when you sit down to draft your speech. This may save you time initially, but it will cost you time later in the process. It is much more efficient to organize your information while you are in the process of collecting it. One of the best ways to do this is by using a filing system. Filing as you go helps you keep track of the information you've already found and ensures that it fulfills the needs you had originally intended for it.

Begin by organizing your materials according to your research inventory. Set up separate files for examples and stories, statistics, testimony, and definitions (Chapter 6) or color-code your materials by type of evidence with a highlighter or system of saving documents by names (statistics, interviews, and so on). Create summaries of your notes and copies, identifying the type of evidence they contain, the date you recorded them, the point the material makes, and where you might use it in your speech (for example, "good for introduction"). As you gather more material, organize it by main points and subpoints (Chapters 3 and 8).

Bookmark Interesting URLs

When you find useful information in the Internet, be sure to bookmark it so you can access it again. Some computers keep an excellent record of the history of your searches, but even with this record, it is often difficult to locate the source you are looking for when it's buried among so many searches. To save time, bookmark the information you think you'll use again so you can find it easily and with minimal frustration. Or, make a separate file with just the URLs of the sites you especially liked, include a short label (most recent data, or excellent story, for example) next to the URL, and you can access this information easily at a later date.

Gather More Material Than You Think You'll Need

We often underestimate the amount of material we need to support our ideas. Or we think we've found the perfect example, only to discover that when we put the speech together, we cannot use it after all. For these reasons, gather more information than you think you'll need. Collect several possibilities for your introduction and conclusion, and if your instructor asks for three sources from one time frame, gather six and use the best three. If you need one great example of what a statistic really means, ask your interviewee for a few and choose the one that best illustrates your point. Although you probably won't use all this information in your speech, having it will help you feel more prepared and thus more confident, and you'll be better able to conduct a question-and-answer session because you'll have a deeper understanding of your topic.

Begin Your Bibliography with Your First Source

A bibliography is a record of each of the sources you use in your speech, and accuracy is the key to a good bibliography. There are many different styles for bibliographies. Two styles that are often used for public speaking are the APA (American Psychological Association) style, which formats the bibliography as a References list, and MLA (Modern Language Association) style, which uses a Works Cited format. Figure 5.3 shows these styles applied to common types of sources. Be sure to check with your instructor, or your employer if a work presentation requires a bibliography, for which academic or professional style to follow.

Start your bibliography the moment you collect your first source, and apply the appropriate style to all your entries consistently. By doing so, you will have the citations you need before you log off the Internet or leave the library or interview.

	MLA style (Works Cited)	APA style (References)
Book	Isaacson, Walter. *Benjamin Franklin: An American Life*. Simon and Schuster, 2004.	Isaacson, W. (2004). *Benjamin Franklin: An American life*. New York, NY: Simon & Schuster.
Edited book	D'Emilio, Sandra, and Sharyn Udall. "Inner Voices, Outward Forms: Women Painters in New Mexico." *Independent Spirits: Women Painters of the American West, 1890–1945*, edited by Patricia Trenton, U of California P, 1995, pp. 153–82.	D'Emilio, S., & Udall, S. (1995). Inner voices, outward forms: Women painters in New Mexico. In P. Trenton (Ed.), *Independent spirits: Women painters of the American West, 1890–1945* (pp. 153–182). Berkeley, CA: University of California Press.
Academic journal	Agyeman, Julian. "Communicating 'Just' Sustainability." *Environmental Communication*, vol. 1, no. 2, 2007, pp. 119–22.	Agyeman, J. (2007). Communicating "just" sustainability. *Environmental Communication*, *1*(7), 119–122.
Magazine	Kristal, Marc. "True Hollywood Story." *Dwell*, 10 Oct. 2007, pp. 199–214.	Kristal, M. (2007, October 10). True Hollywood story. *Dwell*, 199–214.
Newspaper	Parker-Pope, Tara. "A Problem of the Brain, Not the Hands: Group Urges Phone Ban for Drivers." *The New York Times*, 13 Jan. 2009, p. D5.	Parker-Pope, T. (2009, January 13). A problem of the brain, not the hands: Group urges phone ban for drivers. *The New York Times*, p. D5.
Electronic article based on print source	DiFilippo, Dana. "Experts Puzzled, Worried by Youngsters' Suicides." *The Philadelphia Inquirer*, 15 May 2010, articles.philly.com/keyword/suicide-note/recent/4.	DiFilippo, D. (2010, May 15). Experts puzzled, worried by youngsters' suicides. *The Philadelphia Inquirer*. Retrieved from http://www.articles.philly.com/keyword/suicide-note/recent/4
Electronic article from Internet-only publication	Zelman, Kathleen M. "Expert Q&A: Eating with Food Allergies: An Interview with Stanley Cohen, MD." *WebMD*, 30 June 2009, www.webmd.com/diet/features/expert-q-and-a-eating-with-food-allergies.	Zelman, K. M. (2009, June 30). Expert q&a: Eating with food allergies: An interview with Stanley Cohen, MD. Retrieved from http://www.webmd.com/diet/features/expert-q-and-a-eating-with-food-allergies
Electronic article retrieved from database	Grabe, Mark. "Voluntary Use of Online Lecture Notes: Correlates of Note Use and Note Use as an Alternative to Class Attendance." *Computers and Education*, vol. 44, no. 4, May 2005, pp. 409–21. *ACM Digital Library*, doi: 10.1016/j.compedu.2004.04.005.	Grabe, M. (2005, May). Voluntary use of online lecture notes: Correlates of note use and note use as an alternative to class attendance. *Computers and Education*, *44*(4), 409–421. doi: 10.1016/j.compedu.2004.04.005.
Movie	*The Dark Knight*. Directed by Christopher Nolan, performances by Christian Bale, Heath Ledger, Warner Home Video, 2008.	De La Noy, K. (Executive Producer), & Nolan, C. (Director). (2008). *The Dark Knight* [Motion picture]. United States: Warner Brothers Pictures.
Television program	"Beyond Here Lies Nothin'." *True Blood*, HBO, 13 Sept. 2009.	Woo, A. (Writer), & Cuestra, M. (Director). (2009, September 13). Beyond here lies nothin' [Television series episode]. In A. Ball (Producer), *True Blood*. New York, NY: Time Warner/HBO.
Music recording	Nirvana. "Smells Like Teen Spirit." *Nevermind*, Geffen, 1991.	Nirvana. (1991). Smells like teen spirit. On *Nevermind* [CD]. Santa Monica, CA: Geffen.
Personal interview	Sykes, Anna. Personal interview. 19 Feb. 2011.	APA style dictates that no personal interview is included in a reference list. Rather, cite this type of source orally in your speech, mentioning the name of the person you interviewed and the date of the interview.

Figure 5.3   Examples of the MLA and APA bibliographic styles

Figure 5.4 Sample preliminary bibliography

> ## Preliminary Bibliography
>
> Enos, Sandra. _Mothering from the Inside: Parenting in a Women's Prison._ State University of New York Press, 2001.
>
> _Every Door Closed: Facts about Parents with Criminal Records._ Center for Law and Social Policy and Community Legal Services, Inc. 29 Sept. 2003, http://www.clasp.org/publications/EDC_fact_sheets.pdf.
>
> Poehlmann, Julie. "Children's Family Environments and Intellectual Outcomes during Maternal Incarceration." _Journal of Marriage and Family_, vol 67, no. 5, 2005, pp. 1275–1285.
>
> "The Beat Within: A Weekly Publication of Writing and Art from the Inside." _Pacific News Service._ http://thebeatwithin.org/news/view_article.html.

And when you've finished your research, you will have a **preliminary bibliography**, a list of all the potential sources you'll use as you prepare your speech. (Figure 5.4 shows a sample of a preliminary bibliography.) As you organize your speech, you'll decide which information to include or not include and remove entries you don't need. When you finish putting your speech together, you will find your final bibliography is complete, and you won't have to rush to finish it just before your speech.

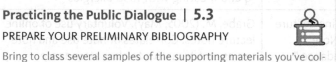

Practicing the Public Dialogue | 5.3

PREPARE YOUR PRELIMINARY BIBLIOGRAPHY

Bring to class several samples of the supporting materials you've collected for your speech, including your Internet research, library research, and interviews. Working as a class, help one another prepare your preliminary bibliography. To format your bibliography correctly, use the citation style required by your instructor.

MindTap

You can use Outline Builder to help you prepare your preliminary bibliography with whatever citation style you are assigned.

preliminary bibliography: List of all the potential sources you'll use as you prepare your speech.

Citing Sources

When you incorporate your sources into your speech to support your ideas, you must cite them properly. There are two reasons to cite sources: it is ethical and it adds credibility to your ideas.

Citing Sources Is Ethical

In public speaking, our own ideas often grow from the ideas of others. When you cite your sources, you acknowledge this debt, fulfilling your ethical responsibilities to give credit to others for their work and their contributions to your own thinking. If you cite your sources properly, there should be no uncertainty among audience members about which ideas are your own and which ideas come from others. If you do not cite your sources, you risk committing plagiarism.

Citing Sources Adds Credibility

When you cite sources in a speech, you indicate that you have done research on your topic, have some understanding of it, and that your ideas about it have the backing of experts. Citing sources also shows your audience that you value the public dialogue and that you recognize others have something to offer to this dialogue. When you want to bolster the credibility of a point you make, cite the source so your audience recognizes the authority from which it came.

Rules for Citing Sources

Although your instructor may have specific rules for the number and format of sources you are to cite in a speech, there are three general guidelines for citing sources during your speech. These guidelines rely on ethical principles and an audience-centered approach.

Give credit to others. When you rely on the specific ideas or words of others, give them credit during your speech. The guideline works like this: the more specifically you rely on someone else's ideas or words, the more responsible you are for citing them. If you use someone's research, quote or paraphrase someone, or share information from a magazine, book, newspaper, or other news source, you need to cite your source in your speech. You can use phrases like the following:

> Last week's *New York Times* tells us that . . .

> According to the 2010 Census, . . .

> The director of the Center for Applied Studies in Appropriate Technology responded to my question in this way . . .

> *The Old Farmer's Almanac* reports that this will be the wettest year this area has experienced since 1938.

> Jane Kneller, professor of philosophy at this university, writes, . . .

Note that even though much of what we already know grows out of the research and work of others, we do not need to provide a citation for every claim we make. Some claims are based on common knowledge, information that is generally known by most people. For example, the statement "Eating a balanced diet is good for your health" is common knowledge and does not require a citation. But the statement "Eat at least three ounces of whole grain bread, cereal, crackers, rice, or pasta every day" requires a source citation such as "according to the U.S. Department of Agriculture's food pyramid."

Give specific information about your source. General phrases such as "research shows," "evidence suggests," and "someone once said" are usually not enough to lend credibility to your speech. If your audience is listening with care, they'll want to know more about your sources. They'll be asking "What research?" "Whose evidence?" and "Who said?" When you cite a source, include the following information:

- The name of the person or the publication
- The credentials of that person or publication
- The date of the study, statistic, or piece of evidence

These three pieces of information generally are enough to show your audience that your source is valid and your statistics are reliable and relevant to your topic. You can usually omit details such as page numbers and place of publication from your actual speech, but you will want to include them in your bibliography.

Deliver all information accurately. When you cite a source, you must do so accurately. This means giving the name and title of the person correctly, pronouncing any unfamiliar words clearly, and delivering all statistics and quotations accurately. Mispronouncing names and titles, stumbling over dates and quotes, and leaving out important elements of a citation can reduce your credibility. It can even alter the facts you are sharing with your audience. So before you give your speech, check to be sure you have all your source citations recorded correctly and rehearse them until they smoothly fit into your speech. (You'll learn more about delivery in Chapter 10.)

Practicing the Public Dialogue | 5.4

CITE YOUR SUPPORTING EVIDENCE

Working in pairs or with a group, practice citing the sources listed in your preliminary bibliography aloud, using the rules provided in this chapter.

MindTap°

Watch video clips of student speakers Tiffany Brisco and Damien Beasley as they cite sources in their speeches. Assess the degree to which they accurately cite their sources and provide information about them. You can upload your own speech and ask others to give you feedback on how you cited your sources.

Chapter Summary

Gathering a wide, relevant range of supporting materials for your speech ensures that you help the public dialogue remain responsive, lively, and healthy.

- You can find information to use as supporting material by consulting your own knowledge and experience, doing research over the Internet and in libraries, and conducting interviews.
- The tools to aid you in the research process include the research inventory, search engines, librarians, catalogs, databases and indexes, government documents, reference works, and professional interviewing practices.
- To present ethical arguments and proposals to your audiences, learn to evaluate the strengths and weaknesses of your sources by assessing their reliability, authoritativeness, currency, completeness, relevance, and consistency.

With a bit of planning, you can make the research process efficient and productive.

- Start your research by filling out your research inventory.
- As you gather materials, take notes, make copies, and download material from the Internet. By accurately recording

the critical details about each of your sources, you can easily avoid plagiarism and get an early start on your preliminary bibliography.

- To give yourself more options when you're in the final stages of preparing your speech, gather more information than you think you'll need.
- Set up a filing system at the start of your research effort to keep careful track of your materials.

Citing sources properly is ethical and adds credibility to your ideas.

- Cite the sources you rely on specifically or quote directly.
- Provide enough specific information about your source so that your audience knows the source is valid, reliable, and relevant.
- Cite sources accurately by recording all your research carefully and practicing your delivery.

Invitation to Public Speaking Online MindTap®

Now that you have read Chapter 5, use your MindTap Communication for *Invitation to Public Speaking* for quick access to the digital resources that accompany this text. These resources include

- **Study tools** that will help you assess your learning and prepare for exams (digital glossary, key term flash cards, review quizzes).
- **Activities and assignments** that will help you hone your knowledge and build your public speaking skills throughout the course, as well as help you explore public speaking

concepts online (web links), give you step-by-step guidance through the research, outline, and note card preparation process (Outline Builder), watch and critique videos of sample speeches (Interactive Video Activities), and allow you to practice and present your presentation online using a speech video delivery, recording, and grading system (YouSeeU).

This chapter's key concepts and review questions are also featured in this end-of-chapter section.

Key Concepts MindTap® Test your knowledge with online printable flash cards.

abstract (87)
bibliographic database (86)
Boolean operators (86)
database (86)
full-text database (86)
global plagiarism (95)
incremental plagiarism (95)
index (87)

information overload (80)
interview (90)
patchwork plagiarism (95)
plagiarism (95)
preliminary bibliography (97)
probe (92)
research inventory (80)

Review Questions

1. Bring the material you have gathered for your next speech to class. Working in pairs or groups, sort the material by the types discussed in this chapter. Do you have a range of evidence types or do you need to diversify? Make a list of the types of evidence you still need.

2. Use the evaluation criteria described in this chapter to evaluate the strengths and weaknesses of the information you have gathered for your next speech. Is it reliable, authoritative, current, complete, relevant, and consistent? Based on your assessment, identify information you might discard, and consider whether you need to do more research for your speech.

3. Identify several of the ideas and actual quotations from your research that you want to use in your next speech. How will you avoid plagiarizing these sources? What strategies will you use for citing them ethically and accurately?

4. Draft a list of questions you would like to ask a personal contact for your next speech. Keep in mind your speech goals, time limitations, and audience. Now organize that list so the most important questions are first and the least important ones are last. Next consider how you will begin your interview. Will you start with your most important questions or some warm-up questions? What questions will you use to close the interview?

5. Bring three or four of the sources you will use in your next speech to class. In small groups, practice delivering the citation of those sources with each other. Focus on those sources with especially long titles, with names that are difficult to pronounce, or names that are just confusing. Work with one another to find the most comfortable way to cite these sources in your next speech.

6 | Developing and Supporting Your Ideas

IN THIS CHAPTER, YOU WILL LEARN TO:

- Explain the importance of supporting materials in a speech

- Identify the five main types of supporting materials

- Evaluate the different strengths of the five types of supporting materials

- Utilize Toulmin's map of reasoning to help you develop and support your ideas

- Apply tips for using each of the five types of supporting materials effectively

In public speaking, a **claim** is an assertion that must be proved. When we make claims, we communicate with others so that we can explore and exchange ideas, respond to one another, and clarify, refine, and revise our positions. When we communicate our claims ethically and effectively, we stimulate and enhance the public dialogue.

MindTap® Start with a quick warm-up activity and review the chapter's learning objectives.

▲ Forensic scientist John Manlove relied on the evidence presented in this image to help overturn a wrongful murder conviction. His careful use of supporting materials significantly changed the course of one man's life. In this chapter, you will explore different types of supporting materials and the ways they can help you strengthen your claims.

We prove our claims with **evidence,** the materials speakers use to support their ideas. Evidence comes from the information you already know and gather in your research on the Internet, at the library, and in interviews. Ethical evidence allows you to explain a process with confidence, share a perspective in a way that encourages understanding, identify a problem and pose a solution, motivate an audience to action, or acknowledge someone's accomplishments. And strong evidence helps build your credibility, or believability. In Chapter 14 you'll learn how you can enhance your personal credibility. In this chapter, you'll learn how to assess the credibility of your evidence. Credible and ethical evidence is the foundation of the common language in the public sphere.

The five most common types of supporting material are examples, narratives, statistics, testimony, and definitions. You are probably familiar with these types of evidence, but you may not be sure when to use them or how to evaluate their strengths and weaknesses. Let's start with examples as evidence.

MindTap®

Read, highlight, and take notes online.

Examples

Examples are specific instances used to illustrate a concept, experience, issue, or problem. Examples can be brief, only a word or a sentence or two, or they can be longer and more richly detailed. Examples can also be real or hypothetical. A **real example** is an instance that actually took place. A **hypothetical example** is an instance that did not take place but could have. Generally, real examples are more credible and convey a sense of immediacy. Consider the following real examples from student speeches:

> In her speech on binge drinking on college campuses nationwide, Eileen used a powerful example of a binge drinker by describing her friend who "consumed twelve to fifteen beers combined with shots of hard liquor each evening, and stopped only because she ran out of alcohol, time, or money."

> In his speech on the dangers of exotic pets, Kyle used an example provided by the head of his city's Pest Control and Wildlife Department: "According to the department's head, one man had a Gaboon viper, a cobra, a black-tailed rattlesnake, a copperhead, three large boas, and a full-grown alligator that acted as a 'guard dog.'" Kyle explained to his audience that these pets were hazardous because the owner was "bitten by his Gaboon viper and died from the bite. The remaining so-called pets? They went to the Humane Society to be adopted by other people or to be euthanized."

These students used examples to help clarify exactly what they meant when they used the terms *binge drinker* and *hazardous pets.*

Occasionally, you can clarify a point with a hypothetical example. A hypothetical example usually begins with words like *imagine, suppose,* or *let's say that.* For example, when Clara addressed a group of teenagers in an after-school program on proper eating, she could have simply said, "Skipping breakfast isn't good for you." Instead, to be a more effective speaker, she supported her claim with a hypothetical example:

> Suppose you skipped breakfast this morning. Let's see what that would do to your energy level by about 9 or 10 o'clock—that's during second period, right? If you haven't eaten by then, you'll probably feel bored or restless, and maybe sad or unmotivated. You might also feel angry or irritable, kind of grouchy and crabby. And maybe you'll feel a little light-headed or dizzy if you stand up fast. You might have a headache. You'll definitely have trouble concentrating on your schoolwork because your blood sugar is low or because all you can think about is how hungry you are. Sound familiar to any of you?

Clara's hypothetical example, although not real itself, grew out of research that was grounded in real experience. It helped her audience understand more clearly why skipping meals isn't good for them.

claim: Assertion that must be proved.

evidence: Materials that speakers use to support their ideas.

example: Specific instance used to illustrate a concept, experience, issue, or problem.

real example: Instance that actually took place.

hypothetical example: Instance that did not take place but could have.

Several criteria can help you decide when using an example would be most effective. Consider the following guidelines, all of which help you answer in advance any questions your audience may have about your topic.

Use Examples to Clarify Concepts

Identify the concepts in your speech that your audience might consider complex or unfamiliar, and then use an example to help you frame those concepts in terms your audience will understand. That is, try to anticipate what parts of your speech might prompt your audience to ask, "What do you mean by that?" Examples frame abstract concepts and experiences in terms of concrete actions, events, people, and things. Thus, an example can make an abstract or complex point clearer.

In Clara's case, she anticipated her audience's question "What does she mean by 'isn't good' for me?" Her detailed example about the physical and mental impacts of skipping breakfast clarified what she meant.

Use Examples to Reinforce Points

What parts of your speech might prompt the audience to say, "I don't see how this point matters"? Examples help an audience see your points in terms of the larger case you're making in your speech. Therefore, examples help audiences recognize the relevance and importance of your points as support for your claims. Kyle used an example of the hazardous potential of exotic pets to reinforce his point that owning exotic pets is a dangerous hobby. By describing what happened to one owner of such pets and then what happened to the animals after the owner died, Kyle encouraged his audience to consider the potentially deadly consequences of this hobby.

Use Examples to Bring Concepts to Life or to Elicit Emotions

When someone says, "I'm not affected by that issue," an example helps bring a concept to life by providing specific images audience members can picture in their minds. When they're able to create a mental picture, one that is filtered through their own thoughts and experiences, they can better understand how an issue affects them or someone they know. Eileen's example of the sheer amount of alcohol consumed by her friend brought the reality of binge drinking to life for her audience. Specifically, Eileen's reference to drinking that "stopped only when [her friend] ran out of alcohol, time, or money" highlighted just how out of control and self-destructive binge drinking can become, adding emotional weight to her claim. Similarly, Kyle's example of the exotic pets being euthanized brought out the emotions in his audience. No longer were the exotic pets curiosities; they became real animals that died through no fault of their own.

Use Examples to Build Your Case or Make Credible Generalizations

When someone says, "It's not as common or prevalent as you say," using a number of examples helps show that it is. A series of examples can help you build a case or help you make a plausible generalization. For example, if Eileen cited numerous examples of binge drinking on college campuses throughout the country, those in her audience who think binge drinking is an isolated problem might be compelled to reconsider their views and see the issue as a nationwide concern.

Not all examples are equal. Some don't illustrate your point well, and others won't resonate with your audience. See Table 6.1 for tips that will help you evaluate an example for its strengths and weaknesses.[1]

Table 6.1 Tips for Using Examples Ethically and Effectively

ASK YOURSELF THIS...	AND DO THIS...	EXAMPLE
Is the example relevant?	Make sure your example refers to the point you are making, not to something else.	In her speech about binge drinking, Eileen offers an example of treatment programs for older adults as her "success story solution." But her example won't be relevant because her target population consists of students in their teens and early twenties, not older adults. It's a great example of a solution but not the solution to her specific problem.
Is the example appropriate?	Avoid examples that are too graphic, emotional, detailed, or personal for an audience. Use caution with examples that contain violent details, the manipulation of emotions, overly technical material, or the use of explicit personal details.	In his speech on the damage caused by the earthquake in Chile, Trenton used many images and verbal descriptions of the devastation caused. As he attempted to persuade his audience to support the relief efforts there, he was careful not to prey on his audience's emotions by showing only overly graphic images of children who had been killed or hurt. Instead, he showed a range of examples of the devastation so that his audience had a realistic sense of the magnitude of the relief efforts needed.
Is the hypothetical example ethical?	Make sure your hypothetical example represents events or information grounded in fact. Audiences should believe it really could be true or have happened. And tell your audience the example is hypothetical. Don't mislead your audience into believing that a made-up example, however plausible, is real when it isn't.	In his speech about humans being able to adapt to and survive in harsh environments, Colin provided a dramatic description of how we would have to adapt to live on Venus. However, it would be impossible for almost all life on Earth to survive on Venus. Its average surface temperature is 860 degrees Fahrenheit, and the clouds rain sulfuric acid. Thus, this example didn't give his audience much insight into how humans have adapted to harsh conditions on Earth, such as barren deserts and ice ages.
Are there enough examples to support your claim?	Determine whether one example is enough or whether you need several: • If you cannot find more than one example to support your point, perhaps your claim is unfounded. • If you want to suggest something is common but cannot find examples of it, it may not be as common as you thought. One example suggests an isolated incident, not a trend, so avoid generalizing from a single example.	When Eileen described the extent of the problem of binge drinking, she used quite a few examples to make her case. But earlier in her speech, when she was simply illustrating what constitutes binge drinking, she knew just one example would be sufficient.
Have you accounted for the counterexamples?	Be sure to consider counterexamples that refute your claims. Counterexamples are specific instances that contradict your claims; they make your assertions appear false or at least weaken them.	If Kyle found that many exotic pets were safe to own, he'd have to explain why this is so. If he cannot explain these counterexamples, he has to adjust his claim to "some exotic pets, such as poisonous snakes, are dangerous to own." He cannot ethically claim that all exotic pets are dangerous because he has counterexamples that refute this claim.

Narratives

A **narrative** is a story that recounts or foretells real or hypothetical events. Narratives help us explain, interpret, and understand events in our lives or the lives of others.[2] Speakers can use **brief narratives**, sometimes called *vignettes*, to illustrate a specific point, or **extended narratives** to make an evolving connection with a broader point. Whatever their length, narratives can be valuable aids to public speakers. When used in speeches, stories can give historical context to events, make strong connections between ideas and experiences, and add emotional depth to characterizations. They can also describe subjects, settings, and actions with sensory details that can captivate an audience.

Stories often reference other stories or rely on parts of other stories to be complete. This process, called **intertextuality**, is very common in television programs, movies, and computer games. For example, one TV show refers to another or relies on part of a narrative from another show to make its point. Today, because many of our stories come from entertainment media, intertextuality in everyday communication is very common. Make sure your audience has the references necessary to follow these types of intertextual narratives.

Because narratives are so appealing to audiences, always search for stories you can use in your speech as you gather your supporting material. A carefully selected and well told story can add a personal touch, make a point, or move an audience in significant ways. There are several criteria to follow when you are thinking about incorporating a narrative into your speech.

One of Ronald Reagan's strengths as a speaker was his ability to personalize his speeches with narratives. For example, he personalized a speech commemorating the Allied soldiers who landed in Normandy, France, during World War II in an effort to defeat the German army in Europe by telling the stories of individual soldiers who exhibited courage and strength during a battle that took many lives. What stories might you use to personalize your ideas and draw your audience into your speech?

Use Narratives to Personalize a Point

Late U.S. President Ronald Reagan was an expert at using stories to make his point in personal ways. An advocate of private initiative rather than government assistance, he told the story of Jose Salcido, whose wife had died of cancer.

> [Her death left Jose] both father and mother of thirteen children. In an accident only the Lord can explain, one day the brakes on his truck didn't hold and he was crushed against a brick wall as he walked in front of the vehicle. The children who had lost their mother now had lost their father. But even they were not orphaned.

Reagan went on to tell of extended family, neighbors, members of their church parish, and even strangers who stepped in to help the Salcido children in the absence of their parents. He finished his story by reading a letter from one of the people who assisted the children: "This is for the children of Jose Salcido. It is for them to know there are always others who care; that despite personal tragedy, the world is not always the dark place it seems to be." In this one story, Reagan drew his audience personally into his argument. As they listened to his story, they actually could see themselves assisting the children.[3]

Use Narratives to Challenge an Audience to Think in New Ways

A narrative can challenge an audience to think differently or to understand the world in new ways. Curtis began his speech on the various kinds of racism in the following way: "Let me tell you the story of Ishmael."

narrative: Story that recounts or foretells real or hypothetical events.

brief narrative: Short story or vignette that illustrates a specific point.

extended narrative: Longer story that makes an evolving connection with a broader point.

intertextuality: Process in which stories reference other stories or rely on parts of other stories to be complete.

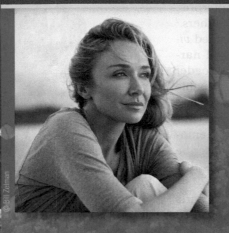

ALEXANDRA COUSTEAU, Explorer and Social Environment Advocate

Can you tell us about the importance of storytelling in communication and the public dialogue?

Sure. My grandfather, Jacques Cousteau, was a communicator. He was not a scientist, although almost everyone thought he was a scientist, actually a marine biologist, and he wasn't. He was a communicator. He was one of the great filmmakers and storytellers of his day. And I think through his exploration, through his discoveries, through his communication on television and radio and books, he shaped the conversation about the ocean. He had an impact on the world and people still remember his stories. So he was one of the great French communicators on water, on oceans, on environment. And that has been the tradition of my family.

Ishmael was sitting at a restaurant in town, minding his own business, eating dinner with some of his friends. At another table nearby, he and his friends heard snickering and laughter but ignored it because they didn't think it related to them. Pretty soon, the laughter got louder, and two guys from that table began to address Ishmael and his friends. At first, they thought it was going to be a friendly exchange but soon realized they were the butt of the jokes being told—racist jokes, about the shape of Ishmael's eyes and the color of his skin. The so-called jokes soon turned to taunts and verbal abuse, with the girlfriends joining in. Not sure what to do, Ishmael and his friends were saved, so to speak, by the owner of the restaurant, who asked Ishmael and his friends to leave.

Curtis paused here to let the story sink in. He began again: "You think I might be making this up? It happened to my best friend a couple of years ago while he was a student at this very university."

With his narrative, Curtis compelled any listeners in his audience who might have believed that racism no longer exists to rethink their views. As we tell a story, we share our perspectives with an audience in personal, yet organized, ways. In listening to our story, an audience may find a commonality not recognized before or gain a new or deeper understanding of an issue.

Use Narratives to Draw an Audience in Emotionally

Facts, statistics, and examples can prove the claims you make in your speech, but they lack the emotional appeal of a story. If your audience cannot connect with your speech on an emotional level, your listeners may not feel that its subject is important enough for them to care whether or not you prove your claims. Use a story, then, when you want to draw your audience into the speech emotionally. Josiah used this brief story, which he found as he gathered materials for his speech on the history of battles portrayed in theatrical productions:

Planned stage combat reduces the level of danger that is part of any battle scene in a play. According to William Hobbs in *Fight Direction for the Stage and Screen*, in early sixteenth-century Stockholm, the actor who played the part of Longinus in *The Mystery of the Passion*, and who had to pierce the crucified Christ, was so carried away with the spirit of the action that he actually killed the other actor. The king, who was present, was so angry that he leapt onto the stage and cut off the head of Longinus. And the audience, who had been pleased with the actor's zeal, were so infuriated with the king that they turned upon him and slew him.

MindTap

Watch a video clip of student speaker Chelsey Penoyer as she uses narratives to bring emotion to her speech. As you watch Chelsey speak, consider how effectively she uses narratives. Do they draw you into her speech?

Josiah could have made his point by offering statistics on the number of deaths and accidents in stage fights over some period of time, but instead he drew his audience in emotionally with a brief story about the implications of unrehearsed fights in theatrical battle scenes.

Use Narratives to Unite with Your Audience

Stories can describe common, profound, or dramatic experiences that you can use to create unity between yourself and your audience. When you share a story about an experience that is just like everyone else's, you establish common ground with your audience. When you relate a powerful moment in your life, you reveal a personal aspect of yourself that allows your audience to identify with you more fully. When you tell dramatic or exciting stories, you can connect with your audience by sharing a way of thinking about the world that may be new to them. Because of their human element and the personalized way they are told, stories can create a sense of togetherness between speakers and their audiences.

In speeches, narratives are more than stories that entertain: they convey something specific to an audience. Table 6.2 has tips that can help you determine whether the narrative you want to use in your speech does more than simply "tell a good story."

Statistics

Statistics are numerical summaries of facts, figures, and research findings. They help audiences understand amounts (100 individuals participated), proportions (that's almost half the people in this organization), and percentages (fully 50 percent said they'd participate again). Numbers summarize and help audiences make sense of large chunks of information (8 glasses of water a day, every day of the year, is the equivalent of almost 3,000 glasses of water a year). They also help people see where something is in relation to other things (he's the third-fastest runner in the world). See Figure 6.1 below for a visual representation of statistics that could help an audience understand how the U.S. government classifies people who immigrate to the United States.

Numbers and statistics may seem less glamorous than a story or a clever example, but relevant, surprising, or little-known statistics can grab an audience's attention. Statistics can help you synthesize large amounts of data, point out exceptions to trends or generalizations, or express the magnitude or impact of an event or issue. Statistics can also help you make and refine your claims, and they can highlight certain aspects of your topic that other types of evidence cannot. According to Cynthia Crossen, author of *Tainted Truth: The Manipulation of Fact in America,* 82 percent of people surveyed said statistics increase a story's credibility.[4] One of the best sources of statistics is the *Statistical Abstract of the United States*. This resource, which you can access online, includes statistics related to crime, population, health, and many other topics.

Types of Statistics

Common statistics include totals and amounts, costs, scales and ranges, ratios, rates, dates and times, measurements, and percentages. Other more technical statistics are the mean, median, and mode—the numbers that summarize sets of

Practicing the Public Dialogue | 6.1

FINDING GOOD STORIES AND EXAMPLES

Stories and examples for your next speech can come from a variety of places. Begin by considering the stories in your own life, or examples of terms or claims you plan to make in your speech that come from your own personal experiences or those of friends and families. Next, do several Google searches on your topic to see if others have written or posted good stories and examples to help you develop your ideas. Now return to Chapter 5 and evaluate the strength and credibility of these stories and examples. Are they credible? Are the realistic? Are they appropriate? Do they actually help you develop your ideas? If you can answer "yes" to all four of these questions, then save these stories and examples as possible material for your next speech.

statistics: Numerical summaries of facts, figures, and research findings.

Table 6.2 Tips for Using Narratives Ethically and Effectively

ASK YOURSELF THIS . . .	AND DO THIS . . .	EXAMPLE
Does your narrative make a specific point?	Have a specific reason for telling a story. For example, you may want to reaffirm values, challenge perspectives, remind your audience of important events and beliefs, or teach ways of being and thinking. Be sure your narrative has a clear point. Remember, there are a lot of great stories, but not every one makes your point well.	President Reagan told the story of the orphaned children in such a way that his point could not be missed—without assistance from everyday people, the children would have suffered more than they already had.
Is the length appropriate?	Make sure your story fits within the time limit for your speech. Brief stories allow you to make your point quickly and often fit better into speeches. But don't discard an extended story without considering how it might fit in your speech. An extended story offers more detail and can keep the audience listening throughout the speech to "hear how the story ends."	In her speech about wildlife conservation, Mariah wanted to use an extended story about Christian the lion, famously purchased from a department store in London, reintroduced to the wild, and then reunited with his former owners.[4] She opened with a part of the story (how Christian came to be purchased from a department store), added pieces of it as she developed her speech (his being raised in London and then reintroduced to the wild), and then concluded with the remainder of the story (the reunion).
Is the language you use vivid?	Use language not only to relate the story's details, but also to bring the story's message to life: • You don't need to use flowery or complicated language to present your story, nor should you exaggerate or change a story to meet your needs. • Rather, think about the language you choose and the images and messages it conveys and creates.	Remember that you have an ethical obligation to tell the truth with your story. Language facilitated the story's message in both Josiah's and Reagan's speeches. When Josiah said the audience "turned upon him and slew him," he created a visual image and evoked sixteenth-century speech. Reagan's phrase the "world isn't always a dark place" conveyed a sense of hope during troubled times.
Is the delivery appropriate to the story?	Ensure that your delivery of the story is appropriate. Practice telling your story several times until you get your pauses, emphasis, gestures, and expressions the way you want them.	When Josiah told the story about stage fighting gone wrong, he was appropriately dramatic yet somber. He didn't tell the story in a flippant or joking way that would have made light of a tragic situation.
Is the story appropriate for my audience?	Consider how your listeners will respond to your story; not all people respond to stories in the same way. How listeners do respond depends on many factors, including their cultural background: • Make sure the stories you tell ring true for your audience. • Your story shouldn't be too graphic, too personal, or simply inappropriate for a particular audience. Some stories don't tell a familiar tale or recount a common experience. If you suspect parts of your story will be too culturally unfamiliar to your audience, make sure you explain those parts. Or choose a different story altogether.	When Marie gave a speech about her experience as an exchange student in Africa, she told the traditional parable of a European missionary who felt guilty that he was able to live in a much nicer house than his African neighbors. One day, the missionary confessed this to one of his neighbors, who responded in surprise, "But, Father, you're the poorest man in the village. You have no grandchildren!" She explained that this story illustrated the importance of family over individual wealth in African culture.

4REAL

Josh Thome, Explorer and New Media Cultural Storyteller

Rebecca Hale/National Geographic Creative

Josh Thome and childhood friend Sol Guy (featured in Chapter 15) want you to hear a story. It is about a trio in South Africa whose hit song is credited with lowering the AIDS rate in their region, about a baby who was left in a box and eventually grew up to run a medical clinic for thousands of people in a slum of East Africa, and about a boy who survived Liberia's brutal civil war, exposed the training of child soldiers, and now builds orphanages and playgrounds for the next generation.[5] These are just some of the stories featured on the television show *4Real*.

Thome expanded what started as a high school environmental club into an international movement of youth engaged in social change. After attending a Global Leadership Jam in 2000, an event that brought together thirty outstanding young leaders from around the world, Thome was inspired to hear more about how young people were creating social change. He contacted childhood friend Guy Sol, and the two developed the idea and eventually coproduced the television show *4Real*.

As the two describe it, *4Real* "spans the globe—from the slums of Nairobi, to the Amazon forest, to the drug-ravaged Lower East Side of Vancouver and a block party in post-conflict Liberia—viewers get a raw and authentic view of life through the eyes of residents, community leaders and the visiting celebrities."[6] Celebrities such as Cameron Diaz, Joaquin Phoenix, Mos Def, and K'naan have traveled with Thome and Sol, creating an instant connection with young viewers.

Thome and Sol share the stories of people who are using music, art, culture, and school programs to inspire youth. The intersection of popular culture with social change has had enormous influences on youth involvement. As Thome writes, "The core of my interest in getting young people involved in social change today is basically my inspiration to see what our human potential is."[7] In fact, Thome knows today's young people are already making a difference. The statistics from the United Nations 2014 Millennium Development Goals reports reveals:

- Since 1990, extreme poverty in the world has been reduced by half.
- Between 2000 and 2010, the percentage of people without access to improved drinking water sources was also reduced by half.
- Between 2000 and 2012, gender parity in primary education was achieved in almost every developing region.
- Between 2000 and 2014, political participation continued to increase globally, with forty-six countries having 30 percent or more female members of parliaments in at least one chamber.
- The proportion of undernourished people in developing regions decreased from 24 percent in 1992 to 14 percent in 2013.

- The mortality rate for children under age five dropped almost 50 percent between 1990 and 2012.
- Maternal mortality dropped 45 percent between 1990 and 2013.

Thome believes humanity is "capable of taking on some of the world's greatest challenges when we prioritize them."[8] As Thome continues to forge relationships with members of different cultures, he reminds us that building trust with others is "as simple as making a connection. We're ultimately not that different."[9] When developing relationships with members of a different culture, Thome is reminded of an aboriginal activists group's key belief: "If you have come here to help me, you are wasting our time. But if you come because your liberation is bound up with mine, then let us work together."[10]

WHAT DO YOU THINK?

1. Josh Thome and his collaborator, Sol Guy, are using innovative methods to share stories. In addition to websites, concerts, and videos, how else can technology share the narratives of today's youth and encourage them to participate in social change?
2. Thome uses statistics to argue that today's youth are making significant social changes. Would one or more of these statistics make an interesting speech? How could you develop one of Thome's statistics on the changes today's youth are making?
3. Thome is interested in exploring our "human potential." Discuss as a class what you think that potential might include.

Jade Thome

Figure 6.1 Visual representation of statistics

Visual representations of statistics help an audience understand complex or abstract information. This graph shows the number of immigrants to the United States who became permanent residents in 2011 and 2013 by class of admission.

Source: U.S. Department of Homeland Security, Office of Immigration Statistics, 2013 Yearbook of Immigration Statistics. See also http://www.dhs.gov/sites /default/files/publications/ois _yb_2013_0.pdf

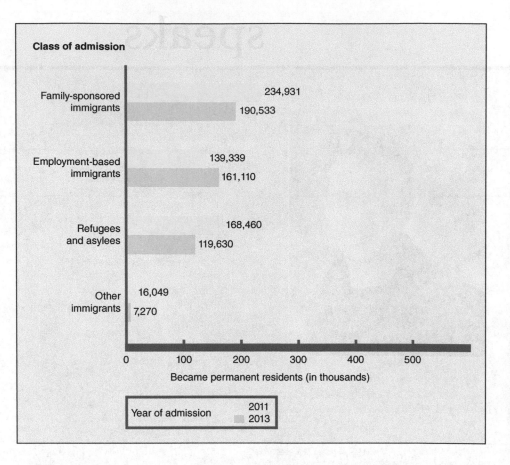

numbers. When you use them correctly, they can be an important source of evidence, but why, how, and when to use them isn't always clear. The descriptions that follow will help you determine the type of statistics you need in your speech. Also see Figure 6.2 for a visual representation of the differences between mean, median, and mode.

The **mean** tells you the average of a group of numbers. Find it by adding all the numbers in your data set and then dividing by the total number of items. Use the mean when you want to describe averages, patterns, tendencies, generalizations, and trends, especially for large groups of data. For example, the mean is what you need if you want to find the average weight of a group of teenagers, like Clara did in her speech to the after-school youth in our earlier example. To find her mean, Clara added together the weight of each of the teens in her audience (they weighed 115, 121, 126, 132, 154, 159, 163, 167, and 170 pounds), and then divided that number by the total number of teens she had weighed (9). This gave her the mean, 145 pounds, the average weight in her audience. She used that average, or mean, to compare her audience's average to the average weight of teenagers fifty years ago and then to teen athletes and nonathletes. She and her audience then entered into a discussion about average weights of teenagers in general.

When your data sets include extreme values, or what are called *outliers*, using the mean to generalize about the data is misleading.[11] A group of students speaking to county commissioners about affordable housing illustrates why this is so. The students presented information about the average cost of housing in their area. Most of the houses rented for $1,100 to $2,500 a month, but one particular home rented for $3,500 a month. In this case, the students couldn't have used the mean because the outlier in this set of data ($3,500) would have distorted the picture of housing costs in their area. To provide a more accurate statistic, the students need to use the median or the mode or leave out the $3,500 rental and explain why.

mean: Average of a group of numbers.

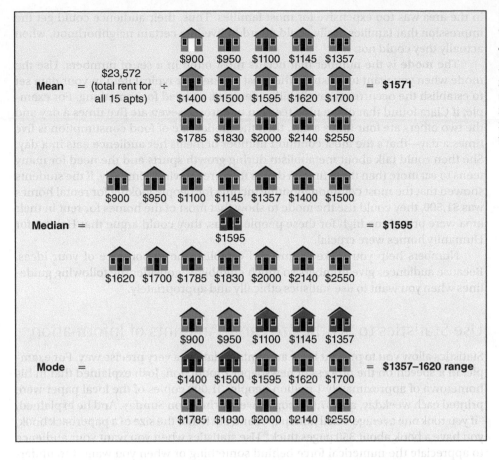

Figure 6.2   **Visual representation of mean, median, and mode**

The mean, median, and mode are numbers that summarize other groups of numbers. This figure shows the mean, median, and mode of the range of rents for fifteen one-bedroom apartments in the Boston area, December 2015.

The **median** is the middle number in a series or set of numbers arranged in a ranked order. A median tells you where the midpoint is in your set of data. It shows you that one-half of your observations will be smaller and one-half larger than that midpoint. Use the median when you want to identify the midpoint and make claims about its significance or about the items that fall above or below it. For example, the median weight of Clara's teens is 154. This means that half the teens weighed more than 154 and half weighed less. Both Clara and her audience now have more information than simply the average weight of teens (145 pounds). For example, Clara can begin to explain weight in relation to body type or height (those below the median ranged in height from 4 feet 11 inches to 5 feet 8 inches and those above the median ranged from 5 feet 6 inches to 6 feet 1 inch).

The students speaking about affordable housing used the median to explain that one-half of the homes they assessed rented for less than $2,000 a month and one-half rented for more than $2,000. They then explained that once the housing that rented for less than the median had been rented, families looking for rentals in their area had to pay more than $2,000 a month. They discussed the monthly income necessary to support such housing costs. Using the median in this way helped them make a case for building Habitat for Humanity homes in a particular neighborhood so more families could afford to live there.

The disadvantage of using the median is that significant numbers below and above the midpoint might not be discussed. For example, is it significant for a teen to weigh 39 pounds less than the median weight, as the lightest person does, or 16 pounds more than the median, as the heaviest does? Similarly, if the students failed to explain that below the median rent of $2,000, houses rented for only as low as $1,100, their audience could get the sense that some housing was much more affordable than that. And if they didn't note that above the median, homes rented for as high as $2,500 their audience might not understand that about half of the housing

median: Middle number in a series or set of numbers arranged in a ranked order.

in the area was too expensive for most families. Thus, their audience could get the impression that families easily could afford to live in a certain neighborhood, when actually they could not.

The **mode** is the number that occurs most often in a set of numbers. Use the mode when you want to illustrate the most frequent or typical item in your data set to establish the occurrence, availability, demand, or need for something. For example, if Clara found that of the nine teens in her group, seven ate five times a day and the two others ate four times a day, then the modal rate of food consumption is five times a day—that's the most common number of meals her audience eats in a day. She then could talk about metabolism during growth spurts and the need for many teens to eat more than three times a day as they are growing. Similarly, if the students showed that the most common monthly income for people looking for rental homes was $1,500, they could use the mode to show that most of the homes for rent in their area were priced too high for these people. Thus, they could argue that Habitat for Humanity homes were crucial.

Numbers help you make claims and establish the importance of your ideas. Because audiences give numbers so much credibility, consider the following guidelines when you want to use statistics ethically and appropriately.

Use Statistics to Synthesize Large Amounts of Information

Statistics allow you to present large amounts of data in a very precise way. For example, in a speech on the process of newspaper production, Josh explained that in his hometown of approximately 1 million people, 31,000 copies of the local paper were printed each weekday, and 37,000 copies were printed on Sunday. And he explained, "if you took one average-sized newspaper and cut it into the size of a paperback book, you have a book about 350 pages thick." Use statistics when you want your audience to appreciate the numerical force behind something or when you want it to understand the size or quantity of an event.

But be careful about using too many statistics. Audiences have a hard time remembering numbers. In fact, the more numbers you use, the fewer that audience members are likely to remember. How difficult do you think it would be to remember the numbers in the following example?

> Based on these 2008 figures, we can say of the 1,393 males between the ages of eighteen and twenty-one with incomes above $24,000 a year and less than two years of training who attended this event more than three times but less than five, 743 drove their own vehicles, 259 rode with friends, 128 took the bus, and 11 walked. This leaves 252 unaccounted for. Now, let's look at the 2010 data. These figures change slightly.

Although this is a hypothetical example, it illustrates how beginning speakers sometimes tend to use too many numbers and use them randomly. The result is more information than audience members can remember, and it is presented without a systematic structure to help them.

Use Statistics When the Numbers Tell a Powerful Story

In a speech on cradle-to-grave marketing, Jess could have told the story of a child heavily influenced by television advertising. Instead, she chose to use statistics:

> The average twelve-year-old spends four hours a day watching television—the equivalent of two months of nonstop TV watching per year. They see 40,000 commercials a year—the equivalent of 100 commercials a day. The result is what marketers call the "nag factor," children badgering their parents to buy products, culminating in 2 billion children-influenced dollars spent on products in 2000. So powerful is the nag factor that U.S families spend 54 billion of their, and their children's, dollars on toys, sweets, food, electronics, shoes, clothes, sports, and movies.

The story Jess told with these numbers—two months total television watching, 100 commercials a day, parents spending an enormous amount of money, and increased

mode: Number that occurs most often in a set of numbers.

focus on this market by advertisers—is far more powerful than the story of one child begging a parent to buy products on a shopping trip.

Use Statistics When Numerical Evidence Strengthens a Claim

Statistics can strengthen a claim, especially one made in an example or a story, because they quantify or measure the impact of an event. They also allow you to make the same claim in a new way. After Rupert gave verbal and visual examples to describe the damage done by Hurricane Katrina, he used statistics to strengthen his claim that the storm, especially when compared to more recent hurricanes, caused an almost incomprehensible amount of damage:

> You can see why this hurricane is still a topic of conversation, concern, and relief efforts today. Katrina flooded fifty-seven miles of coastline along the St. Tammany Parish. The hurricane created a storm surge sixteen feet high, or deep, that traveled a full six miles inland. By August 31, 2005, 80 percent of New Orleans had been flooded, with the famous French Quarter somehow being spared damage.

Rupert's description and examples affected the audience on one level, his visual aids influenced it on another, and his dramatic statistics reinforced his claims about the damage caused by the storm.

There are many ways to misuse statistics. Recall from our housing example that the mean rent misrepresented the affordability of housing in a particular neighborhood. Similarly, if Clara suggested that the modal number of meals for teens is five per day, then we could easily overlook the thousands of teens who go without food each day because of poverty or eating disorders. Because statistics can be manipulated, see Table 6.3 for guidelines that will help you use them responsibly and accurately.

Testimony

When speakers use the opinions or observations of others, they are using testimony as a source of evidence. **Testimony** is sometimes called "quoting others" or "citing the words of others." We usually think of testimony as coming from an authority, an expert, or a person who has professional knowledge about a subject. This is often true, but testimony can also come from average people who have relevant experience with your topic. Speakers sometimes also provide their own testimony—their own words and experiences as sources of evidence.

Testimony often takes the form of a **direct quotation**, an exact word-for-word presentation of another's testimony. At other times, speakers **paraphrase** the words, or provide a summary of another's testimony in the speaker's own words. Direct quotations often are seen as more credible than paraphrasing, but sometimes a person's words or stories are too long, too complex, or contain inappropriate language for a particular audience, making paraphrasing a better option.

Generally, use someone else's testimony when his or her words make your point more clearly, powerfully, or eloquently than your own. When you use the testimony of someone considered an authority in a particular field, you are using **expert testimony**. When you use the testimony of someone who has firsthand knowledge of a topic, you are using **peer testimony**, sometimes called *lay testimony*. You also can use your own testimony to convey your point. This is called **personal testimony**. To use each type of testimony ethically, always give credit to the person you are quoting or paraphrasing, including his or her name and credentials.

Use Testimony When You Need the Voice of an Expert

Sometimes, an audience may be interested in our descriptions of an issue or event, but we might not have enough credibility to make our claims believable. Expert

testimony: Opinions or observations of others.

direct quotation: Exact word-for-word presentation of another's testimony.

paraphrase: Summary of another's testimony in the speaker's own words.

expert testimony: Opinions or observations of someone considered an authority in a particular field.

peer testimony: Opinions or observations of someone who has firsthand knowledge of a topic (sometimes called *lay testimony*).

personal testimony: Your own opinions or observations that you use to convey your point.

Table 6.3 Tips for Using Definitions Ethically and Effectively

ASK YOURSELF THIS . . .	AND DO THIS . . .	EXAMPLE
How accurate are my statistics?	Be certain the sources of your statistics are credible, the data are current, and the statistics represent what you claim they do: • Avoid manipulating a statistic to say what you want. • Be wary when a source that is overly invested in a particular outcome provides a statistic. See if you can find other sources that confirm your statistic, or if that isn't possible, present statistics from various perspectives to make your claim more accurately.	When only 10 percent of those surveyed say they would try a product again but only twenty people were sampled, you don't have a very credible statistic. Using outdated statistics about unemployment rates can mislead the audience into thinking that the economy is better or worse than it actually is. Data on global warming compiled by the petroleum industry are likely to be influenced by the industry's views on the issue.
Can I make my statistics easier to remember by displaying them visually?	Display statistics visually on an overhead, in a PowerPoint slide, in a handout, or on a board or flip chart.	Take another look at Figure 6.1. Imagine a speaker presenting those numbers only verbally. Displaying the immigration statistics visually reinforces the verbal presentation by helping the audience keep track of and visualize the statistics.
Can I make my statistics easier to remember by rounding numbers up or down?	Round your numbers up or down wherever possible, especially when you want to emphasize general size rather than the exact amount.	Rupert rounded his numbers about the damage caused by Hurricane Katrina to whole numbers. He spoke of fifty-seven miles, six miles, and sixteen feet rather than providing the exact measurements of the damage caused.
Can I make my statistics easier to remember by grouping similar numbers together?	When you must present a lot of numbers to make a point, find ways to group similar categories together so your audience can digest them more easily. Although your audience will still have to keep track of quite a few numbers, "chunking" makes them easier to follow.	In our hypothetical example, demographic data, mode of transportation, and insignificant data could be grouped so the audience could remember numbers that are related to one another: "Based on these 2008 figures, we can say that about 1,100 of the 1,400 males under age twenty-one, with basic training and making more than $24,000 a year, traveled to this event. This leaves about 300 unaccounted for."
Can I make my statistics easier to remember by translating them into relatable numbers?	Translate your statistics into numbers that your audience can easily recognize and relate to.	• How long is fifty-seven miles of shoreline? It's the distance between two familiar points, say, your own college campus and the next town or point of significance. It's also the distance of more than two marathons. • What does it mean to say a surge of sixteen feet? Show this distance by asking two members of your audience to stand sixteen feet apart. Or explain that it is the height of approximately three people who are 5 feet 4 inches. • How large is 80 percent of New Orleans? Show a map of the city with that 80 percent shaded in blue. Then explain how much of your own town would have been covered by the same amount of water.

Ethical MOMENT

Master Statuses and Unintended Consequences

How important do you think master statuses are? Consider two examples of students with Arab or Muslim identities. In January 2010, nine students of Arab descent at Dearborn High School in Detroit, Michigan, received national attention when they arrived to school wearing sweatshirts that referenced the September 11, 2001, attacks on the World Trade Center. The group of students, all from the class of 2011, wore sweatshirts that depicted the number 11, representing the twin towers; the school's mascot, a thunderbird, flying directly toward the numerals; and the slogan "You can't bring us down."

After teachers, staff, and other students reported feeling offended by the image, the sweatshirts were confiscated. Dearborn Public Schools spokesperson David Mustonen stated that "teachers and kids were obviously upset," and senior Donovan Golich felt the group should be suspended. The school later held a public meeting for parents, staff, and area residents so they could discuss the situation.

The Dearborn students told school officials that they were simply showing pride for their class of 2011. One of the students, Shiab Mussad, stated that the public was overreacting. He claimed, "[W]e just wanted to show our support (to our class)." Even so, many angry parents called on school officials to suspend the group. However, the administrators determined that the incident was a matter of "kids not thinking, not realizing the consequences of something they thought was pretty innocent," and no disciplinary action was taken against the students. Instead, educators emphasized the need for a public dialogue between parents and the school.

In 2015, Muslim teen, Ahmed Mohamed, created a simple clock from a pencil case. Excited to show his teacher at his school in Irving, Texas, Ahmed took the clock to school and shared his creation with her. To his surprise, the teacher saw the clock as a threat, thinking it was more than a simple clock and possibly a bomb. The teacher called the police, and Ahmed, rather than receiving praise for his innovation, was arrested. Officer James McLellan, spokesperson for the Irving Police department, explained, "We attempted to question the juvenile about what it was and he would simply only tell us it was a clock. The teenager did that because, well, it was a clock," McLellan said.

Ahmed, who has aspirations to become an engineer and attend MIT, shared with the media, "I built a clock to impress my teacher but when I showed it to her, she thought it was a threat to her. . . . It was really sad that she took the wrong impression of it." The incident evoked "outrage" on social media and harsh criticism of the school for racial profiling. It also garnered over 100,000 tweets, as well as support and praise for Ahmed from President Obama, Hillary Clinton, and Mark Zuckerberg.

The shirts and the clock raise questions about master statuses, our ability to acknowledge the many connotative definitions embedded in artifacts, the assumptions we have about individuals and their ethnic and religious backgrounds, and the ethics surrounding those definitions and assumptions.[12]

WHAT DO YOU THINK?

1. What types of evidence and supporting material do you think the administrators used as they made assumptions about the teenagers and the shirts and clock?

2. Evaluate the strength of this supporting material. Were the narratives and examples they relied on credible and ethical? Was there testimony involved? Did they use any statistical data?

3. What assumptions about master statuses led to the administrators' responses to the students in both incidents? Are those assumptions supported well by evidence that is sound, credible, and ethical? Why or why not?

---

testimony can give our ideas an extra boost. Phrases like "according to the surgeon general" add the voice of authority to a speech. Daria enhanced her credibility by using expert testimony in her speech on the shortage of qualified schoolteachers:

> "We have good people coming in," said Sandra Feldman, president of the American Federation of Teachers, "but we lose almost 50 percent of them in the first five years." Why? The reason is money, according to Ms. Feldman: "If someone lasts four or five years, they see that they can teach, but they can't support themselves or their families."[13]

Incorporating the testimony of recognized experts lends an air of credibility to your own testimony and helps you build a stronger case. Just be careful about using testimony from biased sources. **Bias** is an unreasoned distortion of judgment or prejudice about a topic, and a biased source will have an unreasoned personal stake in the outcome of an issue.[14] In contrast, an **objective** source is someone who does not have a personal stake in an issue and can provide a fair, ethical, and undistorted view of a topic. Although objective sources certainly have preferences and feelings, they are not so strongly influenced by their own stake in an issue that they distort information. Obviously, no one can be completely objective. In fact, sometimes we want to use the testimony of someone who has a personal stake in an issue because that person

bias: Unreasoned distortion of judgment or prejudice about a topic.

objective: Having a fair, ethical, and undistorted view on a question or issue.

Mary Barra, the CEO of General Motors, and Anton Valukas, the head of internal recall investigations for GM, field questions and give testimony after GM delayed a recall of defective vehicles. How might you evaluate their testimony and who else would you want to gather testimony from if you were to give a speech on the automobile industry and recalling cars?

understands the issue as an insider. For example, in his persuasive speech on transportation options for people who are legally drunk, Eric cited officer Kirsten Innes as stating, "After 10 o'clock on a weekend evening, almost 50 percent of drivers are alcohol impaired." However, more often, it's preferable to use testimony from sources who are not personally invested in an issue and do not stand to gain from a particular outcome.

Use Testimony to Illustrate Differences or Agreements

Speakers often use testimony when they want to illustrate the range of opinions about a topic. Testimony from several different sources gives an audience a sense of the diversity—or lack of it—on opinions circulating in the public dialogue. If you can cite a variety of expert opinions on your subject, you illustrate the complexity of an issue. Or if all the experts agree and offer a unified voice, you illustrate the strength of a particular opinion. Consider statements like these: "In my review of the minutes for the planning commission meetings from January to September of this year, I found only one person on the nine-member city planning commission who disagreed. Let me share what Joel Phillips, the dissenting voice, said and then tell what the other eight individuals had to say." Or "There seems to be incredible diversity on this issue. Of the five professors I interviewed, none offered the same solution to the problem I posed. Here are some of their suggestions." When used in these ways, testimony sheds light on agreements or disagreements over issues that affect your audience.

Use Your Own Testimony When Your Experience Says It Best

Although the words of an expert can lend credibility to a speech, sometimes your own experiences make a stronger impression. In a speech on the peer pressure that contributes to the prevalence of eating disorders in young women, Rachael used her own testimony. She said to her audience, "No one has ever come up to me and said, 'Wow, Rachael, you look great! Have you gained ten?' It's always the opposite, isn't it? 'Have you lost ten?'" She could have used the testimony of a doctor or a psychologist, but her personal testimony about her own experiences strengthened her point about the peer pressure many young women encounter.

Paraphrase Testimony to Improve Listenability

The exact words of an expert may not always be appropriate for an audience because they may be too complex or too vulgar. However, you can still use that person's words if you paraphrase, summarizing statements rather than repeating them exactly. For example, when Joel Phillips, the dissenting commissioner, explained, "residential zoning factors historically have an inverse effect on the growth this sector of the community feasibly can accommodate," Shatanna paraphrased his words by saying, "Mr. Phillips, the dissenting commission member, explained that, historically, zoning ordinances have a negative effect on the growth of our community." Her paraphrasing allowed her to use the commissioner's testimony without confusing her audience by using his specialized terminology.

Similarly, try paraphrasing when your source uses profanity or vulgar language that may not be appropriate for a particular audience. But note that if your source feels strongly enough about an issue to use profanity, or if the use of profanity is an important part of that person's personality, your paraphrase should reflect this without repeating his or her exact words. Tell your audience that your source feels strongly enough about an idea to swear about it or that the person uses profanity liberally in discussing the idea. Remember, paraphrasing is a summary of what was said, not a recasting of someone's feelings or beliefs. Also note that although profanity may not always be inappropriate in a speech, you should still think carefully about your reasons for including it and your audience's possible reactions to hearing it.

Testimony enhances a claim or adds to a position much like a second opinion would. It brings in outside voices, adds other perspectives, and illustrates what others are thinking and saying about your issue. But to use testimony ethically and effectively, it must meet certain criteria. See Table 6.4 for tips on how to use testimony best.

Definitions

Definitions are essential to public speaking. Without them, the common language shared by speaker and audience breaks down quickly. A **definition** is a statement of the exact meaning of a word or phrase. Definitions can make terms, whether simple or complex, clear and meaningful for your audiences. Provide a definition of a word in a speech when its meaning may be ambiguous and confusing to your audience.

Every word has both a denotative and a connotative definition. The **denotative definition** is the objective meaning you find in a dictionary, the definition of a word on which most everyone can agree. In contrast, a **connotative definition** is the subjective meaning of a word or a phrase based on personal experiences and beliefs. Be aware that providing the dictionary definition of a word may not always be enough to get your point across; definitions come from personal experiences as well as from the dictionary.

An example illustrates how powerful a connotative definition can be. Abolitionist Sojourner Truth, born a slave in New York in approximately 1797 and freed in 1827, focused one of her most famous speeches on the definition of the word *woman*. In "Ain't I a Woman?" she repeatedly questioned the definition of this word, asking her audience to decide whether or not she actually was "a woman."

> That man over there says that women need to be helped into carriages, and lifted over ditches, and to have the best place everywhere. Nobody ever helps me into carriages, or over mud-puddles, or gives me any best place. And, ain't I a woman? Look at me, look at my arm. I have plowed and planted and gathered into barns, and no man could head me—and ain't I a woman? I could work as much and eat as much as a man (when I could get it) and bear the lash as well—and ain't I a woman? I have borne thirteen children and seen them most all sold off into slavery, and when I cried out with a mother's grief, none but Jesus heard. And ain't I a woman?[15]

As this example illustrates, connotative definitions can move an audience in a way that denotative definitions sometimes cannot. However, because connotative definitions are based on emotions and personal experiences, they can cloud an issue or confuse an audience. Therefore, be sure to identify the connotative definitions you use in your speech and take into account the varying connotations one word may have. Truth did this when she questioned the audience's connotative definitions of *woman*.

Although some speeches are built around a definition, as in Truth's example, others incorporate definitions to clarify words for audiences. The guidelines for using definitions in your speeches are as follow.

Use Definitions to Clarify and Create Understanding

Use a definition when you anticipate your audience will say, "I don't know what that word means" or "I've never heard the word used that way before." For technical terms, a denotative definition often suffices. For familiar words used in new ways, connotative definitions are a must. For example, in a speech to students at Moscow

definition: Statement of the exact meaning of a word or phrase.

denotative definition: Objective meaning of a word or a phrase you find in a dictionary.

connotative definition: Subjective meaning of a word or phrase based on personal experiences and beliefs.

Table 6.4 Tips for Using Testimony Ethically and Effectively

ASK YOURSELF THIS...	AND DO THIS...	EXAMPLE
Is the source of your testimony credible?	Determine the credibility of your testimony by asking these questions: • Does it come from people who are knowledgeable about your subject? • Have these people been trained in its particular area? Do they have the proper credentials or experiences? • Have they earned the respect of other experts in their field? Make sure your testimony comes from someone who actually knows about your subject, not just from someone people might like or find interesting. Similarly, when using testimony from a nonexpert, make sure the person has some legitimate connection to the issue you are speaking about.	Advertisements often provide excellent examples of the unethical use of testimony because they rely on how much consumers admire a spokesperson, not on what the spokesperson knows about the product. Yusef noted this fact in his speech about the rise of consumerism in China. He discussed that because it has become a symbol of status to buy celebrity-endorsed products, celebrities are banned from endorsing medical products such as drugs and nutritional supplements.
Is the testimony biased?	To determine if a source is biased, ask these questions about the person: • What is this person's connection to the issue? How does that connection affect her or his perspective? Does he or she have a personal stake in the issue? • Are this person's ideas about this topic so firmly rooted that she or he would be unable to speak credibly on another aspect of the topic? • Are this person's words informed and reasoned? Is he or she making claims based on adequate exposure to the issue?	In his speech about how to cope with depression, Sean used testimony from his sister—an executive at a pharmaceutical company—about how effective a medication her company manufactured was in treating depression. Although his sister wasn't trying to sell the product her company manufactured, Sean's audience was skeptical about her testimony because they perceived it as being biased. Sean could have increased his credibility by also citing unbiased studies that indicated how well the medicine worked. Or he could have discussed the medication his sister's company manufactured as just one of many effective medications on the market.
Have you paraphrased accurately?	Be careful when you paraphrase another person's testimony or change some of the language so it is more suitable to your audience. It is unethical to change the intended meaning of testimony, change its tone, or place it in a context that your source did not intend.	One of the commissioners Shatanna interviewed said, "It's very complicated. Let me outline some of the issues for you." He then described seven distinct issues. Shatanna's paraphrasing reflected this complexity. In her speech, she said, "Commissioner Fields presented seven different issues. The issue that most directly affects my topic today is the first one he mentioned, the conflict between what residents and retailers want."
Is the testimony connected to your point?	When you use personal testimony, make sure it enhances your speech and that you're not using it simply because you want to share your or someone else's perspectives and experiences. If you think testimony about your or someone else's experience fits into your speech perfectly, connect it to the larger issue you are speaking about.	Rachael's testimony about the pressure to be thin was connected to her speech topic. She used her experiences not to draw attention to herself but to illustrate a common experience for many young women. Rachel didn't just tell her own story. She also told the story of other women.

University, Ronald Reagan defined the word *freedom* as the recognition that no single authority has a monopoly on truth. At the time, democracy was new to the Soviet Union, so Reagan's definition helped his audience see more clearly what he believed were the benefits of a democracy.

Use Definitions to Clarify an Emotionally or Politically Charged Word

Many words in our language have become emotionally and politically charged. Words like *racism, sexism, disability, discrimination, equality, freedom, liberal,* and *conservative* have become hotbeds of dispute. When you use words like these, provide a definition. Explain how you are using the word so you can minimize some of the emotions and politics associated with it. Otherwise, your audience may not be able to understand or even listen to you.

Use Definitions to Illustrate What Something Is Not

Definitions also explain to an audience what something isn't. In a student speech on the hostile environment created by sexual harassment, Hillary defined *hostile environment* and *harassment* first by what they are and then by what they are not:

> According to the *Webb Report: A Newsletter on Sexual Harassment,* behavior is sexual harassment if it (1) is sexual in nature, (2) is unwelcome by the person it is directed at, and (3) is sufficiently severe or pervasive that it alters the conditions of that person's employment and creates an abusive working environment. This means it's not sexual harassment nor is it seen as creating a hostile environment if the behavior: (1) isn't sexual in nature, (2) is welcomed by the person it's directed at, and (3) doesn't negatively affect that individual's working environment and create an abusive climate. The behavior may be offensive, unproductive, or even harmful, but if it doesn't meet all three criteria, then it's not considered sexual harassment.

Hillary defined what sexual harassment is by illustrating for her audience what it isn't.

Even familiar terms have both denotative and connotative definitions. As a result, they can convey meanings you may not intend. To minimize this problem, identify some of the familiar terms you plan to use in your speech and look them up. Do you think the connotative meanings of those terms match the dictionary definitions? How will you make sure your own meaning is clear to your audience?

Use Definitions to Trace the History of a Word

The history of a word, called its **etymology**, allows you to trace the original meaning of a word and chart the changes it has undergone over time. In speeches, tracing the history of words offers your audience insight into the words' origins and the ways those origins affect our understanding and use of the words today. Etymologies, then, can help you build an argument for a position or tell a more comprehensive story about an issue. Many dictionaries provide the etymology of words, but The *Oxford English Dictionary* is a particularly good source for tracing a word's origins. Another good resource is the Word Origins website. Both sources define words and give you their original meanings, and they are useful when you want to know why words we use today have the meanings they do.

Using definitions seems fairly straightforward and simple, and it usually is. But as with all forms of evidence, you must consider the credibility, clarity, and accuracy of your definitions. Table 6.5 provides tips to help you ensure that your definitions are ethical and effective.

Practicing the Public Dialogue | 6.2

EVALUATE YOUR SUPPORTING EVIDENCE

Bring the supporting materials you have gathered for your next speech to class. Working in pairs or with a group, separate your materials into categories: examples, narratives, statistics, testimony, and definitions. Discuss how you plan to use each type of evidence in the speech. Using the tips in this chapter to evaluate your evidence, determine whether your audience would see your evidence as credible and ethical. Why would or wouldn't they?

etymology: History of a word.

Table 6.5 Tips for Using Definitions Ethically and Effectively

ASK YOURSELF THIS . . .	AND DO THIS . . .	EXAMPLE
Is the source of the definition credible?	Consider whether the dictionary or other source you are using for your definition is credible: • Some sources are more extensive than others, offering recent definitions as well as a comprehensive history of a word. • Examples of credible sources include encyclopedias, textbooks, and books about specific topics such as music, law, or engineering. If you are using a particular person's definition of a word, make sure that person is a credible and qualified source.	In her speech about the role of the U.S. military in the twenty-first century, Erin didn't rely only on definitions of terms in her regular English dictionary. She confirmed that her definitions were accurate in a military context by using an even more credible source, the U.S. Department of Defense's DOD Dictionary of Military and Associated Terms. With the DOD dictionary, she was able to confirm the meaning of terms such as *health-care provider* and *campaign*, which have specific meanings in military jargon.
Have you avoided *proper meaning superstition*?	If you decide to use a term without defining it, be sure your listeners have the same understanding of the term that you do so you can avoid proper meaning superstition. *Proper meaning superstition,* a term coined by I. A. Richards and C. K. Ogden in the late 1920s, is the belief that everyone attaches the same meaning to a word and that you are using that meaning. With proper meaning superstition, speakers use words believing their audiences will have exactly the same referent, which isn't always the case.	In his speech about feminism in India, Sanjay avoided proper meaning superstition by explaining how the concept of feminism was understood by different people in different contexts and cultures. For example, he provided a basic definition found in most dictionaries—that feminism is a movement for social, cultural, political, and economic equality of men and women. He also defined *feminism* as a global struggle for the end to discrimination and a means for attaining individual liberation.
Have you actually defined the term?	Avoid using a term to define itself, using unfamiliar words in a definition, and using circular definitions. To ensure a fair and ethical public dialogue, our definitions must clarify our arguments rather than confuse our audiences.	• Sharon used a term to define itself when she said, "By *younger* I mean people who aren't very old—they're still young." With this definition, her audience still didn't know what she meant by "young." Is it five years of age, twenty years, or something else? • When Fernando said, "By *septifragal,* I mean to say dehiscing by breaking away from the dissepiments," the words he used were familiar to the scientists in his audience but not to anyone else. • Nelson used a circular definition when he said, "By *masculine,* I'm referring to those traits not feminine, and by feminine, I mean those not masculine." With this definition, his audience still didn't know what he meant by either "masculine" or "feminine."

A Map of Reasoning

Now that you've explored the types of evidence you can use in your speech, it is helpful to begin to think about how you might assemble your ideas logically. Even at this early stage in your speech, you can begin to construct your arguments. In this section, you will begin to develop a map of your reasoning process. A solid argument should follow this map of reasoning, which is adapted from Stephen Toulmin's model of a sound argument (Figure 6.3).[16]

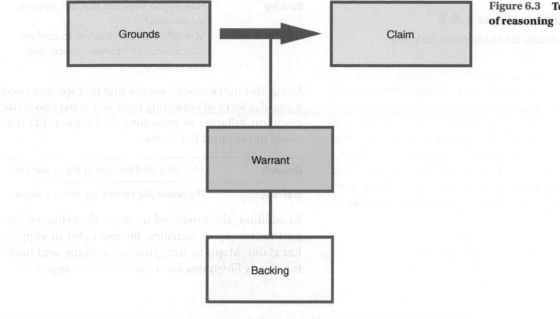

Figure 6.3   Toulmin's model of reasoning

Claim	What do you think or want to propose?
Grounds	Why do you think this or want to propose it?
Warrant	How do you know the grounds support the claim?
Backing	How do you know the warrant supports the grounds?

This model of a sound argument helps you both as a speaker and as an audience member. As a speaker, these questions double-check the logic of your assertions, making a map of your own reasoning. As a listener, the map helps you evaluate the reasons speakers give in support of their claims.

Let's look at a map of the reasoning in Damon's persuasive speech on teen suicide to understand how this model works in an actual argument:

Claim	What do you think or want to propose?
	The high rate of teen suicide for males is now a part of our community.
Grounds	Why do you think this or want to propose it?
	Three boys have committed suicide in our community in the past two months.
Warrant	How do you know the grounds support the claim?
	Three suicides in two months represent a high rate of suicide for male teens in a community of our size.
Backing	How do you know the warrant supports the grounds?
	Research indicates that three suicides in two months are above the average rate for male teens in a community of our size.

This map—a bit like a child's continually asking "why?"—helps speakers and audiences track a line of reasoning and find any flaws or loopholes. The reasoning in Damon's speech is solid, and the map helps us see this. He has acceptable **grounds**, **warrant**, and **backing** for his claim.

The model can also be used to uncover flaws in a speech. Notice how, beginning with the warrant, this speaker's ideas break down:

Claim	What do you think or want to propose?
	Living near power lines increases the risk of cancer.
Grounds	Why do you think this or want to propose it?
	My father died of cancer and we lived near a power line.
Warrant	How do you know the grounds support the claim?
	The reason my father had cancer was because of the power line.

grounds: Why you think something is true or want to propose it.

warrant: The evidence you have to be certain your grounds support your claim.

backing: The evidence you have to be certain your warrant supports your grounds.

APPLY TOULMIN'S MODEL OF REASONING TO YOUR ARGUMENTS

Select one type of evidence you hope to use in your next speech. Map out your reasoning and the claim you want to make with this evidence. Trace each step of your argument with Toulmin's model. Do you find any flaws in your reasoning? Are you able to fix them with additional evidence or more careful claims? To clarify your reasoning, ask yourself the following questions: What am I claiming or proposing? Why do I think or want to propose this? What grounds support my claim? What backing supports the grounds? These questions should help you spot invalid claims and poorly developed arguments and fix them before you give your speech.

Backing	How do you know the warrant supports the grounds?
	Scientific research has yet to confirm the connection between cancer and power lines.

Using Toulmin's model, we see that this speaker used a circular form of reasoning (you will learn about the common fallacies of reasoning in Chapter 14) that could not support her claims:

Grounds	My father died because of the power line.
Warrant	The power line caused my father's death.

In addition, she produced no scientific evidence (expert testimony or statistics, for example) to support her claim. Mapping her grounds, warrant, and backing clearly illustrates the weakness of her argument.

Chapter Summary

Ethical and effective speakers support their claims with evidence that is credible, relevant, appropriate, and organized.

- Each type of supporting material has strengths and weaknesses, and each is important to the common language of public speaking.
- Use a variety of evidence types to build and strengthen your claims, develop your ideas, communicate ethically, and appeal to your audiences.

Examples are specific instances that illustrate a concept, experience, issue, or problem.

- Examples can be real or hypothetical.
- They should help clarify or reinforce a claim or bring an idea to life.

Narratives are stories that recount or foretell real or hypothetical events.

- Narratives can be brief or extended.
- They help you personalize your claims, challenge your audience to think in new ways, evoke emotions, or unite with your audience.

Statistics are numerical summaries of facts, figures, and research findings.

- The three types of statistics most commonly used in speeches are the mean (or average), the median (or middle point), or the mode (or most frequently appearing).
- Use statistics to synthesize large amounts of information, help you tell a powerful story, or strengthen your claims.

Testimony uses your own or others' opinions or observations to support your claims.

- Peer or expert testimony can add the weight of authority to your speech and help you illustrate differences and agreements.
- Use your own testimony (personal testimony) when your voice illustrates your point best.
- Paraphrase complex testimony to improve its listenability.

Definitions are statements of the exact meaning of a word or phrase.

- Definitions can be denotative (commonly agreed on) or connotative (based on personal experiences or beliefs).
- They can clarify or create understanding for your audience or explain an emotionally or politically charged term.
- They also can be used to explain what something is not or to trace the history of a term.

Using Toulmin's model of reasoning, speakers can verify the strength of their arguments.

- The model sets out four questions:
  1. The claim: What do you think or want to propose?
  2. The grounds: Why do you think this or want to propose it?
  3. The warrant: How do you know the grounds support the claim?
  4. The backing: How do you know the warrant supports the grounds?
- Listeners, too, can use this model to assess the strength of a speaker's reasoning.

Invitation to Public Speaking Online MindTap°

Now that you have read Chapter 6, use your MindTap Communication for *Invitation to Public Speaking* for quick access to the electronic resources that accompany this text. These resources include:

- **Study tools** that will help you assess your learning and prepare for exams (*digital glossary, key term flash cards, review quizzes*).
- **Activities and assignments** that will help you hone your knowledge and build your public speaking skills throughout

the course, as well as help you explore public speaking concepts online (web links), give you step-by-step guidance through the research, outline and note card preparation process (Outline Builder), watch and critique videos of sample speeches (Interactive Video Activities), and allow you to practice and present your presentation online using a speech video delivery, recording, and grading system (YouSeeU).

Key Concepts MindTap° Test your knowledge with online printable flash cards.

backing (123)
bias (117)
brief narrative (107)
claim (104)
connotative definition (119)
definition (119)
denotative definition (119)
direct quotation (115)
etymology (121)
evidence (104)
example (104)
expert testimony (115)
extended narrative (107)
grounds (123)

hypothetical example (104)
intertextuality (107)
mean (112)
median (113)
mode (114)
narrative (107)
objective (117)
paraphrase (115)
peer testimony (115)
personal testimony (115)
real example (104)
statistics (109)
testimony (115)
warrant (123)

Review Questions

1. Imagine that you are attempting to support the following argument: Living in the dormitories is the best way for first-year students to adjust to college. In pairs or small groups, create one example, one statistic, one narrative, and one piece of testimony to support this claim. Assess the strength and credibility of your evidence. Which do you think is most convincing? Why?
2. Using any of the following words, find a denotative definition and create a connotative definition for one or more of them: *democracy, free speech, gun control, terrorism,* and *politics*. How might each of these definitions be important in a speech about "the rights and privileges of U.S. citizens"?
3. Consider the examples or narratives you have gathered for your speech. Are they real or hypothetical, brief or

extended? Out loud, practice delivering one of your examples or narratives. Do you feel comfortable with your delivery? Why or why not? Practice delivering this material until it sounds natural and conversational.
4. Bring the statistics you have found in your research to class. In groups, discuss how you might work with these statistics to present them clearly and ethically to your audience. Identify your means, medians, and modes. Discuss what each of these types of statistics tells or illustrates for your audience, including a discussion of how to avoid misrepresenting an issue with your statistics.
5. In what instances might you be an expert and offer your own testimony in a speech? What makes you an expert in this situation and not in others? How could you establish your credibility as an expert if you were to use this testimony?

7 | Organizing and Outlining Your Speech

Organize for Clarity

Main Points

Connectives

The Preparation Outline

The Speaking Outline

Note Cards

....

IN THIS CHAPTER, YOU WILL LEARN TO:

- **Develop the appropriate number of main points for your speech**

- **Organize your main points according to five different patterns**

- **Apply five tips for preparing your main points effectively**

- **Use four different kinds of connectives in your speech**

- **Create a preparation outline**

- **Construct a speaking outline and note cards to use as prompts during a speech**

Once you've gathered the information for your speech, you may be wondering how to organize it into a coherent presentation. You can do this in several ways. In this chapter, you will learn about the role organization plays in clear and effective speeches, how to structure your main points, the different patterns of organization you can use, and effective ways to move from one idea to the next.[1] You also will learn about outlining and how to use this technique to evaluate the organization of

MindTap® Start with a quick warm-up activity and review the chapter's learning objectives.

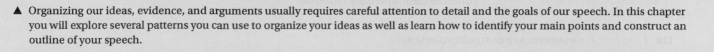

Kentoh/shutterstock.com

▲ Organizing our ideas, evidence, and arguments usually requires careful attention to detail and the goals of our speech. In this chapter you will explore several patterns you can use to organize your ideas as well as learn how to identify your main points and construct an outline of your speech.

your speech and to prepare for its presentation. Once you master the fundamental steps of organization and outlining, you can branch out to more elaborate techniques. For now, use these basic frameworks to help you build speeches that are clear, interesting, and easy to follow.

MindTap®

Read, highlight, and take notes online.

Organize for Clarity

Public speakers usually take considerable time to organize their ideas so that their audiences will find their message logical and easy to follow. Like many other aspects of the speechmaking process, organization is an important audience-centered responsibility. Let's look at an example that illustrates the importance of a well-organized speech. See if you can make sense of the following outline of ideas:

I. Take one of the corners and bring it to the center.
  A. The history of this process is an intriguing one.
  B. My mother had the flag given to her family when her brother died in the Vietnam War.
II. The stars on the edge of the flag are highly symbolic.
  A. It should never touch the ground.
  B. She describes the ceremony as quite beautiful and symbolic.
III. You need two people to fold a flag correctly.
  A. There is a correct way to fold a flag.
  B. The flag should always be displayed behind the speaker's left shoulder.

Can you follow this speaker's organizational logic? Although you begin to realize that the speech is about flags by the second subpoint, are you clear about the speaker's thesis? Is her speech informative, invitational, persuasive, or for a special occasion? Can you tell whether she was asked, required, or decided to speak? It is hard to figure out what this speech is about from the outline just presented.

Now consider this speech organized in a way that is more linear and more appealing to an audience:

MindTap®

Watch a video clip of student speaker Cindy Gardner giving a speech about how to fold an American flag. Notice how she organizes her ideas.

Specific purpose	To inform my audience about the rules and regulations for handling the U.S. flag.
Thesis statement	The flag, a symbol of much that is great about this nation, should be hung, handled, and folded in a specific manner.
Main points	I. Each part of the flag has a specific meaning or purpose dedicated to symbolizing patriotic ideas.
	II. Because of the symbolism of each of these parts, the flag should be hung in a specific manner.
	III. Flag etiquette, more than just stories told from generation to generation, tells us how to handle a flag properly.
	IV. Flags also should be folded in a specific way, with each fold representing important qualities of our country.

Notice how this outline gives you a much clearer sense of what Cindy will cover and how her ideas relate to one another. **Organization**, the systematic arrangement of ideas into a coherent whole, makes speeches listenable. It makes your ideas and arguments clear and easy to follow.

organization: Systematic arrangement of ideas into a coherent whole.

Main Points

One of the first steps in organizing a speech is to identify your main points. **Main points** are the most important, comprehensive ideas you address in your speech. They give your speech focus and help you decide which information to include and which to leave out. They are your overarching themes or subjects.

Identify Your Main Points

You can identify the main points of your speech in two ways. First, take stock of your speech assignment, list of ideas, and research. You will know you have a main point when you realize that if you do not develop a particular idea, your speech topic will seem incomplete, nonsensical, or will not accomplish your goal for the speech.

Second, if you have already written your thesis statement, you should be able to find your main points within it. Notice in the example about folding a flag that Cindy's thesis statement defines her main points: (1) the symbolism in the U.S. flag and how a flag should be (2) hung, (3) handled, and (4) folded. Without a thesis statement (as in the first version of Cindy's outline), a speaker's ideas are simply a random collection of points.

Your thesis statement may not always be as specific as Cindy's, especially if you are giving a process, or how-to, speech. Nonetheless, even with the broad thesis statement in the next speech, Candice used it to develop her main points. Notice how the four steps Candice mentioned in her thesis statement became the four steps she discussed in her speech.

Specific purpose	To inform my audience of the process of making a scrapbook.

Thesis statement	There are four steps to making a quality scrapbook.
Main points	I. Collect the materials you want to put into the book.
	II. Decide on the order of your materials.
	III. Arrange the materials in the book.
	IV. Cover or bind the book.

Your thesis statement and your research should guide your selection of main points for other types of speeches as well. In an invitational speech on the problem of elder abuse, Peter developed the following main points:

Specific purpose	To invite my audience to consider two possible solutions to the problem of elder abuse.

Thesis statement	The problem of elder abuse is quite widespread but may be solved by more thorough background checks of employees in care facilities and increased funding for training and salaries.
Main points	I. More thorough background checks of employees in care facilities may help solve the widespread problem of elder abuse.
	II. Increased funding for training and salaries may also help solve this problem.

In his speech, Peter used his thesis statement to identify the two primary solutions to elder abuse, and he used his research to develop those possibilities.

Use an Appropriate Number of Main Points

Knowing how many main points to include can be difficult because we often gather more information than we need and our subjects can be complex. In addition,

main points: Most important ideas you address in your speech.

classroom speeches often have other requirements, such as incorporating visual aids, citing a specific number of sources, and engaging in a question-and-answer discussion with the audience. So how do you determine the number of main points to include?

In any kind of speech, your time limit is your most important guideline for determining the number of main points. For even a two- to three-minute speech of introduction, you might start with a long list of main points, as May did:

Specific purpose	To introduce myself to my audience.

Thesis statement		I have lived an interesting life thus far and have goals for the future.
Main points	I.	I was born in the air over China, so I have dual citizenship.
	II.	I've lived in many different cities, states, and countries.
	III.	I love to do anything that pertains to water.
	IV.	I'll graduate next June and travel with friends for the summer.
	V.	After that, I'll join the navy.
	VI.	From there, I hope to become an aquatic research scientist for a university.

Although each point is interesting, there are far too many to cover—even if May had ten minutes. Also notice that her thesis statement is quite vague and does not help focus her ideas. When you have a long list of ideas for any kind of speech, recognize that you'll have to reduce your scope. Most classroom speeches are limited to two to four main points depending on the length of your speech and your speaking goals. You can reduce your scope by returning to your thesis statement and tightening it up (as May needs to do) or by focusing on only the main points that best develop your thesis statement. Here's a solution for May's speech:

Specific purpose	To introduce myself to my audience.

Thesis statement		The first twenty-two years of my life have been nomadic ones, and I will most likely continue with this lifestyle for some time.
Main points	I.	My nomadic lifestyle began when I was born in an airplane over an ocean near China.
	II.	I'll continue to nurture my nomadic spirit and love of water by joining the navy when I graduate.

By narrowing her scope and by organizing the six ideas into two main points, May can present a far more coherent and interesting speech. Her audience will be able to follow two main points easily rather than keep track of six points. And by focusing and reducing the number of points, May presents a more memorable image of herself.

Remember, you want to develop your ideas fully, and trying to incorporate too many into one speech only creates problems. If you suspect you have too many main points, review your thesis statement and then consider your time limit. Ask yourself if you can reasonably cover the amount of material you have planned in the time you are allowed. (Tips for managing the length of your main points are offered at the end of this section.) If you have too much information, rewrite your thesis statement to narrow its scope.

Order Your Main Points

Once you've determined the number of main points for your speech, you will want to determine the order in which you discuss them. Although there are numerous organizational patterns, the five covered here are the basic ones: chronological, spatial, causal, problem–solution, and topical. As you become more skilled at speaking, you can adjust these patterns or add patterns that are more complex to your inventory. For now, use these basic patterns to help you improve your organizational skills.

MindTap®

Watch a video clip of student speaker Jeff Malcolm as he gives the introduction to his speech. Jeff uses the chronological pattern to organize his speech.

DIFFERENT GENERATIONS CAN EQUAL DIFFERENT STYLES OF COMMUNICATING

Generation Y (born in the 1980s and 1990s) consists of approximately 71 million young people who are tapped into technology and media, and are now a major part of our workforce. This is the first time in history that four generations—those who lived through World War II, baby boomers (born 1946 to 1964), Generation X (born 1965 to 1980), and Generation Y—are working together (Belkin, 2007). Each generation brings different values, expectations, and styles of communication to the workplace. These differences may be the cause of miscommunication, workplace conflict, and even dissatisfaction with one's job. According to a report by Lee Hecht Harrison, more than 60 percent of employers say they experience tension between employees of different generations.[2] Although the differences in expectations and styles of communication are neither right nor wrong, they do illustrate some of the challenges that multiple generations face when working together.

To help you communicate effectively with your coworkers, members of each generation should:

1. **Learn what each generation values in the workplace.** For example, the World War II generation tends to be more conservative, have a strong work ethic, and value discipline. Generation Yers are connected to technology 24/7, accustomed to instant feedback, and comfortable with virtual problem solving. Recognizing what each generation of workers values can help improve communication and team building. When you give presentations in your workplace, keep in mind the different styles and preferences for communication. Try to incorporate as many of those styles and preferences into your presentations as you can.

2. **Respect the contribution and skills exhibited by each generation.** Harrison found more than 70 percent of older employees are dismissive of younger workers' abilities.[3] And nearly half of employers say that younger employees are dismissive of the abilities of their older coworkers. Acknowledging the different contributions made by each generation can help improve employee relationships. As you prepare your presentations, do your research to discover who has the history or background on an issue or project as well as who can contribute newer perspectives.

3. **Listen to coworkers.** In the workplace, listening is used three times more often than speaking and four to five times more often than reading or writing. Therefore, it's important that employees listen effectively and ethically to their coworkers. When we really listen to what others have to say, we can begin to understand their viewpoint more fully, reduce workplace differences, and show civility to our colleagues.[4]

Chronological pattern. Speeches that trace a sequence of events or ideas follow a **chronological pattern** of organization. If the ideas in your topic extend over a period of time, you may want to use this pattern to organize your speech. In the next example, Serafina used a chronological pattern to discuss the stages of a theory:

Specific purpose	To inform my audience of George Kinder's theory of money maturity.
Thesis statement	The concept of money maturity relates to a person's relationship to money during childhood, adulthood, and on into the future.
Main points	I. Kinder's first stage of money maturity focuses on the relationship to money a person acquires during childhood.
	II. The second stage of money maturity addresses the relationship to money a person has as an adult.
	III. The third stage of money maturity occurs when we set healthy goals for our financial security in the future.

In the next example, Tim uses a chronological pattern to demonstrate and explain a process:

Specific purpose	To inform my audience of how to make a safe ascent during a scuba dive of less than forty feet.
Thesis statement	Safe ascents during scuba diving can be divided into three basic steps.

chronological pattern: Pattern of organization that traces a sequence of events or ideas.

Main points	I.	The first step in making a safe ascent is the preparation step: Signal your buddy and check the time.
	II.	The second step is the "get ready" step: Raise your right hand over your head and hold your buoyancy control device (BCD) with your left hand.
	III.	The third step of the safe ascent is the actual ascent: Slowly rotate upward, breathe normally, and release air from your BCD as you go.

Spatial pattern. When ideas are arranged in terms of location or direction, they follow a **spatial pattern** of organization. For example, arranging ideas from left to right, top to bottom, or inside to outside helps your audience visualize the relationship between ideas or the structure of something. Spatial relationships can be abstract, as in the next example from Terri's speech about eating according to the food pyramid. At other times, they indicate the location of real things or places, as in the second example from Demetrious's speech about five Italian villages.

Specific purpose	To inform my audience of some of the creative ways to eat according to the food pyramid.
Thesis statement	The food pyramid can be used creatively to eat interesting and healthy foods that incorporate whole grains, vegetables and fruits, protein, and even some fats and sugars.
Main points	I. At the foundation of the food pyramid are the grain and vegetable servings that you can combine to make dishes from around the world, such as couscous salad with tomatoes and basil.
	II. You can complement this foundation with the middle level of the pyramid—the dairy, fruit, and protein servings—by making dishes such as curried chicken with apricots.
	III. The top of the pyramid includes the stuff we really like to eat, the fats and sweets that can be made into such delicacies as candied almonds.

In the second example, the spatial pattern describes geographical locations:

Specific purpose	To invite my audience to visit the Cinque Terre five villages along the Mediterranean coast of Italy that are only accessible by boat or by footpath.
Thesis statement	The Cinque Terre contains five villages set into a steep hillside that visitors to the Mediterranean coast of Italy may find enchanting: Monterosso al Mare, Vernazza, Corniglia, Manarola, and Riomaggiore.
Main points	I. The farthest village called Monterosso al Mare is a popular attraction because of the huge statues carved into the rocks overlooking its beaches.
	II. The next two villages, Vernazza and Corniglia, display remarkable vineyards, homes, and a central promenade and piazza.
	III. A hike to the top of the fourth village, Manarola, gives you a stunning view of the ocean and all five of the villages.
	IV. Riomaggiore, the village of love, completes the Cinque Terre or five villages, with its captivating display of homes and shops tucked into the final ravine of this remarkable Italian hillside.

Causal pattern. Speeches that describe a cause-and-effect relationship between ideas or events follow a **causal pattern** of organization. When you use this organizational pattern, you will have two main points: one discussing the cause and the other describing its effects. You can present either the cause first or the effects first, depending on your topic and your speaking goal. In the next example, Jeremy uses a causal pattern to organize the ideas presented in his informative speech on sibling rivalry.

spatial pattern: Pattern of organization that arranges ideas in terms of location or direction.

causal pattern: Pattern of organization that describes a cause-and-effect relationship between ideas or events.

Specific purpose	To inform my audience of the causes and most serious effects of sibling rivalry.
Thesis statement	Sibling rivalry is caused by competition for attention and can become quite severe if not handled properly.
Main points	I. Sibling rivalry is caused by competition for positive attention from parents.
	II. If ignored, sibling rivalry can turn to hatred between siblings.

John Zich/Bloomberg/Getty Images

If the effects have already happened, you might choose to present the effects first followed by the cause. In this next example, Chaundra discusses the effects of worker burnout first, and then she attempts to persuade the audience of one of its possible causes.

Specific purpose	To persuade my audience that the rapid pace of today's workplace is leading to an unusually high level of burnout.
Thesis statement	Today's workers are experiencing high levels of burnout, which is caused by increased demands on their time and energy.
Main points	I. Today's workers display levels of burnout that are higher than ever.
	II. Today's working environments contribute to burnout through a constant demand for more output in shorter amounts of time.

A causal organizational pattern is useful when your topic describes an event or situation and its consequences. It is also helpful when you want to describe an event that might happen and what its effects might be.

Problem–solution pattern. Speeches that identify a specific problem and offer a possible solution follow a **problem–solution pattern** of organization. This pattern is common in persuasive speeches because we can describe a problem and follow with a call to action. The problem–solution pattern has two main points: the description of the problem followed by a description of the solution. Solutions can be general or specific. In the following example, Molly's solution was a general recommendation:

Specific purpose	To persuade my audience that beef by-products have invaded our lives and that awareness is the first step to becoming an educated consumer.
Thesis statement	Becoming aware of the problem of the presence of beef by-products in such common items as deodorants, photographic film, marshmallows, gum, and candles is the first step in a solution of raising our awareness to make educated consumer choices.
Main points	I. Without our knowledge, beef by-products are included in many of the products we put on and in our bodies, as well as in and around our houses.
	II. The solution to this invasion is to become aware of the presence of these beef by-products so we can make informed choices about what we buy and use.

In the next example, Brandon called for a very specific solution:

Specific purpose	To persuade my audience to vote in favor of bond measure 343 in November.
Thesis statement	Money going to support before- and after-school meal programs is at an all-time low, and this measure will ensure the improvement of these services to students in our public schools.

A speech about TSA regulations and security lines at airports could easily be organized around cause-and-effect relationships. What other patterns of organization could you use for a speech about security and traveling? What might your main points be for those speeches?

problem–solution pattern: Pattern of organization that identifies a specific problem and offers a possible solution.

MAIN POINTS / **133**

| **Main points** | I. | There currently is not enough money available to provide adequate before- and after-school meal programs to students in our public schools. |
| | II. | Passing bond measure 343 will provide this necessary money. |

In Chapter 15 you'll learn more about the various types of solutions that speakers can suggest to their audiences.

Topical pattern. Speeches that divide their topics into subtopics, each of which addresses a different aspect of the larger topic, follow a **topical pattern** of organization. When you use a topical pattern, you can organize your ideas by following a progression of ideas that suits your own style. You can use the principle of primacy (putting your most important idea first) or recency (putting what you most want your audience to remember last), or you can arrange the ideas in other ways. In the following example, Justin arranged his ideas topically to address the two major types of phobias:

Specific purpose	To inform my audience of the two major types of phobias.
Thesis statement	Although there are many specific phobias, these "irrational fears and dislikes" can be categorized in two ways: social and specific.
Main points	I. A social phobia is a fear of appearing stupid or being shamed in a social situation.
	II. A specific phobia is a fear of specific objects or situations, like spiders, closed spaces, and so on.

In the following example, Alex uses a topical pattern to persuade her audience that women in "glory sports" are just as talented as the men.

Specific purpose	To persuade my audience that very talented women engage in what are commonly called glory sports.
Thesis statement	We know very little about the women who participate in glory sports, even though they are as talented as the men who participate in the same sports.
Main points	I. Hawaiian surfer Carissa Moore has been difficult to beat for the past seven years, consistently winning world tour and star events, setting a record eleven NSSA Titles, and was "inducted into the Surfers' Hall of Fame in 2014."
	II. Twenty-year-old Lizzie Armanto, from Santa Monica, California, is said to be "rewriting skating history" by dominating women's skateboarding competitions and competing against men in international events.
	III. British sensation, Jenny Jones, a snowboarder who "has done it all," won a bronze at the Sochi Olympics with her "near perfect run," and then headed to Iceland with her split board to "shred" just "for the fun of it."

Topical patterns help you organize a speech that doesn't fit into a chronological, spatial, causal, or problem–solution organizational pattern. If you try to rearrange the examples in this section into one of these other organizational patterns, you'll find that your ideas won't fit well.

Identify when you will use technology. No matter your organizational pattern, technology will help you reinforce your main ideas and keep your audience interested. Here are some tips to help you decide on the type of technology you might use:

Chronological pattern: Images can help you trace the evolution of something or show how ideas have moved forward historically. Time lines presented visually also will help your audience follow your claims.

Spatial pattern: Technology can help you show where things are located in relation to one another. It can also help you bring in interesting photographs, images, and maps.

topical pattern: Pattern of organization that allows the speaker to divide a topic into subtopics, each of which addresses a different aspect of the larger topic.

Causal pattern: Technology can help you organize graphs and charts and present statistics. Simple tools like a few PowerPoint slides or Prezi can help you identify the causes of a problem you are explaining.

Problem-solution pattern: PowerPoint slides or Prezi can help you list the parts or components of a problem or its solution. Appropriate images can help you bring in an emotional aspect of a problem.

Topical pattern: Images and photographs can help you identify your main points clearly as you introduce them. PowerPoint slides or Prezi can help your audience keep track of each of your individual main points.

Tips for Preparing Main Points

There are three keys to developing your main points. First, keep each main point separate and distinct—don't combine points. Second, word your points consistently. Finally, devote appropriate coverage to each main point.

Keep each main point separate and distinct. To be as clear as possible, each main point should be a separate idea. Once you've identified your likely main points, double-check them to be sure you have not combined two ideas into one main point. We may be tempted to combine two ideas to cover as much information as we can. But notice what happened when Aaron combined two ideas into a single point in his second main point:

Ineffective main points	Effective main points
I. Electronic music is produced from a variety of machines that make noise electronically.	I. Electronic music is produced from a variety of machines that make noise electronically.
II. Electronic music has become more popular in recent years and is performed by many well-known artists.	II. Electronic music has become more popular in recent years. Electronic music is performed by many well-known artists.

Although both columns cover the same ground, the points in the right column are clearer because each addresses only one idea. By separating the two points, Aaron can avoid confusing or overwhelming his audience.

Practicing the Public Dialogue | 7.1

SELECT AN ORGANIZATIONAL PATTERN FOR YOUR SPEECH

As a class, brainstorm topics for speeches that could conceivably be arranged according to more than one of the organizational patterns discussed in this chapter. Choose one of these topics and then divide into five groups. Assign a different organizational pattern (chronological, spatial, causal, problem–solution, or topical) to each group. In your group, create a specific purpose, thesis statement, and as many as five main points for the topic using the organizational pattern you were assigned. Have each group present its results to the class. Then, as a class, determine which organizational pattern (or patterns) worked best for the topic. Why was this pattern more successful than the others? Use what you learned from this activity to select the most appropriate pattern for your next speech.

MindTap°

When you're ready to organize the main points of your next speech, you can use Outline Builder to help you.

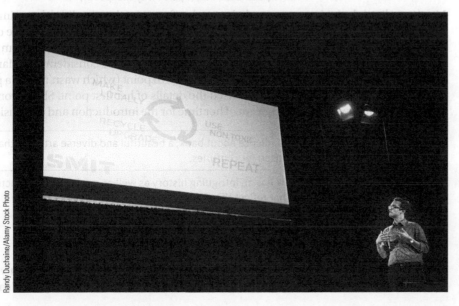

Randy Duchaine/Alamy Stock Photo

Speakers often use technology to help their audience members visualize and recall the ideas they are presenting. As you read about these different types of organizational patterns, begin to think about the kinds of technology you will use to help your audience follow your ideas.

Word your main points consistently. Try to word your main points as consistently as possible. A parallel structure is easier to organize and remember. In the next example, Michael presented an informative speech on the reasons for stop signs. Notice how the parallel main points in the right column are clearer and more memorable than those in the left column:

Ineffective main points	Effective main points
I. Drivers need to know who has the right of way, and a stop sign tells us that.	I. Stop signs assign the right of way to vehicles using an intersection.
II. Stop signs slow down drivers who are traveling at unsafe speeds.	II. Stop signs reduce the problem of speeding in certain areas.
III. Sometimes, pedestrians need protection from vehicles, and stop signs give them that protection.	III. Stop signs protect pedestrians in busy intersections or near schools.

With a simple reworking of phrasing, Michael made his main points parallel: Stop signs assign, stop signs reduce, stop signs protect. Although this kind of parallel structure is not always possible, your ideas will be clearer and more memorable when you can use it.

Devote the appropriate coverage to each main point. Remember that your main points are your most important ideas. Therefore, each point should receive the same level of development and attention in your speech. If you find yourself spending little time developing a particular point, ask yourself whether it really is as important as you thought and whether it should be a main point in your speech. If, on the other hand, you find yourself putting a lot of development into one point, consider if you should divide it into two points. In preparing a speech on the art of batik, Martha discovered the following imbalance:

Specific purpose	To inform my audience about batik, a beautiful and diverse art form that has been practiced for centuries.
Thesis statement	The art of batik has an intriguing history as well as methods of production and designs that reflect the skill and politics of the artisan.
Main points	I. The history of batik (*65 percent of the speech*)
	II. The production of batik (*15 percent of the speech*)
	III. The designs of batik (*15 percent of the speech*)
	IV. Where to purchase batik (*5 percent of the speech*)

Martha realized she had spent so much time on her first point that she didn't have time to cover her remaining points. Although the history of batik is important, it wasn't the only information she wanted to share with her listeners. She also wanted to show them the production process and some of the designs she loved. After some consideration, Martha reduced the scope of her speech by dropping her fourth point (which wasn't really a part of her thesis statement), and she condensed the details of her first point. She reworked her speech as follows, saving 20 percent of her time for the introduction and conclusion:

Specific purpose	To inform my audience about batik, a beautiful and diverse art form that has been practiced for centuries.
Thesis statement	The art of batik has an intriguing history as well as methods of production and designs that reflect the skill and politics of the artisan.
Main points	I. The history of batik (*30 percent*)
	II. The production of batik (*25 percent*)
	III. The designs of batik (*25 percent*)

Your goal, as Martha's revised main points suggest, is not necessarily to spend exactly the same amount of time on each point but to offer a balanced presentation of your ideas.

Extreme Engineering in the "Forbidden Zone"
Albert Yu-Min Lin: Explorer, Research Scientist, and Engineer

Courtesy of Albert Yu-Min Lin

Albert Yu-Min Lin, research scientist, engineer, and Explorer for National Geographic, has a passion for finding and preserving stories, especially as they help us understand our "collective cultural heritage." Lin and his team of explorers believe they may have found the tomb and last resting place of Genghis Khan, a leader the world knows little about but whose influence has been profound. Many Mongolians consider the tomb an extremely sacred place and believe any desecration could trigger a curse that would end the world. According to Lin, the world does not know the full story of Khan's life or contributions.

The tomb, located in Mongolia's "Forbidden Zone," represents a discovery that has eluded historians and scientists for centuries. Yet Lin and his team are not going about this potential discovery with the traditional excavation methods, because, Lin explains, "using traditional archeological methods would be disrespectful to believers." Instead, Lin's team is using advanced technology that "leverages photographs taken firsthand on the ground, images gathered from satellites and unmanned aircraft, GPS tracks from expeditions, and geophysical instruments." Although finding the tomb represents years of attempting to communicate to others that he could indeed find it, honoring cultural beliefs and traditions is also paramount to Lin. As he explains, "there are many ways to look under the ground without having to touch it." Communicating respect for the beliefs and practices of cultures is central, and now:

> the ability to explore in a noninvasive way lets us try to solve this ancient secret without overstepping cultural barriers. It also allows us to empower Mongolian researchers with tools they might not have access to otherwise. Today's world still benefits from Genghis Kahn's ability to connect East with West. He forged international relations that have never been broken.

By locating his tomb, we hope to emphasize how important it is for the world to protect such cultural heritage treasures.

A few years ago, Lin shares, he thought he was destined to be stuck in an office in a job he did not love. Following his family's heritage and his grandfather's words, he left the United States for Mongolia, finding "a world that had changed little in a millennium. And at its core [was] Genghis Khan." Lin states, "Engineers are really just explorers, pushing the limits of what we think we can do." He realized he could be a scientist and still do "crazy extreme things, and that's what I wanted to do."[5]

WHAT DO YOU THINK?

1. Lin uses a different approach to collecting his data. How many of the organizational patterns discussed in this chapter do you think he could use effectively to present his data?

2. Lin and his team are not sure, but they believe they could have found a tomb in the Forbidden Zone that might be Genghis Khan's tomb. Draft a specific purpose and thesis statement for a speech Lin might give about this discovery. How many main points would this speech have? How might he organize them?

Jun Mu/Shutterstock.com

Connectives

Your main points are the heart of your speech. Once you have them on paper and supported them with your research, you must find ways to connect them to enhance the audience's understanding. The words and phrases we use to link ideas in a speech are called **connectives**. They show audiences the relationship between ideas.

Before you read the descriptions of the four types of connectives, consider some of the connectives that speakers use unconsciously: "all right," "next," "now," "um," "and," "so," "so then," and "ah." These words or sounds are often called *fillers* because they tell the audience very little about the relationship between ideas. Fillers can be annoying, especially when the same one is repeated often in a speech. The following section offers four useful alternatives to these fillers. Transitions, internal previews, internal summaries, and signposts add meaning and help your audience remember your ideas.

Transitions

Transitions are phrases that indicate you are finished with one idea and are moving to a new one. Effective transitions restate the idea you are finishing and introduce your next one. In the following examples, the transitions are underlined:

> Now that you understand how our childhood memories influence our relationship to money, let's explore the relationship we have to money as adults.

> Once you've visited Manarola, you're ready to move to the final village, Riomaggiore, also known as "the village of love."

You can consciously insert transitions such as "Let's turn to," "Now that you understand," "In addition to," and "That brings me to my next point." But many will come naturally as you close one point or idea and begin a new one. Use transitions to link ideas within your main points and guide your audience from point to point as you deliver your speech.

Internal Previews

An **internal preview** is a statement in the body of your speech that details what you plan to discuss next. Internal previews focus on what comes next in the speech rather than linking two points as transitions do. Internal previews are very similar to the preview you offer in the introduction of a speech (Chapter 8), but you use them to introduce a new point rather than the entire speech. In the next example, Martha introduces her second point, batik production, with an internal preview:

> In discussing the production of batik, I'll explain the four steps: the preparation of the cloth, the mixing of the dyes, the application of the dye, and the setting of the image in the cloth.

After hearing this preview, the audience is ready for four steps and begins to appreciate the intricacies of the batik process. Internal previews are often combined with transitions, as in Robert's discussion of theatrical lighting:

> As you can see (transition), with the invention of the lightbulb came exciting and safer possibilities for theatrical lighting. And the now familiar lightbulb takes me to my third point (internal preview), the invention of three instruments that revolutionized lighting in the theater: the ellipsoidal, the Fresnel, and the Intellabeam.

Not every main point requires an internal preview, but the unfamiliar terminology in Robert's third point lends itself to a preview. Introducing new concepts or terminology before offering the details enhances your audience's understanding of your topic.

connective: Word or a phrase used to link ideas in a speech.

transition: Phrase that indicates a speaker is finished with one idea and is moving on to a new one.

internal preview: Statement in the body of a speech that details what the speaker plans to discuss next.

Internal Summaries

An **internal summary** is a statement in the body of your speech that summarizes a point you've already discussed. If you've just finished an important or complicated point, add an internal summary to remind your audience of its highlights. In Jeremy's speech on sibling rivalry, he used an internal summary at the end of the first point:

> To summarize, the causes of sibling rivalry—birth order, sex, parental attitudes, and individual personality traits—can cause children to compete for their parents' affection and attention.

Like internal previews, internal summaries can be combined with transitions so you can move efficiently into your next point. Here's an example from Brandon's speech:

> In short (internal summary), the lack of funding for before- and after-school meal programs leads to poor academic performance, increased absences, and behavioral problems. But let's see (transition) what this bond issue will do to remedy many of these problems.

Internal summaries are excellent tools when you want your audience to remember key points before you move on to a new idea. When combined with transitions, internal summaries can help audiences move smoothly from one idea to the next.

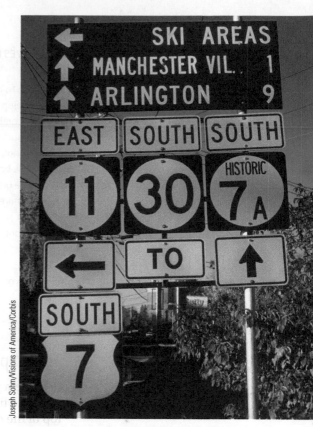

Joseph Sohm/Visions of America/Corbis

Signposts

A **signpost** is a simple word or statement that indicates where you are in your speech or highlights an important idea. Signposts tell your audience where you are in the presentation of your main points and help your listeners keep track of a detailed discussion or list of items. These tools add clarity to a speech and can make it flow. Signposts can be numbers ("first," "second," "third"), phrases ("The most important thing to remember is," "You'll want to make note of this"), or questions you ask and then answer ("So, how do we solve this dilemma?"). In Alex's speech on women in glory sports, she asked questions to introduce each of her main points.

For her first main point, she asked:

"How many of you know who Carissa Moore is?"

For her second, she asked:

"So, you didn't know Carissa Moore. How about Lizzie Armanto? Can anyone tell me her accomplishments?"

And for her third, she asked:

"Okay, I'll give you one more try. Who knows Jenny Jones' contributions to the world of glory sports?"

Although you don't want to overuse these kinds of questions, they can be effective in getting audience members involved in your speech because they will try to answer the questions in their own heads before you do.

The final use of signposts is to mark the most important ideas in your speech. When you hear or use any of the following phrases, it's a signpost asking the audience to pay close attention:

1. The most important thing to remember is . . .
2. If you hear nothing else from today's speech, hear this . . .
3. Let me repeat that last figure for you . . .
4. This next point is crucial to understanding my arguments . . .

Transitions, internal previews, internal summaries, and signposts are like highway signs that help your audience see where you're going in your speech. Where will you include connectives in your next speech to best show your audience how your ideas relate to one another?

internal summary: Statement in the body of a speech that summarizes a point a speaker has already discussed.

signpost: Simple word or statement that indicates where you are in your speech or highlights an important idea.

Practicing the Public Dialogue | 7.2

PREPARE THE MAIN POINTS AND CONNECTIVES FOR
YOUR SPEECH

Bring your thesis statement for your next speech to class. With a partner, discuss the main points you prepared to develop your thesis statement. Are your main points distinct? If you have combined your points,
separate them. Next consider the phrasing of your main points. Have
you used a parallel structure to word each one? If not, revise your wording so your points are parallel. Now consider how balanced your main
points are. If you suspect you're spending too little or too much time on
a point, adjust it so the coverage of each point is more balanced. Finally,
identify the places within or between your main points where a connective would add clarity or help you move from one idea to the next.

MindTap

You can use Outline Builder to help you create your main points and
connectives for your next speech.

You should use this kind of signpost only once in a
speech. If you use it more often, the audience quickly
loses confidence that what you are about to say is really "the most important thing."

The Preparation Outline

The **preparation outline** is a detailed outline of your
speech that helps you evaluate the organization of
your ideas. The preparation outline consists of your
speech's title, specific purpose, thesis statement, introduction, main points and subpoints, connectives,
conclusion, and source citations. It contains enough
detail for you to verify that your speech is fully organized and complete, but it does not include every
word you will say. Note that it's best to begin creating
a preparation outline as soon as you begin working on
your speech.

Title, Specific Purpose, and Thesis Statement

Because a preparation outline helps focus your ideas and organize your materials,
write the title of your speech and your specific purpose and thesis statement at the
top of the outline. The title of a speech usually comes from its specific purpose and
thesis statement because both indicate the theme of your speech. A good title also
reflects the tone of your speech. Let's take a look at how Brooke and Katy titled their
speeches.

Brooke:

Title	The World's Fire
Specific purpose	To inform my audience about the history and legends of the chili pepper.
Thesis statement	The history of the chili pepper includes global, national, and personal stories.

Katy:

Title	Why Pi?
Specific purpose	To inform my audience about the number pi.
Thesis statement	Pi, a fascinating number with an unusual history, has become an obsession for some people.

Both speakers chose simple, yet appropriate, titles for their speeches. Their titles reflect the content of their speeches, which is explicitly stated in their specific purposes
and thesis statements. (Katy's complete preparation outline for her speech "Why Pi?"
is featured at the end of this section.)

Introduction

You'll read much more about introductions in Chapter 8, but here we'll discuss how
to incorporate this part of a speech into an outline. An introduction should do four
things: catch your audience's attention, reveal your speech topic, establish your credibility, and preview your main points. Identify these four steps in your preparation
outline. This will help you be sure you have included each of them in your introduction. Here's how Nathan and Brooke outlined their introductions.

preparation outline: Detailed outline a
speaker builds when preparing a speech
that includes the title, specific purpose,
thesis statement, introduction, main
points and subpoints, connectives,
conclusion, and source citations of the
speech.

Nathan:

  I. How far do you think you can walk? (*catch attention*)

      A. A hike from Georgia to Maine will put you on the Appalachian National Scenic Trail. (*reveal topic*)

      B. I've hiked this trail twice in my life, the most recent time being last summer. (*establish credibility*)

 II. Today, I'd like to share with you a brief history of this trail, some facts about the trail and how it's maintained, and stories from some people who've hiked the trail. (*preview main points*)

Brooke:

  I. The words *chilly*, *chili*, and *Chile* refer to cold weather, spicy beans, and a country in South America. (*catch attention*)

      A. Today, I'm speaking about the chili pepper. (*reveal topic*)

      B. The Chile Today website says the chili pepper has conquered taste buds and cuisines for 10,000 years. (*catch attention and establish credibility*)

      C. To me, the chili pepper is a legend, story, and tale. (*establish credibility*)

 II. The chili pepper legends I'll discuss come from a variety of stories. (*preview main points*)

      A. Some stories are found across the globe.

      B. Others are the national stories originating in our own country.

      C. My final story is a personal one about my grandfather, the person who introduced me to the chili pepper's legacy. (*also establishes credibility*)

In these examples, the speakers summarized their introductions in outline form. These outlines do not include the full text of the speeches but are synopses of the main ideas. By using this format, the speakers could see they included the four components of a strong introduction.

Main Points, Subpoints, and Sub-Subpoints

As you learned earlier in this chapter, the most important ideas in your speech are your main points. Your main points make up the body of your speech. When you want to elaborate on your main points, you use subpoints and sub-subpoints. A **subpoint** develops an aspect of a main point. A **sub-subpoint** goes deeper to develop an aspect of a subpoint. You can think of main points, subpoints, and sub-subpoints as moving from the whole to the parts, or from the general to the specific. Consider the following example from Kameron's speech on zebra mussels:

  I. Zebra mussels cause damage to every aspect of any aquatic ecosystem they encounter.

      A. They destroy the natural balance of the ecosystem.

          1. They consume all the food available to those lower on the food chain.

          2. Larger fish no longer have smaller fish to feed on.

      B. They form large colonies that attach themselves to any solid object, making it difficult for commercial enterprises.

          1. They congregate on buoys and markers, causing them to sink.

          2. They clog intake ports by attaching themselves to anything solid.

Notice that the main point (I) is developed and supported by the two subpoints (A and B). In addition, the subpoints are developed and supported by the sub-subpoints (1 and 2 under subpoints A and B). In addition, notice that the points are organized according to the principle of **coordination**, or arranging your points into successive levels, with the points on a specific level having equal importance.

Remember, a main point is the broadest, most comprehensive idea; a subpoint supports and develops the main idea; and a sub-subpoint supports and develops the subpoint.

subpoint: Point in a speech that develops an aspect of a main point.

sub-subpoint: Point in a speech that develops an aspect of a subpoint.

coordination: Process of arranging points into successive levels, with the points on a specific level having equal importance.

PROOF THAT ONE PERSON DOES COUNT

In the early 1990s, the former nation of Yugoslavia was being torn apart by bitter ethnic conflicts that were collectively known as the Yugoslav Wars. These wars quickly became infamous for the war crimes that were being committed, including mass ethic cleansing and the systematic rape of women as a tool of warfare. In the United States, Zainab Salbi and her new husband, Amjad Atallah, were horrified by media reports of the women who were being victimized during the wars. They wanted to volunteer to help but found that no organization was addressing the problem. So, instead of spending their honeymoon money on a trip, they used it to found Women for Women International, an organization that works to help women survivors of war from all over the world.

Women for Women International focuses on helping women recover from their wartime experiences to become fully participating citizens in their communities. The organization offers both direct aid and more lasting help in the form of job training

Andrew H. Walker/Getty Images

and leadership education. It also puts women in touch with one another with the goal of giving them a voice in regions of the world where women do not traditionally have one. Women for Women's philosophy is that "access of knowledge and expression of voice + access to and control of resources = lasting social and political change."

Salbi's passion for helping women who have survived war stems from her own

experiences. Born and raised in Baghdad, Iraq, she tried to live a normal life during wartime. "I learned to coexist with war," she says, often waking up to the sound of missiles hitting her neighborhood. And just a month after she moved to the United States at nineteen, Iraq invaded Kuwait and she was cut off from her parents. Her inability to help or be with her family during such a crisis motivated her to find a way to help others affected by war. "Yes, I am only one person," she says, "but I am proof that one person does count."[6]

🔄 YOU CAN GET INVOLVED

MindTap Learn more about Women for Women International. You can find many innovative ways to help, including opportunities to volunteer, shop for products made by women the organization helps, and sponsor a "sister." You can also explore Girls Inc., a youth organization that helps U.S. girls "confront subtle societal messages about their value and potential, and prepares them to lead successful, independent, and fulfilling lives."

Conclusion

You'll read much more about conclusions in Chapter 8, but here we'll discuss how to incorporate this part of a speech into an outline. The conclusion has two goals: to signal the end of the speech and to reinforce your thesis statement. As you outline your conclusion, make sure it meets these goals. Like your introduction, the outline of the conclusion isn't a word-for-word transcript. Rather, it's a summary of what you'll say. Let's take a look at how Nathan and Will outlined the conclusions to their speeches.

Nathan:

    I. So, now do you think you could walk from New York to Chicago or from Georgia to Maine? (*bring speech to an end*)

    II. Even if you're not up for the hike, many people have hiked the 2,200-mile-long footpath to raise funds, overcome disabilities, and seek out spiritual insights. (*reinforce thesis statement*)

Will:

    I. As you've seen in these few minutes, ideas that were once regarded as fiction may soon be reality. (*bring speech to an end*)

    II. Although there are ethical questions and concerns, germ-line engineering and cloning may soon be processes that are used every day. (*reinforce thesis statement*)

Connectives

As we discussed earlier, connectives are words and phrases used to link ideas in a speech, and they come in four varieties: transitions, internal previews, internal summaries, and signposts. Because most connectives are only a single sentence, simply write them out rather than outline them. By writing out your connectives, you can easily see if you've overused a phrase (for example, "Now let's" again and again), and you can see which points you might clarify with internal previews, summaries, or both. In her speech on crazy lawsuits, Cassie previewed her main points in her introduction, wrote the connective to her first main point, and then outlined her first main point:

Connective	Let's begin by looking at some definitions.

    I.   Three terms come up in most of these cases.
        A.   The first term is *tort*.
        B.   The second term is *civil suit*.
        C.   The third term is *frivolous lawsuit*.

Similarly, Kelly used a transition in his speech on the Japanese language to get from his first main point to his second:

Connective	Now that I've introduced you to some Japanese body language, I would like to discuss a little bit about spoken Japanese.

And in his speech on germ-line engineering, Will incorporated an internal summary into his preparation outline and then moved on to cloning, his next main point:

Connective	As you've just heard, germ-line engineering combines the age-old idea of manipulating DNA strands through selective breeding of animals and the newer research that is unpacking the human DNA code. But this isn't the only radical idea around today.

Include connectives between the major sections of your preparation outline (introduction, body, and conclusion) and between main points to help track your transitions from one idea to the next.

Works Cited

The final component of your preparation outline is a list of the works you have cited in your speech. Follow the guidelines required by your instructor for preparing a preliminary bibliography, such as the guidelines for the Works Cited list of the Modern Language Association (MLA) or the References list of the American Psychological Association (APA). For guidelines for these bibliographic styles, see Figure 5.3 in Chapter 5.

Unless your instructor indicates otherwise, include only the sources you actually cited orally in your speech. By listing sources, you'll see how many you relied on to build your arguments and establish your credibility. If you discover you have cited only one or two sources and think you need more, you can go back and rework sections of your speech to include additional citations. Remember, citing the work of others not only enhances your ideas and increases your credibility, but it is also ethical.

Tips for the Preparation Outline

There are three keys to building your preparation outline. First, use complete sentences. Second, label the introduction, body, conclusion, and connectives. Third, use a consistent pattern of symbols and indentation.

Keyword outline (incorrect)	Full-sentence outline (correct)

Keyword outline (incorrect)

I. The Tuskegee Airmen
  A. Four squadrons
  B. The elite 332nd
  C. Their names
II. Obstacles
  A. The first
  B. No officers
  C. Recognition

Full-sentence outline (correct)

I. The Tuskegee Airmen were an elite group of African American fighter pilots who fought during the Second World War.
  A. The first five men graduated from four different squadrons at the Tuskegee training center in Alabama.
  B. The Tuskegee Airmen were considered one of the Allies' strongest weapons.
  C. Because of their talents, the Tuskegee Airmen were given nicknames in both German and English.
II. Although history books now recognize these men as heroes, they had to overcome many obstacles to be allowed to fly.
  A. At first, they were not allowed to form a squadron because "no colored squadrons" were needed.
  B. They then were told no such unit was allowed because there were "no commissioned Negro officers" in the Air Force.
  C. Although they never lost a bomber they escorted, it wasn't until 1948 that the first African American pilot received his gold wings.

Figure 7.1 Keyword versus full-sentence outline

Use complete sentences. Always write your ideas in complete sentences. The difference between a full-sentence outline and a keyword outline is obvious when the two are compared, as in Figure 7.1. Although you do get a sense of Javad's topic and ideas in the keyword example, a full-sentence outline is a far more useful tool to help you prepare and track the components of your speech. A keyword outline gives you very little sense of how fully developed your ideas are and whether you have thought them through completely. In contrast, a full-sentence outline clearly shows how well your speech is organized, what the contents of each point are, where there are inconsistencies, and where more development might be needed.

Label the introduction, body, conclusion, and connectives. In addition to labeling the title, specific purpose, and thesis statement in your preparation outline, label the introduction, body, conclusion, and connectives. These labels mark each component of your speech and encourage you to consider each one separately. They also help you see how much time you are devoting to each section and avoid an introduction that is overly long or a conclusion that is too abrupt.

Use a consistent pattern of symbols and indentation. Outlines are based on the principles of **subordination**, or ranking ideas in order from the most to the least important. The most common way to indicate subordination in an outline is to use a traditional pattern of symbols and indentations. Main points are labeled with capital Roman numerals (I, II, III, and so on). Subpoints are labeled with capital letters (A, B, C, and so on). Sub-subpoints are labeled with Arabic numbers (1, 2, 3, and so on). Indentations help you visually indicate the subordination of ideas. Your main points are set farthest left, and each level of subpoints is indented progressively farther to the right. In a complex outline, you may

---

Practicing the Public Dialogue | 7.3

BUILD YOUR PREPARATION OUTLINE

Using the template provided by your instructor or the sample at the end of this section as a guide, build a preparation outline for your next speech. Start by creating a title and indicating your specific purpose and thesis statement. Then outline your introduction, your main points, subpoints, sub-subpoints, and your conclusion. Add connectives that will help you transition from one idea to the next. Finally, add a section of the works you intend to cite in your speech, following the format provided by your instructor or this book. As you prepare your outline, remember to incorporate the tips you've read in this chapter: translate incomplete sentences or keywords into full sentences; label the introduction, body, and conclusion of your speech; use the proper symbols to indicate your main points, subpoints, and sub-subpoints; indent your points properly; and correct any imbalances you discover in your points.

MindTap
You can use Outline Builder to help create your outline.

subordination: Process of ranking ideas in order from the most to the least important.

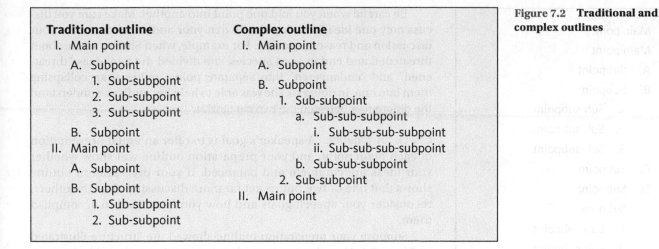

Figure 7.2 **Traditional and complex outlines**

Traditional outline
I. Main point
   A. Subpoint
      1. Sub-subpoint
      2. Sub-subpoint
      3. Sub-subpoint
   B. Subpoint
II. Main point
   A. Subpoint
   B. Subpoint
      1. Sub-subpoint
      2. Sub-subpoint

Complex outline
I. Main point
   A. Subpoint
   B. Subpoint
      1. Sub-subpoint
         a. Sub-sub-subpoint
            i. Sub-sub-sub-subpoint
            ii. Sub-sub-sub-subpoint
         b. Sub-sub-subpoint
      2. Sub-subpoint
II. Main point

need sub-sub-subpoints and even sub-sub-sub-subpoints. Label sub-sub-subpoints with lowercase letters (a, b, c, and so on), and label sub-sub-sub-subpoints with lowercase Roman numerals (i, ii, iii, and so on). Figure 7.2 gives examples of traditional and complex outlines.

When you indent, be sure you indent all the text that corresponds with the point, not just the first line of text. (This type of indent is called a *hanging indent*. You can use Word's numbering formatting feature or the margin tabs in the ruler at the top of your document to help create hanging indents.) This will help you see the ranking of each point clearly and emphasize the relationship your subpoints have to your main points.

Incorrect

  II. Although history books now recognize these men as heroes, they had to overcome many obstacles to be allowed to fly.
     A. At first, they were not allowed to form a squadron because "no colored squadrons" were needed

Correct

  II. Although history books now recognize these men as heroes, they had to overcome many obstacles to be allowed to fly.
     A. At first, they were not allowed to form a squadron because "no colored squadrons" were needed.

Divide points into at least two subpoints. When you support broad ideas with more specific ideas, you divide your points. For example, in Javad's speech about the Tuskegee Airmen, he discussed the three obstacles the men overcame in his second point. He divided this main point about overcoming obstacles into three subpoints: (1) the belief that there was no need for a "colored squadron," (2) the fact that there were "no commissioned Negro officers in the Air Force," and (3) the fact that they were not formally recognized as pilots until 1948.

Common sense tells us that when we divide a point, we must divide it into at least two parts because you cannot divide something into only one part. But what if a point doesn't seem to divide naturally into two or more parts? For example, when Cassie began working on her speech about frivolous lawsuits, she intended to define only one legal term, not three. Thus, she wound up with only one subpoint for her main point about definitions. To solve this dilemma, she could have folded the definition into another point. For example, she could have defined the term *tort* while describing her first crazy lawsuit. Instead, she decided to expand her original point about important definitions and ended up with three subpoints.

I. Main point
II. Main point
   A. Subpoint
   B. Subpoint
      1. Sub-subpoint
      2. Sub-subpoint
      3. Sub-subpoint
   C. Subpoint
   D. Subpoint
   E. Subpoint
      1. Sub-subpoint
      2. Sub-subpoint
      3. Sub-subpoint
      4. Sub-subpoint
      5. Sub-subpoint
III. Main point
   A. Subpoint
   B. Subpoint

Figure 7.3　Imbalanced outline

Be careful when you fold one point into another. Make sure you discuss only one idea in each point so that your audience can follow your discussion and reasoning easily. For example, when Shelley spoke about threatened and endangered species, she divided the two ideas "threatened" and "endangered" into separate points rather than collapsing them into one. In doing so, she was able to help her audience understand the differences between the two categories.

Check for balance. A speaker's goal is to offer an equal presentation of each main point, and your preparation outline will show whether your ideas are complete and balanced. If your presentation outline shows that one or two points get far more discussion than the others, reconsider your speech goals and how you have tried to accomplish them.

Suppose your preparation outline showed the structure illustrated by Figure 7.3. Note that the second main point is developed in far more detail than the first or third main point. In addition, subpoints B and E are more fully developed than the others are. The outline shows an imbalance that needs to be corrected. Either the speech can be refocused to make the second main point the thesis statement, or some material can be eliminated from the second main point and some material added to the other two main points.

PREPARATION OUTLINE WITH COMMENTARY

COMMENTARY

Katy indicates her specific purpose and thesis statement at the beginning of her preparation outline. This helps her stay audience centered, focused on her topic, and reminded of her speech goals.

She labels her introduction to help keep her place as she gives her speech. The outline of her introduction is very detailed to help her account for and identify the four components of a strong introduction.

Katy catches her audience's attention by reciting pi to thirty-one decimal places and by getting them curious about its presence in their lives.

In subpoint E, she reveals the topic of her speech.

Katy adapts her topic to her audience by indicating she knows her audience quite well—she recognizes they are all speech majors. She establishes her

Why Pi?

by Katy Mazz

Specific Purpose: To inform my audience about the number pi.

Thesis Statement: Pi, a fascinating number with an unusual history, has become an obsession for some people.

MindTap˙ Are you ready to build your preparation outline? Use the following outline as a model. The assignment was to give a four- to six-minute informative speech about any topic. Students were asked to create a preparation outline, to cite at least four sources, and to speak from a speaking outline. In addition, they were asked to end on a strong note. (You can read Katy's speaking outline later in this chapter and see a video clip of Katy's speech based on this outline in MindTap.)

Introduction

I.　3.1415926535897932384626433832795. *(catch attention)*
   A.　Most of you know the name of the number I just recited.
   B.　It is found in rainbows, pupils of eyes, sound waves, ripples in the water, and DNA.
   C.　It is a ratio that nature and music understand but that the mind cannot comprehend.
   D.　This number has sparked curiosity over the past 4,000 years.
   E.　I am talking about pi—not the dessert, but the circle ratio. *(reveal topic)*

II. I will try to present pi as the fascinating topic I think it is to a class of speech majors who wonder if they can survive a speech about math.
   A. I have researched this topic, finding information not only technical and historical but also fanatical. (*establish credibility*)
   B. My own interest came about when I was challenged to memorize more digits than a friend of mine.
III. I plan to inform you of what pi is, the history of pi, and how pi has created obsessions in people's lives. (*preview main points*)

Body

I. Even if you don't know what it represents, pi is a number that almost everyone is familiar with.
   A. When you divide the circumference of a circle by its diameter, the result will always equal pi.
      1. No matter the size of the circle, this division results in what is called the circle ratio.
      2. Although we refer to pi as 3.14 or 22/7, it is actually an irrational number, meaning that it cannot be represented as a fraction.
      3. The number pi is never ending—or is it?
      4. For ages, mathematicians have puzzled, and have been almost ashamed, that it is so difficult to find another value as simple as the circle ratio.
   B. Pi is more than just the circle ratio.
      1. According to David Blatner, who wrote *The Joy of Pi*, this value can be found in all fields of math and science, architecture, the arts, and even in the Bible.
      2. The world record for calculating pi to the greatest number of decimal places is 206 billion decimal places, calculated by Dr. Kanada at the University of Tokyo.

Transition: Although 206 billion digits have been calculated thus far, there was a time in antiquity when there was uncertainty about the second decimal place.

I. Woven among pi's infinite digits is a rich history, ranging from the great thinkers of ancient cultures to the supercomputers of the twentieth century.
   A. Four thousand years ago, there was no decimal system, compass, paper, or pencil, yet people still found ways to calculate pi.
      1. The Egyptians used a stake, a rope, and the sand to approximate pi as a little greater than 3.
      2. The Greeks, Babylonians, Israelites, Chinese, and Mesopotamians also studied the circle ratio, yet none of them were certain of the third decimal place.
   B. Whether pi is an infinite number remained a mystery until the sixteenth century.
      1. Petr Beckmann, a former professor of engineering at Colorado University, likes to call this period the age of the digit hunters, with each generation popping out more digits than the next.
      2. Keep in mind that at this point the electronic calculator had not yet been invented.
      3. Famous mathematicians of the time continued to break records for calculating pi.
   C. In the twentieth century, the invention of the computer allowed mathematicians to calculate pi to 16,000 digits, confirming that pi is infinite and totally random.

Transition: What is the fascination with pi that has caused people to be both fanatical and obsessed?

II. Blatner states, "People have calculated, memorized, philosophized, and expounded on" pi more than on any number in history.

credibility by indicating she has researched her topic and is personally interested in it.

In the last point of her introduction, Katy previews the three main points of her speech.

By marking the body of her speech with a heading, she can clearly see where she must shift from her introduction to her first main point.

Notice that she uses complete sentences for each point.

She divides her first main point into two subpoints. In the first one, she explains what pi is and what makes it unusual. Notice how she uses a rhetorical question in her third sub-subpoint to spark her audience's interest.

In subpoint B, Katy continues to explain what pi is. Again, she presents interesting information to help her audience appreciate pi's popularity and intrigue.

In her first transition, Katy briefly restates her last point and introduces her second point, the history of pi. She sets the transition off so she can find it easily and see she is moving on to her second main point.

Katy divides her second main point into three subpoints that help her develop her discussion of pi's rich history. She develops her argument chronologically, from ancient history to the present era. Notice her use of subordination and proper indentation of each new point.

Katy shares interesting historical facts about math that appeal to her audience of speech majors.

Note her interesting language: "the age of the digit hunters" and "each generation popping out more digits." In this point, she uses her research creatively and stays audience centered.

Katy brings her audience up to the present era with subpoint C.

By asking another rhetorical question, she previews her third main point.

In her final point, Katy explains the obsession some people have with the number pi. In her three subpoints, she discusses a different aspect of this obsession.

In subpoint A, Katy tells a story of the Chudnovsky brothers and the lengths to which they went to study pi.

Katy uses Goto as an example of someone obsessed with memorizing pi and then shares some memorization methods that are easier. Notice that subpoint B is slightly more developed than subpoints A or C but that her three subpoints still are fairly evenly balanced.

Her third subpoint wraps up her discussion of the obsession with pi, using a lighthearted story of a tradition she learned on the Ridiculously Enhanced Pi Page website.

Katy includes a transition in her summary by returning to one of her questions from earlier in her speech. Also note that she marks her conclusion as a distinct part of her outline.

Katy begins her conclusion by answering her question about why pi has caused such a craze. She then summarizes her main points.

Notice that the outline of her conclusion includes a lot of detail. This helps her (1) make sure she has incorporated the two aspects of a strong conclusion, and (2) see that her conclusion is shorter than her introduction and will take only a few moments to deliver.

Katy ends her speech with a quotation, leaving her audience with a strong sense of the mystique of the number pi.

Katy includes a bibliography of the specific research she references in her speech, using the MLA style. She prepared this speech in 2000, and note that her sources range from 1970 to 2000, indicating that she did both historical and current research. She also relies on both Internet and print sources, illustrating that she searched in several places for material rather than relying on only one kind of source.

A. The Chudnovsky brothers, Gregory and David, were both mathematicians from Russia who moved to New York to entertain their obsession with pi.
   1. In their own apartment, they built a supercomputer from scrap materials.
   2. With this computer, they were able to calculate more digits and to study its use in various formulas.
B. Other people try to memorize pi.
   1. Some do it for sport or to be silly, but others are more serious.
   2. Blatner states that in 1995, Hiroyuki Goto spent over nine hours reciting 42,000 digits of pi from memory, far exceeding the world record.
      a. This was a rare case, but there are methods of memorization for the average memory.
      b. Some people remember pi through poems, clever mnemonics, and songs.
      c. Some simply memorize the digits in groups of fours, which is the method I've found easiest.
C. So many people are obsessed with pi that the number is celebrated on Pi Day every March 14, or 3/14.
   1. The website Ridiculously Enhanced Pi Page suggests that you gather with friends at 1:59 p.m. to celebrate.
   2. At this time, eat pie and share personal stories about pi.

Summary and transition: So ends my analysis of people's obsessions, but my earlier question was not fully answered.

Conclusion

I. No one knows for sure why pi has caused such a craze or why several books, movies, and web pages have been devoted to this subject. (*bring speech to an end*)
   A. What inspired the Chudnovsky brothers to devote their lives to the search for pi?
   B. What inspired me to write a speech on a silly number?
   C. The answer lies in the mystery of pi: people explore pi because it is an adventure to do so.
II. Remember that pi is not only the circle ratio, not only the biggest influence on math over history, but also a number that has a great effect on people and an influence on everything we do. (*reinforce thesis and summarize main points*)
III. William Schaaf, in "The Nature and History of Pi," concludes that "probably no symbol in mathematics has evoked as much mystery, romanticism, misconception and human interest as the number pi."

Works Cited

Beckmann, Petr. *A History of Pi*. Golem Press, 1970.

Blatner, David. *The Joy of Pi*. Walker Publishing, 1997.

—. "Pi Facts." *The Joy of Pi*, www.joyofpi.com/pifacts.html. Accessed 20 Sept. 2000.

Ridiculously Enhanced Pi Page. *Exploratorium*, 1998, www.exploratorium.edu/pi/pi98/. Accessed 23 Sept. 2000.

Schaaf, William. "The Nature and History of Pi. *The Joy of Pi*, www.joyofpi.com/schaaf.html. Accessed 20 Sept. 2000.

Witcombe, Chris. "Earth Mysteries: Notes on Pi." *Brittania*, www.britannia.com/wonder/pi.html. Accessed 23 Sept. 2000.

National Geographic Explorer

Courtesy of Becca Skinner

BECCA SKINNER, Explorer and Photographer

How much preparation time goes into your presentations? And, how does your preparation time vary between shorter or longer presentations?

I think I have spent more time on the shorter presentations, because it's difficult for me to cut it down and to share the really important parts and all of my favorite photographs. I probably spend anywhere from two to seven hours working on presentations, and then I prep multiple, multiple times before I give them.

When you're actually giving the presentation, what kind of notes do you then use? Do you use bold full outlines or note cards?

I like making outlines with very few words, so when I look at my slide I can have a piece of paper that has maybe a bullet point or a couple of key words that will remind me of what I want to say for that slide. And once I practice, then I tend not to look at the notes; they're there for me just in case. An outline is typically what I use.

The Speaking Outline

The **speaking outline**, sometimes called *speaking notes*, is a condensed form of your preparation outline that you use when speaking. Remember that you will almost never memorize a speech or read it from a manuscript. Most often, you will choose the exact words of your speech as you are giving it. Therefore, you need a speaking outline to help remember specific information that you plan to include in your speech. For example, your speaking outline might include the full text of quotations, statistics, names, and other material you want to remember exactly. It also includes delivery prompts, such as "Make eye contact," "Slow down," and "Breathe."

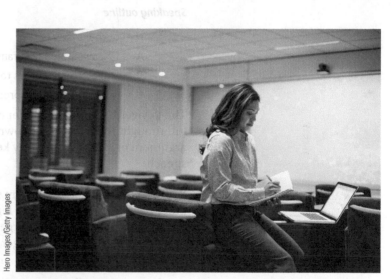

Hero Images/Getty Images

The most effective speakers make frequent eye contact with their audience and speak directly to them. Their speaking outlines encourage them to do this. Because speakers do not have the full text written out in front of them, they are not tempted to read to the audience. Instead, they rely on the ideas, words, and phrases in their speaking outline to remind them of what they want to say.

Although you may feel you will give a better speech if much of it is written out fully on your speaking outline, experienced speakers have found this simply isn't so. The most dynamic speakers are those whose speaking outlines only prompt their memories and enable them to engage their audiences directly.

Speaking outlines are very personalized documents. As you gain experience speaking, you will discover what you need to include in your outline and

You need your speaking outline to remember specific information you plan to use in your speech. Many speakers add delivery cues to their outlines to help them remember to pause, make eye contact, or use a visual aid. What delivery cues do you think you would use in your next speech?

speaking outline: Condensed form of a preparation outline that you use when speaking.

what you can leave out. For now, use the following tips to help build your speaking outline.

Tips for the Speaking Outline

There are three keys to developing your speaking outline. First, include only key words and phrases. Second, write clearly and legibly. Finally, add cues to help you with your delivery.

Use keywords and phrases. When you write your speaking outline, use keywords and phrases or abbreviated sentences. As you prepare this outline, think carefully about what words and phrases will help you remember your complete ideas. In the example here, notice how Graham reduced his full sentences to keywords, working from the larger idea to its most essential component:

Preparation outline

I. Many people are not aware of what a voucher system is.

   A. Voucher programs take taxpayers' money and give it to families.

      1. Families then use money to send children to the school of their choice.

      2. The school of choice could be either a public or private school.

   B. In theory, money that normally goes to public schools now is distributed to a range of schools.

   C. The program is touted as a new solution to the old problem of inadequate public education.

Speaking outline

I. The voucher system

   A. Taxpayers' money to families

   B. Money normally goes to public schools

   C. New solution to old problem

The keywords capture the essence of Graham's ideas and help him remember the full thought when he looks down at his notes. The keywords call to mind the full argument or explanation. They keep him talking and prevent him from reading his speech.

Write clearly and legibly. Many speakers print their speaking outline from a computer because the print is more legible than their handwriting. They also use a plain, easy-to-read font, often in a larger size than normal. (Similarly, speakers who write their outline by hand print larger than they normally do.) Notice the difference between these two font sizes:

Love conquers all.

Love conquers all.

Although in most writing we wouldn't use the larger font size, in a speaking outline the bigger letters make our speech much easier to deliver, especially if we're nervous.

Add cues for delivery. As you practice, notice where you tend to stumble, where you are too tied to the outline and forget to make eye contact, and where you move too quickly or slowly. Also notice where you have trouble with pronunciation or remembering what you want to say. Add cues to help you through these rough spots. Cues are words and phrases like "Slow down," "Pause," "Look up," "Show visual aid," and "Make eye contact." They also include the correct pronunciation of any words that are hard for you to say, especially names, or a word or two to help

MindTap

Use Outline Builder to build your outline.

Note card -9-

-9-

Transition:

What is the fascination with pi that has caused people to be both fascinated and obsessed?

(Pause)

III. As <u>Blatner</u> states, "People have calculated, memorized, philosophized, and expounded on" pi more than on any number in history.

Note card -10-

-10-

A. The Chudnovsky (chud-NOV-sky) brothers, Gregory and David.

  1. In their apartment, built a supercomputer from scrap.

  2. Calculated more digits and studied the use of pi in various formulas.

B. Many other people try to memorize pi.

  1. Some for sport or to be silly; others are more serious.

Note card -11-

-11-

  2. <u>Blatner</u> states that in 1995, Hiroyuko (he-roy-U-ko) Goto spent over nine hours reciting 42,000 digits of pi from memory, far exceeding the world record.

(Make eye contact)

    a. This was a rare case

Figure 7.4 Sample note cards

you remember a complete idea or a part of a story or example you tend to forget. Add this final component of your speaking outline after you've written it and have practiced your speech a few times. If you've printed your outline from a computer, handwrite your cues. If you've handwritten your speaking outline, use a different color for your cues. Be sure to keep the cues brief so they don't distract you from your audience and your speech.

Note Cards

Some speakers prefer note cards to a speaking outline (see Figure 7.4). Note cards (three-by-five or four-by-six inches) are smaller and less obvious than full sheets of paper. They also are sturdier and less likely to shake if a speaker's hands tremble. And they give us something to hold on to, sometimes making us feel a little more secure as we speak. If you feel more comfortable with note cards, follow these guidelines:

- Use keywords and phrases and place no more than five or six lines on each card. As with speaking outlines, do not write the full text of the speech on the cards.
- Write clearly and legibly. Print or type directly on the card, or if you handwrite your notes, use large, clear printing that is easy to read.
- Use only one side of the card. This reduces the likelihood that cards will get out of order during the speech.
- Number each card so you can easily reorder them if they get mixed up.
- Put cues for delivery on your cards so you can see them (use separate cards or different colors for these cues).
- When you deliver the speech, the cards should have a low profile. Try not to gesture with them, play with them, or tap them on the podium. You want the audience to pay attention to you, not the note cards.

COMMENTARY

At the top of her speaking outline, Katy makes notes to herself to breathe and make eye contact with her audience. She knows she'll be nervous, so she uses these notes to remind her to take a breath and look for friendly faces. She also makes a note to pause after she recites the digits of pi and before she goes on with her introduction.

Note that her introduction is an abbreviated version of the introduction in her preparation outline. She gives herself just enough cues to help her remember the four steps of her introduction.

To help with her delivery, Katy reminds herself to pause and make eye contact here before stating the topic of her speech.

She previews her speech in point III, stating her three main points.

Katy titles the body of her speech to remind her that she is moving to the main points. This is also a visual cue to help find her place after she makes eye contact with her audience.

She writes "slow" as she begins her first point to remind her to not rush through this information, which is new for many of her audience members.

Again, Katy gives herself enough text to remember her ideas, but not so much that she can fall prey to reading her speech to her audience.

Katy underlines the names of her sources and sets the numbers she wants to remember in bold so she'll deliver them correctly. Notice

Why Pi?
by Katy Mazz

MindTap® Katy based her speaking outline on her preparation outline, and she modified it in places to account for problems she encountered with her delivery as she practiced her speech. You can use your MindTap for *Invitation to Public Speaking* to watch a video clip of the speech Katy Mazz gave based on this outline.

(Breathe)

(Make eye contact)

Introduction

I.   3.14159265358979323846426433832795

(Pause)

   A. Most of you know the name of this number.
   B. In rainbows, pupils of eyes, sound waves, ripples in the water, and DNA.
   C. Nature and music understand, but the human mind cannot quite comprehend.
   D. 4,000 years of curiosity.

(Pause)

(Make eye contact)

   E. I am talking about pi, the circle ratio.

II. Speech majors may wonder if they can survive a speech about math.

   A. My research turned up technical, historical, and fanatical information.
   B. What sparked my own interest.

III. Today, I'll share with you what pi is, the history of pi, and how pi has created obsessions in people's lives.

Body

I.   Pi is a symbol that most everyone is familiar with.
   A. The circumference of a circle divided by its diameter.

(Slow)

     1. This number is also called the circle ratio.
     2. We refer to pi as 3.14 or 22/7, but it is an irrational number.
     3. Pi's mysticism is due to the fact it's never ending—or is it?
     4. Mathematicians have long puzzled about values as simple as the ratio of a circle.
   B. Pi is more than the circle ratio.
     1. According to David Blatner, who wrote *The Joy of Pi,* this value can be found in all fields of math and science, architecture, the arts, and even the Bible.
     2. The world record for calculating pi to the greatest number of digits is 206 billion decimal places, calculated by Dr. Kanada at the University of Tokyo.

(Pause)

Although 206 billion digits have been calculated thus far, there was a time in antiquity when there was uncertainty of the second decimal place.

II. Pi has a rich history.
   A. Four thousand years ago, people could calculate pi, even without today's resources.
     1. The Egyptians approximated pi as a little greater than 3.
     2. The Greeks, Babylonians, Israelites, Chinese, and Mesopotamians were not certain of the third decimal place.
   B. The infinity of pi remained a mystery until the sixteenth century.
     1. <u>Petr Beckmann</u>, a former professor of engineering at <u>Colorado University</u>, calls this period "the age of the digit hunters, with each generation popping out more digits than the next."

2. Keep in mind there was still no electronic calculator.
3. Famous mathematicians continued to break records.
C. In the twentieth century, the invention of the computer allowed mathematicians to calculate pi to **16,000 digits**.

What is the fascination with pi that has caused people to be both fanatical and obsessed?

(Pause)

III. As Blatner states, "People have calculated, memorized, philosophized, and expounded on" pi more than on any number in history.
   A. The Chudnovsky (Chud-NOV-sky) brothers, Gregory and David.
      1. In their apartment, built a supercomputer from scrap.
      2. Calculated more digits and studied the use of pi in various formulas.
   B. Many other people try to memorize pi.
      1. Some for sport or to be silly; others are more serious.
      2. Blatner states that in 1995, Hiroyuki (He-roy-U-ke) Goto spent over nine hours **reciting 42,000 digits of pi from memory, far exceeding the world record.**

      (Make eye contact)

         a. This was a rare case.
         b. Some people remember pi through poems, mnemonics, and songs.
         c. Some memorize the digits in groups of fours.
   C. The number is celebrated on Pi Day every March 14, or 3/14.
      1. The Ridiculously Enhanced Pi Page suggests gathering at 1:59 p.m.
      2. Eat pie and share stories about pi.

So ends my analysis of people's obsessions, but my earlier question was not fully answered.

Conclusion

(Slow down!)

(Make eye contact)

I. No one knows why pi has caused such a craze.
   A. What inspired the Chudnovsky brothers?
   B. What inspired me?
   C. The answer lies in the mystery and adventure.
II. The biggest influence on math over history and influences everything we do.
III. William Schaaf, in "**The Nature and History of Pi**," concludes that **"probably no symbol in mathematics has evoked as much mystery, romanticism, misconception, and human interest as the number pi."**

Source: Adapted with permission from Katy Mazz.

that she sets entire quotes in bold so she can find them easily and deliver them correctly.

She makes a note to pause before her transition so she can shift her pace a little to signal she is moving to a new point. She also writes out her full transition to remind her to deliver it—she's concerned that her nervousness will cause her to skip it and jump into her second main point.

As she did in her first main point, she underlines sources and sets in bold the facts she wants to remember.

Again, Katy writes out her transition, this time including a signal to pause after the transition before she begins her final main point.

In point III, Katy adds the phonetic spelling (spelled as they should sound) of two names so she will be sure to pronounce them correctly.

Her note to make eye contact signals her to look directly at her audience after she delivers the startling statistics of nine hours and 42,000 digits. This will help emphasize her point that this feat is rare but that people really are obsessed with pi.

When she practiced her speech, Katy noticed she tended to rush through her conclusion. She added notes to slow down and make eye contact so she would take time to wrap up her speech.

Practicing the Public Dialogue | 7.4

BUILD YOUR SPEAKING OUTLINE

Using the template provided by your instructor or the sample at the end of this section as a guide, build a speaking outline for your next speech. Translate the complete sentences of your preparation outline into keywords and phrases that will help you remember key ideas as you give your speech. Review your outline to make sure your ideas are outlined and easy to follow visually. Also make sure your computer-written text or handwriting is easy to read from a distance. If it isn't, adjust your printing, fonts, or type sizes so they are clear and legible. Finally, save a copy of your outline on your computer or make a few photocopies of it.

As you practice your speech, add your delivery cues. If you find your outline is too messy after several rounds of practice and adjustments, print a new one and add only those cues that you find most helpful (or mark up one of your photocopies). Remember, your speaking outline should be legible. Too many notes and changes will make it hard to read.

Chapter Summary

Organization is the systematic arrangement of ideas into a clear and coherent whole.

- To achieve this clarity, you must identify the main points of your speech.
- Main points are the most important ideas in a speech, developed from your research or your thesis statement.
- Use the time limit of your speech as a guideline for determining your number of main points. If you have too many points to cover in the time allotted to speak, return to your thesis statement and narrow the scope of your presentation.
- Be sure each main point is separate and distinct, and that you use consistent wording for each point and devote the appropriate amount of coverage to each point.
- To show the relationships between your main points, use connectives: transitions, internal previews, internal summaries, and signposts.

Main points can be organized in five basic patterns.

1. Chronological
2. Spatial
3. Causal
4. Problem–solution
5. Topical

The preparation outline is the outline you use to prepare a speech.

- It contains your main points, subpoints, and sub-subpoints written out in complete sentences.
- This outline also includes the title of your speech, the specific purpose, and the thesis statement.
- It outlines your introduction and conclusion, labels each part of your speech clearly, and includes your connectives and a list of the research sources you plan to cite in the speech.

The speaking outline is the outline you use when you deliver your speech.

- Speaking outlines contain keywords and phrases rather than full sentences, ensuring that you will deliver your speech in a conversational manner.
- Some speakers prefer note cards to speaking outlines. Note cards are smaller and sturdier than a full sheet of paper.

Invitation to Public Speaking Online MindTap®

Now that you have read Chapter 7, use your MindTap Communication for *Invitation to Public Speaking* for quick access to the digital resources that accompany this text. These resources include

- **Study tools** that will help you assess your learning and prepare for exams (digital glossary, key term flash cards, review quizzes).
- **Activities and assignments** that will help you hone your knowledge and build your public speaking skills throughout the course, as well as help you explore public speaking

concepts online (web links), give you step-by-step guidance through the research, outline and note card preparation process (Outline Builder), watch and critique videos of sample speeches (Interactive Video Activities), and allow you to practice and present your presentation online using a speech video delivery, recording, and grading system (YouSeeU).

Key Concepts MindTap® Test your knowledge with online printable flash cards.

causal pattern (132)
chronological pattern (131)
connective (138)
coordination (141)
internal preview (138)
internal summary (139)
main points (129)
organization (128)
preparation outline (140)

problem–solution pattern (133)
signpost (139)
spatial pattern (132)
speaking outline (149)
subordination (144)
subpoint (141)
sub-subpoint (141)
topical pattern (134)
transition (138)

Review Questions

1. Write a specific purpose, thesis statement, main points, and subpoints for a speech on a topic of your choice. Now mix up those main points and subpoints and try to deliver a sketch of the speech to your classmates. Can they follow your organization? Why or why not?

2. Choose one of the following topics: M&M's candy, Valentine's Day, or finals week. Using each of the five patterns of organization discussed in this chapter, write a specific purpose, thesis statement, and main points for a speech about the topic you chose. What is the

emphasis in each speech, depending on its organizational pattern?

3. In class, write a possible speech topic on a three-by-five-inch card or a strip of paper. Pass your topic to your instructor. Your instructor will select several topics, ask you to get into groups of five, and distribute a topic to each group. With your group, write the specific purpose, thesis statement, and main points for a speech. Also write connectives for the speech, including each of the four types of connectives discussed in this chapter. Now deliver the sketch of your group's speech to the class (be sure to use your connectives).

4. Imagine you're going to give a speech describing your day from breakfast through dinner. Prepare a preparation outline for this speech. Make sure your outline includes the title of your speech, your specific purpose and thesis statement, an introduction, four main points with at least two subpoints per main point, connectives, and a conclusion.

5. Using the preparation outline from question 4, construct a speaking outline for your speech on your day. Add delivery cues as needed. Discuss the differences between your preparation outline and your speaking outline. What are the strengths and weaknesses of each?

8 | Introductions and Conclusions

IN THIS CHAPTER, YOU WILL LEARN TO:

- Explain the four functions of an effective introduction
- Prepare a compelling introduction
- Summarize the two functions of an effective conclusion
- Prepare a compelling conclusion
- Apply the four tips for preparing both an introduction and a conclusion

Introductions, even short ones, make an audience more willing to listen to a speech, think more highly of the speaker, and understand the speech better.[1] At the end of the speech, conclusions reinforce thesis statements, remind listeners of main points, and frame the speaker's ideas and arguments in just the way he or she wants. Because the introduction and the conclusion are such important parts of a speech, they require special consideration. In this chapter, you will learn the basic techniques for developing each. As you read the following discussions, keep in mind that your introduction and conclusion frame the way you enter and exit the public dialogue.

MindTap Start with a quick warm-up activity and review the chapter's learning objectives.

▲ An introduction can draw an audience into a speech and pique their curiosity about your topic. A conclusion can bring closure and even motivate your audience to take action. In this chapter you will find strategies for developing effective introductions and conclusions for your speeches.

The Introduction

Your introduction is your first contact with your audience. In the opening words of your speech, you set the stage for what's to come, connect your audience to your topic, and establish your purpose for speaking. Introductions are like first impressions—they are important and lasting. Because of this, introductions require all of your audience analysis skills (Chapter 4). To develop an introduction that allows you to connect with your audience in the way you want, consider the four functions of any introduction:

1. Catch the audience's attention
2. Reveal the topic to the audience
3. Establish credibility with the audience
4. Preview the speech for the audience

Notice that each objective is highly audience centered. Thus, you need to design your introduction, like the body of your speech, with your audience in mind. In each of the four components of the introduction, you consider the audience's perspectives and the reason the audience is listening to your speech as well as your own goals. Let's take a closer look at each component and then at some techniques for implementing them in your introduction.

Catch the Audience's Attention

One of the most important tasks you have as a speaker is to capture the attention of your audience. You want your audience to listen to you and be intrigued and curious about your topic. When you catch audience members' attention, you not only pique their curiosity but also show them how the topic relates to them. Keep in mind that however you get your audience interested in your topic, to act ethically you must be honest, respectful, and behave in a manner consistent with the principles of an open and healthy public dialogue.

Reveal the Topic of Your Speech

In your introduction, you also want to let the audience know the subject of your speech. Although guessing games can be fun, your audience wants to know what you will be discussing. Keeping them in suspense for a moment or two is fine, but your introduction should reveal your topic before you begin your first main point.

Establish Your Credibility

As you've learned, to be credible is to gain the trust of your audience and to communicate to listeners that you have considerable knowledge of your topic. If audience members regard you as credible and competent, they will believe they have good reasons to listen to your ideas. Establishing credibility contains an ethical dimension. Audiences do not like to be lied to or misled. If you distort your credibility on a subject, then your audience is less likely to believe you or be influenced by your speech.

Preview Your Speech

The fourth component of an introduction is to preview the main points of the speech. In your **preview**, you share with your audience a brief overview of each of the main points in your speech. Previews communicate to your audience that you are organized and competent. In setting the stage for the body of the speech, previews help listeners organize their thoughts about your topic and mentally prepare for what you're going to say next.

preview: Brief overview in the introduction of a speech of each of the main points in the speech.

"Water Is Life"

Alexandra Cousteau, Explorer and Social Environment Advocate

© Bill Zelman

Take a sip of water—what do you taste and see? To Alexandra Cousteau, daughter of Philippe and Jan Cousteau, and granddaughter of the legendary Jacques Cousteau, "Water is life." We must redefine our relationships to it and our decisions around it. Cousteau established the Blue Legacy initiative, and she and her team are in the process of working with people around the world to "help shape society's dialogue to include water as one of the defining issues of our century." Cousteau and her team are also combining the technologies developed in her grandfather's era with new media opportunities to create platforms for individuals concerned about the environment to speak out about water. And she is undertaking an exploration of many of the world's most precious water ecosystems to chronicle their connectivity and link to our own survival.

Cousteau and her team travel around the world telling the story of our water systems and their centrality to sustaining life on this planet. This story includes the Ganges River in India, "the cultural and spiritual lifeblood" of a nation. The Ganges provides water and spiritual cleansing to more than 400 million people, yet it is literally toxic. More than 400 tannery factories along the river pump more than 20 million liters of waste every day, not to mention raw sewage, into this most sacred of rivers. The story continues in Botswana, where, in a land that is mostly desert, she continues to explore the interconnected nature of water. In an interview with Onkokame Kitso Mokaila, Botswanian minister of the environment, wildlife, and tourism, Cousteau asks how Botswana, a landlocked country, views water as its most precious commodity. Mokaila responds: "All living things require water, whether you are in agriculture, tourism, or wildlife. . . . You have to treat it as gold." Cousteau and her team continue their work and their story as they travel to the Middle East, Mississippi, and Cambodia (forty-five major water sources in all) chronicling "the interconnectivity of water . . . what it means to live in a world where water is our most precious resource."[2]

To tell her story, Cousteau relies on the most recent Internet technologies. And even though her father and grandfather were pushing the edge of technological advances, Cousteau explains that where the *Calypso* carried a crew of thirty people in the field for months and sent film back to Los Angeles for development, today she is able to work for three months in the field with a crew of only seven and post her stories immediately. She sees this as truly engaging people and as a truly interactive experience. Working with others and media in this way is very exciting for Cousteau. "From a communication standpoint, to be able to engage people through their networks and give them stories to talk about and start conversations around is one of our greatest opportunities" for change. Where 50,000 people see a movie in a theater, "I can reach 50,000 people in a day and maybe in an hour with this next expedition."[3]

Cousteau and her team present information on panels and at symposiums and even narrate videos and interview individuals who are working in environmental preservation.

WHAT DO YOU THINK?

1. Cousteau uses technology to capture and disseminate her story about the centrality of water in our lives. What are some of the ways you might use technology to capture your audience's attention in your next speech?
2. Identify the topic of your next speech. What compelling story, question, or intriguing statement could you make about that topic as you introduce your speech? Use the example of Cousteau and her passion for water to help you generate interesting and ethical ideas.

Paul Sutherland/National Geographic Creative

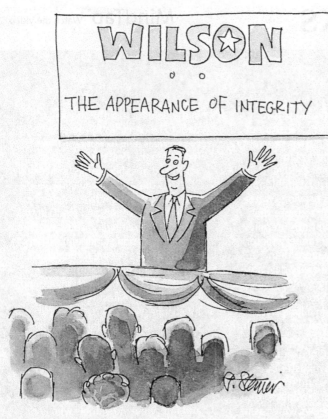

WILSON
o o
THE APPEARANCE OF INTEGRITY

© The New Yorker Collection 2000 Peter Steiner from cartoonbank.com. All Rights Reserved.

Establish your credibility early in your introduction so your audience understands why you're qualified to speak on your topic. But be careful to represent your expertise accurately and ethically. Audiences don't like to be misled.

Preparing a Compelling Introduction

There are several creative ways to gain your audience's attention, reveal your topic, establish your credibility, and preview your speech. Let's look at some techniques that will help you prepare compelling, memorable introductions.

Ask a Question

A question can arouse your listeners' curiosity and capture their attention. A question can also reveal the topic of your speech—the answer should relate to your topic. Sometimes, speakers use a **rhetorical question**, a question, used for effect, that the audience isn't supposed to answer out loud but rather in their own minds. At other times, speakers may ask questions to solicit answers directly from the audience. In the next two examples, Nathan asks rhetorical questions and supplies his own answers, and Cassie solicits answers from her audience before revealing the topic of her speech:

> Do you think you could walk from New York to just beyond Chicago? How about from Georgia to Maine? If you're up for such a hike, take the route from Georgia to Maine—that will put you on the Appalachian National Scenic Trail, a trail that stretches over 2,000 miles and traverses fourteen states. This trail is also the topic of my speech today.

> You've heard of the game "Strange but True"? Play with me for a minute. I'll read the headline, and you tell me if it's true or not. Ready? Okay.
> "Surfer Sues Surfer for Theft of Wave." True or false?
> "Deaf Bank Robber Wins Suit: Courts Say Alarm Exploited His Disability." True or false?
> "College Student Falls Out Fourth-Story Window during Mooning Prank: Sues University for Negligence." True or false?
> Each of these lawsuits is real, and these "crazy lawsuits" are the subject of my speech today.

Beginning a speech with a question, whether or not rhetorical, encourages active listening by your audience. Thus, questions can prevent your audience from sitting back passively as you speak. If you open your speech with a question, be sure it relates directly to your topic, and remember to pause after each question so audience members have time to answer it either aloud or in their heads.

MindTap®

Watch a video clip of student speaker Brandi Lafferty telling a story in her introduction.

rhetorical question: Question, used for effect, that an audience isn't supposed to answer out loud but rather in their own minds.

Tell a Story

A second way to capture your audience's attention and reveal your topic is to tell a story. Remember from Chapter 6 that stories, or narratives, draw an audience into your speech by offering characters and dramas they can relate to. Stories also personalize topics that might seem remote or disconnected to some audience members. Notice how Brandi uses language creatively to draw her audience into her story.

> It seemed like such a harmless thing to do. What could be wrong with putting out a little food to help the foxes and deer make it through a hard winter? Besides, seeing wildlife in your backyard is one of the many benefits to living in Colorado. Or so thought a family who set out dog food, hamburger, and grains for foxes and deer near their home in

the wooded foothills just outside Denver. But guess who also came to dinner? Tasty treats left in the family's backyard lured hungry mountain lions into the neighborhood. Not only did the wild cats like the hamburger, but they also had their eyes on one of their favorite prey, the deer.

It didn't take long for the real trouble to start. Residents' cats and dogs began disappearing from their yards. Fear and anger set in, and people began calling officials to do something about the mountain lions. What started as a well-meaning effort for deer and foxes ended in the death of one of Colorado's favorite wild animals. The mountain lion was killed in a trap set out to make the neighborhood safe again.

Hi, my name is Brandi Lafferty, and today I'd like to describe some of the negative consequences associated with feeding big game wildlife and encourage you to help keep our wildlife wild.

Kathryn Scott Osler/Denver Post/Getty Images

If you use a story in your opening, be sure it relates directly to your topic and clearly connects to the body of your speech. Sometimes, it's tempting to tell a great story just because it's a great story. Avoid this pitfall and use only stories that help introduce your topic.

Most people enjoy a good story, so telling one is a particularly effective way to catch an audience's attention. What are some interesting stories from your life that you could tell in the introduction to a speech? Would one of these stories relate to the topic of your next speech?

Recite a Quotation or a Poem

You also can catch your audience's interest and reveal your topic through a quotation or poem. Quotations lend your speech the credibility of someone more famous or knowledgeable than you are. They also can teach lessons or illustrate perspectives that are relevant to your speech. Quotations can be quite simple or fairly complex. In a speech on adoption, Chad began with a simple quotation:

> Dennis Rainey, author of the book *One Home at a Time,* states, "I have a wife and six children, two of which are adopted—but I can't remember which ones."

Speaking about the terrorist attacks on New York City and Washington, D.C., in September 2001, Mike began with a more complex quotation:

> Mohandas K. Gandhi said, "When I despair, I remember that all through history the way of truth and love has always won. There have been murderers and tyrants, and for a time they can seem invincible. But in the end they always fail. Think of it: always."

In the next example, Jessica begins her speech with a poem to set the tone and reveal her topic:

> May your thoughts be as glad as the shamrocks,
> May your heart be as light as the song.
> May each day bring you bright happy hours,
> That stay with you all year long.
> For each petal on the shamrock,
> This brings a wish your way—
> Good health, good luck, and happiness
> For today and every day.

> When some hear this Irish blessing, they think of a three-leaf clover. Others think of Ireland or St. Patrick. My family has its roots in Ireland, and we always think of all three. The shamrock has a long history of meaning for the Irish, and it represents the magical number 3. To fully understand the importance of the shamrock, though, you need to know how it became the symbol of Ireland. You must also understand how St. Patrick used it, and how it is represented every year by St. Patrick's Day. Even if you're not Irish, a little bit of information about the shamrock will help you enjoy your next March 17 celebration or understand those who make such a big deal of it.

HOW YOUR PUBLIC SPEAKING SKILLS CAN HELP YOU KEEP THAT NEW JOB

According to the PRSA jobcenter, employees need to prove their commitment to a new job, as well as their "fit" with a company in just nine weeks. Employers not only quickly evaluate a new employee's skill set but also consider how compatible the person is with the culture of the workplace and how well they collaborate with coworkers. Rookies make six common mistakes.[4] Fortunately, there are ways to avoid them, and your public speaking skills can help:

1. **Clarify expectations.** Within the first few days, new employees should meet with their managers to learn the priorities of their jobs, how they will be evaluated, and how they should communicate with bosses and coworkers. Use your research skills (Chapter 5) and your interview skills (Chapter 5) to help you to get an overview of the "big picture": How does your job fit into the larger goals and visions of the company? Request "continual feedback" so you can make sure you are performing up to expectations.

2. **Watch others.** Learn and observe from your coworkers. Pay attention to their habits and communication styles and how they collaborate with others. Your listening skills (Chapter 2) will help you learn the norms and practices of your new workplace.

3. **Be enthusiastic.** Even if the job is not your dream job, keep a positive and upbeat attitude. Your enthusiasm will put you in a better light for a future promotion—or help you move to the job you really want. Use your visualization and affirmation skills (Chapter 1) to help you with your attitude.

4. **Make friends.** Take time to get to know your coworkers and socialize a bit with them. Take an interest in them and ask about tips for success. Introduce yourself to project managers and people you will be working closely with or reporting to. These people can help you learn the expectations and culture of your new job. Understanding master statuses, cultural differences, and the role of gender (Chapter 4) will help you get to know people honestly and ethically.

5. **Mind your meeting manners.** At those first meetings, pay attention to the communication styles, leaders, group roles, and culture and climate of the organization. Notice whether people take notes, bring laptops, follow agendas, speak out, or are quiet. Once you know the culture of meetings, take steps to follow that culture so you fit in. Your audience analysis skills (Chapter 4) and your organizational skills (Chapter 7) will be of great help here.

6. **Wait to suggest change.** Unless you have been hired to change an organization, do not suggest changes until you have built relationships and established trust. Rookie employees need to earn the trust and respect of their coworkers and bosses. Take note of things that might be improved but wait until you are a trusted member of the team before you suggest changes. Gather your evidence carefully (Chapter 5), listening (Chapter 2), and effectively introducing your new ideas (Chapter 7) will help you initiate change, when appropriate.

Notice, too, how Jessica establishes her credibility early in the introduction by referring to her family's roots in Ireland. She also connects her topic to her audience in the final sentences of the introduction.

When you use a quotation or poem, be sure it relates directly to your topic or illustrates the importance of your subject. Like stories, there are a lot of great quotations and poems, but you should only use one that sums up your topic and grabs your audience's attention. Also remember to cite the source of the quotation or poem and to deliver it so the audience knows it is a quotation or poem rather than your own words (for tips on delivery, see Chapter 10).

Give a Demonstration

When you demonstrate some aspect of your topic, you can capture your audience's interest and make them want to see or hear more. In the following example, Megan began by singing. After she had captured her audience's attention, she revealed the topic of her speech, the author of her song. In the second paragraph, she previewed her speech so her audience knew exactly what she was going to cover:

(*Begin by singing* "Amazing Grace.") Comfort is what I feel when I hear this song. No matter if I am at a funeral service or singing it in a choir, this song overwhelms me with a sense of peace. I know it has the same effect on others as well. But who was the man behind this song? And isn't it, as some say, a bit overdone? Dr. Ralph F. Wilson states that he used to think "Amazing Grace" was just that, overdone. Wilson says, "'saved a wretch like me,' come on, really now. But the author really was a wretch, a moral pariah." Wilson is the author of *Amazing Grace: The Story of John Newton,* and John Newton is the author of America's most popular hymn, "Amazing Grace."

But what happened to John Newton that made him a "moral pariah"? What happened in this man's life that it was only the "grace of God" that could save him? Well, today I'm going to share with you just how a "wretch" like John Newton wrote such a well-known hymn. I'll begin by telling you a little bit about his early life. Then, I'll tell you how he came to write "Amazing Grace." Finally, I'll conclude by discussing this hymn's legacy.

Although not everyone has the talent to stand up and sing for their audiences, many speeches can be opened with some type of demonstration. Speeches about activities, sports, and art—about how to do anything—offer good possibilities for demonstrations.

When you use a demonstration to introduce your speech, make sure you can complete it in only a few minutes or even seconds. Introductions and conclusions are a relatively small part of the speech. In fact, as you will see later in this chapter, your introduction and conclusion should make up no more than 20 percent of your speech. Time your demonstration to make sure you'll have enough time for the rest of your speech. If your demonstration seems too long, think about using it in the body of your speech instead. In either case, practice your demonstration before the speech so you can make a positive impression on the audience.

Make an Intriguing or Startling Statement

An intriguing or startling statement is an excellent way to draw your audience in with the unknown or the curious. Let's look at a few examples of this technique:

> *Ohayoo gozaimasu.* You probably don't know what I just said. I just gave you the greeting for "good morning" in Japanese, the ninth most spoken language in the world. Having studied Japanese for over three years now, I would like to share a little bit about this intriguing language with you today. I know you're probably wondering, "Why should I care about the Japanese language when I live in the United States?" Well, according to the *Encyclopedia Britannica,* there are currently over 125 million speakers of Japanese worldwide. In today's world, that means you're more than likely to meet a Japanese speaker at least once in your life. Wouldn't it be a good idea to know at least something about his or her language?
>
> Today, I'll share some of what I know about the Japanese language with you. I'll first talk about Japanese body language, which is both similar to and different from American body language. Then, I'll discuss spoken Japanese, which requires a lot of practice to learn. Finally, I'll tell you a little about the written language, which contains over 50,000 characters and three alphabets.

In this example, Kelly illustrates all four criteria for a strong introduction. He catches the audience's interest in the first few lines, establishes his credibility in the third sentence, relates the topic to his audience in his final lines of the first paragraph, and previews his speech in the second paragraph.

As you read this next example, see if you can identify all four of the criteria for a strong introduction. Notice how Katy takes a little extra time in her introduction to relate the topic to her audience and to establish her credibility:

> 3.14159265358979323846264338327950. Most of you know the name of the number I just recited. It's a number found in rainbows, pupils of eyes, sound waves, ripples in the water, and DNA—a ratio that both nature and music understand but that the human mind cannot quite comprehend. This number has sparked curiosity in many minds over the past 4,000 years. I'm talking about pi—not the dessert, but the circle ratio.
>
> Now, a class of speech majors is probably wondering if they can survive a six-minute speech about math. My own interest came about when I was challenged to memorize more digits than a friend of mine could. As a result of that challenge, I have researched this topic, finding information not only technical and historical but also fanatical. Today, I plan to inform you of what pi is, the history of pi, and how pi has created an obsession in people's lives.

When you choose to introduce your speech with a startling statement, use caution. You want to startle rather than offend your audience. Beginning speakers sometimes fall into the trap of thinking that an offensive statement is appropriate because it will, indeed, startle. If you are thinking about using a statement that may be too graphic or inappropriate, find an acceptable alternative. Your startling statement should invite the audience to listen, not shut down communication.

State the Importance of the Topic

Some speakers begin their speeches with clear statements of the significance or magnitude of a topic. When you state the importance of the topic, you tell audience members why they should listen. Tina used this technique to introduce a speech on a topic that seemed fairly ordinary but was actually quite relevant to her audience:

> Okay. Everyone look down at your feet. How many of you have shoes on? Just as I thought. Each of us has a pair of shoes or sandals on our feet. But how many know where those shoes come from? And let's be honest. How many women in the audience have shoes with heels of an inch or more? Um-hmm, don't answer. And for the men, do you steer the women in your lives toward the heels in the shoe stores? Maybe even some of you men own a pair of heels? Well, when I look in my closet, I see one pair of sneakers, two pairs of boots, and a dozen high-heeled shoes. But do I know where these shoes come from or how heels were invented? No. At least not until I did some research into my shoe fetish.
>
> Today, I'd like to share the story of shoes with you. I'd like to discuss the origination of shoes, the changes they've gone through, the invention of high heels (which originally were made for men, by the way), and the troubles those heels have caused.

In this example, Tina states the importance of her topic by reminding her audience that wearing shoes is something almost everyone does but that it can have troubling consequences for some.

You also can state the importance of a topic by showing that although a practice or phenomenon is uncommon, it has a significant impact. Will did this in his speech about germ-line engineering and cloning:

> Imagine a world filled with humans who are genetically perfect, with no flaws or birth defects—humans who are superior to what we know today. Now imagine there's no shortage of body parts for transplants or to repair what we now call "irreparable" injuries, because an exact replica of each person is available—strictly for donation. Although these two notions seem far-fetched, we may be coming closer to this imaginary world than we realize.
>
> The two processes I asked you to imagine are called germ-line engineering and cloning, the topic of my speech. I know most of you are familiar with these ideas from science fiction novels, movies, and television, but in the next few decades, you may be able to visit your local geneticist to create a designer baby or maybe even have yourself cloned. I realize there are serious moral and ethical concerns about genetic engineering. However, I'd like to invite you to consider that the benefits of these two forms of engineering far outweigh the disadvantages. Today, I'll describe the two processes for you, germ-line engineering and cloning, and then share the advantages of these processes. I'll then discuss two ways that those of us in this room are likely to be affected by these forms of genetic engineering and then open the floor for discussion.

Share Your Expertise

Although you know your qualifications for speaking on a subject, your audience may not. Establishing credibility does not mean boasting and bragging. Instead, it means you share your expertise with your audience. Recall how Jessica, Kelly, Katy, and Tina stated their credibility in their introductions:

- *Shamrocks.* My family has its roots in Ireland.
- *Japanese Language.* Having studied Japanese for over three years now, I would like to share a little bit about this intriguing language with you today.

- *Why Pi?* As a result of that challenge, I have researched this topic, finding information not only technical and historical but also fanatical.
- *History of Shoes.* Well, when I look in my closet, I see one pair of sneakers, two pairs of boots, and a dozen high-heeled shoes. But do I know where these shoes come from or how heels were invented? No. At least not until I did some research into my shoe fetish.

Establishing your credibility often is a subtle process. In these examples, the speakers revealed their expertise by illustrating their qualifications to speak about their topics. They referred to family, study, research, and personal experience to communicate their competence. Use these same techniques to establish your credibility in your speeches. And remember, your credibility also comes through your research (Chapter 5), the development of your ideas (Chapter 6), your reasoning (Chapter 14), your organization (Chapter 7), and your delivery (Chapter 10).

State What's to Come

Previewing your speech is a necessary component of your introduction. When you preview your speech, you give your audience an overview of your main points. This is important because even the best listeners need help following and remembering a speaker's ideas throughout a speech. When your listeners hear a preview, they will anticipate your main points, be prepared to listen to them, and not be surprised or confused.

The best previews are brief; they set the audience up for what's to come but do not go into too much detail. Here's how Nathan and Cassie previewed their speeches:

Francois Durand/Getty Images Entertainment/Getty Images

U2 singer Bono is known for giving speeches with particularly memorable introductions, often making intriguing statements to great effect. Think about the last speech you watched or listened to. How well was the introduction presented? Was it interesting or startling or funny? Did it draw you into the speech?

> *Appalachian Trail.* First, I'll give you a brief history of the trail's formation. Then, I'll share some facts with you about the trail itself and how it's maintained. Finally, I'll tell you the stories from some of those who have hiked the trail.

> *Crazy Lawsuits.* In my research, I found many crazy cases that actually have gone to court, and today, I'll discuss some of the craziest. I'll begin with some basic legal terms that come up in these cases so you can follow them more easily. Then I'll share with you some of my favorite cases and give you a sample of the kinds of things that tie up our court system. Finally, I'll persuade you that we should help those who are organizing to control these lawsuits and stop the abuses of our legal system.

In each example, the speakers used variations of "first, then, finally" to identify the order of main points. Although this language might seem unimaginative, spoken language is quite different from written language (Chapter 9). Audience members need extra tools to help them absorb and remember a speaker's ideas. (This is also why connectives are so helpful to audiences.) Explicit language like that used in the previews here increases the likelihood that your audience will understand your ideas, follow them throughout the speech, and remember them when the speech is over.

Tips for Your Introduction

There are four keys to preparing an effective introduction. First, look for material as you do your research. Second, prepare and practice your introduction. Third, make your introduction, brief. Finally, be creative.

TRY TO LIVE A MEANINGFUL LIFE

Yassmin Abdel-Magied defies many people's conscious and unconscious assumptions and biases. Born in Sudan, Abdel-Magied and her family moved to Queensland, Australia, when she was just two. One of the first Sudanese families in Brisbane, the Abdel-Magied family quickly became involved in their community and schools. Both parents, who had worked as an engineer and an architect in Sudan, "were not considered qualified" in Brisbane, so took jobs in the public sector. Abdel-Magied explains, "The dinner table discussion at my house was probably not a typical one," with topics ranging from "current affairs and politics," to Sudan, the Middle East, and "what was happening in Australia . . . talking about public life was something that was just really normal."

In her final year of high school, Abdel-Magied attended an Asia-Pacific City Summit, which gathered young people from around the world to "discuss issues facing them, and the organizations they were working with." Disconcerted by the fact that none of the organizations were actually working together, Abdel-Magied shared her concerns with her mother, who said, "If you've got a problem with something, why don't you do something about it?" And so, at the age of 16, Abdel-Magied created Youth Without Borders, an "umbrella"

Yassmin Abdel-Magied

organization "that works toward positive change for young people of all backgrounds and diversities."[5] An organization led by youth, Youth Without Borders's mission is to "empower young people as leaders of positive change and build capacity through collaborative community-based initiatives." Those initiatives include developing "Kamar Buku," a mobile library that travels on the back of a motor bike, bringing books and other library materials to the villages near Depok, Indonesia; "Masterchef meets the Streets," which brings together elders and leaders of ethnic communities with Brisbane school children, who learn to cook a specific ethnic dish and then distribute the finished product to local homeless people; and "Shinpads and Hijabs," which teaches local

Muslim women to play on and coach their own football teams.[6]

Abdel-Magied describes herself as a combination of a "Mediterranean mongrel" and an "adventure junkie." After high school she studied mechanical engineering in Queensland, getting involved in racecar driving and "running the university's race team." She turned down an offer to receive a master's degree in the UK in motorsport, because, she explains, "At the end of the day I care about being useful to society, I care about improving access to opportunity for other young people, I care about making sure that young people—wherever they're from—don't feel like their opportunities and future are dictated by the circumstances of their birth." Currently, Abdel-Magied works as an engineer on oil and gas rigs; a journalist at Formula One racing events; speaks, writes, and blogs regularly on the "experience growing up migrant and Muslim in a post 9/11 world."[7] Reflecting on her immersion in so many worlds, Abdel-Magied explains that she is committed to being open, honest, and self-reflective concluding, "I try to live a meaningful life."[8]

🔊 YOU CAN GET INVOLVED

MindTap Learn more about Youth Without Borders and how to get involved to help your local community or even the world.

Look for introductory materials as you do your research. As you conduct research on your speech topic, look for stories, quotations, startling facts or statements, and other material for your introduction. If you collect material you might use in your introduction, you will have several options to choose from, so you can select the one that suits your audience and your goals best.

Prepare and practice the full introduction in detail. Introductions represent your first opportunity to connect with your audience, so prepare and practice the introduction completely before you give your speech. If you are opening with a story, practice telling the full story until you can tell it with ease and flair. If you are opening with a quotation, memorize it. If you plan to begin with a demonstration, rehearse it until you have it perfected. Introductions set the stage for what's to come, so you want this

tip
National Geographic Explorer

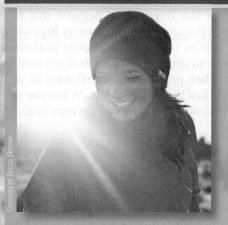

Courtesy of Becca Skinner

BECCA SKINNER, Explorer and Photographer

Do you prepare a special introduction or conclusion for your talk?

Yes, I like to try to get people engaged in the presentation right off the bat. At the very start of my presentation in Montreal, I asked people to raise their hands if they remembered when Hurricane Katrina hit or when the 2004 tsunami struck. I believe that personal stories make a really great starting point for a presentation. People have an easier time connecting with people's personal accounts than to see a picture of a building that has been destroyed. During both of those trips to photograph the rebuilding of post-natural disaster communities, I tried to talk to a lot of people, gather as many stories as I could and record personal accounts to make the story more compelling.

I ended my Indonesia presentation with a photograph of the top of a mosque that had landed nine miles from a village and in the middle of a rice paddy. I went out to the mosque one night and all the stars were out. The photo that I took turned out to be one of my favorites since you can see the stars overhead of the top of the mosque. Since my expedition to Indonesia was my first trip out of the country, it felt like a really big risk for me to go across the world with no idea of what photos I was going to shoot. So I end my presentation by telling the audience that it's okay to fear the unknown but not to let that fear control you.

part of the speech to go flawlessly. Use your notes as infrequently as possible, if at all, and be sure to make maximum eye contact. Practice your full introduction until you can deliver it smoothly and confidently. A well-delivered introduction will not only enhance your credibility but also increase your confidence as you move into the body of your speech.

Be brief. Remember, introductions tell just a little of what's to come and set the stage for the body of the speech. Introductions should be brief, only 10 to 15 percent of the speech. If they are longer, they become tedious. They also cut into the time you need for your main points. If your planned introduction is longer than 10 to 15 percent of your speech, you probably have included too much detail. Remember, your goal is not to give your speech in the introduction but to get the audience ready to hear your speech.

Be creative. Creativity is one of the best ways to capture an audience's attention and reveal your topic. Creative doesn't necessarily mean "elaborate and artistic." In this case, creativity means simply using your imagination to come up with new ideas and perspectives on how to open your speech until you find something that works just right. Trying out several of the techniques in this chapter will help you prepare a creative and effective introduction.

Practicing the Public Dialogue | 8.1

In class, generate a list of six to eight possible speech topics. Divide into groups, one for each topic. In each group, write an introduction for a speech on the topic you've chosen. Be sure to include the four parts of an introduction and one of the techniques for making it compelling. Now share this introduction with the class and get feedback on its effectiveness.

MindTap

You can use Outline Builder to help you create your introduction.

Effective conclusions reinforce your thesis statement and indicate clearly that you are ending your speech. For example, if you were speaking about military rituals, you could describe several traditional rituals, present their history, and discuss their obvious and subtle meanings. When you concluded your speech, you could illustrate your thesis by describing an actual ritual, such as the one shown here that commemorated the 74th anniversary if the attack on Pearl Harbor. In addition, you could use a visual aid, such as a photo like this one, to reinforce the meanings of the ritual.

The Conclusion

Your conclusion is your final contact with your audience. Just as the introduction represents the first impression you make on your audience, the conclusion represents your last impression. Because this last impression will linger with your listeners long after your speech is over, take time to prepare your conclusion so you end your speech with as much care as you began it. Then practice that conclusion so you can deliver it in just the way you want. When you deliver your conclusion, you have two primary goals:

1. Bring your speech to an end
2. Reinforce your thesis statement

End Your Speech

When you end a speech, you are signaling to the audience that your presentation is over. Rather than ending abruptly or just trailing off, you want to communicate clearly that the speech is wrapping up. This signal comes through your words as well as your style of delivery. The more audience centered you are, the more effective your conclusion will be.

Like the close of a conversation, the conclusion of a speech exhibits a shift in style.[9] Generally, closure in conversations is signaled by a pause, a change in the rate of speaking, and even a different tone of voice. In speeches, we use these same cues. When you've concluded your final main point, use these shifts in delivery to signal to your audience that you are about to wrap up.

Another effective way to signal the end of your speech is with a concluding transition. These are simple words and phrases such as "In closing," "In summary," "In conclusion," "Let me close by saying," and "My purpose today has been." Although these transitions seem obvious, they alert your listeners that you are moving from the body of your speech to your conclusion. These transitions also will help you incorporate the techniques discussed in the next section.

Reinforce Your Thesis Statement

The second function of your conclusion is to reinforce the thesis statement of your speech. Recall from Chapter 3 that your thesis statement summarizes, in a single declarative sentence, the main ideas, assumptions, or arguments you want to express in your speech. When you restate or rephrase your thesis statement in your conclusion, you remind your audience of the core idea of your speech. Notice how this reinforcement can be very succinct, as in Chad's speech on adoption, or more elaborate, as in Katy's on pi:

> In my family, I have two parents, an older sister, and two younger brothers. One of them is adopted, but in my heart I could not tell you which one.

> In conclusion, no one knows why pi has caused such a craze or why several books, movies, and fanatical web pages have been produced on this subject. What inspired the Chudnovsky brothers to devote their lives to the search for pi? What inspired me to write a speech on a silly number? The answer lies in the mystery. Exploring pi is an adventure, which is why people do it. I want you to remember pi not only as the circle ratio, not only as the biggest influence on math over the course of history, but as a number that has an influence on everything we do.

Restating your thesis statement reinforces your arguments and encourages your audience to remember your speech.

Preparing a Compelling Conclusion

There are several techniques for signaling the end of a speech and reinforcing your thesis statement. You likely will combine several of these techniques to deliver a comprehensive conclusion. As you develop your conclusion, remember to continually ask yourself, "What final ideas do I want to leave with my audience?"

Summarize Your Main Points

An effective tool for ending your speech and restating your thesis statement is a summary of your main points. A **summary** is a concise restatement of your main points at the end of your speech. You use it to review your ideas and remind your audience of what's important in your speech. Will used this technique in his conclusion:

> As you've seen in these last few minutes, ideas that have been presented to us as fiction may soon be reality. Germ-line engineering and cloning may soon be processes that are used in our everyday life. Both techniques raise ethical questions and concerns, especially as we consider the advantages and disadvantages of each. I have shared some of my own thoughts about these issues in this presentation; I'd now like to open it up for questions and discussion.

When you summarize your main points, remember to do three things. First, offer only a summary—don't restate too much of your speech. The audience has already heard the details, and you are only trying to reinforce the key ideas and help listeners remember what you've said. Second, don't introduce new ideas into the summary. If you didn't bring up an idea in the body of the speech, don't raise it in the conclusion. New ideas in a conclusion will only confuse your audience. Finally, try to use the same kind of language in your summary that you used in the body of your speech. Familiar phrasing will help your listeners recall your main ideas rather than force them to figure out what the new wording means.

Answer Your Introductory Question

If your speech begins with questions, answer them in the conclusion. This technique reminds audience members of what they've learned in the speech. Nathan, who began with questions about hiking the Appalachian Trail, returned to those questions in his conclusion:

> So, now do you think you could walk from New York to Chicago or from Georgia to Maine? Well, even if you're not up for the hike, many others have been. As a result of the efforts to maintain the Appalachian Trail, individuals have hiked the 2,200-mile-long footpath to raise funds, overcome disabilities, and seek out spiritual insights. The next time someone asks you if you want to "take a hike," perhaps you'll say, "why not?"

Refer Back to the Introduction

Occasionally, a speaker opens with a word, phrase, or idea and then returns to it in the conclusion. Like answering introductory questions, this technique brings the speech full circle and provides a sense of completeness. This technique usually is combined with others, such as summarizing the main points. Recall Kelly's speech about the Japanese language. After he summarized his ideas, Kelly returned to his opening as he concluded his speech:

> Thank you for listening, or as they say in Japan, *doomo arigatoo gozaimashita.*

Reggie, who opened his speech with a story of a boy's battles with chronic health problems, finished the story in his conclusion. After restating his thesis, he said,

summary: Concise restatement of the main points at the end of a speech.

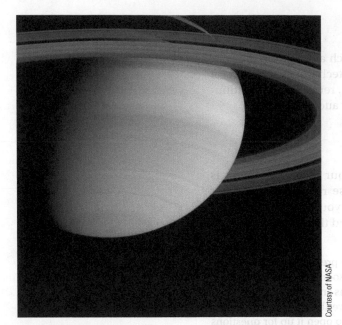
Courtesy of NASA

And that boy I told you about in the opening of my speech? Well, I'm that boy, I'm now nineteen, doing fine, and in fact, I haven't set foot in a hospital for over four years now.

Recite a Quotation

When you conclude with a quotation, you rely on someone else's words to reinforce your thesis statement. A concluding quotation should come from someone you cited in your speech or from a famous person the audience will recognize. In the following example, Tina returns to a source she had cited earlier in her speech:

> As we've heard today, shoes have gone through great changes over time. What started with animal skins and then lace transformed itself into the nineteen-inch heels worn by both men and women and on to the modern look we know today. But as Dr. Rene Caillet says, "Shoes should protect the foot and not disturb it. Having sore feet is not normal. As in any body part, pain is a signal that something is wrong."

Bring your speech around full circle by referring to your introduction in your conclusion. For example, if you were speaking about space exploration, you could begin your speech with the story of Galileo's first vague glimpse of Saturn's rings. You could then end with a description of the Cassini-Huygens mission to Saturn and Titan, which yielded stunning new images of Saturn and its moons unlike any seen before. What ideas do you have for concluding your next speech in a memorable way?

Tips for Your Conclusion

There are four keys to preparing a compelling conclusion. First, look for materials as you do your research. Second, be creative. Third, keep your conclusion brief. Finally, prepare and practice your conclusion carefully ahead of time.

Look for concluding materials. As you research your speech, look for materials you can use in your conclusion. You may find just the right summary or technique if you keep in mind the kind of conclusion you want to create. If you find more quotations than you can use in the body of your speech, try to select one for your conclusion. Or if a story is too long to tell in the introduction, think about saving part of it for the conclusion. As you research and develop your speech, you will come across effective materials for your conclusion. Save them and then draw from these options to create an ending your audience will appreciate.

Be creative. Your conclusion is your last contact with your audience. Your creativity should keep your listeners interested until the very end and help them remember your ideas and arguments after your speech is over. A creative conclusion, like Nathan's or Reggie's, can emerge from a clear summary and a reference back to the introduction. Or it may involve sharing a quotation or finishing a story begun in the introduction. Whatever technique you use, it must suit your audience, speech goals, and the tone of your speech.

MindTap®

To see a good example of a speaker who uses her conclusion to enhance her credibility, watch a video clip of student speaker Chelsey Penoyer. As you watch Chelsey speak, notice the startling statement she makes about her experience with her speech topic. How does her statement enhance her credibility?

Be brief. Conclusions should make up only 5 to 10 percent of the total speech. Remember, conclusions don't introduce new information; they bring closure to the ideas already presented. If you find your conclusion is running too long, you may be finishing a main point you did not cover completely in the body or providing too much detail in your summary. If your conclusion is too long, reduce its scope and detail.

Don't leave the conclusion to chance. Take time to prepare the conclusion carefully before you deliver the speech. Your last contact with your audience should be one that enhances your credibility and strengthens your arguments. Make sure you know what you want to say and rehearse your closing words carefully so you can make eye contact with the audience and end your speech with confidence and assurance.

Foothills Gateway: Vote YES on Referendum 1A

by Mike Piel

Specific purpose: To persuade my audience to vote yes on Referendum 1A.

Thesis statement: Voting yes on Referendum 1A is a good idea because it will save Foot hills Gateway, a community organization that serves people with mental disabilities at little cost to the taxpayer.

MindTap As you craft the introduction and conclusion of your next speech, you can use the following speech as a model. Watch the video clip of Mike Piel's speech. As part of a service learning assignment, Mike gave this speech in an introductory public speaking class. The assignment was to give a four- to five-minute persuasive speech about a local issue.

Introduction

How many of you are planning on having children? How many of you are planning on having a child with a mental disability? None?

Unfortunately, this is a reality that so many people in this world have to face day to day. In fact, one of every four people in Larimer County alone is in some way affected by someone with a mental disability. Luckily for these people, a community organization called Foothills Gateway is here to make their lives a little easier. Unfortunately, this great organization is in danger of losing its funding. The only way to prevent this from happening is to vote yes on Referendum 1A in the upcoming election. To make you more aware of the situation, I'm going to take the next few minutes to inform you of several things. I will let you know what it is exactly that Foothills Gateway does, why passing this referendum is such a good idea, and lastly, how it's going to affect you, the taxpayer.

Conclusion

Now, over the last few minutes, I have tried to inform you about what Foothills Gateway does, why this referendum is a good idea, and a little bit about how it's going to affect you, the taxpayer. I'll try to appeal to your good sense, your good nature as human beings—don't turn your back on people who are less fortunate than you, because if you don't take care of them, nobody else will. So please vote yes when you go to the ballot. Thank you.

COMMENTARY

Mike begins with two rhetorical questions and a compelling statistic that captures the audience's attention and relates his topic to his audience.

He reveals his topic and states his goal. He establishes his credibility by explicitly stating this goal and by stating he will address the impact of this vote on taxpayers.

Mike finishes his introduction by previewing his speech. Notice how he clearly states his three main points and adapts his last point to his audience.

Mike signals the end of his speech with the phrase "over the last few minutes" and by restating his three main points.

He makes a direct appeal to his audience, reinforcing his thesis and reminding his listeners of his purpose for speaking—to persuade them to vote yes on the referendum. Notice how he makes a direct, yet simple, appeal to their emotions, ending his speech on a strong note of human interest and compassion.

Chapter Summary

A speech's introduction is your first contact with your audience.

- An introduction has four objectives:
  1. To catch your audience's attention.
  2. To reveal your topic.
  3. To establish your credibility.
  4. To preview your speech.
- To accomplish these four goals, use a variety of techniques, such as asking a question, telling a story, reciting a quotation or poem, giving a demonstration, beginning with an

intriguing or startling statement, or stating the importance of your topic.

Several tips are useful to remember when you create your introduction.

- Look for introductory materials as you do your research.
- Make the introduction brief, no more than 10 to 15 percent of the speech.
- Be creative.

- Practice the full introduction carefully before you give the speech.

A speech's conclusion expresses the final words in your speech.
- A speech conclusion has two goals:
  1. To signal the end of your speech.
  2. To reinforce your thesis statement.
- To indicate that you have reached the conclusion of your speech, use pauses, shifts in the rate and tone of your delivery, and transitions.
- Several other techniques can help you leave a lasting impression with your audience, including summarizing your main points, providing the ending to a story begun in the introduction, answering a question raised in the introduction, referring back to a comment made in the introduction, and summing up your speech with a quotation.

Several tips will help you with your conclusion.
- As with the introduction, look for effective concluding materials during your research.
- Be creative and brief.
- Conclusions should be no more than 5 to 10 percent of your speech.
- Don't leave your conclusion to chance. Develop it carefully and practice it until you can deliver it with confidence.

To be effective, introductions and conclusions must be audience centered.
- To connect positively with your audience in the opening moments of your speech, consider who your listeners are and what kinds of appeals will be appropriate and interesting to them.
- Similarly, to leave a lasting and effective impression with audience members, consider how they feel about your topic.

Invitation to Public Speaking Online MindTap°

Now that you have read Chapter 8, use your MindTap Communication for *Invitation to Public Speaking* for quick access to the digital resources that accompany this text. These resources include
- **Study tools** that will help you assess your learning and prepare for exams (digital glossary, key term flash cards, review quizzes).
- **Activities and assignments** that will help you hone your knowledge and build your public speaking skills throughout

the course, as well as help you explore public speaking concepts online (web links), give you step-by-step guidance through the research, outline and note card preparation process (Outline Builder), watch and critique videos of sample speeches (Interactive Video Activities), and allow you to practice and present your presentation online using a speech video delivery, recording, and grading system (YouSeeU).

Key Concepts MindTap° Test your knowledge with online printable flash cards.

preview (158)

rhetorical question (160)

summary (169)

Review Questions

1. Name eight different techniques for catching the attention of the audience and revealing the topic of a speech. Identify the strengths of each technique.
2. Why should speakers establish their credibility and preview the main points of a speech? Are these components of an introduction important?
3. Suppose you have been asked to give a speech on the history of bubble gum. How would you establish your credibility on this topic? How creative do you think you could be in introducing this topic? Give

examples of how you would establish your credibility and creativity.
4. Name four different techniques for concluding a speech. Identify the strengths of each technique.
5. In class, write a possible speech topic on a slip of paper and trade that paper with another student. Now write an introduction and a conclusion for a speech on that topic using the techniques discussed in this chapter. Present your introduction and conclusion to the class for feedback on each of their components.

9 | Language

IN THIS CHAPTER, YOU WILL LEARN TO:

- Choose clear and accurate language for your speeches

- Apply the principles for using culturally inclusive and gender-inclusive language

- Compare and contrast the differences between spoken and written language

- Experiment with various ways to use language to create memorable images

- Identify ways to use language to create an interesting rhythm

Language, the system of verbal or gestural symbols a community uses to communicate, is central to the speechmaking process. Yet we often take language for granted, failing to realize how much of our knowledge comes from language rather than from direct experience. Some would say that objects exist in the world around us and that people use language to describe those objects as they truly are. However, most now believe the way we know something is through the words we use to describe it.[1]

MindTap Start with a quick warm-up activity and review the chapter's learning objectives.

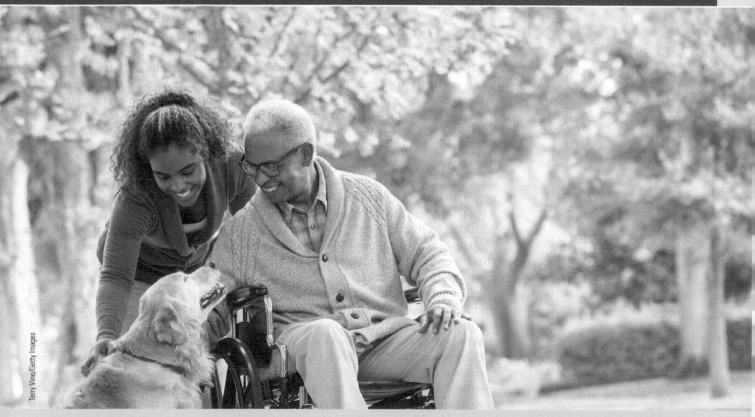

Terry Vine/Getty Images

▲ Although we often take language for granted, it is one of the most important ways we name and organize the world. Understanding the importance of using language carefully and ethically contributes to a productive public dialogue. In this chapter you will find strategies for keeping listeners engaged by selecting words and phrases that are culturally inclusive, appropriate, and accurate.

For example, even though a dog may sit directly in front of a group of people, one person may describe it as a large, clumsy, furry, lovable animal; another as an unpredictable, aggressive, frightening nuisance; and another as a hairy, smelly, extra mouth to feed. Language, it seems, can be a tool we use to shape and describe the world around us. Communication scholars agree that language, the systematic code of a group of people, is central to establishing and maintaining societies.

In the public dialogue, language allows us to share our thoughts, question the ideas of others, and invite our audiences to consider our positions. In Chapter 2, we discussed language as it relates to listening. In this chapter, we explore language as it relates to speaking. Specifically, we discuss the ambiguity of language, culture and language, gender and language, the accurate use of language, the importance of language in public speaking, and several of the linguistic devices public speakers use to create memorable images and a pleasing rhythm.

MindTap®

Read, highlight, and take notes online.

Language Is Ambiguous

If a speaker never utters a word but instead communicates through mime and gesture, how well do you think you would understand the speech? What if a speaker delivered the speech in a different language? Could you grasp the intricacies of the message? Obviously, understanding others when we do not share a common language is difficult. But if we share a common language with our audience, shouldn't communication be easier? Isn't it enough to use the same labels for things to communicate a message? How much attention must we give to the language in our speeches if we speak the same language as our audience? Consider the semantic triangle of meaning, created in 1923 by C. K. Ogden and I. A. Richards,[2] as shown in Figure 9.1.

On the left corner of the triangle is the **symbol**, the word or phrase spoken by the speaker. For example, when a speaker says "freedom," as Martin Luther King Jr. did in his "I Have a Dream" speech, or "health care," as did Barack Obama when he spoke to the nation about his ideas on the necessity of health care for all citizens, those words are the symbols. On the right corner of the triangle is the **referent**, the object, concept, or event the symbol represents. In our two examples, the referent is the actual experience of freedom or the actual health care a person might (or might not) have. You might also think of this as the denotative definition of a word or event. This is the commonly held definition of a word or the actual object or event named by the speaker.

At the top of the triangle is the **thought** or **reference**. This is the memory and past experiences audience members have with an object, concept, or event. When a speaker offers a word or phrase, audience members recall their own experiences with that word or phrase. These are our connotative definitions, our personalized, subjective interpretations of words, objects, or events. So the symbols "freedom" and "health care" call to mind a variety of connotative experiences and memories for the members of an audience.

The semantic triangle of meaning shows us that even though all the audience members might understand the symbol and even have a similar referent for it, they do not have the same thoughts, or references, for the symbol. This difference is what makes language ambiguous. The experience of freedom or the desire for health care (or any referent) differs among people and groups, depending on their culture, geographical location, and master statuses. For some, freedom is a given. For others, freedom is something that has been fought for over the centuries. Similarly, health care means different things to different people, depending on their income levels, personal health, and political views.

language: System of verbal or gestural symbols a community uses to communicate.

symbol: Word or phrase spoken by a speaker.

referent: Object, concept, or event a symbol represents.

thought or reference: Memory and past experiences that audience members have with an object, concept, or event.

When speakers forget that words do not have the same meaning for everyone, they unintentionally create ambiguity for their audiences. When they forget that people may share symbols but not experiences with those symbols, they run the risk of confusing or alienating their audiences. One way to clear up some of this ambiguity is to use concrete language. **Concrete language** refers to a tangible object—a person, place, or thing. For example, rather than talking about politicians, speak about specific politicians: name them or their political parties so your audience knows exactly which politicians you are referring to. This will help you avoid **abstract language**, which refers to ideas or concepts but not to specific objects.

As you think about whether the language you will use in your speech is concrete or abstract, diagram it on Ogden and Richards's semantic triangle of meaning. Ask yourself whether the language you use is as specific as you think it is. If it isn't, search for ways to represent generalized concepts or ideas with specific examples. And if you must use abstract language, take time in your speech to define key concepts or ideas for your audience so your listeners will understand your intended meaning. Review the discussion of definitions in Chapter 6 to familiarize yourself with some of the ways speakers can define words for their audiences to eliminate the ambiguity created by connotations.

Language and Culture

In its most basic sense, language is an organized and learned symbol system. It is used to represent human experiences and to transmit messages. Language allows us to describe, label, and share events with others and to understand each other's perspectives and experiences. However, people in different cultures have different life experiences and thus name and define the world differently.

For example, in American Sign Language, which is a visual rather than spoken language, signs often are subtly altered to reflect the visual aspects of objects and events. The concepts "modest home" and "mansion" begin with the same basic sign for "home" but differ in their execution. In contrast, in spoken English, words are only occasionally modified to emphasize some aspect of appearance (for example, "huuuge house"). Usually, to emphasize some visual aspect, we add more words to the description or choose a different word.

Subcultures, or groups within a larger culture that share its language, may also use the language differently. For example, the language of rap music, which has roots in the African American tradition of "signifying," has clear differences from Standard English. Signifying is governed by its own rules of grammar, semantics, and syntax. It allows people to make statements that have double, and often even multiple, meanings that are not understood by people outside the subculture.[3] The topics of rap music, the words it uses, and the ways those words are put together and delivered reflect these multiple meanings, as well as the experiences and perspectives of members of this subculture.

The culturally bound nature of language requires us to be aware of obvious, as well as subtle, differences. As speakers, we can adapt our language choices to the culture of the people we are addressing, or if we do not know their culture well enough to do so, we can acknowledge the differences as we speak. If we can identify which words our audience might not understand because of cultural or regional differences, then we can offer clarification for those words and promote understanding rather than confusion.

Idioms are especially difficult for people of other cultures to understand. An **idiom** is a fixed, distinctive expression whose meaning is not indicated by its individual words. "I was in stitches" and "They kept me in the dark" are examples of English idioms. In American Sign Language, "The train is gone" is an idiom that means you missed the joke or the heart of the matter. We often use idioms without realizing it:

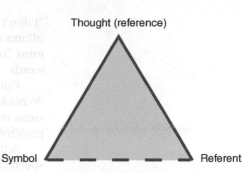

Figure 9.1   Semantic triangle of meaning Notice that the line at the bottom of the triangle is broken, reflecting the arbitrary nature of language. There is not necessarily a connection between a symbol and a referent because the words (symbols) we use to name things (referents) are human inventions. For example, the symbol freedom is just an English word we've come up with to name its referent, the state in which someone lives without undue restraints and restrictions. What other symbols for the experience of "freedom" can you think of?

concrete language: Language that refers to a tangible object—a person, place, or thing.

abstract language: Language that refers to ideas or concepts but not to specific objects.

idiom: Fixed, distinctive expression whose meaning is not indicated by its individual words.

"I don't get it," "It's way over my head," and "Go figure" are three common examples. Idioms can be especially difficult for nonnative speakers. To be fully understood, we must "unpack the meanings" (another idiom) of potentially confusing phrases and words.

Cultural differences can interfere with communication in other ways, too. If we do not know how a cultural group prefers to identify itself, we may accidentally offend some members of our audience. Table 9.1 will help familiarize you with some of the preferred labels for different cultural groups.

Although the use of appropriate labels sometimes is called "politically correct speech," appropriate labels really are about respecting others. Labels help us shape our perceptions of others, and our perceptions affect how we treat other people. Thus, inappropriate labels, such as labels that perpetuate stereotypes, can cause an audience to feel disrespected and stop listening. Groups name themselves because they wish to emphasize aspects of their lives that are important to them. Audience-centered speakers are aware of how cultures and subcultures name themselves and the characteristics or histories they are honoring. We show respect for our audience when we use appropriate labels.

Table 9.1 Appropriate Labels for Diverse Identities

Ethnicity	African American or black
	Asian American, or identify the country of heritage: Chinese American, Japanese American, Korean American. (Note that *oriental* refers to an art object, like a rug, and not a person.)
	Hispanic, Latina or Latino, Chicana or Chicano, or identify the country of heritage: Cuban American, Mexican American
	Native American or American Indian, or identify the specific nation: Sioux, Navajo, Hopi. (Note that just *Indian* more often refers to people from India.)
	European American or white
Physical ability	A person with (name of disability)
	A person who has (name of disability)
Age	Boy or girl (a person under the age of twelve)
	Young woman or young man (a person between the ages of twelve and eighteen)
	Man or woman (a person nineteen years old or older)
	Older person (rather than elderly or senior)
Sexual orientation	Bisexual man or woman
	Gay man or lesbian
	Straight or heterosexual man or woman
Gender identity	Cisgender (a person whose personal identity corresponds to the gender and sex assigned at birth)
	Transgender person (a general term to describe those who have gender identities not traditionally associated with their birth sex)
	Trans man
	Trans woman
	Transsexual (a person who wants to change, or has changed, his or her anatomical sex)
	Cross-dresser (a person who dresses in the clothes of the opposite sex)
	Genderqueer, bigender, androgyny (a person whose identity moves between or even beyond masculinity and femininity)

"Language Hotspots"
Gregory D. S. Anderson: Explorer and Linguist

MARK THIESSEN/National Geographic Creative

Dr. Gregory D. S. Anderson is a linguist and the co-founder of the Living Tongues Institute for Endangered Languages, a not-for-profit organization that documents, revitalizes, and preserves some of the world's vanishing languages. Dr. Anderson has worked in the field with speakers of languages in Siberia (Russia), Kyrgyzstan, Nigeria, India, Bolivia, Australia, Paraguay, Papua New Guinea, and the United States. In the image here, Dr. Anderson (and fellow linguist Dr. K. David Harrison) work with Ichiro John, a Mwoakillese

elder, on Mwoakilloa Atoll, Federated States of Micronesia. More than 40 percent of the world's approximate 7,000 languages are currently at risk of becoming extinct. Anderson helped create a language hotspot map to showcase areas around the world with high linguistic diversity as well as high levels of linguistic endangerment. Cameroon, a country in west-central Africa, is an example of a region with a high level of linguistic diversity: more than 275 indigenous languages are spoken there. Dr. Anderson says it is important to document and preserve Cameroon's indigenous languages now because many are unlikely to survive through the 21 century.

The United States also has many language hotspots. Oklahoma and California are two states of particular interest. The Winnemem Wintu people who live outside of Redding, California, were working to preserve their cultural and linguistic identity when a house fire in 2008 destroyed a large portion of the materials necessary to help their revitalization efforts. They have been struggling ever since to preserve their language. Their leaders contacted Dr. Anderson to seek his assistance with their efforts. With help from the

Enduring Voices project, Dr. Anderson and his team delivered a Language Technology Kit to the Winnemem Wintu and trained them to use audio and video recorders to help record and preserve their language. Projects like these can help promote global awareness and expose the language extinction crisis around the world.[4]

WHAT DO YOU THINK?

1. How important is the preservation of a language? What would the loss of your native language feel like to you and your family?
2. Do you speak more than one language? If so, identify some of the differences in those languages? For example, how are their grammar and vocabulary (the things they name as important) different? What does this tell you about the languages and the cultures they come from?
3. How might technology shape the way language is recorded and preserved for different speakers around the world? Is technology useful and appropriate to use in the efforts to prevent languages from becoming extinct? Why?

Language and Gender

In Chapter 2, you learned that it's important to use gender-neutral language so your speeches address both women and men. To help you do this, consider the guidelines in Table 9.2 for translating some common gender-biased language into gender-inclusive language. These guidelines are from the American Psychological Association.

Increasingly, speakers are using gender-inclusive words and phrases in their speaking. Politicians are regularly referring to men and women as they discuss employment and the impact of policies on workers, daughters and sons as they refer to military personnel, and adjusting phrases and descriptions to reflect gender diversity in the workplace (mail carriers, police officers, and firefighters) and our college campuses (first-year students, faculty and their partners or spouses, and female and male athletes). Using gender-neutral and gender-inclusive language reflects your awareness of both men and women as valued and active participants in the world.

Table 9.2 Guidelines for Gender-Inclusive Language

PROBLEMATIC	PREFERRED
Man, mankind	People, humanity, human beings, humankind, human species
To man a project	To staff a project, hire personnel, employ staff
Manpower	Workforce, personnel, workers, human resources, staff
Man's search for knowledge	The search for knowledge
Chairman	Chair, chairperson, moderator, discussion leader, facilitator
Foreman, mailman	Supervisor or superintendent, postal worker or mail carrier
Salesmanship	Selling ability
Sportsmanship	Teamwork, cooperation, conduct, respect for others, graciousness
He, his, him (universal "he" as a pronoun that refers to both women and men)	They (used with plural nouns), she or he, his or her, him or her
Dear Sir:	Dear Sir or Madam, To whom it may concern, Dear members of the ___ Committee (name the specific group)
Mr. and Mrs. John Smith	John and Jane Smith
Doctors and their wives	Doctors and their partners or significant others
Woman doctor, lady lawyer	Doctor or physician, lawyer or attorney

"It Begins with the Phrase, 'That's So Gay'"

Gay teenagers living in the United States face many challenges, especially during their middle and high school years. In 2010, news broke that five gay or gay-perceived teenagers committed suicide within a three-week span after being taunted, harassed, and shamed for their sexual orientation. These deaths occurred across the United States: from the East Coast to California. Fourteen-year-old Jamey Rodemeyer took his life after claiming he couldn't handle the verbal harassment he was facing at school and online. If we take a closer look at the situations leading to the tragic suicides and assaults, we can discover just how powerful language can be. Let's look at the phrase, "That's so gay." The phrase is commonly used by young and old alike to represent something as "silly," "tacky," "wrong," or "hideous." Although some people say "That's so gay" doesn't really mean anything, others disagree. Freshman student Rebekah Rice discovered just how serious the phrase can be. After being teased for her Mormon background and asked if she had multiple moms, Rebekah replied, "That's so gay." She later found herself in the principal's office for using the phrase and a note was placed in her permanent file. After Rebekah's parents sued the school for violating her First Amendment rights. Rebekah herself claimed that she did not mean to intentionally insult gay people. Instead, she claims that she meant, "That's so stupid, that's so silly, that's so dumb."[5] School officials disagree, arguing that they are taking a strict stand against hurtful language after two boys had been paid to beat up a gay student the previous year.

Teenagers are not the only ones who use the phrase. Celebrity comedian Tracy Morgan faced public ridicule for making anti-gay remarks during his comedy routine. After claiming homosexuality is a choice and that he would kill his son if he came out to him, Morgan issued a public apology and claimed his humor was not meant to hurt anyone.[6] Shannon Gilreath, a law professor at Wake Forest University, disagreed and explained that "physical violence begins with bullying, name-calling and homophobic remarks." When no one intervenes, a situation regularly "escalates to violence." Many public figures agree with Gilreath, among them Judy Shepard, whose son was murdered for being gay, and Ellen Degeneres.[7] These public figures are educating audiences about the powerful impact of uncivil language. Shepard and Degeneres argue that we have the power to shape and alter the meaning of words; we also have the ability to stop using language that can be considered hateful or derogatory.

WHAT DO YOU THINK?

1. Make a list of phrases like "That's so gay" that have been banned from schools or workplaces or that cast people in negative, unflattering, or demeaning ways. What groups of individuals might be harmed by these phrases? How might they be harmed? If you think these phrases "don't mean anything," explain why.

2. If language is as powerful as Shepard and Degeneres argue, what are some other terms we can use in our speeches to replace the derogatory ones?

3. Should comedians like Tracy Morgan have the right to say anything they want and make anti-gay comments in their routines? Why or why not?

Language and Accuracy

Consider the following lists of words:

persecution	prosecution
simple	simplistic
patriarchal	patriarchic
good	well

What are the differences between the words in each column? If someone is *persecuted*, is that the same as being *prosecuted*? If you look in the dictionary, you'll see that to be persecuted is to be subjected to cruel or unfair treatment, whereas to be prosecuted is to be tried in a court of law for a criminal offense. The words have different meanings, yet they often are confused. Similarly, many speakers like to add "-istic" to the end of words because they think it makes a concept sound more complex. Yet *simple* means easy, straightforward, or effortless, and *simplistic* means lacking complexities. Although you should be able to find *patriarchal* in the dictionary, can you find *patriarchic*? It's not a word in the English language, although speakers sometimes use it, confusing it with *patriarchal*. How about *good* and *well*? Do you know the difference between the two? Does your favorite band play good or do they play well? (They should play well and sound good.)

AZIZ ABU SARAH, Explorer and Cultural Educator

Can you tell us about a time when understanding the importance of language, gender, and culture really helped you communicate successfully?

In my work now, I think the trick is learning different cultural styles of communication. I come from a culture where interrupting is normal and everybody says what they think at the moment. Well, in the United States, for example, you can't do that, so I have to adjust and remember what is correct in other cultures. I have to adjust my communication style for each country. And I have to ask questions about what is appropriate. For example, in Spain I had to ask what certain hand gestures meant because I know there are differences internationally, and I don't want to use those gestures that could be offensive. I have to understand cultural differences.

But even with gender, for example, handshakes are important. Sometimes I can shake a woman's hand, and sometimes I can't. And if I did shake a woman's hand in a country where that is not acceptable, I could really offend people. So, although it's acceptable for your own culture and maybe you disagree with the fact that a woman isn't allowed to shake your hand, you still have to respect that cultural practice if you're going to communicate effectively. It takes time to learn and to understand important cultural difference—but you have to if you want to be effective.

Knowing the correct definitions and usage of words is important because accurate language affects not only your meaning but also your credibility. Three tips will help you improve the accuracy of your language:

1. *Check the definitions of the words you are using.* When a word is central to the meaning of a sentence or a claim, look it up in the dictionary to be sure you have the correct word. Looking up words can save you considerable embarrassment. In a commemorative speech, a student described her sister by saying, "She's incredible: She's kind, generous, and always thinks of others; she's notorious for this in my hometown." Although her sister was remarkable, "notorious" means well known for undesirable features, not desirable ones.

2. *If your use of language is not as strong as you'd like, work with someone who has strong language skills.* Most colleges and universities have writing and tutoring labs, with people ready to help students with clarity and grammar. (Ask your instructor about the resources available on your campus if you aren't familiar with them.) If you take time to seek this kind of help, you will find that not only will your speeches be clearer and your credibility enhanced, but also your writing will improve.

3. *Study the language.* American civil rights leader Malcolm X copied the dictionary word by word to improve his language skills, but there are other ways to improve yours. Read books, magazines, and newspapers; take courses that focus on language skills; and practice with language and vocabulary workbooks from the library, bookstores, and teaching supply stores. You can even study a foreign language, which will teach you about your own language in the process. Studying a language systematically will not only increase your vocabulary but also help you develop your arguments and ideas more clearly.

Language and Public Speaking

It may be tempting to write out our entire speeches beforehand to get every word right. And then we may be tempted to read the speech to our audience to avoid the ambiguities and errors of language discussed in this chapter. However, when we speak, we want to use language meant to be spoken, not read. Writing out a speech is appropriate only when speaking from a manuscript (see Chapter 10). Even though every speaker makes a mistake now and then, with care and attention to language, you can learn to address your audience with clarity and vividness most of the time.

The most effective speakers use what is called an **oral style**, a style that reflects the spoken rather than the written word. They "talk" their speeches rather than read them, and this makes them more "listenable" and easier to understand. The differences between the spoken word and the written word are significant: spoken language is more interactive, more casual, and more repetitive than written language.[8]

Spoken Language Is More Interactive

Written messages are fixed messages whose words are already recorded or written down. However, when we speak to others, we interact with them: we make adjustments as we speak, monitor their interest and understanding, and ask or respond to questions. When we speak publicly, our language reflects the shifts, pauses, and adjustments we make for our audience. We carry on a conversation with our audience in ways that we do not when we write to someone.

Our nonverbal communication also reflects this interactive mode. Our expressions and gestures reinforce our words, giving spoken language a different tone than written language. Written prose doesn't lend itself to this spontaneous nonverbal interaction. Speakers who read written-out speeches usually sound as if they're delivering something the audience should be reading rather than listening to. Although speakers might feel more confident delivering a memorized speech, audiences can get restless and irritated with this style. Remember to stay audience centered and use an interactive style of language and delivery.

Spoken Language Is More Casual

Written language tends to be more formal than spoken language, although there are exceptions. If you open almost any book or magazine and read the text out loud, you will notice that the words sound a little formal. Written and spoken languages differ in formality because writing tends to be more rule governed than speaking. When we speak, we use more contractions (for example, "can't" instead of "cannot") and colloquialisms ("No way!" instead of "That simply is not possible"). We also run our words together when we speak (we read, "I'm going to ask" but say, "I'm gonna ask"). A speaker who delivers a speech in a written style sounds more distant and formal than one who talks to the audience.

Spoken Language Is More Repetitive

Written messages do not need the repetition that spoken messages do. When a message is written, readers can go back and reread it if they need help remembering what was said. But because public speaking audiences often need help remembering what they hear, public speakers use more repetition than writers do.

Practicing the Public Dialogue | 9.1

EVALUATE ACCURACY OF THE LANGUAGE IN YOUR SPEECH

Make a list of five to ten words you think everyone in your audience will define in the same way. Exchange lists with a partner in your speech class and write definitions for each other's words, but don't use a dictionary. Share your definitions with each other and see if you agree on them. Now look your words up in a dictionary and see if your and your partner's definitions match the definitions provided in the dictionary.

John Medina/Getty Images

Many public figures, like Oprah, are known for their conversational speaking style and rapport with their audiences. Would you describe your own speaking style as following an oral or a written style? What steps will you take to use an oral style in your next speech?

MindTap

To see a speaker using a casual style, watch the video clip of student speaker Brandi Lafferty.

oral style: Speaking style that reflects the spoken rather than the written word.

Public speakers intentionally repeat main ideas and arguments. They summarize their main points and restate important arguments to help their audiences remember them. Recall from Chapters 7 and 8 that in your speeches you present an overview of your ideas (introduction), state those ideas (body), and then summarize them (conclusion). You also use repetitive tools like transitions, internal summaries, and internal previews to help audiences remember your ideas. This repetitive quality, so necessary to public speaking, is found less often in many forms of written communication. The need for repetition reinforces the importance of speaking rather than reading to audiences.

Language, Imagery, and Rhythm

Because much of what we know comes to us through language rather than direct experience, we want to pay careful attention to the images we create with our words. As you put together the final touches of your speeches, listen to your words and phrases. Do they inspire you? Do they create a picture in your mind of what you are describing? Are they pleasing to your ears? Do they make you want to hear more? If your language draws you into your speech, then it likely will draw in your audience. By carefully choosing the words in your speech, you can use language to create rich images and sensations.

In this section, you will read about a number of verbal techniques that draw your listeners into your ideas. These tools can be divided into two general categories: language that creates memorable imagery and language that creates a pleasing rhythm.

Practicing the Public Dialogue | 9.2
EVALUATE THE STYLE OF THE LANGUAGE IN YOUR SPEECH

Bring the outline and speaking notes from one of your speeches to class. With a partner or in a small group, discuss whether you followed an oral or a written style when you prepared this speech. (*Hint:* If you wrote out your speech word for word, you probably followed a written rather than an oral style.) If you followed an oral style, get feedback from your partner or group about how you might strengthen your oral style to make your speech more listenable. If you followed a written style, share strategies for giving your next speech in an oral style rather than a written one.

MindTap®

To practice comparing an oral style to a written style, watch or listen to a speech by a political figure and then compare the speech with something this person has written.

Language That Creates Memorable Imagery

Our language can call to mind engaging sights, smells, tastes, and sounds. With language, we can bring an idea to life and make abstractions seem concrete. Figures of speech, such as similes, metaphors, and personification, can create powerful images for our audiences, making our speeches appealing, interesting, and memorable. In the examples that follow, notice how these devices blend with the words around them. They call up the images without calling attention to themselves.

Simile. **Simile** makes an explicit comparison of two things that uses the word *like* or *as*. Although the two things we are comparing are different, they are similar in a way that we want to highlight to make a specific point. Consider the following examples of similes from speeches given by Patrick and Haley:

Although he stands only five feet ten to my six feet two, *my father seems like a giant* to me and probably always will. But he's a gentle giant, for the most part, and I look up to him and appreciate many of the lessons he taught me.

From the time you first begin to consume it, the sugar in your body scratches the lining of the arteries leading to your heart. *The process is like sandpaper on wood*, and it never reverses itself.

Through similes, Patrick emphasized his respect for his father, and Haley dramatized the hazards of consuming sugar. Patrick could simply have said he respected his father, and Haley's statement that sugar scratches the lining of the heart was enough to make her point. However, by using similes, their audiences could "see" Patrick's respect for his father and the damage sugar does to arteries.

simile: Figure of speech that makes an explicit comparison of two things using the word *like* or *as*.

Metaphor. **Metaphor** is a comparison between two things that describes one thing as being something else. Aristotle described a command of metaphors as "the greatest thing by far." The word *metaphor* comes from a Greek term meaning "transference."[9] When we use metaphors, we are transferring the qualities of one thing to another, illustrating their similarities.

Although many metaphors create associations that are obvious (for example, "the war on drugs"), some are subtler, such as Guatemalan human rights advocate Rigoberta Menchú's "We are not myths of the past, ruins in the jungle, or zoos."[10] In the "war on drugs," the comparison is explicit—the government is responding to drug trafficking in a warlike manner. In contrast, Menchú's comparison of the Mayan people to myths, ruins, and zoos is subtler. Menchú is arguing for the rights of the Mayan people today by comparing them to what they are not. In both examples, the metaphors make the comparisons memorable. Two student speakers, Silas and Brooke, used metaphors quite successfully in the following ways:

> Melanoma is one of the most common cancers in Americans between the ages of twenty-five and twenty-nine. If it is caught early and removed, a person lives a normal life. Well, maybe it's normal. According to Matthew Brady, now nineteen, after summers on his boogie board and at the age of only fourteen, "they *cut a steak out of my back.*"

> As I ate, my mouth got hotter and hotter . . . and hotter. I took a sip of water. It kept right on heating up. The source of this *fire in my mouth?* The fairly well-known habanero chili.

Like similes, metaphors bring ideas to life with rich associations and comparisons. However, they can go astray sometimes in awkward ways. A **mixed metaphor** makes illogical comparisons between two or more things. When speakers mix their metaphors, they begin with one metaphor and then switch to another midstream. The confusion, if not humor, that results from mixed metaphors is apparent in the following examples:[11]

Art Konovalov/Shutterstock.com

> By my count, the current package has just one major flaw. It could do a lot more to change *how* the government spends its money. It doesn't have nearly the amount of the fresh, reformist thinking as Mr. Obama's campaign speeches and proposals did. Instead, the bill is mostly a *stew of spending* on existing programs, whatever their *warts* may be.[12]

> I wanted all my *ducks in a row,* so if we did *get into a posture,* we could pretty much *slam dunk this thing and put it to bed.*

In the first example, the audience is asked to associate the metaphor of a stew (many items of food mixed together) with warts. However, food does not have warts—animals do. In the second example, the speaker associates a slam dunk (a high probability shot in basketball) with putting something to bed (finishing a task). Combined with the metaphor of ducks in a row (everything in order) and a posture (a bluff), the audience has trouble deciding which image to focus on. In short, mixed metaphors bring together too many or contradictory associations and are difficult to visualize. To avoid mixed metaphors, take a close look at the metaphors you want to use to be sure the words in the phrase refer to the same category, event, or thing.

Personification. When we use **personification**, we attribute human characteristics to animals, objects, or concepts. Personification assigns sight, speech, hearing, thought, emotion, action, or sensation to objects (such as trees, rocks, buildings) or to concepts (such as love, bravery, sadness). "Confusion spoke," "the trees listen," and "the voice of democracy" are examples of personification. In the following examples, notice how easy it is to accept the traits assigned to things we don't typically see as having these human qualities:

> *My bones are tired.* Not tired of struggling, but tired of oppression. (Audley "Queen Mother" Moore, civil rights leader)[13]

Speakers often use language to create powerful visual images for their audiences. Describe this 1959 Chevrolet Corvette using simile, metaphor, and personification. For example, how would you describe what it felt like to drive this car on a scenic highway? What words would you use to describe, say, excitement or apprehension about driving such an expensive car?

metaphor: Figure of speech that makes a comparison between two things by describing one thing as being something else.

mixed metaphor: Metaphor that makes illogical comparisons between two or more things.

personification: Figure of speech that attributes human characteristics to animals, objects, or concepts.

With personification, the ideas expressed here come to life. Bones, which can break or weaken, cannot become tired. However, the image of deep fatigue is highly effective and stays with the audience long after the words are said.

In a speech about losing his job, Carl used personification to describe the letter he received and his reaction to it:

> Those words just sat there staring at me. They wouldn't leave and they wouldn't explain themselves. "You're fired," they said. And they refused to tell me anything else.

The image Carl created conveys the shock of being fired without explanation or recourse. Personification, in sum, can call up vivid images and sensations for your audience.

Language That Creates a Pleasing Rhythm

We can strengthen the images we create with our words by focusing on the way the words sound when put together. When we think of rhythm, we may think of poetry, music, or children's stories, not speeches. However, some of the most effective public speakers in history have used rhythm to strengthen the presentation of their ideas. Consider Jesse Jackson, John F. Kennedy, and Barbara Jordan. These speakers are all known for the power of their ideas and their rhythmic language. In speeches, **rhythm** is the arrangement of words into patterns so the sounds of the words together enhance the meaning of a phrase. Parallelism, repetition, alliteration, and antithesis are four ways to emphasize your ideas with rhythm.

Parallelism. When we arrange related words so they are balanced or arrange related sentences so they have identical structures, we are using **parallelism**. The notion that "beauty is as beauty does" is an example of a simple but effective use of parallelism. Because of its rhythm and symmetry, parallelism helps an audience remember a statement. Here are other, more complex, examples of parallelism:

> *Rich and poor, intelligent and ignorant, wise and foolish, virtuous and vicious, man and woman*—it is ever the same, each soul must depend wholly on itself. (Elizabeth Cady Stanton, nineteenth-century suffragist)

> My parents shared not only an improbable love, they shared an abiding faith in the possibilities of this nation. They would give me an African name, Barack, or "blessed," believing that *in a tolerant America* your name is no barrier to success. They imagined—they imagined me going to the best schools in the land, even though they weren't rich, because in *a generous America* you don't have to be rich to achieve your potential. (Barack Obama, then U.S. Senator Illinois, 2004 keynote address to the Democratic National Convention)

Repetition. When we use **repetition** in a speech, we repeat keywords or phrases at the beginnings or endings of sentences or clauses. President Franklin D. Roosevelt's "I see one-third of the nation ill-housed, ill-clad, and ill-nourished" is an example of repetition. The repetition of the word *ill* creates a rhythm that helped his audience remember his claims. Representative Barbara Jordan used repetition in her 1976 keynote address to the Democratic National Convention:

> *We are a people* in a quandary about the present. *We are a people* in search of our future. *We are a people* in search of a national community.

In the next example, poet Nikki Giovanni used repetition to create a memorable message in her speech "We Are Virginia Tech," given at the close of the memorial ceremony for the 2007 Virginia Tech shooting victims. Notice that in the fourth sentence, "we are" is implied:

> *We are* Virginia Tech. *We are* strong enough to stand tall tearlessly. *We are* brave enough to bend to cry. And sad enough to know we must laugh again. *We are* Virginia Tech.

rhythm: Arrangement of words into patterns so the sounds of the words together enhance the meaning of a phrase.

parallelism: Arrangement of related words so they are balanced or of related sentences so they have identical structures.

repetition: Repeating keywords or phrases at the beginnings or endings of sentences or clauses to create rhythm.

Repetition is one of the easier verbal techniques for beginning speakers to use. Consider these examples from student speeches:

> Let me talk about my experiences as a first-year teacher. I'll tell you now, I loved it, but I was not prepared. For the endless energy of the students? *I was not prepared.* The demands on my time outside the classroom? *Not prepared.* Angry parents? *Not prepared.* Learning disabilities? *Not prepared.* Language differences? Personal tragedies? Trusting faces staring up at me? You got it; *I was not prepared.*
>
> *As students, we need* to respond. *As students, we need* to care. *As students, we need* to step forward and share our positions.

Speakers often combine repetition with parallelism to reinforce messages rhythmically and ensure that their words stay with us long after a speech is over. In the following example, former Massachusetts Congressman Joe Moakley repeats "it is never a crime" and then uses parallelism to end with "It is always a duty":

> *It is never a crime to speak* up for the poor, the helpless, or the ill; *it is never a crime to* tell the truth; *it is never a crime* to demand justice; *it is never a crime* to teach people their rights; *it is never a crime* to struggle for a just peace. *It is never a crime. It is always a duty*.

Alliteration. **Alliteration** is the repetition of the initial sounds of two or more words in a sentence or phrase. We can use alliteration to emphasize an idea, to create a humorous tone, or as a **mnemonic device** (a verbal device that makes information easier to remember).[14] Alliteration is not just for children's rhyming games (such as *P*eter *P*iper and his *p*ickled *p*eppers). Consider these common phrases: the *W*ild *W*est, *f*east or *f*amine, the *b*allot or the *b*ullet, *c*ompassionate *c*onservatism, *s*trong and *s*ilent, and the *M*illion *M*an *M*arch. These phrases have become familiar in part because alliteration has made them more memorable. When used sparingly, alliteration can give a rhythm to your words that audiences find engaging and easy to remember. Consider these examples of alliteration and the ways the repetition of sounds make it easier to remember the ideas in a speech:

AP Images

> We are in a transitional period right now—*f*ascinating and exhilarating times, learning to adjust to *ch*anges and the *ch*oices we—men and women—are facing. (Barbara Bush, former first lady)

> Now is the time for *r*epentance, *r*estitution, and *r*econciliation, and I honor those three functions in the light of the great ethnic, racial diversity in our world today. (Maggie Kuhn, founder of the Gray Panthers)

Antithesis. The word *antithesis* means "opposite." In a speech, you use **antithesis** when you place words and phrases in contrast or opposition to one another. One of the most famous uses of antithesis comes from John F. Kennedy's inaugural address in 1961: "And so, my fellow Americans: *Ask not what your country can do for you—ask what you can do for your country.*" With this simple phrase, he caused those listening to think about their personal responsibility for preserving the freedoms many Americans had begun to take for granted. Kennedy offered a second example of antithesis in that same speech:

> Let us never negotiate out of fear. But let us never fear to negotiate.

Antithesis is perhaps more complex than alliteration and parallelism, but it still is used with great success. As you put together the ideas in your speeches, see if you

John F. Kennedy is renowned for using eloquent language in his speeches. One of the techniques he's most known for is his use of antithesis. Try to incorporate at least one example of antithesis into your next speech.

alliteration: Repetition of initial sounds of two or more words in a sentence or phrase.

mnemonic device: Verbal device that makes information easier to remember.

antithesis: Placement of words and phrases in contrast or opposition to one another.

EVALUATE THE IMAGERY AND RHYTHM OF YOUR SPEECH

As a class, select a speech topic for an imaginary speech. Prepare the general and specific purposes for the speech and the main points. Break into groups and assign each of the following elements to a different group: the introduction, the conclusion, and the main points (one main point per group). In your groups, use as many of the devices for creating memorable images and appealing rhythms as you can for your part of the speech. Make sure your language is culturally inclusive and gender inclusive. Now, in your groups, deliver the parts of the speech to the class and discuss the language strategies you used in your speech part. Why did you make the choices you made? Why were they effective or not?

MindTap°

To see a speaker use linguistic devices in her speech, watch the video clip of student speaker Stacey Newman. Were her uses of these devices effective? Why or why not?

might be able to phrase them using antithesis. Here's how Werner used antithesis in his speech:

> Some say that people with developmental disabilities only *take from* us, but I say they actually *give to us*.

Other speakers also have used antithesis with great impact:

> We can do no *great things—only small things* with great love. (Mother Teresa, humanitarian and Nobel Peace Prize laureate)

> Words *cannot be remote from reality* when they *create reality*. (John Cowper Powys, British novelist)

Antithesis draws an audience into your speech, adding force and rhythm to your ideas.

These seven devices for engaging your audience in your ideas—simile, metaphor, personification, parallelism, repetition, alliteration, and antithesis—can help you create memorable images and appealing rhythms in your speech. Used thoughtfully, they can help your audience recall sensations and experiences and remember your ideas. As you use these linguistic devices, remember the importance of respecting cultural differences and speaking with gender-inclusive language. Similarly, remember that language can be ambiguous, and your linguistic devices should clarify your ideas, not confuse your audience. If you create appropriate and engaging images with your language, you will enhance the public dialogue.

Chapter Summary

Language is the system of symbols we use to communicate with one another.

- Language is complex and ambiguous because of our subjective associations with the meaning of words.

- The semantic triangle of meaning reveals this complexity and ambiguity by illustrating how word meaning derives from the relationships among the symbol, the referent, and the thought (or reference).

Culture also affects language and our understanding of the meaning of words.

- To be audience centered, avoid words that are strictly tied to a single culture or explain the meaning of those words that are.

- To better connect with and avoid alienating the diverse members of an audience, use culturally inclusive and gender-inclusive language.

Accurate use of language communicates your credibility to your audiences.

- Inaccurate use of language can harm your credibility and cause unnecessary confusion.

- To ensure accuracy, check the definitions of keywords before you deliver your speech, or improve your use of language by working with someone who has a strong command of the language or by studying English or even another language.

There are several differences between spoken and written language.

- Spoken language reflects an oral style that is more interactive, casual, and repetitive than written language.

- Because of these differences, avoid writing out your speech and reading it to your audience. Instead, work from an outline so you will deliver your speech in a conversational rather than written style.

Many techniques can make your language more appealing to your audience.

- To create vivid and memorable images, use similes, metaphors, and personification.

- *Similes* are explicit comparisons of two things using the word *like* or *as*.

- *Metaphors* are comparisons of two things that describe one as the same as the other.

- *Personification* ascribes human characteristics to nonhuman objects or ideas.
- To create a pleasing rhythm, use parallelism, repetition, alliteration, and antithesis.
- *Parallelism* balances related words, phrases, or sentences by giving them identical structures.
- *Repetition* emphasizes keywords or phrases at the beginning or ending of a sentence or clause.
- *Alliteration* is the repetition of the initial sounds of two or more words in a phrase or sentence.
- *Antithesis* is the contrast of words or phrases.

Invitation to Public Speaking Online MindTap

Now that you have read Chapter 9, use your MindTap Communication for *Invitation to Public Speaking* for quick access to the digital resources that accompany this text. These resources include:

- **Study tools** that will help you assess your learning and prepare for exams (digital glossary, key term flash cards, review quizzes).
- **Activities and assignments** that will help you hone your knowledge and build your public speaking skills throughout

the course, as well as help you explore public speaking concepts online (web links), give you step-by-step guidance through the research, outline and note card preparation process (Outline Builder), watch and critique videos of sample speeches (Interactive Video Activities), and allow you to practice and present your presentation online using a speech video delivery, recording, and grading system (YouSeeU).

Key Concepts MindTap Test your knowledge with online printable flash cards.

abstract language (175)
alliteration (185)
antithesis (185)
concrete language (175)
idiom (175)
language (173)
metaphor (183)
mixed metaphor (183)
mnemonic device (185)

oral style (181)
parallelism (184)
personification (183)
referent (174)
repetition (184)
rhythm (184)
simile (182)
symbol (174)
thought or reference (174)

Review Questions

1. Look up the dictionary definitions of five to seven keywords you will use in your next speech. Do they mean what you thought they meant? Have you been pronouncing them correctly? If you were using an incorrect word, replace it with a correct one.

2. Bring a newspaper or magazine to class and look for language that is sensitive or insensitive to culture and gender. In what ways is the language appropriate or inappropriate? What mistakes do you think the authors of the articles made, if any? What are the implications of these mistakes? What are the implications of the appropriate choices the authors made?

3. As a class, use a computer or cell phone to look up the following commonly confused pairs of words:

accept/except	compose /comprise	nauseated/nauseous
adverse/averse	explicit/implicit	principal/principle
affect/effect	poured/pored	anxious/eager
fewer/less	reign/rein	appraise/apprise
healthy/healthful	stationery/ stationary	between/among
imply/infer	uninterested/ disinterested	compliment/ complement
lay/lie	who/whom	

How many of these words did you have confused before you began this exercise?

4. Select a topic for an imaginary speech. Write out your introduction or first main point for that speech. Now read that to a small audience. Put the paper aside and talk that part of your speech in an oral style. What differences do you notice? Is the oral style interactive, casual, and repetitive?

5. Divide into groups and select one of the following terms:

smoking	political parties	war
Halloween	vacations	

Using the seven devices for creating imagery and rhythm (simile, metaphor, personification, parallelism, repetition, alliteration, antithesis), write statements about this topic. Share your results with the class. Which devices helped you do a particularly good job conveying your ideas? Why do you think so?

10 | Delivering Your Speech

Methods of Delivery

Verbal Components of Delivery

Nonverbal Components of Delivery

Rehearsing Your Speech

IN THIS CHAPTER, YOU WILL LEARN TO:

- Compare and contrast the four different methods of delivering a speech

- Name and experiment with the verbal components of delivery

- List and experiment with the nonverbal components of delivery

- Test and implement effective strategies for rehearsing your speech

When we deliver our speeches, we share our message with our audience. Our delivery should bring our ideas to life for our audience. However, **delivery** is more complex than simply "giving a speech." It is your way of connecting with your audience and sharing your ideas. Because of the importance of delivery, this chapter covers the verbal and nonverbal components of delivery that will help you present your ideas in the most effective way. In the discussion that follows, you will learn about four methods of delivery, the verbal and nonverbal components of delivery, and strategies for rehearsing your speech.

MindTap® Start with a quick warm-up activity and review the chapter's learning objectives.

Douglas Graham/Roll Call/CQ-Roll Call Group/Getty Images

▲ Chad Pregracke (also featured in Chapter 16) is the founder of Living Lands and Waters. He, his crew, and over 87,000 volunteers have pulled more than 8.4 million pounds of debris from our nation's rivers. Pregracke's successes lie not only in his drive and charisma but also in his ability to deliver his message successfully to diverse audiences. Because delivery is so important to our public dialogue, in this chapter you will explore the ways your delivery can help you engage your audience and express your ideas.

Methods of Delivery

The four types of delivery you use as a public speaker are extemporaneous, impromptu, manuscript, and memorized.[1] Let's look at each of these methods of delivery and the reasons for using them.

Extemporaneous Delivery

Most of your speeches will be extemporaneous. When you give an **extemporaneous speech**, you present a carefully prepared and practiced speech from brief notes rather than from memory or a written manuscript. Because an extemporaneous delivery tends to be more natural than other deliveries, it is one of the more common methods.

An extemporaneous delivery evolves as you work from your preparation outline to your speaking outline. Recall from Chapter 7 that when you work with your preparation outline, you organize all the material you've thoroughly researched. Therefore, you come to know your speech in full detail. You then summarize that detail in the speaking outline. When you practice giving your speech from the speaking outline, words and phrases remind you of the full ideas on the preparation outline. Thus, your speaking outline provides the brief notes you speak from. Because you don't need to read the full text of your speech to remember what you want to say, you can give your speech in a natural way.

The advantages of extemporaneous deliveries are many. The speaking outline or speaking notes prompt your ideas but do not allow you to read every word to your audience. Your eye contact and gestures are natural, and your tone is conversational. Finally, because extemporaneous deliveries encourage direct communication between the speaker and audience, it is easier to stay audience centered.

Delivery tips. Many beginning speakers worry they might forget their speeches if they use an extemporaneous delivery. To help overcome this fear, follow these guidelines:

1. Add more keywords and phrases to your outline (not full sentences). This way, you'll have more cues to aid your memory.
2. Practice your speech often before you give it so you will feel more confident about what you will remember and want to say.

Your goal isn't necessarily to eliminate your fear by reading your speech but to give yourself tools so you can "talk" your speech.

The differences between an extemporaneous delivery and a speech read to an audience are striking. With an extemporaneous delivery, your language follows an oral rather than a written style (Chapter 9). An extemporaneous delivery also follows a **conversational style**, which is more formal than everyday conversation but remains spontaneous and relaxed.[2] In addition, with a conversational style, your posture and gestures are relaxed, and you make frequent eye contact with your audience. In contrast, because reading requires your full attention, you're less able to make eye contact with your audience and gesture spontaneously. Imagine if Dr. Martin Luther King Jr. or Hillary Clinton had read their most famous speeches to their audiences. Their charisma and power would have disappeared.

Impromptu Delivery

When you give an **impromptu speech**, you present a speech that you have not planned or prepared in advance. Although you may be wondering why anyone would

American author and speaker Mark Twain joked, "It usually takes more than three weeks to prepare a good impromptu speech." This isn't true, of course, but with a few minutes of thoughtful organization, you can make it seem as if you took three weeks to prepare.

Bettmann/Corbis

delivery: Action or manner of speaking to an audience.

extemporaneous speech: Speech that is carefully prepared and practiced from brief notes rather than from memory or a written manuscript.

conversational style: Speaking style that is more formal than everyday conversation but remains spontaneous and relaxed.

impromptu speech: Speech that is not planned or prepared in advance.

do this—especially in light of the previous discussions about the importance of preparation, planning, and practice—impromptu speaking is quite common. It occurs in meetings or public gatherings when someone is asked to speak or feels the need to share her or his perspective. When you decide to speak, you have the advantage of having a moment or two to organize your ideas. If you suddenly are asked to speak, you may not be able to jot down notes, but you still can organize your ideas. Consider the following scenario:

> As a senior at the university, José was having trouble registering for the courses he needed to graduate. Enrollment on his campus was at an all-time high, and the number of majors in his own department had grown enormously. As a result, classes filled early. He expressed his frustration to his adviser, who suggested José attend a campus open forum on graduation requirements. José's adviser facilitated the discussion, and during the question-and-answer session, he asked José if he would share his frustrating experiences with the audience. José paused and quickly organized his thoughts about his frustrations and how they related to the discussion. His speech was a success not only because it addressed the discussion directly but also because he was candid about his experiences.

José's quick organization in his head gave him confidence and helped him deliver an audience-centered speech that was easy to follow.

Delivery tips. Although you never have much time to prepare an impromptu speech, you can practice impromptu deliveries. In fact, your speech instructor likely will ask you to give several impromptu speeches during the semester. When you deliver an impromptu speech, use the following guidelines:

1. Quickly but calmly decide on the main points you want to make.
2. Introduce your main points as you would in a speech you had prepared in advance: offer a preview such as "the three things I'd like to cover are" and use signposts such as "first."
3. Support your main points with subpoints and sub-subpoints.
4. Summarize your main points in a brief conclusion.

If you find yourself in an impromptu situation, stay calm. The skills you learn in your public speaking course are invaluable for such situations. Even though you may be nervous, you have learned to organize ideas, relate them to the audience, and deliver various types of speeches. Remember, too, that when you give an impromptu speech, your audience does not expect elaborate source citations, fancy visual aids, or creative introductions. They are looking for immediate clarity or guidance. If you rely on the fundamental skills you have learned in your public speaking course, you can handle impromptu speeches successfully.

Manuscript Delivery

When you give a **manuscript speech**, you read to an audience from a written text. Although most speeches are best delivered extemporaneously, some speeches require a manuscript delivery:

- When detailed and exact information must be reported carefully, such as to a professional board or a formal committee.
- When your speech will be scrutinized word by word, archived, and referred to later (for example, the president's address to the nation).
- When your speech text will be used later for some other purpose (for example, a keynote address at a conference, which often is published).

A manuscript speech is one of the most challenging forms of delivery. Contrary to what most beginning public speakers think, speaking effectively from a manuscript requires more preparation and skill than extemporaneous or impromptu speaking. Two problems are likely when a speaker reads from the full text. First, the speech often sounds like a written text and not an oral text, or a speech that "reads" well but doesn't "talk" well. Second, the speaker may be inclined to read to the

MindTap®

To compare the differences between a speech delivered in a conversational style and one that is read, watch the video clips of student speakers Shelley Weibel and Eric Daley. Which style of delivery do you think is more effective?

manuscript speech: Speech that is read to an audience from a written text.

Practicing the Public Dialogue | 10.1

COMPARE DELIVERY METHODS

In class, take an item out of your backpack or from your pocket. Turn to the person next to you and give an impromptu speech about this item. The speech can be informative, invitational, or persuasive and should be no longer than sixty seconds. Now find an example of something written—a paragraph in this textbook, the newspaper, or the like. Give another sixty-second "speech," reading the written material. With your partner, discuss the differences between the delivery styles. Which did you prefer to deliver? Which did you prefer to listen to?

MindTap®

Learn more about giving impromptu speeches, and also consider the benefits and drawbacks of extemporaneous delivery.

audience rather than talk with the people in it. Let's look at some solutions to these problems.

Delivery tips. When you write your speech in manuscript format, the best way to avoid a written style is to talk the speech aloud as you write it. The following guidelines will help you do this:

1. Working from your preparation outline, sit at your desk and speak the words as you write them on your computer or paper.
2. If you find yourself thinking the speech rather than saying it aloud, go back and speak the part you have just written. You usually will notice that you've slipped into a writer's style instead of a speaker's style.
3. Change the language in these sections to reflect spoken ideas rather than written ideas. Remember, your goal is to write a speech, not an essay.

The second problem with using a manuscript is the temptation to read it to the audience. This will greatly reduce your eye contact with the audience because you are focusing on the manuscript and not your listeners. Also, your words may sound wooden because you are more concerned about reading words accurately than how they might sound to your audience. Finally, your delivery may be too fast because you are more focused on getting the words out than paying attention to how the audience is reacting to you.

The way to overcome the challenges associated with reading a speech is to practice speaking from the manuscript again and again. If you become familiar with your manuscript during practice, you will find your natural rhythm and conversational style. You will notice where you can make eye contact with your audience easily and for extended periods. Like your extemporaneous speeches, you will be able to deliver full ideas or subpoints without reading. You also will discover that you'll want to slow down because, even though the words are in front of you, you feel comfortable enough to speak the words with feeling rather than rush through them.

Memorized Delivery

When you give a **memorized speech**, you present a speech that has been written out, committed to memory, and given word for word. With a memorized delivery, you give the speech without any notes. Orators 2,000 years ago prided themselves on their ability to memorize speeches that were hours long. Today, memorized speeches are usually used only for toasts, blessings, acceptance speeches, introductions, and sometimes in forensics. Use a memorized delivery in these situations:

- When your speech is very short
- When you want to say things in a very specific way
- When notes would be awkward or disruptive

The trick to a memorized delivery is to speak as naturally and conversationally as possible. Rather than focusing on remembering your words, focus on communicating your words to your audience. When you deliver a memorized speech, don't recite it but deliver it as though you were talking to your audience.

Delivery tips. To commit a speech to memory, follow these steps:

1. Write a manuscript of the speech using an oral style, not a written one.
2. Commit each line of your speech to memory.

memorized speech: Speech that has been written out, committed to memory, and given word for word.

"ALRIGHT HEAR THIS"

Founded in 2001 by former Def Jam head Russell Simmons, the Hip-Hop Summit Action Network (HSAN) is dedicated to using hip-hop as a catalyst for education and advocacy related to the well-being of at-risk youth. HSAN focuses on issues of community development, access to high-quality public education and literacy, freedom of speech, voter education, economic advancement, and youth leadership development. Since its beginnings, HSAN has sponsored a number of civic events, such as the 2008 get-out-the-vote campaign to register "50K in one day" (with the Hip-Hop Caucus) and the 2009 national Hip-Hop Summit on Financial Empowerment entitled "Get Your Money Right." In 2013, HSAN also sponsored the Hip-Hop Inaugural Ball II (with PHILANTHROPIK), described as the "hippest and hottest ticket of the inaugural weekend, celebrating the hip-hop community's role in popular culture and the 2012 election" of Barack Obama.[2] HSAN also works with the Recording Industry Association of America on advisory labels that alert parents to explicit content in music. It has defended hip-hop culture before members of the U.S. Congress, the Federal Trade Commission, and the Federal Communications Commission.

HSAN also seeks to harness the immense popularity of hip-hop to educate others about hip-hop music and culture. "Once an underground, controversial style characterized by gangsta mythology and

AP Images/Rob Widdis

all-too-real turf wars," says Nelson George, author of *Hip Hop America*, "rap music is now embraced across the radio dial and across the nation by a diverse, multiracial fan base. . . . Rappers are pop stars, pop stars rap, and the sound is as integral to the cultural landscape as country music or rock." HSAN's goal is to use this mainstream success to encourage the recording industry to establish mentoring programs and forums that will stimulate dialogue between artists, hip-hop fans, and industry leaders and promote understanding and positive change.

In 2007, HSAN entered into dialogue with the recording and broadcast industries with the goal of creating guidelines for lyrical and visual standards, particularly around the words *bitch* and *ho* and *nigger*. HSAN maintained that these words are

utterly derogatory and show complete lack of respect for the history of suffering and oppression that women, African Americans, and other people of color have experienced in the United States. Today, HSAN continues to deliver its message of the importance of engaging the Hip-Hop generation in "issues related to equal access to high quality public education and literacy, freedom of speech, voter registration, and economic empowerment."[3]

⏺ YOU CAN GET INVOLVED

MindTap˙ Learn more about the work of the Hip-Hop Summit Action Network and see how you can become a part of their efforts. You can get involved with issues related to the arts, the media, free speech, and much more.

---

3. Every few lines, set the manuscript aside and practice delivering them to an imaginary audience without reading them. Repeat until you can deliver your entire speech naturally and with confidence.
4. Once you've learned the full speech, practice it over and over, reminding yourself to listen to the meaning of your words. Remember, you want to bring the words to life and connect with your audience.

If you are delivering a long memorized speech, keep your manuscript nearby, if you can, so you can find your place if you get lost. If you cannot keep your manuscript near you, someone else may be able to hold it and prompt you if you lose your place. If you lose your place and have no one to prompt you, continue extemporaneously or

Table 10.1 Advantages and Disadvantages of the Four Delivery Methods

	EXTEMPORANEOUS	IMPROMPTU	MANUSCRIPT	MEMORIZED
Definition	A speech that is carefully prepared and practiced from brief notes rather than from memory or a written manuscript.	A speech that is not planned or prepared in advance and uses few or no notes.	A speech that is written word for word and read to an audience.	A speech that is written word for word, memorized, and given word for word.
Advantages	Combines a conversational style with a speaking outline. Encourages careful organization.	Allows for a conversational style with few or no notes.	Helps present very detailed or specific information exactly as the speaker wants.	Frees the speaker to move about the room. No need for notes.
Disadvantages	Requires practice time. Speakers may be tempted to memorize the speech.	Requires thinking and organizing ideas quickly. No time for preparation.	Requires a conversational style that can be hard to achieve because the speaker reads from a full text.	Requires careful memorization. Speaker must remember important points and details without notes.

MindTap®

Watch the video clips of student speakers Brandi Lafferty, Amy Wood, Carol Godart, and Hans Erian as they deliver parts of their speeches. Each of these speakers used a different method of delivery for her or his speech. Which delivery method do you think was most effective?

pause, backtrack to the last line you remember, repeat it in your head, and you should be able to remember what comes next.

Table 10.1 reviews the advantages and disadvantages of the four delivery methods.

Technology and Delivery

The explosion of technologies to help speakers deliver their messages has far outpaced the research that helps us understand the effectiveness of these aids. In fact, very little research exists to show what works well and what doesn't. In *High-Tech Worship? Using Presentational Technologies Wisely* (2005), Quentin Schultze argues that the latest or even more technology are not necessarily better for our presentations. Rather, wisdom and thoughtfulness about the reason we are using technology are the keys to using technology successfully in our presentations. Schultze suggests that speakers take control of their technology (rather than be controlled by it) and consider how particular kinds of technology will enhance the delivery of a message rather than dictate it.[4] To that end, consider the following questions and their answers as you incorporate different technologies into your delivery:

1. Do I want to move about as I speak? Will I be able to do so with the technology I have selected?
2. Will my technology (images and clips, for example) overpower me? Will I be able to strike a balance of images or clips with my arguments?
3. Does the technology I have chosen to use help me develop my ideas or present them more clearly than if I did not add it to my speech?

Considering the answers to these questions and the kinds of technology that will enhance your delivery (rather than detract or replace it) will help you select technology that assists you rather than constrains or hinders your presentation.

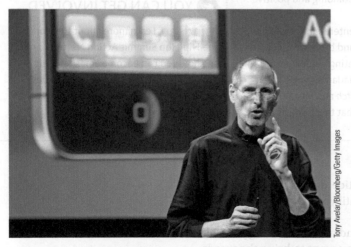

Steve Jobs, and others like him, revolutionized not just cell phone technology but also the options speakers have to deliver their messages to audiences. What do you think are the best aspects of this revolution for speakers? Do you see any drawbacks or disadvantages?

Tony Avelar/Bloomberg/Getty Images

Verbal Components of Delivery

A speech's power comes not only from its words but also from how they are delivered. Speakers known for their delivery—for example, John F. Kennedy, Barack Obama, Ann Richards, and Martin Luther King Jr.—use **vocal variety**, or changes in the volume, rate, and pitch of a speaker's voice that affect the meaning of the words delivered. We achieve vocal variety by consciously using certain verbal components of delivery: volume, rate, pitch and inflection, and pauses. The proper articulation and pronunciation of words and a consideration of dialect are also important components of delivery.

Volume

Volume is the loudness of a speaker's voice. Common sense tells us that we want to speak loudly enough for our audiences to hear us but not so loudly that we make our listeners uncomfortable. Knowing just how loud to speak can be difficult because our own voice sounds louder to us than to the audience and because the appropriate volume varies with each situation. Culture also affects perceptions about appropriate speaking volume. For example, in some Mediterranean cultures, a loud voice signals sincerity and strength, whereas in some parts of the United States, it may signal aggression or anger. In some Native American and Asian cultures, a soft voice signals education and good manners.[6] However, in some European cultures, a soft voice may signal femininity, secrecy, or even fear.

Pay attention to nonverbal cues from your audience to help you adjust your volume. If you are speaking without a microphone, watch the faces and postures of people in the back of the room as well as those in front as you begin to speak. If the people in the back seem confused, straining to hear, or are leaning forward intently, it's a signal to increase your volume. If the people in front move back in their seats and look uneasy, you likely are speaking too loudly. This is a signal to lower your volume.

When you use a microphone, you still need to pay attention to your volume. Before you begin your speech, test your voice with the microphone. Make sure you are the proper distance from it (neither too far nor too close) so the audience can listen comfortably. Don't turn off or avoid a microphone because it makes you nervous or you think people can hear you without one. Microphones exist to help audiences listen (and speakers speak) comfortably. Stay audience centered and use the microphone.

Rate

Rate is the speed at which we speak. There is no formula for the proper rate at which to deliver a speech. For example, Dr. Martin Luther King Jr. began his "I Have a Dream" speech at a rate of 92 words per minute and finished at a rate of 145.[7] The rate at which we speak conveys different feelings. When we speak quickly, we project a sense of urgency, excitement, or even haste. When we speak slowly, we convey seriousness, heaviness, or even uncertainty. Both a rapid rate and a slow rate have their place in a speech. However, too much of one or the other strains the audience's attention and may cause them to stop listening.

To check your rate, tape yourself for several minutes. Then play back the recording and assess your speed. If you are using a manuscript, each page (typed, double spaced, in a twelve-point font) should take two minutes to deliver. If you are much faster or slower, adjust your rate accordingly. You can also use rhythm (Chapter 9) to help you monitor your rate. Arranging your words into patterns so the sounds of the words together enhance meaning can help you vary your rate in an appealing way. Remember, rate is an audience-centered concern. We want to engage our audience, and our rate of speaking helps us in this effort by communicating certain emotions or energies.

vocal variety: Changes in the volume, rate, and pitch of a speaker's voice that affect the meaning of the words delivered.

volume: Loudness of a speaker's voice.

rate: Speed at which a speaker speaks.

Unique Manifestations of the Human Spirit

Wade Davis, Explorer

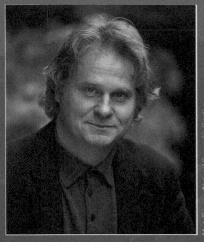

Mark Thiessen/National Geographic Creative

Anthropologist, ethnobotanist, ethnographer, author, filmmaker, and photographer, Wade Davis is described as "a rare combination of scientist, scholar, poet and passionate defender of life's diversity." His work has taken him to East Africa, Borneo, Nepal, Peru, Polynesia, Tibet, Mali, Benin, Togo, New Guinea, Australia, Colombia, Vanuatu, Mongolia, and the high Artic of Nunavut and Greenland. He has catalogued over 6,000 botanical species; studied zombies and the plant preparations that accompany practices; and has published more than a dozen books sharing his research and insights. He holds degrees in anthropology and biology, and a PhD from Harvard in ethnobotany. Davis explains his perspective and one of the guiding principles behind his work: "The world in which you were born is just one model of reality. Other cultures are not failed attempts at being you. They are unique manifestations of the human spirit."

Davis urges students to become "entrepreneurs of knowledge" and skilled public speakers: our knowledge base can be "monetized," he says, if students "learn how to communicate." Davis suggests that one of the biggest challenges of the sciences is "the inability to communicate," in fact, the "disinclination to do so." One of the reasons that "climate change has not really captured the public imagination is, quite simply, that the narrative has not been properly communicated to the public." And, after the horrific events of 9/11, Davis explains, "not a single anthropologist" was interviewed; yet, anthropology is, perhaps, the "one profession that actually could answer that question then on the lips of every American, why do they hate us?" So important are public speaking skills, in Davis's view, that individuals "literally have had their careers transformed by a single TED talk that turns up online."

For Davis, the most important credential for being a communicator "is to have something important to say that the world needs to hear." He explains that before his association with National Geographic, he began speaking publicly about each of the books he wrote. Then, his agent urged him to pull his experiences from his years of work with voodoo and in the Amazon to offer a "global perspective." And, as he did that, Davis recounts, "All that grew out of the process of communication, how the stories morphed" into larger perspectives. He adds, "it's funny how it worked, I mean it kind of grew out of that one speech my agent asked me to do, this sort of greatest hits speech . . . that the Geographic Society heard at a film festival in Telluride . . . that led me to being recruited as an explorer in residence."

In the late 1990s, Davis discovered the work of Michael Krauss and Ken Hale, linguists who shared that of the "7,000 languages of the world, half weren't being taught to children," and added languages and linguistics to his long list of passions. Davis sees language as "not just grammar and vocabulary"; instead, he argues, language is "a flash of the human spirit, a vehicle to the soul of a culture," and the fact that we are losing so many languages so quickly is horrifying. Languages communicate and organize one's culture, Davis explains, and cultures show us possibilities:

"The idea that the world in which you were born, it's just one model of reality, and the people of the world aren't failed attempts at being new or failed attempts at being modern. Each culture, by definition, is a unique answer to a fundamental question, what does it mean to be human and alive? When the people of the world answer that question, they do so in 7,000 different voices, which collectively become the human repertoire for dealing with the challenges that will confront us in the coming millennia . . . every culture has something to say, and each one deserves to be heard. And the great curse of humanity is cultural myopia, the idea that my world is the real world and everybody else is a failed attempt of, of being me."[5]

WHAT DO YOU THINK?

1. Davis encourages students to become "skilled public speakers." Even though many of us are quite nervous thinking about giving speeches, how might you, as a student, take steps to become a skilled public speaker?

2. After 9/11, Davis says, anthropologists might have helped answer the question, "Why do they hate us?" What aspects about connecting with your audience would a student of communication need to consider when helping to answer this question?

3. A speaker presenting a TED Talk usually uses technology such as PowerPoint slides or video to help present the speech. Watch several TED Talk presentations and assess their slides and videos. What makes them effective?

Wade Davis

When members of your audience come from varied cultural backgrounds or are nonnative speakers of your language, try to slow your rate so accents and unfamiliar words are easier to follow. Adjusting your rate in this way communicates an audience-centered stance and adds to your credibility.

Pitch and Inflection

Pitch refers to the position of tones on the musical scale, and in public speaking, it reveals itself in the highness or lowness of a speaker's voice. **Inflection** is the manipulation of pitch to create certain meanings or moods. Together, pitch and inflection help us communicate more effectively with our audience. Consider the word *well* and its different meanings when used in spoken language. The control of pitch and inflection allows us to say "well" in ways that suggest joyful surprise or indecision or indignation or pity. All speakers manipulate their pitch to create meaning during their speeches. All of us alter our pitch to ask a question, express satisfaction or displeasure, convey confidence or confusion, or even communicate threats or aggression. Variations in pitch clarify meaning and help catch and maintain our audience's attention.

Saul Loeb/AFP/Getty Images

Speakers who do not pay attention to their pitch and inflection risk losing their audience. Speakers who do not alter their pitch speak in what is called a **monotone**. Other speakers may say everything in too low or high a pitch. When a speaker says everything in a monotone or a low pitch, the audience senses a lack of interest or energy. When the pitch is too high for too long, every word is communicated with equal enthusiasm, or "excessive zeal,"[8] and the audience begins to wonder which points are the most important. There are solutions to these problems. First, tape yourself so you can hear your pitch. If your pitch is too high, practice breathing more deeply (from the abdomen rather than the throat) and relaxing your throat muscles as you speak. Speak from your diaphragm rather than your throat, and read aloud regularly to practice this technique until you can get your pitch to drop naturally. (Note that proper breathing also helps you increase the volume of your voice and project your voice farther.) If you speak in a monotone or in too low a pitch, practice delivering your speech (or reading something aloud) in an overly dramatic way, using inflection, exclamations, and vocal variation as much as possible. With practice, vocal variation will come naturally and carry over into public speaking situations.

Speakers like Barack Obama incorporate vocal variety in their speeches to engage audiences. Consider the introduction to your next speech. Practice this part of your speech, listening for your vocal variety. Adjust your delivery as needed to make sure you catch your audience's attention and communicate your message clearly.

Pauses

Pauses are hesitations and brief silences in speech or conversation. In speeches, they often are planned, and they serve several useful functions. Pauses give us time to breathe fully and to collect our thoughts during a speech or before we answer a question from the audience. Pauses also give audiences time to absorb and process information—they're like rest stops, giving the audience breathers before continuing. Finally, pauses before or after a climactic word or an important point reinforce that word or point.

Pauses can also add clarity. Read the passage here without stopping to pause after any of the words:

> The back of the eye on which an image of the outside world is thrown and which corresponds to the eye of a camera is composed of a mosaic of rods and cones whose diameter is little more than the length of an average light wave.

Without pauses, it's hard to understand what's being said here, isn't it? Now read the passage again and note where you would naturally pause. Does the meaning of the passage become clearer?

The four pauses that make this passage easier to understand are after *eye, thrown, camera,* and *cones.*[9] These are places in written text where we would add commas to

pitch: Highness or lowness of a speaker's voice.

inflection: Manipulation of pitch to create certain meanings or moods.

monotone: Way of speaking in which a speaker does not alter her or his pitch.

pauses: Hesitations and brief silences in speech or conversation.

indicate meaning. In written text, pauses often are indicated by punctuation, but in speeches, audiences cannot see the punctuation. Pause to punctuate your words as well as to establish mood, indicate a transition, take time to reflect, or emphasize a point. For example, in his speech on the pollution caused by using fossil fuels, Preston used a pause to make a particular impact: "In fact," Preston argued, "according to the Southern California Edison Electric Transportation website, updated only last month, running for half an hour in urban air pollution introduces as much carbon monoxide into your lungs as [pause] smoking a pack of cigarettes."

Learning the art of the pause takes time and practice. Before you become comfortable with the brief moments of silence necessary in a speech, you may have the urge to fill the silence. Avoid **vocalized pauses**, or pauses that speakers fill with words or sounds like "um," "er," or "uh." Vocalized pauses not only are irritating, but they can also create a negative impression of the speaker. When a speaker uses so many vocalized pauses that they intrude into an audience's awareness, listeners may begin to question the speaker's knowledge and speaking capabilities.[10] If you have a habit of vocalizing pauses, try the following process to eliminate them:

1. Listen for vocalized pauses in your daily speech.
2. When you hear one, anticipate the next one.
3. When you feel the urge to say "um" or "er" to fill space, gently bite your tongue and don't let the word escape.
4. Wait until your next word of substance is ready to come out and say it instead.

It may take time to eliminate vocalized pauses from your speech, and you may feel awkward with the silence, but the results are worth the effort.

Articulation

Articulation is the physical process of producing specific speech sounds to make language intelligible to our audiences. Our clarity depends on our articulation—whether we say words distinctly or whether we mumble and slur. Articulation depends on the accuracy of movement of our tongue, lips, jaws, and teeth. This movement produces either "didjago?" or "did you go?" In fact, scholars of performance and delivery argue that poor articulation is a trend across all sectors of U.S. culture.[11]

Audiences expect public speaking to be more clearly articulated than private conversation. Speakers with an audience-centered focus care about clear articulation. Clearly articulated words communicate that you want your audience to understand you and can add to your credibility. For your audience to understand your ideas, they must be able to decipher your words. To improve your articulation skills, try the following exercise:

1. Several days before your speech, select a part of your speech or a short written text you can read aloud.
2. Practice saying each word of your speech excerpt or text as slowly and clearly as possible, exaggerating the clarity of each word.
3. Repeat this exercise once or twice each day before you give your speech.

This exercise will help you recognize how much you slur or mumble and teach you to speak more clearly when you give your speech. Don't worry—you won't speak in this exaggerated way when you finally deliver your speech, but your words will be much clearer.

Pronunciation

Just as you would not turn in an essay you knew was filled with spelling errors, never deliver a speech filled with pronunciation errors. **Pronunciation** is the act of saying words correctly according to the accepted standards of a language. Pronunciation and articulation may seem similar, but pronunciation refers to how *correctly* a word is said, whereas articulation refers to how *clearly* a word is said. For example, saying the word *nuclear* as "nu-cle-ar" (correct) rather than "nu-cu-lar" (incorrect) has to

vocalized pauses: Pauses that speakers fill with words or sounds like "um," "er," or "uh."

articulation: Physical process of producing specific speech sounds to make language intelligible.

pronunciation: Act of saying words correctly according to the accepted standards of a language.

do with pronunciation, and mumbling either pronunciation rather than speaking it clearly has to do with articulation.

Pronouncing words correctly communicates to your audience that you have listened carefully to the public dialogue going on around you. You have taken care to learn the common language and pronounce it correctly. In addition, correct pronunciation of terms and names in a language other than your native one communicates your respect for that culture and enhances your credibility.

Dialect

A **dialect** is a pattern of speech shared by an ethnic group or people from specific geographical locations. Dialects include specific vocabulary that is unique to a group as well as styles of pronunciation shared by members of that group. All people have a dialect, and your own dialect comes from your ethnic heritage as well as the place you grew up. For example, do you say "wash" or "warsh" when you want something clean? How about "soda," "pop," or "coke" when you want a soft drink? Your choices reflect your dialect.

People who use a standard American dialect (the dialect newscasters use when they are on the air) often forget that they, too, have a dialect, and they sometimes view the dialect of others as inferior. For public speaking, dialect is important because speakers need to consider the effect their dialect has on those who are unfamiliar with it. Speakers may use words that aren't familiar to their audience or may pronounce words in ways that sound odd or different.

If you know your dialect will be unfamiliar to your audience, try the following:

1. Acknowledge your region of birth or ethnic heritage.
2. Talk about how that shapes your use of language by giving examples of some of the differences you've encountered between your dialect and those of your audience.
3. Define terms that are unfamiliar to your audience.
4. Soften the accent associated with your dialect if that accent is fairly strong and might hinder understanding.

Practicing the Public Dialogue | 10.2

REFINE THE VERBAL COMPONENTS OF YOUR DELIVERY

If you'd like to get some feedback on the verbal components of your delivery, ask your public speaking class to help you. Here are some exercises you can do in front of the classroom using your classmates as your audience:

- If you are a very quiet speaker, begin speaking as softly as you can and increase your volume until all the people at the back of the classroom nod their heads to indicate they can hear you comfortably.
- If you are a very fast speaker, begin speaking as fast as you can and decrease your rate until your listeners nod to indicate they are comfortable with your rate.
- If you have trouble with vocalized pauses, begin using as many of them as you can while you speak for about sixty seconds. Then continue to speak for another sixty seconds, being careful not to use a single vocalized pause.
- If you struggle with articulation, pronunciation, or dialect, begin speaking as you normally would for about sixty seconds. Then slow your speech and say each word carefully until your listeners nod to indicate they can understand you clearly.

Nonverbal Components of Delivery

The nonverbal components of delivery are those aspects communicated through our bodies and faces. For public speakers, these include personal appearance, eye contact, facial expression, posture, gestures, and proxemics.[12]

Scholars of interpersonal communication recognize that nonverbal communication has a powerful impact on the meanings exchanged between people. Researchers suggest that between 65 and 93 percent of the total meaning of a message comes to us through nonverbal signals.[13] In addition, when nonverbal signals contradict verbal signals (for example, you say you're glad to see someone but your facial expression and physical posture suggest you're not), people tend to believe the nonverbal signals more than the verbal ones.[14]

For public speakers, nonverbal communication is especially important because it conveys meaning and it can either enhance or detract from the overall message. Let's look at how the components of nonverbal communication affect a speech.[15]

dialect: Pattern of speech that is shared by an ethnic group or people from specific geographical locations.

Personal Appearance

Personal appearance, or the way you dress, groom, and present yourself physically, is an important part of delivery. But how important? Consider the following sayings:

You can't judge a book by its cover.

Beauty is in the eye of the beholder.

Looks are everything.

Beauty is as beauty does.

You can never be too rich or too thin.

You can dress him up, but you still can't take him out.

Good-looking lawyers make more money.

Which statements are true? Does physical appearance matter, or is it irrelevant? Studies show that, indeed, personal appearance matters quite a bit. People deemed "more attractive" earn more money than their "less attractive" peers, and personal grooming plays a large part in our perception of a person's attractiveness for both men and women.[16] Attractive characteristics are defined as "those characteristics that make one person appear pleasing to another."[17] Even though we may say we shouldn't judge people by their looks, it seems that is exactly what we do.[18]

Without a doubt, standards for attractiveness and beauty change with generations as well as with cultures and subcultures. Despite these differences, though, there is a basic standard for acceptable personal grooming in public speaking situations: The speaker's dress should be appropriate to the occasion.[19] If the occasion is formal, the speaker is expected to dress formally. If the occasion is casual, the speaker's clothing should be less formal. A speaker who shows up at a formal occasion in a T-shirt and shorts not only displays a lack of audience awareness but also is likely to lose credibility. Similarly, wearing formal business attire to speak at a casual gathering is also inappropriate. In short, be sure your clothing matches the style and tone of the occasion.

Another standard for appropriate grooming in public speaking situations is to wear attire that is neither too revealing nor too restricting. As fashions change, standards for acceptability change. More than 100 years ago, displaying bare skin in public was considered highly unacceptable. Today, the amount of bare skin or body that can be exposed or accentuated is far greater, and many celebrities accept awards and make speeches wearing very little at all. However, most of us aren't movie stars or pop stars, so when giving a speech in public, we want the audience to listen to our message and not be distracted by our appearance. Dressing simply and tastefully does more than help your audience pay attention to your message. It also helps you move about comfortably and freely as you give your speech.

Delivery begins the moment the audience sees you, so pay careful attention to your personal appearance and present yourself appropriately for the occasion at which you are speaking.

personal appearance: Way speakers dress, groom, and present themselves physically.

When does our personal appearance matter, and why? Do you think it will matter to the individual in jeans and a casual shirt in this image? Why might this style of dress be a disadvantage? Are there situations in which it could it be an advantage? Why or why not?

Peter Cade/Getty Images

tip
National Geographic Explorer

BARRINGTON IRVING, Explorer, Pilot, Educator

Can you tell us about the importance of eye contact when giving speeches?
Yes. Great politicians, they're great at looking people in the eye, creating a welcoming environment, and it's as if you're having a conversation with the person and you're not just giving a lecture to them; you are actually talking to the person.

You have to trust yourself and you really have to know what you're talking about, you know. When you write something on a piece of paper, and you put colorful words around it, you can fool anyone. When you're talking from the heart and making eye contact with your audience, you really have to know exactly what you're talking about and it creates an inviting touch, as well. Remember, it's okay to make a mistake and when you do that people recognize that you're not staring at a sheet of paper. You know, people recognize that you're not just reading from a sheet of paper.

Eye Contact

The second essential component of nonverbal delivery is **eye contact**, visual contact with another person's eyes. Like personal appearance, appropriate eye contact is affected by culture and gender. Most North Americans and western Europeans expect a speaker to make extensive eye contact. However, in Native American cultures, as in Japan and parts of Africa, extensive eye contact is considered invasive and disrespectful. Gender, too, affects the meaning of eye contact. For men, direct and extended eye contact with another man may be perceived as a challenge or threat. For women, direct and extended eye contact with a man may be interpreted as an invitation to flirt. So knowing what to do with our eyes as we deliver a speech depends on knowing who is in our audience.

Even though the nuances of eye contact are complex, most cultures expect at least some eye contact during a speech. Eye contact has three functions. First, it is a way to greet and acknowledge the audience before the speech begins. Second, eye contact is a way to gauge and keep our audience's interest. We use eye contact to monitor feedback from our audience and adjust our volume, rate, and pitch accordingly. Third, eye contact is a way to communicate sincerity and honesty.

Audiences rate speakers who make eye contact for less than half their speech as tentative, uncomfortable, and even as insincere and dishonest.[20] In contrast, speakers who make eye contact for more than half their speech are viewed as more credible and trustworthy.[21]

For eye contact to be effective, try to do two things as you look out at your audience. First, make eye contact with many people in the audience rather than a few friendly faces. Make eye contact with people in all parts of the room, not just those immediately in front of you. Gather information about level of comprehension, interest, and agreement from as many people as you can.

Second, look with interest. Rather than scanning faces in the audience or looking over listeners' heads to the back of the room, really look at individual people in the audience. Slow down the movement of your eyes so you actually make a connection

eye contact: Visual contact with another person's eyes.

with people through your eye contact. Looking with interest communicates you are pleased to be speaking to your audience and are interested in their responses.

Facial Expression

Your face plays a central role in communicating with your audience, letting them know your attitudes, emotional states, and sometimes even your inner thoughts. Your **facial expression** is the movement of your eyes, eyebrows, and mouth to convey reactions and emotions. Actors are highly skilled at using their faces to communicate, and audiences appreciate this talent. Although you don't need to be as skilled as an actor, you do need to consider your facial expressions as you deliver your speech. A poker face, although useful in a card game, will not help you communicate your ideas.

You can use your facial expressions to communicate your own interest in your topic, your agreement or disagreement with a point, your openness to an idea, and even your feeling about an issue. Take some time to decide which facial expressions might be useful to include in your speech. If these expressions aren't coming naturally to you, practice them until you are comfortable delivering them.

Posture

Posture is the way we position and carry our bodies, and whether or not we realize it, people assign meaning to our posture. We are perceived as confident and relaxed or tense and insecure based, in part, on our posture. A confident speaker is often called "poised," possessing assurance, dignity, and a sense of calm. Nervousness can affect our posture, making us feel awkward and act in ways we'd never do in other situations: grip the podium with both hands, slouch over our speaking notes, pace back and forth, or stand stuck to one spot. These nervous reactions detract from our delivery and communicate a message we probably don't want to send.[22]

But by paying attention during practice to the way we carry our bodies, we can eliminate some nervous postures. To become aware of your posture during a speech, practice your speech in the way you actually will give it. That is, if you will deliver your speech standing, practice while standing up. Devise a makeshift podium if need be. Or if you are to sit while giving the speech, practice the speech while sitting, with chairs beside you and your notes on a table in front of you. Similarly, if you will use a handheld or attachable microphone, practice with something resembling it so you get the feel of speaking with a microphone.

By practicing the speech in the way you'll actually give it, you can correct your nervous habits before you deliver the speech. For example, if you find that you pace or grip the podium tightly, you can replace the bad habit with a better one. If you discover you stand immobilized when you practice, you can add cues to your speaking outline to remind you to move during your speech. If you slouch, you can practice sitting up straight and looking out at your audience. In sum, your posture during your speech should improve if you pay attention to your body during practice.

Finally, pay attention to the way you begin and end your speech. Wait until you are at the podium or have the microphone in your hand before you begin talking. Don't start speaking until you are facing your audience and have made eye contact. Similarly, don't walk off the stage until you have finished the last word of your conclusion. Finishing your conclusion or your final answer before you leave the spotlight communicates confidence and a willingness to give every word the attention it deserves. These guidelines will help you remain audience centered.

Gestures

Gestures are movements, usually of the hands but sometimes of the entire body, that express meaning and emotion or offer clarity to a message. Students of rhetoric in ancient Greece and Rome spent hours learning specific gestures to accompany

facial expression: The movement of your eyes, eyebrows, and mouth to convey reactions and emotions.

posture: Way speakers position and carry their bodies.

gestures: Movements, usually of the hands but sometimes of the full body, that express meaning and emotion or offer clarity to a message.

MANAGING THOSE NERVES

If you fear public speaking, you are not alone. Speaking in front of others is one of the most common fears of people in the workplace. Some individuals are so fearful, explains anxietycoach.com, that they turn down promotions or change jobs if the position will require giving speeches. Others might not take such extreme measures, but may try to avoid giving even the smallest of speeches by arriving late to a meeting or function so that they can avoid self-introductions. If they cannot avoid these small presentations, they cope by rushing through them, which results in giving others a less than desirable first impression. When speaking is required, fearful individuals often try several unproductive measures, such as skipping parts of their speech, rushing or reading, pretending to be sick so they can shorten their presentation or excuse their delivery, or using excessive slides and images to avoid speaking. Although this may not seem like much of a problem, these behaviors can get in the way of our work performance. Imagine a coworker who avoids, stumbles, rushes, or omits information—it doesn't bode well for the company or the individual. Recall that our nervousness before a speech is called communication apprehension (Chapter 1) and that it can take two forms. Trait anxiety refers to those individuals who are apprehensive about communication in all situations, while situational anxiety refers to apprehension in specific situations, like public speaking (Chapter 1). Take a moment to consider whether you are apprehensive about all communication situations, or mostly apprehensive about public speaking. The suggestions in Chapter 1 can help you manage your nerves and make a good impression in your workplace. Numerous websites offer a range of solutions, most of them involving the relaxation techniques discussed in that chapter. Remember, visualization, breathing, and staying positive can assist you in reducing your apprehension. Writing, exercising, reframing, and working with a therapist are other options to help you stay calm.[24]

specific parts of their speeches. For example, certain gestures were used with transitions, and others signaled specific kinds of main points or ideas. These choreographed gestures were used until the eighteenth century.[23] Today, research on gestures in public speaking indicates that gestures should be as natural as possible rather than memorized.

However, beginning public speakers don't always know what gestures will appear natural in a speech. With only minor variations, natural gestures in a speech are the same as those you normally use in personal conversations to complement your ideas and bring your words to life. The same is true for public speeches. Gestures make our delivery lively, offer emphasis and clarity, and convey our passion and interest. Use these tips to help you with gestures:

1. *Vary your gestures.* Try to use different kinds of gestures rather than repeating only one gesture. Some gestures emphasize (a fist on the podium), clarify (counting first, second, third on your fingers), or illustrate (drawing a shape with your hands in the air). Try to incorporate a variety of these gestures into your speech.
2. *Use gestures that fit your message.* Sometimes, a point needs an extravagant gesture; at other times, a more subtle gesture is much more effective. For example, use a relaxed pattern of hand movement as you explain a point but a larger more vigorous movement when you are emphasizing something quite important.
3. *Stay relaxed.* Your gestures should flow with your words. Try to keep your movements comfortable and effortless. If you find a gesture makes you tense, drop it from the speech and replace it with something more casual and familiar.

You will find that as you relax and gain experience speaking, you will stop thinking about your gestures and simply use them as you normally do in conversation.

Practicing the Public Dialogue | 10.3

REFINE THE NONVERBAL COMPONENTS OF YOUR DELIVERY

As a class, discuss the differences in your styles of nonverbal delivery: Are you someone who likes to dress more formally or more casually? Do you have to make adjustments to your nonverbal style because of your cultural background? How much eye contact are you comfortable with? Do you wish you could stand closer to your audience or farther away? Would you prefer to hold the podium, gesture, or put your hands in your pockets? What about your personal preferences enhances your speaking presence and what might detract from it?

Proxemics

Effective speakers pay close attention to **proxemics**, the use of space during communication. Be mindful of how far away you are from your audience as well as how elevated you are from them (for example, on a platform or a podium). The farther away you are, the stronger the idea of separation. The higher up you are, the more the idea of power is communicated.

You can work with proxemics in your delivery. Recall from Chapter 4 that the Dalai Lama worked without a lectern, sometimes even sitting down on stage. Although you don't want to remain too close to your audience throughout your speech, getting close to them at key points allows for greater connection and communicates a desire to be perceived as more of an equal. Try stepping from behind the lectern or down from the podium and moving closer to your audience. If you cannot do this because you need a microphone or a place to put your notes, you might be able to move closer during a question-and-answer session. Doing so will help you communicate openness and a willingness to engage in conversation with your audience.

Rehearsing Your Speech

Although it may sound odd, the more you practice, the more natural you will sound. This is because you will be familiar with your speech on many levels. You'll not only know the ideas but will also have some of the wording worked out. You will be comfortable with the verbal and nonverbal components of your delivery. And you'll feel more confident during your question-and-answer session, if your speech includes one, because you will have prepared and rehearsed the answers to questions you might be asked. (For information about how to handle question-and-answer sessions, see Chapter 4 and the Appendix.) Take a look at these guidelines for rehearsing your delivery. If you follow them, your delivery will communicate your interest in participating in the public dialogue:

1. Practice giving your speech aloud using your speaking outline (Chapter 7).
2. Practice all stories, quotations, statistics, and other evidence until you can deliver them exactly as you want.
3. When you are comfortable with your material, practice your speech in front of a mirror. Monitor your nonverbal communication and make adjustments as needed so you communicate your message clearly.
4. Now tape your speech and listen for vocal variety. Check your volume, rate, pitch and inflection, pauses, and how you articulate and pronounce words. If you think your dialect will hinder your delivery, make adjustments.
5. Practice your speech again, incorporating the verbal and nonverbal changes you worked out in steps 1 through 4.
6. Now practice a few times in front of a friend. Have the person ask you questions at the end of the speech and practice answering them. Incorporate any useful feedback your friend may offer.
7. Stage a dress rehearsal. Consider your personal appearance by wearing the clothing you will wear on the day you speak. Set up your practice area so it resembles the actual speaking situation as closely as possible. Consider proxemics and the space you want between you and the audience.

proxemics: Use of space during communication.

Chapter Summary

To deliver a speech to an audience is to share your hard work and well-planned ideas.

- Delivering a speech involves many components: delivery type, verbal and nonverbal considerations, and the rehearsal process.
- When we hear or give a carefully prepared and well-articulated speech, we realize that delivery is the art of clarifying issues and engaging audiences.

There are four types of delivery.

- An extemporaneous speech is delivered from brief notes or an outline.
- An impromptu speech is delivered with little or no advance notice or time for preparation.
- A manuscript speech is written out word for word and read aloud.
- A memorized speech has been committed to memory and is delivered without notes.

As you deliver your speeches, pay attention to both verbal and nonverbal components.

- To achieve vocal variety, be mindful of verbal components such as volume, rate, pitch and inflection, pauses, articulation, pronunciation, and dialect.
- To enhance your verbal message, consider the nonverbal components of your speech, including personal appearance, eye contact, facial expressions, posture, gestures, and proxemics.

Be sure to rehearse your speech.

- Rehearsing your speech helps ensure that your delivery will be smooth and comfortable.
- A well-practiced speech also helps you communicate your interest in your topic and in the public dialogue.

Invitation to Public Speaking Online MindTap®

Now that you have read Chapter 10, use your MindTap Communication for *Invitation to Public Speaking* for quick access to the digital resources that accompany this text. These resources include:

- **Study tools** that will help you assess your learning and prepare for exams (digital glossary, key term flash cards, review quizzes).
- **Activities and assignments** that will help you hone your knowledge and build your public speaking skills throughout

the course, as well as help you explore public speaking concepts online (web links), give you step-by-step guidance through the research, outline and note card preparation process (Outline Builder), watch and critique videos of sample speeches (Interactive Video Activities), and allow you to practice and present your presentation online using a speech video delivery, recording, and grading system (YouSeeU).

Key Concepts MindTap® Test your knowledge with online printable flash cards.

articulation (198)
conversational style (190)
delivery (190)
dialect (199)
extemporaneous speech (190)
eye contact (201)
facial expression (202)
gestures (202)
impromptu speech (190)
inflection (197)
manuscript speech (191)
memorized speech (192)

monotone (197)
pauses (197)
personal appearance (200)
pitch (197)
posture (202)
pronunciation (198)
proxemics (204)
rate (195)
vocal variety (195)
vocalized pauses (198)
volume (195)

Review Questions

1. Identify speakers you consider to have a strong delivery. What characteristics make their delivery strong? How many of these characteristics might you incorporate into your style of delivery?

2. Which method of delivery will you choose (or have you been assigned) for your next speech? Why? How will you make that method as audience centered as possible? Now identify the method of delivery that you actually prefer. If the two don't match, what will you do to feel more comfortable with the type of delivery you will use for your next speech?

3. Review the discussion in Chapter 1 about nervousness. Are there any tips that you can incorporate into your delivery? Which ones? Why do you think they are useful?

4. Identify the differences among extemporaneous, impromptu, manuscript, and memorized deliveries. What are the strengths and weaknesses of each type of delivery?

5. Write a quick speech and exchange the speeches among classmates. In groups, give that speech as though it were a tragedy, a surprise, or a hilarious story. Or choose some other approach that will allow you to work on vocal variety. How well are you able to match the verbal aspects of your delivery to the mood you have selected?

11 | Visual Aids

IN THIS CHAPTER, YOU WILL LEARN TO:

- Discuss the importance of using visual aids
- Identify and analyze the different types of visual aids
- Create effective visual aids
- Explain the five guidelines for using visual aids

People have come to accept the information we get from visual messages as casually as we accept the information we hear. So prevalent are these visual images today that when we are asked to listen without a visual stimulus, we often lose interest and become restless. Although people once listened to music and politicians without accompanying images and visual distractions, now we are bored by performances that aren't stimulating to the eyes as well as the ears. But what does our visual culture mean for beginning public speakers? In your speeches for your speech class, you probably will be asked to use visual aids. And in many of your speeches outside the classroom, you will want to display parts of your message visually. How do you compete with the sophistication of the images that come across our computer screens, are

MindTap Start with a quick warm-up activity and review the chapter's learning objectives.

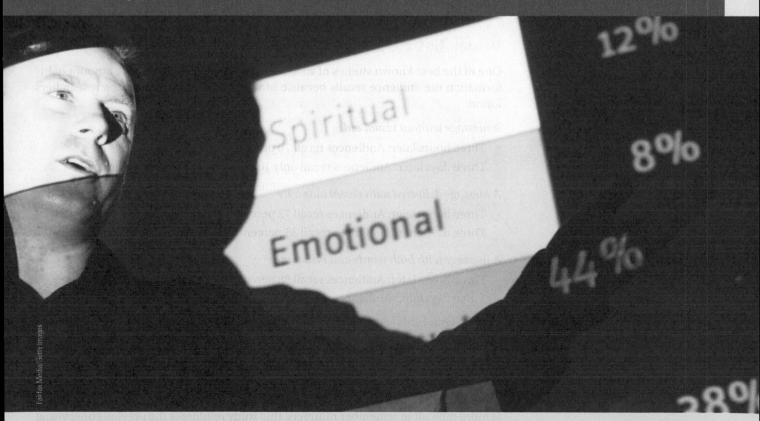

Fairfax Media/Getty Images

▲ Andrew McIntyre, co-founder of the Morris Hargreaves McIntyre market research company, works with museums, galleries, theaters, and art centers helping them connect with audiences and consumers and showcase their organizations. McIntyre shares that he is passionate about the ways audiences and consumers "make meaning" and is a popular speaker, trainer, and product developer. In this chapter you will learn how visual aids can help your audience "make meaning," engage your ideas, and get the most out of your arguments.

displayed throughout live performances, and that we have come to expect in almost every presentation of information? How do you take advantage of technology to craft visual aids that not only enhance your message but also appeal to your audience?

Public speakers need to design effective visual aids. To help you as a public speaker, this chapter discusses the reasons for using visual aids, illustrates the various types of visual aids, helps you decide what to show on a visual aid, how to format your visual aids, and offers guidelines for using them.

MindTap

Read, highlight, and take notes online.

Why Visual Aids Are Important

Although many of the speeches you've read about in this book were given without visual aids, including Martin Luther King Jr.'s famous "I Have a Dream" speech, many types of speeches benefit from effective visual aids. When you are describing a process, explaining complex information, or hoping your message will have a powerful impact, visual aids can help you accomplish these goals. To understand the effects of visual aids, let's first take a look at the important functions of visual aids in a speech.

Visual Aids Help Gain and Maintain Audience Attention

In 1996, when attorney Johnnie Cochran displayed the glove said to belong to accused murderer O. J. Simpson and told the jurors, "If it doesn't fit, you must acquit," he had his audience's full attention. Although his words were compelling and he used a memorable rhyme, the visual aid caught jurors' attention and kept them focused on his argument. A visual aid gives an audience something to focus on, and it reinforces your verbal message. If you want to capture your audience's attention, consider using a visual aid to complement your words.

Visual Aids Help Audiences Recall Information

One of the best-known studies of visual aids in speeches assessed the amount of information the audience recalls because of visual aids. Here is what the researchers found:

A message without visual aids

- Three hours later: Audiences recall 70 percent of the information.
- Three days later: Audiences recall only 10 percent of the information.

A message delivered with visual aids only

- Three hours later: Audiences recall 72 percent.
- Three days later: Audiences recall 35 percent.

A message with both words and visual aids

- Three hours later: Audiences recall 85 percent.
- Three days later: Audiences recall 65 percent.[1]

Clearly, visual aids assist with recall.

In another study, researchers asked people to examine a series of photographs and identify those that were repeated. With as many as 200 photographs in a series, people still could pick out the repeat photographs.[2] However, when recall was tested by listening to series of numbers, people begin to forget which numbers were repeated in series of only six or seven numbers. Although common sense tells us that it often is more difficult to remember numbers, this study reinforces the previous one: visual

tip
National Geographic Explorer

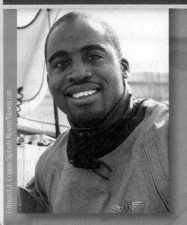

BARRINGTON IRVING, Explorer, Pilot, Educator

What kinds of visual aids do you like to use in your speeches?
When you're talking to young students, I know it's hard for them to picture what you're saying because they're still kids. You have to paint a picture for children because they're not adults and they haven't experienced life yet. So when you're speaking to them, they seem to have more imaginative or creative things going on in their brain: they are trying to picture what you're saying. If the equipment is there, it's much better. It's great for kids to see what a private jet looks like or something that they're not normally exposed to or what some of these places around the world look like. They find that to be fascinating and cool and that's a great attention grabber. So if you can have visual aids in a presentation for children, it helps tremendously.

information greatly improves audience recall. So one of the goals of your visual aids is to help your audience remember information.

Visual Aids Help Explain and Clarify Information

Research also suggests that visual aids can help you explain material and thus enhance the clarity of your information. Complex ideas and numbers can be hard to understand when just heard but are much easier to sort out when displayed visually. Presenting an idea visually makes it more concrete. Visual aids such as simple handouts can also increase audience members' continuity of thought because they can take notes or go back and check their understanding.[3] So the third goal of your visual aids is to help you explain or clarify your ideas.

Visual Aids May Increase Persuasiveness and Enhance Credibility

Research also suggests that visual aids may increase your persuasiveness and enhance your credibility.[4] Here's how:

- Visual aids clarify your message.
- Visual aids organize information.
- Visual aids identify key points.
- Visual aids facilitate the reasoning process.

In addition, images encourage audiences to make associations, so you can use both text and images to move your audiences toward a particular position.

Visual aids also can add to your credibility by bringing an animated and polished dimension to your speech. Professional-looking and creative visual aids can energize your speech, making you appear more prepared, engaging, and lively. For example, an animated graph that displays a trend in people's attitudes, or illustrates changes over time are excellent ways to display the evidence you're using to back up a claim. These dynamic displays of information help you organize and clarify your information, communicating an audience-centered perspective that contributes to your credibility.

Visual Aids May Reduce Nervousness

Finally, visual aids may help reduce your nervousness.[5] When you prepare effective visual aids, you pay more attention to the effectiveness of your speech's organization. Better organization reduces nervousness because you know your ideas are logical and carefully planned. Visual aids also can direct audience attention away from you and give you something to focus on other than your nervousness. In addition, visual aids give you something to do with your hands, helping you relax in front of your audience. For example, in her speech on fitness, Jemma used not only a series of animated slides and short video clips, but she also brought in a fit ball (a large rubber ball used to stretch and strengthen muscles) as a visual aid. A very nervous speaker, Jemma found that as she navigated through her visual aids and demonstrated how to use the ball, her attention was focused on explaining her ideas rather than on her nervousness. Not only was she more relaxed, but the audience also learned a great deal from her demonstrations.

Types of Visual Aids

There are various kinds of visual aids you may be required or choose to use. Every type of visual aid has its strengths and weaknesses, so don't settle on any one kind until you've decided what you want to accomplish with the visual aspect of your speech. Here we'll look at several of the most common visual and presentational aids for speeches: apps and Internet downloads; Prezi, Google, and PowerPoint slides; objects, models, and demonstrations; handouts; whiteboards, and smartboards, and flip charts.

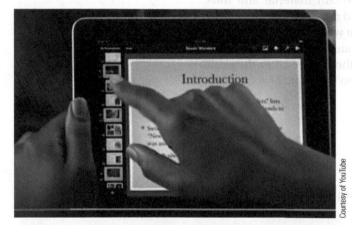

Courtesy of YouTube

Consider the introduction to your next speech. Are there images that can help you capture your audience's attention and gain their interest? Or, is there an image that might help you clarify your thesis or even reduce your level of nervousness? As you explore your app and software options, think about how these images can help you make a positive first impression.

Apps and Internet Software

Our cell phones and computers contain a seemingly endless array of technological options for visual aids. Whether you use an Android or an iPhone, a Mac or a PC, numerous apps and programs are available to assist you in presenting your ideas. Programs such as "Keynote," an app designed for iPhones, will help you arrange objects on slides, add photos and videos, personalize information, and remove unwanted background images that may detract from your message. Connected to an external projector, you can display your work as well as view your presenter notes.

For Androids, the "deck slideshow presentations" app will assist you in developing slides, designing charts and graphs, animating your information and transitioning smoothly from one slide to the next. Other apps for your phone, as well as Internet downloads for your computer, can be used to help you find free artwork to add to your presentation, match images and design features to your content, and even design your own graphs, charts, and flash animations.

But the power of these tools to captivate audiences also carries risks. When you rely too heavily on these visual aids, rather than the ideas you are attempting to communicate, or when you do not use them ethically, they can take over your presentation and diminish your own significance and credibility as a speaker. As you consider the apps and Internet downloads that might best assist you, follow some simple guidelines to get the most out of these technologies.

Balance the visual and the verbal. Regardless of how compelling an image is, or how much dynamism an app will add to a slide, don't let the visual component of your speech overwhelm the verbal. Your audience is interested in what you have to say, and your visual aids should support that message rather than overpower it. Keep the functions of visual aids in mind as you design them. Remember that visual aids should not be the most prominent aspect of your speech, but they will help you gain and maintain your audiences' attention, assist with recalling information, and add clarity, persuasiveness and credibility to your ideas.

Design and edit your visual aids ethically. Computer programs and cell phone apps make the downloading, editing or altering, and even creation of images and animations incredibly easy. This also means that we must be careful that we are ethical in our use and alterations of these images and animations. As you design your visual aids, consider the ethical implications of eliminating a background image, editing someone's photo or data, or superimposing or animating a particular image, idea, or claim. Stay true to the research you have done, and make sure you are presenting your ideas honestly and ethically.

Prezi, Google, and PowerPoint Slides

Similar to apps and software, technologies such as Prezi, as well as Google and PowerPoint slides allow speakers to create slides containing text, diagrams, images, and links to clips or videos you want to include in your speeches. Templates can be created and changed, slides can be edited and reordered, and numerous presenter tools are available for speakers as they deliver their speeches. Unlike Google or PowerPoint, which move your visual aids forward slide by slide, Prezi allows for a very dynamic presentation of your ideas, letting you zoom in and out and move your curser freely around to your various visual images. Both approaches have strengths, and there are speeches in which you want a linear and less fluid presentation, as well as presentations in which moving freely around the screen helps you present your ideas better. These tools can assist us in creative and important ways as public speakers; however, as with all visual aids, you still need to think about what you want to display visually and the best format for that material. When using Prezi, Google, or PowerPoint slides, consider the following guidelines.

EPA/european pressphoto agency b.v./Alamy Stock Photo

Chris Anderson, the curator of TED Talks, used Prezi in his 2010 TED Talk "How Web Video Powers Global Innovation." With this tool, Anderson shared a wide array of images and statistics inspiring his audience to think about how face-to-face communication has been changed by online video. "What Gutenberg did for writing," Anderson states "online video can now do for face-to-face communication."[6]

Understand the purpose of a visual aid. Even though this technology offers a wide variety of design options (such as graphics, overlays, fade-outs, and sound), you may not need to use them all. Consider what will help you focus, clarify, and organize your speech, and incorporate those aspects of this technology. Remember to use this form of visual aid to enhance your message and build your arguments, not to overwhelm your audience with the technology.

Prepare and practice in advance. As with any visual aid, take time to prepare your slides and the accompanying descriptions. Give yourself enough time to reorganize, add slides, animations, and images, and eliminate those that don't seem to contribute to your speech. Use your preparation time to decide which points (if any) lend themselves to fades, overlays, graphics, or sound. And don't forget to check for errors once you've designed your slides. Practice using and describing your slides so your delivery is fluid and extemporaneous. Finally, familiarize yourself with the projection

Petrol/F1online digitale Bildagentur GmbH/Alamy Stock Photo

Displaying an object or a model can engage an audience immediately, and many speeches lend themselves to this type of visual aid. Several of the speakers in Chapter 7 displayed objects. For example, Candice showed a scrapbook, and Martha displayed different batik patterns. The model of the human body shown here is built to scale, but it is quite small. Do you think you could use a model of this size in your next speech? What problems would you need to overcome?

MindTap®

Cindy Gardner demonstrated the process of folding a flag. Watch the video clip of Cindy giving her speech and evaluate how effectively she uses a demonstration.

object: Something that can be seen or touched.

model: Copy of an object, usually built to scale, that represents an object in detail.

demonstration: Display of how something is done or how it works.

equipment before your speech so that you won't run into any problems and can use technology to its fullest.

Although technology can add a very positive element to your speeches, and you often will incorporate the latest tools and approaches to presenting your ideas visually, there are times when simple is best. As you consider the remaining options for visual aids, ask yourself if and when these options might make the most sense for your speech.

Objects, Models, and Demonstrations

An **object** is something that can be seen or touched, and a **model** is a copy of an object, usually built to scale, that represents that object in detail. Objects and models can bring a "real-life" element to an idea. However, objects sometimes are impractical (too big) or impossible (too valuable) to bring to a speaking situation. Models can help you here, because they can be smaller than the objects they represent (a model of a car engine), larger (a model of the mechanics of a wristwatch), or life-sized (a model of a human brain). In all these cases, the models allow you to show an object that otherwise would have been difficult to show.

A **demonstration** is a display of how something is done or how it works. For example, Cindy used her flag to demonstrate the process of folding a flag. Martha displayed various batik styles as she described how batik is produced. You can show a process from a YouTube (or other) video clip. When you display an object or a model or demonstrate a process, consider the following guidelines.

Make sure your visual aids and demonstrations enhance understanding. Some objects or models may be intriguing, but they won't enhance your speech. Choose an object or a model that clarifies information and try to avoid demonstrations that are too complex, require a lot of equipment, or might make you look awkward or unprofessional. If your process is complex, simplify it for your demonstration, show only a part of the process, or use the Internet to help you show your audience the process without having to deal with complex equipment. When Brock gave his speech on emergency rescue services, he wanted to talk about the importance of the equipment used and the knowledge that rescue workers need to use the equipment properly. To demonstrate some of the more complex knots rescue workers often use, Brock brought in ropes with knots already begun. He finished tying the knots for his audience, demonstrating their strength as well as their complexity. Rather than take audience members through the entire process, he helped them understand that process by having a part of it prepared and set up before he began his speech.

Choose objects that are legal and nonthreatening. Many interesting objects are illegal, threatening, or dangerous. Avoid displaying weapons, chemicals, drugs, or animals, all of which can be dangerous or difficult to handle. Although you may know how to handle these items outside a speech situation, you cannot always predict what an animal, a dangerous substance, or other people will do during the speech. If you're not sure whether an object is appropriate for a classroom speech, check with your instructor.

Practice your demonstration before your speech. Don't leave anything to chance with a demonstration. Rehearse it several times before the speech to be sure your equipment works correctly, your steps are smooth and effective, and your words explain what you are showing the audience. If you are using an Internet clip to demonstrate something, download the segment you want before your speech so you can open it without any delays.

Channel Your Inner Mosquito

Asher Jay, Creative Conservationist, Explorer

Rebecca Drobis/National Geographic Creative

"I hope my creativity will inspire each individual to channel their inner mosquito and make an impact with every bite," states Asher Jay, "designer, artist, writer, and activist." Jay puts her artistic skills to use in a range of mediums: she sculpts, designs installations, makes films, advocacy advertising campaigns, and more, to "advance animal rights, sustainable development, and humanitarian causes." Jay, born in India, but "raised by the world," brings attention to the damage done by oil spills, dolphin slaughters, the illegal ivory trade, poaching, diminishing habitats for animals, and the seriousness of the loss of biodiversity. She explains, "The power of art is that it can transcend differences, connect with people on a visceral level, and compel action."

Jay organizes her efforts around two principles: compassion and coexistence. She explains that she chose to focus her efforts in this way because "without compassion and coexistence, we really don't accomplish what is in the best interest of the collective." We are all a part of this earth, and "only when we see things as being a true extension of our being," when we acknowledge there "are no separations," can we achieve empathy and compassion. We must stop "amputating ourselves from the bigger picture," Jay shares, "there is no way in which we can actually save that which we don't think is a part of us. The reason I do what I do is because I think of the world as an extension of who I am." Selfishness, she states, might be a "survival instinct," but we must expand our self-interests to the larger collective level: if we are to survive, we must "make ourselves large enough" to see the world as extensions of who we are.

Technology, Jay explains, creates dichotomies in our efforts toward compassion and coexistence. "I have a huge online tribe that has been of tremendous support to me . . . it's absolutely lovely how people can support you from across the world . . . there's something beautiful there." But, Jay's childhood, growing up without a computer, taking the time to handwrite letters, spending so much time in nature, causes her to reflect: "Now, people are always connected, we take it for granted, the connections don't matter anymore. My mum told me when I was really young, 'if you can do any activity more than once and have the same passion and enthusiasm for it, then do it. But if not, just stop.'" The repetition of this constant connection, she explains, "makes us lose the value of it, we're no longer truly engaged."

When Jay begins work on a new project, she does extensive research. She begins with newspapers and books, "you need to know how the world is in terms of politics and socioeconomics and the like." Then, she continues to research and read about the "particular ecosystem I am focusing on, the particular culture, popular culture references, and—just looking: I go for walks in the cities, to museum exhibits and galleries." Jay looks for shapes, colors, textures, parallels, and "references that could create interesting juxtapositions between what the lay person is comfortable with in their visual vocabulary and then what they need to know." Jay shares, that although she creates a visual story and even "restructures a problem," she does not give her audience the conclusion. She explains, "when they work out the argument behind my compositions, they have figured it out the way I figured it out—that's the moment of epiphany."[7]

WHAT DO YOU THINK?

1. Jay hopes that her work will inspire people to make an impact (channel their inner mosquitoes) in this world. Do you think that art, or even the visual aids you use in a speech, can be a source of such inspiration? Why or why not?
2. When Jay begins a project, she does extensive research in a range of places and from a variety of sources. Could you use some of her places and sources as possible sites for your own research on your next speech? Why or why not?
3. Jay suggests that when we separate ourselves and our thinking from others, we are failing to see that we all are connected and a part of the same planet. Do you agree with Jay? Why or why not?

Whiteboards, Smartboards, and Flip Charts

Whiteboards, smartboards, and even flip charts are very convenient. They allow you to create a visual aid as you speak, clarify concepts during your speech, or keep track of ideas generated during discussions. They also help you when you need to respond immediately to audience confusion or questions. They keep information in front of the audience rather than having to remove it to make space for new information. With the smartboard, you can duplicate what you write on it and make a handout for the audience at the end of your speech.[8] Whiteboards allow you to record and display information, and the pages of a flip chart can be separated and posted around a room for further discussion. Used in these ways, whiteboards, smartboards, and flip charts can help you stay audience centered throughout your speech. If you use these visual aids during a speech, consider the following guidelines.

Write neatly and legibly. What you write on the board is not likely to be as neat as it would be on a prepared visual aid. It also hasn't been proofread for errors in spelling and grammar. So take care to write clearly, use a systematic organizational framework (such as an outline), and watch for spelling errors.

Speak to the audience, not to the board. We sometimes talk while we are writing because we're trying to stay within our time limit and because we're involved in the speech and want to keep the momentum going. However, this means our back is to the audience while we're talking. To avoid this problem, try to stop talking when you turn to the board to write or repeat your comments when you turn to the audience. Although this may feel awkward the first few times, audience members will appreciate the care you take to speak to them directly.

Handouts

Business speakers often use handouts as visual aids. Examples include bound copies of business plans or year-end summaries; agency or product brochures; maps and photographs; and photocopies of graphs, charts, or articles. Many handouts can be displayed on a PowerPoint slide or distributed to your audience electronically beforehand. But there are times when you want your audience to have a hard copy of your information to refer to during a speech, make notes on, or read later and even pass along to others. Before you decide to use a handout, check with your instructor to see if you're allowed to use them in your course. If you can use handouts, consider the following guidelines.

Mark the points you want to emphasize. One problem with handouts is that the audience sometimes has trouble finding the point you want them to focus on. To prevent this confusion, mark the points you want the audience to locate. Use letters or symbols or a more visual device such as color-coded plastic tabs. For example, you want them to turn to specific pages in a report, place tabs on those pages. You also can help your audience locate specific spots in handouts by displaying the page, chart, or map electronically.

Distribute the handout before or after a meeting. To avoid the disruption of passing out material during your speech, distribute your handouts before the meeting begins or your speech starts. This is less distracting for the audience and does not disrupt your speech. Alternatively, distribute a handout after you've finished speaking if your speech includes information you'd like your audience to take away with them.

Remember that the handout supplements the message. A handout should add information to your speech and not become its text. Rather than reading lengthy passages from the handout aloud, refer to its key points during your speech so your audience will be sure to note them when they read the handout after your speech.

What to Show on a Visual Aid

Choosing the best type of visual aid to enhance your speech is your first step in using visual aids effectively. The second is deciding what to show on your visual aids. Remember the purpose of visual aids: to clarify, enhance, and illustrate your ideas and make your key points more memorable. You can accomplish your purpose by using visual aids that are based on text (lists), diagrams (charts and graphs), or images (drawings, photographs, and maps).

Lists

A **list** is a series of words or phrases that organize ideas one after the other. Lists help audiences keep track of material and identify the main points of a speech or discussion. Use lists when your material lends itself to itemizing a group or a series, such as names, key features, or procedures. The animated features of many apps and programs can help you highlight specific words or phrases as you are discussing them. When you use lists, consider the following guidelines.

Make your list brief and balanced. A list is a synopsis, so keep your lists brief. Use keywords or phrases rather than full sentences. Your goal is to prompt the memory of your audience members, not to have them read your full text. Here are some examples showing how to shorten sentences to words or phrases:

Full sentences	List
Visual aids help audiences recall more information.	Recall
Visual aids help explain and clarify information.	Explain
Visual aids can enhance a speaker's persuasiveness.	Persuade
Visual aids can enhance a speaker's credibility.	Enhance credibility
Visual aids can reduce a speaker's nervousness.	Reduce nervousness

Follow the six-word, six-line rule, which suggests you use no more than six words per line and no more than six items per list.[9]

Note that audiences recall lists best if the items are parallel (Chapter 7). As you develop your lists, try to find balance or symmetry in the wording. For example, in a list of tips for using objects as visual aids, here's how you could balance your wording:

Incorrect	Correct
Use objects that illustrate or clarify.	Illustrate or clarify
Illegal and threatening objects may harm your audience.	Legal and nonthreatening

Remember, your goal is to cue your audience visually, not to overload them with text.

Include a heading. To help the audience keep track of your ideas, put a heading in boldfaced type at the top of your list. Because your audience can't go back and reread your written material, as they can with a full text, help them with recall by naming each list.[10] Here's an example:

The Importance of Visual Aids
- Recall
- Explain

list: Series of words or phrases that organize ideas one after the other.

- Persuade
- Enhance credibility
- Reduce nervousness

Charts

Charts show steps in a process or parts of a concept. They can help speakers illustrate the relationship between the steps or parts and how each relates to the whole process or concept. The two most common charts used as visual aids are the flow chart and the organizational chart. A **flow chart** illustrates direction or motion—for example, the unfolding of a process or the steps to a goal. An **organizational chart** illustrates the structure of groups, such as organizations, businesses, or departments. Both flow and organizational charts are well suited to Prezi's fluidity, as you can zoom in and out, and move your visual images around as you discuss the different parts or processes. Use a chart as a visual aid when you want to represent the parts of a whole or to simplify a complex process. Charts are usually created in advance, and if you select a chart as your visual aid, consider the following guidelines.

Emphasize the visual image. When you create a chart, use single words, simple images, or short labels for titles and positions and as few words as possible to describe the steps of a process. Help your audience visualize the process and its parts quickly and clearly by keeping it simple. Figures 11.1 and 11.2 are examples of charts that emphasize the visual.

Use lines, arrows, shading, color, and movement to show relationships and direction. To keep the audience's attention moving in the direction you want, use lines, arrows, shading, color, and movement and animation to help them follow your points as you explain the steps in a process or the structure of an organization. For example, in Figure 11.1, the yellow boxes show the beginning and the end of a fire department's response to an emergency, the green boxes indicate each step of the response process, and the arrows indicate the progression of the steps from beginning to end.

flow chart: Chart that illustrates direction or motion.

organizational chart: Chart that illustrates the structure of groups.

Figure 11.1   Flow chart

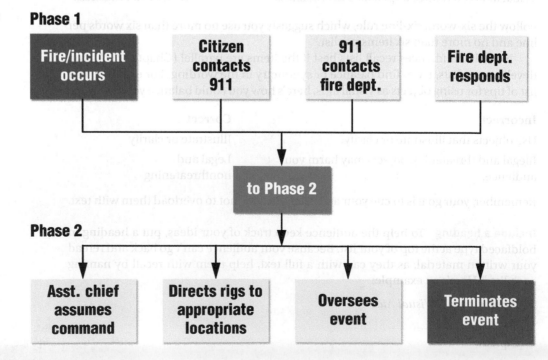

Figure 11.2   Organizational chart

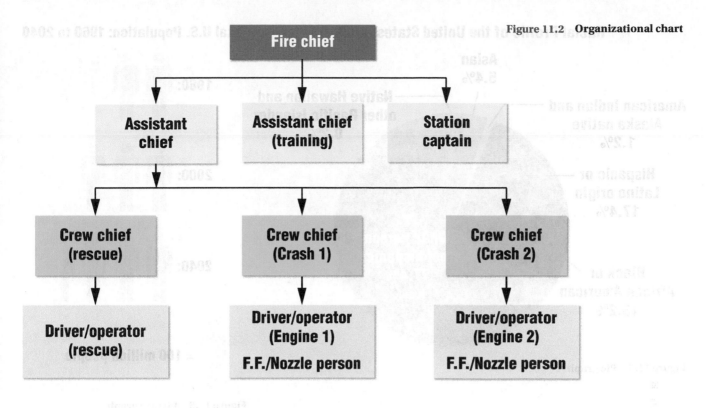

Graphs

When you want to compare numbers, quantities, or statistics, graphs are excellent visual aids. A **graph** is a visual comparison of amounts or quantities. Graphs help audiences see growth, size, proportions, or relationships. You can use different kinds of graphs for different purposes. **Bar graphs** compare quantities at a specific moment in time. **Line graphs** show trends over time. **Pie graphs** show the relative proportions of parts of a whole. **Picture graphs** present information in pictures or images. Apps, such as "live audience poll" make it possible for you to poll your audience in real time and then project a graph of their responses electronically. Figures 11.3, 11.4, 11.5, and 11.6 show how data from the U.S. Census Bureau could be represented using different graphs.

Like charts, graphs are most effective when prepared in advance and when you decide to display the figures you present in a chart, consider the following guidelines.

graph: Visual comparison of amounts or quantities that show growth, size, proportions, or relationships.

bar graph: Graph that compares quantities at a specific moment in time.

line graph: Graph that shows trends over time.

pie graph: Graph that shows the relative proportions of parts of a whole.

picture graph: Graph that presents information in pictures or images.

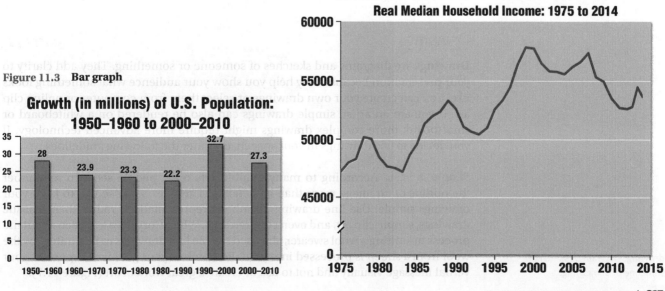

Figure 11.3   Bar graph

Figure 11.4   Line graph

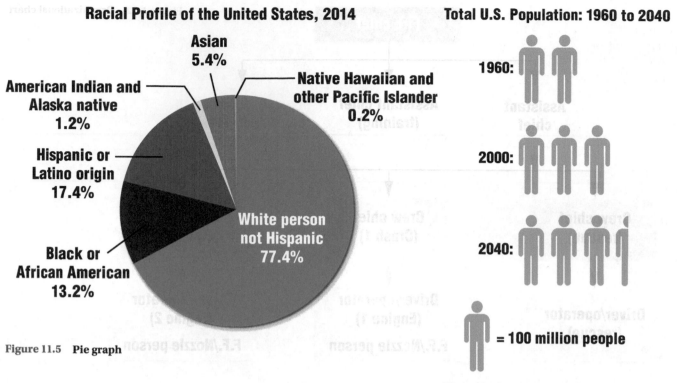

Racial Profile of the United States, 2014

- Asian 5.4%
- American Indian and Alaska native 1.2%
- Native Hawaiian and other Pacific Islander 0.2%
- Hispanic or Latino origin 17.4%
- White person not Hispanic 77.4%
- Black or African American 13.2%

Figure 11.5   Pie graph

Total U.S. Population: 1960 to 2040

1960:
2000:
2040:

= 100 million people

Figure 11.6   Picture graph

Use clear and consistent labels. Use descriptive headings for graphs that contain horizontal and vertical axes—for example, "Year" and "Percentage." For line graphs, mark equal intervals in the graph's grid—for example, numbers by tens, hundreds, or thousands and dates by decades or centuries. Show the numbers of those intervals on the horizontal and vertical axes. For example, the vertical axis in Figure 11.4 indicates dollars earned in intervals of $10,000. The horizontal axis indicates time in intervals of ten years.

Use a computer or app to design your graph. Because graphs display amounts, relationships, and proportions, presenting this information accurately is important. Computer software and various apps can help you represent this information cleanly and precisely, drawing images to scale and marking points on a graph clearly. You can even experiment with different kinds of graphs to see how they show your information.

Drawings

Drawings are diagrams and sketches of someone or something. They add clarity to your presentation because they help you show your audience what something looks like. You can create your own drawings or select them from computer or online clip art. If you are an artist, simple drawings can also be rendered on a whiteboard or smartboard; more complex drawings might require more advanced technology. If you decide to use drawings in your speech, consider the following guidelines.

Simple is best. According to many graphic arts texts, people seem to remember the outline of an image more than its details.[11] These texts advise you to keep your drawings simple. Use line drawings, symbolic representations rather than realistic drawings, simple clip art, and even children's art. When Cory gave a speech about the process of knitting a wool sweater, she used simple line drawings to illustrate how the wool from a sheep is processed into yarn. Remember, your goal is to represent your verbal message visually and not to use or create a great work of art (Figure 11.7).

drawing: Diagram or sketch of someone or something.

Make sure the drawing clarifies the verbal message. Although drawings can be used to set the tone or communicate emotion, more often you will use them to explain your ideas and articulate your message clearly. Use drawings to depict shapes (for example, animals, buildings, symbols, and patterns) and to show details (for example, what someone with dyslexia sees or acupressure points on the body). Before you add a drawing to your speech, think about how it helps communicate your message. Does it clarify a concept? Does it illustrate something your audience may not have seen before? Does it simplify something that is complex? Be sure the drawing will enhance understanding for the audience.

Use audience-centered humor. You can use cartoons and funny or unusual drawings to make a humorous statement. However, first consider how your audience might react to the message sent by a drawing you find humorous. Consider the master statuses, standpoints, attitudes, beliefs, and values (Chapter 4) of your audience members. Be certain a humorous drawing will be funny to everyone. Reject drawings you think might offend or insult members of your audience. For more on the topic of humor in speeches, see Chapter 16.

Figure 11.7   Simple line drawing

Photographs

Photographs help you show your audience exactly what something looks like or what really happened. They can also add color and drama to your speech. If you think a photograph will help clarify your ideas or make your point, consider the following guidelines.

Describe the photograph. To use a photograph successfully, you need to tell audience members what they are seeing. Call their attention to certain aspects of the photograph by describing them or explaining the action captured by the photograph. Don't be tempted to let the image speak for itself. Use the photograph to help you make your point by talking about it with the audience. For example, when Demetrious used photographs to describe the five villages of the Cinque Terre (Chapter 7), he pointed out the unique aspects of each village to help the audience distinguish them.

Maps

Maps are visual representations showing the physical layout of geographical features, cities, road systems, the night sky, and the like. Maps can help you show your audience the physical layout and characteristics of a place, its location in relation to other places, and the route between locations. Use a map to show your audience physical details that are best understood when presented both verbally and visually. If you decide to incorporate a map into your speech, consider the following guidelines.

Identify the map's scale. Because maps help audiences understand relationships, put your scale of measurement on a corner of your map so your audience can gauge the actual distances. For example, in drawing a map of a certain neighborhood, the students from Chapter 6 used the scale of 4 inches = 1 city block. This kind of scale doesn't require precise measurements because the students were mapping something generally. With Google Maps, speakers can easily use a published map to illustrate specific geographical features.

Include the most important details. When you display a map, follow the same design principle you would use for drawings: Simple is best. Eliminate unnecessary details so the most important features will stand out. This will help the audience focus on your points and not get distracted by unrelated details. Mark the parts of the map you want to emphasize using clear identifying features such as animations,

map: Visual representation showing the physical layout of geographical features, cities, road systems, the night sky, and the like.

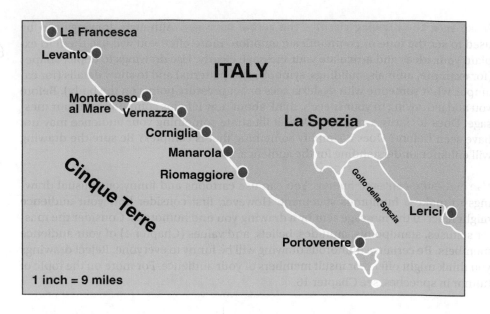

Figure 11.8   Map of the Cinque Terre region in Italy

La Francesca
Levanto
Monterosso al Mare
Vernazza
Corniglia
Manarola
Riomaggiore
Cinque Terre
ITALY
La Spezia
Golfo della Spezia
Lerici
Portovenere
1 inch = 9 miles

Practicing the Public Dialogue | 11.1

IDENTIFY VISUAL AIDS TO USE IN YOUR SPEECH

Identify one or two of the main points you will develop in your next speech. Outline that point and then decide what type of visual aid will help you make that point most clearly. Will it be a list, graph, photograph, video clip, or something else? Now decide how you will show the visual aid to your audience. Will you display an object before your audience or demonstrate a process? Will you show your visual aid in a handout or with a PowerPoint presentation? Discuss these choices as a class or in small groups, keeping in mind the question, "How does this visual aid help me establish my credibility and communicate more clearly?"

MindTap®

As you prepare your own visual aids for your speech, check out a few videos to help you determine what type of visual aid might work best for you. For example, consider whether Carol Godart's PowerPoint presentation helped increase her persuasiveness and credibility in her speech about weight discrimination. Or evaluate whether Chelsey Penoyer's PowerPoint presentation on youth suicide followed the guidelines in this chapter for effective visual aids.

arrows, circles, or color. If you are giving directions or explaining movement, such as the migration of birds, animate the image, or mark the path with numbers or arrows. For example, in Demetrious's speech about the Cinque Terre region in Italy, as he described each village, he could have animated it, or circled it on the map to help the audience see where the villages are in relation to one another (Figure 11.8).

Once you've decided on the type of visual aid you want to use and what you want to show on it, follow some basic principles regarding formats, which are discussed next. These principles will help you design a visual aid that is easy to see and communicates your ideas effectively.

Formats for Visual Aids

Understanding a few basic design principles will help you develop professional-looking visual aids. Understanding a few basic design principles helps enhance your visual message and, by extension, your verbal message.

Font Style and Size

A **font** is a type or style of print. Fonts range from simple to elaborate. As a rule of thumb, ensure the readability of your text by choosing a simple font over a fancy one. You will also need to choose between *serif fonts* and *sans serif fonts*. Serif fonts show small finishing strokes at the ends of the strokes of the letters and so create a baseline for readers' eyes, leading them easily from letter to letter. (The font you're reading now is a serif font.) Most professionally printed materials use serif fonts, and if your visual aid contains a lot of text, this is an excellent font to use. To emphasize words, use a boldfaced version of your font to make the letters heavier and darker. Some common serif fonts are illustrated here, and you will find others on your own computer.

font: Type or style of print.

Times New Roman	**Times New Roman (bold)**
Bookman	**Bookman (bold)**
Palatino	Palatino (bold)

Graphic artists suggest you can add variety to your visual aids by using different fonts in your titles or headings. To do this, use *sans serif fonts,* or fonts without the finishing strokes at the ends of the letter strokes.[12] Because of their straight lines, sans serif fonts create a distinctive, crisp look. Thus, they tend to mark titles or headings as more prominent than the text in serif fonts that follows them. Some common sans serif fonts are shown here, and you will find others on your own computer:

Helvetica	**Helvetica (bold)**
Lucida Sans	**Lucida Sans (bold)**
Univers	**Univers (bold)**

When you create your visual aids, avoid elaborate font styles, including shadow, embossed, engraved, and outline fonts. Although they look fun and interesting, they are more difficult to read and create extra work for your audience. Notice how your eyes have to slow down to identify each letter in the samples here:

Mistral	*Zapf Chancery*
Robotik	*Handwriting*

Save fancy styles for other projects and keep your visual aids simple and easy to read.

Font size is the size of the letters measured in points. The general rules for font size on visual aids are as follows. Note the size for headings, main points, and subpoints:

Headings: 30- to 36-point font

Main points: 24-point font

Subpoints: 18-point font

By varying your font size, you help your audience identify your main points and subpoints. If you plan to use smaller fonts than recommended, make sure your zoom and animation tools increase the size sufficiently so that your audience can read your words and phrases from a distance. If people struggle to see your text, your ideas become difficult to follow. Note that in most classrooms, audiences start sitting at about two or three feet from the speaker, and they are farther if you are speaking, say, on a stage in an auditorium. To test whether your audience will be able to read the text on a projected visual aid, view it from about fifteen feet away. If you strain to read it, your audience probably will, too.

Color

When you add color to your visual aids, you tap into several design principles. First, color helps an audience make associations. For example, soft tones tend to set a calm mood, whereas bright colors tend to set an exciting mood. Note that the meanings of color, and the moods they evoke, vary across cultures. In Western traditions, red

font size: Size of the letters in a particular font measured in points.

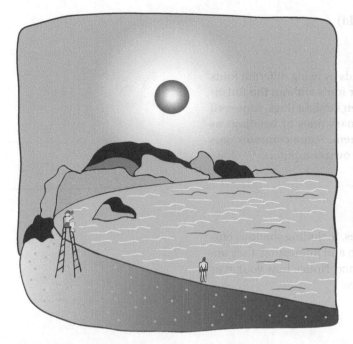

Figure 11.9   Beach in hot colors

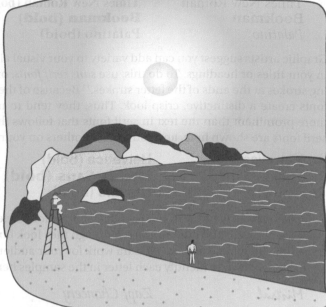

Figure 11.10   Beach in cool colors

can bring to mind anger or passion. But in China, red often symbolizes good fortune, and in ancient Mexico, red symbolized the sun and its awesome power.[13] Second, different colors help your audience differentiate objects or items in a list. Finally, color creates hierarchies. For example, darker to lighter progressions indicate the level of importance, with the darkest the most important. You can use these three design principles to their advantage in your visual aids.

Notice how the addition of color to a visual aid can create a particular mood. In his speech about melanoma, Silas used Figure 11.9 when he discussed the dangers of spending too much unprotected time in the sun. The reds and oranges create an irritating, uncomfortable mood, implying the burning effects of the sun. He used Figure 11.10 with the same basic image, but with blues and greens, to create a cooler, soothing mood that implies shade and protection.

Figure 11.11 shows how dark and light tones can indicate levels of importance. In her speech about dangerous earthquake faults in northern California, Janice displayed a map that shows how intensely certain areas of northern California are likely to shake during a major earthquake. The darker colors indicate more intense shaking, whereas the lighter colors indicate milder shaking.

When you use color in visual aids, establish a contrast between the text and the background so the text is legible. Avoid combinations of colors that are hard to read, such as bright red on dark green or white on light beige. Also, be careful not to overwhelm your audience with too much color. To find the balance you need, follow these suggestions:

Cool colors: Blue, purple, green. Cool colors are calm and relaxing for most people, and they tend to be easier on the eyes. Use no more than two of these colors per page. Use them for text or graphics (as alternatives to black and brown).

Hot colors: Fuchsia, orange, red. Hot colors are stimulating and grab the audience's attention. Use them sparingly to identify keywords or bullet points, create emphasis, or draw the audience's attention to one particular item.

Background colors: Soft yellow, light blue, lavender, light green, soft orange, and beige. Use soft colors such as these to create backgrounds and borders. Background colors also fill in solid areas that otherwise would have no color. Use them to add interest without grabbing the audience's attention. These colors should help the audience better distinguish and focus on foreground elements such as letters or images.

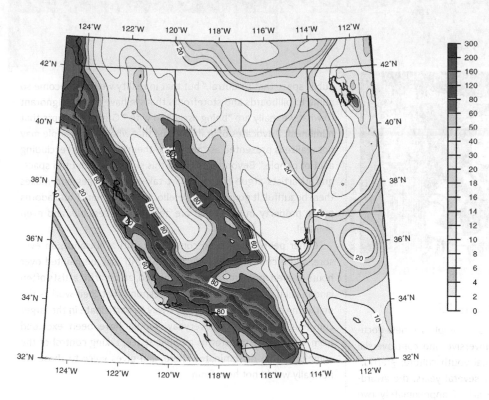

Figure 11.11 Map that shows earthquake intensity with color

Balance

Balance is the visual relationship between the items on your visual aid. You establish balance by the way you use space to arrange your ideas. A balanced visual aid helps your audience find information easily and not feel as if their eyes are tipping in a certain direction. With text, it is easy to achieve balance by using bullets and indentation:

Heading

- First point
- Second point
- Third point

You also can achieve balance by dividing your page (or screen) down the center with an imaginary line. Consider the placement of your information carefully. As you zoom in or out, or manipulate an image, consider the balance (or imbalance) you might be creating. A balanced visual aid sets the audience at ease and makes listening easier. It also helps you communicate your message clearly.

Guidelines for Effective Use of Visual Aids

No doubt you will use many different types of visual aids during your speech class and over the course of your speaking career. As you've read through this chapter, you've probably noticed a few guidelines that came up again and again.

- **Prepare in advance.** By giving yourself adequate time to prepare your visual aids, you will avoid rushing to complete them at the last minute, and you can create visual aids that you can be proud of.

Practicing the Public Dialogue | 11.2

DESIGN YOUR VISUAL AIDS

Begin designing your visual aids for your next speech. Make sure you follow the basic design principles of font style and size, color, and balance. Prepare at least a couple of drafts for each of your visual aids, and then check with friends or classmates about which are most effective in presenting information and promoting recall.

balance: Visual relationship between the items on a visual aid.

culliganphoto/Alamy Stock Photo

Global Graffiti: Whose Space Is It?

The film *Bomb It* (2007) is described as an "explosive new documentary" that "explores the most subversive and controversial art form currently shaping international youth culture: graffiti." Directed by Jon Reiss and filmed over several years, the award-winning documentary showcases the art of approximately two dozen street graffiti artists from around the world, and it makes the argument that public space belongs to the public. In the film, artists argue that "Art is a weapon," that graffiti "represents life"—"It's energy, it's f—n' energy"—and that because it is on walls, in subways, and out in public, "It's alive, it's livin', it's communicatin' to you right now."

Reiss and those featured in *Bomb It* make the argument that graffiti artists are "not asking for the space" and are instead "taking the space." They suggest that "people believe that they live in a public space that's neutral," but that in reality we have become so numb to billboards and storefronts that we have become ignorant to what we really are "being assaulted with." Graffiti disrupts that numbness. Advocates of graffiti argue that what many people may not realize is presented as "neutral to them" actually is "excluding a lot of people." Beyond disrupting this supposedly neutral space, graffiti artists argue that their art takes ugly spaces and makes them beautiful. It goes beyond "Hello, world, I'm here," and adorns public property in ways that are aesthetic, accessible, and even political.

Other people, however, consider graffiti a nuisance, an eyesore, and a crime to be eradicated. Graffiti may be painted over hours or even moments after it is finished, and graffiti artists often land in jail if caught. Graffiti artists respond that their work is the marketing of an idea or an image, a way to participate in the larger conversations they and everyday people have been excluded from. Graffiti art transforms a public space, taking control of the communication disseminated there, and gives voice to those we normally would not hear from.

WHAT DO YOU THINK?

1. What do public space and free speech mean to you? Does graffiti fall into the category of communication? Is it ethical to post graffiti on public buildings and spaces?

2. Do you think that graffiti artists are communicating important messages with their art? Why or why not?

3. Can you think of other visual images that are as controversial as graffiti? Could you develop an ethical and appropriate speech on these visual images?

- **Practice in advance.** Practicing delivering your speech with your visual aids allows you to ensure that they will fit seamlessly into your presentation without any glitches. Practicing also lets you revise or change the order of the visuals if necessary before you give your speech.

- **Use your visual aids only when you discuss them.** When you're through discussing the point that relates to your visual aid, remove it from the audience's attention. This will help shift the audience's focus back to you and your next point.

- **Explain what is shown on each visual aid.** Take the time needed to explain each visual aid fully rather than showing it quickly and moving on to your next point. Audiences will appreciate having each visual aid explained and will have an easier time understanding the relationship between your visual aid and your point.

- **Speak to the audience, not to the visual aid.** Although it's tempting to look at the visual aid while you speak, you want to maintain eye contact with your audience as much as you can. By practicing your speech with your visual aids, you will be better prepared to make eye contact with audience members after they have viewed your visual aids, and as they return their eye contact to you.

Guidelines for Ethical Use of Visual Aids

Another important consideration is the ethical nature of your visual aids. Remember that the goal of your visual aids is to clarify or illustrate your points so your audience will better understand your topic. To stay ethical, follow these guidelines:

- **Stay audience centered.** Avoid visual aids that might shock, disgust, horrify, or offend your audience, particularly within the classroom. One of the best ways to ensure that your visual aids will be appropriate for your audience is to remain audience centered when choosing them. To do so, consider your audience members' master statuses and adapt your visual aids to the needs of not only your speech goal but also your audience.

- **Avoid misleading images.** Be sure to avoid misleading your audience: make sure your visual aids are accurate and do not distort or exaggerate your claims. It may be tempting to jolt your audience with an extreme image or alter a photo, drawing, or graph to gain their attention or make a point, but be careful not to jolt them too much, or to misrepresent an issue, claim, or statistic.

Remember, you want your visual aids to help your audience understand your message more clearly, not to be turned off about your message, or mislead, because of your visual aids.

PREPARATION OUTLINE WITH COMMENTARY

The *Dun Dun* Drum

by Joshua Valentine

Specific purpose: To inform my audience about how and why the dun dun drum is used.

Thesis statement: The dun dun is an African drum with an interesting history that is used both musically and linguistically.

> MindTap This informative speech makes good use of photographs and audio to illustrate and clarify points. Watch a video of Josh Valentine giving this speech, which Josh gave in an introductory public speaking class. The assignment was to give a four- to six-minute speech with visual aids. Students were also asked to create a preparation outline that indicated where in the speech the visual aids were to be displayed, that cited the sources of the visual aids, and that included a bibliography, either as a Works Cited (MLA) or References (APA) list.

COMMENTARY

Josh, a drummer, takes his topic from his interest in music. He catches his audience's attention by asking them to imagine using a musical instrument to communicate language, something people in the United States don't typically do.

In the second main point of his introduction, he introduces his topic. He adapts his topic to his audience by using a familiar source, *Webster's Dictionary*, to define what language is and then explains that although Americans don't use music as language, other cultures do.

He establishes his credibility by indicating that he is a musician and that he learned about his topic in a percussion workshop.

Introduction

I. Imagine that your friend asks you what you did over the weekend, but instead of using words, your friend beats a drum. (*catch attention*)

II. You will probably never have such an encounter, but in some cultures, music is used for purposes that are different from those we are accustomed to. (*reveal topic*)

   A. *Webster's Dictionary* defines language as "any system of symbols, sounds, or gestures used for communication."

   B. Our culture does not have instrumental sounds that represent English words, but in other cultures around the world, sounds have meaning.

III. I have been playing percussion since junior high, and I first learned about the dun dun while attending a percussion workshop two years ago. (*establish credibility*)

IV. Today, I will explain the history of the dun dun as well as its linguistic use and its musical use. (*reveal thesis statement and preview main points*)

Body

I. The Nigerian talking drum, dun dun (pronounced doon doon), actually does talk, in the Yoruba language. [*Display photograph of dun dun drum downloaded and used with permission from http://media.dickinson.edu/gallery/Sect5.html.*]

In the last point of his introduction, Josh previews the two main points of his speech.

Because his audience is unfamiliar with his topic, Josh uses his first main point to explain what the dun dun drum is, where it originated, and what it is used for.

By allowing his audience to see and hear a dun dun drum, Josh helps his audience better understand his topic. In particular, the audio clips let the audience hear what is complicated to explain in words alone.

He kept a careful record of where he obtained his visual and audio aids so he could cite his sources accurately in his speech. Note that he downloaded copyrighted material according to the terms of use posted by the websites he accessed—he requested permission or agreed to use the material only for his speech in class.

The visual aid Josh used for subpoint D of his first main point clarifies how the drum works.

In his second main point, Josh explains how the drum is used to communicate. He continues to use his visual and audio aids to enhance and clarify the information in his speech.

In subpoint B, he provides details that his audience can relate to: "saying hi," "cracking jokes," "telling stories." Notice that he cites his sources simply but effectively.

In point II.B.b Josh uses a specific example to explain how the Yoruba "talk" with the dun dun drum.

In point C.2 he adapts to his audience by explaining how the dun dun drum is used in a way that is familiar to people in the United States, as a musical instrument.

Josh ends the body of his speech with an audio clip that

A. The dun dun originated during the Oyo Empire of Yorubaland in the fifteenth century A.D. for the purposes of worship.

B. Drums are constructed from trees located near roads where many people pass, which allows the tree to hear human speech.

C. The Yoruba language is easily communicated on the dun dun.
 1. Yoruba is a tonal language.
 2. Yoruba speakers use three basic pitches or tones, connected by glides, as an essential element of pronunciation.
  a. Listen to this sound clip and try to identify the three main tones. [*Play a sound clip downloaded for one-time use from the Internet.*]
  b. If you have a sharp ear, you may also be able to pick out some glides essential to the Yoruba language.
 3. Melody is the basis for the Yoruba language because the same word pronounced with a different melody means something different.

D. The dun dun functions by changing the tension of two skin heads using the leather straps that hold the heads in place. [*Point out the straps on the PowerPoint slide.*]

II. The dun dun was originally created to communicate.

A. The Yoruba from southwestern Nigeria have used drums for spiritual communication throughout their history. [*Show photo of carved drum downloaded from www.hamillgallery.com . . . YorubaDrum01.html.*]
 1. The dun dun was originally created as a tool for worship of the gods.
 2. Songs and hymns of praise were created entirely on dun dun drums and are still recited today.
 3. Listen to the intensity of this spiritual worship song played on talking drums. [*Play example downloaded for one-time use from http://www.world-beats.com/instruments/dundun.htm.*]

B. The Yoruba also used drums for social communication.
 1. The dun dun has been part of day-to-day casual conversation.
  a. According to the World Beats website, "A master drummer can maintain a regular monologue on a talking drum, saying hi to different people, cracking jokes, and telling stories."
  b. Dun dun drummers are often heard speaking the names of friends and family on their drums as a greeting and sign of respect.

C. The dun dun's secondary, yet most obvious, use is as a musical instrument.
 1. It became a musical instrument because of its use in worship.
  a. At first it was used mainly to communicate ideas, but because worship in the Yoruba culture is a corporate activity, people began coming together, and music on the dun dun was born.
  b. Religious songs are still recited today, although often only for their musical value.
 2. Even everyday speech becomes song when the Yoruba use the dun dun.
  a. According to the website Drum Talk, the word *kabo*, which means "welcome," is only a two-syllable word, so a more common phrase "spoken" on a dun dun is, "Welcome, we are happy that you arrived safely."
  b. "Speech" on the dun dun is always made rhythmic, even when the spoken word would not be rhythmic.
 3. The dun dun's use as a musical instrument has spread far beyond Nigeria.
  a. Next to the *djembe,* the dun dun is the most well-known and recognizable African drum used in America.
  b. According to African American musician Francis Awe's drum clinic, "[It] fares well in jazz, blues, R&B, rock and roll, reggae, classical music, even choral music."
  c. This clip comes from a song by Francis Awe. [*Play sample clip downloaded from http://www.nitade.com/html/cd1.html.*]

Conclusion

I. Whether in language or song, the *dun dun*'s sound is always unusually beautiful. (*bring speech to an end*)

II. Today, we have seen the origins of the Nigerian talking drum (dun dun), its uses as a linguistic tool, and its uses as a musical instrument. (*reinforce thesis and summarize main points*)

III. So next time you hear music as simple as a beating drum, you might remember that the drummer may be communicating much more than you think.

References

Awe. F. (1999). Drum clinic. Retrieved March 20, 2007, from http://www.after-science.com/awe/clinic.html

De Silva, T. (1997). Lying at the crossroads of everything: Towards a social history of the African drum. *Research, Writing, and Culture: The Best Undergraduate Thesis Essays, 2.* Retrieved March 20, 2007, from http://www.artic.edu/saic/programs/depts/undergrad/Best_Thesis_Essay.pdf

Kernan, M. (2000, June). The talking drums. Retrieved March 20, 2007, from www.smithsonianmag.com/arts-culture/the-talking-drums-29197334/?no-ist

How bata drums talk and what they say. (2002). Retrieved March 21, 2007, from http://www.world-beats.com/instruments/dundun.htm

Nigeria (Africa) *Dun Dun*. (2002). Retrieved March 20, 2007, from http://www.world-beats.com/instruments/dundun.htm

reinforces his final sub-subpoint, that the dun dun drum is now an international instrument.

Josh begins his conclusion by reinforcing that the drum is used for both language and music. He then summarizes his main points.

He ends his speech with an intriguing statement that encourages his audience to remember what he's told them about a particular African drum. Josh uses the APA citation style for his References list.

Chapter Summary

Audiences have come to depend on visual images for both information and entertainment.

- Using simple visual aids in your speech responds to this expectation and helps you clarify and communicate your message.
- In the public dialogue, visual messages are as important as verbal ones.

Visual aids have five purposes.

- They gain and maintain audience attention.
- They aid audience recall of information.
- They help you explain and clarify information.
- They increase your persuasiveness and enhance your credibility.
- They aid your preparation and thereby reduce your nervousness.

You can choose from a variety of visual aids.

- Apps and Internet software
- Prezi, Google, and PowerPoint slides
- Objects, models, and demonstrations
- Whiteboards, smartboards, and flip charts
- Handouts

You can show six different kinds of information on your visual aids.

- Lists of keywords and phrases help you organize ideas sequentially.
- Charts help you break ideas into separate parts.
- Graphs allow you to compare quantities and amounts.
- Drawings show diagrams and sketches of people and things.
- Photographs show audiences how things look in real life.
- Maps help audiences understand places geographically and spatially.

When using any of these types of information on visual aids, pay careful attention to their formatting.

- Use legible font styles and sizes.
- Use color to create a mood that enhances your message; establish a visual hierarchy to help you differentiate among ideas, and create contrast so your visual aids are readable.
- Create visual balance to help your audience find information easily, set them at ease, and make listening easier.

There are several guidelines for using visual aids in speeches.

- Prepare the visual aid in advance. This allows you to make sure the design is effective and to make any necessary changes before the speech.

- Always practice your full speech with your visual aids so you become comfortable using them.
- When you are finished talking about the visual aid, remove it from view so your audience will return their attention to you.
- Always explain each visual aid to your audience so its meaning is clear.

- Speak to the audience when using visual aids so your attention is on them rather than on the visual aid.
- Always consider the ethical nature of your visual aids so that you do not offend or alienate your audience.

Invitation to Public Speaking Online MindTap®

Now that you have read Chapter 11, use your MindTap Communication for *Invitation to Public Speaking* for quick access to the digital resources that accompany this text. These resources include:

- **Study tools** that will help you assess your learning and prepare for exams (digital glossary, key term flash cards, review quizzes).
- **Activities and assignments** that will help you hone your knowledge and build your public speaking skills throughout

the course, as well as help you explore public speaking concepts online (web links), give you step-by-step guidance through the research, outline and note card preparation process (Outline Builder), watch and critique videos of sample speeches (Interactive Video Activities), and allow you to practice and present your presentation online using a speech video delivery, recording, and grading system (YouSeeU).

Key Concepts MindTap® Test your knowledge with online printable flash cards.

balance (223)
bar graph (217)
demonstration (212)
drawing (218)
flow chart (216)
font (220)
font size (221)
graph (217)

line graph (217)
list (215)
map (219)
model (212)
object (212)
organizational chart (216)
picture graph (217)
pie graph (217)

Review Questions

1. Watch a few speakers outside class give speeches, whether live or taped (TED Talks is a good source for this). Which speakers incorporate visual aids and which do not? What are the strengths and weaknesses of each approach?
2. Bring an object or a model to class and practice describing it to your classmates. Try holding it, displaying it, and passing it around. Which techniques work well for you and which do not? Why and why not?
3. Many students believe computer-generated visual aids are superior to other types of visual aids. In addition, many employers want employees to be familiar with this technology. In light of this emphasis on a single type of visual aid, identify the strengths of computer-generated visual aids (such as PowerPoint slides and online images and video). What kind of material is best suited to this form of presentation? Although you may use this type of visual

aid in your future workplace, what other types of visual aids might you also use?
4. Create several drafts of your visual aids using different font styles and sizes, colors, and principles of balance. Bring these to class and, in groups, select those that are most effective. Why are they effective? Why were the others less effective?
5. Select one of the following speech topics. Generate ideas for visual aids you could use for an informative, invitational, or persuasive speech on the topic.

   The Supreme Court

   Musical instruments

   Bubble gum

   Corporate bailouts

   Alexander Graham Bell

12 | Informative Speaking

Types of Informative Speeches

Organizational Patterns for Informative Speeches

Tips for Giving Effective Informative Speeches

Ethical Informative Speaking

IN THIS CHAPTER, YOU WILL LEARN TO:

- Develop the five types of informative speeches

- Apply the four most common patterns of organization for informative speeches

- Implement three tips for giving effective informative speeches

- Utilize three principles for giving ethical informative speeches

Our days are often flooded with information—images, ideas, stories, data, statistics, and more—yet, we don't always receive the full story. We may receive bits of useful information, but we don't always have enough to fully understand an important process, circumstance, or issue. Sometimes, the part of the story we have is inaccurate or incomplete, so our assumptions are skewed, as this quote by Jennifer, a student at Colorado State University, illustrates:

> Sometimes people just need more information. Like the time my friends asked me, "Why can't I just leave my trash here? Isn't that what the staff is paid for, to pick up my trash?" or when they said, "Why does it matter if we lose certain species? I'll never see that animal anyway."

MindTap Start with a quick warm-up activity and review the chapter's learning objectives.

Bloomberg/Getty Images

▲ At a 2016 Facebook F8 Developers Conference, Ime Archibong, Director of Strategic Partnerships for Facebook, shared Facebook's 10-year plan for keeping products relevant and investor's dollars flowing in. Because providing accurate and complete information is so central to the public dialogue, in this chapter you will learn strategies for sharing information with your audience and for giving effective informative speeches.

I knew then that they didn't need persuasion or invitation; they really didn't know why it mattered. They needed information.[1]

To fully understand the world we live in, we need complete and accurate information. To meet that need, speakers in the workplace, in the classroom, and in our communities often speak informatively. An **informative speech** communicates knowledge and understanding about a process, an event, a place or person, an object, or a concept. Informative speakers share what they know or have researched to familiarize audiences with topics they want or need to understand.

Informative speakers create **informative speaking environments**, environments in which a speaker has expertise or knowledge that an audience needs but doesn't already have. When speakers create informative environments, their goal is not to invite (Chapter 13) or persuade (Chapter 15) but rather to illustrate for an audience how something is done or the importance and relevance of a topic. Informative speakers attempt to enhance an audience's understanding of how some part of the world works.

As you enter the public dialogue, you will give many informative speeches.[2] In fact, across professions, demand is growing for employees with strong public communication skills and an ability to share information with others in a wide range of settings.[3] We place such emphasis on informative speaking because we need information every day—for example, to understand how a new medication will affect us, to learn how to parallel park, to deliberate over the governor's proposal for spending a budget surplus, or to complete the complex assignment our boss just gave us.

MindTap®

Read, highlight, and take notes online.

Types of Informative Speeches

The five types of informative speeches most common in public speaking classes and the workplace are speeches about processes, events, places and people, objects, and concepts. Each type of speech has a different focus, and each is suited to a different occasion.

Speeches about Processes

Commonly called a *how-to* or a *demonstration speech*, **speeches about processes** describe how something is done, how something comes to be what it is, or how something works. Process speeches help an audience learn how to complete a task, understand how something develops over time, or comprehend how a process unfolds. The fundamental goal of a process speech is to show your audience how to *perform* a process or how to better *understand* a process. The following are sample topics for process speeches:

- How to get a passport
- How coal is mined in the United States
- How to protect yourself from harmful sunburns
- How to determine how much to tip a server in a restaurant
- How a solar panel converts the sun's heat into energy

Process speeches are common because most people are constantly learning how to perform new tasks. For example, your boss may ask you to explain to a colleague how to fill out and submit an expense report. Or you may be asked to explain to new staff how an employee incentive program came to be implemented, especially if you have a history with that particular program. In the classroom, you may be required to speak about a process that your classmates will benefit from learning more about.

The following two examples illustrate process speeches about a very familiar topic: coffee. In the first example, Tracee describes how coffee came to be a popular drink in North America:

informative speech: Speech that communicates knowledge and understanding about a process, an event, a person or place, an object, or a concept.

informative speaking environment: Environment in which a speaker has expertise or knowledge that an audience needs but doesn't already have.

speech about a process: Informative speech that describes how something is done, how something comes to be what it is, or how something works.

HOW MUCH PUBLIC SPEAKING WILL YOU DO?

According to Susan Ricker at AOL Jobs, at least sixteen different professions, or parts of that profession, make use of employees' public speaking skills on a regular basis. Those occupations include (1) fundraisers who organize events and campaigns that raise money and/or awareness; (2) buyers, managers, and purchasing agents who review products, negotiate contracts, and evaluate materials; (3) training and development specialists who train others, conduct workshops, and plan programs; (4) health educators who teach people about appropriate wellness behaviors and share new information about healthy living with communities; (5) curators who manage art collections and exhibitions and engage in public service activities; (6) teachers who help prepare students for successful lives; (7) actors who work on television, film, or at theme parks or other live events;

HeroImages/Getty Images

(8) writers, producers, and directors who create entertainment and pitch ideas to others; (9) umpires, referees, and other sports officials who preside over sports events, maintain standards of conduct, and communicate those standards to others; (10) mediators who facilitate meetings, negotiations, and dialogue between individuals and parties who cannot come to a decision on their own; (11) judges who apply and communicate the law to others; (12) lawyers who advise and represent people in and out of court; (13) school principles who coordinate and manage school activities, curriculum, and operations and communicate decisions and information to teachers, students, parents, school boards, and their communities; (14) announcers who share music, ideas, stories, and commentary at public and private events; (15) journalists who communicate stories, important events, and breaking news to individuals as well as local and national communities; and (16) construction managers who coordinate and supervise projects from inception to completion.

The Bureau of Labor Statistics adds that those individuals frequently using their public speaking skills also need to be good at listening, decision making, memorization, leadership, negotiating, and interpersonal relationships.[4]

Specific purpose	To inform my audience how coffee became one of the most popular drinks in North America.
Thesis statement	Through a series of historical events beginning in the 1500s, coffee replaced tea as one of the most popular drinks in North America.
Main points	I. Coffee found its way to North America in the 1500s when trade routes opened between coffee-growing countries and Europe and then expanded to North America.
	II. Coffee began to gain in popularity as tensions with England accelerated in the 1700s and imports of tea decreased.
	III. By the 1900s, international commerce, marketing techniques, and individual lifestyles made coffee one of the most popular drinks in North America.

In the second example, Wynton describes how the process of growing and harvesting a particular kind of coffee works:

Specific purpose	To inform my audience how shade-grown coffee is grown and harvested.
Thesis statement	The process of growing and harvesting shade-grown coffee differs from the process used by coffee plantations in three significant ways.
Main points	I. Shade-grown coffee is grown in small plots, quite unlike the more familiar coffee plantation method.
	II. As the plants grow, these plots provide nonchemical forms of fertilizer and pest control.
	III. When the coffee beans are mature, they are harvested and stored in ecologically friendly ways.

Notice how each of these speeches follows a progression of steps, from first to second to third. Because process speeches describe step-by-step progressions, they are almost always organized chronologically. Recall from Chapter 7 that the chronological pattern traces a development or evolution over time. A chronological pattern of organization allows you to develop your speech from the first step to the last or from the earliest signs to the most recent examples. (Later in this chapter, you'll explore organizational patterns for informative speeches more fully.)

Speeches about Events

Speeches about events describe or explain significant, interesting, or unusual occurrences. These speeches help an audience understand what happened, why it happened, and what effect it had. We often describe what happens in our personal lives so we can better understand the influence of events. Similarly, public speakers share what happens with audiences to help them understand a significant event in the context of history or society or community. In some ways, speeches about events are mini history lessons that educate audiences about key moments. Some sample topics for speeches about events are:

- The 2011 Japan tsunami
- The passing of the health-care reform bill
- The death of blues singer Etta James
- Large-scale food recalls

Speakers are often asked to speak about events, usually in professional settings. Consider Thom, whose boss asked him to speak to his fellow employees at a grocery store about the latest recall of beef in their region:

Specific purpose	To inform our staff of the most recent recall of beef and products that contain beef.
Thesis statement	This most recent recall of beef from our store requires that we identify all beef purchased within the last three months, identify all products containing beef purchased within the last three months, and remove and dispose of these products in very specific ways.

In a community setting, people may decide to speak about local events as a way to inform councils, planning boards, or community service agencies and perhaps assist them with the decisions they make:

Specific purpose	To inform the city council about the high rate of accidents at the corner of College and Elm Streets.
Thesis statement	The intersection of College and Elm is the site of an unusually high rate of accidents during certain hours of the day.

When you are required to speak about an event, select a topic your audience will find interesting and relevant. For example, inform your classmates of an event that affects your own campus (a hearing to improve public transportation to the campus), the community that houses your campus (an annual jazz festival that showcases successful musicians from the community), or your state or region (a recognition ceremony for local volunteers who helped collect clothing for flood victims in a nearby community).

Most speeches about events, especially historical events, are arranged chronologically. However, if the way an event unfolds is not the focus of your speech, you can organize your speech topically. Or if you want to analyze why an event occurred and what effect it had, you can use a causal pattern.

speech about an event: Informative speech that describes or explains a significant, interesting, or unusual occurrence.

Speeches about Places and People

Speeches about places and people describe significant, interesting, or unusual places or people. These speeches can be fun to give in a classroom because you can share your experiences with places and people you've visited or have found fascinating. In the workplace or the community, speeches about places and people help audiences understand the importance, nature, appeal, charm, or integrity of a particular place or person or the contributions a particular person has made to an organization or a community. Some sample topics for speeches about places and people are:

Pictorial Press Ltd/Alamy Stock Photo

- Service agencies in your community
- Max Ashton, the youngest blind person to hike to the top of Mount Kilimanjaro
- Sarah Silverman
- LeBron James
- Tanzania
- Supreme Court justices

Because you won't have time in a speech to discuss all there is to know about a place or a person, the goal of this type of speech is to capture the *spirit* of that place or person. You want your audience to understand why this place or person is important or useful to them or their community, important historically, or just interesting and worth learning about. Let's look at an example of a speech that Adrianna gave in her public speaking course:

Historical events are often interesting topics for informative speeches, especially if they relate somehow to an audience's current experience. For example, the invention of the ENIAC computer in 1945 marked the beginning of a revolution in how we distribute, process, and store information. What historical events do you think might make a good topic for an informative speech?

Specific purpose	To inform my audience about the history and features of the Freedom Trail in Boston, Massachusetts.
Thesis statement	The Freedom Trail, which originated in the late 1950s, is a pedestrian path through downtown Boston that links sites of historical importance to the United States, such as our first public school and the site of the Boston Massacre.

In the next example, Garrett informs his classmates about Captain Nicole Malachowski, the first woman selected to join the Thunderbirds, the U.S. Air Force's most elite team of pilots:

Specific purpose	To inform my classmates of Captain Nicole Malachowski, the first woman selected to fly with the Thunderbirds.
Thesis statement	In 2005, the Thunderbirds, a small eight-person team of the best pilots in the Air Force, selected its first woman pilot, Captain Nicole Malachowski, to join them in flying the most advanced aircraft in the world.

Speeches about places or people can be organized topically (how the Freedom Trail was conceived, the importance of the historical sites to which the trail leads), chronologically (events in Captain Malachowski's life that led to her selection), or spatially (Big Bend National Park in Texas features recreational areas in the mountains, the desert, and at the Rio Grande River).

Speeches about Objects

Speeches about objects are about anything that is tangible, that can be perceived by the senses. When we speak informatively about objects, we describe the components or

speech about a place or a person: Informative speech that describes a significant, interesting, or unusual place or person.

speech about an object: Informative speech about anything that is tangible, that can be perceived by the senses.

Practicing the Public Dialogue | 12.1

SELECT AN INFORMATIVE SPEECH TYPE

As a class, brainstorm as many different informative speech topics as you can. Next, group the topics according to the five types of informative speeches you've just read about. Some might fit into several groups depending on how you phrase your thesis statement for a particular topic. Discuss which of these topics you find most interesting and why. Save this list for the next Practicing the Public Dialogue activity.

characteristics of something so an audience can better understand it and why it might be important or valued. Some sample topics for speeches about objects are:

- Meteors
- Honeybees
- Hybrid automobiles
- Poisonous frogs

Speeches about objects are common in the working world. For example, a product development coordinator might speak regularly to his colleagues about new products that come across his desk, describing their qualities, uses, and appeal. Similarly, tour guides often speak about local objects of importance or interest, describing buildings, sculptures, and pieces of art. For a required classroom speech about an object, you might describe something useful, rare, or interesting to your audience. For example, Jun Lee gave a speech about *Mona Lisa*'s mysterious smile:

Specific purpose	To inform my audience about the *Mona Lisa* and the many theories about her famous smile.
Thesis statement	One of the most famous paintings of all time, the *Mona Lisa* has inspired several theories about the reason behind her mysterious smile.

A very popular topic for speeches about *animate* objects is animals and their behaviors, habitats, and ways of interacting with humans and other animals. Here is a sample specific purpose and a thesis statement for Shana's speech about the African serval:

Specific purpose	To inform my audience about keeping the African serval as a house pet.
Thesis statement	Although the African serval's legs, ears, and coloration aid in its survival in the wild, these same adaptations have a whole new meaning when taken into the context of keeping a serval as an exotic house pet.

Many speeches about objects are organized topically (the characteristics of poisonous frogs). Others are organized using a causal pattern (possible causes of the colony collapse disorder plaguing honeybees), and sometimes, a speech about an object can be organized chronologically (hybrid automobiles, from the first to the latest model) or spatially (the different features of a hybrid car). Be sure to select the pattern that helps you express your ideas clearly and efficiently.

Speeches about Concepts

Speeches about concepts are about abstractions, things you cannot perceive with your senses, such as ideas, theories, principles, worldviews, or beliefs. The goal of a speech about a concept is to help your audience understand your subject, its history, its characteristics, and its effect on society or individuals. Some sample topics for speeches about concepts are:

- The new frugality
- Power posing
- The First Amendment
- Theories of adolescent development
- Gun control
- Global citizenship

speech about a concept: Informative speech about an abstraction, something you cannot perceive with your senses, such as an idea, a theory, a principle, a worldview, or a belief.

When you give speeches about concepts, you help audiences more fully understand or appreciate issues, principles, systems, and the like. Consider Tory's speech about "the new frugality":

Ocean Hero
Sylvia Earle: Explorer, Oceanographer

James A. Sugar/National Geographic Creative

Sylvia Earle, an oceanographer for more than 50 years, has written more than 175 publications, lectured in more than 70 countries, and led more than 60 diving expeditions worldwide. She is affectionately known as "Her Deepness" because she holds several world records for depth of diving. Earle has a profound commitment to civic engagement and communicating her insights and passions in as many ways as she can.

An explorer in residence for National Geographic, Earle received the coveted TED Prize (TED stands for Technology, Entertainment, and Design) in 2009 for her proposal to establish Mission Blue, a global network of marine protected areas she dubbed "hope spots." Recipients of the TED Prize are known for their effective communication, commitment to civic engagement, and passion for the work they do. The prize includes $100,000, and the recipient is granted a "wish to change the world." Earle explained her wish as nothing short of saving our oceans. In her book *The World Is Blue: How Our Fate and the Ocean's Are One*, she explains, "My wish is a big wish, but if we can make it happen, it truly can change the world and help ensure the survival of what is actually my favorite species, human beings." She explains,

> Fifty years ago, when I began exploring the ocean, no one—not Jacques Perrin, not Jacques Cousteau, or Rachel Carson—imagined that we could do anything to harm the ocean by what we put into it or by what we took out of it. It seemed, at that time, to be a sea of Eden, but now we know, and now we are facing paradise lost. In fifty years, we've lost—actually, we've taken, we've eaten—more than 90 percent of the big fish in the sea; nearly half of the coral reefs have disappeared; and there has been a mysterious depletion of oxygen in large areas of the Pacific. It really should concern you. It does concern you.

When asked, "if you could have people do one thing to help the ocean, what would it be?" Earle replied,

> Hold up a mirror and ask yourself what you are capable of doing, and what you really care about. Then take the initiative—don't wait for someone else to ask you to act. . . .

Everyone has power. But it doesn't help if you don't use it. Knowing is the key. Become informed! With knowing comes caring, and with caring there is hope that we will find an enduring place for ourselves within the natural—mostly blue—systems that sustain us.

Earle believes that becoming informed is the most important contribution to saving the ocean. And she has made it her mission to help inform people from around the world.[5]

Log on to http://www.ted.com/talks to watch Earle's TED Talks speech. As you listen, consider her speaking goals, how audience centered she is, and her introduction and conclusion.

WHAT DO YOU THINK?

1. Sylvia Earle was asked to speak at the TED2009 Conference. What experiences or expertise does Earle possess that make her a good candidate to speak on changing the world? What are Earle's master statuses?
2. Based on the information presented in Earle's speech introduction, what would her specific purpose and thesis statement be?
3. How does Earle organize her informative speech? Is this a pattern you might use for your own informative speech?

Image getty/Shutterstock.com

Specific purpose	To inform my audience about the new frugality, sometimes called "less is more."
Thesis statement	Because of our recent economic crisis, many people are embracing the values of the new frugality, which involves owning fewer material possessions, being less "possession-identified" and more "self-identified," and of course, spending less money.

Speeches about concepts can be challenging because it might be difficult to explain an abstraction clearly. However, this type of speech is also very helpful because sometimes audiences need to understand concepts before they can understand how something works or why a person is significant.

Speeches about concepts are often organized topically (the various views related to gun control) or chronologically (early theories of adolescent development to the most recent theories). Sometimes, a speech about a concept can be organized causally (the causes of the idea of global citizenship).

Organizational Patterns for Informative Speeches

Informative speeches can be organized in a variety of ways, and you will probably use a wide range of organizational patterns as you become a proficient public speaker. As a beginning speaker, practice using the most common patterns, discussed in Chapter 7 generally and in this section specifically. These organizational patterns are the chronological, spatial, causal, and topical patterns. Using these patterns, you can organize your main points logically.

Chronological Pattern

With a chronological pattern, you can organize your main points to illustrate how a topic has developed over time or what steps an audience must take to complete a task. Most of us are familiar with the chronological pattern because most stories we tell or hear progress from start to finish chronologically. Chronological patterns are especially effective for process speeches, but as you learned earlier in this chapter, they also are well suited for other kinds of informative speeches. In the following example, Alan gives a speech to explain to his audience how the Ford Mustang set the standard for the muscle cars of the 1960s:

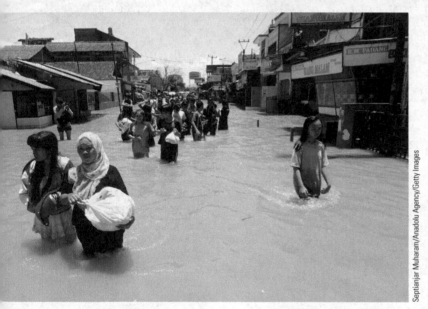

Septianjar Muharam/Anadolu Agency/Getty Images

Many topics of informative speeches can be organized in several different ways. For example, a speech about the effects of extreme geographical events could be organized chronologically (the evolution of a particular geographical event) or spatially (the types of extreme geological events that occur in different parts of the world.) This photograph depicts the March 2016 flooding in Bandung, Indonesia, which displaced more than 10,000 individuals. How might you organize this event topically, chronologically, or causally?

Specific purpose	To inform my audience of the history of the Ford Mustang.
Thesis statement	The Ford Mustang, which quickly became the muscle car to beat in 1964, with its combination of high performance and low cost, continues to be the most popular car of that decade.
Main points	I. Pontiac's GTO—which stands for "gas, tires, oil"—is credited as the first of the muscle cars of the 1960s.
	II. Ford quickly took the top spot among muscle cars, releasing the high-performance, low-cost Mustang to the public on April 17, 1964.
	III. Ford then added new makes with increasingly attractive features and options to maintain its popularity, among them the Fastback, the Grande, the Mach I, the Boss 302, and the Boss 429.

IV. The muscle cars of the 1960s remain some of the most popular cars of that decade, and the newer Mustangs give us a glimpse into why this is so.

Alan takes his audience through the evolution of muscle cars in the 1960s, beginning with the Pontiac GTO; then moving on to Ford's first Mustangs; its release of newer makes, features, and options; and the current influence of those features on today's cars. By using this pattern, he provides his audience with basic information they can build on as he progresses through his speech.

The next example illustrates how Joseph used the chronological pattern to trace the evolution of a concept. He described a spiritual belief system, its evolution, and the ways the system is integrated into every aspect of life:

Specific purpose	To inform my audience how the Kemetic civilizations of ancient Egypt created a holistic view of existence.
Thesis statement	Even though African civilizations are often thought of as pagan, the Kemetic civilizations of ancient Egypt created a holistic view of existence in which a monotheistic spiritual belief system was integrated into every aspect of life, including architecture and astronomy.
Main points	I. This religious belief system began with the observation of heavenly bodies.
	II. The Kemites began to integrate their knowledge of celestial cycles into their religious beliefs and identified many deities, each worshipped as different aspects of one God.
	III. As the Kemites' body of knowledge increased, their society began to integrate their religious beliefs into every aspect of life.

Joseph takes the audience through an evolutionary process, tracing and describing the development of a belief system from its origins to its full development.

Spatial Pattern

The spatial pattern allows you to address topics logically in terms of location or direction. Recall from Chapter 7 that with this pattern you can arrange your main points by the position they represent within a physical space. You can use this pattern to inform your audience of the places that relate to your topic, the activities that occur in those places, or the activities that are necessary to the functioning of your topic. In the following example, Lehla uses a spatial pattern to describe the animal shelter she works for:

Specific purpose	To inform my audience about the animal shelter and the various kinds of animals we care for there.
Thesis statement	Although we care for dogs and cats at the shelter, we also have the capability to care for animals ranging from livestock to fish.
Main points	I. Dogs and cats, which make up most of our clientele, are housed closest to the entrance for ease of care and visitation.
	II. In the cages and containers behind the dogs and cats, we have birds, fish, and small reptiles.
	III. Outside, in back of the shelter, we house the livestock, which need more space and open air.
	IV. At the farthest border of the property, and under tight lock and key, we keep the large reptiles.

By addressing her topic spatially, Lehla guides her audience around the various parts of the shelter. They learn something about the shelter itself as well as about the animals, which was one of her primary speech goals.

In the next example, Scott uses a spatial pattern to describe the different parts of a guitar and how each part works to produce sound:

Specific purpose	To inform my audience of how the different parts of the guitar work together to produce sound.
Thesis statement	The guitar has three main parts—the head, neck, and body—and each works together in intricate ways to produce the sounds we call music.
Main points	I. The top of the guitar is the head, which houses the nut and the tuning pegs.
	II. The next part is the neck, which contains three essential parts: the frets, the truss rod, and the fingerboard.
	III. The bottom part is the body, which is made of a reinforced front, back and side panels, a sound hole, and the bridge and saddle.

The spatial pattern is a clear and effective way to describe the different parts of an object.

Causal Pattern

Causal patterns highlight cause-and-effect relationships. A cause is an event that makes something happen, and an effect is the response, impression, or change that results from that cause. When you use causal patterns, you inform your audience about what causes certain events, places, objects, or concepts to come into being.

In the following example, Kelsey describes how onions cause us to cry and methods to prevent tears when cutting an onion:

Specific purpose	To inform my audience about the cause of an onion's tearful effect and methods used to prevent tears when cutting an onion.
Thesis statement	The internal chemistry of the onion is the cause of its tearful effect when being chopped, but various methods may be used to prevent this occurrence.
Main points	I. The onion's chemical makeup, along with the human eye, combine to induce tears.
	II. The first method to prevent tears is chilling the onion.
	III. The second method involves using an open flame during onion preparation.
	IV. Using water around the onion is a helpful technique to reduce tears as well.
	V. The last method involves cutting the core from an onion, where most lachrymators are thought to be stored.

Kelsey's use of the causal pattern helped her explain what causes the tears and then how you can reduce those tears.

Topical Pattern

The topical organizational pattern allows a speaker to address different aspects of a topic. For example, in Shana's speech about the African serval, she organized her ideas topically to address the physical characteristics that make it so suited to life in the wild. Then she spoke about the consequences of bringing it into a domestic setting. Topical patterns work well for informative speeches when topics can be easily and logically divided into subtopics. Using a topical pattern, you can highlight the aspects of a topic that are most useful and important for an audience to understand. In Lauren's speech about the history of nursery rhymes, she used a topical pattern:

Specific purpose	To inform the audience about the dark history of the origin of nursery rhymes.
Thesis statement	Nursery rhymes are seen as innocent and lighthearted tales because they are always associated with children, but the truth is that stories like "Ring around the Rosie," "Peter, Peter, Pumpkin Eater," and "Mary, Mary, Quite Contrary" have dark and often gruesome origins that would seem anything but child appropriate.
Main points	I. The rhyme "Ring around the Rosie" goes all the way back to the year 1350 in Europe, when the black plague was at its peak. II. The rhyme "Peter, Peter, Pumpkin Eater" is actually a rhyme about a man who forced his mistress to wear a chastity belt. III. "Mary, Mary, Quite Contrary" is actually the most gruesome rhyme of the three.

By using this organizational pattern, Lauren was able to use subtopics to inform her audience of the dark origins of many favorite childhood nursery rhymes.

Practicing the Public Dialogue | 12.2

SELECT AN ORGANIZATIONAL PATTERN FOR YOUR INFORMATIVE SPEECH

Return to the list of possible informative speech topics you prepared in Practicing the Public Dialogue 12.1. In groups, select a single topic and see if you can create a rough thesis statement and main points for four different informative speeches on this topic, using each of the organizational patterns you've just read about. As a class, discuss which of these speeches you would find most interesting and why. As you discuss your favorite topic and organizational pattern, consider the tips for giving effective informative speeches in the next section.

MindTap®

To consider the effectiveness of the organizational pattern one student speaker used for her informative speech, watch a video clip of Shana Moellmer giving her speech about the African serval.

Tips for Giving Effective Informative Speeches

In an informative speaking environment, you contribute to the public dialogue by sharing your knowledge with your audience, illustrating with clarity and detail the relevance of that knowledge to your listeners. Three tips that will help you create informative speaking environments and give effective informative speeches are (1) bring your topic to life, (2) tailor your information to your audience, and (3) use language that is clear and unbiased.

Bring Your Topic to Life

When you give an informative speech, you want your audience to understand your topic in a detailed and dynamic way. Effective informative speakers bring a subject to life for an audience, engaging their listeners so they appreciate the information they receive. Take careful stock of your topic and your audience so you can be sure to share information that is both *engaging* and *relevant*. Engaging material draws listeners in and excites or interests them. Audience members find material relevant if it is useful or something they must know to do their jobs, live in a community, or make informed decisions.

One of the ways to bring a topic to life is to stay audience centered. As you craft your speech, continually ask yourself how your overall topic, main points, and subpoints relate to your audience:

- What does the audience need to know?
- How will audience members use the information you present?
- How can you make the information clear?

If you keep these questions in mind throughout your preparation process, you will be more likely to present your material in an engaging and relevant way. For example, in a speech about school violence, Aaron brought his second point, a perpetrator's manipulation of other students, to life by asking his audience a rhetorical question: "Think back to high school. How many examples of manipulative behavior can you

tip
National Geographic Explorer

BARRINGTON IRVING, Emerging Explorer, Pilot, Educator

How often do you give speeches as an explorer and how did you become an effective speaker?
Oh, goodness, I speak several times a month. My audiences range from educators who want to learn about our practices and our curriculum and what we're doing to speaking with the students who want to become inspired and they're not sure exactly what they want to do in their life. I spend a good amount of time on the road speaking. When young people think of speaking, they think it's easy, right? You just get up on stage and speak. And, although you may have a little bit of talent, there's a lot that goes into it. The traveling and the coordination of the speaking engagement even before you get there. So much work goes into speaking because you're giving your time to others, you're sharing your stories, you're doing the research; but at the same time you have to balance your life, balance your work, balance the research all at the same time that you're giving these talks.

I think my evolution as a speaker came about indirectly—I got so many rejections when I was trying to fly around the world, right? So, I had to communicate to a lot of executives, managers, and so forth, and for two and a half years, people were rejecting me. So it forced me to realize the importance of a number of things, such as introducing yourself, talking to people, sharing information, and when you are talking with someone, really having a conversation with them. And I had to learn those things and I attribute that to the many rejections I got. So I became a better speaker because I listened to what everyone had to say. Now, everyone wasn't right, but when people tell you "no" and they tell you, "Here is why I'm not going to support you," I listened to what they were saying because sometimes they had valid points and I needed to figure out how to convert "no" into "yes."

think of? Probably too many. In my junior year, I remember one group of students who constantly picked on my friends and me. It felt like no matter what we did, we were the brunt of their jokes and the focus of their hostility." By sharing his own experience of manipulation, he touched on an experience common to many members of his audience.

Another way to bring your topic to life is to share the human side of your topic. If you are presenting technical information, explaining intricate details, or carefully outlining a process, try to use examples, images, and descriptions that help your audience connect to your topic personally. If you are presenting numbers or statistics, give the figures a human face. As one student asked after hearing an informative speech about how to avoid the kinds of sunburns that lead to skin cancer, "What do all those SPF factors and fancy names mean for me and my skin tone personally?" As you prepare your speech, anticipate this kind of question and look for opportunities to relate your information to the human experience. For example, in a speech on modern art, you might personalize different techniques and styles by drawing parallels to skills learned in art classes or by asking your audience members to attempt the techniques on their own as you describe them.

Stay Audience Centered

Recall the discussion of information overload from Chapter 5. Just as you can feel overwhelmed by the abundance of information you find in your research, your audiences can be equally overwhelmed by the information you share in your speech—no matter how engaging and relevant you make that information. As an informative speaker, one of your most challenging tasks is to decide how much information to include in a speech and how much to leave out:

- When you present too much information, you run the risk of overwhelming an audience.
- When you present too little information, you run the risk of leaving your audience unclear or confused about your topic.
- If you present material that is too technical, detailed, and complicated, your audience will have a hard time following it.
- If the information in your speech is too simple, audience members will become bored or feel that you are talking down to them.

David MAREUIL/Anadolu Agency/Getty Images

Given these dilemmas, the best way to tailor your information to your audience is to *stay audience centered* throughout the speech process. As you develop and present your speech, continually reflect on the needs and interests of your audience. Include information that you think would be of the greatest educational value for your audience, and adjust your presentation of this information so that it matches your audience's level of knowledge, expertise, and experience.

The decisions about what information to include or exclude can seem very subjective, but if you follow the principles of effective listening (Chapter 2), audience centeredness (Chapter 4), and organizing your speech for clarity (Chapter 7), you will find it easier to determine how much information to include in your speech.

Demonstration speeches are often very engaging because they provide audiences with especially relevant, useful information. When you give this type of speech, remember to avoid overwhelming your audience with too much information. Consider a demonstration speech you might like to give. What is the most important information you think your audience would need?

Use Language That Is Clear and Unbiased

Because informative speeches focus on describing, defining, and explaining, use language that is descriptive and instructive. To ensure your audience can follow you, define all new terminology, break complicated processes into steps, and explain language specific to a particular field or activity. For example, when Wynton spoke about shade-grown coffee, he explained what the terms *shade grown, fair trade, organic*, and *sustainable* mean. Similarly, when Thom spoke to his colleagues about the beef recall affecting their store, he made sure his audience understood the specific dates and exact methods of disposal. You can also make a point of explaining familiar words you use in new ways. For example, Lauren took time to link what her audience thought were lighthearted phrases and words from the nursery rhymes to their darker historical origins.

Informative language should be as objective as you can make it. Focus on presenting your information as clearly and accurately as you can and avoid expressing your own views (as in invitational speaking) or trying to sway your audience (as in persuasive speaking). Remember that the goal of informative speaking is to pass along information your audience needs or wants. Make sure the language of your speech is fair and unbiased. Use phrases like "My research indicates that" or "According to the experts," rather than "I hope I've convinced you that this is the best way."

Similarly, when you incorporate personal knowledge into an informative speech, which is common when you describe or explain something you have experience with, make sure your language reflects your *experience*, not your biases or preferences. For example, phrases like "After spending seven years with these machines, I would recommend the following steps" and "I've been involved in four food recalls since I began in this industry, so I can give you some background and details" are more informative than persuasive.

Adam Radosavljevic/Shutterstock.com

What Might Those Tattoos Be Communicating?

A survey conducted by the Pew Research Center (2013) found that 36 percent of Americans ages eighteen to twenty-five, 40 percent of those twenty-six to forty, and 10 percent of those forty-one to sixty-four have at least one tattoo.[6] Reports vary, but today, among the most popular tattoo designs are tribal, stars, crosses, angels, wings, butterflies, flowers, feathers, text, and fairies.[7] As common as they are, what might all those tattoos be communicating to others? Individuals report that tattoos make them feel rebellious and sexy, but could they also be adding confusion about our identities? Consider the history of tattoos before you answer.

According to the Smithsonian Institution's website, "Humans have marked their bodies with tattoos for thousands of years. These permanent designs—sometimes plain, sometimes elaborate, always personal—have served as amulets, status symbols, declarations of love, signs of religious beliefs, adornments, and even forms of punishment."[8] The earliest examples of tattoos are found on the 5,200-year-old "Iceman" found along the Italian–Austrian border in 1991, and 4,000-year-old Egyptian female mummies. The Iceman's tattoos are thought to be the result of an effort to release pain, as they are found in random spots along his joints. The tattoos on the Egyptian mummies are believed to be artistic markers of status or permanent amulets designed to protect women during pregnancy. Ancient tattoos are thought to have marked status (high or low, depending on the era), and other tattoos were used to identify someone as a slave.

Facial tattoos—most commonly associated with the Maori of New Zealand and some Native American people such as the Cree—were also found on the mummified bodies of six Greenland Inuit women who lived around 1475 A.D. In the Maori culture, the head was considered the most important part of the body, with the face embellished by incredibly elaborate tattoos or "*moko*," which were regarded as marks of high status. Each tattoo design was unique to that individual and since it conveyed specific information about their status, rank, ancestry, and abilities, it has accurately been described as a form of ID card or passport, a kind of aesthetic bar code for the face.[9]

However, tattoos as markers or conveyors of information have also been used by sailors so that they could be easily identified should they drown, to identify prisoners of Nazi concentration camps, and as symbols of gang membership or activities.

Although the excessively tattooed body was once seen as deviant or lower class and was displayed at fairs and circuses, according to communication scholar Mindy Fenske, today's tattoos are a form of "writing on the body" that communicates a challenge to notions of class, acceptability, and even what a body is for and can do. Today's tattooed bodies, Fenske argues, are a "performance of resistance" and often serve as visual statements about someone's identity and the body's ability to speak out about or for something.[10]

WHAT DO YOU THINK?

1. Could the presence of individuals with obvious tattoos be creating confusion about an individual's identity, attitudes, or beliefs in an environment in which tattoos are not the norm? What kind of confusion might be communicated?
2. Although tattoos aren't spoken words or phrases, they do communicate to others. What kinds of tattoos might be unfamiliar, confusing, offensive, or contradictory to someone not familiar with tattoos or tattoo cultures?
3. Are there ways to be audience centered with respect to tattoos? What might audience-centered communication about tattoos involve?

The distinctions here may seem slight, but they are important because they set informative speaking apart from other kinds of speaking. For more information on the effective use of language, see Chapter 2 (how language affects listening) and Chapter 9 (language style).

Ethical Informative Speaking

Ethical informative speakers make sure their speeches are based on careful research, unbiased information, and the honest presentation of information. Let's take a look at each of these components of ethical informative speaking:

- Our audiences expect that we have taken the time to find information that is accurate and complete. So we must carefully research the details of our topic and share the full story with our audiences. If we haven't done this, we may wind up giving our audiences inaccurate or incomplete information. (See Chapter 5 for tips on how to gather accurate and complete supporting materials for your speech.)

- As an informative speaker, present unbiased information to your audience. Recall from Chapter 4 that although we all hold biases, we can take steps to minimize them. You can minimize your biases by presenting examples, statistics, testimony, and other materials as fairly and as neutrally as possible regardless of your personal positions. Save your preferences for your persuasive speeches; use your informative speeches to help your audiences gain a full understanding of your topic.

- Present your information honestly. Don't distort your evidence or make up supporting material as you need it. A healthy public dialogue depends on accuracy. If you misrepresent your speech topic, your audience will come away with an inaccurate view of important issues and situations. Ethical informative speaking relies on the honest and accurate distribution of information, which can happen only if speakers present that information truthfully.

PREPARATION OUTLINE WITH COMMENTARY

The African Serval
by Shana Moellmer

Specific Purpose: To inform my audience about keeping the African serval as a house pet.

Thesis Statement: Though the African serval's legs, ears, and coloration aid in its survival in the wild, these adaptations take on a whole new meaning in the context of keeping a serval as an exotic house pet.

MindTap® You may have already given an informative speech in your class. Whether you have or whether this is the first time you've spoken informatively, you can use the following outline as a model. Watch a video of this speech and see her transcript, speaking outline, and note cards. (In the video, Tim Estiloz delivers Shana's speech.) Shana gave this speech in an introductory public speaking class. The assignment was to give a four- to six-minute speech, with a minimum of four sources cited. Students were also asked to create a preparation outline that included a Works Cited (MLA) or References (APA) section and to use at least one visual aid in their speech.

Introduction

I. By a show of hands, how many of you own a cat? (*attention getter*)
   A. I'm assuming those would be your typical 5- to 15-pound house cats, with the most exotic breeds being a Persian or a sphynx.
   B. What would you say if I told you that you could own a 40-pound cat the size of a Labrador?
II. I'm talking about the African serval, which is native to the grassy savannas of southern and middle Africa. (*reveal topic and relate to audience*)
III. The serval has been domesticated and brought into the homes of about 195 Americans, according to the 2000 cat census by the Long Island Ocelot Club, which is part of the Endangered Species Conservation Federation. (*establish credibility*)
   A. Although the serval can be domesticated, potential owners must know that this feline is well adapted to life in the wild.
   B. Bringing it into a domestic setting can have setbacks.
IV. Though the African serval's legs, ears, and coloration aid in its survival in the wild, these adaptations take on a whole new meaning in the context of keeping a serval as a house pet. (*thesis and preview*)

COMMENTARY

Shana begins her speech with a rhetorical question, engaging her audience early. She piques their curiosity by suggesting they own a typical house cat rather than her unusual subject.

As she reveals her topic, she draws her audience in with a mention of the grassy savannas of Africa and a brief history of the African serval. She also establishes credibility by citing her sources in her introduction.

Shana continues to draw her audience in to her subject with her positive but cautionary language about the drawbacks of keeping a serval as a pet.

At the end of her introduction, Shana clearly reveals her main points. She then uses a transition to signal to her audience that she is beginning her first main point.

Shana clearly states her first main point and uses several sub- and sub-subpoints to develop her ideas.

By citing relevant, reliable sources and providing interesting facts, she boosts her credibility and builds her argument about how the serval is adapted to a life in the wild rather than someone's home.

Shana uses simple, yet interesting, language ("leap," "crash," "crush") to keep her audience interested in her topic.

In points I.C and I.D Shana uses brief transitions ("the next trait," "finally") to indicate that she is shifting her argument to address additional aspects of the serval's life in the wild.

Shana describes the distinctive markings behind the cat's ears, offers the formal name for those markings, and then explains their function. In following this topical pattern, she is able to present her information clearly and maintain her audience's interest.

Shana uses an internal summary and a preview to transition to her second main point. Using both, she is able to remind her audience of what they just learned and to signal them to get ready for her second point. In addition, she ties her main points together by using the material in her first main point to help her develop her discussion of the consequences of keeping an African serval in the home.

In point II.A.1, Shana supports her argument that it's difficult to keep servals as pets by quoting an authority. The quote uses familiar comparisons that her audience can easily relate to.

Transition: First, we'll look at how the serval's physical aspects allow it to survive in the wild.

Body

I. The African serval is a creature that is well adapted for life in the wild.
    A. On average, it stands about two feet tall, is three feet long, and has a ten-inch tail.
        1. Most of the serval's height comes from its long legs.
        2. The serval's legs are "the longest legs relative to its body of any cat species" (Nevada Savannahs).
    B. The serval's legs benefit its survival.
        1. They allow the cat to stand tall in grasses of the African savanna, giving it a height advantage over its prey.
        2. In addition, they allow it to jump up to ten feet straight up into the air, which is a key hunting strategy (Serval Conservation Organization).
            a. Servals will leap up and crash down onto their prey, crushing it instantly or pinning it until they can get it securely into their mouth.
            b. A serval can even "capture . . . birds in flight by leaping . . . into the air and slapping them to the ground."
    C. The next trait of the serval that aids in its survival is its large, rounded ears, which help it locate prey.
        1. The serval's ears are quite mobile and move like satellites to pinpoint the location of a sound.
        2. The size of the serval's ears allows it to take in even the ultrasonic squeaks of savanna rodents.
        3. Without these ears, the rustling of the tall savanna grasses would drown out all evidence of its prey.
    D. Finally, the serval's coloration and spotting pattern provide camouflage and help deter its predators.
        1. The serval's light brown coat with its scattered, dark-spotted pattern break up its profile, allowing the cat to blend into the shadows of the grasses.
        2. In addition, the serval has matching white markings on the backs of its black ears.
            a. These markings are called *ocelli*.
            b. They deter predators, making it seem as if the serval has spotted the threat with eyes in the back of its head (Syminou Exotic Felines).

Transition: Though the legs, ears, and coloration of the serval serve as important tools for survival in the wild, they serve a much different purpose when viewed in the light of keeping the serval as a pet.

II. For those who want to keep the serval as a pet, consider the consequences of bringing its wild adaptations into a domestic setting.
    A. The serval's long legs and jumping capabilities make it difficult to keep it out of unwanted areas.
        1. Jessi Clark-White, webmaster of ExoticCatz.com and avid serval owner, shares an insight into living with this large cat: "Domestic cats jump on your windowsills and the refrigerator, rarely disturbing household objects. Servals jump on your bookshelves, kitchen counters, tables, computer desks, and any other raised surface leaving a trail of destruction in their wake . . . Knickknacks on the bookshelf? Gone, or later discovered buried in the litter box. Stuff on your kitchen counter? Knocked over and sent flying several feet in random directions."
        2. Special precautions must be taken if the serval is kept in an outdoor area.
            a. If the serval is kept in an outdoor enclosure, the enclosure should have a secure roof.
            b. A serval can easily jump and climb out of an inadequate enclosure.

B. The serval's ears, though useful for hunting in the wild, serve as a mood indicator in the domestic setting.
   1. When a house cat is upset, it will hiss and raise the hairs on its back and tail.
   2. But with servals, "these behaviors are just as likely to mean 'I love you, and I'm excited you're home' or 'Cool bird, Mom! Can I chase it?'" (Jessi Clark-White)
      a. The key is how the ears are placed.
         i. An upset serval will have its ears pressed flat against its head as it hisses.
         ii. An interested one will have the ears more erect.
      b. To properly assess the mood of this large pet, it's important to recognize that its body language—especially its ears—is different from a house cat's body language.
C. The serval's coat coloration, which kept it from standing out in the wild, instead draws attention in a domestic setting.
   1. What common city walker wouldn't pause and stare at the spectacle of someone walking a cheetah-like, dog-sized cat on a leash down the street?
   2. That big, colorful coat makes big, colorful hairballs.

Conclusion

I. The African serval's adaptations serve it differently in the wild than in the domestic setting. (*review*)
   - The serval's long legs allow it to leap and catch prey in the wild, and they let the serval get up onto high places around your house.
   - Its ears serve to pinpoint the faint noises of its prey or to let you know how your pet is feeling.
   - The cat's coloration provides camouflage in the wild, while declaring its exotic nature when walking down a suburban street.
II. Although it may seem that keeping a serval is more of a hassle than a privilege, Jessi Clark-White declares that "a well-raised serval really is incredibly sweet and amazing . . . [and] is worth every bit of the time and effort"—as long as you're willing to put up with the obnoxious moments as well as the cute ones. (*closing line*)

Works Cited

"The African Serval." African Servals, *Nevada Savannahs*, www.nevadazatarasavannahs.com /african-servals.html.

Clark-White, Jessi. "African Serval." Small Cat Species, *Exotic Catz.com*, 2005, exoticcatz.com /speciesserval.html.

"LIOC-ESCF 2000 Cat Census." *The Long Island Ocelot Club—Endangered Species Conservation Federation*, efcf.org/Census00.html.

"The Savannah." The Savannah/Serval, *Syminou Exotic Felines, 2007–2008*, www.syminou.com /savannah-en.html.

The Serval Conservation Organization. "Servals in the Wild." Wild, *TSCO*, servals.org/wild.

In point II.B, Shana again compares servals to the more familiar house cat so that she can inform her audience of the challenges of bringing a serval into a home.

She wraps up her second main point with a rhetorical question that again draws her audience into her topic. This question touches on a humorous aspect of owning a serval—big, colorful hairballs.

Shana provides a summary of her first main point, cites one of her authorities to review her second main point, and finishes her speech with an intriguing quotation, keeping her audience's attention until the very last line of her speech. Shana uses the MLA citation style for her Works Cited list.

Chapter Summary

Informative speaking may be the most common form of public speaking.

- To speak informatively is to share knowledge with an audience to increase their understanding of a particular topic.

- To create an informative speaking environment is to bring a topic to life for an audience and to illustrate its relevance so an audience better understands its impact on their world.

The five types of informative speeches are about processes, events, places and people, objects, and concepts.

- Process speeches describe how something is done, how something comes to be what it is, or how something works.
- Speeches about events describe or explain a significant, interesting, or unusual occurrence.
- When you give speeches about places and people, you describe something significant, interesting, or unusual about your topic.
- In speeches about objects, you inform your audiences about anything that can be perceived by the senses.
- Speeches about concepts describe or explain abstractions, things you cannot perceive with your senses, such as ideas, theories, principles, worldviews, or beliefs.
- These five different types of informative speeches can be organized chronologically, spatially, causally, or topically.

Three tips can help you give an effective speech.

- Bring your topic to life: Relate your topic to your audience by sharing the human side of that topic with engaging and relevant details.
- Tailor your information to your audience: Determine how much an audience knows about a topic and thus how much information to present.
- Use language that is clear and unbiased: Use language that focuses on descriptions, definitions, and explanations so audiences can more easily learn new information. This type of language sets informative speaking apart from invitational and persuasive speaking.

Make a point to commit to the principles of ethical public speaking.

- Research the information in your speech carefully.
- Present the information honestly and without bias.

Invitation to Public Speaking Online MindTap

Now that you have read Chapter 12, use your MindTap Communication for *Invitation to Public Speaking* for quick access to the digital resources that accompany this text. These resources include

- **Study tools** that will help you assess your learning and prepare for exams (digital glossary, key term flash cards, review quizzes).
- **Activities and assignments** that will help you hone your knowledge and build your public speaking skills

throughout the course, as well as help you explore public speaking concepts online (web links), give you step-by-step guidance through the research, outline and note card preparation process (Outline Builder), watch and critique videos of sample speeches (Interactive Video Activities), and allow you to practice and present your presentation online using a speech video delivery, recording, and grading system (YouSeeU).

Key Concepts MindTap Test your knowledge with online printable flash cards.

informative speaking environment (230)
informative speech (230)
speeches about concepts (234)
speeches about places and people (233)

speeches about processes (230)
speeches about events (232)
speeches about objects (233)

Review Questions

1. Consider the following as possible informative speaking topics for your next assigned speech:
   - Carpets
   - Making pizza
   - Social media
   - Religion
   - Star Wars movies
   - Subways

   How many different kinds of informative speeches could you give on each topic? What would be the strengths or advantages of choosing one type of speech over another for these topics? How would your speech be relevant to the public dialogue?

2. Create a preparation outline for an informative speech on the topic of the U.S. response to natural disasters. How many different organizational patterns could you use for this topic? How would each pattern highlight a different aspect of this

topic? How would you reduce the scope of your speech to make it manageable for your public speaking course?

3. In groups or as a class, identify five or six of the most commonly used, but poorly defined, terms you hear regularly. Use informative language to define those terms for your classmates. Some terms to define might be:
   - Democracy
   - Socialism
   - Free speech
   - Hate speech
   - Gun control
   - Conservation

4. Select one of the topics from question 3 and write a specific purpose and thesis statement for a speech about that topic. Next choose your organizational pattern and develop the main points for this speech. How might you bring this topic to life and manage the information you have about this topic so it is relevant to the audience?

13 | Invitational Speaking

IN THIS CHAPTER, YOU WILL LEARN TO:

- Describe public deliberation and explain its relationship to public speaking

- Experiment with the three conditions for an invitational speaking environment

- Develop an invitational speech

- Compare and contrast the four most common patterns of organization for invitational speeches

- Apply three tips for giving effective invitational speeches

- Implement two principles for giving ethical invitational speeches

We all have encountered people whose positions on social and political issues are not at all like our own. In such cases, we're not likely to change their views nor are they likely to change ours, no matter how hard both parties try. In fact, in many situations, such as business meetings or community forums, trying to persuade someone that our view is the best is not only unrealistic but also can be inappropriate, especially in a situation where mutual problem solving is

MindTap® Start with a quick warm-up activity and review the chapter's learning objectives.

▲ Alexandra Cousteau is a filmmaker, National Geographic Emerging Explorer, and advocate of water issues that span our globe. She also is known as an expert speaker who regularly invites her audiences to engage complex issues and to consider multifaceted facts and dilemmas. In this chapter, you will begin to learn the skills necessary to engage your audiences in this same manner so that you, too, can enter into a dialogue with your audience over challenging and controversial issues.

Andrew H. Walker/Getty Images Entertainment/Getty Images

the goal. Trying to persuade other people to change their views on a subject can also be inappropriate when we do not have enough information to know what is best for them or when their positions are so personal that it is not our place to ask them to change. For example, issues such as the death penalty, animal rights, and stem cell research are tied to deeply held personal beliefs about politics, economics, and religion that are far beyond any one speaker's area of expertise.

As public speakers, what should we do in these types of situations? Do we simply give up when our audience sees things differently than we do? Or do we forge ahead with our attempts to persuade them even though we do not really understand their perspectives? In this chapter, you will learn a different approach, one that encourages us to explore the many sides of an issue. You will learn that even though you may not be able to change the attitudes of your audience or even want to change them, you can still enter the public dialogue. You'll learn to engage in **invitational speaking**, a type of public speaking that helps us deliberate with others on important matters. In invitational speaking, a speaker enters into a dialogue with an audience to clarify positions, explore issues and ideas, or articulate beliefs and values. To speak invitationally is to do something other than inform or persuade. To speak invitationally is to continue the public dialogue and seek mutual recognition and understanding despite firm differences in opinions, values, and beliefs.

MindTap

Read, highlight, and take notes online.

invitational speaking: Type of public speaking in which a speaker enters into a dialogue with an audience to clarify positions, explore issues and ideas, or articulate beliefs and values.

public deliberation: Engaging in a process that involves the careful weighing of information and views.

Inviting Public Deliberation

Invitational speaking is an important component of what scholars now are calling **"public deliberation."** To deliberate publicly is to engage in a process that "involves the careful weighing of information and views." Deliberation combines "an egalitarian" process that gives people ample time to speak and to listen to others, with "dialogue that bridges differences among participants.[1] When we speak invitationally and deliberate with others, we are speaking because we are well informed or we seek to be well informed, open to different ideas and positions, and respectful of others, even if they hold different views and positions.

Let's look at an example that illustrates the differences between informative, persuasive, and invitational speaking, which sets the stage for deliberation. In a speech proposing that a school district move from a five-day to a four-day school week, an informative speaker might describe the proposal and stop there. We might describe this as a "Here is what the four-day week looks like" speech. A persuasive speaker might ask the audience to support the move to a four-day school week and to possibly take a course of action. This speaker might urge the audience to support the local initiative, to make the change to a four-day week: we could describe this speech as the "I'll convince you that this change is the best for all" speech. However, because issues such as these are complex and often contentious, an invitational speaker would set the stage for the audience to explore and deliberate on the implications of the change to a four-day week and of remaining on a five-day week. We could describe this speech as the "Let's explore the issues related to four- and five-day school weeks" speech.

To summarize, the invitational speaker sets the stage for the audience to explore, discuss, and deliberate on the consequences of an issue so that informed decisions can be made at a later date. The persuasive speaker advocates specific change during the speech. The informative speaker provides facts, figures, and information the audience does not already have about a topic. An invitational speaker encourages a civil and open investigation of a topic and the exploration of its complexities, without trying to persuade the audience of the "right" decision.[2]

The Invitational Speaking Environment

But how does a speaker set the stage for public deliberation in a speech? To speak invitationally, you must try to create an **invitational environment**. In this environment, your highest priorities as a speaker are to:

- Understand the issue fully.
- Respect diverse views.
- Appreciate the range of possible positions on an issue, even if those positions are quite different from your own.
- Engage in a dialogue with your audience.
- Create a space in which your audience and you can express their views.

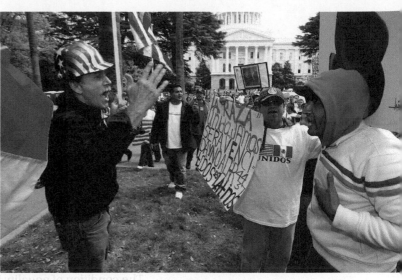

AP Images/Rich Pedroncelli

Although all speakers want to create an environment of respect, doing so is especially important in invitational speaking because the speaker and audience members engage in a dialogue. Because invitational speaking allows for exploration, deliberation, and dialogue, this type of speech is best suited for situations in which speakers have some time with an audience to allow for the fullest expression of the various positions possible.

The Invitational Environment

Invitational deliberations occur at almost every level of our society: local, state, and national. When members of a community gather to examine questions, plans, issues, and policies that affect diverse individuals, they often deliberate on (rather than debate) the impact of those questions, plans, issues, and policies. Topics range from the quality of our lives (parking, housing, transportation, services, and resources) to the impact on our finances (tuition, taxes, zoning ordinances, and city or government services). At the local and state levels, the dilemmas we deliberate over are extensive and complex. However, as a nation, we also deliberate over matters of national concern. After the events of September 11, 2001, members of the Lower Manhattan Development Corporation and the Port Authority of New York and New Jersey undertook lengthy deliberations as they solicited ideas for rebuilding the World Trade Center site.[3] This invitational process involved two public hearings that linked the people of Long Island with New York's five boroughs through videoconferencing technology, allowing thousands of citizens to participate in a dialogue.[4] In addition, when the first round of designs for the memorial failed to inspire New York's citizens, officials initiated a second design competition, receiving a record 5,201 entries from forty-nine U.S. states and sixty-three nations. And when the jury—which included a family member of one of the attack victims, architects, public officials, and a historian—finally reached its decision, and the final design, *Reflecting Absence,* was displayed, the jury avoided suggesting how the audience should think, feel, and react to the memorial. Instead, it acknowledged "that memory belongs primarily to the individual."[5] As Port Authority Executive Director Joseph J. Seymour stated: "The rebuilding of Lower Manhattan has been the most open and accessible process in history."[6]

This example illustrates one of the keys to creating a successful invitational environment: rather than taking on the role of the "expert" and assigning the role of the "listener" to the audience, invitational speakers consider themselves and the audience as both the experts and the listeners. They not only express their views but also listen carefully to their audience's views: they facilitate a discussion of ideas that encourages the exchange of views without risk of attack or ridicule.

Some topics tap into deeply held attitudes, values, and beliefs that audiences are unlikely to change. Yet an audience may be interested in exploring different aspects of an issue with a speaker to gain an understanding or clarify their own positions. For example, the topic of immigration reform in the United States tends to divide audiences into two firm camps: those who want to restrict immigration and those who feel a liberal immigration policy benefits us. How do you think an invitational approach to this topic would affect an audience? Would an invitational approach be more effective than a persuasive approach?

invitational environment: Environment in which the speaker's highest priority is to understand, respect, and appreciate the range of possible positions on an issue, even if those positions are quite different from his or her own.

To build this invitational environment, you must create three conditions: equality, value, and self-determination. These conditions allow you and your audience to see one another as knowledgeable and capable, although perhaps in different ways. These three conditions are interrelated, but they are presented separately here to clarify each condition and its goal. However, all of these conditions help you create an atmosphere of mutual respect, understanding, and exploration. They help you communicate effectively with people who hold positions quite different from your own.[7]

MindTap®

Watch a video clip of student speaker Shelley Weibel as she creates a condition of equality. How does she create this condition?

The Condition of Equality

When you create the **condition of equality**, you acknowledge that there are many good ideas worth considering and your audience members hold valid perspectives worthy of exploration. With the condition of equality, you make a space for all voices to be heard. Communication scholars call this "sufficient opportunity to speak"[8] and note that the "ideas and feelings they share" will be "received with respect and care."[9] The condition of equality is a basic premise of democracy: people with diverse opinions should be heard, and their voices matter even if they are different from our own.

But how do you create this condition? Your language, delivery, and presentation of ideas lets your audience know that you recognize them as people whose knowledge, experiences, and perspectives are as valid for them as yours are for you. Because you and your audience are equal participants in a dialogue (although you still give the speech and lead the discussion), your audience members are able to offer their perspectives, share their experiences, and even question you—in the same way you do with them. A condition of equality creates a sense of safety and welcome that encourages audience members to share their perspectives. The jury who selected the World Trade Center memorial created the condition of equality by making every effort to recognize all community members as equals and to solicit their input.

The Condition of Value

When you create the **condition of value**, you recognize that your audience's views, although they might be different from your own, are worth exploring—they have value. Communication scholars Bone, Griffin, and Scholz explain that when value is present, we communicate to others that we will step outside our own "standpoint in order to understand another perspective."[10] Burkhalter, Gastil, and Kelshaw describe value as the "adequate comprehension and consideration" of another person's ideas.[11]

In creating the condition of value, you let your audience members know that when they express differing views and opinions, those differences will be explored in a spirit of mutual understanding, without judgment or any effort to change them. Value requires that we step outside our own standpoint (Chapter 4) to try to understand another perspective and see the world as someone else sees it. So when disagreement on an issue arises, you and the other participants in the dialogue try to understand the opposing positions and the reasons that people hold their views. The fact that the jury in the World Trade Center example reopened the process after its first attempt illustrates the condition of value and the jury members' willingness to step outside their own standpoints.

The Condition of Self-Determination

As an invitational speaker interested in exploring ideas and deliberation, you also want to create a **condition of self-determination**. This means you recognize that the members of your audience are experts in their own lives—that they know what is best for them and have the right to make choices about their lives based on this knowledge.[12] Although their choices may not be the ones you would make, the members of your audience are free to decide for themselves how to think, feel, and act.

condition of equality: Condition of an invitational environment that requires the speaker to acknowledge that all audience members hold equally valid perspectives worthy of exploration.

condition of value: Condition of an invitational environment that requires the speaker to recognize the inherent value of the audience's views, although those views may differ from the speaker's views.

condition of self-determination: Condition of an invitational environment that requires the speaker to recognize that people know what is best for them and have the right to make choices about their lives based on this knowledge.

The condition of self-determination means you won't close off conversation or try to persuade your audience to do something its members may not feel inclined to do. Rather, you will create an atmosphere in which the members of the audience feel in control of their choices and are respected for their ability to make them. In the real-world example, the jury created a condition of self-determination by displaying all 5,201 entries, allowing people to view each submission and the final selection, and letting them determine for themselves the meaning of each.

In our increasingly diverse and complicated world, invitational speaking is a useful tool in some of the most difficult public conversations and deliberations. When you choose to speak invitationally, you are seeking a full and open exchange of ideas and positions. Creating these three conditions—equality, value, and self-determination—helps you succeed in this exchange. Remember, the goal of invitational speaking is to go beyond informing and to avoid any effort to persuade. Instead, when you speak invitationally, you try to explore issues in a spirit of acceptance, openness, and deliberation.

The Invitational Speech

Although there are several ways to approach the invitational speech, we will explore the most common used by beginning public speakers: the speech to explore an issue.

Speeches to Explore an Issue

When you give an invitational **speech to explore an issue**, you attempt to engage your audience in a discussion about an idea, concern, topic, or plan of action. Your goal is to present an overview of the issue and to gather different perspectives from your audience so you can understand the subject more fully. Quite often, you use what you have learned from your audience to solve problems or plan courses of action that appeal to a broad range of perspectives.

Begin this type of speech by stating your intent to explore the issue. Then lay out the various positions on the issue, going beyond presenting it as having only two sides. When you present three or more perspectives on an issue, you can help your audience understand its complexity and the reasons that making a decision about it may be so difficult. You might also share your opinions about the issue, even if they are tentative. But share your opinions only to help spark dialogue, not with the intent of persuading your audience to agree with you. As an invitational speaker, your goal is to lay the groundwork for an open dialogue and deliberation rooted in equality, value, and self-determination. You want people to feel valued, heard, and respected by one another.

The following examples illustrate invitational speeches to explore issues. In the first, David spoke invitationally about the issue of the federal minimum wage and a group of people known as the working poor. His goal was to get his audience thinking about the amount of money someone earning the minimum wage actually makes, the way of life of the working poor, and possible ways to address this issue:

MindTap®

Watch a video clip of student speaker Melissa Carroll as she creates a condition of self-determination. How does she create this condition?

Specific purpose	To invite my audience to explore with me the federal minimum wage and what some approaches are to assisting the working poor.
Thesis statement	Our current federal minimum wage of $7.25 per hour leaves many working people dependent on public assistance agencies like our county's food bank, but raising the minimum wage creates many problems and may not be the best approach to helping the working poor.
Main points	I. The minimum wage of 25 cents per hour set in 1938 has risen to $7.25 per hour, providing a full-time worker a little over $16,200 annually.

speech to explore an issue: Invitational speech in which the speaker attempts to engage an audience in a discussion about an idea, concern, topic, or plan of action.

II. In recent years, food banks and other public assistance agencies have seen huge growth in the number of working families seeking their aid.

III. Experts suggest that raising the minimum wage may decrease employment opportunities for entry-level employees and create a heavy burden on employers.

IV. Other options exist, but all have their own strengths and limitations.

V. An open discussion about the minimum wage and our working poor can help us gain more insight into this complex issue.

In this speech, David provides some history regarding the federal minimum wage, debunks some of the myths surrounding the working poor, and presents a few of the existing approaches to this issue. He then opens the discussion for exploration and deliberation, knowing that his audience will have strong views. However, throughout his speech, he set the stage for an invitational discussion so that audience members felt free to share their views.

In the next example, Amanda explores the issue of funding HIV and AIDS research and support in both Africa and the United States. She compares and contrasts the AIDS epidemic in both regions, inviting her audience to explore the topic of prioritizing funding and support efforts when there is too little money to fully assist research and support in both parts of the world:

Specific purpose To invite my audience to explore with me the issues involved in funding HIV/AIDS research and support in Africa and the United States.

Thesis statement The HIV/AIDS epidemic significantly affects our local communities as well as communities in Africa, funding is a problem and people are divided over where federal funding should go, but exploring with my audience possible ways to prioritize relief efforts in both regions could give us insight into how to solve this dilemma.

Main points I. Both Africa and the United States are dealing with an AIDS epidemic.
  A. Sub-Saharan Africa has less than 11 percent of the world's population but is home to 70 percent of those living with HIV.
  B. Approximately 1 million people currently living in the United States have HIV/AIDS.

II. Funding is inadequate for both Africa and the United States.
  A. The budget the U.S. Agency for International Development (USAID) set aside for Africa is $15 billion for the next five years, but that barely scratches the surface of the HIV/AIDS problems in Africa's fifteen most affected countries.
  B. The federal HIV/AIDS budget for the United States is $11 billion this year, but that also falls short of the goal of adequate assistance.

III. People are conflicted over where funds to alleviate the HIV/AIDS crisis should go.
  A. Some argue that our money is being wasted on Africa and we should just support the United States.
  B. Others believe that we should give more money to Africa because the problem there is so large.
  C. Yet others believe that we are spending just the right amount of money in both regions.
  D. And some believe that not enough is being spent in either region.

IV. Prioritizing relief funding for HIV/AIDS in Africa and the United States requires careful discussion, and I'd like to now open up the floor to my audience so we can discuss this important issue.

National Geographic Explorer

ALEXANDRA COUSTEAU, Explorer, Social Environment Advocate

Please share a situation in which you spoke to an audience of peers and they held positions of equal merit to you but different than yours. What specific approaches did you use to invite expression of a variety of perspectives?

Because we drink clean water, we can all agree we want the water resources in our own backyard to be unpolluted; we can all agree on a certain number of things no matter who we are. And that aspect of water transcends both politics and religion. I had an experience working with groups in the Middle East made up of Israelis and Arabs, where students from both sides of the conflict would get together and study together and work together and talk together and tell each other their stories. And they realized through this process that they have the same stories. They had a story of conflict, a story of lost loved ones, and a story of fear of others. And because they told each other these stories from their own perspectives, when there was conflict in Gaza, they protested that conflict together and they grieved for each others' losses even though the other was traditionally considered the enemy. So I think we can overcome a lot of those barriers to mutual understanding through effective communication in an unbiased and open way that focuses on our own experiences rather than what we've been taught to believe.

In this example, Amanda presented the controversy fairly and openly. She asked audience members to share their views with her and kept a tone of equality and respect to help them explore the issue. Using an invitational approach, she created an environment in which both she and her audience felt free to express their views openly.

Organizational Patterns for Invitational Speeches

Many organizational patterns are suitable for invitational speaking. The easiest for beginning speakers are the familiar chronological, spatial, and topical, as well as a new pattern called *multiple perspectives*. As your skill at invitational speaking develops, you can modify these patterns and adapt to your audiences and speaking situations as needed.

Chronological Pattern

A chronological pattern of organization allows you to trace a sequence of events or ideas (Chapter 7). In the next example, Jenni uses this pattern to explore the issue of

Practicing the Public Dialogue | 13.1

SELECT AN INVITATIONAL SPEECH TYPE

In class, identify some of the most controversial issues we face today as a society. List these issues on the board. How many of them do you have strong feelings about? How many do you wish you could learn more about in an invitational way? Select two topics from the list and, with a partner, discuss the ways you could frame speeches about these topics invitationally. For each topic, would you want to give a speech to explore an issue or articulate a position? How would you use equality, value, and self-determination to create an invitational speaking environment? Save this list for the next Practicing the Public Dialogue activity.

MindTap®

To see an example of an invitational speech, watch student speaker Cara Buckley-Ott giving a speech and then exploring an issue with her audience.

bilingual education. In this speech, she develops the issue and explores how various thoughts on the issue have changed over time:

Specific purpose	To invite my audience to explore the issues involved in implementing bilingual education in public schools across the United States.
Thesis statement	Bilingual education has a long and controversial history in the United States, and understanding this history's complexity helps us fully understand how the issue is framed today.
Main points	I. Historically, bilingual education was designed to provide a better education for children who emigrated from various countries.
	II. After World War I, legislation changed in many states, reducing the support for bilingual education.
	III. Today's debates over bilingual education center around the cost of this kind of education as well as the right of children whose first language is not English to a quality education.
	IV. Now that we know the complex history of bilingual education, how views of this issue have changed, and its costs and benefits, I'd like to explore this issue with my audience.

Jenni used the chronological pattern to trace the evolution of bilingual education and help her audience understand the issue more fully. In the discussion with her audience, she explored this history, listened to their personal experiences and views, and raised questions of her own. Jenni's audience learned about the complexity of the issue and went beyond the "for" and "against" perspectives so commonly offered. Together, they explored issues and deliberated on solutions that could work for a whole school rather than just one group of individuals.

The next example illustrates how the chronological pattern might work in a business setting. In this example, Shalon addressed colleagues about proposed changes in a parental leave policy to explore whether those changes would work for the employees:

Specific purpose	To invite my audience to work with me to develop a parental leave policy that benefits all employees.
Thesis statement	A discussion with my coworkers could help us develop a parental leave policy that may be more comprehensive, and thus more advantageous, to more employees than the company's original policy, current policy, and the new policy proposed by our employers.
Main points	I. Our company's original parental leave policy, which reflected the demographics and politics of the office at the time it was created, had both strengths and weaknesses.
	A. The policy's strengths lay in the fact that it reflected the demographics and politics of the workplace at the time it was created.
	B. However, the nature of the workplace has changed over the years, highlighting the policy's weaknesses.
	II. Our current policy reflects the fact that the company made changes to the original policy as a result of employee need.
	A. The changes affected women in certain ways.
	B. The changes affected men in certain ways.
	C. The changes also affected our company as a whole.
	III. The new parental leave policy proposed by our employers is both similar to and different from previous policies.
	IV. Given the history of the plan and the new proposal, I'd like to explore with my coworkers the changes to the proposed plan we might want to suggest.

Shalon described past parental leave policies not to bias or sway her colleagues, or to simply educate them, but rather to collect information, stimulate open discussion, and foster self-determination. With this history, audience members could see more clearly how the proposed changes might affect them and could develop an alternative proposal to present to management.

A chronological pattern allows you to share history and offer background information that may help audience members enter a discussion. In the first example, the background information helped Jenni's audience understand the issue more fully and explore possible solutions. In the second, it helped Shalon's audience propose changes that would be in their best interest. By tracing the development of an issue over time, you establish common ground and openness to seeing how the perspective or issue might continue to evolve.

Spatial Pattern

The spatial pattern of organization can help you organize your ideas according to location or geography (Chapter 7). This pattern is helpful when you want to discuss what a topic has in common, or how it differs, across countries, regions, states, or cities. Riley used a spatial pattern to describe the ways communities have responded to hate crimes and to explore how his community might begin to heal from such a crime:

Specific purpose	To invite my audience to visit the scenes of several hate crimes committed across the country so we might know how to begin to heal from what happened in our own town.
Thesis statement	Trying to understand the response to the many hate crimes that have been committed in other communities across the United States might help my own community heal from our recent tragedy.
Main points	I. The response of a Texas community to the hate crime against James Byrd Jr. involved both public and private actions.
	II. Similarly, the response of a Wyoming community to the hate crime against Matthew Shepard was both private and public, bringing in the surrounding areas as well.
	III. The response of a California community to the hate crime against a church with a largely Middle Eastern congregation was far more public in nature.
	IV. With these responses in mind, I'd like to invite the audience to discuss ways we might respond to our own recent tragedy.

By describing how other communities responded to hate crimes, Riley stimulated and encouraged discussion with audience members about the needs of the community and how they felt they might respond to their own tragedy. By exploring this issue, both he and his audience began to formulate a plan of action that helped the community come to terms with a painful event.

You can use a spatial pattern to invite your audience to see how other localities have dealt with many types of public issues, such as transportation, health, poverty, crime, education, and pollution. You can also use this pattern in business speeches to compare how other businesses have dealt with a problem.

Topical Pattern

This pattern allows you to discuss the aspects of your topic point by point (Chapter 7). Here is an example of the topical pattern from Phillip's speech exploring with his audience the implications of sentencing people who commit serious crimes to death or to life in prison:

The life story of Australian aboriginal philosopher and educator Jack Beetson reads like an inspirational movie. The son of a Wongaibon mother and an Ngemba father, he was kicked out of school at thirteen and got into trouble with the police. After spending a few years working in various unfulfilling jobs, he became a street kid in Sydney, Australia. As he neared thirty, he decided to continue his education and started attending Tranby Aboriginal College, an alternative learning environment for adult aboriginal students. He stuck around, and several years later, he became the school's executive director. And in 2001, the Year of Dialogue among Civilizations, he was awarded the Unsung Hero Award by the United Nations, as one of only twelve people in the world to receive this award.

TRESPASSERS WELCOME

Today, Beetson lives on his farm, the Linga Longa Aboriginal Philosophy Farm, in

Bradley Kanaris/Getty Images Sport/Getty Images

New South Wales. A product of Beetson's lifelong efforts to bring indigenous and nonindigenous people together, the farm's workshops and forums provide a rare opportunity for people of all cultures to come together to explore their identities and differences in a friendly, informal environment. He and his wife, Shani, began the farm "so that nonindigenous Australia wouldn't have the excuse that 'there is nowhere we can go to find out'"

about indigenous culture. So welcoming is Beetson that he has said he'd like to put up a "Trespassers Welcome" sign on the front gate in the hopes that people will feel free to stop by for a conversation.

A well-respected community leader, Beetson also travels extensively, speaking out about compassion, justice, and self-determination for aboriginal and indigenous peoples. Summing up his philosophy and approach, he says, "I share this particularly with young people who come out here who are living on the street. . . . There's not a person on the planet who's better than you are, but always remember you're no better than anybody else either. That's how I've tried to live my life."[13]

🔗 YOU CAN GET INVOLVED

MindTap® Increase your cultural awareness and discover opportunities for dialogue with various cultural groups, ethnic and otherwise.

Specific purpose	To invite my audience to explore whether the death penalty is as just and efficient as keeping an inmate in prison for life.
Thesis statement	Although the death penalty is commonly accepted as a just form of punishment, keeping inmates in prison without the possibility of parole may be a better solution, but both approaches present ethical dilemmas.
Main points	I. Life sentences may be a better option than the death penalty, primarily because there have been cases of innocent people being placed on death row and subsequently executed.
	II. The death penalty does not seem to deter people from committing murder—the United States is one of the few first-world countries to practice corporal punishment, yet it still has the highest rate of murder.
	III. Surprisingly, a life sentence is cheaper for taxpayers than an execution.
	IV. However, the suffering caused by a lifetime spent in prison cannot be overlooked.
	V. Because each approach presents moral dilemmas, I'd like to invite my audience to explore the implications of sentencing people who commit serious crimes to life in prison as compared with sentencing them to death.

Using the topical pattern, Phillip shared what he had learned from his research about corporal punishment and life sentencing. However, he did more than inform his audience about these aspects of our penal system; he shared the ethical dilemmas of each and remained open to alternatives, new information, and concerns from his audience.

Multiple Perspectives Pattern

Although you can use this organizational pattern in other types of speeches, it is particularly well suited for invitational speeches. The **multiple perspectives pattern** allows you to systematically address the many sides and positions of an issue before opening up the speech for dialogue, exploration, and deliberation with the audience. You can go beyond dividing an issue into only two opposing sides and illustrate the multiple perspectives that are possible. This approach not only respects a diversity of opinions but also invites your audience to consider even more views than those you covered and makes room for additional perspectives from your audience.

This organizational pattern works well when you want to speak to explore a very complex or contentious issue with an audience. In the next example, Julie invited her audience to explore what to teach in U.S. schools about the creation of the universe. She used the multiple perspectives pattern for her speech, inviting her audience to consider how views from different cultures might fit into an elementary or high school education. The basic outline of her speech looked as follows:

Specific purpose	To invite my audience to explore the many theories of creation and their role in U.S. education.
Thesis statement	Perhaps some of the many theories throughout time and across cultures that explain how the universe was created—particularly creationism, the big bang theory, intelligent design, ancient Egyptian and African theories, and Native American theories—could be taught in U.S. schools.
Main points	I. One of the modern theories of how the universe was created, that God created the universe, comes from the Judeo-Christian tradition.
	II. A second theory, proposed by the Greek philosopher Democritus in 400 B.C., set the stage for the big bang theory of creation proposed by most scientists today.
	III. A third theory, known as the intelligent design theory, accounts for the origins of RNA and DNA and could add yet another perspective to our children's education.
	IV. A fourth theory, offered by ancient Egyptian and African civilizations, presents a holistic view of existence in which many deities are worshipped as different aspects of God.
	V. Yet another theory, advocated by many Native American peoples, suggests that the creator of all, sometimes known as Thought Woman, has both female and male aspects and "thinks" all things into being.
	VI. I'd like to discuss with my audience the possibility that all of these creation theories be taught in U.S. schools to create a more inclusive curriculum.

The next example illustrates how the multiple perspectives pattern can be used in community presentations. In this example, Marko addressed businesspeople

MindTap

Student speaker Chung-yan Man used the topical pattern of organization for her informative speech on Chinese fortune-telling. Although her speech is informative, in some ways it can be considered invitational. Watch her speech and see if you can spot its invitational aspects.

iStockphoto.com/Chris Schmidt

Teachers often frame topics with the multiple perspectives pattern to encourage students to think about an issue in more than one way. Could you use this organizational pattern in your next speech?

multiple perspectives pattern:
Organizational pattern that allows the speaker to address the many sides and positions of an issue before opening up the speech for dialogue with the audience.

and explored the many ways to give to a community, including donating to the United Way:[14]

Specific purpose	To invite my audience to consider the various benefits of donating to the United Way and to value the ways they already give back to their community.
Thesis statement	The United Way, with its overarching view of the community and its needs, is but one of many excellent ways to give back to a community.

Main points

I. Because of its holistic view, contributing to the United Way is a great way to give back to the community.
   A. The United Way brings together key public and private entities to address many of the social ills of our community.
   B. One contribution to the United Way supports forty-one different agencies and projects in this community.
   C. Those who donate can feel confident that their contributions will be wisely distributed because the advisory committee that determines the distribution formula is composed of volunteers from our own community.

II. The United Way also supports other avenues of giving to the community.
   A. Donations to individual agencies and projects are excellent ways to give to the community.
   B. Volunteering is yet another way to support these agencies and projects.
   C. When time or money is tight, simply speaking highly of the United Way and other forms of giving is a third positive act.

III. I'd like to discuss with my audience the idea of donating to the United Way and to other community-based agencies.

Although a persuasive speech might seem most appropriate to solicit donations, Marko uses an invitational approach with great success. He uses the multiple perspectives pattern in a unique way. He not only articulates his position on why he believes the United Way is a fine charitable organization worthy of support but also explores with his audience the other ways to contribute to one's community, thereby examining his topic from different perspectives. By doing this, Marko validates the various perspectives audience members may hold on his topic, encouraging their self-determination. Audience members will appreciate Marko's efforts to examine his topic from so many perspectives and likely be more open to dialogue about the numerous possibilities for giving back to one's community.

To use a multiple perspectives organizational pattern, you must follow three guidelines:

- Do your research so you can explain the various sides to your audience.
- Present each perspective fairly so the audience members can make their own assessment of them all.
- Make room for even more perspectives to be offered from the audience when you open your speech up for dialogue, exploration, and deliberation.

In this diverse world, invitational speaking is an option that allows you to continue the public dialogue and explore with an audience even about the most controversial issues. With care and respect, you can establish the conditions of equality, value, and self-determination even when you disagree with someone. These three conditions

---

Practicing the Public Dialogue | 13.2

SELECT AN ORGANIZATIONAL PATTERN FOR YOUR INVITATIONAL SPEECH

Return to the list of possible invitational speech topics you prepared in Practicing the Public Dialogue 13.1. In groups, select a single topic and see if you can create a rough thesis statement and main points for four different invitational speeches on this topic, using each of the organizational patterns you've just read about. As a class, discuss which of these speeches you would find most interesting and why. As you discuss your favorite topic and organizational pattern, consider the tips for giving effective invitational speeches in the next section.

become increasingly important because, as cultural critic bell hooks explains, if "a person makes a unilateral decision that does not account for me, then I feel exploited by that decision because my needs haven't been considered. But if that person is willing to pause, then at that moment of pause there is an opportunity for mutual recognition because they have at least listened to and considered, honestly, my position."[15]

Tips for Giving Effective Invitational Speeches

Like informative and persuasive speaking, invitational speaking has specific guidelines to follow so you can give a more effective speech. Three tips will help you give effective invitational speeches and create a speaking environment of equality, value, and self-determination: (1) use invitational language, (2) allow time for discussion, exploration, and deliberation, and (3) show respect for diverse positions.

Use Invitational Language

One way you can create an effective invitational speaking environment and encourage deliberation is to use invitational language. Phrases like "You should," "The correct position is," and "Anyone can see," which advocate one position over others, only reduce your chances of creating the condition of equality. *Equality* means that all positions have merit; they are viable for the people who hold them, even if they may not be for you. Invitational language offers your view as one possible view but not as "the best" view. When you present many perspectives, use fair and unbiased adjectives and a respectful tone of voice that showcases the range of ideas and does not belittle or minimize the potential of any of them.

During the dialogue and deliberative parts of your speech, you can use phrases such as "I came to this view because" or "Because of that experience, I began to see this issue as" to help identify your views as your own. Use phrases such as "What are other views or positions we need to consider?" "That's a new perspective, let's explore that more," and "Who haven't we heard from yet?" to communicate to your audience that you value them and welcome views different from yours or even ones already on the table for discussion. Encourage those views and dialogue about those differences and disagreement rather than silencing or censoring them. Offer positive reinforcement to the ideas of others so the dialogue and deliberation can develop openly and freely. Respond with phrases like "Can you elaborate on that idea?," "How might that work?," "Why do you think so?," "Can you explain why you prefer that solution?," and "What benefits do you see with that position?" As you engage audience members in the exploration of an issue, draw them out and get them to elaborate on their views. If the discussion becomes heated, keep track of ideas you want to return to later by writing notes on a whiteboard or flip chart.

Finally, if you encounter a hostile audience member, your language can help manage and even reduce some of that hostility (consider Aziz Abu Sarah's tip from Chapter 2). When audience members respond with anger, the reason usually is that the speaker has touched a sensitive nerve. But your language can defuse the situation and reestablish value. Use words and phrases that acknowledge your audience member's position, express your desire to understand that position more fully, and even apologize for upsetting that person. Rather than responding with angry words or denying that the person has reason to be angry, use language that communicates your respect for him or her as someone with views that may be different from yours.

Allow Time for Discussion

Exploring ideas and deliberating with an audience take time. This means you must be patient and not rush through your presentation or hurry the discussion with your audience. If we are to create the conditions of equality, value, and self-determination and make a space for others in the public dialogue, we must be willing to take the time necessary to do so. Sometimes, this can seem inefficient. Western culture encourages us to get things done quickly and to make decisions without delay. Efficient presentations are often seen as brief, to the point, and tightly organized. However, in invitational speaking, brevity and efficiency may work against you—especially if you become overly controlling and unwilling to explore someone's position. Invitational speakers must allow time for the exploration of ideas.

When time is limited, finding the time for invitational speeches can be challenging. If you are required or choose to speak invitationally, there is a solution to these time constraints. Begin by considering your time frame carefully. If you have only a small amount of time, reduce the scope of your presentation. Decide what you can address in a shorter amount of time and restructure your invitation. For example, instead of covering five different cultural views of creation, Julie could have named as many different theories of creation as she had been able to discover and then explained two of those views in detail. With this reduced scope, Julie still could have offered an invitation but with less detail than the presentation she first chose. By reducing the scope of your presentation, you respect the opinions of the audience and make it possible to engage in a discussion of the larger issue.

Respect Diverse Positions

One of the most important aspects of invitational speaking is to show respect for a diverse range of positions. This means you must research an invitational speech as thoroughly as you would any other type of speech. When you speak invitationally, you want to support each of your main ideas with evidence to the fullest extent possible. To explore an issue fully and respect diverse positions, you cannot just ramble on about different perspectives. You must take time to understand what each position is, why people have that view, and why it is correct for them. You will discover that your attempts to create conditions of value and self-determination will be enhanced if you speak with accuracy, clarity, and detail about the various views and their strengths as well as their weaknesses.

Ethical Invitational Speaking

Ethical invitational speakers must be sure that their purpose is mutual understanding, exploring a range of ideas, and healthy deliberation and that they are speaking on a topic they are open to discussing.

Stay True to Your Purpose

It is tempting to try to give an invitational speech while at the same time having an underlying goal of persuading them that your view really is best. To speak ethically, you truly must have invitation as your goal. Although you can create the conditions of equality, value, and self-determination in other types of speaking, in invitational speaking you create these conditions because your fundamental goal is the exchange and appreciation of perspectives, not persuasion. Invitational speeches are the heart of deliberation and mutual exploration: if you really want to change your audience, do not pretend you are offering an invitational approach. Save that topic for persuasive speech instead.

Share Your Perspective and Listen Fully to the Perspectives of Others

If you are not able to listen to perspectives that are incompatible with your own or to grant them value, then it would be unethical for you to give an invitational speech.

MindTap® Watch the video

Throwing Stones

Aziz Abu Sarah, Explorer and Cultural Educator

DAN WESTERGREN/National Geographic Creative

Have you ever felt animosity toward someone or even a group of people that you had little or no actual interaction with? Have you ever had a neighbor you rarely spoke to yet did not particularly care for? Did your high school have a rival school? Did you or any of your classmates pull pranks against students at this rival school? If you answered yes to any of these questions, you have something in common with Aziz Abu Sarah.

Aziz Abu Sarah was born in Jerusalem. He was only nine years old when he watched Israeli soldiers storm into his home and arrest his eighteen-year-old brother, Tayseer, for allegedly throwing stones at Israeli cars. Tayseer was kept without a trial, interrogated, and beaten for fifteen days until he was finally coerced into admitting he had thrown the stones. Tayseer was held for eleven months, beaten repeatedly, and finally died within weeks of being released from prison. Aziz describes the pain he felt for losing his closest brother and how angry and bitter he felt toward Israelis. He wanted someone to be held responsible for his brother's death. He wanted revenge.

Aziz spent his adolescence and teenage years writing angry articles for a youth magazine. He describes how he used his "pain to spread hatred against the other side." Aziz refused to learn Hebrew because it was considered the "enemy's language." However, he knew that to attend college or obtain a good job, he would have to put his anger aside and study Hebrew. So he attended an institute that taught Hebrew to Jewish newcomers to Israel. Aziz recalls, "It was the first time I had sat in a room of Jews who were not superior to me. It was the first time I had seen faces different from the soldiers at checkpoints. Those soldiers had taken my brother; these students were the same as me. My understanding of the Jewish people started to collapse after just a few weeks of the Ulpan. I found myself confused, thinking 'How can they be normal human beings just like me?'"

Aziz soon discovered that he had a few things in common with his Jewish classmates, and he eventually formed friendships with them. Aziz believes, "As humans, we try to rationalize our hatred. In our minds we demonize the enemy, and discredit their humanity. This is the lie that fires the conflict between Israel and Palestine." Aziz now works as a lecturer and speaks in churches, synagogues, and mosques on the subject of Israeli-Palestinian conflict, peace, reconciliation, and interfaith dialogue. Aziz has won numerous awards for his work in the Israeli–Palestinian peace movement.[16]

WHAT DO YOU THINK?

1. In what ways does Aziz's story illustrate an invitational approach?
2. How does a civil approach to handling conflict help explain Aziz's ability to resolve his feelings toward the Israeli people?
3. How do cultural differences influence conflict between two cultural groups such as the Palestinians and Israelis? In what ways can using invitational approaches to understanding different cultural (and religious) norms begin the process for open and productive communication?

MICHAEL MELFORD/National Geographic Creative

Ethical speakers stay true to their beliefs and values, and they do not pretend they are open to views when they are not. Thus, your topic in an invitational speech must be one about which you truly are open to exploring. This doesn't mean you have to be willing to change your view, but it does mean you have to be willing to listen with respect to other views. If you cannot grant value and self-determination to someone who disagrees with you on a topic, then give an informative or a persuasive speech on that topic. Religion, sexuality, and instances of oppression are three topics that may be especially difficult for invitational speeches because people have such strong beliefs about them. But they also are excellent choices because they are topics about which we truly need to deliberate. So, before you select a topic about which you have very strong feelings and beliefs, be sure you really can be open to and respectful of views that do not match your own.

STUDENT SPEECH WITH COMMENTARY

Four-Day School Week: An Invitational Dialogue
by Courtney Felton

Specific Purpose: To explore with my audience the idea of changing the five-day high school week to a four-day week.

Thesis Statement: Today I want to explore with you the idea of high schools changing from a regular five-day week schedule to a four-day schedule with longer days.

MindTap° Are you ready to give an invitational speech? You can use the following speech as a model. Courtney Felton gave this speech in an introductory public speaking class. The assignment was to give a five- to seven-minute invitational speech, manage a five- to seven-minute dialogue with the audience, and wrap up with a one-minute conclusion. Courtney was also asked to provide at least four sources, meet the objectives of an effective introduction and conclusion, and provide relevant information. Notice how she created the conditions of equality, value, and self-determination and remained invitational throughout her dialogue with the audience. Watch a video clip of this speech (in the video, Eric Rollins delivers Courtney's speech), see the accompanying outline, and read the discussion that followed the speech. You can also access videos of other invitational speeches, including David Barworth's "Federal Minimum Wage" and Cara Buckley-Ott's "Creationism versus the Big Bang Theory."

COMMENTARY

Courtney begins her speech with two simple words and a series of intriguing possibilities for what might take seven hours to do. In this way, she draws her audience into her topic and relates it to their lives.

Courtney cites a credible source (National Conference of State Legislatures) and uses a quotation that begins to introduce her topic. She then shares her own interest in the topic, relates her topic to her audience again, and reveals her specific purpose.

Courtney openly shares that she has no firm position and that she is interested in her audience's feedback. Although she offers only two positions on her subject, she is clear that there are many more. In doing so, she begins to establish an invitational environment for her audience.

Seven hours! That's almost enough sleep for a night. Or perhaps a solid day's worth of skiing. Or the time it takes to travel by plane across the country. Seven hours is also roughly the amount of time high school students spend in school in one school day. Take a second to imagine what it would have been like not having school on Fridays when you were in high school. This would have you with an extra seven hours you hadn't had before! That would have been seven hours to do countless activities.

The National Conference of State Legislatures (NCSL) states, "Supporters of the shortened week also boast of improved morale and increased attendance (by both students and teachers), open Fridays for sporting events and doctor appointments, and more time to spend with loved ones."

This idea of having a shorter high school week has been a topic of interest for me. Since all of us go to school—even though now it's college—I have a feeling it may be a topic that you might want to explore as well. Today I want to explore with you the idea of schools changing from the normal schedule of a five-day week to a four-day week with longer school days. Since I don't have a solid opinion on whether or not this would be beneficial to all schools, I'd like to share two of the many perspectives on this issue, one for and one against. I'd also like to hear your feedback on the issue.

I'd like to start by addressing the pros of a four-day school week. Perhaps the most significant issue right now in education is the idea of budget cuts. Cutting back on one day of school per week saves on expenses such as transportation, utilities such as heat for the school, food expenses, and the other costs to keep a school open.

Another advantage to having only four days of school is the option to hold sporting events on Fridays. And if students are free on Fridays, the attendance at games could increase. A March 12, 2009, Associated Press article from FoxNews.com, accessed on March 9, 2010, explains that "about 85 percent of the district's athletic events are scheduled on Fridays, so a Monday-to-Thursday school week means fewer Friday absences as students and teachers prepare for or travel to games."

A third advantage to the shortened schedule is the idea of having more time to spend with family or friends, taking care of doctor appointments, or being able to schedule any other weekday activity that one may not have time for on a five-day school schedule.

Exactly how many schools are actually doing this, though? An article from the *Wall Street Journal*, accessed on March 9, 2010, states, "Of the nearly 15,000-plus districts nationwide, more than 100 in at least 17 states currently use the four-day system, according to data culled from the Education Commission of the States."

While, in my opinion, all of these aspects seem appealing, I want to address another side of the issue and consider the views of those opposing the change. Each of the articles I looked at on FoxNews.com as well as the NCSL site discussed the following issues.

While the shorter week appears to be helpful in saving money, it may cause parents to take on the cost burden. With their children home during a normal workday, parents have to find extra child care.

Another important problem opponents of the four-day schedule discuss is the increased length of the school day. As current students, some of us may feel like the school day is already long enough. Adding to the length may make high school students even more tired, less able to concentrate, and could hinder their learning time while at school. And extending school further into the day cuts into students' time for extracurricular activities on days other than Friday.

In addition, while an extra day off leaves time for family time and other activities, some parents—and even students—are afraid of how students will actually use this time off.

Finally, it is important to consider the current school reform movement. A research brief prepared by the Principles Partnership of the Union Pacific Foundation explains, "Some educators are concerned that the four-day week may appear to be inconsistent with the new emphasis for more time in school."

Now that we have explored both sides of the issue, as well as opinions of students, teachers, and parents, I think it is important to hear your opinions as well as ideas that I may not have addressed yet.

Courtney and her audience discussed the issues related to moving from a five-day to a four-day week in high schools. To encourage audience members to share their views, she prepared the following questions in advance:

- To begin, by a show of hands, who would like the keep the current school schedule?
- And who would want to change the high school week to four longer days rather than five?
- For those of you who want to change, what aspect of changing is most appealing to you?
- For those of you who think the current schedule should stay, what isn't appealing about changing for you?
- For those of you who were athletes in high school, how do you think changing this schedule would have affected your athletic schedule? Practice time, game time, and so on?
- As a high school student, would you personally have been able to concentrate and work at the level you did on a five-day week for a longer amount of time at school?
- If you had had one extra free day, do you feel like you would have worked better as a student?
- What types of things would you have done with an extra day?
- What aspects of the four days of the week would have been hindered by your longer day at school?
- Are there any other drawbacks or benefits you want to share that I didn't cover?

When the discussion was over, Courtney concluded her speech.

Courtney shares the advantages and disadvantages of the shorter week in a fair and unbiased way. She cites her sources, is open about the pros and cons, and uses statistics and examples to explain some of the advantages of the shorter week.

Courtney continues to establish an invitational environment by clearly pointing out the exact number of schools that are adopting this plan.

Because she is exploring the issue with her audience, she then shares the disadvantages of the four-day week, presenting her evidence clearly and fairly.

She presents the cons of the four-day week invitationally, being open and nonjudgmental so that her audience can hear the evidence and make their own decisions about it. Notice that her language is unbiased.

Using a signpost ("Finally, it is important to consider"), Courtney addresses one final point before she opens the speech up to dialogue with her audience. In this point, she cites experts to enhance her credibility and to illustrate that she has done her research. She then closes with an invitation to her audience to explore the issue with her openly.

Just in case her audience was hesitant to participate, she prepared a list of questions she could use to encourage dialogue. Preparing like this helped her feel more confident and gave her a wide platform from which to begin the invitational dialogue.

Although she didn't need the questions, they reminded her to remain neutral during the discussion and address the many aspects of her topic.

Courtney closes her invitational speech by expressing her appreciation to her audience members for sharing their views. She summarizes the dialogue in a fair and neutral way, restates that there are many ways to think about her topic, and ends in a respectful tone.

> Thanks for sharing your ideas and opinions. I think that really helped shed some more light on the situation and how students really feel about the issue.
>
> We've heard today some of the views in favor of and some against changing the current five-day high school week to a four-day week with longer days. For students, perhaps a shorter week would allow for more time outside school, but it could also cut into sports practice time and extracurricular activities. For parents, finding day care could be an issue, but for the schools, it could be a way to save money.
>
> On the whole, though, I think there are multiple perspectives to consider, and I've enjoyed being able to talk about some of them with you.

Chapter Summary

When you speak invitationally, you are inviting others to deliberate with you.

- You set the stage for an open dialogue, despite differences in beliefs or values.
- You explore many sides of an issue and continue the public dialogue, even when seemingly insurmountable differences of opinion, value, and belief exist.
- Invitational speakers must be ethical and choose topics about which they truly want to invite an exchange of perspectives, rather than inform or persuade their audience.

When speaking invitationally, it is important to create an invitational speaking environment.

- In an invitational environment, the speaker gives top priority to understanding, respecting, and appreciating the range of positions possible on an issue.
- You create this environment by developing conditions of equality, value, and self-determination in your speeches.
- The condition of equality entails recognizing that both you and your audience hold equally valid perspectives that are important to explore.
- The condition of value involves recognizing that audience members' positions have merit, even if they differ from your own.
- The condition of self-determination involves recognizing that your audience members have the right to choose what is best

for them, even if those choices are not the ones you would make.

The invitational speech engages your audience in an exploration of an idea, concern, topic, or plan of action.

- Your goal is to lay the groundwork for an open dialogue and deliberation rooted in equality, value, and self-determination.
- You want people to feel valued, heard, and respected by one another.

The four most common organizational patterns for invitational speeches are:

- Chronological
- Spatial
- Topical
- Multiple perspectives

Three tips are useful for invitational speakers:

- Use invitational language that encourages the respect and expression of different views and that helps you have an open discussion of those views.
- Allow time for dialogue and discussion in your speeches.
- Show respect for the diverse range of positions.

Invitation to Public Speaking Online MindTap®

Now that you have read Chapter 13, use your MindTap Communication for *Invitation to Public Speaking* for quick access to the digital resources that accompany this text. These resources include

- **Study tools** that will help you assess your learning and prepare for exams (digital glossary, key term flash cards, review quizzes).
- **Activities and assignments** that will help you hone your knowledge and build your public speaking skills throughout

the course, as well as help you explore public speaking concepts online (web links), give you step-by-step guidance through the research, outline and note card preparation process (Outline Builder), watch and critique videos of sample speeches (Interactive Video Activities), and allow you to practice and present your presentation online using a speech video delivery, recording, and grading system (YouSeeU).

Key Concepts MindTap® Test your knowledge with online printable flash cards.

condition of equality (250)
condition of self-determination (250)
condition of value (250)
invitational environment (249)

invitational speaking (248)
multiple perspectives pattern (257)
public deliberation (248)
speech to explore an issue (251)

Review Questions

1. Can you identify situations when you might have preferred giving an invitational speech but gave another type instead? What might have been different if you had given an invitational speech rather than the type of speech you did give?
2. Imagine you are giving an invitational speech exploring some of the issues individuals face when fleeing their home countries during times of war and violent conflict. How might you create conditions of equality, value, and self-determination for your audience in this speech?"
3. Identify a person or a group with whom you strongly disagree. Consider whether you might speak invitationally with that person or group and what benefits or disadvantages might result from such an interaction.
4. Suppose that while you are giving the speech you developed in question 3, a member of your audience strongly disagrees with one of the opinions or ideas you explored. What kind of language could you use to acknowledge this anger and frustration but also continue to have a productive dialogue with this person and other members of the audience? (You might role-play this scenario with members of your class.)

14 | Reasoning

IN THIS CHAPTER, YOU WILL LEARN TO:

- Compare and contrast Aristotle's three modes of proof

- Explain the five patterns of reasoning used to construct sound arguments

- Apply tips for reasoning ethically

- Avoid seven of the most common fallacies in persuasive arguments

MindTap Start with a quick warm-up activity and review the chapter's learning objectives.

Whether your speaking goal is to inform, invite, or persuade, sound reasoning plays a central role in your preparations to enter the public dialogue. Only through sound reasoning can you ensure that you have fully and ethically supported your claims. Speakers accomplish sound reasoning when they use the three forms of proof that the Greek philosopher Aristotle labeled *logos*, *ethos*, and *pathos*. **Logos** refers to the logical arrangement of evidence in a speech, **ethos** to the speaker's credibility, and **pathos** to the emotional appeals made by a speaker.[1]

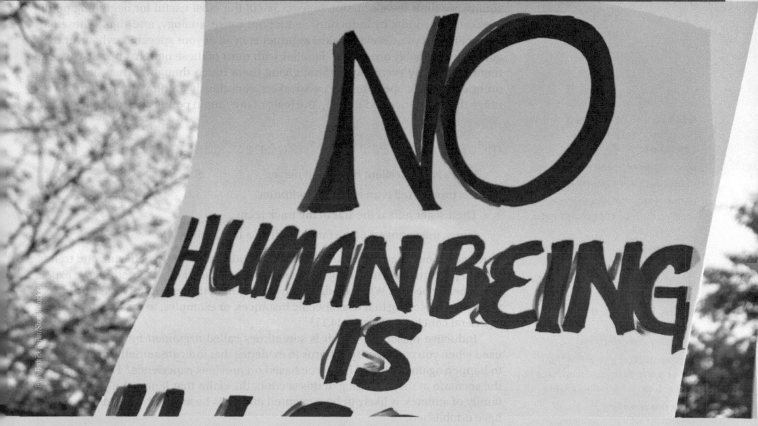

▲ When we make a claim that something is or is not true, that claim must be supported by sound reasoning. What evidence would you need to support or negate this claim? How would you present that evidence? Because there are several patterns of reasoning a speaker could use to make or reject this claim, in this chapter you will explore those different patterns. You will also be exposed to fallacies in reasoning to help you avoid making flawed and unethical arguments.

In the public dialogue, we share our knowledge and views most effectively when we reason with our audience. Reasoning helps an audience make **inferences**, the mental leaps we make when we recognize that a speaker's evidence supports his or her claims. When you reason logically, you offer evidence that you think most people in your audience would accept as legitimate and appropriate.[2] **Evidence** is the material you use to support your ideas, and it consists of the examples, narratives, statistics, testimony, and definitions you gather through research and interviews (Chapter 6). This evidence helps you develop what is often called an *argument*. Although the term *argument* may bring to mind an angry dispute, in the public dialogue, an **argument** is a set of statements that allows you to develop your evidence to establish the validity of your claim.[3]

Each time you develop a main point or link ideas together logically in a speech, you use evidence and reasoning to develop an argument for your perspective. Just as you use organizational patterns to arrange your main points in a speech, you use patterns of reasoning to help you organize your evidence and claims. In this chapter, you'll learn more about these three components of reasoning, specifically as they relate to persuasive speaking. This chapter also examines fallacies, which are errors in logic and reasoning commonly made in persuasive speaking. However, you will use these strategies for reasoning in all of your speeches, so keep in mind that they are important whenever we enter the public dialogue.

MindTap°

Read, highlight, and take notes online.

logos: Logical arrangement of evidence in a speech; the first of Aristotle's three types of proof.

ethos: Speaker's credibility; the second of Aristotle's three types of proof.

pathos: Emotional appeals made by a speaker; the third of Aristotle's three types of proof.

inferences: Mental leaps we make when we recognize that a speaker's evidence supports his or her claims.

evidence: Material you use to support your ideas, and it consists of the examples, narratives, statistics, testimony, and definitions.

argument: Set of statements that allows you to develop your evidence to establish the validity of your claim.

inductive reasoning: Process of reasoning that uses specific instances, or examples, to make a claim about a general conclusion.

Patterns of Reasoning

Although scholars have developed more than twenty-five different patterns of reasoning, we limit the discussion here to five of the most useful for beginning public speakers: reasoning by induction, deduction, cause, analogy, and sign.[4] These patterns can help you develop logical arguments in all of your speeches, whatever their goals. You probably are already familiar with most of these patterns because we use them commonly every day without giving them much thought. What makes them unique in public speaking is that speakers consciously employ the patterns to arrange their evidence and develop the logic of their main points and subpoints.

Induction, or Reasoning from Specific Instances

James is an excellent basketball player.

His brother Jeff is an excellent swimmer.

Their sister Julia is the star of the track team.

Jenny, the youngest of the family, will be a fine athlete, too.

Throughout our lives, we often observe regularities, patterns of behavior, and trends. We can point to these repeating patterns to make a claim about something we expect to happen or be true. When we do so, we reason inductively. **Inductive reasoning** is a process of reasoning that uses specific instances, or examples, to make a claim about a general conclusion (Figure 14.1).[5]

Inductive reasoning, which is sometimes called *argument by example,* is best used when you can identify patterns in evidence that indicate something is expected to happen again or should hold true based on previous experience.[6] For example, in the scenario at the beginning of this section, the claim that Jenny, the youngest in a family of athletes, is likely to be a talented athlete is based on the trend her siblings have established.

Let's look at how inductive reasoning can be used in a speech. In her invitational speech on becoming a vegetarian, Karyl used inductive reasoning to describe her

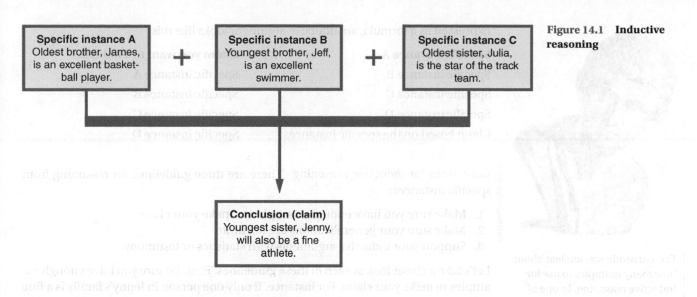

Figure 14.1 **Inductive reasoning**

| Specific instance A
Oldest brother, James, is an excellent basketball player. | + | Specific instance B
Youngest brother, Jeff, is an excellent swimmer. | + | Specific instance C
Oldest sister, Julia, is the star of the track team. |

Conclusion (claim)
Youngest sister, Jenny, will also be a fine athlete.

switch from eating meat to avoiding it. She gave examples from six slaughterhouses to illustrate the treatment of the animals and the reasons she chose to stop eating meat. This series of examples allowed Karyl to reason as follows:

> Animals in the six slaughterhouses I researched experience harsh conditions and unnecessary cruelty (*her series of specific examples*). Animals in slaughterhouses throughout the United States are treated inhumanely (*her generalization based on her examples*), and I decided not to support this treatment by not eating animals (*her personal decision based on her inductive reasoning*).

When you reason from specific instances, you can state your claim (general observation) first and then offer your supporting instances, or you can present the instances first and then make your claim. In the following example, Ruby stated her claim first and then provided specific instances:

> The amount of privacy we are allowed to keep is under siege every day (*claim*). Beverly Dennis, an Ohio grandmother, completed a questionnaire to get free product samples. Instead, she got a sexually graphic and threatening letter from a convict in Texas who was assigned the task of entering product data into computers for the company (*specific instance*). Similarly, the dean of the Harvard Divinity School was forced to resign after downloading pornography to his home computer. He asked a Harvard technician to install more memory to his computer at home, and in the process of transferring files, the technician discovered, and reported, the pornography (*specific instance*).

Ruby used inductive reasoning again later in her speech. In the following example, she withheld her claim until after she had described her specific instances. Also notice how she used statistics to reinforce the pattern in her specific instances:

> Like many of you, I thought my own life was safe because I do not download pornography or request free product samples. But as I continued to do research for my speech, I learned that my medical records, phone calls, and text messages aren't as private as I thought. Nor are my e-mails at work. Medical records are passed along to numerous individuals and recorded or filed electronically—accessible to any determined employee or computer hacker (*specific instance*). And phone calls and text messages can be monitored by anyone from the office staff to our government (*specific instance*).

> And according to this year's report by the American Management Association, nearly three-quarters of U.S. companies say they are monitoring employees electronically. In fact, according to *The Unwanted Gaze,* some companies even use computer software that monitors and records every keystroke an employee makes. Using this software, called Spector, an employee at a Nissan dealership was fired after her employer opened one of her e-mails, a sexually explicit note to her boyfriend (*specific instance*). Can you imagine your boss reading your e-mails to your boyfriend? Our privacy has gone public in ways we are only beginning to imagine (*claim*).

North Wind Picture Archives

Even Aristotle was unclear about how many examples to use for inductive reasoning. In one of the oldest surviving treatises on rhetoric, he stated, "If you put your examples first you must give a large number of them; if you put them last, a single one is sufficient; even a single witness will serve if he is a good one."[7]

Expressed as a formula, an inductive argument looks like this:

Specific instance A	or	Claim you want to establish
Specific instance B		Specific instance A
Specific instance C		Specific instance B
Specific instance D		Specific instance C
Claim based on the specific instances		Specific instance D

Guidelines for inductive reasoning. There are three guidelines for reasoning from specific instances:

1. Make sure you have enough examples to make your claim.
2. Make sure your generalizations are accurate.
3. Support your inductive arguments with statistics or testimony.

Let's take a closer look at each of these guidelines. First, be sure you have enough examples to make your claim. For instance, if only one person in Jenny's family is a fine athlete, you cannot claim she likely will be because you do not have enough specific instances to back that claim. Similarly, if only one or two slaughterhouses treat animals inhumanely, you cannot claim that most of them do.

Therefore, to reason ethically, avoid *anomalies*. Anomalies are exceptions to a rule, unique instances that do not represent the norm. When speakers rely on anomalies or use too few examples to make a claim, they may be guilty of making **hasty generalizations**, or reaching a conclusion without enough evidence to support it. To support your claim, find more than three instances before you make any inferences about larger patterns. However, your audience probably needs no more than four specific instances, even if you have identified far more than that.

Second, make sure your generalizations are accurate. Although it can be tempting to make a claim about only a few instances, be careful not to overgeneralize. For example, if people in your community are buying hybrid vehicles and this trend seems to be catching on in your region, you can predict that many people in your community will replace their current vehicles with a hybrid in the coming year. But you probably cannot extend that prediction to other parts of the country unless you have specific examples to support your claim. Don't be too hasty in extending examples from one area or group to another unless your data support that claim.

Third, support your inductive arguments with statistics or testimony. Although you cannot produce an endless list of examples without boring your audience, you can develop your case by supplementing your examples with statistics or testimony. For example, if you want to explain that organic farms produce competitively priced, high-quality crops, offer examples of two or three farms that do so. Then strengthen your inductive process with statistics showing that organic farmers are successfully competing with nonorganic farms at a county, state, or national level. You also could support your examples with testimony from the head of the Department of Agriculture, validating the profitability of organic farming. Statistics and testimony help your audience better understand the validity of the larger trend you are describing.

Deduction, or Reasoning from a General Principle

Grade inflation negatively affects all college students.

Jody is a college student.

Jody is affected negatively by grade inflation.

When speakers reason from general principles to specific instances (the opposite of inductive reasoning), they reason deductively. **Deductive reasoning** is a process of reasoning that uses a familiar and commonly accepted claim to establish the truth of a very specific claim (Figure 14.2). The first statement, "Grade inflation negatively affects all college students," is called the **major premise**, or the *general principle*, and

hasty generalization: Error in reasoning in which a speaker reaches a conclusion without enough evidence to support it.

deductive reasoning: Process of reasoning that uses a familiar and commonly accepted claim to establish the truth of a very specific claim.

major premise: Claim in an argument that states a familiar, commonly accepted belief (also called the general principle).

Figure 14.2 **Deductive reasoning**

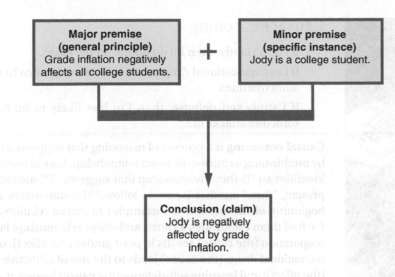

states a familiar, commonly accepted belief. The combination of the major premise with the second statement, "Jody is a college student," called the **minor premise**, or the *specific instance,* establishes the truth of the third statement, "Jody is negatively affected by grade inflation," which is called the **conclusion**.

Expressed as a formula, a deductive argument looks as follows:

Major premise, or general principle

Minor premise, or specific instance of the general principle

Conclusion based on the combination of the major and minor premises

Guidelines for deductive reasoning. Reasoning from general principles to specific instances is an effective way to build a case for your claims. When your general principle is firmly established or commonly accepted, your reasoning should unfold smoothly. For example, some clearly established and commonly accepted general principles are that asbestos causes lung cancer, driving drunk is dangerous, and elected officials should act with integrity.

Sometimes, audiences won't accept your general principle. When they don't, you will need to strengthen it with additional evidence or reasoning. This process is called *establishing the validity of the major premise.* For example, if you assert that raising cattle for beef consumption is cruel and unethical, juvenile crime is out of control, or pornography is a violation of women's rights, your audience is more likely to need proof. If your audience does not accept your major premise, they are less likely to accept your conclusion. You will need to use careful reasoning to develop your case.

We often enter the public dialogue precisely because we want to establish the truth of a general principle. Let's see how one very famous speaker, Susan B. Anthony, worked from a controversial general principle. Anthony spoke in favor of women's right to vote in the 1870s. She built her reasoning for women's right to vote on the premise that the U.S. Constitution guarantees all citizens the right to vote. Her full line of reasoning looked as follows:

Major premise: The U.S. Constitution guarantees every citizen the right to vote.

Minor premise: Women are U.S. citizens.

Conclusion: The U.S. Constitution guarantees women the right to vote.

Although this deductive argument makes sense to us today, Anthony's major and minor premises were open to dispute more than 140 years ago. People did not agree that the Constitution guaranteed all citizens the right to vote, nor did they agree about who was a citizen. Anthony and many other suffragists devoted much of their speeches to trying to convince their audiences of their major and minor premises. Despite their passionate efforts, women did not get the right to vote in the United States until 1920.[8]

minor premise: Claim in an argument that states a specific instance linked to the major premise.

conclusion: Logical outcome of an argument that results from the combination of the major and minor premises.

Causal Reasoning

NIKLAS HALLE'N/AFP/Getty Images

If I don't study, then I'll do poorly on my exam.

If I use recreational drugs, then I'll eventually turn to more addictive ones.

If I study self-defense, then I'm less likely to be hurt if someone attacks me.

Causal reasoning is a process of reasoning that supports a claim by establishing a cause-and-effect relationship. Causal reasoning identifies an "if-then" relationship that suggests "if" one factor is present, "then" another is sure to follow.[9] The statements at the beginning of this section are examples of causal relationships. Each of them establishes a cause-and-effect relationship: lack of preparation (the cause) results in poor grades (the effect); use of recreational drugs (the cause) leads to the use of addictive ones (the effect); and learning self-defense (the cause) lessens the risk of harm in the event of an attack (the effect).

Speakers often use causal reasoning to develop their ideas with great success. In the following example, Kameron uses causal reasoning to develop his argument that zebra mussels, native to the Caspian Sea in Europe but not to the waters of the United States, are seriously damaging the aquatic environment:

> Zebra mussels cause damage to every aspect of any aquatic ecosystem they encounter. They destroy the natural balance of the ecosystem by filtering the food from water at an insane rate of one liter of water each day. Not much you think? Well, these mollusks can live in colonies of up to 70,000 mussels. That's 70,000 liters of water cleared of all food each day. This means the zebra mussels consume all the food usually eaten by animals lower in the food chain. The result is catastrophic repercussions on down the line. For example, a body of water whose food is filtered away cannot support any kind of life. The larger fish then have nothing to eat, resulting in fewer fish for anglers.

Kameron's causal reasoning allows him to argue compellingly that zebra mussels (the cause) lead to aquatic devastation (the effect).

Guidelines for causal reasoning. Causal reasoning is an effective form of reasoning because it allows you to link two events together. But because causal relationships are sometimes difficult to prove, select your causal evidence carefully. Consider the following three guidelines:

- Avoid false causes.
- Avoid assuming an event has only one cause.
- Cite supporting evidence to strengthen your cause-and-effect relationships.

Let's take a closer look at each of these guidelines. First, avoid false causes.[10] A **false cause** is an error in reasoning in which a speaker assumes that one event caused another simply because the first event happened before the second. It can be easy to assume a false cause. You pick up your "lucky" pen from your desk, and five minutes later, you get a creative brainstorm for the project you are working on.

Did the lucky pen cause the creative brainstorm? Perhaps, but it's hard to tell. Similarly, your nephew watches two hours of violent cartoon programming in the morning. When he sits down to lunch, he points his hot dog at his sister and makes shooting noises. Did the violence in the cartoons cause the behavior? Perhaps his behavior was prompted by the game he played with neighbors the day before or the joke his father told while making similar gestures. Again, the connection is not certain.

Although it is tempting to assume direct causes when one event happens shortly after another, the two events may not be directly related. When one event happens

Although both of these protesters are arguing against fracking—a process of fracturing rock deep under the earth's surface to force gas to escape—are they using the same pattern of reasoning? Can you identify the pattern of reasoning they are using? What claims are they making to develop their arguments against fracking? Is it hard or easy for their audience to follow their reasoning? Should our reasoning be easy for our audiences to follow? Why or why not?

causal reasoning: Process of reasoning that supports a claim by establishing a cause-and-effect relationship.

false cause: Error in reasoning in which a speaker assumes that one event caused another simply because the first event happened before the second.

immediately after another, there may be a link, but you would need to investigate further to be sure. To remain ethical, if you make a causal claim in a speech, you must be certain one event did in fact cause the other.

Second, avoid assuming that an event has only one cause. Events often have many causes, especially those that become topics in the public dialogue. For example, it is unrealistic to try to pin the cause of teen suicide on one factor. It is far more appropriate to address the multiple factors that contribute to teen suicide: the home and school environment, social pressures, individual personality traits, and the teen's support system and friendships. Similarly, it is inaccurate to suggest that watching violent television is the sole cause of violence in children. Many other factors contribute to violent behaviors, and a speaker's reasoning must address all these causes.

Third, strengthen your cause-and-effect relationships by citing strong supporting evidence. For example, in his informative speech about zebra mussels, Kameron identified a very strong connection between the overpopulation of zebra mussels and the damage done to boats, buoys, docks, and anchors. He was able to support his connection by providing testimony from local fishers who had seen buoys sink from the weight of too many mussels! However, in a persuasive speech about the relationship between power lines and cancer in people who live close to them, Christina could make only a very weak connection: Her father, who died of cancer, had lived near power lines for years. However, the scientific evidence she provided to establish a strong link between cancer and proximity to power lines was sketchy and inconclusive. Thus, no matter how hard she tried, her audience would not accept her claim that power lines caused her father's cancer.

Analogical Reasoning

> The American Academy of Pediatrics, partnering with First Lady Michelle Obama, is urging its doctors to write exercise and eating "prescriptions" for their patients. "Just as we give immunizations," says AAP president Judith Palfrey, "we're going to give healthy eating and exercise advice at every visit."
>
> Public health advocates are taking on Big Food just as their predecessors took on Big Tobacco. Dr. David Kessler, the former head of the FDA, argues that the fattening of America has happened by design as food companies intentionally manufactured irresistible cocktails of sugar, fat, and salt. Manufacturers' efforts to do better don't assuage Kelly Brownell, head of Yale's Rudd Center for Food Policy and Obesity. "The country defaults to giving industry the benefit of the doubt," he says. "Industry says you don't need to regulate us; we'll police ourselves." The tobacco industry abused that with [who knows] how many lives as a consequence. To expect the food industry to be different may be wishful thinking.[11]

When we compare two similar things and suggest that what is true for the first will be true for the second, then we are reasoning analogically. **Analogical reasoning**, or reasoning by way of comparison and similarity, implies that because two things resemble each other in one respect, they also share similarities in another respect. For example,

> when *Newsweek* writers compare the U.S. food industry to the so-called Big Tobacco corporations, the writers argue that the food industry, like major tobacco companies before they began to be regulated in the late 1990s, cannot be trusted to put the health of consumers before its own profits.

We also reason analogically when we contrast different approaches to events and draw inferences about the harms and/or benefits of those approaches. Consider this example, from the *Economist*, which uses the analogies of a staircase and a hospital to contrast approaches to responding to people who are homeless:

> The standard way to help them has long been the "staircase" approach: requiring them to quit drink and drugs before shepherding them through emergency shelters and temporary lodging . . . [but in] what has come to be known as "housing first" . . . [h]omeless people are triaged much like arrivals at a hospital emergency room: those deemed most at risk of dying on the street go to the top of the queue [for homes].[12]

analogical reasoning: A process of reasoning by way of comparison and similarity that implies that because two things resemble each other in one respect, they also share similarities in another respect.

When *Economist* writers compare the "triage" approach, which gives homeless individuals houses first, to the "staircase" approach, which requires that individuals climb "staircases" to be clean and sober before receiving homes, they are suggesting that not only is the "triage" approach more effective in saving lives, but it also saves communities money.

Analogies also can be short and straightforward. For example, when speaking to her audience about the importance of more than direct care, physician Deborah Prothrow-Stith used this simple and effective analogy: "We were just stitching them up and sending them back out on the streets, back to the domestic equivalent of a war zone."[13]

Guidelines for analogical reasoning. To increase the effectiveness of analogical reasoning, be sure what you are comparing is truly alike. When you compare two things that don't share characteristics, your analogy is invalid and will seem illogical to your audience. Most of us have heard invalid analogies and thought to ourselves, "That's like comparing apples to oranges." For example, it is invalid to suggest that proposed nonsmoking ordinances will succeed in Kentucky, Tennessee, and North Carolina because they succeeded in California, Oregon, and Washington. This analogy is invalid because the public attitudes toward smoking in the three tobacco-growing Southern states are different from those in the three Western states whose economies do not depend on tobacco. If you make an analogy between two things, they must share true similarities for the analogy to be valid.

Reasoning by Sign

> Even watching their seismographs jump—even if they could have measured the height of the waves at their origin—geologists couldn't have predicted with any certainty that the sea would rise up in Sri Lanka, a thousand miles away from the fault line.[14]

A **sign** is something that represents something else. It is one of the most common forms of reasoning we use in our daily lives: Dark clouds are a sign of a storm rolling in; a decrease in the number of applications for a certain academic program is a sign of declining interest; the bailiff's command "all rise" is a sign that the judge is about to enter the courtroom.[15] Signs have an important function in the reasoning process because they prompt us to infer what is *likely* to be. They help speakers establish relationships and draw conclusions for their audiences based on those relationships. However, as the example about the tsunami that struck Sri Lanka in 2004 suggests, sometimes the connection between a sign—the movement on a seismograph or the height of waves at their origin—that is needed to infer the likelihood of an event—a devastating tsunami in Sri Lanka—cannot be made or just isn't there. **Reasoning by sign** assumes something exists or will happen based on something else that exists or has happened.

Signs, like causal relationships, can have strong or weak relationships. Reasoning by sign is strengthened when you can point to the repetition of one example to build a case. For example, *every* time the Richter scale registers above a certain level for an undersea earthquake, a tsunami occurs. Scientists have accurately predicted all five of the significant ocean-spanning tsunamis since 1950, but they also predicted fifteen that turned out to be false alarms.[16] So note that few signs are infallible, and most are open to question.

Guidelines for reasoning by sign. Because signs are fallible, consider three guidelines for using them:

- Think about whether an alternative explanation is more credible.
- Make sure a sign is not just an isolated instance.
- If you can find instances in which a sign does not indicate a particular event, you do not have a solid argument.

sign: Something that represents something else.

reasoning by sign: Process of reasoning that assumes something exists or will happen based on something else that exists or has happened.

Let's take a closer look at each of these guidelines. First, is an alternative explanation more credible? In a speech on the standards for licensing teachers, Seogwan suggested that the low test scores in the nation's public schools were a sign of poorly trained teachers. He reasoned that low scores represented, or signaled, poor teaching. However, when his audience questioned him, they raised a number of equally credible explanations. Could the lower scores be a sign of outdated or biased tests? Of overcrowded classrooms? Of the need to restructure our classrooms? Of poor testing skills? Each of these explanations is as likely as the one Seogwan offered, and much evidence supports each of them. As a result, his audience thought Seogwan's reasoning was flawed. To avoid this pitfall, be sure that when you claim one thing is a sign of another, an alternative explanation isn't equally valid or better.

Second, when you reason by sign, make sure the sign is not just an isolated instance. Speaking in favor of gun control, Mark argued that all of his friends supported stricter gun control laws, even those who hunted. This, he claimed, was a sign that most people support stricter gun control legislation. He ignored the nationwide debate on gun control measures and the many people who oppose them. He mistakenly assumed that one instance (his friends' support of gun control legislation) represented a larger pattern.

Third, when you reason by sign, you are suggesting the sign almost always indicates a particular event. If you can find instances in which the sign does not indicate that event, you do not have a solid argument. In his speech on our ability to predict natural disasters, Tim offered the evidence that not every undersea earthquake of a certain magnitude results in a tsunami. He added that, in fact, a few quakes of a lesser magnitude did. Thus, blaming scientists for not notifying countries about tsunamis was unreasonable. However, Tim argued, the occurrence of that tsunami and the tragedies left in its wake are signs that warning systems, regardless of their overprediction rates, are imperative.

> ### Practicing the Public Dialogue | 14.1
>
> TEST THE REASONING OF YOUR ARGUMENTS
>
> Bring one of the main arguments of your speech to class. Present this argument to the class and determine which pattern of reasoning will help you develop this argument most fully (inductive, deductive, causal, analogical, or by sign). After each person has presented her or his argument and selected a pattern of reasoning to support it, discuss the strengths and weaknesses of each person's approach.
>
> ## MindTap®
>
> To see examples of two types of reasoning, deductive and causal, used in a speech, watch video clips of student speakers Lisa Alagna and Brent Erb. Consider how effectively Lisa uses deduction, paying particular attention to how she establishes the major premise of her argument. Consider how Brent makes a causal claim. Is the stated cause-and-effect relationship accurate or inaccurate?

Tips for Reasoning Ethically

Evidence, reasoning, logic, and arguments are powerful tools in the public dialogue. With them, we can share information, express our perspective and invite dialogue on an issue, make a case for a certain position, and even celebrate someone's accomplishments. However, we can also manipulate, confuse, and misrepresent events, issues, and people. Thus, we must carefully consider the ethics of reasoning. Speaking ethically requires our commitment to giving speeches that are accurate and well reasoned. The following tips will help you reason ethically in your speeches.

Build Your Credibility

The reasoning in your speech helps you build credibility with your audience. **Credibility** is the audience's perception of a speaker's competence and character. **Competence** is the audience's view of a speaker's intelligence, expertise, and knowledge of a subject. As a speaker, you express your competence through reasoning, organization, and delivery of your speech. **Character** is the audience's view of a speaker's sincerity, trustworthiness, and concern for the well-being of the audience. You show your character through the honesty and regard you display for the audience.[17]

credibility: Audience's perception of a speaker's competence and character.

competence: Audience's view of a speaker's intelligence, expertise, and knowledge of a subject.

character: Audience's view of a speaker's sincerity, trustworthiness, and concern for the well-being of the audience.

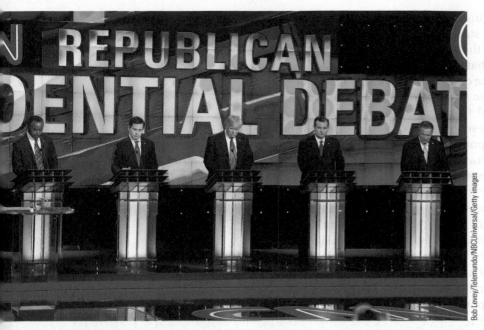

When political candidates participate in a debate, they must make sure the evidence they present is accurate, particularly about issues of national interest. Otherwise, voters will doubt their credibility. How might you verify the accuracy of evidence in your speech? What implications for the public dialogue result from the misuse of evidence?

Through ethical reasoning, as discussed throughout this chapter, you communicate to an audience that you are competent and you care about them. You convey to the audience that you have thought about the best way to express your ideas and you want others to understand them. In short, a careful reasoning process communicates an audience-centered stance that enhances your credibility. This credibility is a critical component of the ethical reasoning process. (For more about credibility, especially in regard to persuasive speaking, see Chapter 15.)

Use Accurate Evidence

Because speakers are adding to the ongoing discussion of issues that affect us all, they want to use accurate evidence. It is just as easy to find examples, statistics, and testimony from unreliable sources as it is to find them from credible sources. It is also possible to misrepresent or alter any statistic, example, narrative, or testimony you do find. However, a healthy public dialogue depends on legitimate evidence to build sound reasoning.

As a speaker, you are ethically obligated to use accurate evidence in all of your reasoning, no matter what pattern you use to present it. Although you may be able to present a fully developed inductive argument based on fabricated examples or a compelling analogy that is false, you would be deceiving your audience.

Verify the Structure of Your Reasoning

Applying Stephen Toulmin's model of reasoning to your arguments is the final way you can ensure the ethical nature of your reasoning (see Chapter 6). In fact, Toulmin developed this framework to assist average people in discovering weaknesses in their reasoning processes. By using this model as you develop your speech, you can check the warrants, grounds, and backing for your claims and ensure their accuracy. Note that it is unethical to assert a claim is true if you do not have evidence to support that claim. Similarly, it is unethical to make unfounded arguments that could alarm audiences (recall Christina's speech about power lines and cancer). When you correct weaknesses and potentially disturbing claims before presenting them to your audiences, you are acting ethically.

Fallacies in Reasoning

Whether or not you intend to, you can make inaccurate arguments, called fallacies. A **fallacy** is an argument that seems valid but is flawed because of unsound evidence or reasoning. Fallacies are a problem in persuasive speeches not only because they undermine speakers' arguments but also because, despite their factual or logical errors, they can be quite persuasive. Fallacies can seem reasonable and acceptable on the surface, but when we analyze them, we see that their logic is flawed. Although there are more than 125 different fallacies, a discussion of the most common types is adequate for beginning public speakers. These are ad hominem, bandwagon, either-or, false cause, hasty generalization, red herring, and slippery slope.[18] At the end of the discussion of these fallacies, also see Table 14.1, which provides brief descriptions of other fallacies often heard in speeches.

fallacy: Argument that seems valid but is flawed because of unsound evidence or reasoning.

tip
National Geographic Explorer

AZIZ ABU SARAH, Explorer And Cultural Educator

Is there a particular kind of reasoning that you enjoy the most when you are speaking to persuade your audience? I do define the bulk of the speaking that I do as persuasive. And that goal—persuading people—can be a challenge. Normally I use quite a bit of emotional communication, and I focus on personal narratives and storytelling. But I also use what I call public narratives, which include defining where you are coming from and finding a way to actually connect to the values of the group you're speaking to. For me, this means making my story a story that everyone in the audience can relate to, empathize with, and understand. From there, I can take the story and connect it to the other issues we're dealing with. When I speak to an audience, the story is not the goal; the goal is actually to use that story to move people from point A to point B. I try to show them a new narrative or an alternative that they hadn't considered before, and, through that narrative, I can try to change their perspective on the issue we are talking about.

Ad Hominem: Against the Person

Ad hominem is a Latin term that means "against the person." Perhaps one of the most familiar fallacies, an **ad hominem fallacy** is an argument in which a speaker attacks a person rather than that person's arguments. By portraying someone with an opposing position as incompetent, unreliable, or even stupid, you effectively silence that person and discredit her or his arguments or ideas. Here are some other examples of ad hominem fallacies:

> Of course Obama worked so hard to pass the health-care bill—he's a liberal democrat who only wants to create a socialist country.

> Well, sure, Bush wanted to open up lands for drilling. Isn't that how he got into office, with the financial support of his oil buddies?

Ad hominem fallacies are persuasive because they turn the audience's attention away from the content of an argument and toward the character and credibility of the person offering that argument. They cloud an issue, making it hard for an audience to evaluate the ideas the speaker challenges. But more important, ad hominem fallacies make erroneous claims. The argument against Obama's character clouds the issue of whether providing health care for American citizens is the right thing to do. Similarly, Bush may have indeed received campaign financing from oil companies, but that fact does not prove his drilling policy was suspect.

Listen carefully for arguments against a person's character and avoid them in your own speeches. They do little to build your credibility or help your audience see that your ideas are preferable to someone else's.

Bandwagon: Everyone Else Agrees

When you fall prey to the **bandwagon fallacy**, you are suggesting that something is correct or good because everyone else agrees with it or is doing it. In public speaking, this translates to making statements like these:

> Many other communities are adopting this nonsmoking ordinance in restaurants. It's a perfect solution for us as well.

ad hominem fallacy: Argument in which a speaker attacks a person rather his or her arguments.

bandwagon fallacy: Argument that suggests something has merit because everyone else agrees with it or is doing it.

How can we adopt a zero-tolerance policy? Other schools in our area aren't, so why should we?

The bandwagon fallacy works a little like group pressure: it's hard to say no to something everyone else is doing. But the logic of the bandwagon is flawed for two reasons. First, even though a solution or a plan might work well for some, it might not be the best solution for your audience. You need to do more than argue "it will work for you because it worked for others." You need to explain exactly why a plan might work for a particular group of people, community, or organization. Second, just because "lots of others agree" does not make something "good." Large groups of people agree about many things, but those things aren't necessarily appropriate for everyone. When you hear the bandwagon fallacy, ask yourself two questions: (1) If it is good for them, is it good for *me*? (2) Even if many others are doing something, is it something I support?

Either–Or: A False Dilemma

A dilemma is a situation that requires you to choose from options that are all unpleasant or that are mutually exclusive. When we're facing a dilemma, we feel we must make a choice even if it is not to our liking. In persuasive speeches, an **either–or fallacy**, sometimes called a *false dilemma,* is an argument in which a speaker claims our options are "either A or B," when actually more than two options exist. To identify a *false dilemma,* listen for the words *either* and *or* linked together as a speaker presents an argument. Consider these two examples:

> Either we increase access to our before- and after-school meal programs or our students will continue to fail.

> Either we increase our candidate's appeal to women or we don't get elected.

In both examples, the audience is presented with a false dilemma. Intuitively, we know there must be other options. In the first example, there are other ways to respond to poor student performance—better nutrition is only one part of the solution. In the second, there likely are other ways to increase a candidate's appeal and chances of success. Sometimes, it's hard to see the other options immediately, but they are usually there.

Either–or arguments are fallacious because they oversimplify complex issues. Usually, the speaker has created an atmosphere in which the audience feels pressured to select one of the two options presented. Even if those options may be good choices, an either–or argument prevents us from considering others that may be even better.

False Cause (Post Hoc): Mistaking a Chronological Relationship

A **false cause fallacy** is an argument that mistakes a chronological relationship for a causal relationship. There are two types of false cause fallacies. The first type occurs when a speaker assumes that one event *caused* the second to occur. Notice how the speaker in the following example mistakenly assumes that the first event caused the second:

> After the state passed legislation in favor of the death penalty, violent crimes decreased. The new legislation has deterred criminal activity.

Criminal activity may have declined after the state implemented the new legislation, but the speaker has not proven that the legislation caused the decline. Other factors may have influenced the decline, such as methods of reporting violent crimes, rehabilitation programs in prisons, and even educational opportunities for individuals at risk of committing violent crimes.

The second type of false cause fallacy is known as a *single cause fallacy*. This fallacy occurs when speakers oversimplify and assume a particular effect has only one cause.

either–or fallacy: Argument that presents only two options—"either A or B"—when actually more than two options exist; also known as a *false dilemma.*

false cause fallacy: Argument that mistakes a chronological relationship for a causal relationship.

Create the Best Educated Leadership

Shabana Basij-Rasikh, Educator and Explorer

From the age of six until she was eleven, Shabana Basij-Rasikh dressed as a boy so that she could escort her sister, who was too old to go out in public alone, to a secret school in Afghanistan. Knowing that they would likely be killed if they were caught, the two girls disguised their books as groceries, took a different route each day to the secret school, and shared a small living-room-turned-schoolroom with 100 other girls. They knew that everyone there—teachers, students, and even the families who saw their education as so important—was at risk of death. Under Taliban rule, it was illegal for girls to receive an education. Basij-Rasikh recounts, "[F]rom time-to-time, the school would suddenly be canceled for a week because Taliban were suspicious. We always wondered what they knew about us. Were we being followed? Do they know where we live? We were scared, but still school was where we wanted to be."

Basij-Rasikh considers herself lucky because she grew up "in a family where education was prized and daughters were treasured." She describes her grandfather as an "extraordinary man for his time." He was disowned by his own father for educating his daughters. Basij-Rasikh's father was the first in his family to receive an education, and despite "the Taliban, despite the risks," Basij-Rasikh explains, to her father, "there was greater risk in not educating his children." He supported the education of his daughters, and she says, "During Taliban years I remember I would get so frustrated by our life and always being scared and not seeing a future. I would want to quit, but my father, he would say, 'Listen my daughter, you can lose everything you own in your life. Your money can be stolen. You can be forced to leave your home during a war, but the thing that will always remain is [your education], and if we have to sell our blood to pay your school fees, we will, so do you still not want to continue?'"

Basij-Rasikh states: "I was raised in a country that has been destroyed by decades of war. Fewer than six percent of women my age have made it beyond high school, and had my family not been so committed to my education, I would be one of them." Because of this support, she attended high school and college in the United States and graduated from Middlebury College in Vermont. At the age of eighteen, she cofounded School of Leadership Afghanistan (SOLA), and established HELA, "a nonprofit organization to empower Afghan women through education." She returned to Kabul after graduation to "turn SOLA, into the nation's first boarding school for girls." However, Basij-Rasikh shares that it is still very dangerous for girls to go to school. And, without their fathers they likely would not go. One of her students and her father, walking home from school, narrowly missed being killed by a bomb, a bomb that exploded minutes after they passed. Basij-Rasikh says, "As he arrived home the phone rang, a voice warning him that if he sent his daughter back to school, they would try again. 'Kill me now, if you wish,' he said, 'but I will not ruin my daughter's future because of your old and backward ideas.'"

Because of SOLA, young women now can take college preparatory courses and "enter universities worldwide." More than this, however, the 3 million young girls who now receive an education "return to substantive careers in Afghanistan," and become the "first women to enter certain fields." Basij-Rasikh shares her belief that "The most effective antidote to the Taliban is to create the best educated leadership generation in Afghanistan's history."[19]

WHAT DO YOU THINK?

1. Basij-Rasikh and her family, and families like them, face an incredibly difficult problem: going against Taliban rule and educating girls. What patterns of reasoning might families like these use in making such a dangerous decision?
2. When Basij-Rasikh's father claimed "there was greater risk in not educating his children," what pattern reasoning is he using to support his claim?
3. Basij-Rasikh states, "The most effective antidote to the Taliban is to create the best educated leadership generation in Afghanistan's history," what patterns of reasoning is she using to make this assertion?

New York City Department of Health and Mental Hygiene

10 Tips for Safer Use

1. Prevent Overdose
2. Treat Overdose
3. Don't Share
4. Use New Syringes
5. Prepare Drugs Carefully
6. Take Care of Your Veins
7. Know Your HIV Status
8. Get Tested and Treated for Hepatitis
9. Get Help for Depression
10. Ask for Help to Stop Using

What Are Good Reasons?

In 2010, the New York City Department of Health and Mental Hygiene angered some New York City residents after publishing a pamphlet for drug users. Because accidental drug overdose is reportedly the fourth leading cause of early adult death in New York City, the agency hoped the pamphlet would help save lives. The pamphlet consists of ten tips to help users reduce the harms associated with injecting drugs. These tips included information about how to "prepare drugs carefully" and advised people to use new syringes every time and to make sure to find a vein before injecting drugs. This detailed advice left some city residents questioning whether the pamphlet was a helpful pamphlet or a how-to guide.

John P. Gilbride, a federal Drug Enforcement Administration official, "expressed his concern that the pamphlet could send a message that leads individuals to believe they can use heroin in a safe manner" and that "heroin can never be safe." Similarly, New York City Council Representative Peter F. Vallone, Jr., said he was unhappy that taxpayer money was used to produce the pamphlet and asked the health commissioner to stop circulating it.

Don Des Jarlais, a research director for the Chemical Dependency Institute, offered a different view of the pamphlet. He believes it can save lives. Des Jarlais claims that after New York City implemented a needle-exchange program, the city saw an 80 percent reduction in new HIV reports for new drug users. He believes the advice in the pamphlet could reduce the number of deaths associated with heroin overdose.[20]

WHAT DO YOU THINK?

1. Are there good reasons to try to prevent HIV infections or deaths among drug users, even though users engage in an illegal activity? What are those reasons?

2. Do you think the pamphlet is unethical and a misuse of taxpayer money? Why or why not?

3. Are there other ways the Health Department could use ethos, pathos, and logos to inform drug users about the risks associated with drug use? What other kinds of evidence could the Health Department use to reduce rates of HIV infection and overdose?

This is misleading because many problems are complex, resulting from multiple causes. Notice how the following example blames only one cause for childhood obesity:

> The number of obese children in the United States has significantly increased over the past decade. According to pediatric experts, approximately 30 percent of children under the age of thirteen are obese. This problem is caused by the unhealthy school lunches being served in schools across the nation. We need legislation mandating more nutritious lunches to solve the obesity epidemic.

This example assumes that there is only one cause to the problem of childhood obesity—unhealthy school lunches. In fact, there are a number of reasons American children are obese: fast food, junk food, and trans fats consumed outside of school; lack of physical exercise inside and outside school; and possibly genetic factors.

Hasty Generalization: Too Few Examples

A **hasty generalization fallacy** is an argument based on too few cases, or examples, to support a conclusion. For example, when speakers rely only on personal experiences to draw conclusions, they may fall into the trap of a hasty generalization because personal experiences often are not enough to prove a claim is true. Notice how the following speaker relies only on her personal experience to support a larger claim:

> The School of Business and Finance is the hardest program to be accepted into at our university. I have applied three times and still have not been admitted.

Although this particular speaker may have been denied admittance into the School of Business and Finance many times, it does not prove that the program is the toughest for *all* students.

In addition to relying solely on personal experience, hasty generalization fallacies also consist of too few external cases, or examples, to support a claim. The following example illustrates an argument based on too few examples:

hasty generalization fallacy:
Argument based on too few cases or examples to support a conclusion.

Bilingual teachers will be hired before monolingual teachers. After all, Mr. Montoya and Ms. Morale were both recently hired, and they speak two languages.

This example relies on too few examples at only one school to prove that bilingual teachers are hired before monolingual teachers. Speakers using examples to support a claim must provide enough specific instances to convince their audience that the claim is true.

Red Herring: Raising an Irrelevant Issue

The term *red herring* comes from the foxhunting tradition in England. Before a hunt began, farmers often dragged a smoked herring around the perimeter of their fields. The strong odor from the fish masked the scent of the fox and threw the hounds off its trail, keeping the hounds from trampling the farmers' crops. Although this worked well for the farmers, trailing the equivalent of a red herring around an argument is not such a good idea. When we make use of the **red herring fallacy**, we introduce irrelevant information into an argument to distract an audience from the real issue. The following example illustrates the red herring fallacy:

> How can we worry about the few cases of AIDS in our town of only 50,000 when thousands and thousands of children are dying of AIDS and AIDS-related illnesses in other countries?

In this example, the speaker turns the argument away from her own community and toward the international problem of AIDS. The audience then becomes more concerned about AIDS in other countries. Undoubtedly, this is an important issue, but it is not the one under discussion, which is equally important. Because of the red herring, the audience is less inclined to move toward a solution for the local situation.

Red herring arguments are fallacious because they turn the audience's attention from one issue to another. This type of fallacy can be hard to spot because both issues usually are important, but the audience feels pulled toward the most recently raised issue. As an audience member, listen carefully when a speaker introduces a new and important topic in a persuasive speech; you might be hearing a red herring fallacy.

Slippery Slope: The Second Step Is Inevitable

A **slippery slope fallacy** is an argument in which a speaker claims that taking a first step in one direction will inevitably lead to undesirable further steps. Like a skier speeding down a hill without being able to stop, a slippery slope fallacy suggests the momentum of one decision or action will cause others to follow. Here is an example of a slippery slope fallacy:

> If we allow our children to dress in any way they want at school, they soon will be wearing more and more outrageous clothing. They'll start trying to outdress one another. Then it'll be increasingly outrageous behaviors inside and outside the classrooms. Soon they'll turn to violence as they try to top one another.

The speaker is making a slippery slope argument by suggesting that if one unwanted thing happens, others certainly will follow. The audience gets caught up in the momentum of this "snowball" argument. Slippery slope arguments can be persuasive because the speaker extends the first claim (for example, the dress codes) to a larger issue (violence) even though the two may not be linked. Before you accept the full claim made with a slippery slope argument, stop and consider whether the chain of events really is inevitable.

As you listen to speeches, and as you put your own arguments together, keep in mind that a fallacy is an error in logic. When we persuade others, we want to be sure our logic is

---

Practicing the Public Dialogue | 14.2

CONSIDERING LOGICAL FALLACIES

Using your speech topic and research for your next persuasive speech, convert the arguments you plan to make in your speech to logical fallacies. Write one example of each of seven of the logical fallacies you've just read about. Bring your fallacies to class and present each of them to your classmates. See if they can identify the type of fallacy you are committing. After every student has presented her or his fallacies, discuss which were the hardest to spot and which were the most "persuasive." Now revise those fallacies, correcting their flawed reasoning.

---

red herring fallacy: Introduction of irrelevant information into an argument to distract from the real issue.

slippery slope fallacy: Argument that claims a first step in a certain direction will inevitably lead to undesirable further steps in that direction.

Table 14.1 Additional Fallacies Often Heard in Speeches

FALLACY	WHAT IT DOES	EXAMPLE
Ad populum ("to the people")	Convinces the audience that because something is popular, it must be correct or right.	Nearly 75 percent of children in our community take advantage of YMCA programs. The Y programs must be the best for keeping children active and safe.
Appeal to fear	Seeks to gain support based on deception or a threat.	Even though you told me that your class is full, I would like to take it this semester. I spoke to my mother, who is one of the university's attorneys, and she said overrides can be granted.
Appeal to ignorance	Assumes that a lack of evidence proves (or disproves) the speaker's claim.	Because there is no concrete evidence that civilizations exist on planets other than Earth, they must not exist.
Appeal to tradition	Argues for the continuation of a practice because it has always been done that way.	The college should continue to require that students have 120 credits to graduate because the college has always required students to take 120 credits.
Begging the question	Makes a circular argument whereby the speaker uses the same argument as both the evidence and claim.	Hormone-free meat products are the healthiest because they do not contain hormones.
False analogy	Presents an analogy based on two things that are not essentially alike.	Because the state banned texting while driving to reduce accident rates, the state should also ban eating while driving.
False authority	Cites a well-known person rather than evidence to prove a claim.	The NBA commissioner said that athletes drafted into the NBA right out of high school will not face any future repercussions for not having a college degree. He must be right.
Non sequitur ("it does not follow")	Makes a conclusion that does not follow logically from the premises.	The federal government needs to raise the national minimum wage if it wants to help put unemployed workers back into the workforce.
Straw man	Attributes a weak argument to the opposition and then demolishes it (rather than addressing the opposition's real argument).	Politicians who want to tax candy and soda are not concerned about the working class. These politicians are only worried about making money, not about how struggling families will be impacted by the additional tax. We need to help working-class families, not hurt them by creating another tax!

sound and not based on error or deception. The fallacies that commonly occur in persuasive speeches are easy to spot if you understand how they work. Those discussed in this chapter and presented in Table 14.1, are easy to avoid if you take time to lay out your arguments carefully. By avoiding fallacies, you will enhance your persuasive efforts, increase your credibility, and contribute positively to the public dialogue.

Staying Audience Centered

With so many kinds of reasoning to consider and fallacies to avoid, how do public speakers create effective speeches that appeal to their audiences? Fortunately, you can do several things to ensure that the reasoning in your speeches is appropriate and of interest to your audience. First, take a moment to think about who is in your audience and what kinds of reasoning you have used to present your ideas. Have you used a variety of patterns of reasoning? Will they appeal to your audience? And do those patterns of reasoning help you develop your ideas clearly? Then, return to your arguments and check for any fallacies you might have constructed. Are there any slippery slope claims? Have you used an ad hominem or either–or argument? Do you make hasty generalizations or raise irrelevant arguments? If you find some of these fallacies, take time to correct them so that your audience can see your arguments clearly and follow your logic. Finally, stay audience centered by asking yourself, "Have I presented my arguments carefully, fully, and fairly?"

PREPARATION OUTLINE WITH COMMENTARY

You Have My Deepest Sympathy: You Just Won the Lottery
by Maria DiMaggio

Specific Purpose: To persuade my audience that winning the lottery is not as great as it's perceived to be and that they should invest their money in alternative ways.

Thesis Statement: Lottery participants could avoid the financial and personal problems that often accompany lottery winnings by finding alternatives to this form of gambling.

MindTap Now that you've explored how to use logos (evidence), ethos (credibility), pathos (emotion), and mythos (cultural beliefs) in persuasive speaking, how to avoid some common fallacies, and how to persuade audiences effectively and ethically, create your own persuasive speech. Use the following speech as a model. Watch a video clip of this speech and see Maria's transcript and speaking outline. Maria gave this speech in an introductory public speaking class. The assignment was to give a five- to seven-minute persuasive speech with a minimum of four sources cited. Students were also asked to create a preparation outline that included a Works Cited (MLA) or References (APA) section. (You can watch videos of other persuasive speeches, including "Colorado Prison Reform: A Solution to Reduce Recidivism and Overcrowding" by Jessica Fuller, "Fat Discrimination" by Carol Godart, and "Stop Animal Testing" by Amanda Konecny.)

COMMENTARY

Maria begins her speech by combining antithesis with an intriguing statement. She then reveals the topic and problem of her speech.

She creates common ground by telling her audience that she used to think she'd be happy if she won the lottery, a common dream. She also establishes her credibility by stating that she's researched her topic.

Maria hopes to persuade her audience to immediate action. She alludes to her solution throughout her introduction and states it explicitly here: people should seek happiness in other ways and find alternative ways to spend their money.

Maria uses her first main point to describe the evolution of lotteries. She defines lotteries as a form of gambling, evoking a negative connotation. However, she takes her definition from a highly credible source.

Introduction

I. You have my deepest sympathy; you just won the lottery. (*catch attention*)
II. Most of us would be shocked if someone said we'd won $20 million and then offered us condolences; however, hundreds of lottery winners have discovered the downside of winning big.
III. I used to think I'd be the happiest person in Brooklyn if I could just win a million dollars, but my research about the lottery winners convinced me to spend my money elsewhere—and I hope you'll follow my example. (*establish credibility*)
IV. Lottery participants can avoid problems that often accompany lottery winnings by finding alternatives to this form of gambling.
V. Today I'll explain that the lottery is a form of gambling that raises money for good causes; however, winners often end up with financial and personal problems, and you are better off spending your money elsewhere. (*preview main points*)

Body

I. Lotteries are a form of gambling that raise money for good causes.
    A. The *World Book Encyclopedia* identifies lotteries as a popular form of gambling.
        1. Winners pay to participate, generally by purchasing tickets at a uniform price.
        2. According to a 2002 article in *The Detroit News*, winners are determined by random drawings; unfortunately, you are sixteen times more likely to get killed driving to buy the ticket than you are to win a record amount.

In her subpoint I.B, Maria acknowledges that lotteries also generate revenue for good causes. The examples touch on two iconic American events, the American Revolution and France's gift of the Statue of Liberty. These examples and Maria's acknowledgment that lotteries are used for good causes set the stage for her appeal to mythos later in the speech.

Reasoning deductively, Maria makes a broad claim that supports her thesis: "unexpected problems arise for lottery winners." Her supporting examples establish her claim as viable.

Organized according to the problem–solution pattern, Maria's speech focuses on a question of policy. In her second main point, she states the problem: winning the lottery often causes misery. By appealing to emotions and citing statistics and examples from her research, she establishes the scope of the problem.

In her third main point, Maria explicitly proposes her solution: invest your disposable income in ways that will generate a greater return or that will be more fulfilling. Her suggestions are reasonable, and her audience will probably be open to considering them.

Also notice that she makes an indirect appeal to mythos by asking her audience to spend money on pursuits that define the American way of life: endorsing capitalism by investing in the stock market, supporting altruism by donating to charity, and indulging in luxuries that we've earned through our hard work.

3. Lotteries were popular in the United States in the 1700s.
4. However, several states made them unconstitutional in the 1880s due to fraud by lottery companies and pressure from social reformers.
5. New Hampshire reinstated the lottery in 1963; now, more than half the states have state-run lotteries.

B. Lotteries generate revenue for good causes.
   1. The earliest lottery, organized in London in 1680, raised money for a municipal water supply.
   2. A French lottery helped pay for the Statue of Liberty.
   3. Closer to home, a national lottery helped support the American Revolutionary War.
   4. In 1772, one lottery's proceeds were divided among a Presbyterian church, a German Lutheran church, the Newark Academy, and three Philadelphia schoolmasters.
   5. Current lotteries in New Hampshire and Oregon, among other states, provide educational funding.

Transition: Now that we know a bit about the history of lotteries, you'd think your life would be great if you could only win big. Right? Well, there can be major problems for winners and their heirs.

II. Unexpected problems arise for lottery winners.
   A. First, their dreams of instant riches are not always fulfilled.
      1. Unless winners take a much lower lump sum, funds are distributed over twenty to twenty-five years.
      2. A lottery "millionaire" is really a "thousandaire" who gets about $50,000 annually before taxes, delinquent taxes, past-due child support, and student loans are taken out.
      3. Winners cannot draw cash from winnings, use them as collateral for loans, or liquidate future payments.
   B. In addition, many suffer personal loss and rejection.
      1. William "Bud" Post won $16.2 million but watched his brother go to jail, convicted of hiring a hit man to kill him.
      2. Debbie won $6.58 million but lost contact with her sisters, who stopped speaking to her when she declined to pay their debts.
      3. Bernice took a day off work to claim her $1 million; her job was given to someone else.
      4. Daisy won $2.8 million but went through a painful lawsuit.
         a. Her son's friend sued for half the winnings because she asked the friend to pray that she'd win.
         b. He prayed, she won, so he thought he was entitled to some of her money.
         c. The court ruled against him, saying he couldn't prove his prayers caused her to win.
   C. Lottery winnings don't necessarily bring happiness.
      1. A study conducted by the *Journal of Personality and Social Psychology* of people with the best of luck and those with the worst of luck supported this conclusion.
      2. Accident victims weren't as unhappy as expected; however, lottery winners were unhappier and took less pleasure in life than expected.
   D. Finally, heaven help the heirs if a lottery-winning relative dies and leaves them with a fortune.
      1. They must immediately pay estate taxes on the unpaid total, with monthly penalties added after nine months.
      2. According to the article, "Lottery Players ad Winners," Johnny Ray Brewster won $12.8 million, taking it in annual payments. His sister Peggy inherited the payments, but upon inheritance she immediately owed $3.5 million in taxes.

Transition: Given the low probability of winning and the many problems winners face, there surely must be other solutions if you have money to burn.

III. Use your extra money in far more profitable expenditures.
   A. Invest in the stock market; investing just $10 to $20 monthly can pay off immensely by the time you retire.
   B. Donate your extra money to a charitable organization and claim a tax deduction.
   C. Indulge yourself: buy cable, eat lobster occasionally, buy season tickets to a sporting or a cultural event, or get an exotic pet.
   D. Finally, if you like to think your lottery money supports education, you can donate to my college fund!

Conclusion

I. I hope I've convinced you that playing the lottery is not all it's advertised to be.
II. I've explained what the lottery is, the problems it can cause, and some alternative ways to get rid of the money.
III. So the next time you see a new lottery millionaire, consider sending your sympathies rather than your congratulations.

Works Cited

Associated Press. "Compare the Odds." *The Detroit News*, 2002, http://www.detnews.com/2002/metro/0204/16/b01-446437.htm. Accessed 2 June 2005.

Beyer, Gerry W., and Jessica Petrini. "Lottery Players and Winners: Estate Planning for the Optimistic and the Lucky." *The Website of Gerry W. Beyer*, 2002, www.professorbeyer.com/Archives/new_wite/Articles/Lottery.html. Accessed 2 June 2005.

Brickman, Philip, et al. "Lottery Winners and Accident Victims: Is Happiness Relative?" *Journal of Personality and Social Psychology*, vol. 36, no. 8, Aug. 1978, pp. 917–27.

Findlay, John M. *People of Chance*. Oxford UP, 1986.

Goodman, Ellen. "8 Lottery Winners Who Lost Their Millions." *MSN Money*, 18 Nov. 2004, moneycentral.msn.com/content/Savinganddebt/Savemoney/P99649.asp. Accessed 2 June 2005.

"Lottery." *The World Book Encyclopedia*, Rev. ed., Vol. 14, World Book, 2007, p. 183.

Sanford, Rob. *Infinite Financial Management: What to Do before and after You Win the Lottery*. Titlewaves Publishing, 1994.

Von Herrmann, Denise. *Their Big Gamble: The Politics of Lottery and Casino Expansion*. Praeger, 2002.

Maria could have strengthened this portion of her speech by spending as much time discussing her solution as she did discussing the problem. For example, she could have told a brief story about how spending her own money on small luxuries has brought her fulfillment. Overall, she could have provided much more evidence to convince her audience that her solutions would result in happiness.

She uses a common phrase to signal the end of a speech. She then provides a nice, succinct summary of her main points, and she reinforces her thesis.

Maria concludes her speech by circling back to the intriguing statement she made in her introduction. Maria uses the MLA style of citation for her Works Cited.

Chapter Summary

The process of sound reasoning is basic to all speeches.

Sound reasoning is one of the most powerful aspects of a healthy public dialogue.

- When we reason, we use Aristotle's three types of proofs—logos, ethos, and pathos—to offer explanations and justifications for our ideas and positions.

- The logic of our reasons depends on our evidence—the examples, narratives, statistics, testimony, and definitions we gather during our research process.

- This logic helps our audience make inferences and see the connections between our evidence and claims. Our goal is to develop an argument that our audience will find credible.

Beginning speakers use five common patterns of reasoning.

1. Inductive reasoning, or reasoning from specific instances, relies on a series of examples to develop a claim we expect to be true.

   - When you reason inductively, have enough examples to support your claim.

   - Make sure your generalizations are accurate.

   - Use statistics and testimony to support your arguments.

2. Deductive reasoning, or reasoning from a general principle, begins with a commonly accepted major premise. In combination with a specific instance, or minor premise, it then establishes the truth of a specific claim or conclusion. If your general principle is one the audience will not accept immediately, you will need to establish its validity.

3. Causal reasoning establishes an "if–then" relationship, suggesting that if one event happens (a cause), then another is sure to follow (an effect).
   - When you use causal reasoning, be careful not to claim a causal relationship if it cannot be proved.
   - Also be careful not to assume mistakenly there is only one cause for an event.
   - In addition, try to identify the strength or weakness of the relationship you are establishing.
4. Analogical reasoning is a process of reasoning by way of comparison and similarity. It implies that because two things resemble each other in one respect, they also share similarities in another respect. However, be sure the two things you are comparing truly are alike.
5. Reasoning by sign assumes something exists or will happen based on something else that exists or has happened. A sign represents something else, and when the sign is present, speakers reason that the other thing will be, too.
   - When you reason by sign, be sure there isn't a more credible explanation for your claim.
   - Also be sure that the sign is not an isolated instance. The sign should always be present alongside what it represents.

Like all other aspects of public speaking, reasoning has an ethical component.
- To be ethical during the reasoning process is to establish strong credibility with your audience through sound reasoning.
- Ethical speakers use their evidence accurately and do not make claims their evidence does not support.
- They also take time during the speech writing and research process to verify the structure of their reasoning so they will not confuse or alienate their audience.

Fallacies are errors in an argument that result from flawed reasoning. The most common fallacies are
- Ad hominem (against the person)
- Bandwagon (everyone else does it)
- Either–or (false dilemma)
- False cause (mistaking a chronological relationship)
- Hasty generalization (providing too few examples)
- Red herring (raising a distracting new issue)
- Slippery slope (one step will lead to others)

Invitation to Public Speaking Online MindTap®

Now that you have read Chapter 14, use your MindTap Communication for *Invitation to Public Speaking* for quick access to the digital resources that accompany this text. These resources include:

- **Study tools** that will help you assess your learning and prepare for exams (digital glossary, key term flash cards, review quizzes).
- **Activities and assignments** that will help you hone your knowledge and build your public speaking skills throughout

the course, as well as help you explore public speaking concepts online (web links), give you step-by-step guidance through the research, outline and note card preparation process (Outline Builder), watch and critique videos of sample speeches (Interactive Video Activities), and allow you to practice and present your presentation online using a speech video delivery, recording, and grading system (YouSeeU).

Key Concepts MindTap® Test your knowledge with online printable flash cards.

ad hominem fallacy (277)
analogical reasoning (273)
argument (268)
bandwagon fallacy (277)
causal reasoning (272)
character (275)
competence (275)
conclusion (271)
credibility (275)
deductive reasoning (270)

either–or fallacy (278)
ethos (268)
evidence (268)
fallacy (276)
false cause (272)
false cause fallacy (278)
hasty generalization (270)
hasty generalization fallacy (280)
inductive reasoning (268)
inferences (268)

logos (268)
major premise (270)
minor premise (271)
pathos (268)
red herring fallacy (281)
reasoning by sign (274)
sign (274)
slippery slope fallacy (281)

Review Questions

1. Bring a copy of the newspaper to class. In groups, identify as many different types of reasoning as you can find in the text, photographs, and advertisements. Label each item you find inductive, deductive, causal, analogical, or sign and evaluate the strength of each item's reasoning according to the guidelines discussed in this chapter.
2. This chapter suggests that a speaker's credibility is an important part of the ethical process of using reasoning. Do you agree? Why or why not? Can you identify speakers you have

heard or read about who do not have much credibility and you would deem unethical? Compare those speakers lacking credibility to a speaker you find credible. Whose arguments do you find more ethical?
3. Bring a copy of the morning newspaper or your favorite magazine to class. In groups, identify as many different types of fallacies as you can find. Now that you recognize these fallacies, evaluate the strength of the argument being advanced.

15 | Persuasive Speaking

IN THIS CHAPTER, YOU WILL LEARN TO:

- Compare and contrast the three types of persuasive speeches

- Apply the most common patterns of organization for persuasive speeches

- Apply the three tips for giving effective persuasive speeches

- Utilize the principles for giving ethical persuasive speeches

Throughout history, people have given persuasive speeches in political arenas, courtrooms, workplaces, community settings, social gatherings, and classrooms. Today, just as our ancestors have, we use persuasive speech in the public dialogue to influence and alter the perspectives, the positions, and even the lives of others. When you understand the principles of persuasive speaking, you too can add your voice to the public dialogue

MindTap° Start with a quick warm-up activity and review the chapter's learning objectives.

Ben Baker/Redux

▲ Community organizers Alicia Garza (center), Patrisse Cullors (left), and Opal Tometi (right) founded Black Lives Matter to call attention to political and social injustices and the devaluation of the lives of black people. They used social media to raise awareness about an important issue and to persuade people to take action. In this chapter you will find strategies for developing and organizing persuasive speeches and adding your voice to the public dialogue in civil and ethical ways.

as a persuasive speaker whether you decide to speak, are asked to speak, or are required to speak.

A **persuasive speech** is one whose message attempts to change or reinforce an audience's thoughts, feelings, or actions. To ask an audience to see things the way we do is quite different from speaking informatively (Chapter 12) or invitationally (Chapter 13). When we speak to persuade, we ask an audience to think as we do about a topic, to adopt our position, or to support our actions and beliefs. In that sense, we act as advocates for a particular issue, belief, or course of action.

This chapter discusses several aspects of speaking that are central to persuasion. You will explore the three major types of persuasive speeches, the organizational patterns best suited to persuasive speeches, the role of evidence and emotions in persuasion, and some ethical considerations that persuasive speaking presents.

MindTap°

Read, highlight, and take notes online.

Types of Persuasive Speeches

Attempts at persuasion generally address questions of fact, questions of value, or questions of policy. Each category concerns a different type of change sought from an audience. Knowing which type of change you want to request from your audience members helps you develop a listenable message for them.

Questions of Fact

When we want to persuade an audience about debatable points, we are speaking about questions of fact. A **question of fact** addresses whether or not something is verifiably true. For example, we can determine with certainty who won the last New York City Marathon by consulting a yearbook or looking up marathon records online, and so the facts concerning this topic are not open to debate. But we cannot absolutely determine the training schedule that will produce the fastest marathon runners in the future. Any claim to such knowledge is speculative and therefore open to dispute. An audience can be persuaded to accept one opinion or another about the best training method by a speaker's use of arguments, evidence, and reasoning (Chapter 14).

Our understanding of many topics today derives from theories that have not yet been conclusively proven. Whether it is the reason dinosaurs became extinct, the original purpose of Stonehenge, the techniques used to construct the Egyptian pyramids, the way to end the HIV and AIDS crisis, or the most effective methods to improve student reading skills, the facts about these issues are not absolute and leave room for competing theories. Therefore, they make excellent topics for speeches in which you try to persuade audiences that you have the correct answers.

Questions of Value

When we want to persuade an audience about what is good or bad, right or wrong, we are speaking about questions of value. A **question of value** addresses the merit or morality of an object, action, or belief. Is it right to continue offshore drilling for oil even though drilling presents risks to the environment? Is it moral to punish certain crimes with death? Is it ethical to require all children to say the Pledge of Allegiance in school? These are questions of value, as are debates over what constitutes "good" and "bad" art, music, or theater.

When you attempt to persuade your audiences about questions of value, you move from asserting that something is true or false to advocating that one thing is better or worse than another. Questions of value cannot be answered simply by analyzing facts.

persuasive speech: Speech whose message attempts to change or reinforce an audience's thoughts, feelings, or actions.

question of fact: Question that addresses whether or not something is verifiably true.

question of value: Question that addresses the merit or morality of an object, action, or belief.

question of policy: Question that addresses the best course of action or solution to a problem.

tip
National Geographic Explorer

AZIZ ABU SARAH, Explorer and Cultural Educator

Tell us about a persuasive speech you gave and how you used evidence fairly and ethically without compromising the power of persuasion. Was the speech about a statement of "fact" that you questioned, proved, or disproved; a speech based on a question of values or an issue of policy?

I always start with the personal level; then I move to a value that people agree on. The main thing is to understand who you're speaking to and to understand your crowd and what statistics and what facts would speak to them. In every situation, it's not always useful to just recount multiple facts. I try to show many studies to prove a point. And even if you are successful, sometimes facts alone don't always move people and their ideals. There are also values. Let me give you an example. If I'm speaking to a religious Jewish group, what I try to do is to understand that their values have a lot to do with the Torah and their Holy Bible. So I try to relate to that as much as possible. I try to use stories from the Torah as much as possible. I will share with them the story of the burning tree, for example, one of the things that I happen to know, and I'll share the scripture that they relate to. Then the fact becomes related to their value. That's my strategy for connecting these two—fact and value—together.

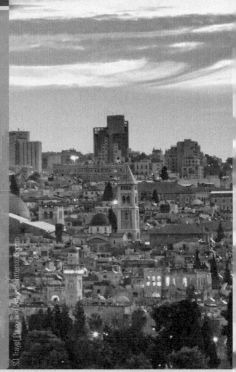

Rather, they are grounded in what people believe is right, good, appropriate, worthy, and ethically sound. Thus, it can be difficult to persuade audiences about questions of value. This is because when we speak on questions of value, we must *justify* our claims. We must provide suitable reasons for accepting a particular action or view. When we justify a claim, we set standards and we argue that our view satisfies certain principles or values generally regarded as correct and valid by most people. So when we try to persuade an audience that drilling for oil is worth the risk to the environment, we justify that claim by arguing that the oil from offshore drilling meets a certain standard of necessity that warrants risks to the environment. Or when we attempt to persuade our audience that it is moral to punish certain crimes with death, we try to justify our claim on the basis of a particular standard: that certain actions fall into a specific category that warrants this kind of punishment.

Persuasive speakers often ask audiences to take a course of action that will solve a problem or otherwise benefit a particular community. Around the world, speakers—like this speaker in Paris—mobilized support for victims of a mass shooting at a gay nightclub in Orlando, Florida. What problem do you feel needs to be addressed in your community? What course of action could you suggest that would motivate an audience to help you address that problem?

Questions of Policy

When we want to persuade an audience about the best way to act or solve a problem, we are speaking about questions of policy. A **question of policy** addresses the best course of action or solution to a problem. What form of support should employers provide for veterans with disabilities? How should the federal government implement mandatory drug testing? How many credits for graduation should the university require? At what age should people be legally allowed to drink alcoholic beverages? Each of these questions focuses on an issue that cannot be resolved solely by answering a question of absolute fact or debating the morality of an issue.

Practicing the Public Dialogue | 15.1

SELECT A PERSUASIVE SPEECH TYPE

As a class, brainstorm as many different persuasive speech topics as you can. Next, group the topics according to the three types of persuasive speeches you've just read about. Some might fit into more than one group depending on how you phrase your thesis statement for a particular topic. Discuss which of these topics you find most interesting and why. Save this list for the next Practicing the Public Dialogue activity.

MindTap°

To see an example of a good persuasive speech, watch a video clip of Hans Erian giving his speech about the dangers of sugar.

Although questions of policy might address the facts about the contributions veterans make in the workplace or the morality of mandatory drug testing, they go beyond these questions to offer solutions and plans of action. In sum, speeches about questions of policy present audience members with a specific solution or plan to a problem and try to persuade them that the solution or plan will eliminate the problem satisfactorily.

Because each type of persuasive speech—questions of fact, value, or policy—focuses on different issues and goals for change, each requires a different type of organizational pattern to be most effective. Many persuasive speeches can be organized according to the patterns discussed in Chapter 7, particularly speeches about questions of fact and value. However, because speeches about questions of policy often call on an audience to take a specific action, they sometimes require unique organizational patterns.

Organization of Speeches on Questions of Fact

Speeches on questions of fact can be organized chronologically, spatially, and topically. To help you decide which organizational pattern is best, ask yourself the following questions: can you achieve your goals best by describing the issue as it developed over time, by describing a spatial arrangement, or by covering distinct topics?

Thomas used the spatial pattern to organize his speech about campus lighting. He traced the layout of the campus from its center to its perimeter to make the case that it is not adequately lit for safety:

Specific purpose	To persuade my audience that the lighting on campus is not adequate
Thesis statement	From the library to the farthest parking lot, the lighting on campus is not adequate to ensure safety after dark.
Main points	I. Lighting near the center of the campus casts many shadows in which someone can hide.
	II. Around the perimeter of this center, the lighting is spaced too far apart to offer adequate protection.
	III. The lighting in the parking lots that border the campus should be much brighter than it currently is.

In the next example, Jacki used the topical pattern to develop her speech about the benefits of the school voucher system:

Specific purpose	To persuade my audience that the United States should implement more school choice through the voucher system as a way to increase performance and satisfaction for students.
Thesis statement	Although there are arguments against it, implementing vouchers to increase school choice encourages schools to use resources more effectively, resulting in a better education for students.
Main points	I. A private school choice system means that the federal government gives vouchers or money to students to help pay for the cost of attending private schools.
	II. The Milwaukee Parental Choice Program (MPCP), which has been in place since 1990, currently serves 127 schools in Milwaukee, Wisconsin, and benefits both private and public schools.

III. Vouchers encourage competition and break the stranglehold of teachers' unions, resulting in better education for students.

IV. Although critics say vouchers pull the brightest students away from our public schools, the benefits and opportunities for all students outweigh this risk.

By organizing her speech topically, Jacki was able to discuss the main issues related to a school voucher system, including its benefits.

Organization of Speeches on Questions of Value

Like speeches on questions of fact, speeches on questions of value can be organized chronologically, spatially, or topically. In the following example, Eiji used the chronological pattern to develop her speech about the value of encouraging girls to participate in the sciences:

Specific purpose	To persuade my audience that encouraging girls to participate in the sciences is of value to us all.

Thesis statement	Throughout history, when women have been encouraged to participate in the traditionally male-dominated world of science, they have made significant contributions that have benefited all of us.

Main points	I. In the late 1700s, Caroline Lucretia Herschel's father and brother encouraged her interest in astronomy, and she developed the modern mathematical approach to astronomy.
	II. In the late 1800s, with the support of her husband and colleagues, botanist Elizabeth Knight Britton built impressive botanical collections and is said to be the first person to suggest the establishment of the New York Botanical Garden.
	III. In the early 1900s, Maria Goeppert Mayer was encouraged by her university professors to pursue her interest in science, which led to her winning the 1963 Nobel Prize in physics for her groundbreaking work in modeling the nuclei of atoms.

principigalli/Getty Images

The next example illustrates a question of value organized spatially. In this speech, Trevor arranged his main points so they followed specific locations within a city:

Specific purpose	To persuade my audience that the preservation of open space within and between communities should take priority in city planning.

Thesis statement	Open space both within and along the perimeter of a city is crucial for a healthy community.
Main points	I. Open space in the heart of a city creates a friendlier, more relaxed city center.

Persuading an audience on a question of value can be a challenge, especially if audience members have different opinions about what is good or moral. Therefore, selecting an effective organizational pattern is important. For example, would it be more effective to persuade a group of teenagers that smoking is dangerous by discussing the diseases that smokers typically die of (topical) or by discussing the debilitating progression of a particular disease (chronological)?

A FEW CITIZEN ACTIVISTS WITH BUCKETS

When activist Erin Brockovich and attorney Edward Masry—both made famous by the movie *Erin Brockovich*—became ill in 1995 from fumes emitted by an oil refinery that Masry was suing, the bucket brigade movement was born. Bucket brigades are community-based groups that use specially designed buckets, commissioned by Masry, to gather and test air samples in neighborhoods near state-owned oil refineries, chemical plants, and similar facilities that emit toxins into the environment. When people in these neighborhoods experience health problems they suspect are caused by pollution, they form bucket brigades to help crack down on facilities that are violating environmental laws.

The bucket brigade movement achieved one of its most important successes in 1999 when a Louisiana brigade successfully monitored emissions from more than fifty industrial facilities around Mossville, Louisiana, including vinyl plastic manufacturers, chemical production facilities, oil refineries, and a coal-fired power plant. Mossville residents had long complained of numerous illnesses but were repeatedly told by industry representatives that the facilities' emissions were not harmful. "I've asked [the refinery officials] to solve their problems, but they deny, deny, deny," explained Ken Ford, president of St. Bernard Citizens for Environmental Quality.

Fed up with the companies' total lack of response to their complaints, the community decided to make their problem a "national issue," says Anne Rolfes, director of the Louisiana Bucket Brigade. Mossville residents formed their own bucket brigade and began taking samples of air around the facilities, which revealed extraordinarily high levels of contaminants. Those levels were verified by the Environmental Protection Agency, and offending companies were forced to pay fines and upgrade to state-of-the-art monitoring equipment. In addition, other towns in Louisiana's "cancer alley" took Mossville's cue and formed their own bucket brigades, leading to the establishment of the Louisiana Bucket Brigade. As a result, reports the Louisiana

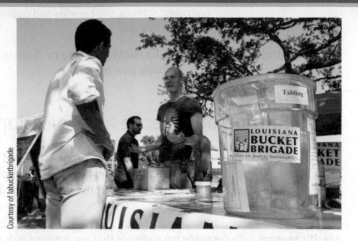

Bucket Brigade's website, "Pollution has been significantly reduced, all of which stemmed from a few citizen activists with their buckets."

Recently, the brigade has partnered with Grassroots Mapping, a group of Gulf Coast residents and activist mappers, who are documenting the effects of the BP oil spill in the Gulf Coast. Their goal is to collect data that will assist in the federal government's assessment and response to the disaster, as well as in the coming litigation over the spill.[1]

🔗 YOU CAN GET INVOLVED

MindTap Check out an online hub that launches and promotes movements for social change on the web.

II.	Open space in identifiable areas or districts within a city brings people together, resulting in more familiarity with one's neighbors and safer neighborhoods.

III.	Open space between two cities reduces urban sprawl and strengthens people's attachment to their own city.

When we give persuasive speeches on questions of fact or value, we may ask our audience members to change their view or agree on what is right or wrong, but we do not ask them to do anything. Therefore, the chronological, spatial, and topical patterns work well for these types of speeches. However, for persuasive speeches about questions of policy, we also ask our audience to agree on what must be done to solve a problem. Thus, we must rely on different types of organizational patterns.

Organization of Speeches on Questions of Policy

Persuasive speeches about questions of policy usually require organizational patterns that clearly define a problem and then offer a well-developed solution. Determining the best pattern for your speech depends on the kind of change you are hoping to get

"Apathetic is Pathetic"
Sol Guy, Explorer, New Media Cultural Story Teller

Rebecca Hale/National Geographic Creative

As an artist, social entrepreneur committed to ethical business practices, former manager of some of today's highest-profile hip-hop artists, and a film and TV producer, Canadian-born Sol Guy was "[r]iding the wave of the hip-hop music explosion" and "on track to becoming a top recording industry executive." However, "at the height of his success, he grew disillusioned with the North American hip-hop scene's increasing emphasis on violence and materialism." In 2000, he traveled to Africa to be a part of the award-winning documentary *Musicians in the War Zone*. The trip, Guy states, changed his life: "I can't really explain why that happened, but it was this thing where I saw something that I couldn't look away from. And then, in fact, I saw there was a way I could influence it. And then I saw the power of storytelling." Returning from the trip, Guy "adopted a new focus." He explains, "Acknowledging my success and experience in the music industry I began to realize the power I possessed in creating media.

I decided that I wanted to create a new hybrid that connects the worlds of entertainment and activism." He and long-time friend Josh Thome coproduced *4REAL*, a television series that introduces celebrities, such as Cameron Diaz, Joaquin Phoenix, and others, to young people "creating real social change using music, art, and culture to propel communities forward. They've been through some of the most horrible experiences imaginable, yet have come out shining with phenomenal passion and power."

What makes these young people so exceptional, Guy explains, is "their desire to radically change their community and their inability to see any obstacle as an obstacle." What some of us might see as "insurmountable odds," these young leaders see as something to be pushed through. What is missing, he says, is "the can't, the idea of cannot. Instead, it's just, like 'well, why not?' And that's a really interesting thing because the only barriers to any entry to radically changing something are the thoughts you have and what you believe yourself to be capable of." He continues, "The people, the things they've seen, the world," don't stop them; instead, these young leaders from some of the harshest conditions imaginable "are just like . . . well, why not? And I know that feeling because I share it with them. You see something that you want to do, and you're passionate about it, you go for it. And that's how you create things. That's how you create change. That's how new things come about."

Guy has delivered speeches and presentations "from boardrooms to primary schools, community centers, jails, reservations, wherever I am invited." We all have stories to tell, he says; what we must do is "create space for important stories to be told . . . and whatever the medium is, if the story is told and the storyteller is good, it'll find its way." He continues, "apathetic is pathetic"; people have to stop blaming one another and take action. He sees all of us living in a "time of urgency" and believes there is no time to "play it safe." Guy concludes, humans are "an extraordinary animal, you know? And we stifle ourselves and our potential only because we forget that we created everything that we are living in. These are all ideas. Our thoughts created reality. And that's our power of manifestation. And, wow, imagine when we all recognize that collective power."[2]

WHAT DO YOU THINK?

1. Sol Guy suggests that "apathetic is pathetic." As a class, discuss what you think he means by this. How might this influence your persuasive speech topic?
2. Guy urges young people to say "Why not?" rather than "I can't." Reflect on times you have said "I can't." What would change if you had said "Why not?" instead?
3. Log on to TEDxToronto and watch Guy's presentation and delivery. What are the strengths of his presentation? In what ways can you incorporate some of these strengths into your own speech?

Courtesy of 4REAL

from your audience: *immediate action* or *passive agreement*. The differences between the two are simple, yet the impact they have on a speech is significant.

When you attempt to **gain immediate action**, your goal is to encourage an audience to engage in a specific behavior or take a specific action. You want to move beyond simply asking your audience to alter a belief. When you seek immediate action, you want to be as specific as possible in stating what you want your audience to do. You need a clear **call to action**, an explicit request that an audience engage in some clearly stated behavior. For example, rather than asking audience members to simply agree with you that the lighting on campus is inadequate, you ask them to contact the school administration and urge its staff to provide the funds needed to improve campus lighting in next year's budget.

In contrast, when you want to **gain passive agreement**, your goal is to ask an audience to adopt a new position without asking them to act in support of that position. When you seek passive agreement, you still advocate a solution to a problem, but you don't call the members of your audience to action. Instead, you simply encourage them to adopt a new position or perspective. Consider the differences between requesting immediate action and passive agreement in the following specific purpose statements:

Immediate action

To persuade my audience to vote against placing vending machines in our public schools

To persuade my audience to adopt my aerobics training program

Passive agreement

To persuade my audience that open space in a city benefits that city and its residents by making it more attractive and livable

To persuade my audience that childhood obesity is a serious problem

Notice how the requests for immediate action focus on asking an audience to do something specific, whereas the requests for passive agreement simply ask an audience to alter a belief. Let's look at some organizational patterns that will help you meet your speech goals whether you request immediate action or passive agreement.

Problem–Solution Organization

Speeches that follow a **problem–solution organization** focus on persuading an audience that a specific problem exists and can be solved or minimized by a specific solution. These types of persuasive speeches are generally organized into two main points. The first point specifies a problem, and the second proposes a solution to that problem. In the problem component of your speech, you must define a problem clearly, and the problem must be relevant to your audience. In the solution component, you must offer a solution that really does help solve the problem and that an audience can reasonably support and implement.

Consider the following example of a problem–solution speech given by Sheri on the issue of light pollution. Notice how she used her thesis statements to state a problem clearly and then how she communicated that problem to her audience in her first main point. Also notice how she related the problem to her audiences directly and personally:

gain immediate action: Encourage an audience to engage in a specific behavior or take a specific action.

call to action: Explicitly request that an audience engage in some clearly stated behavior.

gain passive agreement: Asks audience members to adopt a new position without also asking them to act in support of that position.

problem–solution organization: Organizational pattern that focuses on persuading an audience that a specific problem exists and can be solved or minimized by a specific solution.

Specific purpose	To persuade my audience that although light pollution is a problem that affects us increasingly every day, we can implement simple solutions to reduce the effects of this pollution.
Thesis statement	Light pollution disrupts ground-based astronomy, is a costly energy waste, and affects our health and safety, but there are simple solutions to the problem of light pollution.
Main points	I. Light pollution poses three significant problems. A. In cities, light pollution causes urban sky glow, which disrupts ground-based telescopes.

    B. Light pollution represents an extreme waste of energy, and that waste is costly to all of us

    C. Light pollution causes mild to severe medical conditions and so is unsafe for our communities.

II. The problem of light pollution can be alleviated in two ways.

    A. Light pollution can be controlled through government regulations, such as light codes, which are similar to noise codes.

    B. Light pollution can be reduced through personal actions, such as using less unnecessary light and purchasing equipment that reduces light directed toward the sky.

Notice how Sheri's first main point clearly defines the specific problems created by light pollution and how her second main point offers reasonable solutions. Also note that she requests both passive agreement and immediate action. She asks for passive agreement when she states that supporting government regulations is a good idea, and she asks for immediate action when she suggests audience members modify the lights in their homes. Because problem–solution speeches pose a problem while simultaneously offering a solution, they are excellent vehicles for persuading an audience to support a cause or take an action.

Problem–Cause–Solution Organization

The problem–cause–solution pattern of organization is a slight variation of the problem-solution pattern. Speeches that follow a **problem–cause–solution organization** focus on identifying a specific problem, the causes of that problem, and a solution to the problem. This type of speech is especially effective when you think you will be more persuasive if you explain how a problem came about. Explaining the causes of a problem can help your audience better see the merits of a proposed solution. Describing causes also allows you to clarify any misconceptions members of an audience may have about a topic. In either case, you are sometimes more persuasive if you provide an audience with more information about a problem.

    Problem–cause–solution speeches generally have three main points: the first identifies a clear and relevant problem, the second identifies the relevant causes of that problem, and the third details a clear and appropriate solution to the problem. Two examples illustrate this pattern of organization:

Specific purpose	To persuade my audience that the problems caused by feeding big game wildlife can be easily solved.
Thesis statement	The problems of wildlife overpopulation, the spread of disease, and other negative consequences caused by feeding big game wildlife can be solved by keeping food away from wild animals.
Main points	I. In many areas where people and big game wildlife live near each other, there is overpopulation in certain species, outbreaks of disease, and a decrease in our acceptance of hunters and hunting.
	II. These problems are caused by well-meaning people leaving food out for wildlife in the winter and by campers who are not careful to keep their food and food smells away from wild animals.
	III. These problems can be solved by simply not feeding wildlife; by protecting our food, washing our dishes, and washing our faces and hands when camping; and by putting our garbage in sealed containers.

Notice how Brandi was able to make a stronger case for her solution by identifying the specific causes of wildlife overpopulation, the spread of disease, and other wildlife-related problems. Once audience members knew the reasons for the problems, they could see the merits of a solution that might have seemed too simple to be effective.

MindTap®

Watch a video clip of student speaker Brent Erb giving a persuasive speech and urging immediate action from his audience. Pay attention to the solutions he proposes. Could you implement them?

problem–cause–solution organization: Organizational pattern that focuses on identifying a specific problem, the causes of that problem, and a solution to the problem.

MindTap

Watch a video clip of student speaker Brandi Lafferty giving a persuasive speech. Did her decision to include a discussion of the problem's causes make the speech more effective?

A second example illustrates a different purpose for addressing a cause of a problem:

Specific purpose	To persuade audience members to manage their privacy settings on their social networking sites to ensure fairer treatment in the hiring process.
Thesis statement	Managing privacy settings on social networking sites can reduce the likelihood that employers will unfairly base hiring decisions on applicants' personal and private information online.
Main points	I. Many employers unfairly use personal and private information obtained on social networking sites to make hiring decisions.
	II. Teenagers and young adults often do not set privacy restrictions on their social networking sites, making themselves vulnerable to repercussions in the hiring process.
	III. Setting privacy controls on social networking sites will prohibit employers from accessing personal and private information about employees and ensuring fairer and more equitable treatment in the hiring process.

Problem–cause–solution organizational patterns are useful when you think that providing information about the cause of a problem will help persuade members of your audience to change their views or beliefs.

Causal Organization

When a problem is based on a cause-and-effect relationship, a causal pattern of organization will work well to persuade an audience. Speeches that follow a **causal organization** can develop in two ways: moving from cause to effect or from effect to cause. For example, Eli wanted to discuss the effects of reintroducing wolves in several Western states. He first described the process of reintroducing the wolves (cause) and then focused on the decline in wildlife population (effect):

Specific purpose	To persuade my audience that the reintroduction of the gray wolf has significantly decreased the elk population in Idaho, Montana, and Wyoming.
Thesis statement	Since the reintroduction of wolves in Western regions, the elk population has declined dramatically and farmers' cattle sheep and dogs have been killed.
Main points	I. In 1995 gray wolves were reintroduced to Yellowstone National Park and the surrounding states of Montana and Idaho.
	II. Since the reintroduction of wolves in Western regions, the elk population has declined dramatically, forcing some regions to ban elk hunting.
	III. Other animals, including cattle, sheep, and dogs, have also been impacted by the reintroduction of wolves.

A cause-to-effect pattern worked well for Eli's topic because it emphasized that the wolves were the main reason for the decline in elk populations. In contrast, Rupa chose to arrange her speech using the effect-to-cause pattern of organization. She wanted to make her point by first capturing her audience's attention with some troubling statistics and data, and then explaining what those data mean for drivers and their passengers:

Specific purpose	To persuade my audience that using a cell phone while driving can lead to serious and even fatal accidents.
Thesis statement	When drivers use cell phones while driving, they are putting their lives, and their passengers' lives, in danger.

causal organization: Organizational pattern that is based on a cause-and-effect relationship that can develop in two ways: moving from cause to effect or from effect to cause.

Main points
I. In 2013, drivers distracted by their phones were involved in approximately 1.2 million accidents, at least 341,000 of these occurred while drivers were texting, and over 3,300 of these caused fatalities for the drivers, passengers, or individuals walking across the street.

II. When drivers text, their attention is taken from the road for a minimum of 5 seconds. At 55 miles an hour, that's like driving the length of a football field without paying attention.

III. Even though the majority of teens recognize the danger of using cell phones and social media apps while driving, almost half of them do it anyway.

In this speaking situation, Rupa believed that reminding her audience of the dangers of driving while using a cell phone would help persuade them that using cell phones while driving is a serious issue.

Narrative Organization

Speeches can also be organized using one or more stories to construct an argument. This pattern is called a **narrative organization**. Depending on the topic, a speaker may share an extended narrative to help personalize an argument that may seem difficult for some audience members to fully comprehend. Razz implemented this strategy in his speech on the problem of children being abducted and forced to work as child soldiers in countries such as Sierra Leone in Africa. Razz wanted to share Ishmael Beah's story as an extended narrative to reveal the thoughts, reactions, and experiences of one boy's journey from abduction to rehabilitation:

Specific purpose To convince my audience that rehabilitation programs work to change child soldiers' lives for the better.

Thesis statement Ishmael Beah is a former child soldier from Sierra Leone, Africa, and his story teaches us that rehabilitation programs can work to give child soldiers a new life.

Main points
I. Ishmael Beah was a young boy when his village was attacked and burned, forcing him and several other children to wander from place to place to survive.

II. At the age of twelve, Beah was captured by the Revolutionary United Front (RUF) and forced to become a child soldier.

III. Beah was rescued by UNICEF, was given counseling and rehabilitation services, and received the opportunity to start a new life in the United States.

By using Beah's story to personalize the problem of child soldiers, Razz made his topic more accessible for his audience. This strategy helped him convince his audience that rehabilitation programs sponsored by UNICEF can work to provide these young children with a better life.

Comparative Advantages Organization

When your audience agrees with you about a problem but feels the solution is up for debate, a comparative advantages speech is often an excellent choice. Speeches that follow a **comparative advantages organization** illustrate the advantages of one solution over others. In this type of speech, use each main point to explain why your solution is preferable to other possible solutions. If you must criticize alternative solutions to strengthen your explanations, simply explain why the alternatives will not work, taking care not to degrade or belittle them.

Consider Angela's situation. Her coworkers and bosses already knew a problem existed: sales were down, and they were beginning to lose what had once

narrative organization: Organizational pattern that uses one or more stories to construct an argument.

comparative advantages organization: Organizational pattern that illustrates the advantages of one solution over others.

been faithful customers. Therefore, Angela chose to give a comparative advantages speech so she could focus on illustrating the strengths of her proposed training program:

Specific purpose   To persuade my coworkers that my new training program will increase our sales and enhance our public profile.

Thesis statement   My proposed training program—which includes a longer initial training period, a more detailed assessment and understanding of the strengths of our products, and a stronger mentoring component than our current program—will turn our sales around.

Main points
I.   A longer initial training program will give our staff more time than our current program allows to develop a working knowledge and appreciation of the company and its mission.

II.   A more detailed knowledge of our products and their value will enable our staff to work with our clientele more expertly than our current training allows.

III.   A stronger mentoring program will improve the communication style of our new sales staff and help them respond to unfamiliar situations more effectively than our current mentoring program does.

Angela did not spend time outlining the problem because her audience already knew the training program needed improvement. Instead, she compared the advantages of her program to the weaknesses of the company's current program. She was careful to avoid criticizing the current program too heavily because her boss had been instrumental in bringing that model to the company. Rather, she simply said, "Our current program no longer is meeting our needs. If we make these changes, we'll be back on top."

Monroe's Motivated Sequence

Monroe's motivated sequence is an organizational pattern that helps you address an audience's motives and how those motives could translate into action. Developed in 1935 by Alan Monroe, **Monroe's motivated sequence** is a step-by-step process used to persuade audiences by gaining attention, demonstrating a need, satisfying that need, visualizing beneficial results, and calling for action. Monroe maintained that this pattern satisfies an audience's desire for order and helps a speaker focus on what motivates an audience to action. Monroe's motivated sequence organizes the entire speech, not just the body, and takes listeners through a step-by-step process of identifying a problem and resolving to help solve that problem:[3]

1.   **Attention**. In this step, you catch audience members' interest so they take notice of an issue. Your goal is to motivate the people in the audience to listen and see the personal connection they have to a topic. Using statistics or a story can accomplish this task. For example, Sierra began her speech by telling a story to capture her audience's attention. She began, "I was only ten years old when I found my mother sitting on her bed crying. Not knowing how to react, I sat down beside her and grabbed her hand. When I asked her what was wrong, she replied, 'I am sick and hope that I can hold your hand for many, many more years.' I soon learned my mother had breast cancer and that she would not be able to hold my hand much longer."

2.   **Need**. In this step, you identify the need for a change, meaning a problem that can be solved. You define the problem and how it directly or indirectly affects the audience. Your goal is to encourage your audience to become invested in the problem, feel affected by it, and want to find a solution. Sierra began the need section by proving the severity of the problem. She stated, "The latest study on breast cancer indicates that one in eight women will be diagnosed with breast cancer in her lifetime! That means two of you in this room will be

Monroe's motivated sequence:
Step-by-step process used to persuade audiences by gaining attention, demonstrating a need, satisfying that need, visualizing beneficial results, and calling for action.

directly affected, and almost everyone else will likely know someone affected by breast cancer."

3. **Satisfaction.** In this step, you define what the specific solution is and why it solves the problem. In doing so, you show the members of the audience how the "need" is "satisfied." Sierra argued in her speech that the Susan G. Komen Breast Cancer Foundation was making important strides in finding a cure for breast cancer and needed more national, state, and local funding to support its research efforts.

4. **Visualization.** In this step, you describe the benefits that will result from the audience's need to be satisfied. You can describe what life will be like once the solution is in place, or you can remind the audience what it would be like if the solution were not implemented. Either way, you help audience members visualize how the solution will benefit them. Sierra achieved the visualization step by asking her audience to imagine life without the fear of breast cancer. She described, "Imagine one day you're standing in your bedroom and your daughter walks in and takes your hand. Now imagine being able to tell her that you want to be able to hold her hand for many years in the future, and this time, you can. Reducing the rates of breast cancer will ensure longer, healthier lives for women."

5. **Action.** In this final step, you outline exactly what the audience should do. This is your call to action, the plea for the audience to take immediate action or make a personal commitment to support the changes you're advocating. Sierra asked her class to join her for a breast cancer walk being held in their community. She concluded, "This Saturday at 9 A.M., a walk to raise money for breast cancer research will take place right here on campus. I ask that you join me in this fight and join me on the walk."

Practicing the Public Dialogue | 15.2

SELECT AN ORGANIZATIONAL PATTERN FOR YOUR PERSUASIVE SPEECH

Return to the list of possible persuasive speech topics that you prepared in Practicing the Public Dialogue 15.1. In groups, select a single topic and determine whether you want to work on a question of fact, value, or policy. See if you can create a rough thesis statement and main points for a persuasive speech on this topic using one of the organizational patterns you've just read about. Select the pattern that would best help you persuade the members of your audience to take action or modify their thinking about a topic. As you discuss your organizational pattern, consider the tips for giving effective persuasive speeches in the next section.

MindTap®

To see another example of a persuasive speech that you can use as a model, watch the video clip of Sheri's speech about light pollution. Consider the effectiveness of the organizational pattern she uses for her speech. If you had given a speech on this topic, would you have used the same pattern? Why or why not?

Connecting with Your Audience

The **elaboration likelihood model (ELM),** developed by psychology professors Richard Petty and John Cacioppo, explains that receivers process persuasive messages in either a *central processing* or a *peripheral processing* route depending on how motivated the audience is to think critically about a message. The more a speaker encourages listeners to become consciously engaged to think about a persuasive message, the more likely listeners are processing information in the central route. This means listeners are evaluating the overall quality of the argument, evidence and supporting material included, and any call for action presented in the speech. In this situation, listeners may research additional information on the topic after they listen to the speech because they want more details before deciding if they will support the speaker's argument.

When listeners lack motivation to think critically about a topic, they move toward using the peripheral route. In this situation, listeners consume messages in a passive manner. They may focus on parts of the speech without thinking critically about the message in its entirety. In addition, listeners may be influenced by the speaker's style of dress or delivery, not the quality of speech structure and content.

To encourage listeners to process information in the central route, speakers should connect their topic to their audience, explain the reasons that the audience should be concerned about the speech topic, and continuously work toward keeping

elaboration likelihood model (ELM): Explains that receivers process persuasive messages in either a *central processing* or a *peripheral processing* route depending on how motivated the audience is to think critically about a message.

the audience actively and critically thinking about the speech information. Listeners using the central processing route tend to be more heavily influenced by a speaker than those using the peripheral route.

Evidence and Persuasion

When you speak persuasively, you use evidence in much the same way you use it in other types of speeches. However, for persuasive speeches, three aspects of the effective use of evidence are especially important: the use of specific evidence, novel information, and credible sources.

Use Specific Evidence

When you want to convince your audience that something is true, good, or appropriate, you will be more successful if you use evidence that is *specific* rather than *general*.[4] Your evidence should support your claims as explicitly as possible. For example, in a speech persuading her audience not to smoke, Shannan used the following specific evidence to describe the toxic ingredients in cigarettes:

> You want to make a cigarette? According to Dr. Roger Morrisette of Farmington State College, a single cigarette contains over 4,000 chemicals. If you want the recipe, well, this is what you'll need. You'll need some carcinogens, or cancer-causing agents; some formaldehyde, or embalming fluid; some acetone, which is paint stripper or nail polish remover; benzene or arsenic; pesticides such as fungicides, herbicides, and insecticides; and toxins like hydrogen cyanide, ammonia, and nicotine.

Shannan could have argued "Cigarettes are toxic and contain thousands of poisonous chemicals," but that is far less specific than her list of ingredients. She is more persuasive because she uses specific evidence rather than simply making a general claim.

Present Novel Information

In this age of information overload, it seems that audiences have already heard "all the reasons" to support (or oppose) a position. Still, research indicates that you will be more persuasive when you present new, rather than well-known, information to your audience.[5] When you go beyond what audience members already know, you capture their attention and cause them to listen more carefully to your ideas.

In a speech on pet overpopulation, Malachi produced new information that was quite persuasive. His audience already knew that unspayed animals cause pet overpopulation, so he presented some novel information on this familiar topic:

> According to the Humane Society of the United States in seven years, one unspayed female cat and her unspayed offspring can theoretically produce 420,000 cats. In six years, one unspayed female dog and her offspring can produce 67,000 dogs.

Malachi used information that was new to his audience as well as specific evidence (the exact figures). He took a familiar topic, pet overpopulation, and helped his audience take notice in new ways.

Use Credible Sources

Recall that in research, credibility relates to the potential bias of a source, whereas in reasoning, it relates to the trustworthiness of a source. When you want to persuade your audience, you must use evidence that comes from dependable sources.

There are two guidelines for using credible sources persuasively. First, provide enough information about your source so that your audience can assess its credibility.[6] This means that rather than saying "a lot of research supports this idea," you want to cite as much specific source information as you can: dates of publication, authors' credentials, organizational affiliations, and other significant information. Second, select sources your audience will see as trustworthy and fair. Although every source has a perspective, use sources your audience will see as relatively unbiased. For example, even though the Humane Society has a position on animal overpopulation, it also has a reputation for being credible and fair. To be persuasive, choose sources that are reliable and known for expertise in your subject. Avoid sources that may be seen as extreme or overly biased.

Your audience is more likely to consider your persuasive arguments when you strengthen your reasoning with specific evidence, novel information, and credible sources. However, you must go beyond using evidence effectively in a persuasive speech. You must also make appropriate use of ethos, or your credibility as a speaker.

Credibility and Persuasion

A speaker's **credibility** comes from the audience's perception of a speaker's competence and character. The most important aspect of credibility is that an audience attributes it to a speaker. No matter how talented, prepared, or polished you are as a speaker, if the audience does not see you as credible, you simply aren't credible.[7]

The two most important factors in credibility are the audience's perception of your competence and character. **Competence** is the audience's view of a speaker's intelligence, expertise, and knowledge of a subject, and **character** is the audience's view of a speaker's sincerity, trustworthiness, and concern for the well-being of the audience.[8] You express your competence through your research, your organization, and your delivery. Competence also comes from your personal talents and expertise, the experience and knowledge you bring to the speech before your research. You communicate your character by taking the time to understand who is in your audience and tailor your speech to meet their needs, using inclusive language and convincing logic to express your integrity, values, principles, and attitudes toward others. These actions let audience members know you care about them and can be trusted to give a speech that is thoughtful and worth listening to.

You can manage your credibility by understanding the three types of credibility and when they are established in a speech and by knowing how you can enhance your credibility.

Types of Credibility

Three types of credibility exist in any speech: initial, derived, and terminal. **Initial credibility** is the credibility a speaker has before giving a speech, **derived credibility** is the credibility a speaker develops during a speech, and **terminal credibility** is the credibility given to the speaker at the end of a speech. The following scenario illustrates how these three types of credibility develop.

You've been assigned to speak to a group of high school students and persuade them to volunteer in their community. When you arrive at the high school auditorium to speak, you've brought your initial credibility with you—what the students think about you before you even begin your speech. Their impression might be based on very little information (you're a college student) or on some specific information (their teachers told them who you are, why you're coming to speak, and what you'll be talking about).

You begin your speech. It's well researched and you've thought carefully about audience members and how your topic is relevant to them. You've developed a style of delivery that you think the students will appreciate. You've worked hard on your

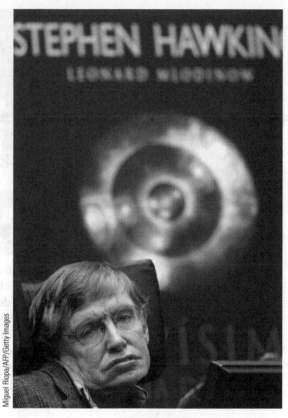

Miguel Riopa/AFP/Getty Images

Audiences consider sources that are well respected in their field to be credible. For example, British astrophysicist Stephen Hawking is almost universally seen as a trustworthy and credible source because his research is solid and validated by his peers and because he has the integrity to admit when he has made a mistake. What evidence from a well-respected source could you use to lend credibility to your next speech?

credibility: An audience's perception of a speaker's competence and character.

competence: An audience's view of a speaker's intelligence, expertise, and knowledge of a subject.

character: An audience's view of a speaker's sincerity, trustworthiness, and concern for his or her well-being.

initial credibility: The credibility a speaker has before giving a speech.

derived credibility: Credibility a speaker develops during a speech.

terminal credibility: Credibility given to a speaker at the end of a speech.

RosaIreneBetancourt 10/Alamy Stock Photo

Do you see this speaker as credible? Do you think his audience sees him as credible? What do you think this speaker can do to establish common ground with his audience?

introduction, knowing you need to catch their attention right away. You've also decided to share your own volunteer experiences with them. As you give your speech, you are establishing *derived credibility*—what you say and do throughout your speech to cause students to see you as competent and trustworthy.

You finish your speech and open up the floor for questions and discussion. At the end of your time with the students, you close your presentation and say good-bye. When the students leave their interaction with you, they've assigned what's called *terminal credibility;* they walk away with some conception of your level of knowledge, expertise, sincerity, and trustworthiness.

As you can see from this scenario, credibility evolves during a speech. You may start your speech with high initial credibility, but if you don't follow through on this by building your derived and terminal credibility throughout your speech, your overall credibility with your audience will drop. Or you may begin with low initial credibility because an audience does not know you but wind up with excellent overall credibility because you worked diligently to build your derived and terminal credibility during your speech. Because credibility is a process, you must work to enhance or maintain it throughout your speech.

Enhancing Your Credibility

If you begin a speech with little initial credibility because the audience does not know you, you need to build credibility during the speech. You can build your credibility in three ways: explain your competence as you begin your speech, establish common ground with your audience, and deliver your speech fluently with expression and conviction.

Establish your competence. Your introduction (Chapter 8) is an ideal place to establish your competence. Here you can reveal any credentials, training, or experiences that make you competent to speak on your topic. Or you can explain that although you may not be specifically trained, you have done extensive research on the topic. Throughout the speech, you can increase your credibility by citing sources, sharing your experiences, and offering insights based on your background and research. In her speech on teen suicide, Chelsey enhanced her credibility right away by citing statistics and credible sources. Throughout her speech, she used narratives and visual aids to increase her credibility. And at the end of her speech, she used personal testimony to great effect:

> I've been a member of the Yellow Ribbon Organization [a suicide prevention program] for three years now and a survivor for five years. I found this organization at the worst stage of my life when I had completely hit rock bottom. With their help, I recovered and now have made it one of my missions in life to speak out about youth suicide.

At first, Chelsey seemed to be just another speaker with the usual amount of initial credibility. But as she spoke, her research, evidence, and preparation increased her credibility quite effectively. Her startling personal testimony at the end of her speech enhanced her terminal credibility, bringing a personal note to the speech that moved audience members and kept them interested to the end.

Establish common ground. A second way to build your credibility is to establish common ground with your audience. To establish **common ground** is to identify similarities, shared interests, and mutual perspectives with an audience. You can establish

common ground: Similarities, shared interests, and mutual perspectives held by a speaker and his or her audience.

common ground by showing audience members that you share values, experiences, and group memberships with them.[9] You can do so by stating that you belong to similar organizations, appreciate the same activities, or hold certain values as important. You can also establish common ground when you explain your views and positions and why they are in harmony with those held by audience members. When you take time to establish a friendly bond (often called *rapport*) with audience members, they will begin to like, trust, and respect you. Audiences attach higher credibility to speakers they see as similar to themselves.

Deliver your speech effectively. A third way to enhance your credibility is through your delivery. Research indicates that speakers who are prepared, energetic, speak moderately fast, and appear comfortable in front of their audience are seen as credible.[10] If you practice your speech and work on your delivery (Chapter 10), your credibility should increase.

Remember that the audience assigns credibility to a speaker. Speakers with high credibility tend to be more persuasive than those with low credibility, so give this component of your speech careful consideration. You can also strengthen your persuasive message by making appropriate use of pathos, or appeals to emotion.

Emotion and Persuasion

Emotional appeals, or pathos, can be one of the most challenging aspects of persuasion. On the one hand, research suggests that speakers persuade only when they appeal to emotions because they encourage the audience to relate to an issue on an internal, personal level. On the other hand, because emotions are so personal and powerful, research also suggests that an inappropriate appeal to emotions can cause an audience to shut down in an instant.[11] Appeals to emotions can be complicated, so it's useful to understand what emotions are and which emotions people most commonly experience.

Emotions are "internal mental states" that focus primarily on feelings. Research distinguishes emotions (internal states such as fear, anger, sadness) from bodily states (tiredness, hunger), cognitive states (confusion, uncertainty), and behavioral states (timidity, aggressiveness).[12] Communication research has identified six primary emotions that tend to be expressed similarly across cultures and three secondary emotions that are expressed differently depending on age, gender, and culture.[13] The following are primary emotions:

- *Fear:* an unpleasant feeling of apprehension or distress; the anticipation of danger or threat
- *Anger:* a feeling of annoyance, irritation, or rage
- *Surprise:* a feeling of sudden wonder or amazement, especially because of something unexpected
- *Sadness:* a feeling of unhappiness, grief, or sorrow
- *Disgust:* a feeling of horrified or sickened distaste for something
- *Happiness:* a feeling of pleasure, contentment, or joy

The following are secondary emotions:

- *Pride:* an appropriate level of respect for a person, character trait, accomplishment, experience, or value; feeling pleased or delighted
- *Guilt:* an awareness of having done wrong, accompanied by feelings of shame and regret
- *Shame:* a feeling of dishonor, unworthiness, and embarrassment

The following is another emotion common to persuasive speeches but not identified among the primary or secondary emotions:

- *Reverence:* a feeling of deep respect, awe, or devotion

In persuasive speaking, you make appeals to emotions to accomplish the following goals:

- *Gain attention and motivate listening.* You often catch an audience's attention and motivate members to listen by appealing to their emotions with a compelling short story, testimony, or examples.
- *Reinforce points.* You can use emotional appeals to reinforce main points or subpoints. For example, when you support a point with a statistic and then reinforce the statistic with an example of how some aspect of the statistic has affected a specific person, an audience can understand your point on a more personal level.
- *Express personal commitment.* When you care deeply about an issue and want your audiences to recognize this depth of commitment, you may appeal to emotions by shifting your delivery to a more passionate or intense tone, or you may personalize your claims and arguments.
- *Call to action or conclude memorably.* You can often move audience members to action by asking them to envision the result of that action and how it could affect them personally. You might end your speech with a compelling story or quote and so conclude memorably.

Because emotional appeals engage an audience personally, you'll want to consider a few aspects of emotional appeals to use them effectively: audience centeredness, vivid language, and a balance of emotion and reason.

Stay Audience Centered

Perhaps the most important component of a persuasive emotional appeal is how appropriate that appeal is for the audience. Consider your audience very carefully before you decide what kinds of appeals to use. For example, almost every one of our master statuses (Chapter 4) affects how we respond to the emotional side of an issue; our age, gender, physical ability, religion, ethnicity, and culture greatly influence how we see an issue and thus the acceptability of an emotional appeal. As you consider the emotional appeals you want to make to your audience, ask yourself the following questions:

- What kinds of experiences will audience members have had with your topic?
- What emotions might be associated with those experiences? If they haven't had direct experiences, why not?
- In what ways might you be able to draw them into your topic emotionally without offending anyone?

Although no speaker can predict with total accuracy how an audience will respond to an emotional appeal, you can consider your audience carefully and select those appeals to emotions that seem most appropriate. When speakers misjudge the appropriateness of an appeal to an emotion, they generally make one of three errors.

Overly graphic and violent appeals. An overly graphic visual or verbal appeal is one that describes wounds and injuries, deaths, attacks, or harm to another being in extensive detail. The speaker generally is hoping to impress the audience with the horror of an act but carries the description too far and causes audience members to shut down or feel overwhelming revulsion.

Overly frightening or threatening appeals. When a speaker describes something so frightening or threatening that people in the audience feel helpless or panicked, they will stop listening or they will feel immobilized. These kinds of appeals tend to stay with audience members long after a speech is over and cause them to feel unnecessarily fearful. In contrast, an appropriate fear appeal is one that moves audience members to act but does not immobilize or terrorize them. A common overly frightening appeal is one in which a speaker argues that if members of the audience don't prevent something from happening or stop some behavior, they or someone they care about will die.

Overly manipulative appeals. An appeal to an emotion, either positive or negative, that relies on theatrics, melodrama, and sensation rather than on fact and research is overly manipulative. Such appeals encourage the audience to feel pity, shame, guilt, or humiliation about something or to become overly excited or enthusiastic. Speakers may make overly manipulative appeals when they want their audience to see a person in a certain way, donate time or money to a cause, or act in a particular way.

By staying audience centered, you can make appropriate appeals to emotions. If you keep the people in your audience in the front of your mind, you will recognize which appeals are appropriate for them and which ones aren't.

Use Vivid Language

Appeals to emotions ask listeners to recall some of their most profound experiences. You can use vivid descriptions and examples to help your audience connect with those experiences. One reason that Martin Luther King Jr. is considered one of the most influential speakers of the twentieth century is the vivid language he used to create images for his audiences. In his "I Have a Dream" speech on the steps of the Lincoln Memorial, his language helped his audience "see" his vision and connect to it emotionally as well as rationally. When he spoke of freedom, he described the "chains of discrimination" and the "manacles of segregation" that "crippled." He used evocative words and phrases, such as "languishing" and "exile," the "magnificent words of the Constitution," and a "promise to all" for the "riches of freedom."[14]

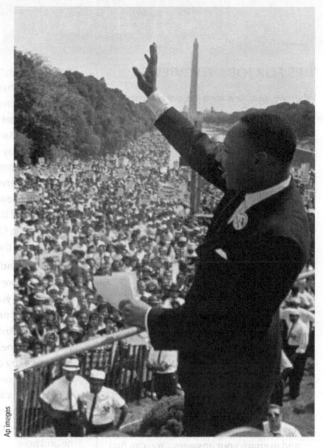

Ap images

Martin Luther King Jr. is particularly well known for his powerful use of language to inspire and motivate his audiences. Consider your next persuasive speech. What are some images you can use to help your audience see what you're talking about and make an emotional connection to your topic?

The world's most profound speakers have been trained to make the most of vivid language, but even novice speakers can use language to move and inspire. In a speech on American veterans that was both persuasive and commemorative, Darrin created the following emotional appeal through his vivid language:

> Imagine sitting down to a peaceful meal with your wife, husband, or children. A "ring," "ring," "ring" is heard, interrupting you like an unwanted guest. The distinct sound of this ring suspends all talk. It's like this illusionary figure drifts across the room, touching the souls of those dear to you. Even before you pick it up, you know your country has gone to war, and this is your call to duty.

Vivid language helps your listeners create images that are rich with feeling. When you speak persuasively, try to find words and phrases that tap into your audience's memories. If you do so, you will have an easier time drawing your audience in emotionally to your claims and arguments.

Balance Emotion and Reason

When you speak persuasively, seek a balance between reason and emotion. Overly emotional speeches may stimulate audience members, but without sound reasoning, they are less likely to be persuaded by your arguments. Use appeals to emotion to elaborate on your reasons or to show the more personal side of your evidence. If you make a claim with statistics or offer an example of the impact of a plan, support it by drawing out the emotional aspects. Similarly, if you make an appeal to emotions, back it up with sound reasoning. When you balance emotion and reason, your audience will see more than one dimension of your persuasive appeals and can be persuaded on more than one level.

Appeals to emotion are necessary parts of persuasive speeches. If you can avoid overly graphic, frightening, or manipulative appeals, you can tap into powerful emotions. By staying audience centered, paying careful attention to your language, and

TIPS FOR JOB INTERVIEWS

When we interview for a job, we are using our persuasive speaking skills to a very specific end: securing a job offer. According to Randall Hanson, of Quint Careers, professional and polished résumés, applications, and cover letters are a must, but your speaking skills are what will secure the position once you get that interview. Hanson offers several tips for job seekers once the interview is scheduled, all of them involving strong communication, and even persuasive speaking, skills:

1. **Research your prospective employer.** Take time before the interview to find out as much as you can about the company or organization, the people who work there, and the requirements of the job. The research skills you learned in Chapter 5 will help you answer the questions you are asked during the actual interview.

2. **Review common interview questions and prepare your answers.** You can find examples of the most common interview questions asked specific to the job you are applying for online. Because you want "concise responses, focus[ed] on specific examples and concise responses," you can practice your answers beforehand so that you sound prepared and professional. The skills you learned in Chapters 6 (Developing and Supporting Your Ideas) and 10 (Delivering Your Speech) will help you here.

3. **Dress and sit for success.** Select your interview clothes with an eye toward fitting in to the organizational culture and style of dress. Avoid excessive accessories, attend to personal hygiene,

and remember, "it's always better to be overdressed than under." Monitor your posture, gestures, facial expressions, and other nonverbal cues. If you slouch, fidget, avoid eye contact, or play with a pen or hair, you may send the message that you are uninterested, unprofessional, or excessively nervous and even unprepared for the interview and the job. Chapter 10 (Delivery) and the material on managing your nerves in Chapter 1 will help you with this aspect of the interview.

4. **Be on time and prepared.** Arrive fifteen minutes before the scheduled interview. This will give you time to fill out paperwork, if necessary, and to observe the office culture and dynamics. Turn off your cell phone. Before the interview, print out extra copies of your résumé and your references to leave or to share with individuals who may not have them. The discussions throughout this book on staying audience centered will be very helpful here.

5. **Be authentic and ethical.** Respond truthfully to questions, stay focused and offer concise examples of your skills and talents, and never talk negatively about your previous employers or coworkers. Showcase your true skills and talents and how they match the job description rather than trying to make yourself look good by putting others down. Chapter 4 (Listening) and Chapter 6 (Developing and Supporting Your Ideas) will give you excellent strategies for responding to interview questions.

6. **Ask appropriate questions.** If you've prepared for the interview and done your research, you should have a number

of questions that you want to ask the prospective employer. These may relate to job expectations ("What is the most important trait or skill necessary for this position?"), the importance of teamwork ("How often do your teams meet?"), the need to work independently ("When employees are working independently on a project, how often do they check in with their supervisor?"), and the culture of the organization ("Can you describe what a typical day or week might look like?"). Your questions indicate that you are interested in the position and are thinking professionally. Chapter 4 (Your Audience and Speaking Environment) and the information on interviewing in Chapter 5 will help you develop appropriate questions.

7. **Say thank you.** Before you leave, thank the prospective employer for the interview, ask about next steps and timelines ("Do you know what your next steps will be?" or "Do you know when will a decision be made?"), close by stating that you look forward to hearing from them again or in the near future. Shortly after the interview (no more that twenty-four hours later), write thank you emails to each of the individuals involved in the interview process, thanking them for their time and reiterating your interest in the job. Keep these short and professional—even if you felt comfortable and established a good rapport in the interview, avoid getting too casual at this early stage. Chapter 4 (Your Audience and Speaking Environment) and Chapter 9 (Language) will assist you in saying "thank you" professionally and appropriately.[15]

---

balancing reason and emotion, you will be able to craft persuasive arguments that encourage your audience to think differently about issues.

Tips for Giving Effective Persuasive Speeches

Most people are deeply committed to certain things in life, such as their spiritual or political beliefs. Or because of deeply held convictions, they feel a strong sense of right and wrong about certain issues. It's natural to want others to share our commitments and beliefs, and most of us can think of many times we wanted to convince others to think, feel, and act as we do.

To help you give persuasive speeches, remember the following tips to increase your chances for successful persuasion: (1) be realistic about changing your audience's views, and (2) use your evidence fairly and strategically for the best results.

Be Realistic about Changing Your Audience's Views

Researchers generally agree that for persuasion to succeed, an audience must be open to change. If an audience is not open to change, even your best persuasive efforts are likely to fail. This means you must consider your audience's perspectives carefully and frame your persuasive attempts around issues that your audience will be open to considering. Think carefully about the position audience members hold and choose a realistic argument before you attempt to change their views. It is often tempting to ask them to change their views completely, especially if you don't agree with those views. However, successful persuasion involves advocating a position, or some *aspect* of a position, that your audience can be open about. For example, it may be unrealistic to think you can change your audience's views on legalizing certain drugs if audience members have had bad experiences with drugs or people who use drugs. But you may be able to persuade them to see the benefits that some of these drugs offer in medical treatments—that is, you may be able to persuade them to reconsider some part of their position rather than undertake a radical change.[16] Rather than asking for radical changes, approach your speech goals and your audience with some restraint.

Use Evidence Fairly and Strategically

Research on evidence and persuasion suggests that besides carefully researching, organizing, and delivering your speech, you can use some strategies to help construct effective persuasive arguments. These strategies involve two-sided messages, counterarguments, and fear appeals.

Because persuasive speakers advocate one position over others, they often frame an issue as two-sided, even if there are multiple perspectives on the issue (Chapter 13). A **two-sided message** addresses two sides of an issue, refuting one side to prove the other is better. Research suggests that when speakers discuss two sides of an issue, they are more persuasive if they actively refute the side they oppose rather than simply describe it without providing evidence for why the audience should share the speaker's views on it.[17]

Similarly, addressing **counterarguments**, arguments against the speaker's own position, enhances a speaker's credibility. For example, when Tony advocated a policy of controlled burns to prevent forest fires, he increased his believability when he also discussed the argument that controlled burns can get out of control and cause major damage. By acknowledging this counterargument, Tony illustrated why the concerns it raises are unfounded, strengthening his position that controlled burns prevent other fires from burning out of control.

Note, however, that you must use two-sided messages and counterarguments with care. In persuasion, credibility is important, and you must take care that your opposing comments are not too judgmental or inflammatory. If you unfairly attack someone else's view or refute an opposing position too harshly, audiences may perceive you as less likable—and audiences find unlikable speakers less persuasive. In addition, audience members will focus their attention on assessing the merit of your judgmental claim rather than attending to the rest of your message.[18]

Speakers can also use fear appeals to persuade audiences to change or take action. A **fear appeal** is the threat of something undesirable happening if change does not occur. In political ads, politicians frequently employ fear appeals as a way to motivate voters. Research suggests that fear appeals may motivate audiences who are not initially invested in your topic to *become* invested.[19] A fear appeal

two-sided message: Persuasive strategy that addresses both sides of an issue, refuting one side to prove the other is better.

counterarguments: Arguments against the speaker's own position.

fear appeal: Threat of something undesirable happening if change does not occur.

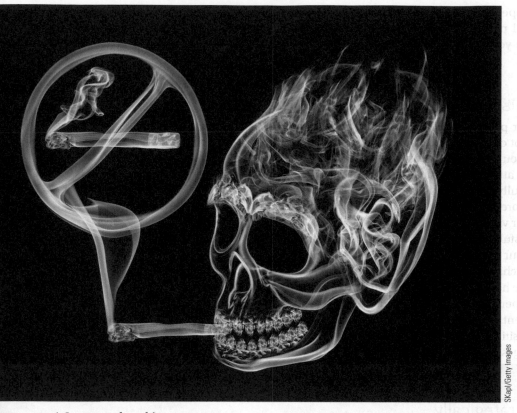

causes audience members to take notice of an issue and see how it relates to them personally. When audiences already feel connected to the topic, fear appeals simply reinforce that connection. However, if a fear appeal is so extreme that audience members feel immobilized, imagining that there is nothing they can do to solve the problem, they may simply avoid or deny the problem.[20] Thus, if you use fear appeals, temper them so your audience feels there is a solution to the problem that will actually work. For example, if your speech is about the risk of violent crime in your community, speak honestly about it but do not exaggerate it. Then offer practical steps that audience members can take to reduce their risk so they feel hopeful and empowered rather than defeated.

SKapl/Getty Images

Images such as this one are often displayed on billboards in Australia, Portugal, and Spain in an attempt to persuade people to stop smoking, or to never begin. Do you think this fear appeal might have persuasive power? Why or why not?

Ethical Persuasive Speaking

Have you ever noticed that sometimes when you try to change someone, that person regularly resists your attempts?[21] Can you recall when your parents tried to persuade you to do (or not do) something, like dress a certain way, date a certain kind of person, or attend a certain function? For many people, as soon as the persuasion began, so did the resistance. Why did this happen when our parents likely had our best interests at heart?

Research and personal experience tell us that when others try to persuade us, we can feel that our freedom to choose our own path is threatened. In addition, the issues we try to persuade others about are often complicated, making the process of persuasion even more challenging. Questions of fact, value, and policy are rarely simple or clear-cut. When beliefs, preferences, experiences, and habits come into play, these questions can get clouded and emotional, and people often become invested in particular outcomes.

Given these characteristics of persuasion, be sure you request change ethically. To persuade ethically is to persuade others without threatening or challenging their sense of freedom to choose what is best for them. Ethical persuasion also requires you to recognize the complexity of the issues you speak about and the possible impact of your proposed solutions on your audience. As you prepare your persuasive speech, keep the following four questions in mind. The first three address the complexity of audiences and issues, and the fourth helps you consider the effect of the changes you request:

1. What is my position on this topic, and why do I hold this position?
2. What positions do my audience members hold on this topic—and why?
3. Why am I qualified to try to persuade my audience on this issue?
4. Is my request reasonable for audience members, and how will they be affected by the change?

As an ethical persuasive speaker, you must understand your own position and the positions of your audience. Acknowledge your own master statuses, standpoints, and unique experiences as well as those of each member of your audience.

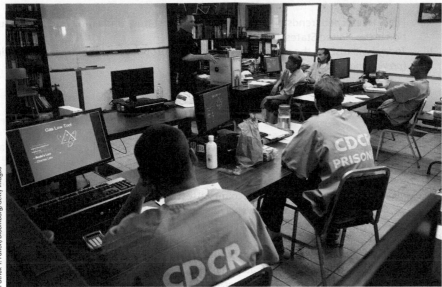

Patrick T. Fallon/Bloomberg/Getty Images

Be realistic about what you can or cannot persuade an audience to think, feel, or do. For very personal or controversial issues, focus on some aspect of the issue that an audience could reasonably consider. For example, some audience members may have been victims of crime and may not be receptive to the notion of "prisoners' rights." In this case, you might focus on aspects of prison reform, such as education, that keep prisoners occupied in a constructive way while they're serving their sentences. How can you frame the topic of your next persuasive speech to be realistic about asking your audience to change?

Similarly, you must tell the truth, avoid distorting or manipulating evidence, and present information accurately and completely. To ensure that you present your evidence ethically, review the research tips in Chapter 5. Remember, audiences dislike being manipulated and misled. Even if a speaker gains support through the unethical manipulation of evidence or ideas, that support is usually lost when the audience discovers the deceit. Gaining support through ethical means will only increase your credibility.

PREPARATION OUTLINE WITH COMMENTARY

No Child Left Behind: Addressing the School Dropout Rate among Latinos

by Dana Barker

Specific purpose: To persuade my audience that our nation must address the high dropout rate among Latinos.

Thesis statement: The dropout rate among Latinos in high schools and colleges, caused by low economic status and lack of family support, is too high, and this problem must be addressed with increased funding and teacher training.

MindTap Are you ready to practice your powers of persuasion by giving an effective persuasive speech? Use the following speech as a model. Watch a video clip of this speech and see Dana's transcript and speaking outline. Dana gave this speech in an introductory public speaking class. The assignment was to give a four- to six-minute speech with a minimum of four sources cited. Students were also asked to create a preparation outline that included a Works Cited (MLA) or References (APA) section. (You can access videos of other persuasive speeches, including "The U.S. and the World Peace Crisis" by Renee DeSalvo.)

Introduction

I. I'll begin with a story from the *Santa Fe New Mexican* about Mabel Arellanes. (*catch attention*)
   A. After becoming pregnant and dropping out of school at sixteen, Mabel has reenrolled in high school and is the junior class president.
   B. Her change in attitude has led her to the hope of becoming a lawyer.
   C. But Mabel's story is not representative of the current trends among Latinos.

COMMENTARY

Dana begins her speech by sharing an inspiring story about Mabel, a young Latina high school dropout.

With this story, she reveals the topic and problem of her speech: Latino dropout rates. She then establishes her credibility by explaining that she has conducted extensive research on her topic. She completes her introduction by previewing the main points of her speech.

I have researched trends in Latino socioeconomic status, graduation rate, and population in the United States. (*establish credibility*)

III. Today I will discuss the problem of a high Latino dropout rate and suggest a solution. (*preview main points*)

Transition: Let me begin by discussing the problem.

Body

I. The dropout rate among Latinos in secondary schools and colleges is too high and must be addressed.

A. The dropout rate is excessive.

1. Statistics and firsthand accounts attest to the high dropout rate.

a. According to the *News & Observer*, one in twelve Latino students dropped out of high school in North Carolina during the 2003–2004 school year.

b. This statistic does not account for the 47.5 percent of Latino students who have not graduated in four years since the beginning of the 1999–2000 academic year.

c. Gamaliel Fuentes, who dropped out of school at fifteen, said, "We have no money; that's why I dropped out of school. [My father] asked me, but I decided. Now, if I could go back in time, I would stay still in school."

2. The tendency for Latinos to drop out is triggered by low socioeconomic status and a lack of family support.

a. The *Hispanic Outlook in Higher Education* explains that students coming from families of lower socioeconomic status are less likely to succeed in college because high schools do not prepare them well.

b. Latino families expect their young people to contribute economically, and work schedules often conflict with studies.

Transition: Next, I will discuss the importance of addressing the Latino dropout rate.

B. Addressing the dropout rate will keep Latinos from remaining at a generally low economic status.

1. Income is heavily dependent on education level.

a. According to the *Daily Evergreen* newspaper, a person with a bachelor's degree can earn almost one million dollars more over the course of their lifetime than someone with no college education.

b. A census report in the San *Antonio Express-News* found that Latinos earned merely 6.2 percent of the bachelor's degrees awarded in 2001.

c. Yet, the U.S. Census Bureau found that Latinos made up 12 percent of the national population in 2000 and 13.3 percent in 2002.

d. In her essay "Canto, Locura, y Poesia," Olivia Castellano of California State University, Sacramento, writes, "They [Latinos] carry a deeply ingrained sense of inferiority, a firm conviction that they are not worthy of success."

2. Ultimately, all who hold the belief that our country is the "land of opportunity" are affected by the Latino dropout rate.

a. The U.S. Census Bureau states that in 2001 two out of ten Hispanics lived below the poverty line, while only one out of four earned a yearly salary of $35,000 or more.

b. Comparatively, around 50 percent of non-Hispanic whites earned $35,000 or more that year.

c. These figures are far from exemplifying opportunity for Latinos.

Transition: But what will happen if the problem is not solved?

C. Since the percentage of Latinos in our population is still climbing, ignoring this issue will lead to a greater gap between the life of the typical American and the life of the Latino American.

Dana begins the body of her speech by clearly stating her argument: the dropout rate for Latinos in secondary schools must be addressed.

She supports her proposition by citing recent statistics about the North Carolina school system. Additionally, she uses peer testimony to explain why Latino students are dropping out of high school and to establish pathos.

To support her point that dropout rates contribute to the generally low economic status of U.S. Latinos, Dana provides a source that describes the discrepancy of income levels between high school dropouts and university graduates. She also provides statistics to highlight the low number of Latinos graduating from college.

Next, Dana uses expert testimony to explain why such low graduation rates exist for the Latino population.

Dana also provides statistics from a highly credible source to illustrate the typical disparity between the income level of Hispanics and non-Hispanic whites.

Dana's transition between her points I.B and I.C tells her audience that she is about to explain the consequences of not addressing the problem of Latino dropout rates.

Before moving to her solution, Dana draws audience members in personally by asking them to consider the urgency of the problem. Then Dana presents her solution, explaining that teacher training and educational success programs will help Latinos succeed in school and will help change the Latino mind-set about education.

Transition: As I proceed to discuss the solutions for this problem, are you beginning to sense the urgency of this situation?

II. To solve the problem of a high dropout rate, we must fund teacher sensitivity training and programs that help Latinos succeed in education, and Latinos must change their perspective on the importance of education and their ability to succeed.

    A. Programs that educate teachers about Latino culture and beliefs and that help Latino students succeed in education will have the most impact on the dropout rate.

        1. Properly educated teachers will become aware of how they are able to meet the needs of Latino students.

        2. The *Santa Fe New Mexican* reported on the success of a program called AVID, which boasts a 95 percent college entrance rate among its Latino students.

Transition: What can we expect from this solution?

    B. This solution, which can be implemented at the national, state, and local levels, is dependent on increased funding and the efforts of educators with experience in Latino culture.

        1. Increased funding will help reform educational budgets for Latino communities and fund college success programs like AVID.

        2. This solution also requires the collective efforts of highly knowledgeable professionals with experience in education and Latino culture who can train other educators.

    C. Given proper attention and execution, the plan to address the Latino dropout rate will help the dropout rate begin to fall and will instill pride in the Latino community.

        1. Although it will take at least a decade before results are fully apparent, perhaps even a generation, ideally the plan will result in an increase in Latinos earning bachelor's, master's, and doctoral degrees.

        2. The sense of accomplishment gained by furthering education will change the typical Latino mind-set regarding education and instill an overall sense of pride in the U.S. Latino community.

Conclusion

I. I have discussed the problem of high dropout rate among Latinos, and I have discussed a possible solution for addressing the issue. (*summarize main points*)

II. Hopefully, you can clearly see that the high Latino dropout rate is an issue of great concern, one that requires prompt and thorough attention. (*reinforce thesis*)

Works Cited

Castellano, Olivia. "Canto, Locura, y Poesia." *Race, Class, and Gender: An Anthology,* compiled by Margaret L. Andersen, and edited by Patricia Hill Collins, Wadsworth, 1997.

Ferry, Barbara. "High School Program Gives Students a Fighting Chance." *Santa Fe New Mexican,* 15 Feb. 2005, p. B1.

Hannah-Jones, Nikole. "School an Elusive Dream: For Latino Students, Desire for Diploma Often Clashes with Needs of Families." *News & Observer,* 18 Feb. 2005, p. A1.

McGlynn, Angela Provitera. "Improving Completion Rates for Hispanic Students: 'Best Practices' for Community Colleges." *Hispanic Outlook in Higher Education,* vol. 14, no. 4, 2003, pp. 21–25.

Ramirez, Roberto R., and G. Patricia de la Cruz. *The Hispanic Population in the United States: March 2002.* United States, Department of Commerce, Economics and Statistics Administration, Census Bureau, June 2003, www.census.gov/prod/2003pubs/p20-545.pdf. Accessed 14 Mar. 2005.

Silva, Elda. "Latino Grad Rate Still Lags across U.S.: Finances Often Hinder Earning a Four-Year Degree." *San Antonio Express-News,* 6 June 2004, p. 1K.

Turner, Drew. "Four Year Degree Worth the Wait." *The Daily Evergreen,* 10 Jan. 2005, www.dailyevergreen.com/.

She uses an example of a successful program, AVID, to support her claim. Note how with this example Dana uses analogical reasoning (Chapter 14) to convince her audience that her solution will be successful, suggesting that the success of this program could be repeated with similar programs. Additionally, in point II.B, she succinctly states how her solution could be implemented.

Dana explains the potential results of implementing her plan. She informs her audience that the results will take time, but the plan could produce a newfound sense of accomplishment and pride among the U.S. Latino community.

Dana completes her speech with a brief conclusion that summarizes her main points and reinforces her thesis.

Dana's bibliography of the specific research she references in her speech shows the currency of her sources. (She created the speech in 2008.) She relies on a variety of sources, including books, newspapers, and the Internet, and she uses the MLA style of citation.

Chapter Summary

When you speak persuasively, you often address questions that are complex and not easily resolved.

- Your goal with a persuasive speech is to alter or influence an audience's thoughts, feelings, or actions about issues that are not easily resolved.

Persuasive speeches generally fall into three categories.

- Questions of fact address the verifiable truth of an issue.
- Questions of value refer to the appropriateness of an action or belief.
- Questions of policy focus on the best solution to a problem.

There are several organizational patterns you can use for persuasive speeches.

- Persuasive speeches on questions of fact and value can be organized with chronological, spatial, and topical patterns.
- Persuasive speeches on questions of policy can be organized with the problem–solution, problem–cause–solution, causal, narrative, comparative advantages, and Monroe's motivated sequence patterns.
- All of these organizational patterns provide different ways to present information about a problem and proposed solutions.
- Which pattern you select depends on your audience and your speech goals.

For policy speeches, you can request immediate action or passive agreement.

- When you seek to gain immediate action, you attempt to encourage members of an audience to engage in a specific behavior or take a specific action.

- When you seek to gain passive agreement, you try to persuade audience members to adopt a new position without asking them to act in support of that position.

Three important tips will help you give an effective persuasive speech.

- Use persuasion realistically. Don't ask for radical changes if members of an audience aren't likely to support your proposals. Adapt your request for change to your audience's ability to change.
- Use evidence fairly and strategically to strengthen your arguments and increase your chances for audience support. Address complex issues with two-sided messages and counterarguments so you can refute opposing positions and appear more credible to your audience.
- Similarly, use fear appeals to motivate your audience to change, but don't overuse this strategy to the point of immobilizing your audience with fear.
- Use language that will motivate audience members to change but will not threaten or insult them.

Do your best to give ethical persuasive speeches.

- Request change without threatening or manipulating your audience.
- Make an effort to understand audience members' positions on an issue as well as you understand it.
- Present information that is honest, accurate, and fair.

Invitation to Public Speaking Online MindTap®

Now that you have read Chapter 15, use your MindTap Communication for *Invitation to Public Speaking* for quick access to the digital resources that accompany this text. These resources include

- **Study tools** that will help you assess your learning and prepare for exams (digital glossary, key term flash cards, review quizzes).
- **Activities and assignments** that will help you hone your knowledge and build your public speaking skills throughout

the course, as well as help you explore public speaking concepts online (web links), give you step-by-step guidance through the research, outline and note card preparation process (Outline Builder), watch and critique videos of sample speeches (Interactive Video Activities), and allow you to practice and present your presentation online using a speech video delivery, recording, and grading system (YouSeeU).

Key Concepts MindTap® Test your knowledge with online printable flash cards.

call to action (294)
causal organization (296)
character (301)
common ground (302)
competence (301)
comparative advantages organization (297)
counterarguments (307)

credibility (301)
derived credibility (301)
elaboration likelihood model (ELM) (299)
fear appeal (307)
gain immediate action (294)
gain passive agreement (294)
initial credibility (301)

Review Questions

1. With other members of your class, develop an imaginary speech to persuade lawmakers to lower the voting age to sixteen. As you develop this speech, consider the implications of the requested change for as many constituencies as possible: sixteen-year-olds, parents, lawmakers, voter-registration workers, voting sites, mail ballots, candidates, teachers, the structure of education, and the like. What are the implications of this persuasive request?

2. You have just been informed you have only five minutes of the legislator's time to present your persuasive appeal developed in question 1. How will you revise your speech to account for this time frame? How will you determine what information to keep in and what to leave out?

3. Consider the speeches you have heard that changed your mind or actions regarding an issue. How were you persuaded to change? Can you incorporate any techniques from these speeches into your own persuasive speeches?

4. Your topic is public transportation. Develop a specific purpose statement, thesis statement, and main points for the following three types of persuasive speeches: a question of fact, a question of value, and a question of policy. Use the discussion of organizational patterns in this chapter to help organize your speech.

5. Write an outline for a persuasive speech on the subject of physical education in schools. Organize this speech according to Monroe's motivated sequence. Pay careful attention to each of the steps in this organizational pattern. What are the advantages of this pattern over, say, a comparative advantages pattern or a problem–solution pattern? What are the disadvantages?

6. Search for "graphic Australian anti-smoking ad" on YouTube. Are the fear appeals used in this antismoking campaign legitimate? Do they motivate an audience to action, or are they so strong that they immobilize an audience? Why?

16 | Speaking on Special Occasions

Speeches of Introduction

Speeches of Commemoration

Speeches of Acceptance

Speeches to Entertain

IN THIS CHAPTER YOU WILL LEARN TO:

- Create any of the four types of special occasion speeches

- Make use of at least four tips for giving effective special occasion speeches

People give special occasion speeches when they come together to celebrate, reflect, remember, or establish a common purpose or goal. We give these speeches when we want to acknowledge someone's accomplishments or celebrate events or transitions. We also give them when we come together after difficult events. Special occasion speeches are given at weddings, awards ceremonies, banquets, and funerals. These speeches often bring an audience together and remind people of what they have in common. They also mark certain occasions as special, as uniquely apart from the familiar events of our lives.

MindTap® Start with a quick warm-up activity and review the chapter's learning objectives.

▲ When we speak at special occasions, such as this *quinceañera* celebration of a young woman's fifteenth birthday, we share why an occasion is important, bring our audience together as a community, and even identify common values. In this chapter you will find strategies for marking moments as important, valuable, and unique in special occasion speeches.

This chapter introduces you to four types of special occasion speeches: speeches of introduction, speeches of commemoration, speeches of acceptance, and speeches to entertain. Each speech recognizes a different kind of special occasion. Therefore, each has a slightly different goal. You will learn about these different goals as well as specific guidelines to help you prepare and deliver effective special occasion speeches.

MindTap®

Read, highlight, and take notes online.

Speeches of Introduction

When you give an **introductory speech**, you provide an audience with a unique perspective on the person you are introducing. Introductory speeches are given for two reasons: to introduce yourself, such as at a job interview or in a newly formed group, or to introduce someone else, usually at a formal event before that person gives a speech. Regardless of whom you're introducing, introductory speeches tend to be brief and tightly organized. The principle of "less is more" applies because the audience is often more interested in what follows the introduction than in the introduction itself.[1] Listeners want you to be brief and to give them specific, interesting, and useful information. Introductory speeches are organized around three goals:

1. Acquaint the audience with a person.
2. Establish the credibility of the person.
3. Generate enthusiasm for the person.

To accomplish these goals, do the following in your speeches of introduction:

Introducing Yourself

- State your name and any of your credentials or titles.
- Identify any qualifications, experiences, or expertise you possess that relates directly to why you're giving your speech. ("I've worked in the insurance business for four years as a . . . during which I learned . . . ")
- State your pleasure at being invited to speak or for the opportunity to participate in the task at hand.

Introducing Another Person

- State your own name and credentials. ("Hello, I'm Mary Brown, director of the Office of Volunteer Programs.")
- Indicate that you will introduce the other person. (For example, "It is my privilege tonight to introduce our speaker, Dr. Robert Gonzales.")
- Provide accurate, relevant details about the person, including credentials, accomplishments, activities, personality traits, personal stories, or even a quote from something the person has said. ("Dr. Gonzales holds a Ph.D. from Harvard University and currently is working as a consultant for . . . He also has experience in . . . He has received numerous awards, some of which include . . . He describes his life as . . . ")
- Identify the topic of the person's speech by describing the general topic or simply by giving the title of the presentation. ("The title of Dr. Gonzales's presentation this evening is . . . He plans to share with us some highlights of his most recent research in . . . ")
- Provide closure to your remarks and welcome the person to the podium or the front of the room. ("Please join me in welcoming Dr. Robert Gonzales.")

When you introduce yourself or another person, your goal is to create a sense of respect, an eagerness to hear more, and an understanding of what to expect. To give an effective speech of introduction, consider the following guidelines.

MindTap®

To see these tips applied in an introductory speech, watch the speech given by Wolf Blitzer at the HeForShe Campaign 2014.

introductory speech: Speech that provides an audience with a unique perspective on the person introduced.

Be Brief

When you introduce yourself, be brief and concise. It can be tempting to share a lot of details about yourself, recount past experiences, and tell personal stories, but doing so can take a lot of time. A successful introductory speech rarely lasts more than three to four minutes. If you do opt to share a past experience or personal story, make sure you can tell it within a minute or two and that it clearly relates to the subject of the introduction.

When you introduce another person, remember you are giving an introduction, not a full-length speech. Avoid lengthy stories and drawn-out explanations. Try instead to share enough information so audience members are eager to hear from the speaker but not so much information that they feel overwhelmed.

Be Accurate

Introductory speeches can require considerable background information on the person being introduced. If you are introducing yourself, you already have the information you need. If you're introducing someone else, there is a good chance you will need to do some research on the person unless you are already well informed about him or her. If you must conduct research on a person, you have a number of options. You can do your research on the Internet or at the library, interview the person you are introducing, or obtain a copy of his or her résumé or biography to get the information you need. Being accurate in your speech means that you state all dates, titles, and awards the person has received correctly and cite the original source of all quotes and personal stories. Being accurate also means you pronounce all information correctly, right down to the speaker's name. If you take time to get your details correct, not only do you show respect for the person you introduced, but also you enhance your own credibility.

Be Appropriate

Use your skills at analyzing an audience to present a speech that is appropriate to the occasion. Remember, your goal is to enhance your own or another person's credibility and build enthusiasm for what's to come. If your remarks are too personal, irrelevant to the occasion, or too informal, you will not only affect your own image but also damage the credibility of the person you are introducing. Share only information that fits the occasion.

Ask for permission before you share anything personal about the person you are introducing. What may seem like trivial details or interesting anecdotes to you may embarrass or disturb the person you are introducing. If the person asks you not to share that information, don't do so, even if it's one of your favorite stories.

Speeches of Commemoration

Commemorative speeches praise, honor, recognize, or pay tribute to a person, an event, an idea, or an institution. The two most common types are speeches of tribute and speeches of award. A **speech of tribute** is given to honor someone. A **speech of award** is given to present a specific award and describe why that person is receiving the award. Both highlight a person's exceptional value, qualities, contributions, or accomplishments. Commemorative speeches are usually given in formal settings, such as banquets, receptions, retirement parties, special birthdays,

Peter Steiner/Alamy Stock Photo

When introducing another speaker, acquaint your audience members with this person and generate their enthusiasm for hearing his or her speech. If you could introduce anyone for any type of speaking occasion, whom do you think you'd like to introduce? What could you say in your speech to help your audience get excited about hearing what this person has to say?

commemorative speech: Speech that praises, honors, recognizes, or pays tribute to a person, an event, an idea, or an institution.

speech of tribute: Speech given to honor someone.

speech of award: Speech given to present a specific award to someone and describe why that person is receiving the award.

memorial services, and rallies. Speeches of commemoration are organized around two goals:

1. Help an audience appreciate the importance of a person, an event, an idea, or an institution.
2. Illustrate for an audience a person's unique achievements or the special impact of an event, idea, or institution.

To accomplish these goals, a speech of commemoration should do the following:

- Identify who or what you are commemorating. Name the person, event, idea, or institution being celebrated.
- Identify and describe the qualities or activities that make this person, event, idea, or institution special. Clearly state the unique characteristics or actions being commemorated.
- Identify and describe the contributions made by the person, event, idea, or institution.
- Identify and describe any obstacles the person, event, idea, or institution had to overcome to be successful.
- Identify and describe your relationship to the person, event, idea, or institution being commemorated.

Marmaduke St. John/Alamy Stock Photo

A speech of tribute is a common type of commemorative speech used to honor a particular person or a group, such as fallen soldiers. Think about a particularly moving speech of tribute you've heard. What about it was special and inspirational? What would you like to hear in a speech of tribute given for you?

Effective commemorative speeches also include a specific kind of language. Commemorative speakers tell compelling stories and anecdotes, use rich language that brings to mind vivid images, and when appropriate, express deep emotion. They also recite special phrases, sayings, or quotations used by the person being commemorated or attributed to an event, idea, or institution.

In the next example, Molly Botswick commemorates her friend, Samantha Spady, a young college student who died from drinking too much alcohol:

> "A memory is what is left when something happens and does not completely unhappen." This quote by Edward de Bono makes me think of one girl. A girl like no other, a girl so beautiful she captured the attention of every person she passed, a girl that changed my life in countless ways, without even knowing it. That girl was Samantha Spady. I'm sure many, if not all, of you have several thoughts running through your mind when you hear her name. Unfortunately, those who weren't touched with the presence of Sam in their lives only know her through the media. I'm here today to tell you that Sam isn't just a statistic; she isn't the girl who drank too much, or the college student who made a deadly mistake. Maybe you knew her, maybe you didn't, but one thing is for sure, Sam was a person with incredible beauty, God-given talents, and an unexplainable innocence that touched the lives of thousands.[2]

Notice how Molly uses a powerful quotation to begin her speech. She also uses descriptive and emotional language to highlight Samantha's positive affect on those around her.

The next example illustrates a speech of award. In 1999, Representative Bobby Rush, a U.S. congressman from Chicago and a former Black Panther, encouraged his audience to support legislation to award the Congressional Gold Medal to Rosa Parks for her remarkable role in the civil rights movement:

> Mr. Speaker, I rise today in support of legislation to award a Congressional Gold Medal to Rosa Parks.
>
> Occasionally in our nation's history there are pivotal moments and indispensable individuals that move America away from its divisive past and closer to its imagined promise. December 1, 1955, produced such a moment and such a person.

Rosa Parks grew up in segregation. Every day she was forced to deal with the violation of America's constitutional guarantees. On December 1, 1955, this American woman exacted of this country the freedom and equality the Constitution promises.

Tired, like most citizens after a hard day's work, Rosa Parks refused to obey a shameful law that required her to sit at the back of a Montgomery, Alabama, bus. Her actions set the stage for the civil rights movement of a people who were unfairly and unjustly living under racist law.

Because of this brave American woman, segregation laws around the nation began to crumble and our nation began to respond to the call for African-American equality. Because of her invaluable contribution to our nation, every American lives a better life today. For that reason, it is quite appropriate that Mrs. Rosa Parks receive the Congressional Gold Medal.

But I must add, Mr. Speaker, that today, our nation continues to call for equality and freedom. There are still issues in our America that were issues in 1955. There are still Americans who do not enjoy the promises enumerated in the Constitution.

So, if we are to truly honor this great woman, we must do so, not only with a Gold Medal, but also with actions that further her purpose. We must all become individuals working to end the discrimination and inequalities that exist in our great nation.

I urge my colleagues to support this legislation and honor the mother of the civil rights movement, Mrs. Rosa Parks. Thank you.[3]

When you give a commemorative speech, you are responsible for conveying the significance of a person, event, idea, or institution to an audience. And if you're commemorating a person, you also want him or her to feel a sense of pride for having been praised and commemorated. To give an effective commemorative speech, consider the following guidelines.

Share What Is Unique and Special

Do not assume the audience already knows the exceptional qualities of who or what you are commemorating. It is your job to inform your listeners of these qualities by offering specific praise for your subject that consists of representative examples of successes, talents, accomplishments, special characteristics, and significant impacts. Be specific about the importance and meaning of who or what you are commemorating.

Express Sincere Appreciation

Express sincere appreciation for all that a person, event, idea, or institution has given or made possible. Speeches of commemoration, whether tributes or awards, praise and honor some person or some thing. Include in your speech sincere recognition of the ways in which who or what you're commemorating has affected a community. Your words should be genuine and express respect and gratitude.

Tell the Truth

Be certain the facts, stories, and traits you attribute to the subject of your commemoration are all accurate. Do not alter the truth to make a story more exciting. Instead, make an effort to find unique and special qualities and experiences that make your speech especially compelling.

When you commemorate a person, share your personal experience with that person so your audience can appreciate his or her exceptional qualities. When you commemorate an event, idea, or institution, share the characteristics that make your subject special in a way that appeals to your audience. Remember, when you give a commemorative speech, you want your audience to feel inspired and appreciative and to respect and admire who or what you are honoring.

MindTap®

Watch student speaker Tara Flanagan share what is unique and special about her grandfather in a commemorative speech.

Cleaning Up Our Rivers
Chad Pregracke: Environmentalist

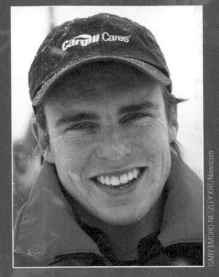

GARY EMORD-NETZLEY KRT/Newscom

Chad Pregracke grew up with the Mississippi River steps from his backyard at his home in Hampton, Illinois. He started exploring the river as soon as he was old enough to swim; when he was in high school, he started earning money for college by diving for mussel shells with his brother. Pregracke soon became outraged at the condition of the river, which was full of trash—from discarded bowling balls to abandoned cars and rusted appliances. At age 17 he started removing trash from the river and riverbanks by himself, but he was soon joined by other volunteers. At age 22,

watching NASCAR races, he had the idea to contact a few companies to see if he could get sponsorship—and sure enough, companies from Alcoa to Coca-Cola to Budweiser soon sponsored his cleanup efforts. He also attracted the attention of news organizations and appeared on several television programs and also became the subject of a few documentaries. Through these efforts he was able to acquire a barge, from which he and his crew still operate, and to form a not-for-profit organization called Living Lands & Waters (LL&W). Years—and hundreds of community river cleanups—later, Pregracke and his crew, aided by more than 70,000 volunteers across the country, have removed more than 8 million pounds of garbage from the Mississippi and other major rivers in the United States.

LL&W's mission is to protect, preserve, and restore the nation's rivers through its four components of community river cleanups, reforestation project, educational outreach, and Adopt-a-River Mile program. More than twenty-seven cities along the Mississippi, from St. Louis, Missouri, to St. Paul, Minnesota, have joined in the campaign to clean up the river. LL&W has now extended its efforts to other river systems such as the Ohio, Missouri, and the Potomac.

Although public speaking was never his goal, Pregracke has of

necessity become an experienced public speaker who has delivered more than 300 presentations to corporate, public, and student audiences. His favorite form of speaking is in informal presentations to elementary school children, teaching them about preserving the environment. He also speaks to the groups of volunteers who assemble for cleanups, who include "people from six years old to 60." In 2011 Chad was honored at the Points of Light Institute, where he was introduced by former President Jimmy Carter with former Presidents George H. W. Bush and Bill Clinton in the audience.[4]

WHAT DO YOU THINK?

1. If you were going to give a speech of introduction for Chad Pregracke, what accomplishments of his would you highlight?
2. If Pregracke were to give a speech commemorating the rivers, what do you think he might include? What stories might his audience want to hear?
3. Review the material in Chapter 4 on master statuses and standpoints. What master statuses do you think Pregracke brings as a speaker? How do you think they help or hinder his credibility as a speaker?

Wayne Kennedy/The LIFE Images Collection/Getty Images

Speeches of Acceptance

In an **acceptance speech**, you express your gratitude, appreciation, and pleasure at receiving an honor or a gift. Speeches of acceptance are organized around three goals:

1. Thank the audience and the organization that has presented you with the award.
2. Show your awareness of the significance of the award.
3. Acknowledge the people who helped you accomplish what you're being honored for.

Professor Katherine Rowell, who received the Council for Advancement and Support of Education and the Carnegie Foundation for the Advancement of Teaching "U.S. Professors of the Year" award, used her acceptance speech to express her gratitude to those who supported her in her journey as a first-generation college student who went on to earn a PhD and receive this prestigious award:

> I am greatly humbled and honored to be receiving this award. I would like to offer my sincerest gratitude to the Council for Advancement and Support of Education as well as the Carnegie Foundation for the Advancement for Teaching for this honor.
>
> I did not make the journey here alone. Numerous people have supported me along the way. First, I learned early on the value of a solid education from my parents. I grew up in a family that had limited educational opportunities. My Grandpa Teater never went to school. He signed his name with an X because he could not read or write. Two of my grandparents had less than an eighth-grade education. My mother never graduated from high school, although she finished her GED when she was 35 years old. My father worked his whole life on an assembly line, making just enough money for our family to have the basics but too much for our family to qualify for federal financial aid. Growing up, I was taught that without an education you really could not make it in the United States. Education was the key to the future. . . . Even though I was an excellent student in high school, I was terrified of college. I had only known a couple of people who had gone to college. I still remember raising my hand in my first class and asking what a "syllabus" was. Fortunately, I was privileged to have amazing college professors and mentors—in fact, some are here today. Their guidance, encouragement, and mentoring have helped make me the person I am today. I am eternally grateful for their support. I had no idea that graduate school could ever be a possibility; I wasn't aware that such things as assistantships and fellowships were available. They convinced me that I was capable of this achievement and opened doors that I did not even know existed. . . .
>
> Many of the students I teach today are up against some of the very same challenges that I faced as a student. That's why I work hard every day to make a difference in my students' lives. I know their struggles. Because of this, I am very proud to be part of the community college movement in the United States and proud to receive this award as a community college teacher.[5]

Sometimes, speakers use the significance of an award to call attention to larger issues. In the 2015 Oscars, for example, Patricia Arquette used a portion of her acceptance speech to make a plea for equal pay for women, while Julianne Moore spoke of Alzheimer's disease. In 2016, Leonardo DiCaprio urged his audience to pay attention to the real effects of climate change.

Although the main focus of a speech of acceptance is to express your thanks for receiving an award or gift, it can have other purposes, as well. To give an effective speech of acceptance, consider the following guidelines.

Practicing the Public Dialogue | 16.1

DESIGN A SPEECH OF COMMEMORATION

Choose a person, event, idea, or institution you would like to commemorate. In class, design a one-minute speech of commemoration. Begin by making a list of the accomplishments, qualities, or influences you wish to recognize. Select two or three that you feel you can talk about comfortably and make them the main points of your speech. Decide how you will describe these characteristics, paying special attention to the language you will use. Be sure your descriptions and praise are specific, your speech expresses sincere appreciation and respect, and your facts are accurate. Now deliver this speech to your classmates and ask them to give you feedback. Did your speech follow the guidelines outlined in this chapter?

MindTap®

To see examples of another common type of commemorative speech, a speech given at a memorial service, watch videos of Professor Nikki Giovanni's inspiring convocation address at the memorial held for the victims of the shootings at Virginia Tech and Oprah Winfrey's eulogy for civil rights activist Rosa Parks.

acceptance speech: Speech that expresses gratitude, appreciation, and pleasure at receiving an honor or a gift.

MANDEL NGAN/Staff/AFP/Getty Images

Ethical Moment: President Obama's Call to Action and the Sandy Hook Tragedy

After the tragic and violent loss of lives at Sandy Hook Elementary School in Newtown, Connecticut, President Barack Obama addressed the nation on December 16, 2012. He delivered his address at the interfaith vigil in Newtown, and began his remarks by commemorating the "20 beautiful young children" and the "6 remarkable adults" who had been senselessly murdered just two days earlier. His address communicated "the love and prayers of a nation" directed to the families who lost loved ones, and conveyed the deep sadness felt, the horrific loss, and the profound tragedy of the event. Obama spoke of the heroic efforts of the staff who urged the children to "wait for the good guys, they're coming" and who protected them by barricading their doors. He commemorated the first responders who "raced to the scene, helping to guide those in harms' way to safety . . . holding at bay their own shock and trauma because they had a job to do and others needed them more." And he spoke of togetherness and community, sharing that the "quiet town full of good and decent people" was not alone, indeed "whatever portion of sadness that we can share with

you to ease this heavy load, we will gladly bear it. Newton—you are not alone."

In a rare move, President Obama made a call for action, stating, "We can't tolerate this anymore. These tragedies must end. And to end them, we must change. We will be told that the causes of such violence are complex, and that is true. No single law—no set of laws can eliminate evil from the world, or prevent every senseless act of violence in our society." He continued, "Surely, we can do better than this. If there is even one step we can take to save another child, or another parent, or another town from the grief that has visited Tucson, and Aurora, and Oak Creek, and Newtown, and communities from Columbine to Blacksburg . . . then surely we have an obligation to try."

As he concluded his remarks, President Obama promised that he would "use whatever power this office holds" to engage citizens, "from law enforcement to mental health professionals to parents and educators—in an effort aimed at preventing more tragedies like this." He asked his audience, "What choice do we have? . . . Are we prepared to say that such violence visited on our children year after year after year is somehow the price of our freedom?"

WHAT DO YOU THINK?

1. What emotional and logical appeals did President Obama make in his address at the interfaith vigil? Do you think these appeals were appropriate and ethical? Why or why not?

2. The controversy around gun control and the right to bear arms is complex and related to many ethical questions. As a class, make a list of those ethical questions. Do you think Obama and other political officials are addressing these ethical questions openly and fairly? Why or why not?

3. President Obama used a commemorative moment to address a very divisive issue—guns. What are the positive and negative ethical implications of his choice of the interfaith vigil to raise the issue of guns, who can and should own them, how they should be regulated, or whether they should be regulated at all?

Understand the Purpose of the Award

Be familiar with the background, history, and unique characteristics of the award. To receive an award is to receive an honor. Be certain you understand the honor you are receiving so you can speak intelligently about what the award means to you. You may even choose to organize your acceptance speech around the specific qualities of the award, or you can use your understanding of the meaning and purpose of the award to encourage others to act, to remind the audience of larger social issues, or simply to reinforce shared values and principles.

Recognize Others

Although you are being recognized as an outstanding individual, give credit and thanks to those who have contributed to your success. Verbally acknowledge their influence, support, and the ways they helped you succeed. Use caution here because it is tempting to try to thank everyone to whom you are close. Avoid this pitfall and thank only those people or groups who have been especially supportive, helpful, or pivotal to your success.

Robert Sullivan/AFP/Getty Images

tip
National Geographic Explorer

BARRINGTON IRVING, Explorer, Pilot, Educator

Can you tell us about occasions when you were speaking to inspire others or to celebrate someone? How did you deliver those speeches?

When you're talking from the heart, I think you really have to know exactly what you're talking about. That creates an inviting touch. And it's okay to make a mistake when you speak from the heart because people recognize that you're not staring at a sheet of paper. I think you just really have to know what you're talking about and this gives you your key points in your speech that you can be certain of. That way, even if you get lost, you can remember those key points so that you don't ramble on.

Edmund J. Coppa/Splash News/Newscom

Respect Time Limitations

The length of your acceptance speech will vary depending on the situation. When you are invited to receive an award and give a speech, ask how long your speech should be. If the award committee requests a short speech, plan to be brief. If they want a longer speech, respect this request. A longer speech suggests your audience is interested in hearing a little more about you. For example, they may want to hear what you plan to do with a monetary award or what your future plans are.

Practicing the Public Dialogue | 16.2

DESIGN A SPEECH OF ACCEPTANCE

Design a one- to two-minute speech of acceptance for an imaginary award you've just received—be creative (and appropriate). In your speech, express your gratitude for receiving the award, acknowledge the purpose of the award, and recognize the people who helped you achieve the award. Conclude by explaining what you will do with the award and what your future plans are. Now deliver this speech to your classmates and ask them to give you feedback. Did your speech follow the guidelines outlined in this chapter?

Speeches to Entertain

Sometimes called *after-dinner speeches,* speeches to entertain are often given after a formal meal, usually a dinner, but also after a lunch or a breakfast meeting.[6] Those who give speeches to entertain usually are more experienced at speaking. However, even a novice speaker may be asked to deliver a speech to entertain at a luncheon for a service group or after a formal dinner at a club. A **speech to entertain** is lighthearted and addresses issues or ideas in a humorous way. But don't mistake these speeches for comedic acts. They do more than just provide the audience with a series of jokes, and they follow many of the basic principles of other special occasion speeches. Speeches to entertain have a specific purpose, thesis statement, and main points. They may be informative, invitational, or persuasive and are organized in specific patterns, just like other speech types. Speeches to entertain have two goals:

1. Entertain the audience.
2. Make the audience think.

When you give a speech to entertain, you want to make the audience laugh and smile as you give your speech. You also want the audience to "entertain" the issue—to look at it carefully and explore its implications. This balance between humor and presenting issues can be a tricky one. Let's take a closer look at each of these components of a speech to entertain.

speech to entertain: Lighthearted speech that addresses issues or ideas in a humorous way.

Humor is perhaps one of the most complicated communication phenomena. What is funny to one person isn't always funny to another. You might tell a joke or story to two people and only one laughs. Then there are times when you tell a joke in the right environment and everyone thinks it's funny. If you repeat that joke in the wrong context, no one will find it the least bit amusing. And if subjectivity and context weren't enough to consider, delivery is also a tricky matter. If you rearrange the wording of a joke just a bit or forget to tell a line, no one will understand what is supposed to be so funny. Predicting what will make people laugh is a bit like predicting the weather—we're often wrong. However, research tells us that what makes something funny is a combination of these elements:

- Timing
- Your objective in telling the joke
- The members of your audience

Timing is the way you use pauses and delivery for maximum effect. Research suggests that timing is a critical element in humor.[7] Personal experiences also tell us that timing is integral to how a joke is received and understood. Pauses to set a mood, before punch lines, or before key phrases can make the difference between a successful joke and one that falls flat. In a now-famous joke, Barbara Bush, in her 1990 speech to the graduating class of Wellesley College, told her audience, "Who knows, somewhere out in this audience may even be someone who will one day follow in my footsteps and preside over the White House as the president's spouse." She paused and added, "I wish him well."

Sometimes, not using a pause when you ordinarily might can also be funny because it can catch the audience off guard. When Ellen DeGeneres delivered the 2009 commencement address at Tulane University, she didn't pause at all when she said, "Follow your passion. Stay true to yourself. Never follow someone else's path unless you're in the woods and you're lost and you see a path. Then by all means you should follow that."[8] She got a big laugh from her audience when she suddenly switched gears from talking about a metaphorical path to giving advice about a very literal one.

The second aspect of successful humor is the objective of the joke. Appropriate jokes for speeches to entertain should strive to make light of something, remind us of our humanity, highlight the silly or the bizarre, tease others playfully, and even relieve tension in difficult times. Although humor can be used to make fun of others and put them down,[9] avoid this type of negative humor because it will likely offend audience members. Appropriate humor stands a greater chance of truly entertaining the audience.

The third component of successful humor is the audience. Of course, no two audiences will respond to the same joke in the same way. Still, when you know your audience well, you should have a better sense of what your listeners will find funny. Remember, one of the most common reasons a joke backfires is that a speaker may have failed to consider the group memberships as well as the individual or collective experiences of the audience.[10] This can lead to you telling a joke that "isn't funny" or that "goes too far" for the members of your audience.[11] So before you select the amusing stories and jokes for your speeches to entertain, consider the master statuses, standpoints, values, and background of your audience carefully.[13]

Research over the past twenty-five years suggests a number of interesting differences related to master statuses. Although men often find humor that shows contempt for others to be funny, women are far less likely to appreciate jokes of this sort. In contrast, women tend to find self-directed humor funnier than do men—but not when it's too harsh. In addition, ethnic minorities may enjoy in-group humor but often take offense at out-group humor—that is, when people from a particular group make jokes about their own group, those jokes may be seen as funny. However, when people outside that group make jokes about the group, those jokes are far less likely to be perceived as funny and may be considered offensive.[14] As a rule, then, when the master statuses of

Ricky Gervais hosted the Golden Globe Awards for the second time in 2016. The *Hollywood Reporter* noted that "no one was safe from becoming a punchline."[12] How is Gervais, known for pushing the margins on humor, a useful role model for incorporating jokes into your speeches? Pay attention to his timing, style of humor, and even his master statuses as you consider your answer.

Paul Drinkwater/NBCUniversal /Getty Images

timing: Way a speaker uses pauses and delivery for maximum effect.

your audiences are quite varied, try to avoid jokes that make fun of people or groups in harsh or mean-spirited ways.

Although funny, speeches to entertain are also about issues that are relevant to a particular audience or community. Some issues that might be relevant to audiences today are how the government spends or doesn't spend tax dollars, the environment, and family life in the new millennium. Speeches to entertain help listeners make sense of what is happening around them or come to terms with issues and dilemmas that affect their lives.[15] They often put things into a new perspective and add humor to situations that may have been difficult or drawn out. They can also introduce new ideas, giving audience members something to think about that may not have occurred to them before.

As you consider the issues you might address in your speech to entertain, identify those topics that may be particularly relevant to members of the audience. Once you've identified several possibilities, narrow these general topics and formulate a thesis statement. Check to be sure your approach has a humorous side to it and will appeal to your audience. From there, you can begin to develop the main points of your speech.

To help you balance the delivery of humor and relevant information to your audience and give a speech that entertains rather than offends or bores, consider the following guidelines.

Use Humor Carefully

Always err on the side of caution when you use humor in your speech. Although it is easy to get caught up in the moment, don't let your jokes run away from you. Remember, jokes often have more than one interpretation, and what may be funny to some can be offensive to others.[16] Most people don't find being made fun of publicly to be humorous. If you think a joke might offend or put someone down, leave it out of the speech. Remember, your goal is to entertain, not to alienate, the audience. When you offend an audience, you lose credibility and respect, which are difficult to regain.

Speak about Meaningful Issues

Remember, a speech to entertain is also about issues. Although it is meant to be funny, your goal is not to provide the audience with a continual stream of jokes. Rather, your goal is to develop an argument or an idea in an amusing way. As you select your topic and decide how you will frame it, consider your audience carefully. Although they do want to be entertained, they also want to hear a speech that is interesting and insightful. Before you finalize the topic of your speech, make sure it truly is relevant, is appropriate, and will hold the interest of your audience.

Pay Careful Attention to Your Delivery

Although delivery is a key component of any speech, a skilled delivery is paramount in a speech to entertain. Practice your speech many times so you can deliver your stories, jokes, and anecdotes smoothly and flawlessly. Work out the timing of your jokes well in advance and practice them until they feel like second nature. Your words and ideas will be even funnier if you can deliver your humor eloquently, in a relaxed style, and with the appropriate timing.[17]

Practicing the Public Dialogue | 16.3

DESIGN A SPEECH TO ENTERTAIN

Identify three local or national issues you think would be appropriate topics for a speech to entertain. Is there a lighter side of these topics, something that makes them humorous or conveys them in a humorous light? Now consider a possible audience for each topic. Be sure that what you find humorous about these topics also will be funny to the audience. Select one of the three topics you feel has the strongest potential to be a successful speech to entertain and prepare a thesis statement and an outline for it. Share these with your class and ask them to give you feedback. Does the class feel your speech would be appropriate and interesting for its intended audience?

MindTap

Politicians often use humor to address (or deflect) issues for particular audiences. Watch an example of President Barack Obama using humor at the 2016 White House Correspondents' Dinner. Humor is also often used in speeches meant to criticize politicians. A good example is the speech comedian and satirist Stephen Colbert gave at the 2006 White House Correspondents' Association Dinner. Why did each of these speakers use humor in their speeches? What was the effect of their humor?

COMMENTARY

By asking a series of questions, Brandon piques his listeners' curiosity and draws them in. He then reveals the topic of his speech.

In his introduction Brandon indicates how he appreciates his topic by describing some of water's virtues. In addition, by talking about water's "strength," "flexibility," and "beauty," he previews his main points.

He connects to his audience by linking his topic to human senses—he asks his audience to think about, move toward, and listen to the sounds of water.

The use of alliteration ("the regenerator, the reviver, the reliever") helps make the speech appealing to listeners.

Brandon includes an anecdote about playing in the snow to relate to his audience of college-aged students.

In using personification ("the clouds that crowd and bustle . . . , giving inspiration"), he helps bring life to his topic.

Notice the vivid imagery and rhythm Brandon uses in this paragraph to describe water's beauty.

In his conclusion, Brandon provides a short summary of the three virtues he admires most about water.

Water

by Brandon Perry

Specific Purpose: To commemorate the strength, flexibility, and beauty of water.

Thesis Statement: I'm thankful for all that water's enduring strength, everlasting flexibility, and exciting beauty have done for us and given us.

MindTap® Are you ready to give a special occasion speech? Use the following speech as a model. Brandon gave this speech in an introductory public speaking class. The assignment was to give a three- to five-minute speech commemorating a special person, place, or thing in the speaker's life. Watch a video of Brandon's speech (delivered by Keith in the video).

It is in the sky. It is on the ground. It is in us. Do you know what IT is? Father Time has no control over it, weapons weep at its power, and like an architect, it chisels and creates. Do you know what IT is? Water is what I speak of, and nowadays we view water passively—nothing more than a convenience—but it is more than that. Every day I see the strength of water in how it shapes the landscape of this Earth. I see its flexibility in giving me the ability to shape snow to throw. And I see a beauty that competes with the most beautiful sunset.

Discovering the amazing strength of water doesn't require going halfway across the Earth. Think about the strange and mysterious creatures of the deep blue sea. Turn your head toward the purple majestic skyscrapers of the West. Listen to the sounds of a roaring old-man-winter blizzard in Colorado. Take a walk down the hallway, then a right, arrive at the fountain, and take a nice long relaxing cool drink. Water, like a lifelong friend, is the regenerator, the reviver, the reliever of your life that you can't live without.

Water is uniquely flexible to many contexts. Little kids throwing water balloons and running through sprinklers would be unheard of without water. College students, enjoying a day off from classes, throwing snowballs at each other and building snowmen, would be unimaginable without water. The clouds that crowd and bustle through our bright blue sky, giving inspiration to artists and kids alike, would be unthinkable without water. The water we use every day once quieted the cries of an early Earth, quenched the thirst of a dinosaur, and gave blood to the mighty trees of the past and present of our world.

Beauty, they say, is in the eye of the beholder. But for those who claim they cannot see water's beauty, they need to look again. The glistening songs of blooming flowers in a midday spring afternoon are water's beauty transformed. Stand by a remote mountain lake, and a perfect, clear reflection of the mighty trees and peaks in the crystal clear water might just say hello. What makes water's beauty more unique and special, though, than any other is its ability to pass it on. The mighty Amazon rain forest or slopes covered in twenty feet of snow are just a couple examples. This beauty also allows all of us to view ourselves in a different light, like a mirror—it tells no lies. So when you stop and stare into a reflection that water gives you, do you see just yourself, or can you see deeper things, deeper ideas, deeper emotions?

Water was here long before and will be here long past our deaths, on this planet or the next. Life without water's enduring strength, everlasting flexibility, and exciting beauty would be all but impossible for most living things on this Earth. Be thankful for all that water has done for us; it has given us ALL that we see before us, in one form or another.

Chapter Summary

Generally, there are four types of special occasion speeches.

1. Speeches of introduction
2. Speeches of commemoration
3. Speeches of acceptance
4. Speeches to entertain

Each type of speech contributes to the public dialogue by calling attention to meaningful and honorable traits or encouraging audiences to reflect on issues in lighthearted ways.

Speeches of introduction provide an audience with a unique perspective on the person introduced.

- The person introduced can be either the speaker or another person.
- When you give a speech of introduction, remember to be brief, accurate, and appropriate.

Speeches of commemoration praise, honor, recognize, or pay tribute to a person, event, idea, or institution.

- When you give this type of speech, share what is unique or special about who or what you are commemorating.
- Also express your sincere appreciation and tell the truth about the person or thing you are commemorating.

In speeches of acceptance, the speaker expresses gratitude, appreciation, and pleasure at receiving an award, honor, or gift.

- The main goal of an acceptance speech is to express thanks.
- However, speakers also should understand the purpose of the award, recognize others for their assistance, and respect any time limitations that have been placed on the speech.

Speeches to entertain are lighthearted speeches that address issues and ideas in humorous and appropriate ways.

- Because what makes people laugh is quite complicated, be sure to use humor carefully in your speeches to entertain.
- Also speak about meaningful issues and pay careful attention to your delivery.

Invitation to Public Speaking Online MindTap

Now that you have read Chapter 16, use your MindTap Communication for *Invitation to Public Speaking* for quick access to the digital resources that accompany this text. These resources include:

- **Study tools** that will help you assess your learning and prepare for exams (digital glossary, key term flash cards, review quizzes).
- **Activities and assignments** that will help you hone your knowledge and build your public speaking skills

throughout the course, as well as help you explore public speaking concepts online (web links), give you step-by-step guidance through the research, outline and note card preparation process (Outline Builder), watch and critique videos of sample speeches (Interactive Video Activities), and allow you to practice and present your presentation online using a speech video delivery, recording, and grading system (YouSeeU).

Key Concepts MindTap Test your knowledge with online printable flash cards.

acceptance speech (321)
commemorative speech (317)
introductory speech (316)
speech of award (317)

speech to entertain (323)
speech of tribute (317)
timing (324)

Review Questions

1. Pair up with someone in class you do not know well. Talk with each other for ten minutes to discover answers to these questions: Who is this person? What are his or her accomplishments? What makes those accomplishments significant? Now write a one-minute speech to introduce your partner. Share your speeches with each other and discuss whether your introductions are accurate and appropriate.
2. Identify an award you would like to receive during your lifetime. What is the purpose of this award? If you were to receive this award, whom would you identify as playing a significant role in assisting you in getting the award?
3. Identify your favorite public figure and write an outline for a speech to commemorate this person. Check that your

outline identifies the traits that make this person unique and special. Identify the places in your speech where you express your sincere appreciation for this person. Finally, check to be sure your representation of this person is true and that your facts and stories about him or her are correct.

4. Bring a newspaper or magazine to class. In groups, select a topic from one of these sources and use it to write an outline for a speech to entertain. Identify your audience and the occasion and then make a list of the ways you could remain audience centered by using humor carefully and appropriately. Make another list of the ways the topic you have selected is meaningful to your audience and the public dialogue.

Glossary

abstract: Summary of the text in an article or publication.

abstract language: Language that refers to ideas or concepts but not to specific objects.

acceptance speech: Speech that expresses gratitude, appreciation, and pleasure at receiving an honor or a gift.

ad hominem fallacy: Argument in which a speaker attacks a person rather his or her arguments.

affirmations: Positive, motivating statements that replace negative self-talk.

alliteration: Repetition of initial sounds of two or more words in a sentence or phrase.

analogical reasoning: A process of reasoning by way of comparison and similarity that implies that because two things resemble each other in one respect, they also share similarities in another respect.

antithesis: Placement of words and phrases in contrast or opposition to one another.

argument: Set of statements that allows you to develop your evidence to establish the validity of your claim.

articulation: Physical process of producing specific speech sounds to make language intelligible.

attitude: General positive or negative feeling a person has about something.

audience: Complex and varied group of people the speaker addresses.

audience centered: Acknowledging your audience by considering and listening to the unique, diverse, and common perspectives of its members before, during, and after your speech.

backing: The evidence you have to be certain your warrant supports your grounds.

balance: Visual relationship between the items on a visual aid.

bandwagon fallacy: Argument that suggests something has merit because everyone else agrees with it or is doing it.

bar graph: Graph that compares quantities at a specific moment in time.

behavioral objectives: Actions a speaker wants the audience to take at the end of a speech.

belief: Person's idea of what is real, not real, true, or not true.

bias: Unreasoned distortion of judgment or prejudice about a topic.

bibliographic database: Database that indexes publishing data for books, periodical articles, government reports, statistics, patents, research reports, conference proceedings, and dissertations.

Boolean operators: Words you can use to create specific phrases that broaden or narrow your search on the Internet.

brainstorming: Process of generating ideas randomly and uncritically, without attention to logic, connections, or relevance.

brief narrative: Short story or vignette that illustrates a specific point.

call to action: Explicitly request that an audience engage in some clearly stated behavior.

careful listener: Listener who overcomes listener interference to better understand a speaker's message.

causal organization: Organizational pattern that is based on a cause-and-effect relationship that can develop in two ways: moving from cause to effect or from effect to cause.

causal pattern: Pattern of organization that describes a cause-and-effect relationship between ideas or events.

causal reasoning: Process of reasoning that supports a claim by establishing a cause-and-effect relationship.

channel: Means by which the message is conveyed.

character: Audience's view of a speaker's sincerity, trustworthiness, and concern for the well-being of the audience.

chronological pattern: Pattern of organization that traces a sequence of events or ideas.

civility: Care and concern for others, the thoughtful use of words and language, and the flexibility to see the many sides of an issue.

communication apprehension: Level of fear or anxiety associated with either real or anticipated communication with another person or people.

claim: Assertion that must be proved.

closed-ended question: Question that requires the respondent to choose an answer from two or more alternatives.

cognitive restructuring: Process that helps reduce anxiety by replacing negative thoughts with positive ones, called affirmations.

colloquialism: Local or regional informal dialect or expression.

commemorative speech: Speech that praises, honors, recognizes, or pays tribute to a person, an event, an idea, or an institution.

common ground: Similarities, shared interests, and mutual perspectives held by a speaker and his or her audience.

comparative advantages organization: Organizational pattern that illustrates the advantages of one solution over others.

competence: An audience's view of a speaker's intelligence, expertise, and knowledge of a subject.

conclusion: Logical outcome of an argument that results from the combination of the major and minor premises.

concrete language: Language that refers to a tangible object—a person, place, or thing.

condition of equality: Condition of an invitational environment that requires the speaker to acknowledge that all audience members hold equally valid perspectives worthy of exploration.

condition of self-determination: Condition of an invitational environment that requires the speaker to recognize that people know what is best for them and have the right to make choices about their lives based on this knowledge.

condition of value: Condition of an invitational environment that requires the speaker to recognize the inherent value of the audience's views, although those views may differ from the speaker's views.

confirm: To recognize, acknowledge, and express value for another person.

connective: Word or a phrase used to link ideas in a speech.

connotative definition: Subjective meaning of a word or phrase based on personal experiences and beliefs.

considerate speech: Speech that eases the audience's burden of processing information.

context: Environment or situation in which a speech occurs.

conversational style: Speaking style that is more formal than everyday conversation but remains spontaneous and relaxed.

coordination: Process of arranging points into successive levels, with the points on a specific level having equal importance.

counterarguments: Arguments against the speaker's own position.

credibility: An audience's perception of a speaker's competence and character.

critical listener: Listener who listens for the accuracy of a speech's content and the implications of a speaker's message.

culturally inclusive language: Language that respectfully recognizes the differences among the many cultures in our society.

database: Collections of information stored electronically so they are easy to find and retrieve.

decoding: Translating words, sounds, and gestures into ideas and feelings in an attempt to understand the message.

deductive reasoning: Process of reasoning that uses a familiar and commonly accepted claim to establish the truth of a very specific claim.

definition: Statement of the exact meaning of a word or phrase.

delivery: Action or manner of speaking to an audience.

demographic audience analysis: Analysis that identifies the particular population traits of an audience.

demonstration: Display of how something is done or how it works.

denotative definition: Objective meaning of a word or a phrase you find in a dictionary.

derived credibility: Credibility a speaker develops during a speech.

dialect: Pattern of speech that is shared by an ethnic group or people from specific geographical locations.

dialogue: Interaction, connection, and exchange of ideas and opinions with others.

direct quotation: Exact word-for-word presentation of another's testimony.

drawing: Diagram or sketch of someone or something.

either–or fallacy: Argument that presents only two options—"either A or B"—when actually more than two options exist; also known as a *false dilemma*.

elaboration likelihood model (ELM): Explains that receivers process persuasive messages in either a *central processing* or a *peripheral processing* route depending on how motivated the audience is to think critically about a message.

empathy: Trying to see and understand the world as another person does.

encoding: Translating ideas and feelings into words, sounds, and gestures.

ethical listener: Listener who considers the moral impact of a speaker's message on one's self and one's community.

ethical public speaker: Speaker who considers the moral impact of his or her ideas and arguments on others when involved in the public dialogue.

ethnocentrism: Belief that our own cultural perspectives, norms, and ways of organizing society are superior to others.

ethos: Speaker's credibility; the second of Aristotle's three types of proof.

etymology: History of a word.

euphemism: Word or phrase that substitutes an agreeable or inoffensive expression for one that may offend or suggest something unpleasant.

evidence: Materials that speakers use to support their ideas, such as examples, narratives, statistics, testimony, and definitions.

example: Specific instance used to illustrate a concept, experience, issue, or problem.

expert testimony: Opinions or observations of someone considered an authority in a particular field.

extemporaneous speech: Speech that is carefully prepared and practiced from brief notes rather than from memory or a written manuscript.

extended narrative: Longer story that makes an evolving connection with a broader point.

eye contact: Visual contact with another person's eyes.

facial expression: The movement of your eyes, eyebrows, and mouth to convey reactions and emotions.

fallacy: Argument that seems valid but is flawed because of unsound evidence or reasoning.

false cause: Error in reasoning in which a speaker assumes that one event caused another simply because the first event happened before the second.

false cause fallacy: Argument that mistakes a chronological relationship for a causal relationship.

fear appeal: Threat of something undesirable happening if change does not occur.

feedback: Verbal and nonverbal signals an audience gives a speaker.

flow chart: Chart that illustrates direction or motion.

font: Type or style of print.

font size: Size of the letters in a particular font measured in points.

full-text database: Database that indexes the complete text of newspapers, periodicals, encyclopedias, research reports, court cases, books, and the like.

gain immediate action: Encourage an audience to engage in a specific behavior or take a specific action.

gain passive agreement: Asks audience members to adopt a new position without also asking them to act in support of that position.

gender-inclusive language: Language recognizing that both women and men are active participants in the world.

general purpose: Speech's broad goal: to inform, invite, persuade, introduce, commemorate, or accept.

gestures: Movements, usually of the hands but sometimes of the full body, that express meaning and emotion or offer clarity to a message.

global plagiarism: Stealing an entire speech from a single source and presenting it as your own.

graph: Visual comparison of amounts or quantities that show growth, size, proportions, or relationships.

grounds: Why you think something is true or want to propose it.

group communication: Communication among members of a team or a collective about topics such as goals, strategies, and conflict.

hasty generalization: Error in reasoning in which a speaker reaches a conclusion without enough evidence to support it.

hasty generalization fallacy: Argument based on too few cases or examples to support a conclusion.

hearing: Vibration of sound waves on our eardrums and the impulses then sent to the brain.

hypothetical example: Instance that did not take place but could have.

idiom: Fixed, distinctive expression whose meaning is not indicated by its individual words.

impromptu speech: Speech that is not planned or prepared in advance.

incremental plagiarism: Presenting select portions from a single speech as your own.

index: Alphabetical listing of the topics discussed in a specific publication, along with the corresponding year, volume, and page numbers.

inductive reasoning: Process of reasoning that uses specific instances, or examples, to make a claim about a general conclusion.

inferences: Mental leaps we make when we recognize that a speaker's evidence supports his or her claims.

inflection: Manipulation of pitch to create certain meanings or moods.

information overload: When we take in more information than we can process but realize there still is more information we are expected to know.

informative speaking environment: Environment in which a speaker has expertise or knowledge that an audience needs but doesn't already have.

informative speech: Speech that communicates knowledge and understanding about a process, an event, a person or place, an object, or a concept.

initial credibility: The credibility a speaker has before giving a speech.

interference: Anything that stops or hinders a listener from receiving a message.

internal preview: Statement in the body of a speech that details what the speaker plans to discuss next.

internal summary: Statement in the body of a speech that summarizes a point a speaker has already discussed.

interpersonal communication: Communication with other people that ranges from the highly personal to the highly impersonal.

intertextuality: Process in which stories reference other stories or rely on parts of other stories to be complete.

interview: Planned interaction with another person that is organized around inquiry and response, with one person asking questions while the other person answers them.

intrapersonal communication: Communication with ourselves via the dialogue that goes on in our heads.

introductory speech: Speech that provides an audience with a unique perspective on the person introduced.

invitational environment: Environment in which the speaker's highest priority is to understand, respect, and appreciate the range of possible positions on an issue, even if those positions are quite different from his or her own.

invitational speaking: Type of public speaking in which a speaker enters into a dialogue with an audience to clarify positions, explore issues and ideas, or articulate beliefs and values.

jargon: Technical language used by a special group or for a special activity.

language: System of verbal or gestural symbols a community uses to communicate.

line graph: Graph that shows trends over time.

list: Series of words or phrases that organize ideas one after the other.

listenable speech: Speech that is considerate and delivered in an oral style.

listening: Process of giving thoughtful attention to another person's words and understanding what you hear.

logos: Logical arrangement of evidence in a speech; the first of Aristotle's three types of proof.

main points: Most important ideas you address in your speech.

major premise: Claim in an argument that states a familiar, commonly accepted belief (also called the general principle).

manuscript speech: Speech that is read to an audience from a written text.

map: Visual representation showing the physical layout of geographical features, cities, road systems, the night sky, and the like.

mass communication: Communication generated by media organizations that is designed to reach large audiences.

master statuses: Significant positions occupied by a person within society that affect that person's identity in almost all social situations.

mean: Average of a group of numbers.

median: Middle number in a series or set of numbers arranged in a ranked order.

memorized speech: Speech that has been written out, committed to memory, and given word for word.

message: Information conveyed by the speaker to the audience.

metaphor: Figure of speech that makes a comparison between two things by describing one thing as being something else.

minor premise: Claim in an argument that states a specific instance linked to the major premise.

mixed metaphor: Metaphor that makes illogical comparisons between two or more things.

mnemonic device: Verbal device that makes information easier to remember.

mode: Number that occurs most often in a set of numbers.

model: Copy of an object, usually built to scale, that represents an object in detail.

monotone: Way of speaking in which a speaker does not alter her or his pitch.

Monroe's motivated sequence: Step-by-step process used to persuade audiences by gaining attention, demonstrating a need, satisfying that need, visualizing beneficial results, and calling for action.

multiple perspectives pattern: Organizational pattern that allows the speaker to address the many sides and positions of an issue before opening up the speech for dialogue with the audience.

narrative: Story that recounts or foretells real or hypothetical events.

narrative organization: Organizational pattern that uses one or more stories to construct an argument.

noise: Anything that interferes with understanding the message being communicated.

object: Something that can be seen or touched.

objective: Having a fair, ethical, and undistorted view on a question or issue.

open-ended question: Question that allows the respondent to answer in an unrestricted way.

oral style: Speaking style that reflects the spoken rather than the written word.

organization: Systematic arrangement of ideas into a coherent whole.

organizational chart: Chart that illustrates the structure of groups.

parallelism: Arrangement of related words so they are balanced or of related sentences so they have identical structures.

paraphrase: Summary of another's testimony in the speaker's own words.

patchwork plagiarism: Constructing a complete speech that you present as your own from portions of several different sources.

pathos: Emotional appeals made by a speaker; the third of Aristotle's three types of proof.

pauses: Hesitations and brief silences in speech or conversation.

peer testimony: Opinions or observations of someone who has firsthand knowledge of a topic (sometimes called *lay testimony*).

personal appearance: Way speakers dress, groom, and present themselves physically.

personal testimony: Your own opinions or observations that you use to convey your point.

personification: Figure of speech that attributes human characteristics to animals, objects, or concepts.

persuasive speech: Speech whose message attempts to change or reinforce an audience's thoughts, feelings, or actions.

picture graph: Graph that presents information in pictures or images.

pie graph: Graph that shows the relative proportions of parts of a whole.

pitch: Highness or lowness of a speaker's voice.

plagiarism: Presenting another person's words and ideas as your own.

posture: Way speakers position and carry their bodies.

preliminary bibliography: List of all the potential sources you'll use as you prepare your speech.

preparation outline: Detailed outline a speaker builds when preparing a speech that includes the title, specific purpose, thesis statement, introduction, main points and subpoints, connectives, conclusion, and source citations of the speech.

preview: Brief overview in the introduction of a speech of each of the main points in the speech.

probe: Question that fills out or follows up an answer to a previous question.

problem–cause–solution organization: Organizational pattern that focuses on identifying a specific problem, the causes of that problem, and a solution to the problem.

problem–solution organization: Organizational pattern that focuses on persuading an audience that a specific

problem exists and can be solved or minimized by a specific solution.

problem–solution pattern: Pattern of organization that identifies a specific problem and offers a possible solution.

pronunciation: Act of saying words correctly according to the accepted standards of a language.

proxemics: Use of space during communication.

public communication: Communication in which one person gives a speech to other people, most often in a public setting.

public deliberation: Engaging in a process that involves the careful weighing of information and views.

public dialogue: Ethical and civil exchange of ideas and opinions among communities about topics that affect the public.

question of fact: Question that addresses whether or not something is verifiably true.

question of policy: Question that addresses the best course of action or solution to a problem.

question of value: Question that addresses the merit or morality of an object, action, or belief.

rate: Speed at which a speaker speaks.

real example: Instance that actually took place.

reasoning by sign: Process of reasoning that assumes something exists or will happen based on something else that exists or has happened.

red herring fallacy: Introduction of irrelevant information into an argument to distract from the real issue.

referent: Object, concept, or event a symbol represents.

repetition: Repeating keywords or phrases at the beginnings or endings of sentences or clauses to create rhythm.

research inventory: List of the types of information you have for your speech and the types you want to find.

rhetorical question: Question, used for effect, that an audience isn't supposed to answer out loud but rather in their own minds.

rhythm: Arrangement of words into patterns so the sounds of the words together enhance the meaning of a phrase.

sign: Something that represents something else.

signpost: Simple word or statement that indicates where you are in your speech or highlights an important idea.

simile: Figure of speech that makes an explicit comparison of two things using the word *like* or *as*.

slang: Informal nonstandard vocabulary, usually made up of arbitrarily changed words.

slippery slope fallacy: Argument that claims a first step in a certain direction will inevitably lead to undesirable further steps in that direction.

spatial pattern: Pattern of organization that arranges ideas in terms of location or direction.

speaker: Person who stimulates public dialogue by delivering an oral message.

speaking environment: Time and place in which a speaker will speak.

speaking outline: Condensed form of a preparation outline that you use when speaking.

specific purpose: Focused statement that identifies exactly what a speaker wants to accomplish with a speech.

speech about a concept: Informative speech about an abstraction, something you cannot perceive with your senses, such as an idea, a theory, a principle, a worldview, or a belief.

speech about an event: Informative speech that describes or explains a significant, interesting, or unusual occurrence.

speech about an object: Informative speech about anything that is tangible, that can be perceived by the senses.

speech about a place or a person: Informative speech that describes a significant, interesting, or unusual place or person.

speech about a process: Informative speech that describes how something is done, how something comes to be what it is, or how something works.

speech of award: Speech given to present a specific award to someone and describe why that person is receiving the award.

speech of tribute: Speech given to honor someone.

speech to entertain: Lighthearted speech that addresses issues or ideas in a humorous way.

speech to explore an issue: Invitational speech in which the speaker attempts to engage an audience in a discussion about an idea, concern, topic, or plan of action.

speech topic: Subject of your speech.

spotlighting: Practice of highlighting a person's race or ethnicity (or sex, sexual orientation, physical disability, and the like) during a speech.

standpoint: Perspective from which a person views and evaluates society.

state or situational anxiety: Apprehension about communicating with others in a particular situation.

statistics: Numerical summaries of facts, figures, and research findings.

stereotype: Broad generalization about an entire group based on limited knowledge or exposure to only certain members of that group.

sub-subpoint: Point in a speech that develops an aspect of a subpoint.

subordination: Process of ranking ideas in order from the most to the least important.

subpoint: Point in a speech that develops an aspect of a main point.

summary: Concise restatement of the main points at the end of a speech.

symbol: Word or phrase spoken by a speaker.

systematic desensitization: Technique for reducing anxiety that involves teaching your body to feel calm and relaxed rather than fearful during your speeches.

terminal credibility: Credibility given to a speaker at the end of a speech.

testimony: Opinions or observations of others.

thesis statement: Statement that summarizes in a single declarative sentence the main ideas, assumptions, or arguments you want to express in your speech.

thought or reference: Memory and past experiences that audience members have with an object, concept, or event.

timing: Way a speaker uses pauses and delivery for maximum effect.

topical pattern: Pattern of organization that allows the speaker to divide a topic into subtopics, each of which addresses a different aspect of the larger topic.

trait anxiety: Apprehension about communicating with others in any situation.

transition: Phrase that indicates a speaker is finished with one idea and is moving on to a new one.

two-sided message: Persuasive strategy that addresses both sides of an issue, refuting one side to prove the other is better.

value: Person's idea of what is good, worthy, or important.

verbal clutter: Extra words that pad sentences and claims but don't add meaning.

visualization: Process in which you construct a mental image of yourself giving a successful speech.

vocalized pauses: Pauses that speakers fill with words or sounds like "um," "er," or "uh."

vocal variety: Changes in the volume, rate, and pitch of a speaker's voice that affect the meaning of the words delivered.

volume: Loudness of a speaker's voice.

warrant: The evidence you have to be certain your grounds support your claim.

References

Chapter 1

1. Harold Barrett, *Rhetoric and Civility: Human Development, Narcissism, and the Good Audience* (Albany: State University of New York Press, 1991), 147.
2. Deborah Tannen, *The Argument Culture: Moving from Debate to Dialogue* (New York: Random House, 1998), 1–4.
3. See, for example, Stephen Yarbrough, "On 'Getting It': Resistance, Temporality, and the 'Ethical Shifting' of Discursive Interaction," *Rhetoric Society Quarterly* 40 (2010): 1–22; Jennifer Emerling Bone, Cindy L. Griffin, and T. M. Linda Scholz, "Beyond Traditional Conceptualizations of Rhetoric: Invitational Rhetoric and a Move Toward Civility," *Western Journal of Communication* 72 (October–December 2008): 434–62; Shawn Spano, *Public Dialogue and Participatory Democracy: The Cupertino Community Project* (Cresskill: Hampton Press, 2001); William Isaacs, *Dialogue and the Art of Thinking Together* (New York: Currency, 1999); Stephen L. Carter, *Civility: Manners, Morals, and the Etiquette of Democracy* (New York: Basic Books, 1998); Linda Ellinor and Glenna Gerard, *Dialogue: Rediscover the Transforming Power of Conversation* (New York: Wiley, 1998); Jeffrey C. Goldfarb, *Civility and Subversion: The Intellectual in the Democratic Society* (Cambridge: Cambridge University Press, 1998); Josina M. Makau and Ronald C. Arnett, *Communication Ethics in an Age of Diversity* (Chicago: University of Illinois Press, 1997); Ivana Markova, Carl F. Graumann, and Klaus Foppa, eds., *Mutualities in Dialogue* (Cambridge: Cambridge University Press, 1995); Douglas N. Walton and Erik C. W. Krabbee, *Commitment in Dialogue: Basic Concepts of Interpersonal Reasoning* (Albany: State University of New York Press, 1995); Rob Anderson, Kenneth N. Cissna, and Ronald C. Arnett, *The Reach of Dialogue: Confirmation, Voice, and Community* (Cresskill: Hampton Press, 1994); Harold Barrett, *Rhetoric and Civility: Human Development, Narcissism, and the Good Audience* (Albany: State University of New York Press, 1991).
4. For an excellent discussion of the public dialogue, see Spano, *Public Dialogue and Participatory Democracy.*
5. Adapted from Kenneth Burke, *The Philosophy of Literary Form: Studies in Symbolic Action*, 3rd ed. (Berkeley: University of California Press, 1973, original work published 1941), 110–11.
6. Melbourne S. Cummings, "Teaching the African American Rhetoric Course," in *African American Communications: An Anthology in Traditional and Contemporary Studies*, ed. James W. Ward (Dubuque: Kendall/Hunt, 1993), 241.
7. Adapted from Janice Walker Anderson, "A Comparison of Arab and American Conceptions of 'Effective' Persuasion," *Howard Journal of Communications* 2 (Winter 1989–1990): 81–114; Larry A. Samovar and Richard E. Porter, eds., *Intercultural Communication: A Reader*, 10th ed. (Belmont: Wadsworth, 2003); A. J. Almaney and A. J. Alwan, *Communicating with the Arabs: A Handbook for the Business Executive* (Prospect Heights: Waveland, 1982), 79.
8. Bonnie Dow, "Ann Willis Richards: A Voice for Political Empowerment," in *Women Public Speakers in the United States, 1925–1993*, ed. Karlyn Kohrs Campbell (Westport: Greenwood Press, 1994), 456.
9. Material for this section is from David Niven and Jeremy Zilber, "Elite Use of Racial Labels: Ideology and Preference for African American or Black," *Howard Journal of Communications* 11 (2000): 267–77; Ward, *African American Communications*; Mary Jane Collier, "A Comparison of Conversations among and between Domestic Culture Groups: How Intra- and Intercultural Competencies Vary," *Communication Quarterly* 36 (1988): 122–44; Larry A. Samovar and Richard E. Porter, *Communication between Cultures* (Belmont: Wadsworth, 2007); Anderson, "A Comparison of Arab and American Conceptions of 'Effective' Persuasion"; Samovar and Porter, *Intercultural Communication*; Almaney and Alwan, *Communicating with the Arabs.*
10. Charmaine Shutiva, "Native American Culture and Communication through Humor," in *Our Voices: Essays in Culture, Ethnicity, and Communication*, 3rd ed., ed. Alberto Gonzalez, Marsha Houston, and Victoria Chen (Los Angeles: Roxbury, 2000), 113–17.
11. Bonnie J. Dow and Mari Boor Tonn, "'Feminine Style' and Political Judgment in the Rhetoric of Ann Richards," *Quarterly Journal of Speech* 79 (1993): 286–302; Julia T. Wood, *Gendered Lives: Communication, Gender, and Culture*, 9th ed. (Belmont: Wadsworth, 2011); Marsha Houston, "When Black Women Talk with White Women: Why the Dialogues Are Difficult," in *Our Voices*, ed. Gonzalez, Houston, and Chen, pp. 98–104.
12. T. T. R. Culhane, "Urban Planner," *National Geographic*, accessed December 2011, http://www.nationalgeographic.com/explorers/bios/culhane-thomas/.
13. T.T.R. Culhane, "The Great Conversation: Solar CITIES" (speech, Abu Dhabi, United Arab Emirates,

October 2010), posted on *Solar Cities Blog*, March 4, 2011, accessed December 27, 2011, http://solarcities .blogspot.com/2011/03/great-conversation-solar -cities.html.

14. James C. McCroskey, "Oral Communication Apprehension: A Summary of Recent Theory and Research," *Human Communication Research* 4 (1977): 78 (italics added). See also Amber N. Finn, Chris R. Sawyer, and Paul Schrodt "Examining the Effect of Exposure Therapy on Public Speaking State Anxiety," *Communication Education* 58 (January 2009): 92–109; Paul L. Witt, Mendy L. Roberts, and Ralph R. Behnke, "Comparative Patterns of Anxiety and Depression in a Public Speaking Context," *Human Communication* 11 (Summer 2008): 219–30; Jessica J. Winters et al., "Affect Intensity of Student Speakers as a Predictor of Anticipatory Public Speaking Anxiety," *Texas Speech Communication Journal* 31 (Winter 2007): 44–48.

15. Ralph R. Behnke and Chris R. Sawyer, "Milestones of Anticipatory Public Speaking Anxiety," *Communication Education* 48 (1999): 164–72; Amy M. Bippus and John A. Daly, "What Do People Think Causes Stage Fright? Naïve Attributions about the Reasons for Public Speaking Anxiety," *Communication Education* 48 (1999): 63–72; Thomas E. Robinson II, "Communication Apprehension and the Basic Public Speaking Course: A National Survey of In-Class Treatment Techniques," *Communication Education* 46 (1997): 190–97.

16. Michael J. Beatty, "Situational and Predispositional Correlates of Public Speaking Anxiety," *Communication Education* 37 (January 1988): 29–30; Bippus and Daly, "What Do People Think Causes Stage Fright?"

17. Paul L. Witt and Ralph R. Behnke, "Anticipatory Speech Anxiety as a Function of Public Speaking Assignment Type," *Communication Education* 55 (April 2006): 167–77; Shannon C. McCullough et al., "Anticipatory Public Speaking State Anxiety as a Function of Body Sensations and State of Mind," *Communication Quarterly* 54 (February 2006): 101–09; Murray B. Stein, John R. Walker, and David R. Forde, "Public-Speaking Fears in a Community Sample: Prevalence, Impact on Functioning, and Diagnostic Classification," *Archives of General Psychiatry* 53 (1996): 169–74.

18. John A. Daly, Anita L. Vangelisti, and David J. Weber, "Speech Anxiety Affects How People Prepare Speeches: A Protocol Analysis of the Preparation Processes of Speakers," *Communication Monographs* 62 (December 1995): 383–97.

19. See Tony E. Smith and Ann Bainbridge Frymier, "Get 'Real': Does Practicing Speeches Before an Audience Improve Performance?" *Communication Quarterly* 54 (February 2006): 111–25; Karen Kangas Dwyer, *Conquer Your Speechfright: Learn How to Overcome the Nervousness of Public Speaking* (Fort

Worth: Harcourt, 1998); Karen Kangas Dwyer, "The Multidimensional Model: Teaching Students to Self-Manage High Communication Apprehension by Self-Selecting Treatments," *Communication Education* 49 (2000): 72–81; James C. McCroskey, "The Implementation of a Large Scale Program of Systematic Desensitization for Communication Apprehension," *Speech Teacher* 21 (1972): 255–64.

20. Joe Ayres and Theodore S. Hopf, "Visualization: A Means of Reducing Speech Anxiety," *Communication Education* 34 (1985): 318–23; Joe Ayres and Theodore S. Hopf, "Visualization: Is It More Than Extra-Attention?" *Communication Education* 38 (1989): 1–5; Joe Ayres and Theodore S. Hopf, "The Long-Term Effect of Visualization in the Classroom: A Brief Research Report," *Communication Education* 39 (1990): 75–78; Joe Ayres, Tim Hopf, and Debbie M. Ayres, "An Examination of Whether Imaging Ability Enhances the Effectiveness of an Intervention Designed to Reduce Speech Anxiety," *Communication Education* 43 (1994): 252–58; Robert McGarvey, "Rehearsing for Success: Tap the Power of the Mind through Visualization," *Executive Female* (January–February 1990): 34–37.

21. Adapted from Ayres and Hopf, "Visualization: Is It More Than Extra-Attention?" 2–3.

22. Joe Ayres, "Coping with Speech Anxiety: The Power of Positive Thinking," *Communication Education* 37 (October 1988): 289–96.

23. William J. Fremouw and Michael D. Scott, "Cognitive Restructuring: An Alternative Method for the Treatment of Communication Apprehension," *Communication Education* 28 (1979): 129–33.

24. Compiled from *Converging Voices, LLC*, accessed June 12, 2007, http://www.convergingvoices.com /oband; "Orangeband," *KaiDegner.com*, accessed April 23, 2010, http://www.orangeband.org/; "The Orangeband Initiative," *Idealist*, accessed August 3, 2016, *http://www.idealist.org/view/nonprofit /mKjmnjBHKGBD/*.

Chapter 2

1. See Laura Ann Janusik and Andrew D. Wolvin, "24 Hours in a Day: A Listening Update to the Time Studies," *International Journal of Listening* 23 (2009): 104–20, doi: 10.1080/10904010903014442.

2. Richard Emanual et al., "How College Students Spend Their Time Communicating," *The International Journal of Listening* 22 (2008): 26.

3. Lyman K. Steil, Larry L. Barker, and Kittie W. Watson, *Effective Listening: Key to Your Success* (New York: McGraw-Hill, 1993), 51.

4. Martin Buber, "Distance and Relation" in *The Knowledge of Man*, trans. Ronald Gregor Smith (London: George Allen and Unwin, 1965), 71, quoted in *The Reach of Dialogue: Confirmation,*

Voice, and Community, ed. Rob Anderson, Kenneth N. Cissna, and Ronald C. Arnett (Cresskill: Hampton Press, 1994), 23.

5. Michael P. Nichols, *The Lost Art of Listening* (New York: Guilford Press, 1995), 3.

6. This definition is adapted from Donald L. Rubin, "Listenability = Oral-Based Discourse + Considerateness," in *Perspectives on Listening*, ed. Andrew D. Wolvin and Carolyn Gwynn Coakley (Norwood: Ablex, 1993), 261–81.

7. Adapted from Arthur K. Robertson, *Listen for Success: A Guide to Effective Listening* (New York: Irwin, 1994), 25–26.

8. Mihir Patkar, "30 Trendy Internet Slang Words and Acronyms You Need to Know to Fit In," accessed November 23, 2015, www.makeuseof.com/tag/30 -trendy-internet-acronyms-slang-need-know-fit/.

9. Patkar, "30 Trendy Internet Slang Words and Acronyms You Need to Know to Fit In."

10. Adapted from "Examples of Euphemism," *YourDictionary*, accessed November 23, 2015, http:// examples.yourdictionary.com/examples-of -euphemism.html.

11. "Examples of Euphemism."

12. Julia Wood, *Gendered Lives: Communication, Gender, and Culture*, 9th ed. (Belmont: Wadsworth, 2011), 118.

13. Wood, *Gendered Lives,* 118.

14. Diana K. Ivy and Phil Backlund, *Exploring GenderSpeak: Personal Effectiveness in Gender Communication,* 2nd ed. (Boston: McGraw-Hill, 2000), 175–76.

15. See Manual Carreias et al., "The Use of Stereotypical Gender information in Constricting a Mental Model: Evidence from English and Spanish," *Quarterly Journal of Experimental Psychology* 49 (1996): 639–66; Friederike Braun et al., "Konned Geophysider Frauen sein? Generische Personenbezeichnungen im Deutschen [Can Geophysicians be Women? Generic Terms in German]," *Zeitschrift fur Germanistische Lingistic* 26 (1998): 265–83.

16. Pascal Gyagz et al., "Generically Intended, but Specifically Interpreted: When Beauticians, Musicians, and Mechanics Are All Men," *Language, and Cognitive Processes* 23 (2008): 464–84.

17. Adapted from Amy Einsohn, *The Copyeditor's Handbook: A Guide for Book Publishing and Corporate Communications*, 2nd ed. (Berkeley: University of California Press, 2006), 404–16.

18. U.S. Bureau of Labor Statistics, "Highlights of Women's Earnings in 2014," Report 1058, *BLS Reports,* November 2015, www.bls.gov/opub/reports/cps /highlights-of-womens-earnings-in-2014.pdf.

19. Andrew Wolvin and Carolyn Gwynn Coakley, *Listening*, 5th ed. (Madison: Brown and Benchmark, 1996), 232.

20. Don Gonyea and Domenico Montanaro, "Trump On His Plan to Ban Muslims: 'Not Politically Correct, But I Don't Care,'" *NPR*, December 15, 2015, www.npr .org/2015/12/08/458875362/trump-on-his-plan-to -ban-muslims-not-politically-correct-but-i-don-t-care.

21. Nina Bahadur, "18 Real Things Donald Trump Has Actually Said about Women," *Huffington Post,* August 19, 2015, www.huffingtonpost.com/entry/18-real -things-donald-trump-has-said-about-women _55d356a8e4b07addcb442023.

22. Todd Van Luling, "Hey Politicians. It's the 21st Century. Time to Stop Being Sexist Idiots," *Huffington Post,* October 8, 2013, www.huffingtonpost.com/2013/10/08 /sexist-politician-quotes_n_4038199.html.

23. "Explorers/Bio: K. David Harrison," *National Geographic,* http://www.nationalgeographic.com/explorers/bios /david-harrison/.

24. "Explorers/Bio: K. David Harrison."

25. K. David Harrison, "The Tragedy of Dying Languages," *BBC,* February 5, 2010, http://news.bbc.co.uk/2 /hi/8500108.stm.

26. Harrison, "The Tragedy of Dying Languages."

27. Harrison, "The Tragedy of Dying Languages."

Chapter 3

1. Maya Eliahou, "University of Missouri Protests and Their Effect on Education across the Nation," *The Daily Californian*, November 17, 2015, http://www .dailycal.org/2015/11/17/university-of-missouri -protests-and-their-effect-on-education-across-the -nation.

2. Tom Hayden, "Participatory Democracy: From the Port Huron Statement to Occupy Wall Street," *The Nation*, April 16, 2012, http://www.thenation.com /article/167079/participatory-democracy-port -huron-statement-occupy-wall-street.

3. "Explorers/Bio: Becca Skinner," *National Geographic,* accessed May 27, 2013, http://www.nationalgeographic .com/explorers/bios/becca-skinner/.

4. Alfred Rosa and Paul Escholz, *The Writer's Brief Handbook,* 2nd ed. (Scarborough, Ontario, Canada: Allyn and Bacon, 1996), 7.

5. Compiled from Wangari Maathai, *The Green Belt Movement: Sharing the Approach and the Experience* (New York: Lantern Books, 2003); Wangari Muta Maathai, *Unbowed* (New York: Knopf, 2006); "Wangari Maathai Quotes," http://womenshistory .about.com/od/quotes/a/wangari_maathai.htm; and *The Green Belt Movement*, http://www .greenbeltmovement.org.

Chapter 4

1. For an excellent summary and discussion of the various theories that attempt to explain social development, see Julia T. Wood, *Gendered Lives: Communication, Gender, and Culture,* 12th ed. (Belmont: Wadsworth, 2017), 35–54.

2. Gordon Marshall, ed., *The Concise Oxford Dictionary of Sociology* (New York: Oxford University Press, 1994), 315.

3. See, for example, Samia Ula Nur Alhabib and Roger Jones, "Domestic Violence Against Women: Systematic Review of Prevalence Studies." *Journal of Family Violence* 25, no. 4 (2010): 369–82; "Demographics," United States Department of Labor, Bureau of Labor Statistics, http://www.bls.gov/cps/demographics.htm#race; Alex Kingsbury, "Fighting Violence with Words and Deeds," *U.S. News & World Report* 146, no. 10 (November 2009): 53; "A Policy Maker's Guide to Hate Crimes," United States Department of Justice, Bureau of Justice Assistance, http://www.ncjrs.gov/pdffi les1/bja/162304.pdf; "Victims," Office of Justice Programs, Bureau of Justice Statistics, http://www.bjs.gov/index.cfm?ty=tp&tid=9; William B. Weeks and Amy E. Wallace, "Race and Gender Differences in General Internists' Annual Income," *Journal of General Internal Medicine* 21 (November 2006): 1167–71; Meagan Meuchel Wilson, "Hate Crime Victimization, 2004–2012—Statistical Tables," NCJ 244409, Office of Justice Programs, Bureau of Justice Statistics, (February 20, 2014), http://www.bjs.gov/index.cfm?ty=pbdetail&iid=4905; Jesse Bennett and Jessica Ellison, "Tracking the Wage Gap: In Honor of Equal Pay Day, 12 Sobering Figures about Men, Women and Work," *Newsweek,* April 10, 2010, http://www.newsweek.com/2010/04/19tracking-the-wage-gap.html.

4. Katharine Etsy, Richard Griffin, and Marcie Schorr-Hirsh, *Workplace Diversity: Managers Guide to Solving Problems and Turning Diversity into a Competitive Advantage* (Avon: Adams Media Corporation, 1995); Keli A. Green et al., "Diversity in the Workplace: Benefits, Challenges, and the Required Managerial Tools," (EDIS Publication #HR022, University of Florida, 2012); David Ingram, "Advantages and Disadvantages of Diversity in the Workplace," *Chron*, accessed February 10, 2015, http://smallbusiness.chron.com/advantages-disadvantages-diversity-workplace-3041.html.

5. University of California, San Francisco, Human Resources, "Chapter 12: Managing Diversity in the Workplace," in *Guide to Managing Human Resources*, accessed February 10, 2015, http://ucsfhr.ucsf.edu/index.php/pubs/hrguidearticle/chapter-12-managing-diversity-in-the-workplace/.

6. University of California, San Francisco, "Managing Diversity in the Workplace"; Green et al., "Diversity in the Workplace."

7. Kim Abreu, "The Myriad Benefits of Diversity in the Workplace," *Entrepreneur,* December 9, 2014, http://www.entrepreneur.com/article/240550; Sophia Kerby and Crosby Burns, "Top 10 Economic Facts of Diversity in the Workplace: A Diverse Workforce is Integral to a Strong Economy," *Center for American Progress,* July 12, 2012, https://www.americanprogress.org/issues/labor/news/2012/07/12/11900/the-top-10-economic-facts-of-diversity-in-the-workplace/.

8. Abreu, "The Myriad Benefits of Diversity in the Workplace"; Kerby and Burns, "Top 10 Economic Facts of Diversity in the Workplace."

9. Abreu, "The Myriad Benefits of Diversity in the Workplace."

10. Kerby and Burns, "Top 10 Economic Facts of Diversity in the Workplace."

11. Kerby and Burns, "Top 10 Economic Facts of Diversity in the Workplace."

12. Alice H. Eagly and Shelly Chaiken, "The Advantages of an Inclusive Definition of Attitude," *Social Cognition* 25, no. 5 (2007): 582–602; Alice Egly and Shelly Chaiken, "Attitude Structure and Function," in *Handbook of Social Psychology* 1 (1998): 323–90; James M. Olson and Mark P. Zanna, "Attitudes and Attitude Change," *Annual Review of Psychology* 44 (1993): 117–54.

13. Rushworth M. Kidder, *How Good People Make Tough Choices: Resolving the Dilemmas of Ethical Living,* (New York: Harper Collins, 2003, original work published in 1995); Kidder, *Shared Values for a Troubled World* (San Francisco: Jossey-Bass, 1994); Milton Rokeach, *Beliefs, Attitudes, and Values: A Theory of Organization and Change* (San Francisco: Jossey-Bass, 1970); Milton Rokeach, *The Nature of Human Values* (New York: Free Press, 1973); Shalom H. Schwartz and Wolfgang Blisky, "Toward a Theory of the Universal Content and Structure of Values: Extensions and Cross-Cultural Replications," *Journal of Personality and Social Psychology* 58 (1990): 878–91.

14. Compiled from Raghava KK, personal interview, January 13, 2015; "Explorers/Bio: Raghava KK," Explorers Bio," *National Geographic*, accessed February 4, 2015, www.nationalgeographic.com/explorers/bios/raghava-kk/; and Raghava KK, "My 5 Lives as an Artist," filmed February 2010, TEDTalk, 17:55, posted February 2010, accessed February 4, 2015, www.ted.com/talks/raghava_kk_five_lives_of_an_artist.

15. His Holiness the Dalai Lama and Howard C. Cutler, *The Art of Happiness: A Handbook for Living* (New York: Riverhead Books, 1998), 1–2.

16. Compiled from *United Nations*, http://www.un.org/works; Hillary Mayheux, "Angelina Jolie on Her UN Refugee Role," *National Geographic News*, June 18, 2003, http://news.nationalgeographic.com/news/2003/06/0618_030618_angelinajolie.html and "Goodwill Ambassadors," *UNHCR: The UN Human Refugee Agency*, http://www.unhcr.org/cgi-bin/textis/vtx/home.

17. Kenneth Burke, *Counter-Statement* (Berkeley: University of California Press, 1968), 31.

18. Lyman K. Steil, Larry L. Barker, and Kittie W. Watson, *Effective Listening: Key to Your Success* (New York: McGraw-Hill, 1993), 91.

Chapter 5

1. Alvin Toffler, *Future Shock* (New York: Random House, 1970), 350.

2. Roger Bohn and James Short, "Measuring Consumer Information," *International Journal of Communication* 6 (2012): 980–1000, http://ijoc.org /ojs/index.php/ijoc/article/viewFile/1566/743 (citation is from note 2, page 983).

3. Patricia Senn Breivik, *Student Learning in the Information Age* (Phoenix: Oryx Press, 1998), xi.

4. Adapted from Myrtle S. Bolner and Gayle A. Poirier, *The Research Process: Books and Beyond*, 2nd ed. (Dubuque: Kendall/Hunt, 2002), 144–45; Shirley Duglin Kennedy, *Best Bet Internet: Reference and Research When You Don't Have Time to Mess Around* (Chicago: American Library Association, 1998), 144–45.

5. Adapted from Bolner and Poirier, *The Research Process*, 168; Christine A. Hult, *Researching and Writing across the Curriculum* (Boston: Allyn and Bacon, 1996), 28–29.

6. "Shakira's Biggest Hit," *CBS News*, March 23, 2014, accessed April 6, 2016, www.cbsnews.com/news /shakiras-biggest-hit/.

7. "Shakira's Biggest Hit"; "Shakira and Gerard Piqué Host World Baby Shower to Support UNICEF's Work for Children," *UNICEF*, January 19, 2015, accessed April 4, 2016, www.unicef.org/media/media_78722 .html.

8. Compiled from *All You Give Returns*, http://www .fundacionalas.org/en; *The Barefoot Foundation*, http://www.barefootfoundation.com/; Dan Kimpel, "Shakira's Songs Are the Heart of Her Success," *BMI.*, July 30, 2007, www.bmi.com/news/entry/535199; "Shakira says Slim, Buffet Donating 200M to Poor Latin American Children," *News*, May 16, 2008, accessed April 5, 2016, http://www.ngnews.ca /Entertainment/2008-05-16/article-324078/Shakira -says-Slim-Buffett-donating-200M-to-poor-Latin -American-children/1; "Shakira Shakes It at Charity Event," *Entertainment*, May 20, 2008, accessed April 5, 2016, www.stuff.co.nz/entertainment/451545/Shakira -shakes-it-at-charity-event-pics; "Shakira at Oxford: Excerpts from the Pop Star's Speech," *Wall Street Journal*, December 8, 2009, accessed April 5, 2016, http://on.wsj.com/178gSXa; and Amy Turner, "Shakira: Every Little Thing She Does Is Magic," *Sunday Times*, March 1, 2009, http://www.thesundaytimes.co.uk /sto/culture/music/article152524.ece.

9. Shel Israel, "9 Tips on Conducting Great Interviews," *Forbes*, April 14, 2012, www.forbes.com/sites /shelisrael/2012/04/14/8-tips-on-conducting-great -interviews/#48b148a7387a.

10. Adapted from Charles J. Stewart and William B. Cash, Jr., *Interviewing: Principles and Practices*, 11th ed. (Boston: McGraw-Hill, 2006), 1.

11. Larry King, *The Best of Larry King Live: The Greatest Interviews* (Atlanta: Times, 1995). Review this book and notice the depth of knowledge King has of a wide range of subjects and topics. His preparation enables him to ask relevant, informed questions of each of his interviewees.

Chapter 6

1. Adapted from Edward S. Inch and Barbara Warnick, *Critical Thinking and Communication: The Use of Reason in Argument*, 3rd ed. (Boston: Allyn and Bacon, 1989), 194–97.

2. Walter R. Fisher, *Human Communication as Narration: Toward a Philosophy of Reason, Value, and Action* (Columbia: University of South Carolina Press, 1987), 58.

3. Kathleen Hall Jamieson, *Eloquence in the Electronic Age: The Transformation of Political Speechmaking* (New York: Oxford University Press, 1988), 140.

4. Cynthia Crossen, *Tainted Truth: The Manipulation of Fact in America* (New York: Simon and Schuster, 1994), 42.

5. From "Explorers/Bio: Sol Guy and Josh Thome," *National Geographic*, accessed February 8, 2015, http://www.nationalgeographic.com/explorers/bios /guy-thome/.

6. From "Explorers/Bio: Sol Guy and Josh Thome."

7. Josh Thome, personal communication, February 10, 2015.

8. Thome, February 10, 2015.

9. Thome, February 10, 2015.

10. Thome, February 10, 2015.

11. Reza Fadaei, ed., *Applied Algebra and Statistics* (Needham Heights: Simon and Schuster Custom Publishing, 2000), 544, 545.

12. Compiled from "Offensive WTC Shirts Get Mich. Students in Trouble," *Newsday*, January 6, 2010, http:// www.newsday.com/news/nation/offensive-wtc -shirts-get-mich-students-in-trouble-1.1686517; Eric D. Lawrence, "Hundreds Attend Dearborn Meeting about Twin Towers Shirts," *Detroit Free Press*, January 6, 2010, accessed December 31, 2015, http://www .wzzm13.com/news/news_story.aspx?storyid=117250; Ashley Fantz, Steve Almasy, and AnneClaire Stapleton, "Muslim Teen Ahmed Mohammed Creates Clock, Shows Teacher, Gets Arrested," *CNN*, September 16, 2015, accessed December 31, 2015, http://www.cnn .com/2015/09/16/us/texas-student-ahmed-muslim -clock-bomb/.

13. Barbara Kantrowitz and Pat Wingert, "Teachers Wanted," *Newsweek*, October 2, 2000, 40.
14. Adapted from Inch and Warnick, *Critical Thinking and Communication*, 154.
15. The discussion over the type of language used by Truth, and whether or not she actually repeated the phrase "ain't I a woman," is nicely summarized in Suzanne Pullon Fitch and Roseann M. Mandziuk, *Sojourner Truth as Orator: Wit, Story, and Song* (Westport: Greenwood Press, 1997).
16. Stephen Toulmin, *The Uses of Argument* (London: Cambridge University Press, 1969); Stephen Toulmin, Richard Rieke, and Allan Janik, *An Introduction to Reasoning* (New York: Macmillan, 1979). See also Mary M. Gleason, "The Role of Evidence in Argumentative Writing," *Reading & Writing Quarterly* 14 (1999): 81–106.

Chapter 7

1. For a historical overview of the research on organizing speeches, see Ernest Thompson, "Some Effects of Message Structure on Listeners' Comprehension," *Speech Monographs* 34 (1967): 51–57; James C. McCroskey and R. S. Mehrley, "The Effects of Disorganization and Non-Fluency on Attitude Change and Source Credibility," *Communication Monographs* 36 (1969): 13–21; Arlee Johnson, "A Preliminary Investigation of the Relationship between Organization and Listener Comprehension," *Central States Speech Journal* 21 (1970): 104–07; Christopher Spicer and Ronald E. Bassett, "The Effect of Organization on Learning from an Informative Message," *Southern Speech Communication Journal* 41 (1976): 290–99. For more recent discussions of the importance of organization in speeches, see Patricia R. Palmerton, "Teaching Skills or Teaching Thinking," *Journal of Applied Communication Research* 20 (1992): 335–41; Robert G. Powell, "Critical Thinking and Speech Communication: Our Teaching Strategies Are Warranted—Not!" *Journal of Applied Communication Research* 20 (1992): 342–47.
2. "Managing Today's Multigenerational Workforce," *Lee Hecht Harrison*, accessed November 3, 2011, http://marketing.adeccona.com/lhh_enewsq2/pdf/lhh_wp_multigen.pdf.
3. "Managing Today's Multigenerational Workforce."
4. Compiled from Lisa Belkin, "Life's Work: When Whippersnappers and Geezers Collide," *New York Times*, July 26, 2007, accessed March 25, 2016 http://www.nytimes.com/2007/07/26/fashion/26work.html?pagewanted=all&_r=0; Allene Grognet and Carol Van Duzer, "Listening Skills in the Workplace," Technical Assistance for English Training Projects, 2002–2003, Spring Institute for International

Studies, accessed December 21, 2014, http://www.spring-institute.org/pdf/ListeningWkplc.pdf; "Managing Today's Multigenerational Workforce."
5. Compiled from "Explorers/Bio: Albert Yu Min-Lin," *National Geographic*, accessed January 32, 212, http://www.nationalgeographic.com/explorers/bios/albert-lin/.
6. Compiled from Caroline Kennedy, "Zainab Salbi Helps Women Recover," *Time*, May 1, 2008, http://content.time.com/time/magazine/article/0,9171,1736706,00.html; Pati Poblete, "Profile: Zainab Salbi: One Mission, Thousands of Lives," *San Francisco Chronicle*, January 27, 2002, E5; *Women for Women International*, http://www.womenforwomen.org.

Chapter 8

1. Bas A. Andeweg, Jaap C. de Jong, and Hans Hoeken, "'May I Have Your Attention?' Exordial Techniques in Informative Oral Presentations," *Technical Communication Quarterly* 7 (1998): 281.
2. Steve Boyes, "Crossing the Okavango Delta for World Heritage Status: Celebrating Botswana's Wetland Wilderness," *National Geographic*, December 22, 2011, accessed December 27, 2011, http://voices.nationalgeographic.com/2011/12/22/crossing-the-okavango-delta-for-world-heritage-status-celebrating-botswanas-wetland-wilderness/.
3. Compiled from Fred Cochran, "Alexandra Cousteau's Blue Planet," *National Geographic*, September 2, 2009, accessed December 27, 2011, http://voices.nationalgeographic.com/2009/09/02/alexandra_cousteaus_blue_plane/; "Expedition Blue Planet," *Alexandra Cousteau*, accessed December 27, 2011; Alexandra Cousteau, telephone communication, January 17, 2012.
4. The Creative Group, "New Job? Avoid Those Rookie Mistakes," *PRSA jobcenter*, accessed April 2, 2015, www.prsa.org/jobcenter/career_resources/issues_and_trends/careerarticleemployment120507.
5. Geoff Hutchison and Chloe Papas, "Yassmin Abdel-Magied: Engineer, Social Activist, and Formula One Obsessive," *ABC News*, March 25, 2015, accessed March 7, 2016, www.abc.net.au/news/2015-03-25/who-are-you-yassmin-abdel-magied/6347566.
6. *Youth without Borders*, http://youthwithoutborders.com.au/category/opportunities/#.
7. Yassmin Abdel-Magied, "Le Blog," *Yassmin Abdel-Magied*, http://www.yassminam.com/rtn; Yassmin Abdel-Magied, "What Does My Headscarf Mean to You?" filmed December 2014, TEDTalk, 14:01, posted May 2015, https://www.ted.com/talks/yassmin_abdel_magied_what_does_my_headscarf_mean_to_you?language=en.

8. Hutchison and Papas, "Yassmin Abdel-Magied: Engineer, Social Activist, and Formula One Obsessive."
9. Mark L. Knapp, et al., "The Rhetoric of Goodbye: Verbal and Nonverbal Correlates of Human Leave-Taking," *Speech Monographs* 40 (1973): 182–98.

Chapter 9

1. The debate over the role of language in constructing or reflecting reality is centuries old, beginning with Plato and Aristotle. For a summary of this debate and the implications of the many positions, see Ann Gill, *Rhetoric and Human Understanding* (Prospect Heights: Waveland Press, 1994). James L. Golden, Goodwin F. Berquist, and William E. Coleman offer an anthology of some of the primary texts in this debate in their book *The Rhetoric of Western Thought*, 10th ed. (Dubuque: Kendall/Hunt, 2011).
2. C. K. Ogden and I. A. Richards, *The Meaning of Meaning: A Study of the Influence of Language upon Thought and of the Science of Symbolism* (New York: Harcourt, Brace and World, 1930, original work published 1923).
3. For an excellent discussion of signifying, see Henry Louis Gates, *The Signifying Monkey: A Theory of Afro-American Literary Criticism* (New York: Oxford University Press, 1988); Geneva Smitherman, *Talkin' and Testifying: The Language of Black America* (Boston: Houghton Mifflin, 1977).
4. Compiled from "Explorers/Bio: Gregory Anderson," *National Geographic*, accessed January 27, 2015, http://www.nationalgeographic.com/explorers /bios/gregory-anderson/; and Gregory Anderson, personal interview, January 2015; "Enduring Voices: Western North America Trip, June 2009," *National Geographic*, accessed January 27, 2015, http://www .livingtongues.org/enduringvoicesreports/Enduring _Voices_-_Wintu_final_print.pdf.
5. "'That's So Gay' Prompts a Law Suit," *Life on NBC News.com*, February 29, 2007, accessed November 16, 2010, http://www.nbcnews.com/id/17388702/ns /us_news-life/t/thats-so-gay-prompts-lawsuit/# .V4mbkJMrKqC.
6. Steven Petrow, "'That's So Gay' Is Not So Funny," *Huffington Post*, February 9, 2009, accessed November 16, 2010, http://www.huffingtonpost .com/steven-petrow/sthats-so-gay-is-not-so-fu_b _165109.html.
7. Judy Shepard, "Judy Shepard on Gay Suicides," *Advocate*, October 2, 2010, accessed. November 11, 2011, http://www.advocate.com/news/daily-news /2010/10/02/judy-shepard-gay-suicides; "Ellen Degeneres and Anderson Cooper on the term 'GAY,'" filmed October 8, 2010, YouTube video, 2:08, posted October 2010, accessed April 11, 2013, https://www .youtube.com/watch?v=OTCJQgSbiLQ.

8. Jennifer Steinhauer, "Verdict in Myspace Suicide Case," *New York Times*, November 26, 2008, http:// www.nytimes.com/2008/11/27/us/27myspace.html.
9. The material in this section is from Khosrow Jahandarie, *Spoken and Written Discourse: A Multi-Disciplinary Perspective* (Stamford: Ablex, 1999), 131–50; Eckart Scheerer, "Orality, Literacy, and Cognitive Modeling," in *Communicating Meaning: The Evolution and Development of Language*, ed. Boris M. Velichkovsky ad Duane M Rumbaugh (Mahwah: Erlbaum, 1996), 211–56; M. A. K. Halliday, "Spoken and Written Modes of Meaning," in *Comprehending Oral and Written Language*, ed. Rosalind Horowitz and S. Jay Samuels (New York: Harcourt Brace Jovanovich, 1987), 55–82; Wallace Chafe and Jane Danielewicz, "Properties of Spoken and Written Language," in *Comprehending Oral and Written Language*, ed. Rosalind Horowitz and S. Jay Samuels (New York: Harcourt Brace Jovanovich, 1987), 83–113.
10. "Interview with Rigoberta Menchú Tum: Five Hundred Years of Sacrifice before Alien Gods," *Indians.org*, 1992, http://www.indians.org/welker /menchu2.htm.
11. Eric Partridge, *Usage and Abusage: A Guide to Good English* (New York: Norton, 1995, original work published 1942), 182.
12. David Leonhardt, "A Stimulus with Merit, and Misses Too," *New York Times,* January 27, 2009, accessed April 11, 2013, http://www.nytimes.com/2009/01/28 /business/economy/28leonhardt.html?_r=0.
13. Richard Lederer, *The Bride of Anguished English: A Bonus of Bloopers, Blunders, Botches, and Boo-Boos* (New York: St. Martin's Press), 33, 44.
14. Compiled from, *HSAN*, http://www.hsan.org; Joan Anderman et al., "Hip-Hop Setting the Beat in First: Black Artists Hold Billboard's Top 10," *Boston Globe*, October 4, 2003, http://archive.boston.com/news /local/articles/2003/10/04/hip_hop_setting_the _beat/; "Industry Insiders Call for Limits on Rap Lyrics: Group Seeks Voluntary Standards for Language," *Houston Chronicle*, April 25, 2007, 2; "Zip Un-Hip Lyrics: Rap Bigs Say Industry Should 'Bleep' Out Three Dirty Words," *Daily News* (New York), April 24, 2007, 4; The Smiley Group, *The Covenant with Black America* (Chicago: Third World Press, 2006).

Chapter 10

1. Herbert W. Hildebrant and Walter W. Stevens suggest that no one method is better than another. Rather, "it is the ability of the individual speaker in using a particular method" that is influential. See Hildebrant and Stevens, "Manuscript and Extemporaneous Delivery in Communicating Information," *Speech Monographs* 30 (1963): 369–72.

2. "La La Anthony to Host Russell Simmons' Hip-Hop Inaugural Ball," *Look to the Stars: The World of Celebrity Giving*, January 18, 2013, accessed July 20, 2016, https://wwwlooktothestars.org/news/9576-la-la-anthony-to-host-a russell-simmons-hip-hop-inaugural-ball.

3. "Hip Hop Summit Action Network (Russell Simmons' and Dr. Benjamin Chavis' Foundation)," *LinkedIn*, accessed July 20, 2016, https://www.linkedin.com/company/hip-hop-summit-action-network-russell-simmons'-and-dr.-benjamin-chavis'-foundation-.

4. Quentin J. Schultze, *High Tech Worship? Using Presentational Technologies Wisely* (Grand Rapids: Baker Books, 2005).

5. Compiled from Wade Davis, personal interview, 2015.

6. Peter A. Andersen, Michael L. Hecht, and Gregory D. Hoebler, "The Cultural Dimension of Nonverbal Communication," in *Handbook of International and Intercultural Communication*, ed. William B. Gudykunst and Bella Moody (Thousand Oaks: Sage, 2002), 89–106; Larry A. Samovar and Richard E. Porter, *Communication between Cultures* (Belmont: Wadsworth, 1991), 205–06.

7. Stephen E. Lucas, *The Art of Public Speaking*, 7th ed. (New York: McGraw-Hill, 2001), 290.

8. Paul L. Soper, *Basic Public Speaking*, 2nd ed. (New York: Oxford University Press, 1956), 151. Soper also cites Ambrose Bierce as suggesting, with regard to too high a pitch, that positive is "being mistaken at the top of one's voice" (150).

9. Adapted from Soper, *Basic Public Speaking*, 143.

10. Nicholas Christenfeld, "Does It Hurt to Say Um?" *Journal of Nonverbal Behavior* 19 (Fall 1995): 171–86. Christenfeld's study also found that audiences prefer no pauses to empty pauses.

11. See, for example, Stephanie Martin and Lyn Darnley, *The Teaching Voice* (San Diego: Singular Publishing Group, 1996), 60; Patsy Rodenburg, *The Need for Words: Voice and the Text* (New York: Routledge, 2001); Linda Gates, *Voice for Performance* (New York: Applause, 2000); Richard Dowis, *The Lost Art of the Great Speech: How to Write One, How to Deliver It* (New York: American Management Association, 2000).

12. Many communication scholars define nonverbal communication as all aspects of communication other than words. In a public speaking course, the distinction between vocalized communication as verbal and nonvocalized communication as nonverbal seems pedagogically useful. A similar distinction is made in many other public speaking texts.

13. Ray Birdwhistell, *Kinesics and Context* (Philadelphia: University of Pennsylvania Press, 1970); Albert Mehrabian, *Silent Messages: Implicit Communication of Emotion and Attitudes*, 2nd ed. (Belmont: Wadsworth, 1981).

14. See, for example, April R. Trees and Valerie Manusov, "Managing Face Concerns in Critics: Integrating Nonverbal Behaviors as a Dimension of Politeness in Female Friendship Dyads," *Human Communication Research* 24 (1998): 564–83; James C. McCroskey, et al., "Nonverbal Immediacy and Cognitive Learning: A Cross-Cultural Investigation," *Communication Education* 45 (1996): 200–11; Mary Mino, "The Relative Effects of Content and Vocal Delivery during a Simulated Employment Interview," *Communication Research Reports* 13 (1996): 225–38. See also Julia T. Wood, *Interpersonal Communication: Everyday Encounters*, 2nd ed. (Belmont: Wadsworth, 1999), 148.

15. For an excellent discussion of variations in nonverbal expectations across cultures, see Gudykunst and Moody, eds., *Handbook of International and Intercultural Communication*.

16. For example, see "Good-Looking Lawyers Make More Money, Says a Study by Economists," *Wall Street Journal*, January 4, 1996, A1; Patricia Rozell, David Kennedy, and Edward Grabb, "Physical Attractiveness and Income Attainment among Canadians," *Journal of Psychology* 123 (1989): 547–59; Tracy L. Morris, et al., "Fashion in the Classroom: Effects of Attire on Student Perceptions of Instructors in College Classes," *Communication Education* 45 (1996): 135–48.

17. Arthur J. Hartz, "Psycho-Socionomics: Attractiveness Research from a Societal Perspective," *Journal of Social Behavior and Personality* 11 (1996): 683.

18. Anthony C. Little, Benedict C. Jones, and Lisa M. DeBruine, "Facial Attractiveness: Evolutionary Based Research," *The Royal Society* 366, no. 1571 (2011): 1638–59; Ulrich Rosar, Markus Klein, and Tilo Beckers, "Magic Mayors: Predicting Electoral Success from Candidates' Physical Attractiveness under the Conditions of a Presidential Electoral System," *German Politics* 21, no. 4, (2012): 372–91; Timothy A. Judge, Charlice Hurst, and Lauren S. Simon, "Does It Pay to Be Smart, Attractive, or Confident (or All Three)? Relationships among General Mental Ability, Physical Attractiveness, Core Self-Evaluations, and Income," *Journal of Applied Psychology* 94, no. 3, (2009): 742–55, doi: 10.1037/a0015497.

19. Paula Morrow writes that even though physical attractiveness is difficult to "quantify," "people within a given culture tend to agree with each other regarding whether a person's facial appearance is physically attractive or not and they tend to be consistent in their judgments over time." See Morrow, "Physical Attractiveness and Selection Decision Making," *Journal of Management* 16 (1990): 45–60, esp. p. 47. See also Ruth P. Rubinstein, *Dress Codes: Meanings and Messages in American Culture*, 2nd ed. (Boulder: Westview, 2001); C. Peter Herman, Mark

P. Zanna, and E. Tory Higgins, *Physical Appearance, Stigma, and Social Behavior: The Ontario symposium,* vol. 3 (Hillsdale: Erlbaum, 1986).

20. Mark T. Palmer and Karl B. Simmons, "Communicating Intentions through Nonverbal Behaviors," *Human Communication Research* 22 (1995): 128–60.

21. Steven A. Beebe, "Eye Contact: A Nonverbal Determinant of Speaker Credibility," *Speech Teacher* 23 (1974): 21–25; Steven A. Beebe, "Effects of Eye Contact, Posture and Vocal Inflection upon Credibility and Comprehension," *Australian Scan Journal of Nonverbal Communication* 7–8 (1979–1980): 57–70; Martin Cobin, "Response to Eye Contact," *Quarterly Journal of Speech* 48 (1963): 415–19.

22. See, for example, Peter E. Bull, *Posture and Gesture* (New York: Pergamon, 1987).

23. See, for example, Gilbert Austin, *Chironomia or A Treatise on Rhetorical Delivery,* ed. Mary Margaret Robb and Lester Thonssen (Carbondale: Southern Illinois University Press, 1966, original work published 1806); John Bulwer, *Chirologia: Or the Natural Language of the Hand, and Chiromomia: Or the Art of Manual Rhetoric,* ed. James W. Cleary (Carbondale: Southern Illinois University Press, 1974, original work published 1644).

24. Compiled from Margarita Tartskovsky, "9 Ways to Reduce Anxiety Right Here, Right Now," *PsychCentral,* http://psychcentral.com/lib/9-ways-to-reduce -anxiety-right-here-right-now; David Carbonell, "The Anxiety Trick," *AnxietyCoach.com,* updated July 3, 2016, www.anxietycoach.com/anxietytrick.html; and "How to Stop Feeling Nervous from Anxiety," *CalmClinic,* June 17, 2016, www.calmclinic.com /anxiety/symptoms/nervous.

Chapter 11

1. Will Linkugel and D. Berg, *A Time to Speak* (Belmont: Wadsworth, 1970), 68–96. See also Elena P. Zayas-Bazan, "Instructional Media in the Total Language Picture," *International Journal of Instructional Media* 5 (1977–1978): 145–50; Emil Bohn and David Jabusch, "The Effect of Four Methods of Instruction on the Use of Visual Aids in Speeches," *Western Journal of Speech Communication* 46 (1982): 253–65.

2. Raymond S. Nickerson, "Short-Term Memory for Complex Meaningful Visual Configurations: A Demonstration of Capacity," *Canadian Journal of Psychology* 19 (1965): 155–60.

3. Bohn and Jabusch, "The Effect of Four Methods of Instruction on the Use of Visual Aids in Speeches," 254.

4. William J. Seiler, "The Effects of Visual Materials on Attitudes, Credibility, and Retention," *Speech Monographs* 38 (1971): 331–34.

5. Joe Ayres, "Using Visual Aids to Reduce Speech Anxiety," *Communication Research Reports* 8 (1991): 73–79.

6. Chris Anderson, "How Web Video Powers Global Innovation," filmed July 2010, TEDTalk, posted September 2010, https://www.ted.com/talks/chris _anderson_how_web_video_powers_global _innovation?language=en.

7. Compiled from Asher Jay, personal interview, 2015; and "Explorers/Bio: Asher Jay," *National Geographic,* accessed April 10, 2015 www.nationalgeographic .com/explorers/bios/asher-jay.

8. Myles Martel, *Before You Say a Word: The Executive Guide to Effective Communication* (Upper Saddle River: Prentice Hall, 1984).

9. Wilma Davidson and Susan J. Kline, "Ace Your Presentation," *Journal of Accountancy* 187 (1999): 61–63.

10. For a nice discussion of using lists as visual aids, see Margaret Y. Rabb, *The Presentation Design Book: Tips, Techniques and Advice for Creating Effective, Attractive Slides, Overheads, Multimedia Presentations, Screen Shows and More* (Chapel Hill: Ventana, 1993).

11. For example, see Lynn Kearny, *Graphics for Presenters: Getting Your Ideas Across* (Menlo Park: Crisp Publications, 1996); Claudyne Wilder, *The Presentations Kit: Ten Steps for Spelling Out Your Ideas* (New York: Wiley, 1994); Rabb, *The Presentation Design Book.*

12. For example, see Rabb, *The Presentation Design Book*; Wilder, *The Presentations Kit*; Russell N. Baird, et al., *The Graphics of Communication: Methods, Media and Technology* (New York: Harcourt Brace Jovanovich, 1993).

13. Hans Biedermann, *Dictionary of Symbolism: Cultural Icons and the Meanings behind Them,* trans. James Hulbert (New York: Facts on File, 1992).

Chapter 12

1. Conversation with Jennifer McMartin, student at Colorado State University, June 6, 2001.

2. John R. Johnson and Nancy Szczupakiewicz, "The Public Speaking Course: Is It Preparing Students with Work Related Public Speaking Skills?" *Communication Education* 36, no. 2 (1987): 131–37.

3. See, for example, Deanna P. Dannels, "Time to Speak Up: A Theoretical Framework of Situated Pedagogy and Practice for Communication across the Curriculum," *Communication Education* 50 (2001): 144–58; Sherwin Morreal, Michael Osborn, and Judy Pearson, "Why Communication Is Important: A Rationale for the Centrality of the Study of Communication," *Journal of the Association for Communication Administration* 29 (2000):

1–25; Andrew D. Wolvin, "The Basic Course and the Future of the Workplace," *Basic Communication Course Annual* 10 (1989): 1–6; National Association of Colleges and Employers, *Job Outlook 2010* (Bethlehem, PA: National Association of Colleges and Employers, November 2009), NACE Research, PDF Report, http://www.eng.fiu.edu/mme/robotics/info/how_employers_see_candidates_nace2010.pdf.

4. Susan Ricker, "Skills Spotlight: Public Speaking and 16 Related Jobs," *AOL.*, August 1, 2014, accessed December 29, 2014, www.aol.com/article/2014/08/01/skills-spotlight-public-speaking-jobs/20940624/.

5. Compiled from Sylvia Earle, *The World is Blue: How Our Fate and the Ocean's Are One* (Washington, DC: National Geographic Books, 2009); "National Geographic Explorer-in-Residence Sylvia Earle Spotlights Crisis Facing Our Seas in New Book," *Underwater Times.com*, October 9, 2009, accessed December 27, 2011, http://www.underwatertimes.com/news.php?article_id=82639710504; "Ocean Hero: Sylvia Earle," *National Geographic*, accessed December 27, 2011, http://ocean.nationalgeographic.com/take-action/ocean-hero-sylvia-earle/.

6. "Tatoo Statistics," *Statistic Brain*, September 27, 2015, http://www.statisticbrain.com/tattoo-statistics/.

7. Dennis G, "50 Most Popular Tattoo Designs," *Rank My Tattoos Magazine*, accessed November 18, 2014, http://mag.rankmytattoos.com/top-50-most-popular-tattoo-designs.html; Michelle Keldgord, "Most Popular Tattoos of 2014: Cutest Tattoo Ideas of the Year," *YouQueen*, July 22, 2014, accessed November 18, 2014, http://youqueen.com/beauty/most-popular-tattoos-2014/.

8. Cate Lineberry, "Tattoos: The Ancient and Mysterious History," *Smithsonian.com*, January 1, 2007, accessed June 24, 2010, http://www.smithsonianmag.com/history/tattoos-144038580/; Cate Lineberry, "Today's Tattoos: Making Your Mark," *Smithsonian.com*, January 1, 2007, accessed June 21, 2010, http://www.smithsonianmag.com/arts-culture/todays-tattoos-143959362/.

9. Lineberry, "Tattoos: The Ancient and Mysterious History."

10. Mindy Fenske, "The Aesthetics of the Unfinished: Ethics and Performance." *Text and Performance Quarterly*, 24, no. 1 (2004): 1–19.

Chapter 13

1. Stephanie Burkhalter, John Gastil, and Todd Kelshaw, "A Conceptual Definition and Theoretical Model of Public Deliberation in Small Face-to-Face Groups," *Communication Theory*, 12 (2002): 416.

2. The theory of invitational rhetoric was initially proposed by Sonja K. Foss and Cindy L. Griffin in "Beyond Persuasion: A Proposal for an Invitational Rhetoric," *Communication Monographs* 62 (1995): 1–18. That theory has been modified here so it is applicable to public speaking practices.

3. This excerpt comes from Jennifer Emerling Bone, Cindy L. Griffin, and T. M. Linda Scholz, "Beyond Traditional Conceptualizations of Rhetoric: Invitational Rhetoric and a Move toward Civility," *Western Journal of Communication* 72 (2008): 434–62. Thanks go to Jennifer Emerling Bone for her work on this portion of the manuscript.

4. "World Trade Center Site Memorial Competition Jury Statement," *New York Times*, accessed November 19, 2003, http://www.nytimes.com/2003/11/19/nyregion/19WTC-JURY-TEXT.html.

5. "Memorial—Reflecting Absence: WTC Memorial Jury Statement for Winning Design," *Lower Manhattan Development Corporation*, accessed January 13, 2004, http://www.renewnyc.com.

6. "Memorial—Reflecting Absence: WTC Memorial Jury Statement for Winning Design."

7. For more discussion on the conditions of equality, value, and self-determination, see Harold Barrett, *Rhetoric and Civility: Human Development, Narcissism, and the Good Audience* (Albany: State University of New York Press, 1991); Seyla Benhabib, *Situating the Self: Gender, Community, and Postmodernism in Contemporary Ethics* (New York: Routledge, 1992); Linda Ellinor and Glenna Gerard, *Dialogue: Creating and Sustaining Collaborative Partnerships at Work* (New York: Wiley, 1998); William Isaacs, *Dialogue and the Art of Thinking Together* (New York: Currency Doubleday, 1999); Paul Rogat Loeb, *Soul of a Citizen: Living with Conviction in a Cynical Time* (New York: St. Martin's Griffin, 1999); M. Scott Peck, *The Different Drum: Community-Making and Peace* (New York: Simon and Schuster, 1987); Carl R. Rogers, "The Interpersonal Relationship: The Core of Guidance," *Harvard Educational Review* 32 (1962): 416–29; Margaret Urban Walker, "Moral Understandings: Alternative 'Epistemology' for a Feminist Ethics," *Hypatia* 4 (1989): 15–28.

8. Burkhalter, Gastil, and Kelshaw, "A Conceptual Definition and Theoretical Model of Public Deliberation in Small Face-to-Face Groups," 416.

9. Foss and Griffin, "Beyond Persuasion: A Proposal for an Invitational Rhetoric," 10.

10. Bone, Griffin, and Scholz, "Beyond Traditional Conceptualizations of Rhetoric: Invitational Rhetoric and a Move toward Civility," 437.

11. Burkhalter, Gastil, and Kelshaw, "A Conceptual Definition and Theoretical Model of Public Deliberation in Small Face-to-Face Groups," 416.

12. Foss and Griffin, "Beyond Persuasion: A Proposal for an Invitational Rhetoric," 12; Bone, Griffin, and Scholz, "Beyond Traditional

13. Compiled from *United Nations Year of Dialog among Civilizations 2001*, http://www.un.org/Dialogue/heroes.html; *Message Stick*, "Remember Finis," ABC1, March 10, 2002, special guest Jack Beetson, http://www.messagestick.com.au/awareness/jbeetson/index.html; "Trespassers Will Be Welcome," *Sidney Morning Herald*, September 21, 2002, http://www.smh.com.au/articles/2002/09/20/1032054956049; *Living Black*, season 5, episode 12, SBS Australia, May 24, 2006, starring Karla Grant, http://news.sbs.com.au/livingblack/index.php?action=proginfo&id=345; Andrew Dunkley, "Literacy Levels in Aboriginal Communities on the Rise," *ABC Western Plains,* March 13, 2015, accessed April 25, 2016, www.abc.net.au/local/stories/2015/03/13/4197172.htm; *Literacy for Life Foundation*, http://www.lflf.org.au.

14. My thanks to Marko Mohlenhoff, former campaign associate at the Fort Collins Area United Way, for sharing his approach to public speaking and working with me on this example.

15. bell hooks, *Outlaw Culture: Resisting Representations* (New York: Routledge, 1994), 241.

16. azizabussarah, "A Conflict Close to Home," *Aziz Abu Sarah: A Blog for Peace in Israel-Palestine*, May 6, 2009, accessed November 29, 2014, http://azizabusarah.wordpress.com/2009/05/06/a-conflict-close-to-home/.

Chapter 14

1. For a nice discussion of the importance of maintaining Aristotle's distinction between *logos* and *logic,* see Joseph Little, "Confusion in the Classroom: Does Logos Mean Logic?" *Journal of Technical Writing and Communication* 29 (1999): 349–53. Aristotle suggested that *logos* refers to the process of reasoning as well as establishing credibility, or *ethos,* and using emotional appeals, or *pathos*. See also Aristotle, *On Rhetoric: A Theory of Civic Discourse*, trans. George Kennedy (Oxford: Oxford University Press, 1991), 37.

2. See Chaim Perelman and Luce Olbrechts-Tyteca, *The New Rhetoric: A Treatise on Argumentation,* trans. John Wilkinson and Purcell Weaver (Notre Dame: University of Notre Dame Press, 1969), 31–35, for a discussion of the universal audience, or that group of imagined listeners to whom we submit claims and test their "logic."

3. Adapted from Stephen Toulmin, Richard Rieke, and Allan Janik, *An Introduction to Reasoning* (New York: Macmillan, 1979).

4. Perelman and Olbrechts-Tyteca identify approximately twenty-two different argument schemes *The New Rhetoric*, and Douglas N. Walton offers twenty-five different argumentation schemes in *Argumentation Schemes for Presumptive Reasoning* (Mahwah: Erlbaum, 1996). Although all of these schemes are important, students in a beginning public speaking course do well to rely on the five basic types discussed in this chapter and in most other public speaking texts.

5. The material in this section and the section on deductive reasoning is from Lester Faigley and Jack Selzer, *Good Reasons* (Needham Heights: Allyn and Bacon, 2000); Howard Kahane and Nancy Cavender, *Logic and Contemporary Rhetoric: The Use of Reason in Everyday Life*, 11th ed. (Boston: Wadsworth, 2010); Stephen Toulmin, *The Uses of Argument* (London: Cambridge University Press, 1969).

6. See, for example, David Vancil, *Rhetoric and Argumentation* (Boston: Allyn and Bacon, 1993), 134, who suggests that argument by example is "one of the archetypal forms of the inductive process"; David Zarefsky, *Public Speaking: Strategies for Success* (Needham Heights: Allyn and Bacon, 2002), 153–54.

7. Aristotle, *Rhetoric*, II, 20, 1394a, cited in Perelman and Olbrechts-Tyteca, *The New Rhetoric*, 358. See also Aristotle, *The "Art" of Rhetoric*, trans. John H. Freese (Cambridge, MA: Harvard University Press, 1982), 265, for a slightly different translation of Aristotle's view on examples.

8. For an excellent compilation of women's speeches related to their right to vote, as well as other rights, including Anthony's speech, see Karlyn Kohrs Campbell, ed., *Man Cannot Speak for Her: Key Texts of the Early Feminists* (New York: Praeger, 1989).

9. See Faigley and Selzer, *Good Reasons;* Kahane and Cavender, *Logic and Contemporary Rhetoric;* Edward S. Inch and Barbara Warnick, *Critical Thinking and Communication: The Use of Reason in Argument*, 3rd ed. (Boston: Allyn and Bacon, 1998).

10. False causes are also known by their Latin name, *post hoc, ergo propter hoc,* which means "after this, therefore because of this." For a succinct discussion of false causes, see Inch and Warnick, *Critical Thinking and Communication*, 208–09.

11. Compiled from Claudia Kalb, "Culture of Corpulence: American Innovations in Food, Transportation, and Technology are Threatening to Supersize Us All," *Newsweek*, March 22, 2010, 42–48; Michelle Obama, "Michelle on a Mission: How We Can Empower Parents, Schools, and the Community to Battle Childhood Obesity," *Newsweek*, March 22, 2010, 40–41.

12. "One Home at a Time: How to Cut the Number of Street Dwellers—and Save Money Too," *Economist*, November 15, 2014, 64.

13. Cited in Paul Rogat Loeb, *Soul of a Citizen: Living with Conviction in a Cynical Time* (New York: St. Martin's Griffin, 1999), 68–69.

14. Jerry Alder and Mary Carmichael, "The Tsunami Threat," *Newsweek*, January 10, 2005, 42.

15. Inch and Warnick call reasoning by sign "coexistential" reasoning, suggesting "an argument from coexistence reasons from something that can be observed (as a sign) to a condition or feature that cannot be observed." See Inch and Warnick, *Critical Thinking and Communication*, 201.

16. Alder and Carmichael, "The Tsunami Threat," 42.

17. For a discussion of the characteristics of credibility, see James B. Stiff, *Persuasive Communication* (New York: Guilford Press, 1994), 89–98.

18. See Frans H. van Eemeren and Rob Grootendorst, *Argumentation, Communication, and Fallacies: A Pragma-Dialectical Perspective* (Hillsdale: Erlbaum, 1992); Howard Kahane and Nancy Cavender, *Logic and Contemporary Rhetoric: The Use of Reason in Everyday Life*, 8th ed. (Belmont: Wadsworth, 1998).

19. Compiled from Shabana Basij-Rasikh, "Dare to Educate Afghan Girls," filmed December 2012, TEDTalk, 9:36, posted February 2013, accessed April 9, 2015, www.ted.com/talks/shabana _basij_rasikh_dare_to_educate_afghan_girls /transcript?language=en "Explorers/Bio: Shabana Basij-Rasikh," *National Geographic*, accessed April 9, 2015, www.nationalgeographic.com/explorers/bios /shabana-basij-rasikh/.

20. Evan Buxbaum, "NYC Heroin Pamphlet—Is It a Help or a How-to Guide?" *CNN*, January 4, 2010, www.cnn .com/2010/CRIME/01/04/ny.heroin.pamphlet/.

Chapter 15

1. Compiled from *Louisiana Bucket Brigade*, http:// www.labucketbrigade.org; The Smiley Group, *The Covenant with Black America* (Chicago: Third World Press, 2006); "Watchdog Group to Protest Refinery: Activists to Mix with Exxon Stockholders," *Times-Picayune* (New Orleans), May 24, 2005, 1; "Two Groups Suing Refinery: They Claim Plant Violates Clean Air Act," *Times-Picayune* (New Orleans), February 13, 2004, 1; "Group Plans to File Suit against Refinery: They Allege Pollution Violations," *Times-Picayune* (New Orleans), December 5, 2003, 1; "Refinery Emissions Too High, Groups Say: Chalmette Residents Fear for Their Health," *Times-Picayune* (New Orleans), September 24, 2003, 1; "Residents to Learn to Test Air Quality: Devices to Check for Chemicals on Display," *Times-Picayune* (New Orleans), October 18, 2002, 1; and "Neighbors Seeking Proof of Pollution," *Times-Picayune* (New Orleans), July 20, 2000, 1.

2. Compiled from "Explorers/Bio: Sol Guy and Josh Thome," *National Geographic*, accessed March 24, 2015, http://www.nationalgeographic.com /explorers/bios/guy-thome/; personal interview, March 3, 2014; and Sol Guy, "How to be Powerful," filmed September 30, 2010, TEDTalk, 7:12, posted October 2010, accessed October 2, 2014, https:// www.youtube.com/watch?v=DyGiGevmupk.

3. Adapted from Bruce E. Gronbeck, et al., *Principles and Types of Speech Communication*, 11th ed. (Glenview: Scott, Foresman/Little, Brown Higher Education, 1990), 180–205.

4. John C. Reinhard, "The Empirical Study of the Persuasive Effects of Evidence: The Status after 50 Years of Research," *Human Communication Research* 15 (1988): 3–59.

5. Donald Dean Morely and Kim B. Walker, "The Role of Importance, Novelty, and Plausibility in Producing Belief Change," *Communication Monographs* 54 (1987): 436–42.

6. See Edward S. Inch and Barbara Warnick, *Critical Thinking and Communication: The Use of Reason in Argument*, 3rd ed. (Boston: Allyn and Bacon, 1998), 159.

7. See, for example, Peter A. Andersen and Laura K. Guerrero, eds., *Handbook of Communication and Emotion: Research, Theory, Applications, and Contexts* (San Diego: Academic Press, 1998), especially Chapters 16 and 17; Kathleen Kelley Reardon, *Persuasion in Practice* (Newbury Park: Sage, 1991), 108–10; James B. Stiff, *Persuasive Communication* (New York: Guilford Press, 1994), 119–31.

8. Laura K. Guerrero, Peter A. Andersen, and Melanie R. Trost, "Communication and Emotion: Basic Concepts and Approaches," in *Handbook of Communication and Emotion*, ed. Andersen and Guerrero, 6.

9. Richard E. Porter and Larry A. Samovar, "Cultural Influences on Emotional Expression: Implications for Intercultural Communication," in *Handbook of Communication and Emotion*, ed. Andersen and Guerrero, 452.

10. For a sample of speakers who possess these traits, see "Top 100 American Speeches of the 20th Century," *News*, University of Wisconsin–Madison, http://www .news.wisc.edu/misc/speeches/.

11. See Richard M. Perloff, *The Dynamics of Persuasion* (Hillsdale: Erlbaum, 1993), 136–55; Stiff, *Persuasive Communication*, 89–106.

12. Stiff, *Persuasive Communication*, 102–04.

13. Perloff, *Dynamics of Persuasion*, 170–79.

14. "Top 100 American Speeches of the 20th Century."

15. Compiled from Randall S. Hansen, "Ten Best Job Interview Tips for Job-Seekers," *QUINTESSENTIAL*, accessed February 10, 2016, https://www.livecareer .com/quintessential/job-interview-tips.

16. Numerous scholars, beginning with Aristotle, define persuasion as a process, as something that takes place over time. For example, see Gerald R. Miller and Michael E. Roloff, eds., *Persuasion: New Directions in Theory and Research* (Beverly Hills: Sage, 1980); Kathleen Kennedy Reardon, *Persuasion in Practice* (Newbury Park: Sage, 1991); James B. Stiff, *Persuasive Communication* (New York: Guilford Press, 1994) for three examples of this processual definition of persuasion.

17. See Stiff, *Persuasive Communication*, 117–19.

18. Bryan B. Whaley and Lisa Smith Wagner, "Rebuttal Analogy in Persuasive Messages: Communicator Likability and Cognitive Responses," *Journal of Language and Social Psychology* 19 (2000): 66–84.

19. Connie Roser and Margaret Thompson, "Fear Appeals and the Formation of Active Publics," *Journal of Communication* 45 (1995): 103–21, doi: 10.1111/j.1460-2466.1995.tb00717.x.

20. Patricia A. Rippetoe and Ronald W. Rogers, "Effects of Components of Protection-Motivation Theory on Adaptive and Maladaptive Coping with a Health Threat," *Journal of Personality and Social Psychology* 53 (1987): 596–604; Mary K. Casey, et al., "Response and Self-Efficacy of Condom Use: A Meta-Analysis of this Important Element of AIDS Education and Prevention," *Southern Communication Journal* 74, no. 1 (January 2009): 57–78, accessed May 27, 2010, doi: 10.1080/10417940802335953; Donna C. Jessop and Jennifer Wade, "Fear Appeals and Binge Drinking: A Terror Management Theory Perspective," *British Journal of Health Psychology* 13, no. 4 (November 2008): 773–88, accessed May 27, 2010, doi: 10.1348/135910707X272790; Robin L. Nabi, David Roskos-Ewoldsen, and Francesca Dillman Carpentier, "Subjective Knowledge and Fear Appeal Effectiveness: Implications for Message Design," *Health Communication* 23, no. 2 (2008): 191–201, accessed May 27, 2010, doi: 10.1080/10410230701808327; Roser and Thompson, "Fear Appeals and the Formation of Active Publics," *Journal of Communication* 45 (1995): 103–21, doi: 10.1111/j.1460-2466.1995.tb00717.x; Carol L. Schmitt and Thomas Blass, "Fear Appeals Revisited: Testing a Unique Anti-Smoking Film," *Current Psychology* 27, no. 2 (2008): 145–51, accessed May 27, 2010, doi: 10.1007/s12144-008-9029-7; and Norman C. H. Wong and Joseph N. Cappella, "Antismoking Threat and Efficacy Appeals: Effects on Smoking Cessation Intentions for Smokers with Low and High Readiness to Quit," *Journal of Applied Communication Research* 37, no. 1 (February 2009): 1–20, accessed May 27, 2010, doi: 0.1080/00909880802593928.

21. Jack W. Brehm, *A Theory of Psychological Reactance* (New York: Academic Press, 1996); Patricia Kearney, Timothy G. Plax, and Nancy F. Burroughs, "An Attributional Analysis of College Students' Resistance Decisions," *Communication Education* 40, no. 4, (September 1991): 325–42, doi: 10.1080/03634529109378858.

Chapter 16

1. "Ludwig Mies van der Rohe," *Saylor.org Academy*, 1, http://www.saylor.org/site/wp-content/uploads/2011/05/Ludwig-Mies-van-der-Rohe.pdf. Architect Ludwig Mies van der Rohe (1886–1969) is credited with using the phrase "less is more" to describe his "skin and bones" architecture.

2. "Commemorative Speech Written by Molly Botswick," Memories, Commemorative Speeches, *Sam Spady Foundation*, accessed May 2010, http://www.samspadyfoundation.org/pdf/mollysspeech.pdf.

3. *Consideration of H.R. 573 to Award the Congressional Gold Medal to Rosa Parks, United States House*, 106th Cong. (April 20, 1999) (testimony supporting H.R. 573 in tribute to Rosa Parks, Bobby L. Rush, U.S. Rep., Washington, D.C.), capitolwords.org/date/1999/04.20/H2150-6_authorizing-awarding-of-gold-medal-to-rosa-parks/.

4. "National Geographic Events: Speaker's Bureau: Chad Pregracke: Environmentalist," *National Geographic*, accessed May 27, 2013, http://events.nationalgeographic.com/events/speakers-bureau/speaker/chad-pregracke/; Jerry Palmer, *Taking Humor Seriously* (London: Routledge, 1994), 161.

5. Katherine R. Rowell, "Acceptance Speech, Outstanding Community Colleges Professor of the Year, National Winner," *U.S. Professors of the Year Awards Program*, accessed May 2, 2016, http://www.usprofessorsoftheyear.org/Winners/Previous_Natl_Winners/Rowell_Acceptance_Speech.html#.V5wBDpMrKqA.

6. Stephen E. Lucas, *The Art of Public Speaking*, 7th ed. (Boston: McGraw-Hill, 2001), 445.

7. Jerry Palmer, *Taking Humor Seriously* (London: Routledge, 1994), 161.

8. Ellen DeGeneres, Commencement Address (Tulane University, New Orleans, LA, May 11, 2009), *Graduation Wisdom*, accessed May 2010, http://www.graduationwisdom.com/speeches/v0041-4-ellen.html.

9. See, for example, Charles R. Gruner, "Advice to the Beginning Speaker on Using Humor—What the Research Tells Us," *Communication Education* 34 (1985): 142–47; Christie McGufee Smith and Larry Power, "The Use of Disparaging Humor by Group Leaders," *Southern Speech Communication Journal* 53 (1988): 279–92; Elizabeth E. Grahm, Michael J. Papa, and Gordon P. Brooks, "Functions of Humor in Conversation: Conceptualization and Measurement," *Western Journal of Communication* 56 (1992):

161–83; Frank J. MacHovec, *Humor: Theory, History, Applications* (Springfield: Charles C Thomas, 1988); Palmer, *Taking Humor Seriously*.

10. Jeffrey H. Goldstein, "Theoretical Notes on Humor," *Journal of Communication* 26 (1976): 104–12. See also Barry Alan Morris, "The Communal Constraints on Parody: The Symbolic Death of Joe Bob Briggs," *Quarterly Journal of Speech* 73 (1987): 460–73.

11. Even experienced comedians can go too far for their audiences. Consider the example of Joe Bob Briggs in Morris, "The Communal Constraints on Parody," 460–73.

12. Jackie Strause, "Golden Globes: Host Ricky Gervais Pokes Fun at NBC Zero Nominations," *Hollywood Reporter*, January 10, 2016, http://www.hollywoodreporter.com/news/golden-globes-2016-ricky-gervais-854016.

13. For an interesting discussion of gender differences in humor, see M. Alison Kibler, "Gender Conflict and Coercion on A&E's *An Evening at the Improv*," *Journal of Popular Culture* 32 (1999): 45–57.

14. See Joan B. Levine, "The Feminine Routine," *Journal of Communication* 26 (1976): 173–75; Lawrence La Fave and Roger Mannell, "Does Ethnic Humor Serve Prejudice?" *Journal of Communication* 26 (1976): 116–23; Dolf Zillmann and Holly Stocking, "Putdown Humor," *Journal of Communication* 26 (1976): 154–63.

15. See Palmer, *Taking Humor Seriously*; Joseph Alan Ullian, "Joking at Work," *Journal of Communication* 26 (1976): 129–33.

16. Victor Raskin, *Semantic Mechanism of Humor* (Dordrecht, the Netherlands: D. Reidel, 1985).

17. Sylvia Simmons, *How to Be the Life of the Podium: Openers, Closers and Everything in Between to Keep Them Listening* (New York: AMACOM, 1991).

Index

Page numbers followed by "t" and "f" represent tables and figures respectively; page numbers A1–A14 are available in MindTap Reader only.